THE FIN...
STATEMENTS

Fundamental Accounting Principles uses a colour scheme to help students differentiate among the four key financial statement

Organico's Income Statement
For Month Ended March 31, 2017

Revenues:		
Food services revenue	$ 3,800	
Teaching revenue	300	
Total revenues		$ 4,100
Operating expenses:		
Rent expense	$ 1,000	
Salaries expense	700	
Total operating expenses		1,700
Profit		$ 2,400

Organico Statement of Changes in Equity
For Month Ended March 31, 2017

Hailey Walker, capital, March 1		$ -0-
Add: Investments by owner	$ 10,000	
Profit	2,400	12,400
Total		$ 12,400
Less: Withdrawals by owner		600
Hailey Walker, capital, March 31		$ 11,800

Organico Balance Sheet
March 31, 2017

Assets		Liabilities		
Cash	$ 8,400	Accounts payable	$ 200	
Supplies	3,600	Notes payable	6,000	
Equipment	6,000	Total liabilities		$ 6,200
		Equity		
		Hailey Walker, capital		11,800
Total assets	$18,000	Total liabilities and equity		$ 18,000

Organico Statement of Cash Flows
For Month Ended March 31, 2017

Cash flows from operating activities		
Cash received from clients	$ 4,100	
Cash paid for supplies	(3,400)	
Cash paid for rent	(1,000)	
Cash paid to employee	(700)	
Net cash used by operating activities		$ (1,000)
Cash flows from investing activities		-0-
Cash flows from financing activities		
Investment by owner	$10,000	
Withdrawal by owner	(600)	
Net cash provided by financing activities		9,400
Net increase in cash		$ 8,400
Cash balance, March 1		-0-
Cash balance, March 31		$ 8,400

The arrows are provided for education purposes only to emphasize the link between statements.

Fundamental
ACCOUNTING PRINCIPLES

Volume

Fifteenth Canadian Edition

Kermit D. Larson
University of Texas—Austin

Tilly Jensen
Athabasca University—Alberta

Heidi Dieckmann
Kwantlen Polytechnic University—British Columbia

McGraw Hill Education

Fundamental Accounting Principles
Volume 1
Fifteenth Canadian Edition

The Internet addresses listed in the text were accurate at the time of publication. The inclusion of a Web site does not indicate an endorsement by the authors or McGraw-Hill Ryerson, and McGraw-Hill Ryerson does not guarantee the accuracy of the information presented at these sites.

ISBN-13: 978-1-25-908727-1
ISBN-10: 1-25-908727-1

2 3 4 5 6 7 8 9 0 TCP 1 9 8 7

Printed and bound in Canada.

Care has been taken to trace ownership of copyright material contained in this text; however, the publisher will welcome any information that enables them to rectify any reference or credit for subsequent editions.

Director of Product Management: Rhondda McNabb
Product Manager: Keara Emmett
Executive Marketing Manager: Joy Armitage-Taylor
Product Developer: Sarah Fulton
Senior Product Team Associate: Stephanie Giles
Supervising Editor: Jessica Barnoski
Photo/Permissions Editor: Tracy Leonard
Copy Editor: Karen Rolfe
Plant Production Coordinator: Scott Morrison
Manufacturing Production Coordinator: Emily Hickey
Cover Design: Michelle Losier
Cover Image: Rachel Idzerda
Interior Design: Michelle Losier
Page Layout: Aptara®, Inc.
Printer: Transcontinental Printing Group

About the Authors

Kermit D. Larson, University of Texas–Austin

Kermit D. Larson is the Arthur Andersen & Co. Alumni Professor of Accounting Emeritus at the University of Texas at Austin. He served as chair of the University of Texas, Department of Accounting, and was visiting associate professor at Tulane University. His scholarly articles have been published in a variety of journals, including *The Accounting Review, Journal of Accountancy, and Abacus*. He is the author of several books, including *Financial Accounting* and *Fundamentals of Financial* and *Managerial Accounting*, both published by Irwin/McGraw-Hill.

Professor Larson is a member of the American Accounting Association, the Texas Society of CPAs, and the American Institute of CPAs. His positions with the AAA have included vice president, southwest regional service president, and chair of several committees, including the Committee of Concepts and Standards. He was a member of the committee that planned the first AAA doctoral consortium and served as its director.

Tilly Jensen, Athabasca University–Alberta

Tilly Jensen graduated from the University of Alberta with a Bachelor of Commerce and later attained the designation of Certified Management Accountant. She worked in private industry for a number of years before making teaching her full-time career. Tilly was an accounting instructor at the Northern Alberta Institute of Technology (NAIT) in Edmonton, Alberta, for a number of years and is now an Assistant Professor of Accounting at Athabasca University, Canada's open, online university. She obtained her M.Ed. at the University of Sheffield in Britain while travelling abroad and completed her doctoral studies at the University of Calgary focusing on how educational technologies might be used to enhance critical thinking. Tilly spent four years in the Middle East teaching at Dubai Men's College of the Higher Colleges of Technology in the United Arab Emirates. While overseas, she also taught financial accounting to students enrolled in the Chartered Institute of Management Accountants (CIMA) program, a British professional accounting designation. During a sabbatical, Tilly also taught accounting in China to ESL students at Shenyang Ligong University. She authored LIFA—Lyryx Interactive Financial Accounting—a dynamic, leading-edge, Web-based teaching and learning tool produced by Lyryx. Tilly has also authored material for CGA-Canada. In addition to her professional interests, Tilly places a priority on time spent with her family and friends.

Heidi Dieckmann, Kwantlen Polytechnic University–British Columbia

Heidi Dieckmann graduated from Simon Fraser University in Burnaby, BC with a BBA in Accounting and carried on her studies in the Masters of Professional Accountancy Program at the University of Saskatchewan. Heidi attained her CA designation while working in public practice at KPMG in Burnaby before beginning her career in education as an Accounting instructor at Kwantlen Polytechnic University. While at KPU, Heidi has served as Department Chair and has sat on several committees. Her major initiatives at KPU included spearheading the Accounting Society of Kwantlen, an impressive accounting student club that has created opportunities for students to network with professional accountants in industry and public practice. She was also actively involved in the redesign of KPU's new BBA program and managed the detailed competency mapping for the new CPA designation. She is currently involved as a CPA Mentor, coaching upcoming CPAs through the new CPA education and experience requirements.

Heidi has a passion for student engagement and learning outcomes and is inspired by Eric Mazur's research on the Flipped Classroom and Peer Instruction, and Dee Fink's research in Creating Significant Learning Experiences. Heidi is a member of the Canadian Accountants Academics Association and has presented at the Learning Strategies Exchange for her work in student engagement through online education. She has been inspired to embrace international education through participating in the award-winning Canadian Academics Studying Europe conference led by Catherine Vertesi and Robert Buttery; visiting the European Union and the Council of Europe; and studying Swiss Banking at the University of Zurich, and political and education systems at the University of Applied Sciences and Arts Northwestern Switzerland. In her spare time Heidi enjoys volunteering through teaching art classes at her children's school. She loves to create new dishes; travel; and, most of all, spending time with her husband Andrew, her two children, and her close family and friends.

Brief Contents

Contents

CHAPTER 6
Inventory Costing and Valuation 390

CHAPTER 7
Internal Control and Cash 459

CONTENTS

Preface

A Note About Our Cover

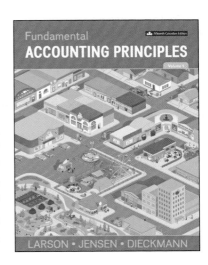

The cover of the Fifteenth Canadian Edition is the work of Rachel Idzerda. Rachel's playful illustration spotlights many of the companies, entrepreneurs, and organizations featured in *Fundamental Accounting Principles'* 17 chapter opening vignettes. See if you can spot the images representing Zane Caplansky's food truck (Chapter 1), Frogbox's green moving supplies (Chapter 3), Kicking Horse Coffee (Chapter 11), or ZooShare (Chapter 14). Rachel is a freelance illustrator specializing in editorial illustration and portraiture. She combines clean, delicate linework with bold colours and graphic elements to create a sense of energy and mood in her work. Rachel received her BAA in Illustration from Sheridan College in 2012, and currently lives and works in Montreal, QC with her partner and their two pampered dogs.

Inside the Chapters

As educators, instructors strive to create an environment that fosters learning and provides students with the tools they need to succeed. The Fifteenth Canadian Edition continues to meet and surpass the high standards the market expects from *Fundamental Accounting Principles*. We continue to put learning first, with student-centred pedagogy and critical thinking lessons throughout the text.

All the pedagogical tools are carefully designed for ease of use and understanding, helping the instructor teach and giving the students what they need to succeed.

Pedagogy

STUDENT SUCCESS CYCLE

Student success at the post-secondary level is not measured by how much knowledge a student has acquired, but rather by how well a student can *use* knowledge. The Student Success Cycle, illustrated by a circular icon, reinforces decision-making skills by highlighting key steps toward understanding and critically evaluating the information the student has just read. **Read–Do–Check–Apply** reinforces active learning rather than passive learning. This tool is integrated throughout the text, including the chapter opening page, Checkpoint questions, Demonstration Problems, and end-of-chapter material.

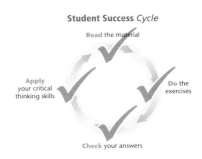

Student Success *Cycle*

Read the material

Do the exercises

Check your answers

Apply your critical thinking skills

CRITICAL THINKING CHALLENGE

An essential element of critical thinking is the ability to ask questions while reading (or listening or speaking). These exercises are designed to help students develop the skills related to questioning. Suggested answers are posted on **Connect**.

CRITICAL THINKING CHALLENGE Would Amazon have a merchandise turnover similar to Lululemon Athletica's? Explain why or why not. What does "inventory demand planning" refer to? What would the effect be of cost-saving strategies on the weighted average cost of inventory?

IFRS AND ASPE—THE DIFFERENCES

IFRS AND ASPE—THE DIFFERENCES		
Difference	International Financial Reporting Standards (IFRS)	Accounting Standards for Private Enterprises (ASPE)
Recording adjusting entries	• IFRS require that financial statements be presented at least annually*; therefore, adjustments would be prepared at least annually. However, for publicly listed companies, Securities Commissions' Law requires publicly listed companies to present quarterly financial statements, which, in turn, would require that adjusting entries be prepared at least quarterly.	• Unlike IFRS, ASPE does not explicitly require that financial statements be presented at least annually although it is implied given that financial statements must be presented in a timely manner** and items must be presented consistently from period to period.*** Financial statements are prepared at least annually for tax purposes and, for example, to meet any banking requirements.
	• Both public and private enterprises may prepare adjusting entries more frequently, such as monthly, to enhance the accuracy of information required for decision making.	
Depreciation vs. amortization	• IFRS uses the term *depreciation***** (although it uses *amortization* for intangible assets).*****	• ASPE uses the term *amortization*.******

*IFRS 2014, IAS 1 Para. 36.
**ASPE, Accounting Standards, Section 1000.17(b).
***ASPE, Accounting Standards, Section 1000.19–20.
****IFRS 2014, IAS 16 Para. 6.
*****IFRS 2014, IAS 38 Para. 8.
******ASPE, Accounting Standards, Section 3061.16.

This box appears at the end of every chapter to highlight any differences or important points about reporting and terminology as they relate to the financial accounting course. The chapter content is IFRS 2014 compliant for Volume I and IFRS 2015 compliant throughout Volume 2; references are provided where appropriate.

REAL-WORLD FOCUS

The Fifteenth Canadian Edition has increased the use of real business examples to reflect the most current information available. This continues the text's strong ties to the real world of accounting, be it through detailed interviews with businesspeople for the chapter opening vignettes, examples of ethical standards and treatments, or annual reports for both in-chapter example disclosures and end-of-chapter material. When an actual business is used, its name is highlighted in **bold magenta** for emphasis. This integration with real-world companies helps engage students while they read.

> A **business** is an entity represented by one or more individuals selling products or services for profit. Products sold include anything from athletic apparel (**CCM, Bauer, Lululemon, NIKE, Reebok**), to electronic devices (**Apple, Dell, Hewlett-Packard, Samsung**), and clothing (**Abercrombie and Fitch, GAP, Zara**). Service providers such as data communication providers (**Bell, Rogers,** and **Telus**), food services (**McDonald's, The Keg, Starbucks, Tim Hortons**), and internet services (**Google, Twitter, Skype, Facebook, Instagram**) make our lives more connected. A business can be as small as an in-home

Food Truck Frenzy

Across the country, major urban centres are experiencing an industry trend to go to the street to entice customers with a wide range of made-to-order food options. In Canada, the street vendor industry is in the growth phase of its industry life cycle, according to IBISWorld, a global market research firm. IBISWorld estimates the market for street vendors in Canada to be strong over the next five years with revenues expected to reach $281 million in 2018 and expected annual growth to cap out at 4.2% in 2015. The market is dominated by new market entrants—in most cases individual owners operating as sole proprietors. The most successful street vendors will take advantage of effective marketing and branding toward health-conscious consumers looking for unique dining options.

Thundering Thelma received her initial debut on CBC's *Dragons' Den* when owner Zane Caplansky decided to expand his famous brick-and-mortar deli in downtown Toronto and enter the trendy urban food truck business. After being labelled "insane Zane" by Kevin O'Leary, and the other Dragons balking at the 15% ownership interest at a proposed cost of $350,000, Zane decided to continue his new business venture on his own. A year later, Caplansky returned on *Dragons' Den* and boasted achieving profit margins between 30 and 40% and achieving $110,000 in sales in his first six months of operation. Caplansky's business continues to thrive with two new locations opening at the Toronto Pearson Airport, one modelled after his brick-and-mortar restaurant and the other modelled after his food truck.

Sources: http://clients1.ibisworld.ca/reports/ca/industry/industryoutlook.aspx?entid=1683, accessed April 15, 2014; http://www.torontolife.com/daily-dish/people-dish/2011/11/03/zane-capjansky-on-dragons-den, accessed April 15, 2014; http://www.postcity.com/Eat-Shop-Do/Eat/November-2013/Weekly-Restaurant-Recap-Harvest-Kitchen/;CBC Dragon's Den, Season 7, Episode 11, aired January 7, 2013.

Video Link: http://www.cbc.ca/dragonsden/episodes/season-7/episode-11-season-7

NEW VIDEO LINKS

This text features interactive digital links directing students and instructors to helpful videos to provide students with real world application of the chapter content and enhance student exposure to valuable online resources.

NEW: A LOOK BACK, A LOOK AT THIS CHAPTER, A LOOK AHEAD

In these brief paragraphs, students are directed to reflect on their learning from previous chapters; provided with a high-level summary of the current chapter; and introduced to the concepts covered in the following chapter. These helpful learning summaries help students focus on how their learning ties into big-picture objectives.

Receivables

A Look Back

Chapter 7 provides an introduction to Internal Control and Cash with a detailed analysis of internal control guidelines, banking activities, accounting for petty cash funds, and reconciling the differences between cash reported in the bank account and cash in the company's accounting records.

A Look at This Chapter

Chapter 8 takes a look at accounting for customer accounts receivable and short-term notes receivable, specifically investigating tools such as initial recognition of the receivables and subsequent measurement at the end of the accounting period. Valuation is assessed through methods to estimate bad debts, including the benefits of an A/R aging report, and using the accounts receivable turnover ratio and days' sales uncollected ratios to evaluate financial statements.

A Look Ahead

Chapter 9, the first chapter of Volume 2, investigates accounting issues for fixed assets under the following major categories: property, plant and equipment, and intangible assets. The chapter focuses on identifying all items that are included in their asset cost and analyzes options for matching their usage costs over their useful lives. Other considerations such as how to handle asset disposals, exchanges, and sales are analyzed.

LEARNING OBJECTIVES

Learning Objectives have long been a standard in the Larson textbook. By giving students a head start on what the following material encompasses, the text readies them for the work ahead.

CHECKPOINT

This series of questions within the chapter reinforces the material presented immediately before it. These questions allow students to "Do" problem material by referencing what they

CHECKPOINT

5. What is the difference between private and public accountants?
6. What are the four broad fields of accounting?
7. What is the purpose of an audit?
8. Distinguish between managerial and financial accounting.
9. What is the difference between external and internal users of accounting information?
10. Why are internal controls important?

Do Quick Study question: QS 1-5

have just learned. Answers at the end of each chapter will then allow them to "Check" their work, further supporting the Student Success Cycle. Under each set of Checkpoints is a reference to the Quick Study questions (single-topic exercises) available at the end of each chapter. Students can go ahead and try them at this point. Checkpoint solutions are at the end of the chapter. Quick Study solutions are available on **Connect.**

Important Tip: Ensure you know the following rules as illustrated in Exhibit 2.7 before reading Chapter 3. For a helpful learning tool, review the following video by Colin Dodds, an educational music video enthusiast.
Video Link: https://youtu.be/7EuxfW76BWU

NEW: IMPORTANT TIPS

Important tip boxes have been incorporated throughout the text to direct students' attention to critical concepts that students often miss in their initial reading of the text.

DECISION INSIGHT

Social responsibility continues to be important for students to learn early in their accounting courses. Through the Decision Insight feature, accounting's role in ethics and social responsibility is described by both reporting and assessing its impact. Relating theory to a real-life situation piques interest and reinforces active learning.

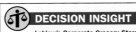

DECISION INSIGHT

Loblaw's Corporate Grocery Stores Go Perpetual

Loblaw Companies Limited, identifies its upgrade of its IT infrastructure as a positive move to enable the company to develop a more precise estimate through a "system-generated average cost." The company estimates "the impact of this inventory measurement and other conversion differences associated with implementation of a perpetual inventory system to be a $190 million decrease to the value of the inventory."

DECISION MAKER   Answer—End of chapter

Inventory Manager—Ethical Dilemma

You are the inventory manager for a trendy urban retail inventory merchandiser. Your compensation includes a bonus plan based on the amount of gross profit reported in the financial statements. Your supervisor comes to you and asks your opinion about changing the inventory costing method from moving weighted average to FIFO. Since costs have been rising and are expected to continue to rise, your superior predicts the company will be more attractive to investors because of the reported higher profit using FIFO. You realize this proposed change will likely increase your bonus as well. What do you recommend?

DECISION MAKER

This feature requires students to make accounting and business decisions by using role-playing to show the interaction of judgment and awareness, as well as the impact of decisions made. Guidance answers are available at the end of each chapter.

EXTEND YOUR KNOWLEDGE (EYK)

Supplementary material has been developed to explore some topics in more detail than the textbook can allow. A list of EYKs relevant to each chapter is presented at the end of the chapter, alerting students to visit **Connect** if they choose to delve deeper into the material.

For further study on some topics of relevance to this chapter, please see the following Extend Your Knowledge supplements:

EYK 4-1	Work Sheet Demonstration
EYK 4-2	Corporate Supplement
EYK 4-3	Summary of Business Activities
EYK 4-4	Examples of Classified Balance Sheets

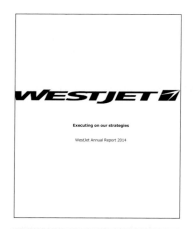

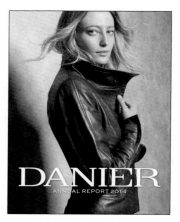

FINANCIAL STATEMENTS

Features and assignments that highlight companies such as **WestJet** (a company that provides services) and **Danier** (a merchandiser) show accounting in a modern and global context. Because students go directly to the financial statements of real companies, they remain engaged in the active learning process. The audited annual financial statement section of these annual reports (with notes to the financial statements), as well as those of **Indigo Books & Music**, and **Telus** (without the notes), are reproduced at the end of Volume 1. In Volume 2, the annual audited financial statements, **excluding** notes to the financial statements, for WestJet, Danier, Indigo, and Telus are included.

End-of-Chapter Material

Fundamental Accounting Principles sets the standard for quantity and quality of end-of-chapter material.

SUMMARY

Each chapter includes a Summary of the chapter by Learning Objective, to reinforce what students have just learned.

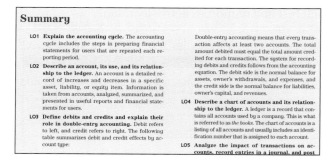

GUIDANCE ANSWERS TO DECISION MAKER

These discuss the Decision Maker boxes presented earlier in the chapter, and reinforce the need for decision making and critical thinking skills. This feature fits into the Student Success Cycle by reinforcing the "Apply" step.

GUIDANCE ANSWERS TO CHECKPOINT

Guidance Answers to CHECKPOINT

1. Best Buy.
2. Total cost is $12,180, calculated as:
   $11,400 + $130 + $150 + $100 + $400.
3. The matching principle.
4. Businesses that sell unique, high dollar–value merchandise in relatively low volume levels might choose specific identification. Car dealerships are a good example because each car received as merchandise inventory is unique in terms of both features and identification number. Using specific identification allows the business to accurately tag each item coming in and going out.
5. Moving weighted average gives a lower inventory figure on the balance sheet as compared to FIFO. FIFO's inventory amount will approximate current replacement costs. Moving weighted average costs increase but more slowly because of the effect of averaging.
6. Because these units are the same ones that were originally written down, a reversal is appropriate and would be recorded as:

Merchandise Inventory	2,000	
Cost of Goods Sold		2,000

$1,800 − $1,300 = $500/unit original write-down; $500 × 4 = $2,000 maximum reversal

7. The reported inventory amount is $540, calculated as (20 × $5) + (40 × $8) + (10 × $12).
8. Cost of goods sold is understated by $10,000 in 2017 and overstated by $10,000 in 2018.
9. The estimated ending inventory (at cost) is $327,000 and is calculated as:
   Step 1: ($530,000 + $335,000) − $320,000 = $545,000
   Step 2: $\dfrac{\$324,000 + \$195,000}{\$530,000 + \$335,000} = 60\%$
   Step 3: $545,000 × 60% = $327,000
10. Company B is more efficient at selling its inventory because it has higher merchandise turnover.

GUIDANCE ANSWERS TO CHECKPOINT

The Checkpoint material throughout the chapter allows students to pause and check their progress. This feature reinforces the "Do," "Check," and "Apply" steps of the Student Success Cycle.

GLOSSARY

All terms highlighted in the chapter are included.

Glossary

Consignee One who receives and holds goods owned by another party for the purpose of acting as an agent and selling the goods for the owner. The consignee gets paid a fee from the consignor for finding a buyer.

Consignor An owner of inventory goods who ships them to another party who will then find a buyer and sell the goods for the owner. The consignor retains title to the goods while they are held offsite by the consignee.

Consistency principle The accounting requirement that a company use the same accounting policies period after period so that the financial statements of succeeding periods will be comparable.

Days' sales in inventory A financial analysis tool used to estimate how many days it will take to convert the inventory on hand into accounts receivable or cash; calculated by dividing the ending inventory by cost of goods sold and multiplying the result by 365.

Faithful representation The accounting principle that requires information to be complete, neutral, unbiased, and free from error.

First-in, first-out (FIFO) The pricing of an inventory under the assumption that inventory items are sold in the order acquired; the first items received are the first items sold.

Problem Material

DEMONSTRATION PROBLEM

This Demonstration Problem is based on the same facts as the Demonstration Problem at the end of Chapter 1 except for two additional items: (b) August 1 and (k) August 18. The following activities occurred during the first month of Joanne Cardinal's new haircutting business called The Cutlery:

a. On August 1, Cardinal put $16,000 cash into a chequing account in the name of The Cutlery. She also invested $10,000 of equipment that she already owned.
b. On August 1, Cardinal paid $2,400 for six months of insurance effective immediately.
c. On August 2, she paid $2,000 cash for furniture for the shop.
d. On August 3, she paid $3,200 cash to rent space in a strip mall for August.
e. On August 4, she furnished the shop by installing the old equipment and some new equipment that she bought on credit for $21,000. This amount is to be repaid in three equal payments at the end of August, September, and October.

DEMONSTRATION PROBLEMS

These problems reinforce the chapter material and further bolster the Student Success Cycle.

ANALYSIS COMPONENT

An analysis component is included in each Mid- and End-of-Chapter Demonstration Problem, as well as several Exercises, Problems, and Focus on Financial Statements questions. These promote critical thinking and give students opportunities to practise their analytical skills.

Analysis Component:
Refer to The Cutlery's August 31, 2017, financial statements. What do each of *equity* and *liabilities* represent?

Concept Review Questions

1. What tasks are performed with the work sheet?
2. What two purposes are accomplished by recording closing entries?
3. What are the four closing entries?
4. Daniel is having trouble determining whether withdrawals, the owner's capital, interest income and prepaid insurance are temporary or permanent accounts. Explain to him the difference between a temporary and a permanent account in accounting and classify the accounts into each category.
9. Refer to Danier's income statement in Appendix III at the end of the book. What journal entry was recorded as of June 28, 2014, to close the revenue account?
10. What is a company's operating cycle?
11. Why is a classified balance sheet more useful to financial statement users than a non-classified balance sheet?
12. What classes of assets and liabilities are shown on a typical classified balance sheet?

CONCEPT REVIEW QUESTIONS

These short-answer questions reinforce the chapter content by Learning Objective.

QUICK STUDY

These single-topic exercises give students a quick test of each key element in the chapter and are referenced to Learning Objectives. Answers to these items are available on **Connect.**

Quick Study

QS 6-1 Inventory ownership LO1

1. At year-end Carefree Company has shipped, FOB destination, $500 of merchandise that is still in transit to Stark Company. Which company should include the $500 as part of inventory at year-end?
2. Carefree Company has shipped goods to Stark and has an arrangement that Stark will sell the goods for Carefree. Identify the consignor and the consignee. Which company should include any unsold goods as part of inventory?

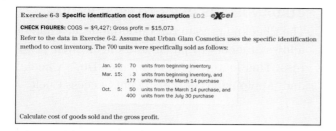

Exercise 6-3 Specific identification cost flow assumption LO2 e**X**cel

CHECK FIGURES: COGS = $9,427; Gross profit = $15,073

Refer to the data in Exercise 6-2. Assume that Urban Glam Cosmetics uses the specific identification method to cost inventory. The 700 units were specifically sold as follows:

Jan. 10:	70	units from beginning inventory
Mar. 15:	3	units from beginning inventory, and
	177	units from the March 14 purchase
Oct. 5:	50	units from the March 14 purchase, and
	400	units from the July 30 purchase

Calculate cost of goods sold and the gross profit.

EXERCISES

Exercises provide students with an additional opportunity to reinforce basic chapter concepts by Learning Objective. Note: Selected end-of-chapter exercises and problems are marked with this icon: e**X**cel. These have Excel templates located on **Connect**.

PROBLEMS

Problems typically incorporate two or more concepts. As well, there are two groups of Problems: A Problems and Alternate or (B) Problems. B Problems mirror the A Problems to help improve understanding through repetition.

Problems

Problem 1-1A Identifying type of business organization LO2

Complete the chart below by placing a checkmark in the appropriate column.

	Type of Business Organization		
Characteristic	Sole Proprietorship	Partnership	Corporation
Limited liability			
Unlimited liability			
Owners are shareholders			
Owners are partners			
Taxed as a separate legal entity			

Ethics Challenge

EC 5-1

Claire Phelps is a popular high school student who attends approximately four dances a year at her high school. Each dance requires a new dress and accessories that necessitate a financial outlay of $100 to $200 per event. Claire's parents inform her that she is on her own with respect to financing the dresses. After incurring a major hit to her savings for the first dance in her second year, Claire developed a different approach. She buys the dress on credit the week before the dance, wears it to the dance, and returns the dress the next week to the store for a full refund on her charge card.

Required

1. Comment on the ethics exhibited by Claire and possible consequences of her actions.
2. How does the store account for the dresses that Claire returns?

ETHICS CHALLENGE

Each chapter includes at least one Ethics Challenge to reinforce critical thinking skills for students and open up discussion about various ethical topics.

FOCUS ON FINANCIAL STATEMENTS

Each chapter includes two technical and analytical questions that incorporate into the financial statements all major topics covered up to that point. Additional questions are available online on **Connect**.

Focus on Financial Statements

FFS 2-1

Travis McAllister operates a surveying company. For the first few months of the company's life (through April), the accounting records were maintained by an outside bookkeeping service. According to those records, McAllister's equity balance was $75,000 as of April 30. To save on expenses, McAllister decided to keep the records himself. He managed to record May's transactions properly, but was a bit rusty when the time came to prepare the financial statements. His first versions of the balance sheet and income statement follow. McAllister is bothered that the company apparently operated at a loss during the month, even though he was very busy.

McAllister Surveying
Income Statement
For Month Ended May 31, 2017

Revenue:		
Investments by owner	$	3,000
Unearned surveying fees		6,000
Total revenues	$	9,000

Critical Thinking Mini Case

Prairie Insurance sells life insurance, disability insurance, vehicle insurance, crop insurance, and homeowners' insurance. You are employed by Prairie Insurance and have been promoted to sales division manager for the Western Canadian division. You will be supervising approximately 25 salespeople, along with five administrative assistants at various locations. The salespeople travel extensively and submit expense reports along with sales information monthly. A sample expense report for September shows:

Prairie Insurance—Western Canadian Division
Sales Report: John Bishop
Month Ended September 30, 2017

Sales revenue*	$56,000
Expenses**	34,000

*Sales invoices attached
**Receipts attached

CRITICAL THINKING MINI CASES

These cases give students the opportunity to apply critical thinking skills to concepts learned in the chapter, thus further reinforcing the "Apply" step of the Student Success Cycle.

HELP ME SOLVE IT

New *Help Me Solve It* tutorials are available on **Connect** for Larson's *Fundamental Accounting Principles*. The tutorials guide students through one or two of the more challenging end-of-chapter problems per chapter, providing them with an engaging visual and audio walkthrough of the problem.

Help Me
SOLVE IT

What's New

The Accounting Standard

We listened! Through extensive reviewing and consultations with the market, we have heard the issues and concerns instructors like you have about the materials you use to teach introductory financial accounting. Here you will find a list of new changes to specific chapters that our author has made to ensure the content of Larson's *Fundamental Accounting Principles* remains current and fresh. Whether you are new to using *Fundamental Accounting Principles* or new to this edition, you can see that McGraw-Hill Education and Larson/Jensen/Dieckmann are setting the accounting standard in *Fundamental Accounting Principles*. We know you'll like what you see.

General Updates

- Appendix III for Volume 1 includes the complete annual audited financial statements, including notes to the financial statements, for WestJet and Danier Leather, as well as the audited financial statements *without* the notes for Indigo Books & Music and Telus. Appendix II for Volume 2 includes the annual audited financial statements, *excluding* notes to the financial statements, for WestJet, Danier Leather, Indigo, and Telus.

- Throughout Volumes 1 and 2, the exercises and problems have been refreshed in terms of numbers and/or business name/owner with a focus on providing relevant company examples to connect with today's students. Company scenarios have been expanded and updated to provide students with more information and updated examples to enhance student engagement. Volume 1 end-of-chapter content was revised by Praise Ma of Kwantlen Polytechnic University, and Volume 2 by Laura Dallas, also of Kwantlen Polytechnic University.

- Various end-of-chapter exercises/problems have been adjusted to incorporate instructor and reviewer suggestions.

- The chapter content is IFRS 2014 compliant throughout Volume I and IFRS 2015 compliant throughout Volume 2; IFRS 2014/2015 references are included where appropriate.

- The 15th edition includes 14 exciting *new* chapter opening vignettes, featuring a range of engaging topics, and including inspiring stories from company startups to success stories of well-known businesses and not-for-profit organizations. Additionally, Chapter 7's vignette features an analysis titled "What Is Cash?" outlining the vast array of Canadian payment options available today. Nearly all of the vignettes now include relevant video links for students to broaden their real-world exposure to critical business decisions.

- Actual businesses used as examples throughout Volumes 1 and 2 are bolded and highlighted in magenta at first mention to emphasize integration of accounting concepts with actual business practice.

- IFRS and ASPE differences are identified at the end of each chapter.

- Important tip boxes have been incorporated throughout the text to direct students' attention to critical concepts that students often miss in their initial reading of the text.

- Many new exhibits have been added, including several new learning summaries to assist students in tying together chapter concepts. Many existing exhibits have been refreshed as appropriate with updated information.

- Several new excerpts have been added to direct students' attention to real-company example disclosures in their most recent published annual financial statement reports.

- The number of actual business examples has increased based on review requests; these have been bolded and highlighted in magenta at first mention for emphasis.
- NEW presentation displays all formulas students need to pay attention to in purple boxes.

Chapter-by-Chapter Updates

CHAPTER 1

- New chapter opening vignette featuring entrepreneur Zane Caplansky, founder of Caplansky's Deli and the food truck "Thunderin' Thelma" as featured on CBC's the *Dragons' Den*. A new video link provides students with access to the *Dragons' Den* episode.
- Introduction of new chapter demonstration company, *Organico,* a food truck business.
- New *Decision Insight* on the Chartered Professional Accountants of Ontario's Approach to Ethical Conflict Resolution.
- New *Decision Insight* on the Vancouver Portland Hotel Society's employee travel expenses scandal.
- Updated Exhibit 1.5 charting average annual salaries for accounting positions.
- New Exhibit 1.6: Summary Model of GAAP Framework.
- New Exhibit 1.12 summarizing the elements of financial statements.
- Refreshed section on ethics.

CHAPTER 2

- New chapter opening vignette featuring Olympic double gold medalist, Alexandre Bilodeau. New video link provides a motivating interview with Alexandre Bilodeau.
- Updated transaction analysis chapter demonstration company, *Organico,* linked to Chapter 1.
- Updated presentation and approach to mid-chapter demonstration problem makes the transaction analysis section easier to follow.

- Important Tips boxes added to provide extra support in topic areas where students typically struggle.
- Updated Exhibit 2.8 presentation of revenue and expenses in relation to equity.
- Reordered chapter presentation on recording and posting transactions, and accounting transactions in action, to improve student connections of material to real-world application.

CHAPTER 3

- Updated chapter opening vignette featuring green moving box supplier, Frogbox. New video link features the company's *Dragons' Den* debut and *Dragons' Den* Update episodes.
- Updated adjusting entry analysis chapter demonstration company, *Organico,* linked to preceding chapters.
- Simplified descriptions of each current asset item.
- Updated *Decision Insight* on the Chris Brown concert scam impacting the Chronico Music Group.
- Important Tip boxes added regarding requirement to use accrual accounting, reminding students that adjusting entries do not affect cash, and drawing students' attention to techniques to determine the ending capital balance.

CHAPTER 4

- New chapter opening vignette features founders of BC startup Cupcakes, as featured on their reality series *The Cupcake Girls* on W, We TV, and the Oprah Network (OWN). Vignette includes a link to an interview with the founders discussing entrepreneurship and leadership advice.
- Important Tip box added, emphasizing that the closing process involves only temporary accounts.
- Updated mid-chapter Demonstration Problem to Melodies Piano School.
- Updated terminology for long-term liabilities section of the classified balance sheet to non-current liabilities.
- New Exhibit 4.15 featuring example presentation of current assets for Apple Inc.

- New section on Financial Statement Analysis moving coverage of current ratio from Appendix A to body of chapter. In addition, the quick ratio and debt to equity ratio were added to chapter content.

CHAPTER 5

- Updated chapter opening vignette featuring Mountain Equipment Co-op (MEC), including a new video link to demonstrate MEC's business structure.
- New effective summary table outlines Merchandising Inventory Journal Entries— Perpetual and Merchandising Inventory Journal Entries—Periodic.
- New *Decision Insight* covers Loblaw Companies' transition from periodic to perpetual inventory system.
- New Exhibit 5.18: Gross Margin Snapshot by Company.
- Several new Important Tip boxes on accounting for periodic and perpetual inventory sales and purchases.
- New Financial Statement Analysis sections added for Gross Margin and how markups are calculated.
- New terminology for trade discounts provided for volume purchases and purchase discounts for early payment.
- New *Decision Insight* discusses inventory shrinkage.
- Enhanced discussion covering inventory shrinkage for merchandising adjusting entries.
- Enhanced Appendix 5B discussion on PST, GST, and HST.
- New Exhibit 5B.1 summarizing zero-rated and exempt products for GST.
- Updated Exhibit 5B.2, organizing Sales Tax Rates for rate changes, and restructured into a more student-friendly format.

CHAPTER 6

- New chapter opening vignette features inventory innovation at Amazon.com, including

video links outlining Amazon's warehouse operations, demonstrating its kiva robots, and demonstrating the company's octocopter drones.

- New *Decision Insight* addresses Loblaw Companies' move to perpetual inventory.
- New section highlights inventory costing policies for four companies: Amazon.com, Lululemon Athletica, Proctor & Gamble, and Tiffany & Co.
- New Important Tip boxes regarding accounting for perpetual inventory systems, and calculating the gross profit method.
- New examples providing accounting policy disclosures for Amazon.com Inc., Lululemon Athletica, Procter & Gamble Company, Tiffany & Co., illustrating the various inventory costing alternatives.
- Enhanced coverage of Advantages and Disadvantages of Cost Flow Assumptions.
- New note disclosure for TJX Companies Inc. illustrating the retail method of inventory.
- Expanded coverage of Retail Inventory Method.
- New Financial Statement Analysis section added, bringing inventory turnover and day's sales in inventory into chapter discussion.

CHAPTER 7 (FORMER CHAPTER 8)

- New chapter opening vignette features an analysis of "What Is Cash?" investigating today's payment options in Canada, and outlining the important role of the Canadian Payments Association. New video links are provided for students who want to learn more about how the complex payment system functions in Canada.
- New Important Tip box addresses CAR principle to simplify understanding of control issues and provide students with an approach to responding to identified control weaknesses, demonstrating understanding of debits and credits from the bank's perspective.
- Enhanced discussion of controls to clarify identification and implications of control weaknesses and provide guidance on how to develop recommendations for improvements.

- Enhanced chapter demonstration of steps in reconciling a bank balance, and an improved summary of required adjustments to the bank's balance and the cash book balance.
- New section on the Fraud Triangle and the Drivers of Fraud (includes two new exhibits).
- New *Decision Insight* covers ATM hacker cybercriminals.
- New description of cash and cash equivalents and example disclosure of accounting policy for Amazon.
- New *Decision Insight* on Bank of Canada controls over currency, including a video link to a Bank of Canada video on identifying counterfeit currency.
- New Financial Statement Analysis section for Quick Ratio highlights differences with Current Ratio in body of text (moved from appendix).

CHAPTER 8 (FORMER CHAPTER 9)

- New chapter opening vignette discussing BC–based WN Pharmaceuticals, including insight into the company's approach to the management of customer receivables.
- Coverage of quick ratio moved from appendix into chapter.
- New *Decision Insight* box covers recent applications from Rogers Canada and Walmart Canada to operate as financial institutions in Canada.
- Updated Exhibit 8.1: Accounts Receivable Analysis for Selected Companies as a Percentage of Total Assets.
- New excerpt from Canadian Tire's annual report describing its risk management process for customers.
- New section on Accounts Receivable with Revenue recognition criteria.
- Updated coverage of store-issued credit cards to reflect current approach used by companies.

- New section on Credit Risk Analysis.
- New Important Tip box on calculating interest for Short-Term Notes Receivable.
- New section on Accounts Receivable Control Considerations to reinforce Chapter 7 control concepts and integrate into Accounts Receivable.
- Added a Financial Statement Analysis section incorporating A/R turnover and days' sales (moved from appendix).
- New Exhibit 8.21: Comparison of Accounts Receivable Turnover and Days' Sales Uncollected for High Liner Foods Incorporated and Maple Leaf Foods Inc.

APPENDIX I

- All rates (i.e., EI, CPP, Provincial Tax, Federal Tax) updated to 2015.

APPENDIX II (FORMER CHAPTER 7)

- Responding to reviewer feedback, the former Chapter 7, Accounting Information Systems, has been relocated to an online appendix.

APPENDIX III (FORMER APPENDIX II)

- Volume 1 includes annual audited financial statements (including notes to the financial statements) for WestJet and Danier Leather and annual audited financial statements (excluding notes to the financial statements) for Telus Corporation and Indigo Books & Music.
- Volume 2 includes annual audited financial statements (***excluding*** notes to the financial statements) for WestJet, Danier Leather, Telus Corporation, and Indigo Books & Music.

APPENDIX IV (FORMER APPENDIX III)

- Sample chart of accounts updated to reflect textbook content.

Market Leading Technology

connect

Learn without Limits

McGraw-Hill Connect® is an award-winning digital teaching and learning platform that gives students the means to better connect with their coursework, with their instructors, and with the important concepts that they will need to know for success now and in the future. With Connect, instructors can take advantage of McGraw-Hill's trusted content to seamlessly deliver assignments, quizzes and tests online. McGraw-Hill Connect is the only learning platform that continually adapts to each student, delivering precisely what they need, when they need it, so class time is more engaging and effective. Connect makes teaching and learning personal, easy, and proven.

Connect Key Features:

SMARTBOOK®

As the first and only adaptive reading experience, SmartBook is changing the way students read and learn. SmartBook creates a personalized reading experience by highlighting the most important concepts a student needs to learn at that moment in time. As a student engages with SmartBook, the reading experience continuously adapts by highlighting content based on what each student knows and doesn't know. This ensures that he or she is focused on the content needed to close specific knowledge gaps, while it simultaneously promotes long-term learning.

CONNECT INSIGHT®

Connect Insight is Connect's new one-of-a-kind visual analytics dashboard—now available for both instructors and students—that provides at-a-glance information regarding student performance, which is immediately actionable. By presenting assignment, assessment, and topical performance results together with a time metric that is easily visible for aggregate or individual results, Connect Insight gives the user the ability to take a just-in-time approach to teaching and learning, which was never before available. Connect Insight presents data that empowers students and helps instructors improve class performance in a way that is efficient and effective.

SIMPLE ASSIGNMENT MANAGEMENT

With Connect, creating assignments is easier than ever, so instructors can spend more time teaching and less time managing.

- Assign SmartBook learning modules
- Instructors can edit existing questions and create their own questions
- Draw from a variety of text specific questions, resources, and test bank material to assign online
- Streamline lesson planning, student progress reporting, and assignment grading to make classroom management more efficient than ever

SMART GRADING

When it comes to studying, time is precious. Connect helps students learn more efficiently by providing feedback and practice material when they need it, where they need it.

- Automatically score assignments, providing students immediate feedback on their work and comparisons with correct answers
- Access and review each response, manually change grades, or leave comments for students to review

- Track individual student performance—by question or assignment, or in relation to the class overall—with detailed grade reports.

- Reinforce classroom concepts with practice tests and instant quizzes.

- Integrate grade reports easily with Learning Management Systems including Blackboard, D2L, and Moodle.

INSTRUCTOR LIBRARY

The Connect Instructor Library is a repository for additional resources to improve student engagement in and out of the class. It provides all the critical resources instructors need to build their course. Instructors can

- Access Instructor resources

- View assignments and resources created for past sections

- Post their own resources for students to use

Instructor Resources

Instructor supplements are available within **Connect**.

SOLUTIONS MANUAL

Fundamental Accounting Principles continues to set the standard for accuracy of its problem material. The Solutions Manual has been revised by Praise Ma, Kwantlen Polytechnic University (Volume 1) and Laura Dallas, Kwantlen Polytechnic University (Volume 2). Additional accuracy checking was provided by Rhonda Heninger, SAIT Polytechnic, Elizabeth Hicks, Douglas College, and Michelle Young, CPA. Available in both Microsoft Word and PDF format, solutions for all problem material are included.

COMPUTERIZED TEST BANK

The test bank has been revised and technically checked for accuracy to reflect the changes in the Fifteenth Canadian Edition. Carol Tristani, Mohawk College, revised the test bank for this edition. Grouped according to Learning Objective, difficulty level, and by level of Bloom's Taxonomy, the questions in the computerized test bank include true/false, multiple choice, matching, short essay, and problem material.

POWERPOINT® PRESENTATIONS

These presentation slides, revised by Betty Young, Red River College, are fully integrated with the text to visually present chapter concepts.

INSTRUCTOR'S MANUAL

The Instructor's Manual, revised by Denise Cook, Durham College (Volume 1) and Joe Pidutti, Durham College (Volume 2), cross-references assignment materials by Learning Objective and also provides a convenient chapter outline.

FOCUS ON FINANCIAL STATEMENTS

These include technical and analytical questions that incorporate major topics covered. These, and accompanying solutions in the Solutions Manual, have been revised by Stephanie Ibach, MacEwan University. Two additional Focus on Financial Statement exercises for each chapter are included on Connect.

EXTEND YOUR KNOWLEDGE

This supplemental material has been developed to delve into more detail for specific topics. These have been revised by Stephanie Ibach, MacEwan University.

EXCEL TEMPLATE SOLUTIONS

Solutions to the problems using Excel templates are available for instructors. These have been revised by Ian Feltmate, Acadia University.

IMAGE BANK

All exhibits and tables displayed in the text are available for your use, whether for creating transparencies or handouts, or customizing your own PowerPoint presentations.

Other Supplements for Students

WORKING PAPERS

Available for purchase by students, printed Working Papers for Volumes 1 and 2 match the end-of-chapter material. They include papers that can be used to solve all of the Quick Study questions, Exercises, and A and B Problem sets. The Working Papers for the Fifteenth Canadian Edition have been revised by Praise Ma, Kwantlen Polytechnic University (Volume 1) and Laura Dallas, Kwantlen Polytechnic University (Volume 2). Additional technical checking was completed by Michelle Young.

Superior Learning Solutions and Support

The McGraw-Hill Education team is ready to help instructors assess and integrate any of our products, technology, and services into your course for optimal teaching and learning performance. Whether it's helping your students improve their grades, or putting your entire course online, the McGraw-Hill Education team is here to help you do it. Contact your Learning Solutions Consultant today to learn how to maximize all of McGraw-Hill Education's resources.

For more information, please visit us online: http://www.mheducation.ca/highereducation/educators/digital-solutions

Developing a Market-Driven Text

The success of this text is the result of an exhaustive process, which has gone beyond the scope of a single edition. Hundreds of instructors and educators across the country have been involved in giving their feedback to help develop the most successful accounting fundamentals text in the country. We owe thanks to all of those who took the time to evaluate this textbook and its supplemental products.

Fifteenth Canadian Edition Reviewers

Joan Baines	*Red River College*	Rod Delcourt	*Algonquin College*
Les Barnhouse	*Grant MacEwan University*	Kevin deWolde	*University of the Fraser Valley*
Maria Belanger	*Algonquin College*	Han Donker	*University of Northern British*
Robert Briggs	*New Brunswick Community*		*Columbia*
	College	David Fleming	*George Brown College*
Lewis Callahan	*Lethbridge College*	Brent Groen	*University of Fraser Valley*
Barb Chapple	*St. Clair College*	Kerry Hendricks	*Fanshawe College*
Shiraz Charania	*Langara College*	Rhonda Heninger	*Southern Alberta Institute of*
Denise Cook	*Durham College*		*Technology*
Derek Cook	*Okanagan College*	Elizabeth Hicks	*Douglas College*
Heather Cornish	*Northern Alberta Institute of*	Darcie Hillebrand	*Capilano University*
	Technology	Gwen Hoyseth	*Grande Prairie Regional College*

Yvonne Jacobs	*College of the North Atlantic*	Doug Ringrose	*Grant MacEwan University*
Lauren Kirychuk	*Bow Valley College*	Pina Salvaggio	*Dawson College*
Laurette Korman	*Kwantlen Polytechnic University*	David Scott	*Niagara College*
Michelle Nicholson	*Okanagan College*	Glen Stanger	*Douglas College*
Tariq Nizami	*Champlain Regional College*	Doug Thibodeau	*Nova Scotia Community College*
Joe Pidutti	*Durham College*	Peggy Wallace	*Trent University*
Traven Reed	*Canadore College*	Patricia Zima	*Mohawk College*
James Reimer	*Lethbridge College*		

Fundamental Accounting Principles continues to set the bar in terms of its leading-edge approach to educating today's students through outstanding quality, dependable accuracy, and state-of-the-art supplemental resources.

This has been possible only because of the outstanding efforts and contributions of a dedicated team of exceptional individuals. I owe many thanks to their expertise and commitment as it was extensively drawn upon during the process of writing this textbook. Particular thanks go out to Maria Belanger, Shannon Butler, Denise Cook, Ian Feltmate, Rhonda Heninger, Elizabeth Hicks, Stephanie Ibach, Joe Pidutti, Don Smith, Carol Tristani, Betty Young, and Michelle Young. A big thanks to the many entrepreneurs, financial experts, and business owners that devoted their precious time to making our chapter opening vignettes compelling and captivating. Thanks also to our brilliant illustrator, Rachel Idzerda (www.rachelidzerda.com), for sharing our vision and for her tireless efforts in crafting our cover illustration with creativity and vibrant energy. A special thanks to my close friends and colleagues Praise Ma and Laura Dallas for approaching the project with a fresh perspective. Their innovative spirits and their outstanding dedication ensure the end-of-chapter questions are accurate, relevant and engaging for today's students. I am thankful to McGraw-Hill Ryerson's exceptional team, including Rhondda McNabb, Joy Armitage Taylor, Keara Emmett, Sarah Fulton May, Jessica Barnoski, and freelance copyeditor Karen Rolfe, who have been exceptionally responsive, supportive and dedicated to producing a phenomenal product.

I am incredibly appreciative to my colleagues across Canada and current and past students who have inspired enhancements for this edition. Their knowledge and expertise in identifying student learning hurdles in the classroom and suggestions for enhancing student comprehension are invaluable in our continuous improvement initiative to maintain this textbook as the industry standard.

With heartfelt appreciation,
Heidi Dieckmann

Accounting in Business

A Look at This Chapter

Accounting is crucial in our information age. In this chapter, we discuss the importance of accounting to different types of organizations and describe its many users and uses. We explain that ethics are essential to accounting. We also explain business transactions and how they are reflected in financial statements.

© Rene Johnston/GetStock.com

LEARNING OBJECTIVES

LO1 Describe the purpose and importance of accounting.

LO2 Describe forms of business organization.

LO3 Identify users and uses of, and opportunities in, accounting.

LO4 Identify and explain why ethics and social responsibility are crucial to accounting.

LO5 Identify, explain, and apply accounting principles.

LO6 Identify and explain the content and reporting aims of financial statements.

LO7 Analyze business transactions by applying the accounting equation.

LO8 Prepare financial statements reflecting business transactions.

Food Truck Frenzy

Across the country, major urban centres are experiencing an industry trend to go to the street to entice customers with a wide range of made-to-order food options. In Canada, the street vendor industry is in the growth phase of its industry life cycle, according to IBISWorld, a global market research firm. IBISWorld estimates the market for street vendors in Canada to be strong over the next five years with revenues expected to reach $281 million in 2018 and expected annual growth to cap out at 4.2% in 2015. The market is dominated by new market entrants—in most cases individual owners operating as sole proprietors. The most successful street vendors will take advantage of effective marketing and branding toward health-conscious consumers looking for unique dining options.

Thundering Thelma received her initial debut on CBC's *Dragons' Den* when owner Zane Caplansky decided to expand his famous brick-and-mortar deli in downtown Toronto and enter the trendy urban food truck business. After being labelled "insane Zane" by Kevin O'Leary, and the other Dragons balking at the 15% ownership interest at a proposed cost of $350,000, Zane decided to continue his new business venture on his own. A year later, Caplansky returned to *Dragons' Den* and boasted achieving profit margins between 30 and 40% and achieving $110,000 in sales in his first six months of operation. Caplansky's business continues to thrive with two new locations opening at the Toronto Pearson Airport, one modelled after his brick-and-mortar restaurant and the other modelled after his food truck.

Sources: http://clients1.ibisworld.ca/reports/ca/industry/industryoutlook.aspx?entid=1683, accessed April 15, 2014; http://www.torontolife.com/daily-dish/people-dish/2011/11/03/zane-caplansky-on-dragons-den, accessed April 15, 2014; http://www.postcity.com/Eat-Shop-Do/Eat/November-2013/Weekly-Restaurant-Recap-Harvest-Kitchen/;CBC Dragon's Den, Season 7, Episode 11, aired January 7, 2013.

Video Link: http://www.cbc.ca/dragonsden/episodes/season-7/episode-11-season-7

CRITICAL THINKING CHALLENGE	What questions might Caplansky need to answer in order to get a loan from a bank? Who else might require accounting information from Caplansky's business?

 An essential element of critical thinking is the ability to ask questions while reading (or listening or speaking). This exercise is designed to help students develop the skills related to questioning. Suggested answers are available on Connect.

CHAPTER PREVIEW

 A chapter preview introduces the importance and relevance of the material, and also links these materials to the opening article to help you understand how what you are learning in the chapter relates to the real world through practical examples.

Accounting is at the heart of business: accounting information pulsates throughout an organization, feeding decision makers with details needed to give them an edge over competitors. Whether you have your sights set on a career in the field of accounting, human resources, finance, marketing, or entrepreneurship, you will find the study of financial accounting integral to your ability to communicate successfully in the world of business. Through your study of this book, you will learn about key accounting concepts and develop an ability to interpret financial information that is essential for making sound business decisions.

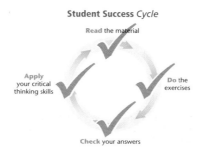

Student Success *Cycle*

This first chapter accomplishes three goals. First, it introduces the subject of accounting, providing a foundation for those students who have little or no understanding of business or the role of accounting in business.

ORGANICO

Second, it focuses on how accounting information is created and communicated in the form of *financial statements*, which report on the financial performance and condition of an organization. This chapter will illustrate how transactions are reflected in financial statements by illustrating chapter concepts through an in-depth demonstration of entrepreneur Hailey Walker, who decides to start up a new food truck business called Organico, specializing in fresh, organic Mexican burritos. The illustration begins with Walker registering her business name and commencing her first month of operations on March 1, 2017.

Third, it introduces you to each of the learning features found in most chapters. For example, a note above explains the purpose of the chapter preview, and three additional features (Learning Objectives, boldfaced terms, and company names) are described below. Some of the features refer to Connect, located on the web. Take the time in this chapter to explore and learn the value of these additional resources.

What Is Accounting?

LO1 Describe the purpose and importance of accounting.

↑ Each chapter is separated into chunks of information called learning objectives (LO). Each LO tells you what needs to be mastered in that section of reading.

Accounting knowledge is a powerful tool; it provides you with essential information to make critical business decisions. How does accounting knowledge give you power? What exactly is the focus of accounting? This section answers these fundamental questions.

Power of Accounting

Accounting is an information system that identifies, measures, records, and communicates *relevant* information that *objectively and correctly represents* an organization's economic activities,[1] as shown in Exhibit 1.1. Its objective is to help people make better decisions. It also helps people better assess opportunities, products, investments, and social and community responsibilities. In addition to reporting on the performance of a business, what the business owns, and what it owes, accounting opens our eyes to new and exciting possibilities. Put more simply, accounting involves collecting relevant information, recording it, and then reporting it to various decision makers. In the chapter opening story, for example, **Caplansky's Food Truck** collects and records accounting information so that it could be reported to Zane Caplansky, the business owner, and other investors, to help them make important decisions—such as those involved in setting selling prices for his deli sandwiches—and develop an effective expansion strategy.

↑ Boldfaced words or phrases represent new terminology that is explained here and defined in the glossary at the end of the chapter.

Real company names are printed in bold magenta.

---

1 When information makes a difference in the decisions made by users, it is *relevant*. For information to possess the quality of *faithful representation*, it must be complete, neutral, and free from error, IFRS 2014 "The conceptual framework for financial reporting: para. QC5-QC6, QC 12. These primary qualitative characteristics of useful accounting information will be discussed in more detail later in this chapter.

EXHIBIT 1.1

Accounting Activities

Identifying	Recording	Communicating

© Diane Diederich/istockphoto.com   © JGI/Tom Gril/Blend Images LLC   © shironosov/istockphoto.com

Focus of Accounting

Accounting for our personal finances enables us to better manage and plan for our future. Some examples of common personal contacts with financial accounting include applying for credit approvals, opening bank accounts, choosing a career path, filling out student loan forms, and making decisions regarding whether to purchase a new or a used car. These experiences are limited and tend to focus on the *recordkeeping* (or *bookkeeping*) parts of accounting. **Recordkeeping**, or **bookkeeping**, is the recording of financial transactions, either manually or electronically, for the purpose of creating a bank of data that is complete, neutral, and free from error. Accounting *involves* the recordkeeping process but *is* much more.

Accounting also involves designing information systems to provide useful reports that provide relevant information in monitoring and controlling an organization's activities. In order to use the reports effectively, decision makers must be able to interpret the information. The skills needed to understand and interpret accounting information are developed through building a foundation in accounting concepts and developing an understanding of recording transactions through the recordkeeping process. The use of technology in recordkeeping reduces the time, effort, and cost of accounting while improving accuracy. As technology has changed the way we store, process, and summarize masses of data, financial analysis tools have improved, resulting in improved decision making. Consulting, planning, and other financial services are now closely linked to accounting. These services require sorting through data, interpreting their meaning, identifying key factors, and analyzing their implications. Because accounting is part of so much that we do in business and our everyday lives, you can enjoy greater opportunities if you understand and are able to use accounting information effectively.

 **CHECKPOINT**

1. What is the major objective of accounting?
2. Distinguish between accounting and recordkeeping.

Do Quick Study questions: QS 1-1, QS 1-2

↑ A series of Checkpoint questions in the chapter reinforces the immediately preceding materials. It gives you feedback on your comprehension before you go on to new topics. Answers to these Checkpoint questions are available for you at the end of each chapter.

↑ Answers to the Quick Study (QS) questions are available on Connect.

Forms of Organization

LO2 Describe forms of business organization.

A **business** is an entity represented by one or more individuals selling products or services for profit. Products sold include anything from athletic apparel (**CCM, Bauer, Lululemon, NIKE, Reebok**), to electronic devices (**Apple, Dell, Hewlett-Packard, Samsung**), and clothing (**Abercrombie** and **Fitch, GAP, Zara**). Service providers such as data communication providers (**Bell, Rogers, and Telus**), food services (**McDonald's, The Keg, Starbucks, Tim Hortons**), and internet services (**Google, Twitter, Skype, Facebook, Instagram**) make our lives more connected. A business can be as small as an in-home tutoring business or as large as **George Weston Ltd**, the food processing company known for its President's Choice and no name brands, owner of the clothing label Joe Fresh, and holder of a significant investment in the supermarket chain **Loblaws Company Ltd**. Nearly 100,000 new businesses are started in Canada each year, with most of them being founded by people who want freedom from ordinary jobs, a new challenge in life, or the potential of earning extra money.

Most organizations engage in economic activities, such as the business activities of purchasing materials and labour, and selling products and services. They can also involve activities for non-business organizations, more commonly referred to as not-for-profit organizations, such as government, schools, and health care and charities. Non-business organizations do not plan and operate for profit, but rather for other goals such as health, education, and cultural and social activities. A common feature in all organizations, both business and non-business, is the reliance on reported financial information to successfully run the organization.

Business Organizations

When a business is initially established, the owner(s) need to select one of the three legal business structures: sole proprietorship, partnership, or corporation.

SOLE PROPRIETORSHIP

A **sole proprietorship**, or **proprietorship**, is a business owned by one person. Initial setup of a sole proprietorship is relatively easy and inexpensive. No special legal requirements must be met in order to start this form of business, other than to file for a business licence and register the business name. While it is a separate entity[2] for accounting purposes, it is *not* a separate legal entity from its owner. This means, for example, that a court can order an owner to sell personal belongings to pay a proprietorship's debt. An owner is even responsible for debts that are greater than the resources of the proprietorship; this is known as **unlimited liability**, and is a clear disadvantage of a sole proprietorship. Because tax authorities do not separate a proprietorship from its owner, the profits of the business are reported and taxed on the owner's personal income tax return. Small retail stores and service businesses often are organized as proprietorships.

PARTNERSHIP

A **partnership**[3] is owned by two or more persons called *partners*. Similar to a proprietorship, no special legal requirements must be met in order to start a partnership, other than to register the business

---

2 The *business entity principle* is one of a group of accounting rules, the *generally accepted accounting principles (GAAP)*, which are discussed later in this chapter. This principle states that each economic entity or business of the owner must keep accounting records and reports separate from the owner and any other economic entity of the owner.

3 Partnerships are discussed in greater detail in Chapter 11 in Volume 2 of the textbook.

name and obtain a business licence. To run the business together, the partners need an oral or written agreement that usually indicates how profits and losses are to be shared, referred to as a partnership agreement. A partnership, like a proprietorship, is not legally separate from its owners; therefore each partner's share of profits is reported and taxed on that partner's tax return. Partners are usually subject to *unlimited liability,* meaning they are personally responsible for the debts of the business.

CORPORATION

A **corporation**[4] is a business that is set up as a separate legal entity chartered (or *incorporated*) under provincial or federal laws. A corporation is responsible for its actions and any debts incurred. It can enter into its own contracts, and it can buy, own, and sell property. It can also sue and be sued. Separate legal status not only gives a corporation an unlimited life, but also entitles the corporation to conduct business with the rights, duties, and responsibilities of a person. As a result, a corporation files a tax return and pays tax on its profits. A corporation acts through its managers, who are its legal agents. Separate legal status also means that the shareholders are not personally liable for corporate acts and debts. Shareholders are legally distinct from the business and their loss is limited to what they invested. This **limited liability** is a key to why corporations can raise resources from shareholders who are not active in managing the business. Ownership, or equity, of all corporations is divided into units called **shares**. Owners of shares are called **shareholders** (the American term for shares is *stock* and for shareholders, *stockholders*). A shareholder can sell or transfer shares to another person without affecting the operations of a corporation. When a corporation issues (or sells) only one class of shares, we call them **common shares**. A corporation that sells its shares to the public is called a **publicly accountable enterprise (PAE)**. The **public sale of shares** refers to the trading of shares in an organized stock market such as the Montreal or Toronto stock exchanges. A **private enterprise (PE)** is a corporation that does not offer its shares for public sale. **Shoppers Drug Mart** is an example of a publicly accountable enterprise. Its shares are available on the Toronto Stock Exchange, and as of December 31, 2013, Shoppers Drug Mart had issued a total of 25 million common shares to the public. This means that Shoppers Drug Mart's ownership is divided into 25 million units. **David's Tea** is a Canadian corporation that is a private enterprise. David's Tea's shares are held by a small group of individuals and are not for sale to the public.

Exhibit 1.2 lists some of the characteristics of each business form.

EXHIBIT 1.2

Characteristics of Business Organizations

	Sole Proprietorship	Partnership	Corporation
Separate business entity	yes	yes	yes
Separate legal entity	no	no	yes
Limited owner liability	no	no	yes
Unlimited life	no	no	yes
Business profit is taxed separate from owner(s)	no	no	yes
One owner allowed	yes	no	yes

---

4 Corporations are discussed in greater detail in Chapter 12 in Volume 2 of the textbook.

CHECKPOINT

3. Identify examples of non-business organizations.
4. What are the three common forms of business organization?

Do Quick Study questions: QS 1-3, QS 1-4

Users of Accounting Information

LO3 Identify users and uses of, and opportunities in, accounting.

Accounting is a service activity that serves the decision-making needs of *external* and *internal* users, as shown in Exhibit 1.3.

External Information Users

An **external user** of accounting information is any party outside the company who requires access to the company's accounting information. They include shareholders, lenders, directors, customers, suppliers, regulators, lawyers, brokers, and media agencies. Each external user has special information needs that depend on the kind of decision to be made. To make decisions, these individuals do not have access to internal records of the company but rely on information presented in financial reports, known widely as financial statements.

EXTERNAL REPORTING

Financial accounting is the area of accounting aimed at serving external users. Its primary objective is to provide external reports called *financial statements* to help users analyze an organization's operations and assess performance. Because external users have limited access to an organization's information, their own success depends on getting external reports that communicate relevant information that is truthfully represented. Some governmental and regulatory agencies have the power to get reports in specific forms, but most external users must rely on *general-purpose financial statements*. The term *general purpose* refers to the broad range of purposes for which external users rely on these statements. *Generally accepted*

EXHIBIT 1.3

Users of Accounting Information

External users

© Photolink/Getty Images

- Lenders   • Consumer groups
- Shareholders   • External auditors
- Governments   • Customers

Internal users

© Yuri_Arcurs/istockphoto.com

- Officers   • Sales staff
- Managers   • Budget officers
- Internal auditors • Controllers

accounting principles (GAAP) are important in increasing the usefulness of financial statements to users. GAAP are the underlying concepts that make up acceptable accounting practices. GAAP for public companies in Canada follow International Financial Reporting Standards (IFRS). IFRS are the "accounting laws" that must be applied by accountants to public companies in Canada, when recording and reporting accounting information. We discuss GAAP and IFRS along with the financial statements in more detail later.

Internal Information Users

Internal users of accounting information are those individuals directly involved in managing and operating an organization's day-to-day activities. The internal role of accounting is to provide information to help internal users improve the efficiency and effectiveness of an organization in delivering products or services.

INTERNAL REPORTING

Managerial accounting is the area of accounting aimed at serving the decision-making needs of internal users. Managerial accounting provides special-purpose reports customized to meet the information needs of internal users. An example of such a report is a monthly sales report for each **David's Tea** location to be used to monitor performance of the store's managers in leading their team. Another example would be a report showing suppliers owed money by David's Tea for food purchases. Internal reports aim to answer questions such as:

- What are the manufacturing expenses per unit of product?
- What is the most profitable mix of goods and/or services?
- What level of revenues is necessary to show profit income?
- Which expenses increase with an increase in revenues?

This book will help you to learn the skills needed to record accounting information effectively to provide answers to questions like these and others.

INTERNAL OPERATING FUNCTIONS

The responsibilities and duties of internal users extend to every function of an organization including human resources, sales, marketing, purchasing, production, distribution, and research and development. Accounting is essential to the smooth operation of each.

To monitor operating functions, managers rely on **internal controls**—procedures set up to protect assets (like cash, equipment, and buildings); ensure that accounting reports are free from error, neutral, and complete; promote efficiency; and ensure that company policies are followed. For example, certain

⚖ DECISION INSIGHT

In September 2011, the federal Competition Bureau, after conducting a joint investigation with the RCMP, charged four Montreal-based telemarketing companies—Mega Byte Information Inc., Express Transaction Services Inc., International Business Logistics Inc., and Comexco Management Inc.—with fraud. It is alleged that after falsely claiming to be regular suppliers, the telemarketers tricked customers into believing that a purchase order had already been pre-authorized. As a result, more than $172 million worth of supplies changed hands between 2001 and 2007 at prices inflated up to 10 times the market value. This situation occurred because of inadequate internal controls.

actions require verification, such as a manager's approval before materials enter production. Internal controls are crucial if accounting reports are to provide relevant and trustworthy information.

Accounting Opportunities

Exhibit 1.4 identifies some of the countless job opportunities in accounting by classifying accountants according to the kind of work that they perform. In general, accountants work in four broad fields:

- Financial
- Managerial
- Taxation
- Accounting related

[handwritten: accountants may works as:
- Private Accountants
- Public "
- Govt "]

Another way to classify accountants is to identify the kinds of organizations in which they work. Most accountants are **private accountants** and work for a single employer, which is often a business. **Public accountants** are licensed and regulated by their professional accounting bodies in the provinces in which they work. For example, the Chartered Professional Accountants of Ontario provides licencing and regulation over CPAs working in Ontario. Exhibit 1.5 shows the average annual salaries for various accounting groups.

Financial Accounting

Financial accounting serves the needs of external users by providing standardized financial reports referred to as financial statements. Public companies are required to issue annual financial reports that are audited by a professional accountant. An **audit** is an independent review of an organization's accounting systems and records; it is performed to add credibility to the financial statements. **External auditors** perform the audit at the request of the board of directors to protect investor interests.

EXHIBIT 1.4

Opportunities in Practice

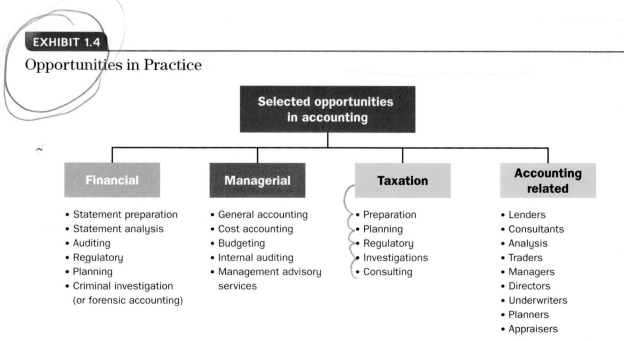

Selected opportunities in accounting

Financial	Managerial	Taxation	Accounting related
• Statement preparation • Statement analysis • Auditing • Regulatory • Planning • Criminal investigation (or forensic accounting)	• General accounting • Cost accounting • Budgeting • Internal auditing • Management advisory services	• Preparation • Planning • Regulatory • Investigations • Consulting	• Lenders • Consultants • Analysis • Traders • Managers • Directors • Underwriters • Planners • Appraisers

EXHIBIT 1.5

Average Annual Salaries for Accounting Positions

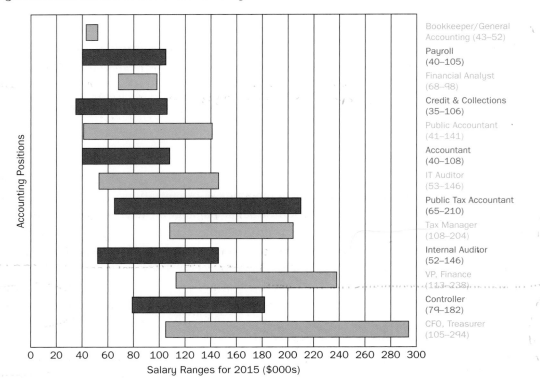

* These values do not include benefits/bonuses.
SOURCE: *2015 Salary Guide* from Robert Half.

Managerial Accounting

Managerial accounting serves the needs of internal users by providing special-purpose reports. These special-purpose reports are the result of general accounting, cost accounting, budgeting, internal auditing, and management consulting.

General accounting	The task of recording transactions, processing the recorded data, and preparing reports for members of the management team such as the **controller** (the chief accounting officer of an organization).
Cost accounting	The process of accumulating the information that managers need about the various **costs** within the organization.
Budgeting	The process of developing formal plans for an organization's future activities.
Internal auditing	Function performed by auditors employed within the organization for the purpose of evaluating the efficiency and effectiveness of procedures.
Management consulting	Service provided by external accountants who suggest improvements to a company's procedures; suggestions may concern new accounting and internal control systems, new computer systems, budgeting, and employee benefit plans.

Taxation

Income tax raised by federal and provincial governments is based on the profit (income) earned by taxpayers. These taxpayers include both individuals and corporate businesses. Sole proprietorships and partnerships are not subject to income tax, but owners of these two non-corporate business forms must pay tax on profit earned from these business forms. The amount of tax is based on what the laws define to be profit for tax purposes. In the field of **taxation**, tax accountants help taxpayers comply with these laws by preparing their tax returns and providing assistance with tax planning for the future. The government (specifically, the **Canada Revenue Agency (CRA)**) employs tax accountants for collection and enforcement.

Professional Certification

Accounting is a profession, like law and medicine, because accountants have special access to confidential matters and the responsibility to adhere to the rules of the profession. The professional status of an accountant is often indicated by one or more professional certifications. In Canada, professional certification has recently transformed. Historically, several provincial accounting organizations provided the education and training required in order to obtain professional certification. These included the Certified General Accountants' Association (for the designation of Certified General Accountant **(CGA)**), the Society of Management Accountants (for the Certified Management Accountant **(CMA)** designation), and the Institute of Chartered Accountants (for the designation of Chartered Accountant **(CA)**). The CGA, CMA, and CA organizations are working together in each province to unite the Canadian accounting profession under the new Canadian Chartered Professional Accountant **(CPA)** designation. The new CPA certification program was launched in Canada in September 2013. At the time of writing, unification is complete in several provinces, and it is expected that soon legislation will pass to unify accountants under the CPA banner in the remaining regions [5]

> For detailed information regarding professional accounting education programs and journals, refer to the following websites: www.cpacanada.ca, www.cga-canada.org.

The preceding discussions illustrate how critical the accounting function is for all organizations. You can be certain that wherever your future career path leads you, an understanding of accounting will be critical because it is integrated deeply into the language of business. A study of this text will help you to develop the foundational skills required to succeed in using this new language and to consider how it relates to your future career.

CHECKPOINT

5. What is the difference between private and public accountants?
6. What are the four broad fields of accounting?
7. What is the purpose of an audit?
8. Distinguish between managerial and financial accounting.
9. What is the difference between external and internal users of accounting information?
10. Why are internal controls important?

Do Quick Study question: QS 1-5

---

[5] https://www.cpacanada.ca/en/the-cpa-profession/uniting-the-canadian-accounting-profession/unification-status (accessed May 2015).

Ethics and Social Responsibility

LO4   Identify and explain why ethics and social responsibility are crucial to accounting.

Ethics and ethical behaviour are important to the effectiveness of the accounting profession and to those who use accounting information. If trust is missing in the accounting profession, shareholders lose confidence in the financial markets and will refrain from investing in businesses. This will make it very difficult for businesses to grow, survive, and be successful in Canada. An important goal of accounting is to provide useful information for decision making. For information to be useful it must be trusted; this demands ethics in accounting. Closely related to ethics is social responsibility. Both are discussed in this section.

Understanding Ethics

Ethics are beliefs based on our value system that enable us to differentiate right from wrong. Business ethics involves producing safe, quality products and treating customers responsibly, understanding the impact of one's actions to the environment, society, and the employees of the company. An ethical dilemma occurs when an individual comes across a situation and needs to make a decision about a right or wrong course of action. Factors impacting the individual making the decision include society's legal framework, the individual's personal value and belief system, and his or her ability to see the impact of a decision on all individuals that are affected by the decision. Companies can encourage employees to uphold corporate values by ensuring employees are properly trained and that their compensation systems are aligned with these values. Examples of ethical issues in the world of business include:

- Proper labelling of products for consumers to make informed decisions (such as "organic" or "genetically modified," and accurate calorie labelling.
- Recording sales made to customers in the appropriate year. GAAP requires companies to follow principles in determining when to recognize revenue as earned from the customer.
- Publicly funded charities utilizing their resources for the end benefit of their stated purpose. The charity directors would need to develop a policy against utilization of charity funds for personal uses such as vacations, personal gifts, etc.
- Companies specifically designing products to break down some time after the elapsed warranty period to require customers to replace the product.
- Universities redirecting monies donated for scholarships and bursaries for capital expansion or employee compensation.

Identifying the optimal ethical decision can be very difficult. The preferred ethical path is to decide on a course of action that maximizes the benefit to the largest number of stakeholders and one that enables you to sleep at night.

ORGANIZATIONAL ETHICS

Organizational ethics are influenced through management example and leadership and are reinforced through the design of compensation systems. Companies that are concerned about their public image in the area of sustainability report their annual performance in a sustainability report. This report is geared to communicate company initiatives in the area of social, environmental, and corporate governance programs to external and internal users. A growing body of research indicates that there is a strong link between companies that adopt sustainable business practices and their financial

Resolving Ethical Dilemmas

The Chartered Professional Accountants of Ontario's Rules of Professional Conduct—Approach to Ethical Conflict Resolution states that part of the resolution process members should consider:

- Relevant facts;
- Ethical issues involved;
- Fundamental principles and rules applicable to the matter in question;
- Established internal procedures; and
- Alternative courses of action.

After considering the above issues, an appropriate course of action needs to be considered that is consistent with the key principles and rules identified as being relevant. The accountant should also assess the consequences of each possible course of action. If the accountant is having difficulty determining the right course of action, the member should consult with other appropriate persons within the firm or employing organization for help. Where a matter involves a conflict with, or within, an organization, the accountant should also consider consulting with those responsible for the governance of the organization, such as the board of directors or the audit committee.

SOURCE: http://www.icao.on.ca/resources/membershandbook/1011page2635.pdf (accessed April 2014).

performance.[6] Companies like **Dell**, **Zara**, **Best Buy**, **Telus**, and **BMW** were recognized as part of *Maclean's* Magazine's Top 50 Socially Responsible Companies for 2013.[7]

Ethical practices build trust, which promotes loyalty and long-term relationships with customers, suppliers, employees, and investors. Good ethics add to an organization's reputation and its success.

Corporate Governance Promotes Corporate Good

Ethical companies are said to have excellent **corporate governance**, the mechanism by which individuals in a company, in particular the board of directors, are motivated to align their behaviours with the overall corporate good. Since the demise of corporations like Enron and WorldCom, caused by fraudulent accounting activities, corporate governance is in the spotlight. Companies with strong corporate governance develop a formal set of policies that their board of directors and executives/employees of the companies will adhere to. Goldcorp, a Canadian gold mining company, with its headquarters in Vancouver, B.C. and mining operations throughout North and South America, has among its corporate governance guidelines an environment and sustainability policy detailing Goldcorp's commitment to life, health, and the environment, an excerpt of which follows:

> We will focus our resources to achieve shareholder profitability in all of our operations without neglecting our commitment to sustainable development.

SOURCE: http://www.goldcorp.com/files/docs_governance/Environmental%20and%20Sustainabiilty%20Policy.pdf (accessed April 2014). Used with permission from Goldcorp.

ACCOUNTING ETHICS

A high commitment to ethics is crucial in the field of accounting due to the confidential nature of information accountants are exposed to and the massive financial and social impact if ethics are neglected. If

---

6   http://www.cga-canada.org/en-ca/ResearchReports/ca_rep_2011-12_informed-view.pdf (accessed April 2014).

7   http://www.macleans.ca/canada-top-50-socially-responsible-corporations-2013/

accounting information is fraudulently presented, shareholders, employees, and many other parties can experience significant consequences. Misleading information can result in many people losing their life's savings when they make investment decisions based on falsified information.

Professional accountants have ethical obligations in at least four general areas: they are expected to maintain a high level of professional competence, treat sensitive information as confidential, exercise personal integrity, and be objective in matters of financial disclosure. These expectations are outlined in a formal code of ethics that is established and monitored by the provincial professional accounting bodies—the Provincial Chartered Professional Accountants, the Provincial Certified General Accountants' Associations, the Provincial Societies of Management Accountants, and the Provincial Institutes of Chartered Accountants. The codes of all Canadian professional accounting bodies state that accountants have a responsibility to society, they must act in the interest of their client or employer, they must exercise due care and professional judgment and continually upgrade their skills, and they must not be associated with deceptive information. These codes can help when one confronts ethical dilemmas.

Ethics codes are also useful when one is dealing with confidential information. For example, auditors have access to confidential salaries and an organization's strategies. Organizations can be harmed if auditors pass this information to others. To prevent this, Canadian Professional Accounting bodies require all accountants to maintain confidentiality of information about their client or employer.

DECISION INSIGHT

Vancouver Portland Hotel Society—Accused of Unethical Practices

The Portland Hotel Society is a government-funded organization that runs a safe injection site for those suffering from addictions in Vancouver's Downtown Eastside. KPMG's audit of expense claims found that when out of town on business, employees were abusing company resources by staying in luxury hotel rooms, ordering flowers and alcoholic beverages, riding in limousines, taking personal vacations, and dining in expensive restaurants. If you were an executive at a charity, what would prevent you from involvement in a similar scandal?

SOURCE: http://fullcomment.nationalpost.com/2014/03/22/national-post-editorial-board-the-emirs-of-vancouvers-portland-hotel-society, April 2014. Material republished with the express permission of: National Post, a division of Postmedia Network Inc.

ETHICAL CHALLENGE

In our lives, we encounter many situations requiring ethical decisions. We need to remember that accounting and other business activities must be practised ethically to maintain the value of the financial reporting process, and we must always ensure that our actions and decisions are ethical.

Social Responsibility

Social responsibility is a concern for the impact of our actions on society as a whole. It requires that an organization identify issues, analyze options, and make socially responsible decisions.

Socially conscious employees, customers, investors, and others see to it that organizations follow claims of social awareness with action, by placing significant pressure on organizations to contribute positively to society. Organizations such as **WestJet** and **Danier Leather** take social responsibility seriously. WestJet invests in the community through WestJet Cares, a program that supports ten national charities including the Boys and Girls Clubs of Canada, Big Brothers Big Sisters Canada, CNIB, Kids Help Phone Canada, KidSport Canada, and Make-A-Wish Canada. Danier Leather sponsors not only Because I Am a Girl, a campaign to fight global gender inequality, but also the construction of the Barlonyo Trade and Vocational Institute in Uganda, and supports more than 150 children through Plan Canada.

> Appendix III at the end of the text includes four sets of real-life financial statements to provide you with a frame of reference.

CHECKPOINT

11. What are the guidelines to use in making ethical and socially responsible decisions?
12. Why are ethics and social responsibility valuable to organizations?
13. Why are ethics crucial to accounting?

Do Quick Study question: QS 1-6

Generally Accepted Accounting Principles (GAAP)

LO5 Identify, explain, and apply accounting principles.

As has already been stated, the goal of accounting is to provide useful information for decision making. For information to be useful, it must be relevant and trustworthy. The accounting profession has created a framework and set of principles to ensure accounting is valuable and can be relied on when making important decisions. The underlying concepts that make up acceptable accounting practices are referred to as **generally accepted accounting principles (GAAP)**.

GAAP for Public vs. Private Enterprises

Canada currently has two main sets of accounting standards. Publicly accountable enterprises (PAEs), including companies that have stock trading on Canadian stock exchanges, are required to meet **International Financial Reporting Standards (IFRS)**. Additionally, the **Accounting Standards Board (AcSB)**, the body that originally governed accounting standards in Canada, has issued a set of "made in Canada" **Accounting Standards for Private Enterprises (ASPE)**.

	Publicly Accountable Enterprises (PAEs)	Private Enterprises (PEs)
GAAP to be used	IFRS	ASPE or IFRS

Why IFRS? Although professional accountants around the world all follow GAAP, how GAAP are interpreted and applied in the recording and reporting of accounting information differs from country to country. These differences can prevent investors, creditors, and other users of global accounting information from making the most informed decisions possible. To improve the comparability of accounting information, the **International Accounting Standards Board (IASB)** was established to try to achieve global agreement on the use of a common set of accounting standards, namely, IFRS.

Why ASPE? Private enterprises are privately owned so have some different reporting needs than public enterprises. For example, a small sole proprietorship might incur significant costs if it had to comply with the complexities of the related IFRS. The AcSB developed ASPE to meet the need for simplification in areas where the adoption of IFRS might have caused significant cost/benefit concerns for private enterprises. Private enterprises can choose whether to follow ASPE or IFRS.

Although these two sets of standards—ASPE and IFRS—are developed by different standard setters, the underlying accounting principles and framework upon which the standards have been developed have many similarities. The differences, within the scope of an introductory financial accounting textbook, are identified and briefly discussed in the IFRS and ASPE—The Differences section at the end of each chapter. This textbook focuses on GAAP as they relate to IFRS and we begin emphasizing these in the early chapters of this book.

PURPOSE OF GAAP

The primary purpose of GAAP is to ensure the usefulness of financial information for external users. The main objective of financial reporting is to provide useful information to external users including existing and potential investor groups, banks, and other lenders to make decisions about providing the entity with resources. For financial information to be useful, it must possess the primary qualitative characteristics of *relevance* and *faithful representation*.[8] Information that has **relevance** is capable of making a difference in the decisions made by users.[9] When information is **faithfully represented**, it is complete, neutral, and free from error.[10] Usefulness is enhanced if the financial information is *comparable, verifiable, timely,* and *understandable*. If companies use a similar framework for accounting, users are able to compare the performance of two different companies or compare the company's performance in different fiscal years, enhancing **comparability**.[11] **Verifiability** means that different knowledgeable individuals would reach consensus that the number represented in the financial statements is reasonable.[12] Information has **timeliness** if it is available to decision makers in time to influence their decisions.[13] Presenting information clearly and concisely gives it **understandability**.[14]

In the next section of the chapter, we highlight some of the fundamental accounting principles that all companies must follow.

FUNDAMENTAL BUILDING BLOCKS OF ACCOUNTING

The following discussion and Exhibit 1.6 summarize the core accounting principles that form the framework of GAAP. Note that the primary objective of GAAP is to provide financial information that is useful for external users. Professional judgement is often required to achieve the right balance in satisfying the various elements of the framework with the focus on meeting the needs of external users.

BUSINESS ENTITY PRINCIPLE

The **business entity principle** requires that each separate economic entity or business of the owner must keep accounting records apart from those of the owner and any other company owned by the owner. To maximize the usefulness of information presented, users want information about the performance of a specific entity.

Example: Looking at David's Tea, owner David Segal must not include personal expenses, such as personal clothing and the cost of going to the movies, as expenses of his business.

---

8   IFRS 2014, "The conceptual framework for financial reporting," para. QC5.
9   IFRS 2014, "The conceptual framework for financial reporting," para. QC6.
10 IFRS 2014, "The conceptual framework for financial reporting," para. QC12.
11 IFRS 2014, "The conceptual framework for financial reporting," para. QC20.
12 IFRS 2014, "The conceptual framework for financial reporting," para. QC26.
13 IFRS 2014, "The conceptual framework for financial reporting," para. QC29.
14 IFRS 2014, "The conceptual framework for financial reporting," para. QC30.

EXHIBIT 1.6

Summary Model of GAAP Framework[15]

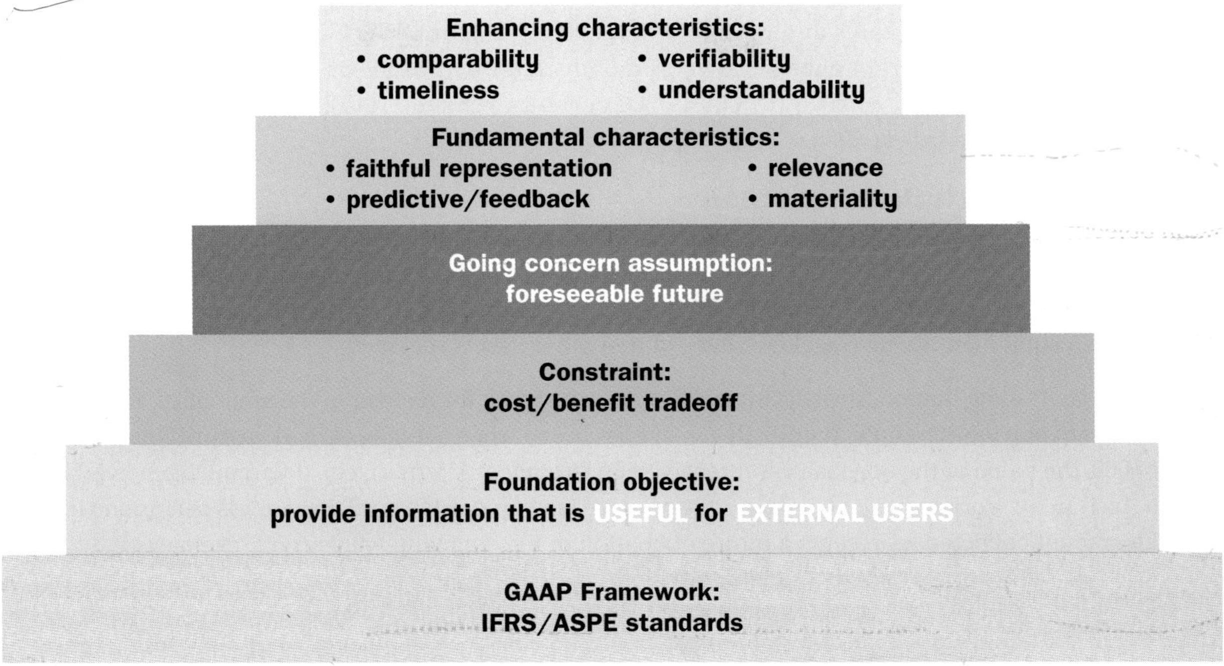

Enhancing characteristics:
- comparability
- timeliness
- verifiability
- understandability

Fundamental characteristics:
- faithful representation
- predictive/feedback
- relevance
- materiality

Going concern assumption:
foreseeable future

Constraint:
cost/benefit tradeoff

Foundation objective:
provide information that is USEFUL for EXTERNAL USERS

GAAP Framework:
IFRS/ASPE standards

Note: Trade-offs between elements require professional judgment to achieve appropriate balance.

COST CONSTRAINT → for small business

The **cost constraint** indicates that the costs incurred in reporting financial statement information must not outweigh the benefits received from the value of the reported information to external users.

GOING CONCERN ASSUMPTION

According to the **going concern assumption**, financial statement users can safely assume that the statements reflect a business that is going to continue its operations at least 12 months into the future unless clearly notified. Therefore, assets are maintained in the accounting records at original cost and not reduced to a liquidation value as if the business were being bought or sold. Companies are required to inform users about material uncertainties that cast significant doubt on their ability to continue on in the foreseeable future.[16]

> *Example:* It is assumed from a review of Organico's financial statements that the business is continuing its operations, because there is no information presented in the audited statements notifying the users that the company is experiencing financial hardships.

CURRENCY

Transactions are to be expressed using units of money in the currency of the country in which the company primarily operates[17] as the common denominator. It is assumed that the monetary unit is stable; therefore, a transaction is left at its originally recorded cost and is not later adjusted for changes in

---

15 Based on IFRS 2014 "The conceptual framework for financial reporting."
16 IFRS 2014, IAS 1, para. 25.
17 IFRS 2014, IAS 21, para. 9.

currency value or inflation. The greater the changes in currency value and inflation, the more difficult it is to use and interpret financial statements across time.

> *Example:* Assume that in August 2017 Organico, a Canadian company, purchased equipment from a supplier in the United States at a total cost of $1,000 (U.S.), or $950 (Cdn) ($1,000/1.0526 exchange rate). If the exchange rate changes several months later to 1.0256, Organico does not restate the value of the equipment to $975 ($1,000/1.0256 current exchange rate). The equipment remains in the accounting records at $950 (Cdn).

REVENUE RECOGNITION PRINCIPLE

The **revenue recognition principle** requires that revenue be recorded at the time that it is earned (generally triggered when the service is performed or product has been delivered), regardless of whether cash or another asset has been exchanged.[18] The amount of revenue to be recorded is the cash received plus the cash equivalent value (market value) of any other assets received.

> *Example:* Assume that on April 3, Organico performed work for a client in the amount of $600. The client did not pay the $600 until May 15. Revenue is recorded when actually earned on April 3 in the amount of $600, the value of the noncash asset received by Organico. Alternatively, if Organico received $1,000 on April 15 for work to be done next month, revenue is *not* recorded until the work is performed in May. The amount collected represents a future obligation of the company—unearned revenue.

MEASUREMENT

Within the accounting standards there are four key methods used to determine the dollar value at which to capture/record a transaction in the financial accounting records[19]:

1. **Historical cost**. Historical cost is the *most commonly adopted method* to record accounting transactions. It requires that all transactions be recorded based on the actual cash amount received or paid. In the absence of cash, the cash equivalent amount of the exchange is recorded.[20]

   > *Example:* If Organico purchased used equipment for $5,000 cash, it is recorded in the accounting records at $5,000. It makes no difference if Hailey Walker thinks that the value of the equipment is $7,000.

2. **Current cost.** Current cost indicates the amount of cash it would cost to acquire that asset/settle the liability today. For example, investments in actively traded corporate stock are reported at their current cost at the year-end date.

3. **Realizable value.** The asset or liability is reported at the amount of cash that would be obtained by selling the asset or paying off the liability in the normal course of business. For example, inventory is reported at the lower of historical cost and realizable value.

4. **Present value.** Assets are reported at the present value of future expected cash flows, after discounting to reflect the time value of money in terms of expected interest/inflation. For example, long-term debt instruments (corporate bonds) sold are reported at the present value of future cash payments, as described in Chapter 14.

Unless otherwise indicated, assume the measurement method used is *historical cost,* which is the amount paid/payable or the amount collected/collectible. In future chapters you will be informed of the specific measurement method to be used for specific assets or liabilities.

---

18 IFRS 2014, IAS 18, para. 9–34; "The conceptual framework for financial reporting," para. 4.37–4.39; IFRS 2015, IFRS 15, para. 9 and 31.
19 IFRS 2015, "The conceptual framework for financial reporting"), para. 4.54–4.56.
20 IFRS 2014, IAS 16, para. 23.

CHECKPOINT

14. Why is the business entity principle important?

15. Describe the historical cost measurement method and explain why it might be considered verifiable.

16. A customer pays cash today for a product that is to be delivered to her next month. When should revenue be recognized?

Do Quick Study questions: QS 1-7, QS 1–8

Communicating Through Financial Statements

LO6 Identify and explain the content and reporting aims of financial statements.

Financial statements are an organization's primary means of financial communication and are the end result of a process, or cycle, that begins with a business transaction like a sale. These transactions are recorded, classified, sorted, and summarized in order to produce the statements.

Previewing Financial Statements

We will begin our study of the four major financial statements—the income statement, balance sheet, statement of changes in equity, and statement of cash flows—with a brief description of each. How these statements are linked is shown in Exhibit 1.7. Examples of financial statements are illustrated in the following pages using Organico.

EXHIBIT 1.7

Links Between Financial Statements

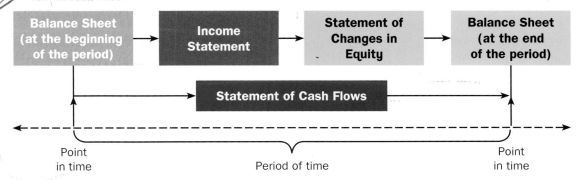

Transactions occur over a period of time, or during the accounting period, and are reported on the income statement, statement of changes in equity, and statement of cash flows. These transactions result in a new balance sheet at the end of the period.

NOTE: Flexibility is permitted in the naming of financial statements. For example, the *statement of financial position* is another name for the *balance sheet*. In Appendix III at the end of the textbook, notice that WestJet uses the term *statement of financial position*, while Danier Leather uses *balance sheet*. The *statement of profit and loss (P&L)*, *statement of earnings*, and other names are used instead of *income statement*. For consistency, the financial statements will be named throughout this textbook as introduced in Exhibit 1.7.

A balance sheet reports on an organization's financial position at a *point in time*. The income statement, statement of changes in equity, and statement of cash flows report on performance over a *period of time*.

Selection of a reporting period is up to preparers and users (including regulatory agencies). A one-year, or annual, reporting period is common, as are semi-annual, quarterly, and monthly periods. The one-year reporting period is also known as the accounting or **fiscal year**. Businesses whose reporting period follows the **calendar year** begin on January 1 and end on December 31. Many companies choose a fiscal year based on their **natural business year** that ends when sales and inventories are low. For example, Lululemon Athletica Inc.'s fiscal year-end is the Sunday closest to January 31, after the holiday season, reporting operating results as at February 3, 2013, January 29, 2012, and January 30, 2011 respectively.[21]

Revenues	−	Expenses	=	Profit or Loss
For example:				
$100	−	$75	=	$25
Revenues		Expenses		Profit
	OR			
$300	−	$360	=	$60
Revenues		Expenses		Loss

INCOME STATEMENT

An **income statement** reports *revenues* earned less *expenses* incurred by a business over a period of time.

Revenues are the value of assets exchanged for products and services provided to customers as part of a business's main operations. Assets are economic resources held by a business and include cash, equipment, buildings, and land. Later in the chapter, we will define assets more precisely. The income statement for Organico's first month of operations is shown in Exhibit 1.8. It shows that Organico earned total revenues of $4,100 during March: $3,800 from teaching revenue plus $300 from equipment rental revenue.

Expenses are costs incurred or the using up of assets from generating revenue. The income statement in Exhibit 1.8 shows that Organico used up some of its assets in paying for rented space. The $1,000 expense for rental space is reported in the income statement as rent expense. Organico also paid for an employee's salary at a cost of $700. This is reported on the income statement as salaries expense. The income statement heading in Exhibit 1.8 identifies the business, the type of statement, and the time period covered. Knowledge of the time period is important for us in judging whether the $2,400 profit earned in March is satisfactory.

Profit, or income, means that revenues are more than expenses. A **loss** means that expenses are more than revenues.

An income statement lists the types and amounts of both revenues and expenses to help users understand and predict company performance. This detailed information is more useful for making decisions than a simple profit or loss number would be.

STATEMENT OF CHANGES IN EQUITY

Equity is equal to total assets minus total liabilities; it represents how much of the assets *belong* to the owner. Equity increases with *owner investments* and profit and decreases with *owner withdrawals* and losses. **Owner investments** occur when the owner transfers personal assets, such as cash, into the business. Since owner investments do not result from the sale of a product or service, they are *not* revenue and *not* reported on the income statement. **Owner withdrawals**, or **withdrawals**, occur when the owner takes cash or other assets from the business. Withdrawals represent a distribution of profit to the owner. Since withdrawals do not help to create revenue, they are *not* expenses and therefore are not reported on the income statement.

The **statement of changes in equity** reports on changes in equity over the reporting period. This statement starts with beginning equity and adjusts it for transactions that (1) increase it (investments by the owner and profit), and (2) decrease it (owner withdrawals and losses).

The statement of changes in equity for Organico's first month of operations is shown in Exhibit 1.9. This statement describes transactions that changed equity during the month. It shows $10,000 of equity created

---

21 Lululemon Athletica Inc. Form 10-K Annual Report, for the period ending 02/03/13, Note 1, par 3 Nature of Operations and Basis of Presentation.

EXHIBIT 1.8 Income Statement for Organico **O**RGANICO

Organico's Income Statement For Month Ended March 31, 2017		
Revenues:		
Food services revenue	$ 3,800	
Teaching revenue	300	
Total revenues		$ 4,100
Operating expenses:		
Rent expense	$ 1,000	
Salaries expense	700	
Total operating expenses		1,700
Profit		$ 2,400

EXHIBIT 1.9 Statement of Changes in Equity for Organico

Organico Statement of Changes in Equity For Month Ended March 31, 2017		
Hailey Walker, capital, March 1		$ -0-
Add: Investments by owner	$ 10,000	
Profit	2,400	12,400
Total		$ 12,400
Less: Withdrawals by owner		600
Hailey Walker, capital, March 31		$ 11,800

if net loss it would go here

EXHIBIT 1.10 Balance Sheet for Hailey Walker

Organico Balance Sheet March 31, 2017			
Assets		**Liabilities**	
Cash	$ 8,400	Accounts payable	$ 200
Supplies	3,600	Notes payable	6,000
Equipment	6,000	Total liabilities	$ 6,200
		Equity	
		Hailey Walker, capital	11,800
Total assets	$18,000	Total liabilities and equity	$ 18,000

EXHIBIT 1.11 Statement of Cash Flows for Organico

Organico Statement of Cash Flows For Month Ended March 31, 2017		
Cash flows from operating activities		
Cash received from clients	$ 4,100	
Cash paid for supplies	(3,400)	
Cash paid for rent	(1,000)	
Cash paid to employee	(700)	
Net cash used by operating activities		$ (1,000)
Cash flows from investing activities		-0-
Cash flows from financing activities		
Investment by owner	$10,000	
Withdrawal by owner	(600)	
Net cash provided by financing activities		9,400
Net increase in cash		$ 8,400
Cash balance, March 1		-0-
Cash balance, March 31		$ 8,400

The arrows are provided for education purposes only to emphasize the link between statements.

by Hailey Walker's initial investment. It also shows $2,400 of profit earned during the month. The statement also reports the owner's $600 withdrawal. Organico's equity balance at the end of the month is $11,800.

BALANCE SHEET

The **balance sheet**, or **statement of financial position**, reports the financial position of a business at a point in time, usually at the end of a month or year. It describes financial position by listing the types and dollar amounts of *assets, liabilities,* and *equity*. **Assets** are the properties or economic resources held by a business. A common characteristic of assets is their ability to provide future benefits to the company.[22] Cash is an asset that businesses can easily exchange for goods and services. **Accounts receivable** is an asset created by selling products or services to customers on credit. It reflects amounts owed to a business by its credit customers. Other common assets include merchandise inventory held for sale, supplies, equipment, buildings, and land. Discussed in Chapter 4 are other assets having intangible rights, such as those granted by a patent or copyright.

Liabilities are debts or obligations of a business. They are claims of others against the assets of the business. A common characteristic of liabilities is their capacity to reduce future assets or to require future services or products.[23] Typical liabilities include *accounts payable* and *notes payable*. An **account payable** is a liability created by buying products or services on credit. It reflects amounts owed to others. A **note payable** is a liability expressed by a written promise to make a future payment at a specific time. Other common liabilities are salaries and wages owed to employees, interest payable, and money collected from customers in advance of providing a service called unearned revenues (further described in Chapter 2).

Individuals and organizations that own the right to receive payments from a business are called its **creditors**. Customers that owe money for services performed are called **debtors**. One entity's payable is another entity's receivable. If a business fails to pay its obligations, the law gives creditors a right to force sale of its assets to obtain the money to meet their claims. When assets are sold under these conditions, creditors are paid first but only up to the amount of their claims. Any remaining money goes to the owner(s) of the business. Creditors often compare the amounts of liabilities and assets on a balance sheet to help them decide whether to lend money to a business. A loan is less risky if liabilities are small in comparison to assets, because there are more resources than claims on resources. A loan is more risky if liabilities are large compared to assets.

Equity is the owner's claim on the assets of a business. It represents the assets that remain after deducting liabilities,[24] also called **net assets**. We explained that income is the difference between revenues and expenses of a business over a period of time. Income on the income statement results in an increase in equity on the balance sheet due to profitable operating activities over a period of time. An operating loss on the income statement results in a decrease in equity on the balance sheet in an accounting period. In this way, the income statement links to the balance sheet at the end of a reporting period. The causes of changes in equity are highlighted in the learning summary box in the margin. Changes in equity are reported in the statement of changes in equity, and give us the ending balance of equity that is reported in the balance sheet. Exhibit 1.12 provides a brief summary of the elements of the financial statements.

Exhibit 1.10 shows the balance sheet as of March 31, 2017. The balance sheet heading lists the business name, the statement, and the specific date on which assets and liabilities are identified and measured. The amounts in the balance sheet are measured as of the close of business on that specific date.

The balance sheet for Organic shows that it has three different assets at the close of business on March 31, 2017. The assets are cash, supplies, and equipment, for a total dollar amount of $18,000. The

---

22 IFRS 2014, "The conceptual framework for financial reporting," para. 4.8.
23 IFRS 2014, "The conceptual framework for financial reporting," para. 4.15.
24 IFRS 2014, "The conceptual framework for financial reporting," para. 4.20.

EXHIBIT 1.12

Elements of Financial Statements Summary[25]

Element of F/S	Definition	Characteristics	Example
Assets	Properties or economic resources held by a business.	The resource: 1) Will result in a future financial benefit 2) Is owned by the business 3) Transaction/exchange to acquire the item has occurred.	By purchasing a food truck, Organico acquires an asset that will provide a future benefit. It will enable Organico to make and distribute its burritos to customers.
Liabilities	Debts or obligations of a business	Present obligation requiring future payment resulting from a past event.	Organico purchases $1,100 of biodegradable food packaging supplies from CanFood Supply Co. and agrees to pay cash for the items in 30 days.
Equity/ Net Assets	The owner's claim on the assets of the business.	Represents the residual interest of the owner(s) in the assets of the company after deducting liabilities	Hailey Walker had $11,800 of equity/capital at the end of the first month of operations (Exhibit 1.9).
Profit	The difference between revenues and expenses of a business during a specific period of time.	Represents the increase in financial benefits earned in an accounting period Results from revenues earned less expenses incurred.	Organico earned $2,400 in its first month of operations (Exhibit 1.8).
Expenses	Costs incurred or the using up of assets as a result of the operations of the business.	Represents decreases in economic benefits in an accounting period	Organico pays for fuel to operate its food truck.
Revenue	The value of assets received or receivable as a result of selling goods or services to customers.	Must be: 1) **Earned**, meaning the asset/service has been transferred/provided to the customer. 2) Expect to **collect** from the customer. 3) Be able to quantify or **measure** the transaction in terms of value expected from the sale/service based on the terms of the contract with the customer.	Organico sells a burrito to a customer.

Learning Summary: Changes to Equity

Increases in equity are caused by:	Decreases in equity are caused by:
• Owner investments	• Owner withdrawals
• Profit (excess revenue over expenses)	• Losses (expenses exceed revenue)

Ending Owner's Equity = Beginning Owner's Equity + Owner Investments + Profit − Withdrawals by Owner

balance sheet also shows total liabilities of $6,200. Equity is $11,800. Equity is the difference between assets and liabilities. The statement is named a *balance sheet* because (1) the total amounts on both sides of the statement are equal; and (2) the reporting of assets, liabilities, and equity is in *balance*.

STATEMENT OF CASH FLOWS

The **statement of cash flows** describes the sources and uses of cash for a reporting period. It also reports the amount of cash at both the beginning and the end of a period. The statement of

---

25 IFRS 2014, "The conceptual framework for financial reporting, Chapter 4.

cash flows is organized by a company's major activities: operating, investing, and financing. Since a company must carefully manage cash if it is to survive and prosper, cash flow information is important.

As an example, the statement of cash flows for Organico is shown in Exhibit 1.11 (notice that Organico shows both operating and financing activities but it had no investing activities during March). To fully appreciate this financial statement, a solid understanding of some basic accounting concepts is required. Therefore, a detailed discussion has been left to Chapter 16.

FINANCIAL STATEMENTS AND FORMS OF ORGANIZATION

Earlier in the chapter, three different forms of business organization were described: sole proprietorships, partnerships, and corporations. Exhibit 1.13 summarizes key differences among these three forms of business ownership. While many differences exist, financial statements for these three types of organizations are very similar.

EXHIBIT 1.13

Financial Statement Differences Based on Type of Business Organization

Difference	Type of Business Organization		
	Sole Proprietorship	Partnership	Corporation
Equity on the balance sheet belongs to:	Sole owner	Partners	Shareholders
Distributions to owners are called:	Withdrawals	Withdrawals	Dividends
When managers are also owners, their salaries are:	Not an expense	Not an expense	Expense

---

The emphasis in the early chapters of this book is on sole proprietorships. This allows us to focus on important measurement and reporting issues in accounting without getting caught up in the complexities of additional forms of organization. We do discuss other forms of organization, however, and provide examples when appropriate. Chapters 11 and 12 return to this topic and provide additional detail about the financial statements of partnerships and corporations.

CHECKPOINT

17. What are the four major financial statements?
18. Describe revenues and expenses.
19. Explain assets, liabilities, and equity.
20. What are three differences in financial statements for different forms of organization?

Do Quick Study question: QS 1-9

The Accounting Equation

LO7 Analyze business transactions by applying the accounting equation.

Notice in Exhibit 1.10 that there are two main sections of the balance sheet: assets on one side and liabilities and equity on the other side. Observe that the total assets of $18,000 equal the total liabilities and equity of $18,000. This equality is known as the *accounting equation*. This equation is based on relationships fundamental to accounting.

EXHIBIT 1.14

The Accounting Equation

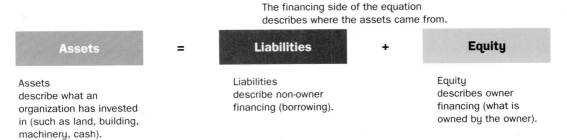

The financing side of the equation describes where the assets came from.

Assets	=	Liabilities	+	Equity

Assets describe what an organization has invested in (such as land, building, machinery, cash).

Liabilities describe non-owner financing (borrowing).

Equity describes owner financing (what is owned by the owner).

When an organization invests in assets, it is the result of an equal amount of financing. This relationship is expressed in the following equation:

$$\text{Investing} = \text{Financing}$$

Since invested amounts are referred to as *assets*, and financing is made up of owner and non-owner financing, we can also express this equality as:

$$\text{Assets} = \text{Non-Owner Financing} + \text{Owner Financing}$$

Non-owners are creditors. Creditors and owners hold claims or rights in the assets. Creditors' claims are called *liabilities* and the owner's claim is called *equity*. The equation can be rewritten as shown in Exhibit 1.14.

It is called the **accounting equation** or **balance sheet equation** because of its link to the balance sheet. It describes the relationship between a company's assets, liabilities, and equity. To demonstrate, assume you want to buy a car that costs $25,000. The bank lends you $15,000 and you pay $10,000 out of your personal savings account.

Assets	=	Liabilities	+	Equity
$25,000	=	**$15,000**	+	**$10,000**

You have invested in a car that costs $25,000.

Borrowing $15,000 from the bank has financed part of your investment.

You, the owner, have financed part of the investment in the car; you own $10,000 of the car; in other words, your equity in the car is $10,000.

The accounting equation can be changed by moving liabilities to the left side of the equation:

$$\underbrace{\text{Assets} - \text{Liabilities}}_{\textit{Net assets}} = \text{Equity}$$

Assets less liabilities equal *net assets*, another name for equity.

CAUTION: The illustration of transaction analysis on the following pages is a learning tool to demonstrate the effects of transactions on the accounting equation. How transactions are recorded in the real world is the topic of Chapter 2.

Transaction Analysis

Business activities can be described in terms of **transactions** and **events**. A **business transaction** is an exchange of *economic consideration* between two parties that causes a change in assets, liabilities, or equity. An **economic consideration** is something of value, and examples include products, services, money, and rights to collect money. These transactions cause changes in the accounting equation. **Source documents** identify and describe transactions entering the accounting process. They are the *source* of accounting information, and can be in either paper or electronic form. Source documents, especially if obtained from outside the organization, provide objective evidence about transactions and their amounts, making information more reliable and useful. Examples of source documents are sales invoices, cheques, purchase orders, charges to customers, bills from suppliers, employee earnings records, and bank statements.

Not all business activities are transactions. **Business events** are activities that do not involve an exchange of economic consideration between two parties and therefore do not affect the accounting equation. Examples include placing an order for supplies, interviewing job applicants, signing a contract, and making a hotel reservation for an out-of-town business trip.

Every transaction recorded must leave the accounting equation in balance. Total *assets* always *equal the sum of total liabilities and total equity.* We show how this equality is maintained by looking at the activities of Organico, a new food truck business that focuses on making organic Mexican burritos, in its first month of operations.

1. Investment by Owner. On March 1, 2017, Hailey Walker registered her business name and began setting up her new food truck business Organico as a sole proprietorship. Walker is the owner and manager of the business. The marketing plan for Organico is to focus primarily on providing fresh, organic, Mexican fast food with a focus on quality and taste. Walker invests $10,000 cash in the new company, which she deposits in a bank account opened under the name Organico. By moving her personal money into the business, an exchange of resources has taken place, so this is classified as a transaction. Transactions affect the accounting equation. As shown, this transaction affects both Organico's cash (an asset) and equity (called *Hailey Walker, Capital*), each for $10,000.

ORGANICO

	Assets	=	Liabilities	+	Equity	Explanation
					Hailey Walker,	
	Cash	=			Capital	
(1)	+$10,000	=			+$10,000	Investment by Owner

This specific increase in equity is identified as an investment by the owner, differentiating it from other transactions affecting equity.

2. Purchase Supplies for Cash. Organico uses $2,500 of its cash to purchase organic food supplies. This is a transaction because it involves an exchange of cash, an asset, for another kind of asset, supplies. The transaction produces no expense because no value is lost. The decrease in cash is exactly equal to the increase in supplies. The equation remains in balance.

	Assets			=	Liabilities	+	Equity	Explanation
	Cash	+	Supplies	=			Hailey Walker,	
							Capital	
Old Bal.	$10,000			=			$10,000	
(2)	−$ 2,500		+$2,500				_____	Purchased Supplies
New Bal.	$ 7,500	+	$2,500	=			$10,000	
		$10,000		=		$10,000		

3. Purchase Equipment and Supplies on Credit. Hailey Walker finds a used food truck from a supplier that specializes in restaurant equipment supplies, CanFood Supply Co. Walker is able to negotiate a deal with the same supplier on biodegradable food packaging supplies; these purchases total $7,100. As we see from the accounting equation in (2) above, however, Organico has only $7,500 in cash. Concerned that these purchases would use nearly all of Organico's cash, Walker arranges to purchase the items on credit from CanFood Supply Co. This is a transaction because an exchange has occurred: Organico has acquired items in exchange for a promise to pay for them later. Supplies cost $1,100, and the equipment costs $6,000. The total liability to CanFood Supply is $7,100. Organico will pay for the supplies in 30 days, but has arranged to pay for the equipment by signing an agreement called a **note**. The effects of this transaction on the accounting equation are:

	Assets					=	Liabilities			+	Equity	Explanation
	Cash	+	Supplies	+	Equipment	=	Accounts Payable	+	Notes Payable	+	Hailey Walker, Capital	
Old Bal.	$7,500		$2,500								$10,000	
(3)			+$1,100	+	+$6,000		+$1,100	+	+$6,000			Purchased Supplies and Equipment
New Bal.	$7,500	+	$3,600	+	$6,000	=	$1,100	+	$6,000	+	$10,000	
			$17,100						$17,100			

This purchase increases assets by $7,100, while liabilities (called *accounts payable* and *notes payable*) increase by the same amount. Both of these payables are promises by Organico to repay its debt, where the note payable reflects a more formal written agreement. We will discuss these liabilities in detail in later chapters.

4. Services Rendered for Cash. A primary objective of a business is to increase its owner's wealth. This goal is met when a business produces a profit, also called *profit*. Profit is reflected in the accounting equation as an increase in equity. Organico earns revenue by selling fresh, organic, Mexican burritos and providing cooking demonstrations. On March 10, Organico sets up the truck outside a concert facility before a sold-out show and sells $2,200 worth of burritos for cash. This is a transaction since an exchange of resources has taken place. When revenue is earned in exchange for cash, it affects the accounting equation by increasing cash and equity. Organico's cash increases by $2,200 and equity also increases by $2,200, identified in the far right column as revenue.

	Assets					=	Liabilities			+	Equity	Explanation
	Cash	+	Supplies	+	Equipment	=	Accounts Payable	+	Notes Payable	+	Hailey Walker, Capital	
Old Bal.	$7,500		$3,600		$6,000		$1,100		$6,000		$10,000	Food Services
(4)	+$2,200			+		=		+			+$ 2,200	March 10 Revenue
New Bal.	$9,700	+	$3,600	+	$6,000	=	$1,100	+	$6,000	+	$12,000	
			$19,300						$19,300			

CHAPTER 1 Accounting in Business

5. and 6. Payment of Expenses in Cash. On March 10, Organico pays its landlord rent on its downtown parking space at a cost of $1,000 for March. Since an exchange has taken place, this is a transaction and affects the accounting equation as shown below in line (5). On March 14, Organico pays the $700 salary of the business's only employee—Brooke. This is also a transaction because an exchange has occurred, and it is therefore reflected in the accounting equation in line (6).

	Assets					=	Liabilities			+	Equity	Explanation
	Cash	+	Supplies	+	Equipment	=	Accounts Payable	+	Notes Payable	+	Hailey Walker, Capital	
Old Bal.	$9,700	+	$3,600	+	$6,000	=	$1,100	+	$6,000	+	$12,200	
(5)	−$1,000										−$ 1,000	Rent Expense
Bal.	$8,700	+	$3,600	+	$6,000	=	$1,100	+	$6,000	+	$11,200	
(6)	−$ 700										−$ 700	Salaries Expense
New Bal.	$8,000	+	$3,600	+	$6,000	=	$1,100	+	$6,000	+	$10,500	
			$17,600						$17,600			

Both (5) and (6) produce expenses for Organico as noted in the far right column. They use up cash for the purpose of providing services to clients. Unlike the asset purchase in (2), the cash payments in (5) and (6) acquire services. The benefits of these services do *not* last beyond the end of this month. The accounting equation remains in balance, and shows that both transactions reduce cash and Walker's equity.

7. Service Contract Signed for April. On March 11, the accounting club at the local university and Hailey Walker sign a $2,700 contract that requires Organico to provide food for a group of graduating students at a CPA recruitment event. Organico has agreed to attend the event to be held next month.

	Assets					=	Liabilities			+	Equity	Explanation
	Cash	+	Supplies	+	Equipment	=	Accounts Payable	+	Notes Payable	+	Hailey Walker, Capital	
Old Bal.	$8,000	+	$3,600	+	$6,000	=	$1,100	+	$6,000		$10,500	
(7)												
New Bal.	$8,000	+	$3,600	+	$6,000	=	$1,100	+	$6,000	+	$10,500	
			$17,600						$17,600			

This is a business event and *not* a business transaction because there was no economic exchange (nothing has yet been received by Organico *and* nothing has been provided to the club (the customer) as of March 11). Therefore, this has no effect on the accounting equation.

8. Services and Rental Revenues Rendered for Credit. On March 17, Organico taught a Mexican cooking class as a team-building exercise for a group of HR professionals for $300 and sold an additional $1,600 in food services at the conference. The group's coordinator is billed for $1,900 for both activities. This is a transaction because an exchange has occurred: Organico provided services to a customer and in exchange received an asset, an account receivable, from the customer. The $1,900 increase in assets produces an equal increase in equity. Notice that the increase in equity is identified as two revenue components in the far right column of the accounting equation:

Assets				=	Liabilities		+	Equity	Explanation
								Hailey Walker,	
	Accounts				**Accounts**	**Notes**		**Walker,**	
Cash	**+ Receivable +**	**Supplies +**	**Equipment =**		**Payable +**	**Payable +**		**Capital**	
Old Bal. $8,000		+ $3,600 +	$6,000 =		$1,100 +	$6,000 +		$10,500	Food Services
(8)	+$1,900							+$1,600	Revenue
				=		+	+	+$ 300	Teaching Revenue
New Bal. $ 8,000 +	$ 1,900 +	$3,600 +	$6,000		$1,100	$6,000		$12,400	

$19,500 $19,500

9. Receipt of Cash on Account. The amount of $1,900 is received from the client on March 27, ten days after the billing for services in (8). This exchange between Organico and the customer represents a transaction and therefore affects the accounting equation. This transaction does not change the total amount of assets and does not affect liabilities or equity. It converts the receivable to cash and *does not* create new revenue. Revenue was recognized when Organico provided the services on March 17. Therefore, revenue is *not* recorded on March 27 when the cash is collected. The new balances are:

Assets				=	Liabilities		+	Equity	Explanation
								Hailey Walker,	
	Accounts				**Accounts**	**Notes**		**Walker,**	
Cash	**+ Receivable +**	**Supplies +**	**Equipment =**		**Payable +**	**Payable +**		**Capital**	
Old Bal. $8,000 +	$1,900 +	$3,600 +	$6,000 =		$1,100 +	$6,000 +		$12,400	Collected Payment
(9) +$1,900	−$1,900								
New Bal. $ 9,900 +	$ -0- +	$3,600 +	$6,000 =		$1,100 +	$6,000 +		$12,400	

$19,500 $19,500

10. Payment of Accounts Payable. Organico pays $900 to CanFood Supply on March 27. This is a transaction since an exchange has occurred between Organico and CanFood Supply. It therefore affects the accounting equation. The $900 payment is for the earlier $1,100 purchase of supplies from CanFood, leaving $200 unpaid. The $6,000 amount due to CanFood for equipment remains unpaid. The accounting equation shows that this transaction decreases Organico's cash by $900 and decreases its liability to CanFood Supply by the same amount. As a result, equity does not change. This transaction does not create an expense, even though cash flows out of Organico.

Assets				=	Liabilities		+	Equity	Explanation
								Hailey Walker,	
	Accounts				**Accounts**	**Notes**		**Walker,**	
Cash	**+ Receivable +**	**Supplies +**	**Equipment =**		**Payable +**	**Payable +**		**Capital**	
Old Bal. $9,900 +	$ -0- +	$3,600 +	$6,000 =		$1,100 +	$6,000 +		$12,400	Paid Supplier
(10) −$ 900					−$900				
New Bal. $ 9,000 +	$ -0- +	$3,600 +	$6,000 =		$ 200 +	$6,000 +		$12,400	

$18,600 $18,600

11. Withdrawal of Cash by Owner. Walker withdraws $600 in cash from Organico for personal living expenses. An exchange has taken place between the owner and the business, so this is a transaction and affects the accounting equation. Withdrawals are not expenses because they are not part of the company's earnings process. Therefore, withdrawals are not used in calculating profit.

	Assets							=	Liabilities			+	Equity	Explanation
	Cash	+	Accounts Receivable	+	Supplies	+	Equipment	=	Accounts Payable	+	Notes Payable	+	Hailey Walker, Capital	
Old Bal.	$9,900	+	$ -0-	+	$3,600	+	$6,000	=	$ 200	+	$6,000	+	$12,400	Withdrawal
(11)	−$600												−$ 600	by Owner
New Bal.	$8,400	+	$ -0-	+	$3,600	+	$6,000	=	$ 200	+	$6,000	+	$11,800	
			$18,000								$18,600			

Summary of Transactions

Summarized in Exhibit 1.15 are the effects of all of Organico's March transactions using the accounting equation. Five points should be noted.

1. The accounting equation remains in balance after every transaction.

2. Transactions can be analyzed by their effects on components of the accounting equation. For example, total assets and equity increase by equal amounts in (1), (4), and (8). In (2) and (9), one asset increases while another decreases by an equal amount. For (3), we see equal increases in assets and liabilities. Both assets and equity decrease by equal amounts in (5), (6), and (11). In (10), we see equal decreases in an asset and a liability.

3. Transactions cause assets, liabilities, or equity to change. Notice in Exhibit 1.15 that (1)–(6) and (8)–(11) caused changes to the accounting equation because each transaction involved an exchange; (7) did not involve an exchange and so did not affect the accounting equation.

4. The format of the preceding analysis was used to demonstrate the effects of transactions on the components of the accounting equation; transactions in the real world are not recorded in this manner.

5. The equality of effects in the accounting equation is fundamental to the *double-entry accounting system* that is discussed in the next chapter.

It is important to recognize that the accounting equation is a representation of the balance sheet. Therefore, we can take the information in Exhibit 1.15 and prepare financial statements for Organico. This will be done in the next section.

CHECKPOINT

21. How can a transaction *not* affect liability and equity accounts?
22. Describe a transaction that increases equity and one that decreases it.
23. Identify a transaction that decreases both assets and liabilities.
24. When is the accounting equation in balance, and what does it mean?
25. Explain the difference between a transaction and an event.
26. Identify examples of accounting source documents.
27. Explain the importance of source documents.

Do Quick Study questions: QS 1-10, QS 1-11, QS 1-12, QS 1-13, QS 1-14

EXHIBIT 1.15

Summary Analysis of Organico's Transactions Using the Accounting Equation

			Assets			=	Liabilities		+	Equity	Explanation of Equity Transaction
	Cash	+ Accounts Receivable +	Supplies	+ Equipment =			Accounts Payable +	Notes Payable +		Hailey Walker, Capital	
(1)	$10,000									$10,000	Investment by Owner
(2)	− 2,500		+$2,500								Purchased Supplies
Bal.	$ 7,500		$2,500							$10,000	Purchased Supplies and Equipment
(3)			+1,100	+$6,000			+ 1,100	+$6,000			
Bal.	$ 7,500		$3,600	$6,000			$1,100	$6,000		$10,000	Food Services Revenue
(4)	+ 2,200									+ 2,200	Revenue
Bal.	$ 9,700		$3,600	$6,000			$1,100	$6,000		$12,200	
(5)	− 1,000									− 1,000	Rent Expense
Bal.	$ 8,700		$3,600	$6,000			$1,100	$6,000		$11,200	
(6)	− 700									− 700	Salaries Expense
Bal.	$ 8,000		$3,600	$6,000			$1,100	$6,000		$10,500	
(7)	No entry*										Food Services
(8)		+$1,900								+ 1,600	Revenue
										+ 300	Teaching Revenue
Bal.	$ 8,000	$ 1,900	$3,600	$6,000			$1,100	$6,000		$12,400	
(9)	+ 1,900	−1,900									Collected Payment
Bal.	$ 9,900	$ -0-	$3,600	$6,000			$1,100	$6,000		$12,400	
(10)	+ 900						− 900				Paid Supplier
Bal.	$ 9,000	$ -0-	$3,600	$6,000			$ 200	$6,000		$12,400	
(11)	− 600									− 600	Withdrawal by Owner
Bal.	$ 8,400 +	$ -0- +	$3,600 +	$6,000 =			$ 200 +	$6,000 +		$11,800	

$18,000 $18,000

*Note: (7) did not involve an economic transaction between two parties, so it is an event and does not affect the accounting equation.

MID-CHAPTER DEMONSTRATION PROBLEM

↑ All chapters have a Mid-Chapter and End-of-Chapter Demonstration Problem to illustrate and reinforce important topics.

Part A

Bob Delgado founded a new moving company as a proprietorship on May 1. The accounting equation showed the following *balances* after each of the company's first five transactions. Analyze the equations and describe each of the five transactions with their amounts.

Transaction	Cash	+	Accounts Receivable	+	Office Supplies	+	Truck	+	Office Furniture	=	Accounts Payable	+	Bob Delgado, Capital
1	$10,000		$ -0-		$-0-		$45,000		$ -0-		$ -0-		$55,000
2	9,000		-0-		-0-		45,000		1,000		-0-		55,000
3	9,000		-0-		-0-		45,000		6,000		5,000		55,000
4	9,000		3,000		-0-		45,000		6,000		5,000		58,000
5	11,000		1,000		-0-		45,000		6,000		5,000		58,000

Part B

During June, Bob Delgado's second month of operations, transactions occurred, resulting in a $68,000 balance in the column Bob Delgado, Capital. Calculate the profit or loss for June under each of the following independent situations:

1. Bob made no investments or withdrawals during June.
2. Bob invested $15,000 during June and made no withdrawals.
3. Bob withdrew a total of $5,000 during June and made no additional investments.
4. Bob invested $5,000 during June and made withdrawals of $3,000.

Analysis Component:

Several activities cause equity to change. Of those activities, which one will help build equity over the long term?

Solution

Part A

1. Started the business by investing $10,000 cash and a $45,000 truck.
2. Purchased $1,000 of office furniture by paying cash.
3. Purchased $5,000 of office furniture on account.
4. Billed a customer $3,000 for services performed.
5. Collected $2,000 from a credit customer.

Part B

1.

Assets	=	Liabilities	+	Equity	
$63,000		$5,000		$58,000	Beginning assets, liabilities, and capital on June 1
			+	0	Plus owner investments during June
			−	0	Less owner withdrawals during June
			+ 10,000		**Plus profit (less loss) realized during June**
			=$68,000		Equals ending capital on June 30

Calculations: $68,000 − $58,000 = $10,000 profit.

2.

Assets	=	Liabilities	+	Equity	
$63,000		$5,000		$58,000	Beginning assets, liabilities, and capital on June 1
				+ 15,000	Plus owner investments during June
				– 0	Less owner withdrawals during June
				– 5,000	**Plus profit (less loss) realized during June**
				=$68,000	Equals ending capital on June 30

Calculations: $68,000 − $15,000 − $58,000 = <u>$5,000 loss.</u>

3.

Assets	=	Liabilities	+	Equity	
$63,000		$5,000		$58,000	Beginning assets, liabilities, and capital on June 1
				+ 0	Plus owner investments during June
				– 5,000	Less owner withdrawals during June
				+ 15,000	**Plus profit (less loss) realized during June**
				=$68,000	Equals ending capital on June 30

Calculations: $68,000 + $5,000 − $58,000 = <u>$15,000 profit.</u>

4.

Assets	=	Liabilities	+	Equity	
$63,000		$5,000		$58,000	Beginning assets, liabilities, and capital on June 1
				+ 5,000	Plus owner investments during June
				– 3,000	Less owner withdrawals during June
				+ 8,000	**Plus profit (less loss) realized during June**
				=$68,000	Equals ending capital on June 30

Calculations: $68,000 + $3,000 − $5,000 − $58,000 = <u>$8,000 profit.</u>

Analysis Component:

Equity increases because of owner investments and profit (when revenues are greater than expenses) and decreases because of owner withdrawals and losses (when expenses are greater than revenues). Recurring profit will help build (or grow) equity over the long term.

Financial Statements

LO8   Prepare financial statements reflecting business transactions.

We illustrated financial statements earlier in this chapter. These statements are required under GAAP. In this section, we describe how the financial statements shown in Exhibits 1.8 to 1.10 were prepared from the business transactions summarized in Exhibit 1.15. The analysis of the statement of cash flows, Exhibit 1.11, is left to Chapter 16.

Income Statement

Organico's income statement is shown on the right side of Exhibit 1.16. It was prepared using revenue and expense information taken from the equity column in Exhibit 1.15, copied in Exhibit 1.16 on the left side.

EXHIBIT 1.16

Organico's Financial Statements

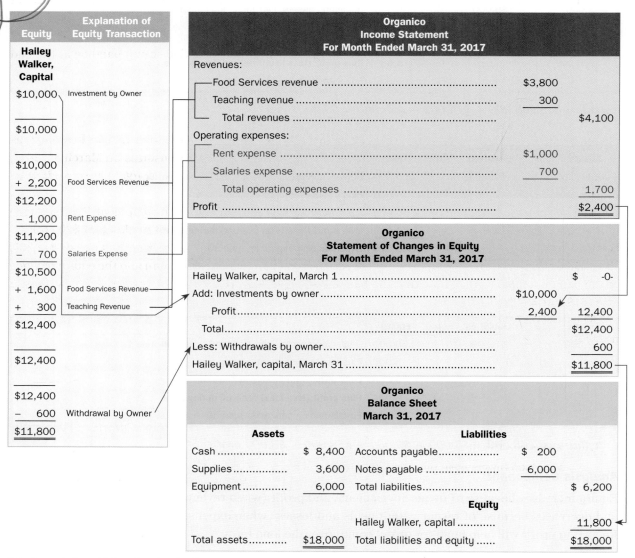

Note: Arrows in the exhibit are for educational purposes only.

Revenues of $4,100 are reported first and include food services revenues of $3,800 ($2,200 + $1,600) plus teaching revenue of $300. Expenses follow revenues, and can be listed in different ways. For convenience in this chapter, we list larger amounts first. Rent of $1,000 and salaries expenses of $700 result in total operating expenses of $1,700. Profit is reported at the bottom and is the amount earned during March. Owner's investments and withdrawals are *not* part of measuring profit; they are shown on the statement of changes in equity.

Statement of Changes in Equity

The second report in Exhibit 1.16 is the statement of changes in equity for Organico. Its heading lists the month as March 2017 because this statement describes transactions that happened during that month. The beginning balance of equity is measured as of the start of business on March 1. It is zero because Organico did not exist before then. An existing business reports the beginning balance as of the end of the prior reporting period. Organico's statement shows that $10,000 of equity is created by Hailey Walker's initial investment. It also shows the $2,400 of profit earned during the month. This item links the income statement to the statement of changes in equity as shown in Exhibit 1.16. The statement also reports the owner's $600 withdrawal and Organico's $11,800 equity balance at the end of the month.

Balance Sheet

The balance sheet in Exhibit 1.16 is the same statement that we described in Exhibit 1.10. Its heading tells us that the statement refers to Organico's financial position at the close of business on March 31, 2017. *Notice that the amounts appearing on the balance sheet came from the column totals summarized in Exhibit 1.15.*

The left side of the balance sheet lists Organico's assets: cash, supplies, and equipment. The right side of the balance sheet shows that Organico owes $6,200 to creditors, an amount made up of $200 for accounts payable and $6,000 for notes payable. The equity section shows an ending balance of $11,800. Note the link between the ending balance from the statement of changes in equity and the equity balance of the capital account. Also, note that the balance sheet equation, Assets = Liabilities + Equity, is still true ($18,000 = $6,200 + $11,800).

The financial statements for Organico can be useful to both internal and external users for making decisions.

DECISION MAKER

Answer—End of chapter

Extending Credit

You open a wholesale business selling entertainment equipment to retail outlets such as **Future Shop**, **Leon's**, and **Best Buy Canada**. You find that most of your customers demand to buy on credit. How can you use the balance sheets of these customers to help you decide which ones are worthy of credit?

CHECKPOINT

28. Explain the link between a profit statement and the statement of changes in equity.
29. Describe the link between a balance sheet and the statement of changes in equity.

Do Quick Study questions: QS 1-15, QS 1-16, QS 1-17, QS 1-18

CRITICAL THINKING CHALLENGE

Refer to the Critical Thinking Challenge questions at the beginning of the chapter. Compare your answers to those suggested on Connect.

IFRS AND ASPE—THE DIFFERENCES

Difference	International Financial Reporting Standards (IFRS)	Accounting Standards for Private Enterprises (ASPE)
Financial statements	• IFRS refers to the financial statements as: statement of financial position (or balance sheet), statement of income, statement of changes in equity, and statement of cash flows.*	• ASPE refers to the financial statements as: balance sheet, income statement, statement of retained earnings (or statement of changes in equity), and cash flow statement.***
GAAP	• Publicly accountable enterprises must use IFRS.	• Private enterprises can choose between ASPE and IFRS but once the choice is made, it must be applied consistently.
	• IFRS does not use the terms *reliability* and *conservatism*.**	• ASPE includes conservatism as a measure of reliability.****

*IFRS 2014, IAS 1, para. 10.
**IFRS 2014, "the conceptual framework for reporting entities," para. 4.1–4.39.
***ASPE, Accounting Standards, General Accounting, Section 1000.04 and Section 1400.10.
****ASPE, Accounting Standards, Section 1000.18(d)

↑ Each chapter identifies the primary differences between IFRS and ASPE at the introductory level of accounting.

A LOOK Ahead

Chapter 2 describes and analyzes business transactions. We explain the analysis and recording of transactions, the ledger and trial balance, and the double-entry system. More generally, Chapters 2 through 4 use the accounting cycle to show how financial statements reflect business activities.

For further study on some topics of relevance to this chapter, please see the following Extend Your Knowledge supplements:

EYK 1-1 External Accounting Information Needs
EYK 1-2 Internal Operating Functions
EYK 1-3 Applying the 4-Way Test
EYK 1-4 Corporate Governance—Example
EYK 1-5 Return and Risk
EYK 1-6 Corporate Supplement
EYK 1-7 Examples of Source Documents
EYK 1-8 Case Study: Transaction Analysis Using Source Documents

↓ Each chapter includes a summary of the chapter by learning objective.

Summary

LO1 Describe the purpose and importance of accounting. Accounting is an information and measurement system that aims to identify, measure, record, and communicate relevant information that faithfully represents an organization's economic activities. It helps us better assess opportunities, products, investments, and social and community responsibilities. The power of accounting is in opening our eyes to new and exciting opportunities. The greatest benefits of understanding accounting often come to those outside accounting, because an improved understanding of accounting helps us to compete better in today's globally focused and technologically challenging world.

LO2 Describe forms of business organization. Organizations can be classified either as businesses or as non-businesses. Businesses are organized for profit, while non-businesses serve us in ways not always measured by profit. Businesses take one of three forms: sole proprietorship, partnership, or corporation. These forms of organization have characteristics that hold important implications for legal liability, taxation, continuity, number of owners, and legal status.

LO3 **Identify users and uses of, and opportunities in, accounting.** There are both internal and external users of accounting. Some users and uses of accounting include (a) management for control, monitoring, and planning; (b) lenders for making decisions regarding loan applications; (c) shareholders for making investment decisions; (d) directors for overseeing management; and (e) employees for judging employment opportunities. Opportunities in accounting encompass traditional financial and managerial accounting, and taxation, but also include accounting-related fields such as lending, consulting, managing, and planning.

LO4 **Identify and explain why ethics and social responsibility are crucial to accounting.** The goal of accounting is to provide useful information for decision making. For information to be useful, it must be trusted. This demands ethics and socially responsible behaviour in accounting. Without these, accounting information loses its reliability.

LO5 **Identify, explain, and apply accounting principles.** Accounting principles aid in producing relevant information that faithfully represents an organization's economic activities. The general principles described in this chapter include business entity, cost, going concern, monetary unit, and revenue recognition. We will discuss others in later chapters. The business entity principle requires that a business be accounted for separately from its owners. The cost principle requires that financial statements be based on actual costs incurred in business transactions. The going concern principle requires that financial statements reflect an assumption that the business continues to operate. The monetary unit principle assumes that transactions can be captured in money terms and that the monetary unit is stable over time. The revenue recognition principle assumes that revenue is recognized when earned, assets received from selling products and services do not have to be in cash, and revenue recognized is measured by cash received plus the cash equivalent (market) value of other assets received.

LO6 **Identify and explain the content and reporting aims of financial statements.** The major

financial statements are: income statement (shows a company's profitability determined as revenues less expenses equals income or loss), statement of changes in equity (explains how equity changes from the beginning to the end of a period), balance sheet (reports on a company's financial position, including assets, liabilities, and equity), and statement of cash flows (identifies all cash inflows and outflows for the period). The differences in financial statements across forms of business organization are (1) the equity on the balance sheet belongs to the sole owner in a sole proprietorship, to the partners in a partnership, and to the shareholders in a corporation; (2) distributions of assets to the owner(s) are called withdrawals for both a sole proprietorship and a partnership, and dividends for a corporation; (3) when the owner of a proprietorship or partnership is its manager, no salary expense is reported, while in a corporation, salaries paid to managers who are also shareholders are reported as expenses.

LO7 **Analyze business transactions by applying the accounting equation.** Investing activities are funded by an organization's financing activities. An organization's assets (investments) must equal its financing (from liabilities and from equity). This basic relation gives us the accounting equation: Assets = Liabilities + Equity. A transaction is an exchange of economic consideration between two parties and affects the accounting equation. The equation is always in balance when business transactions are properly recorded. An economic consideration is something of value; examples include products, services, money, and rights to collect money. Source documents are the source of accounting information. An event does not involve an economic exchange; it has no effect on the accounting equation.

LO8 **Prepare financial statements reflecting business transactions.** Using the accounting equation, business transactions can be summarized and organized so that we can readily prepare the financial statements. The balance sheet uses the ending balances in the accounting equation at a point in time. The statement of changes in equity and the income statement use data from the equity account for the period.

Guidance Answer to DECISION MAKER

Extending Credit

You can use the accounting equation (Assets = Liabilities + Equity) to help identify risky customers to whom you would likely not want to extend credit. A balance sheet provides amounts for each of these key components.

The lower a customer's equity is relative to liabilities, the less likely you would be to extend credit. A low equity means the business has little value that does not already have creditor claims to it.

Guidance Answers to CHECKPOINT

1. Accounting is an information and measurement system that identifies, measures, records, and communicates relevant and faithfully representative information to people that helps them in making better decisions. It helps people in business to identify and react to investment opportunities, and better assess opportunities, products, investments, and social and community responsibilities.

2. Recordkeeping is the recording of financial transactions and events, either manually or electronically. While recordkeeping is essential to ensuring data is complete, free from error, and neutral, accounting is this and much more. Accounting includes identifying, measuring, recording, reporting, and analyzing economic events and transactions. It involves interpreting information, and designing information systems to provide useful reports that monitor and control an organization's activities.

3. Non-business organizations may include public airports, libraries, museums, religious institutions, municipal governments, law enforcement organizations, postal services, colleges, universities, highways, shelters, parks, hospitals, and schools.

4. The three common forms of business organization are sole proprietorships, partnerships, and corporations.

5. Private accountants work for a single employer, which is often a business. A public accountant is available to the public, which means that services are provided to many different clients.

6. The four broad fields of accounting are financial, managerial, taxation, and accounting related.

7. The purpose of an audit is to add credibility to the financial statements.

8. Managerial accounting is for internal users, while financial accounting is for external users.

9. External users of accounting information are not directly involved in running the organization. Internal users of accounting information are those individuals directly involved in managing and operating an organization.

10. Internal controls are procedures set up to protect assets; ensure that accounting reports are complete, free from error, and neutral; promote efficiency; and encourage adherence to company policies. Internal controls are crucial if accounting reports are to provide relevant and trustworthy information.

11. The guidelines for ethical and socially responsible decisions are threefold: (1) identify the ethical and/or social issue; (2) analyze options, considering both good and bad consequences for all individuals affected; and (3) make an ethical/socially responsible decision, choosing the best option after weighing all consequences.

12. Ethics and social responsibility are important for people because, without them, existence is more difficult, inefficient, and unpleasant. They are equally important to organizations, for this same reason. In addition, they often translate into higher profits and a better working environment.

13. Accounting aims to provide useful information for decision making. For information to be useful, it must be trusted. Trustworthiness of information demands ethics in accounting.

14. The business entity principle is important to the usefulness of accounting. Users desire information about the performance of a *specific* entity. If information is mixed between two or more entities, its usefulness decreases. It is imperative that the business entity principle be followed.

15. The cost principle determines that financial statements are based on actual costs incurred in business transactions. Information prepared using the cost principle is considered verifiable because it can be confirmed and is not subject to arbitrary manipulation.

16. Revenue should be recognized next month when the product is delivered, according to the revenue recognition principle. This principle states that revenue is recognized when the product has been provided and not necessarily when cash has been received. In this case, the business has received the cash from the customer without providing the product. Therefore, the business has not realized revenue but instead has incurred a liability; it owes the customer the product.

17. The four major financial statements are income statement, statement of changes in equity, balance sheet, and statement of cash flows.

18. Revenues are the value of assets received in exchange for products or services provided to customers as part of a business's main operations. Expenses are costs incurred or the using up of assets that results from providing products or services to customers. Expenses also can arise from increases in liabilities.

19. Assets are the properties or economic resources owned by a business. Liabilities are the obligations of a business, representing the claims of others against the assets of a business. Equity is the owner's claim on the assets of the business. It is the assets of a business that remain after deducting liabilities.

20. Three differences in financial statements for different forms of organization are (1) proprietorship's equity belongs to one owner. A partnership's equity belongs to the partners. A corporation's equity belongs to the shareholders. (2) Distributions of cash or other assets to owners of a proprietorship or partnership are called withdrawals. Distributions of cash or other assets to owners of a corporation are called dividends. (3) When the owner of a sole proprietorship is also its manager, no salary expense is reported on the income statement. The same is true for a partnership. In a corporation, however, salaries paid to all employees, including managers who are shareholders, are reported as expenses.

21. A transaction, such as (2) that involves changing the form of one asset for another asset would *not* affect any liability and equity accounts.

22. Performing services for a customer, such as in (4) increases the equity (and assets). Incurring expenses while servicing clients, such as in (5) and (6) decreases the equity (and assets). Other examples include owner investments, such as (1) those that increase equity, and owner withdrawals, such as (11) those that decrease equity.

23. Payment of a liability with an asset reduces both asset and liability totals. An example is (10) where an account payable is settled by paying cash.

24. The accounting equation is Assets = Liabilities + Equity. It is in balance when the sum of the assets is equal to the sum of the liabilities and equity accounts. This equation is always in balance, both before and after every transaction. Balance refers to the equality in this equation, which is always maintained.

25. Business transactions are exchanges between two parties and affect the accounting equation. Events do not involve an exchange and therefore do not affect the accounting equation.

26. Examples of source documents are sales invoices, cheques, purchase orders, charges to customers, bills from suppliers, employee earnings records, and bank statements.

27. Source documents serve many purposes, including recordkeeping and internal control. Source documents, especially if obtained from outside the organization, provide evidence about transactions and their amounts for recording. Evidence is important because it makes information more reliable and useful.

28. An income statement describes a company's revenues and expenses along with the resulting profit or loss. A statement of changes in equity describes changes in equity that *include* profit or loss. Also, both statements report transactions occurring over a period of time.

29. A balance sheet describes a company's financial position (assets, liabilities, and equity) at a point in time. The equity account in the balance sheet is obtained from the statement of changes in equity.

DEMONSTRATION PROBLEM

After several months of planning, Joanne Cardinal started a haircutting business called The Cutlery. The following business activities occurred during its first month, August 2017:

a. On August 1, Cardinal put $16,000 cash into a chequing account in the name of The Cutlery. She also invested $10,000 of equipment that she already owned.

b. On August 2, she paid $2,000 cash for furniture for the shop.

c. On August 3, she paid $3,200 cash to rent space in a strip mall for August.

d. On August 4, she equipped the shop by installing the old equipment and some new equipment that she bought on credit for $21,000. This amount is to be repaid in three equal payments at the end of August, September, and October.

e. On August 5, The Cutlery opened for business. Receipts from services provided for cash in the first week and a half of business (ended August 15) were $1,100.

f. On August 15, Cardinal provided haircutting services on account for $750.

g. On August 17, Cardinal received a $750 cheque in the mail for services previously rendered on account.

h. On August 17, Cardinal paid wages of $250 to an assistant for working during the grand opening.

i. On August 18, Cardinal interviewed a job applicant. The applicant was successful in getting the position and will receive $750 per week for part-time work starting in September.

j. Cash receipts from services provided during the second half of August was $1,950.

k. On August 31, Cardinal paid an installment on the account payable created in (d).

l. On August 31, the August hydro bill for $450 was received. It will be paid on September 14.

m. On August 31, Cardinal withdrew $500 cash for her personal use.

Required

1. Arrange the following asset, liability, and equity titles in a table similar to the one in Exhibit 1.15: Cash; Accounts Receivable; Furniture; Store Equipment; Accounts Payable; and Joanne Cardinal, Capital. Show the effects of each transaction on the equation. Explain each of the changes in equity.

2. Prepare an income statement for August.

3. Prepare a statement of changes in equity for August.

4. Prepare a balance sheet as of August 31.

Analysis Component:

a. Identify how much of the assets held by The Cutlery are owned by the owner, Joanne Cardinal.

b. How much of the total assets are financed by equity? By debt? Explain what it means to "finance assets by equity: and to "finance assets by debt."

Planning the Solution

- Set up a table with the appropriate columns, including a final column for describing the transactions that affect equity.

- Identify and analyze each transaction and show its effects as increases or decreases in the appropriate columns. Be sure that the accounting equation remains in balance after each transaction.

- To prepare the income statement, find the revenues and expenses in the Explanation of Equity Transaction column. List those items on the statement, calculate the difference, and label the result as *profit* or *loss*.

- Use the information in the Explanation of Equity Transaction column to prepare the statement of changes in equity.

- Use the information in the last row of the table to prepare the balance sheet.

- Prepare an answer to each part of the analysis component question.

Solution

1.

	Cash	+	Accounts Receivable	+	Furniture	+	Store Equipment	=	Accounts Payable	+	Joane Cardinal, Capital	Explanation of Equity Transaction
												(Assets = Liabilities + Equity)
a.	$16,000						$10,000				$26,000	Investment by Owner
b.	− 2,000				+$2,000							
Bal.	$14,000				$2,000		$10,000				$26,000	
c.	− 3,200										− 3,200	Rent Expense
Bal.	$10,800				$2,000		$10,000				$22,800	
d.							+21,000		+$21,000			
Bal.	$10,800				$2,000		$31,000		$21,000		$22,800	
e.	+ 1,100										+ 1,100	Haircutting Services Revenue
Bal.	$11,900				$2,000		$31,000		$21,000		$23,900	
f.			+ $750								+ 750	Haircutting Services Revenue
Bal.	$11,900		$750		$2,000		$31,000		$21,000		$24,650	
g.	+ 750		− 750									
Bal.	$12,650		$ -0-		$2,000		$31,000		$21,000		$24,650	
h.	− 250										− 250	Wages Expense
Bal.	$12,400				$2,000		$31,000		$21,000		$24,400	
i.	No entry*											
j.	+ 1,950										+ 1,950	Haircutting Services Revenue
Bal.	$14,350				$2,000		$31,000		$21,000		$26,350	
k.	− 7,000								− 7,000			
Bal.	$ 7,350				$2,000		$31,000		$14,000		$26,350	
l.									+ 450		− 450	Hydro Expense
Bal.	$ 7,350				$2,000		$31,000		$14,450		$25,900	
m.	− 500										− 500	Withdrawal by Owner
Bal.	$ 6,850	+	$ -0-	+	$2,000	+	$31,000	=	$14,450	+	$25,400	

= $39,850   = $39,850

*Note: (i) does not involve an economic exchange between two parties; therefore, it does not affect the accounting equation.

2.

The Cutlery
Income Statement
For Month Ended August 31, 2017

Revenues:		
Haircutting services revenue...		$ 3,800
Operating expenses:		
Rent expense	$3,200	
Hydro expense	450	
Wages expense	250	
Total operating expenses		3,900
Loss..		$ 100

3.

The Cutlery
Statement of Changes in Equity
For Month Ended August 31, 2017

Joanne Cardinal, capital, August 1...		$ –0–
Add: Investments by owner..		26,000
Total		$26,000
Less: Withdrawals by owner..	$500	
Loss...	100	600
Joanne Cardinal, capital, August 31..		$25,400

4.

The Cutlery
Balance Sheet
August 31, 2017

Assets		Liabilities	
Cash	$ 6,850	Accounts payable...........................	$14,450
Furniture..........................	2,000		
Store equipment	31,000	**Equity**	
		Joane Cardinal, capital	25,400
Total assets......................	$39,850	Total liabilities and equity	$39,850

The arrows are imaginary but they emphasize the link between statements.

Analysis Component:

a. $25,400 or 64% ($25,400/$39,850 × 100% = 63.74% or 64%) of the total assets are owned by the owner, Joanne Cardinal.

b. $25,400 or 64% ($25,400/$39,850 × 100% = 63.74% or 64%) of the total assets are financed by equity. $14,450 or 36% ($14,450/$39,850 × 100% = 36.26% or 36%) of the total assets are financed by debt.

To *finance assets by equity* means that the equity transactions of owner investment, plus profit(or less loss), and less owner withdrawals resulted in a portion of the assets. In the case of The Cutlery, 64% of the assets at August 31, 2017, resulted from these equity transactions.

To *finance assets by debt* (or liabilities) means that a portion of the assets resulted from borrowings. In the case of The Cutlery, 36% of the assets at August 31, 2017, resulted from, specifically, accounts payable.

↓ The glossary includes terms and phrases explained in the chapter

Glossary

Accounting An information system that identifies, measures, records, and communicates relevant information that faithfully represents an organization's economic activities.

Accounting equation A description of the relationship between a company's assets, liabilities, and equity; expressed as Assets = Liabilities + Equity; also called the *balance sheet equation*.

Accounting Standards Board (AcSB) Prior to Canada's adoption of IFRS, the AcSB was the authoritative body that set accounting standards for Canada. With IFRS being set by the IASB, the AcSB's new role is evolving.

Accounting Standards for Private Enterprises (ASPE) Rules created by the Accounting Standards Board to govern accounting for Canadian private enterprises.

Account payable A liability created by buying goods or services on credit.

Accounts receivable Assets created by selling products or services on credit.

AcSB See *Accounting Standards Board*.

ASPE See *Accounting Standards for Private Enterprises*.

Assets Properties or economic resources owned by the business; more precisely, resources with an ability to provide future benefits to the business, results from a past transaction.

Audit An independent, external check of an organization's accounting systems and records.

Balance sheet A financial statement that reports the financial position of a business at a point in time; lists the types and dollar amounts of assets, liabilities, and equity as of a specific date; also called the *statement of financial position*.

Balance sheet equation Another name for the *accounting equation*.

Bookkeeping The part of accounting that involves recording economic transactions electronically or manually; also called *recordkeeping*.

Budgeting The process of developing formal plans for future activities, which often serve as a basis for evaluating actual performance.

Business One or more individuals selling products or services for profit.

Business activities All of the transactions and events experienced by a business.

Business entity principle The principle that requires every business to be accounted for separately from its owner or owners. It is based on the goal of providing relevant information about each business to users

Business events Activities that do not involve an exchange of economic consideration between two parties and therefore do not affect the accounting equation.

Business transaction An exchange of economic consideration between two parties that causes a change in assets, liabilities, or equity. Examples of economic considerations include products, services, money, and rights to collect money.

CA Chartered Accountant; an accountant who has met the examination, education, and experience requirements of the Institute of Chartered Accountants for an individual professionally competent in accounting.

Calendar year An accounting year that begins on January 1 and ends on December 31.

Canada Revenue Agency (CRA) The federal government agency responsible for the collection of tax and enforcement of tax laws.

CGA Certified General Accountant; an accountant who has met the examination, education, and experience requirements of the Certified General Accountants' Association for an individual professionally competent in accounting.

CMA Certified Management Accountant; an accountant who has met the examination, education, and experience requirements of the Society of Management Accountants for an individual professionally competent in accounting.

Common shares The name for a corporation's shares when only one class of share capital is issued.

Comparability Similarity; ability to be compared with other information.

Controller The chief accounting officer of an organization.

Corporate governance The mechanism by which individuals in a company, in particular the board of directors, are motivated to align their behaviours with the overall corporate good.

Corporation A business that is a separate legal entity under provincial or federal laws with owners who are called shareholders.

Cost accounting A managerial accounting activity designed to help managers identify, measure, and control operating costs.

Cost constraint The accounting standard that requires the benefits obtained from financial statement information to be justifiable based on costs incurred in financial reporting.

Costs The expenses incurred to earn revenues (or sales).

CPA Chartered Professional Accountant, the newly formed accounting body with the mandate to merge the three legacy accounting designations (CA, CMA, CGA).

Creditors Individuals or organizations entitled to receive payments from a company.

Currency Transactions are to be expressed in money units based on the main currency used in operations; examples include units such as the Canadian dollar, American dollar, peso, and pound sterling.

Debtors Individuals or organizations that owe amounts to a business.

Economic consideration Something of value (e.g., products, services, money, and rights to collect money).

Equity The owner's claim on the assets of a business; more precisely, the assets of an entity that remain after deducting its liabilities. Equity increases with owner investments and profit and decreases with owner withdrawals and losses, also called *net assets*.

Ethics Beliefs that differentiate right from wrong.

Events See *business events*.

Expenses Costs incurred or the using up of assets as a result of the major or central operations of a business.

External auditors Accountants outside the company who examine and provide assurance that financial statements are prepared according to generally accepted accounting principles (GAAP).

External users Persons using accounting information who are not directly involved in the running of the organization. Examples include shareholders, customers, regulators, and suppliers.

Equipment Tangible asset intended to be used in the business with an expected life of more than one year.

Faithful representation A quality of information that is complete, neutral, and free from error.

Financial accounting The area of accounting that reports on the financial performance and condition of an organization. It is aimed at serving external users.

Financial statements The products of accounting that report on the financial performance and condition of an organization. They include the income statement, statement of changes in equity, balance sheet, and statement of cash flows.

Fiscal year A one-year (12-month) reporting period.

GAAP See *generally accepted accounting principles*.

General accounting The task of recording transactions, processing data, and preparing reports for managers; includes preparing financial statements for disclosure to external users.

Generally accepted accounting principles (GAAP) The underlying concepts adopted by the accounting profession that make up acceptable accounting practices for the preparation of financial statements.

Going concern assumption The rule that requires financial statements to reflect the assumption that the business will continue operating instead of being closed or sold, unless evidence shows that it will not continue.

IASB See *International Accounting Standards Board*.

IFRS See *International Financial Reporting Standards*.

Income Another name for *profit*.

Income statement The financial statement that shows, by subtracting expenses from revenues, whether the business earned a profit; it lists the types and amounts of revenues earned and expenses incurred by a business over a period of time.

Internal auditing Function performed by employees within organizations who assess whether managers are following established operating procedures and evaluates the efficiency of operating procedures.

Internal controls Procedures set up to protect assets, ensure reliable accounting reports, promote efficiency, and encourage adherence to company policies.

Internal users Persons using accounting information who are directly involved in managing and operating an organization; examples include managers and officers.

International Accounting Standards Board (IASB) The body responsible for setting IFRS.

International Financial Reporting Standards (IFRS) The standards for financial reporting that came into effect January 2011 in Canada for publicly accountable entities.

Liabilities The debts or obligations of a business; claims by others that will reduce the future assets of a business or require future services or products, resulting from a past transaction.

Limited liability The owner's liability is limited to the amount of investment in the business.

Loss The excess of expenses over revenues for a period.

Management consulting Activity in which suggestions are offered for improving a company's procedures; the suggestions may concern new accounting and internal control systems, new computer systems, budgeting, and employee benefit plans.

Managerial accounting The area of accounting aimed at serving the decision-making needs of internal users.

Natural business year A 12-month period that ends when a company's sales activities are at their lowest point.

Net assets Assets minus liabilities; another name for *equity*.

Note payable A liability expressed by a written promise to make a future payment at a specific time.

Owner investments The transfer of an owner's personal assets to the business.

Owner withdrawals See *withdrawals*.

Partnership A business owned by two or more people that is not organized as a corporation.

Private accountants Accountants who work for a single employer other than the government or a public accounting firm.

Private enterprise (PE) A corporation that does not offer its shares for public sale.

Profit The excess of revenues over expenses for a period; also called *income*.

Public accountants Accountants licensed and regulated by their professional accounting bodies in the provinces in which they work. They provide professional services such as audit, tax, and consulting to many different clients.

Publicly accountable enterprise (PAE) A corporation that sells its shares to the public.

Public sale of shares The issuance of shares by a corporation in an organized stock exchange.

Recordkeeping The recording of financial transactions manually or electronically; also called *bookkeeping*.

Relevance Information must make a difference in the decision-making process.

Revenue recognition principle Provides guidance on when revenue should be reflected on the income statement; the rule states that revenue is recorded at the time it is earned regardless of whether cash or another asset has been exchanged.

Revenue The value of assets received or receivable as a result of selling goods or services to customers.

Shareholders The owners of a corporation; also known as stockholders.

Shares Units of ownership in a corporation; also known as stocks.

Social responsibility A commitment by an organization to consider the impact and being accountable for the effects that actions might have on society.

Sole proprietorship A business owned by one person that is not organized as a corporation; also called a *single proprietorship*.

Source documents Original documents that identify and describe transactions within the organization. These documents provide information to be recorded in the accounting information system and can be in paper or electronic form. An example of a source document is an invoice used to record a sale of merchandise to a customer.

Statement of cash flows A financial statement that describes the sources and uses of cash for a reporting period, i.e., where a company's cash came from (receipts) and where it went during the period (payments); the cash flows are arranged by an organization's major activities: operating, investing, and financing activities.

Statement of changes in equity A financial statement that reports the changes in equity over the reporting period; beginning equity is adjusted for increases such as owner investment or profit and for decreases such as owner withdrawals or a loss.

Statement of financial position See *balance sheet*.

Supplies Consumable items that are purchased by the business to carry out its recurring activities. Examples include stationary, printer ink, flour used by a bakery, milk/coffee beans purchased by a café, nails purchased by a carpenter. Classified as a current asset. Consumed supplies become supplies expense.

Taxation The field of accounting that includes preparing tax returns and planning future transactions to minimize the amount of tax paid; involves private, public, and government accountants.

Timeliness A characteristic of accounting information that ensures it is available to decision makers in time to influence their decisions.

Transaction See *business transaction*.

Understandability A quality of information that is useful to users with reasonable knowledge of accounting and business and economic activities.

Unlimited liability When the debts of a sole proprietorship or partnership are greater than its resources, the owner(s) is (are) financially responsible.

Verifiability A quality of information that different knowledgeable users could agree was faithfully represented.

Withdrawals The distributions of cash or other assets from a proprietorship or partnership to its owner or owners.

↓ Short-answer questions reinforce key chapter concepts in order of learning objectives.

Concept Review Questions

1. The chapter's opening vignette describes Zane Caplansky's success with his food truck, Thundering Thelma. Explain why accounting is critical for Caplansky's business and for his expansion strategy.

2. Think about the businesses that you encounter in your everyday life. Identify three real product-based businesses and specify the product that each provides. Name three real service-based businesses and specify the service that each provides.

3. Your friends are studying marketing and human resources and another is undecided on his major.

They say, "This accounting course is a waste of my time when I don't even want to be an accountant!" Explain to your friends how accounting is important and relevant to all students, including those studying marketing and human resources.

4. You have decided to start a business. What would you sell? Identify the three forms of business organization you could choose and describe their characteristics. Which form of business is best for your business and why?

5. Review Organico's financial statements presented in the chapter for the month ended March 31, 2017. Review the balance sheet and determine the business form Hailey Walker has chosen to organize her business.

6. Identify two organizations for which accounting information is available in Appendix III at the end of the book.

7. Identify three types of organizations that can be formed as either profit-oriented businesses, government entities, or not-for-profit organizations.

8. Identify four external and internal users and their uses of accounting information.

9. Describe the internal role of accounting for organizations.

10. Tyler is considering a career in accounting, but is not sure what career options are available within accounting. Help Tyler with his decision by identifying three main areas of accounting for accounting professionals. For each accounting area, identify three accounting-related career opportunities.

11. Identify the auditing firm that audited the financial statements of WestJet in Appendix III.

12. What is the purpose of accounting in society?

13. What ethical issues might accounting professionals face in dealing with confidential information?

14. Why does the user of an income statement need to know the time period that it covers?

15. Why is the revenue recognition principle needed? What does it require?

16. Identify four financial statements that a proprietorship presents to its owner and other users.

17. Jordan thinks the income statement and the balance sheet look the same. Explain to Jordan what information is presented on the income statement and what is presented on the balance sheet.

18. Assets are resources that provide future benefit to a business. Explain how cash, accounts receivable, and supplies provide future benefit to a business.

19. Rachel believes that the terms *accounts receivable* and *accounts payable* can be used interchangeably. Rachel says, "They both show up on the balance sheet and they both are in the accounting equation." Do you agree with Rachel? Explain.

20. In the first year of selling frozen yogurt, the owner of Swirl invested $10,000 into the business and sold $5,000 of frozen yogurt. The accountant has recorded $15,000 of revenue. What do accountants mean by the term *revenue*? Has the accountant at Swirl recorded revenue correctly or incorrectly? Explain.

21. What transactions increase and decrease equity?

22. Your favourite celebrity has asked you to prepare a personal balance sheet for her. Define (a) assets, (b) liabilities, and (d) equity. Identify some of her personal assets and liabilities. Explain to her what her equity represents.

23. Why is it important to prepare the financial statements (statement of changes in equity, balance sheet, income statement and the statement of cash flows) in a specific order? Identify the specific order. Identify how the financial statements are interrelated.

↓ Quick Study questions are single-topic exercises that give the reader a brief test of each key element in the chapter. Answers to the Quick Study (QS) questions are available on Connect.

Quick Study

↓ Each Quick Study, Exercise, and Problem is referenced to a learning objective in the chapter.

QS 1-1 **Uses of accounting** LO1

You have just graduated from the finance program at a local postsecondary institution. An opportunity to become the marketing manager for a medium-sized florist chain is available to you. You are concerned because you know that accounting plays a major role in the successful execution of this role and accounting was not your best subject. Identify at least two questions or issues for which the marketing manager would require accounting information.

QS 1-2 Determining when to record accounting transactions LO1

Determine whether each of the following events should be recorded in the accounting records.

    a. Meeting with the mechanical staff to determine new machine requirements for next year.

    b. Receiving the company's utility bill detailing the usage for the past month.

    c. Analyzing last year's sales report to determine if the discount policy is effective in getting customers to buy in multiple quantities.

    d. Downloading the online bank statements and identifying customer payments.

    e. After an employee is interviewed, hiring him for the accounting position.

QS 1-3 Business vs. non-business organizations LO2

Identify whether each of the following represents a business or non-business organization.

Hint: *Enhance your research skills and check the Internet to confirm your answers.*

    a. Highlands United Church   **d.** University of Toronto

    b. Royal Alexandra Hospital   **e.** Loblaw Companies Limited

    c. Toronto-Dominion Bank   **f.** World Vision

QS 1-4 Financial statements and forms of organization LO2

    SP – Sole proprietorship

    P – Partnership

    C – Corporation

Identify the type of business organization based on the following independent financial statement findings:

    _____ **1.** The equity section of the balance sheet has one capital account.

    _____ **2.** The owners receive dividends, a distribution of earnings, in the form of cash.

    _____ **3.** There are two capital accounts: Tara Davis, Capital, and Sheila Kelton, Capital.

    _____ **4.** The one owner receives distributions of earnings in the form of withdrawals.

    _____ **5.** A manager, also the owner of the business, is paid a salary that is recorded as an expense.

    _____ **6.** The equity on the balance sheet is held by shareholders.

    _____ **7.** The five owners receive distributions of earnings in the form of withdrawals.

QS 1-5 Describing accounting responsibilities LO3

Many accounting professionals work in one of the following three areas:

    a. Financial accounting

    b. Managerial accounting

    c. Taxation accounting

For each of the following responsibilities, identify the area of accounting that most likely involves that responsibility:

    _____ **1.** Auditing financial statements.

    _____ **2.** Planning transactions to minimize taxes paid.

_M_____ **3.** Cost accounting.

_M_____ **4.** Preparing financial statements.

_F_____ **5.** Reviewing financial reports for compliance with provincial securities commissions requirements.

_M_____ **6.** Budgeting.

_M_____ **7.** Internal auditing.

_T_____ **8.** Investigating violations of tax laws.

QS 1-6 Ethics in Accounting: Applying the Chartered Professional Accountants of Ontario's Rules of Professional Conduct—Approach to Ethical Conflict Resolution. LO4

You are a student taking an introductory accounting course. In week two of the course, your girlfriend broke up with you. You missed the lecture on debits and credits and were lost in week three. You did not pass your midterms and desperately need to pass the final. During the final, you go to the bathroom where you take a look at the accounting notes you "threw away" in the garbage. You remember your professor's speech on academic dishonesty. You have always valued honesty, but this situation is your ex-girlfriend's fault. Using Ontario's Rules of Professional Conduct, determine whether your behaviour is ethical.

QS 1-7 Identifying accounting principles LO5

Identify which GAAP most directly describes each of the following correct practices:

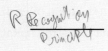

a. Tracy Regis owns two businesses, Second Time Around Clothing and Antique Accents, both of which are sole proprietorships. In having financial statements prepared for the antique store, Regis should be sure that the revenue and expense transactions of Second Time Around are excluded from the statements of Antique Accents.

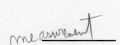

b. In December 2016, Classic Coverings received a customer's order to install carpet and tile in a new house that would not be ready for completion until March 2017. Classic Coverings should record the revenue for the order in March 2017, not in December 2016.

c. If $30,000 cash is paid to buy land, the land should be reported on the purchaser's balance sheet at $30,000 although the purchaser was offered $35,000 the following week.

QS 1-8 Identifying accounting principles LO5

For each of the following, identify which GAAP, if any, has been violated.

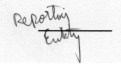

1. A customer called and made arrangements for Jay's Plumbing to provide $6,000 of services *next month*. Jay, the owner, recorded revenue of $6,000 *this month*. No cash was exchanged.

2. Land was purchased for $50,000. The bank appraised it for loan purposes at $68,000. Therefore, the owner of the land recorded it on the balance sheet at $68,000.

3. The owner of Dallas Pizza and Don's Deli combines all transactions by keeping only one set of accounting records for both businesses.

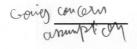

4. The owner of Guu Japanese Eatery has become ill suddenly and is unable to continue the business. The owner's spouse, in need of cash to finance growing personal expenses, took the business's most recent financial statements to the bank and was granted a loan. She did not inform the bank of her husband's inability to work.

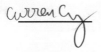

5. Dale's Consulting Services completed a contract with an organization located overseas. Dale included the revenue on the income statement without converting the foreign currency to Canadian dollars.

QS 1-9 Identifying accounting principles LO5

For each of the following, identify which GAAP was violated by Delco Consulting. In cases where more than one GAAP applies, name the primary GAAP that was not followed.

_____ a. Delco performed work for a client located in China and collected 8,450,000 RMB (renminbi, the Chinese currency), the equivalent of about $1,320,000 Canadian. Delco recorded it as 8,450,000.

_____ b. Delco collected $180,000 from a customer on December 20, 2017, for work to be done in February 2018. The $180,000 was recorded as revenue during 2017. Delco's year-end is December 31.

_____ c. Delco's December 31, 2017, balance sheet showed total assets of $840,000 and liabilities of $1,120,000. The income statements for the past six years have shown a trend of increasing losses.

_____ d. Included in Delco's assets was land and a building purchased for $310,000 and reported on the balance sheet at $470,000.

_____ e. Delco's owner, Tom Del, consistently buys personal supplies and charges them to the company.

QS 1-10 Applying the accounting equation LO7

Determine the missing amount for each of the following equations:

	Assets	=	Liabilities	+	Equity
a.	$ 75,000		$ 40,500		?
b.	$300,000		?		$85,500
c.	?		$187,500		$95,400

QS 1-11 Applying the accounting equation LO7

Use the accounting equation to determine:

a. The equity in a business that has $374,700 of assets and $252,450 of liabilities.

b. The liabilities of a business having $150,900 of assets and $126,000 of equity.

c. The assets of a business having $37,650 of liabilities and $112,500 of equity.

QS 1-12 Applying the accounting equation LO7

The balance sheet is a more detailed presentation of the accounting equation. The income statement and statement of changes in equity are linked to the balance sheet (by the accounting equation). Calculate the missing amounts below.

a.

Allin Servicing Income Statement For Month Ended April 30, 2017	
Revenues	$300
Expenses	?
Profit (loss)	?

Allin Servicing Statement of Changes in Equity For Month Ended April 30, 2017		
Tim Allin, capital, April 1		$ 50
Add: Investments by owner..........	$ 30	
Profit	?	?
Total		$255
Less: Withdrawals by owner.........		?
Tim Allin, capital, April 30		?

Allin Servicing Balance Sheet April 30, 2017			
Assets		**Liabilities**	
Cash	$ 60	Accounts payable....	$ 25
Equipment	?	**Equity**	
		Tim Allin, capital......	?
		Total liabilities	
Total assets.......	$265	and equity	?

b.

Allin Servicing Income Statement For Month Ended May 31, 2017	
Revenues	?
Expenses	$ 85
Profit (loss)...	?

Allin Servicing Statement of Changes in Equity For Month Ended May 31, 2017		
Tim Allin, capital, May 1		?
Add: Investments by owner..........	$ 60	
Profit	?	$110
Total		?
Less: Withdrawals by owner.........		75
Tim Allin, capital, May 31		?

Allin Servicing Balance Sheet May 31, 2017			
Assets		**Liabilities**	
Cash	$120	Accounts payable....	$ 45
Equipment	?	**Equity**	
		Tim Allin, capital......	?
		Total liabilities	
Total assets........	?	and equity	?

QS 1-13 Applying the accounting equation LO7

Using the accounting equation provided, calculate:

1. Beginning capital on January 1, 2017, and

2. Ending capital at December 31, 2017.

Assets	=	Liabilities	+	Equity	
$20,000		$15,000		?	Beginning capital on January 1, 2017
				+3,000	Plus owner investments during the year
				+8,000	Plus profit earned during the year
				−4,000	Less owner withdrawals during the year
				?	Equals ending capital on December 31, 2017

***Hint:** Review Part B of the Mid-Chapter Demonstration Problem before trying this question.*

QS 1-14 Transaction analysis LO7

For each transaction described, identify which component of the accounting equation increases and/or decreases. The first one is done as an example.

Example: Services were performed for a client on credit.

    a. A credit customer paid his account.

    b. Supplies were purchased on credit.

    c. The balance owing regarding the supplies purchased in part (b) was paid.

d. Last month's telephone bill was received today. It will be paid on the due date, which is 10 days from now.

e. Paid the employees their weekly wage.

Assets	=	Liabilities	+	Equity
Example: Increase				Increases
a.				
b.				
c.				
d.				
e.				

QS 1-15 Identifying financial statement items LO5,8

Tim Roadster began Roadster Servicing on April 1, 2017, and showed the following items after the first month of operations. Match each of these items with the financial statement or statements on which it should be presented. Indicate your answer by writing the letter or letters for the correct statement(s) in the blank space next to each item.

a. Income statement **b.** Statement of changes in equity **c.** Balance sheet

____ **1.** Supplies	$10	____ **8.** Utilities expense	$10
____ **2.** Supplies expense	22	____ **9.** Furniture	20
____ **3.** Accounts receivable	25	____ **10.** Revenue	70
____ **4.** Accounts payable	12	____ **11.** Rent revenue	35
____ **5.** Equipment	40	____ **12.** Salaries expense	45
____ **6.** Tim Roadster's withdrawals in April	35	____ **13.** Tim Roadster's investments in April	60
____ **7.** Notes payable	30	____ **14.** Profit	?

QS 1-16 Calculating financial statement elements LO5,8

Using the information provided in QS 1-15, calculate each of the following financial statement elements.

1. Total revenues
2. Total operating expenses
3. Profit
4. Total assets

5. Total liabilities
6. Tim Roadster, capital (April 30, 2017)
7. Total liabilities and equity

QS 1-17 Balance sheet LO5,8

Joan Bennish began Bennish Consulting on May 1, 2017, and reported the items below at May 31, 2017. Match each numbered item with the part of the balance sheet on which it should be presented. If the item does not appear on the balance sheet, choose (d) and identify on which financial statement(s) the item would appear.

a. Asset **b.** Liability **c.** Equity **d.** Does not appear on the balance sheet

1. Loss	$?	**8.** Repair supplies	$ 5
2. Rent expense	22	**9.** Notes payable	25
3. Rent payable	6	**10.** Joan Bennish's withdrawals in May	5
4. Accounts receivable	14	**11.** Truck	15
5. Joan Bennish's investments in May	30	**12.** Consulting revenue	18
6. Interest income	2	**13.** Joan Bennish, capital, May 31, 2017	?
7. Joan Bennish, capital, May 1, 2017	0	**14.** Cash	20

QS 1-18 Calculating financial statement elements LO5,8

Using the information in QS 1-17, prepare an income statement and statement of changes in equity for the month ended May 31, 2017, and a balance sheet at May 31, 2017.

↓ Exercises provide you with an additional opportunity to reinforce basic chapter concepts.

Exercises

Exercise 1-1 **Distinguishing business organizations** LO2

Presented below are descriptions of several different business organizations. Determine whether the situation described refers to a sole proprietorship, partnership, or corporation.

    a. Ownership of Cola Corp. is divided into 1,000 shares.

    b. Text Tech is owned by Kimberly Fisher, who is personally liable for the debts of the business.

    c. Jerry Forrentes and Susan Montgomery own Financial Services, a financial and personal services provider. Neither Forrentes nor Montgomery has personal responsibility for the debts of Financial Services.

    d. Nancy Kerr and Frank Levens own Runners, a courier service. Both Kerr and Levens are personally liable for the debts of the business.

    e. MRS Consulting Services does not have a separate legal existence apart from the one person who owns it.

    f. Biotech Company has one owner and does not pay income taxes.

    g. Torby Technologies has two owners and pays its own income taxes.

Exercise 1-2 **Users of accounting information** LO3

You are working part-time at **Starbucks** while you are taking an introductory accounting course. You have learned that accounting information is useful to many users. Identify four external and four internal users for Starbucks' financial information. For each user, describe what decisions accounting information can help them make specific to Starbucks.

Exercise 1-3 **Accounting and accounting-related opportunities** LO3

You have decided to pursue a career in accounting. However, you do not know what area of accounting you want to focus on. Based on your readings and performing some additional research online (job postings, accounting firm websites, and other resources), describe what you think a typical day would be like for an (1) external auditor, (2) controller, and (3) tax specialist.

Exercise 1-4 **Applying the Chartered Professional Accountants of Ontario's Rules of Professional Conduct—Approach to Ethical Conflict Resolution** LO4

Required For each situation described below, apply the Chartered Professional Accountants of Ontario's Rules of Professional Conduct—Approach to Ethical Conflict Resolution as identified earlier in the chapter to determine whether the behaviour is ethical or not.

    a. In performing your job, you and a colleague often need to use your cell phones to make long distance calls to suppliers. Your employer allows you to submit business calls for reimbursement. Your colleague has mentioned that he likes the perk of getting the company to pay for a few of his personal long distance calls.

b. You and a friend go to the movie theatre and purchase tickets. As you and your friend approach the ticket-taker, you both notice that the three people ahead of you have no tickets. The group and the ticket-taker, who appear to know each other, have a brief conversation and the group is admitted without having purchased tickets.

c. To use the facilities at the local fitness centre, clients can pay a $5 drop-in fee each visit or they can purchase an annual pass for unlimited access. The cashier collects the $5 from drop-in clients and provides them with a cash register receipt only if they ask.

Exercise 1-5 Accounting principles LO5

Match each of these numbered descriptions with the term it best describes. Indicate your answer by writing the letter for the correct principle in the blank space next to each description.

a. Cost principle   **c.** Revenue recognition principle

b. Business entity principle   **d.** Going concern principle

_____ **1.** Requires every business to be accounted for separately from its owner or owners.

_____ **2.** Requires financial statement information to be based on costs incurred in transactions.

_____ **3.** Requires financial statements to reflect the assumption that the business will continue operating instead of being closed or sold.

_____ **4.** Requires revenue to be recorded only when the earnings process is complete.

Exercise 1-6 Classifying accounts LO6

Kate is having a difficult time differentiating all of the account names. "My head is spinning when all the accounts sound the same to me! Does unearned revenue belong on the income statement or the balance sheet?" Create a study sheet by categorizing all of the following accounts into a table with the following headings. Some accounts may be used more than once.

Accounts Payable	Prepaid Rent	Supplies	Equipment
Accounts Receivable	Vehicle Expenses	Wages Expense	Maintenance Expense
Advertising Expense	Furniture	Fuel Expense	Land
Insurance Expense	Salaries Expense	Notes Payable	Unearned Revenue
Owner's Capital, Ending balance	Service Revenue	Merchandise Inventory	Rent Revenue
Interest Payable	Other Expenses	Utilities Expense	Supplies Expense
Prepaid Expenses	Interest Income	Vehicles	Interest Receivable
Interest Expense	Cash	Salaries Payable	Rent Expense
Withdrawals	Telephone Expense	Building	
Owner's Capital, Beginning balance	Investment by Owner	Profit/Loss	

Balance Sheet			Income Statement		Statement of Changes in Equity
Assets	Liabilities	Owner's Equity	Revenues	Expenses	

Exercise 1-7 **Determining profit** LO6

CHECK FIGURE: d. $36,000 net loss

Profit (loss), owner withdrawals, and owner investment cause equity to change. We also know that revenues less expenses equals profit (loss). Using the following information, calculate profit (loss) for each independent situation.

   a. The business earned revenues of $516,000 and had expenses of $492,000.

   b. The business showed expenses of $240,000 and revenues of $165,000.

   c. The equity at the beginning of the month was $32,000. During the month, the owner made no investments or withdrawals. At the end of the month, equity totalled $86,000.

   d. The equity at the beginning of the month was $48,000. During the month, the owner made an investment of $40,000 but made no withdrawals. Equity at the end of the month totalled $52,000.

Exercise 1-8 **Missing information** LO6 e**X**cel

This symbol means that an Excel template is available on Connect to help you solve this question. ↑

CHECK FIGURE: e. $102,000

Referring to Exhibit 1.9, calculate the amount of the missing item in each of the following independent cases:

	a	b	c	d	e
Equity, January 1	$ -0-	$ -0-	$ -0-	$ -0-	$?
Owner's investments during the year	60,000	?	31,500	37,500	140,000
Profit (loss) for the year	15,750	30,500	(4,500)	?	(8,000)
Owner's withdrawals during the year	?	(27,000)	(20,000)	(15,750)	(63,000)
Equity, December 31	56,000	49,500	?	32,000	171,000

Exercise 1-9 **Income statement** LO6

CHECK FIGURE: Profit = $11,110

On November 1, 2017, Jean Higgins started a wedding planning company, Extraordinary Studios. On November 30, 2017, the company's records showed the following items. Use this information to prepare a November income statement for the business, similar to Exhibit 1.8.

Cash	$16,000	Owner's withdrawals..	$ 3,360
Accounts receivable...	17,000	Wedding consulting revenue	22,000
Office supplies..	5,000	Rent expense	2,550
Automobiles..	36,000	Salaries expense	6,000
Office equipment	25,250	Telephone expense	1,680
Accounts payable...	7,500	Utilities expenses	660
Owner's investments	84,000		

Exercise 1-10 **Statement of changes in equity** LO6

CHECK FIGURE: Jean Higgins, Capital, November 30 = $91,750

Use the facts in Exercise 1-9 to prepare a November statement of changes in equity for Extraordinary Studios, similar to Exhibit 1.9.

Analysis Component: What activities caused equity to increase during the month of November 2017?

Exercise 1-11 **Balance sheet** LO6

CHECK FIGURE: Total assets = $99,250

Use the facts in Exercise 1-9 to prepare a November 30 balance sheet for Extraordinary Studios, similar to Exhibit 1.10.

Analysis Component: Identify how much of the assets held by Extraordinary Studios are financed by the owner, Jean Higgins.

Exercise 1-12 **Income statement** LO6

CHECK FIGURE: Loss = $220

On July 1, 2017, Windsor Learning Services entered its second month of operations. On July 31, 2017, Milton Windsor, the owner, finalized the company's records that showed the following items. Use this information to prepare a July income statement similar to Exhibit 1.8.

Accounts payable	$1,500	Owner's investments during	
Accounts receivable	2,000	July 2017	$1,200
Cash	1,600	Owner's withdrawals	1,000
Computer equipment	2,200	Supplies	1,280
Furniture	1,800	Textbook rental revenue	300
Milton Windsor, capital,		Tutoring revenue	4,200
June 30, 2017*	7,400	Tutors' wages expense	1,540
Office rent expense	2,500	Utilities expense	680

***Hint:** The ending capital balance for one period is the beginning capital balance for the next period.*

Exercise 1-13 **Statement of changes in equity** LO6

CHECK FIGURE: Milton Windsor, Capital, July 31 = $7,380

Use the facts in Exercise 1-12 to prepare a July statement of changes in equity for Windsor Learning Services, similar to Exhibit 1.9.

Analysis Component: Identify those activities that caused equity to decrease during July 2017.

Exercise 1-14 **Balance sheet** LO6

CHECK FIGURE: Total assets = $8,880

Use the facts in Exercise 1-12 to prepare a July 31 balance sheet for Windsor Learning Services, similar to Exhibit 1.10.

Analysis Component: Identify how much of the assets held by Windsor Learning Services are financed by debt.

Exercise 1-15 **Determining profit** LO6,7

CHECK FIGURE: b. $86,000 profit

A business had the following amounts of assets and liabilities at the beginning and end of a recent year:

	Assets	Liabilities
Beginning of the year	$ 75,000	$30,000
End of the year	$120,000	46,000

Determine the profit earned or loss incurred by the business during the year under each of the following unrelated assumptions:

a. The owner made no additional investments in the business and withdrew no assets during the year.

b. The owner made no additional investments in the business during the year but withdrew $4,750 *per month* to pay personal living expenses.

c. The owner withdrew no assets during the year but invested an additional $80,000 cash.

d. The owner withdrew $3,500 *per month* to pay personal living expenses and invested an additional $75,000 cash in the business.

Hint: Review the Mid-Chapter Demonstration Problem before trying this question.

Exercise 1-16 Accounting equation LO7
CHECK FIGURE: b. Equity Aug. 31, 2017 = $6,000

In the following table, the accounting equation is applied to Business A:

	Assets	=	Liabilities	+	Equity
At August 1, 2017....................	?		$10,000		?
At August 31, 2017..................	$25,000		?		?

Calculate the missing amounts assuming that:

a. Assets decreased by $15,000 during August, and

b. Liabilities increased by $9,000 during August.

Exercise 1-17 Effects of transactions on the accounting equation LO5,7 eXcel
CHECK FIGURE: Total assets = $29,350

Wesson Servicing provides support to customers in the area of ecommerce. Using the format provided, show the effects of the activities listed in (a) through (f).

Assets					=	Liabilities	+	Equity
Cash	+	Accounts Receivable	+	Office Supplies	=	Accounts Payable	+	Marnie Wesson, Capital

a. Marnie Wesson, the owner, invested cash of $25,000 into the business.

b. The owner purchased office supplies on credit; $600.

c. Wesson Servicing did work for a client and received $7,000 cash.

d. Completed an application form for a $10,000 government grant.

e. The owner paid her assistant's salary; $4,500 cash.

f. Completed work for a customer on credit; $1,250.

Exercise 1-18 Effects of transactions on the accounting equation LO6,7 eXcel
CHECK FIGURE: Total assets = $15,600

DigiCom repairs electronic devices. Using the format provided below, show the effects of the activities listed in (a) through (i).

	Assets				=	Liabilities	+	Equity
Cash +	Accounts Receivable +	Parts Supplies +	Equipment	=		Accounts Payable	+	Stacey Crowe, Capital

a. Stacey Crowe, owner of DigiCom, invested cash of $14,000 into her business.

b. DigiCom paid $2,500 to cover rent for the current month.

c. DigiCom purchased supplies on credit; $800.

d. DigiCom completed work for a client on credit; $3,400.

e. DigiCom purchased a new piece of equipment by paying cash of $1,950.

f. DigiCom hired a technician, to start next month, who will get paid $5,000 per month.

g. DigiCom paid for the supplies purchased in (c).

h. DigiCom performed work for a client and received cash of $3,400.

i. DigiCom paid the administrative assistant's salary of $2,700.

Exercise 1-19 Analyzing the accounting equation LO6,7

Elena Bellisario began a new consulting firm on January 3. The accounting equation showed the following transactions. Analyze the equation and describe each of the transactions with their amounts. Transaction (a) has been done as an example for you.

	Assets				=	Liabilities	+	Equity
Transaction	Cash +	Accounts Receivable +	Office Supplies +	Office Furniture	=	Accounts Payable	+	Elena Bellisario, Capital
Beginning Balances	-0-	-0-	-0-	-0-		-0-		-0-
a.	+15,000							+15,000
b.	− 500		+500					
c.	− 8,000			+8,000				
d.		+1,000						+ 1,000
e.			+400			+400		
f.	− 250					−250		
g.	+ 750	− 750						
Totals	7,000	250	900	8,000		150		16,000

Description of transaction (a):

a. The owner invested $15,000 cash into the business.

Exercise 1-20 Effects of transactions on the accounting equation LO6,7 eXcel

CHECK FIGURE: Mailin Moon, Capital = $13,650

Mailin Moon is a freelance writer who submits articles to various magazines and newspapers. She operates out of a small office where she employs one administrative assistant. The following activities occurred during March 2017, her first month of business:

a. Moon invested $2,500 worth of equipment into her business along with $3,000 cash.

b. Submitted a series of articles to *The Globe and Mail* and received $6,500 cash.

c. Purchased supplies on credit; $600.

d. Paid the part-time administrative assistant's salary of $1,450.

e. Moon ordered $3,000 of office equipment from the IKEA catalogue. It is scheduled to arrive in April or May.

f. Paid the rent for the first month; $1,400.

g. Submitted an article to *Report on Business*; will receive $4,500 next month.

Using the format provided below, show the effects of the activities listed in (a) through (g). For each transaction that affects equity, include a brief description beside it (owner investment, owner withdrawal, revenue, expense).

Assets				=	Liabilities	+	Equity	
	Accounts				Accounts		Mailin Moon,	Explanation of Equity
Cash +	Receivable +	Supplies +	Equipment	=	Payable	+	Capital	Transaction

Exercise 1-21 **Financial statements** LO8   e**X**cel

CHECK FIGURES: Profit = $8,150; Total assets = $14,250

Using your answer from Exercise 1-20, prepare an income statement, a statement of changes in equity, and a balance sheet using the formats provided.

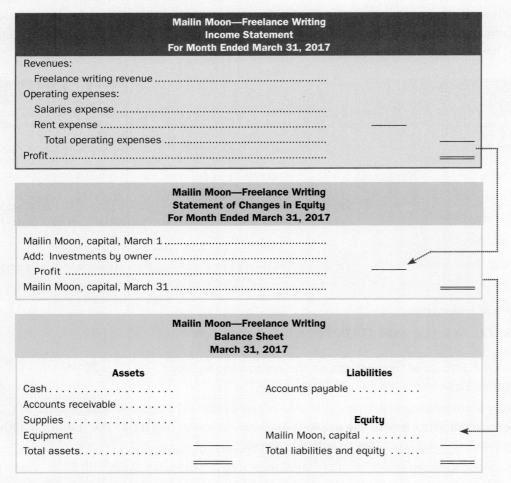

Analysis Component: Identify which assets were financed by:

      a. Liabilities   **b.** Owner investment   **c.** Profit

Also identify the amount(s) for each.

Exercise 1-22 Effects of transactions on the accounting equation LO6,7 eXcel

CHECK FIGURE: Accounts payable, March 31, 2017 = $2,350

    a. Ali invested $4,300 cash and $15,000 of equipment into his business.

    b. Purchased various supplies on account; $1,600.

    c. Bought supplies on credit; $950.

    d. Ali signed a $4,000 contract to do yard work beginning in May.

    e. Did work for a client on account; $550.

    f. Performed services for a customer on credit; $600.

    g. Paid $200 for the supplies purchased in (c).

    h. Paid $250 for advertising online.

    i. Collected the amount owed from the customer in (f).

Using the format provided below, show the effects of the activities listed in (a) through (i). For each transaction that affects equity, include a brief description beside it (owner investment, owner withdrawal, revenue, expense).

Assets					=	Liabilities	+	Equity	
Cash	+ Accounts Receivable	+ Supplies	+ Equipment		=	Accounts Payable	+	Omar Ali, Capital	Explanation of Equity Transaction

Exercise 1-23 Financial statements LO8

CHECK FIGURE: Omar Ali, Capital, March 31, 2017 = $20,200

Using your answer from Exercise 1-22, prepare an income statement, statement of changes in equity, and balance sheet for March 2017.

Analysis Component: Review Omar's income statement. Does the profit of $900 represent $900 of cash? Explain.

Exercise 1-24 Effects of transactions on the accounting equation LO6,7 eXcel

CHECK FIGURE: Natalie Gold, Capital, July 31, 2017 = $11,550

Natalie Gold is the owner of the marketing agency Vivid Voice. The company focuses on online consulting services, such as online marketing campaigns and blog services. The June transactions for Vivid Voice resulted in totals at June 30, 2017, as shown in the following accounting equation format:

Assets					=	Liabilities	+	Equity	
Cash	+ Accounts Receivable	+ Supplies	+ Equipment		=	Accounts Payable	+	Natalie Gold, Capital	Explanation of Equity Transaction
$6,000	+ $1,200	+ $1,900	+ $6,500		=	$4,000	+	$11,600	

During July, the following occurred:

    a. Collected $800 from a credit customer.

    b. Paid $2,500 for equipment purchased on account in June.

    c. Did work for a client and collected cash; $1,100.

    d. Paid a part-time consultant's wages; $950.

    e. Paid the July rent; $1,200.

    f. Paid the July utilities; $600.

g. Performed services for a customer on credit; $1,600.

h. Called an information technology consultant to fix the agency's photo editing software in August; it will cost $350.

Using the format provided above, show the effects of the activities listed in (a) through (h). For each transaction that affects equity, include a brief description beside it (owner investment, owner withdrawal, revenue, expense).

Exercise 1-25 Financial statements LO8

CHECK FIGURES: Loss = $50; Total assets = $13,050

Using your answer from Exercise 1-24, prepare an income statement, a statement of changes in equity, and a balance sheet for July 2017.

Analysis Component: Review Gold's balance sheet. How much of the assets are financed by Gold? How much of the assets are financed by debt?

> ↓ Problems typically incorporate two or more concepts. There are two groups of problems: A problems and Alternate or B problems. B problems mirror the A problems to help you improve your understanding through repetition.

Problems

Problem 1-1A Identifying type of business organization LO2

Complete the chart below by placing a checkmark in the appropriate column.

	Type of Business Organization		
Characteristic	Sole Proprietorship	Partnership	Corporation
Limited liability			
Unlimited liability			
Owners are shareholders			
Owners are partners			
Taxed as a separate legal entity			

Problem 1-2A Understanding assets LO6

You are an accountant at Bright Consulting. The CEO tells his employees, "People are our greatest assets." When you show him the financial statements, he becomes very angry and demands, "Why do we not have our employees on this balance sheet? You better fix these statements or you are fired!"

Required Write an email to the CEO explaining whether employees should be recorded as assets on the balance sheet. Ensure to explain your reasoning based on the definition of an asset.

Problem 1-3A Financial statements: analysis of statement of changes in equity LO6

CHECK FIGURE: Profit 2016 = $60,000

Blue Water Kayak began operations on January 1, 2016. The owner invested $10,000 during the first year and was able to withdraw cash of $42,000 after a successful first year.

During 2017, the second year of operations, the business reported profit of $175,000, owner withdrawals of $78,000, and no owner investments.

In 2018, the third year, Blue Water Kayak incurred a loss of $5,000. The owner made no withdrawals and no owner investments during this period. At the end of 2018, owner's capital was $120,000.

Required Calculate the profit or loss for 2016.

Problem 1-4A **Financial statements** LO6

CHECK FIGURES: Profit = $23,700; Total assets = $86,400

On August 1, 2016, Cross Fitness entered its second year of operations. Cross Fitness provides high-performance group and personal training courses that have been derived from scientific research and exercises used by professional athletes. On July 31, 2017, Jay-Jay Grey, the owner, finalized the company's records, which showed the following items.

Accounts payable	$ 9,400	Workout equipment	$ 19,200
Accounts receivable	42,000	Prepaid rent	4,000
Jay-Jay Grey, capital, July 31, 2016*	79,300	Rent expense	14,000
Jay-Jay Grey, withdrawals	46,000	Personal training revenue	2,500
Cash	5,600	Group training revenue	131,000
Furniture	13,200	Supplies	2,400
Interest expense	2,100	Supplies expense	15,900
Notes payable	20,000	Utilities expense	9,800
		Wages expense	68,000

***Hint:** The ending capital balance for one period is the beginning capital balance for the next period. There were no owner investments during the year ended July 31, 2017.*

Required Prepare an income statement and statement of changes in equity for the year ended July 31, 2017, and balance sheet at July 31, 2017, similar to Exhibits 1.8, 1.9, and 1.10.

Analysis Component: Analyze the balance sheet and calculate what percentage of the assets at July 31, 2017, were financed by (a) debt and (b) equity.

Problem 1-5A **Calculating and interpreting profit and preparing a balance sheet** LO6,7,8

Help Me
SOLVE IT

CHECK FIGURES: 1. Total assets 2016 = $138,750; Total assets 2017 = $235,200

The accounting records of LeClaire Delivery Services show the following assets and liabilities as of the end of 2017 and 2016:

This icon indicates that there is a video tutorial available on Connect to assist you with completing this question.

	December 31	
	2017	**2016**
Cash	$ 9,375	$26,250
Accounts receivable	11,175	14,250
Office supplies	1,650	2,250
Trucks	27,000	27,000
Office equipment	73,500	69,000
Land	22,500	
Building	90,000	
Accounts payable	18,750	3,750
Notes payable	52,500	

During December 2017, the owner, Jess LeClaire, purchased a small office building and moved the business from rented quarters to the new building. The building and the land it occupies cost $112,500. The business paid $60,000 in cash and a note payable was signed for the balance. LeClaire had to invest

$17,500 cash in the business to enable it to pay the $60,000. The business earned a profit during 2017, which enabled LeClaire to withdraw $1,500 per month from the business for personal expenses.

Required

1. Prepare balance sheets for the business as of the end of 2016 and the end of 2017.

2. Prepare a calculation to show how much profit was earned by the business during 2017.

Analysis Component: Assets increased from $138,750 at December 31, 2016, to $235,200 at December 31, 2017. Using numbers wherever possible, explain how these assets were financed.

Problem 1-6A Missing information LO7   e**X**cel

The following financial statement information is known about five unrelated companies:

	Company A	Company B	Company C	Company D	Company E
December 31, 2016:					
Assets	$90,000	$105,000	$58,000	$160,000	$246,000
Liabilities	38,000	45,000	28,000	76,000	?
December 31, 2017:					
Assets	96,000	82,000	?	250,000	225,000
Liabilities	?	55,000	38,000	128,000	150,000
During 2017:					
Owner investments	10,000	19,000	15,500	?	9,000
Profit (loss)	(16,000)	?	18,000	24,000	36,000
Owner withdrawals	5,000	6,000	7,750	-0-	18,000

Required

1. Answer the following questions about Company A:

    a. What was the equity on December 31, 2016?

    b. What was the equity on December 31, 2017?

    c. What was the amount of liabilities owed on December 31, 2017?

2. Answer the following questions about Company B:

    a. What was the equity on December 31, 2016?

    b. What was the equity on December 31, 2017?

    c. What was the profit (loss) for 2017?

3. Calculate the amount of assets owned by Company C on December 31, 2017.

4. Calculate the amount of owner investments in Company D made during 2017.

5. Calculate the amount of liabilities owed by Company E on December 31, 2016.

Problem 1-7A Analyzing transactions and preparing financial statements LO6,7,8   e**X**cel

CHECK FIGURES: 2. George Littlechild, Capital, March 31, 2017 = $175,100
3. Loss = $1,300; Total assets = $743,100

Littlechild started a new kitchen and bath design business called Littlechild Enterprises. The following activities occurred during its first month of operations, March 2017:

    a. Littlechild invested $160,000 cash and office equipment valued at $20,000 in the business.

    b. Purchased a small building for $600,000 to be used as an office. Paid $100,000 in cash and signed a note payable promising to pay the balance over several years.

c. Purchased $3,000 of office supplies for cash.

d. Purchased $72,000 of office equipment on credit.

e. Littlechild made reservations at a hotel hosting a kitchen and bath design conference in August 2017. He will send a $1,000 deposit on July 1, 2017.

f. Completed a project on credit and billed the client $5,200 for the work.

g. Paid a local online newspaper $3,500 for an announcement that the office had opened.

h. Completed a project for a client and collected $4,000 cash.

i. Made a $4,000 payment on the equipment purchased in (d).

j. Received $2,500 from the client described in (f).

k. Paid $7,000 cash for the office secretary's wages.

l. Littlechild withdrew $3,600 cash from the company bank account to pay personal living expenses.

Littlechild Enterprises
Income Statement
For Month Ended March 31, 2017

Revenues:
  Service revenue ....
Operating expenses:
  Wages expense ....
  Advertising expense..
    Total operating expenses .... _____
Loss.. _____

Littlechild Enterprises
Statement of Changes in Equity
For Month Ended March 31, 2017

George Littlechild, capital, March 1 ....
Add: Investments by owner ....
  Total ....
Less: Withdrawals by owner
      Loss.. _____
George Littlechild, capital, March 31 ....

Littlechild Enterprises
Balance Sheet
March 31, 2017

Assets		Liabilities	
Cash		Accounts payable	
Accounts receivable..................		Notes payable	_____
Office supplies..........................		Total liabilities	
Office equipment			
Building.....................................		**Equity**	
		George Littlechild, capital	
Total assets.............................. _____		Total liabilities and equity......... _____	

Required

1. Create a table like the one in Exhibit 1.15, using the following headings for the columns: Cash; Accounts Receivable; Office Supplies; Office Equipment; Building; Accounts Payable; Notes Payable; and George Littlechild, Capital. Leave space for an Explanation of Equity Transaction column to the right of the Capital column. Identify revenues and expenses by name in the Explanation of Equity Transaction column.

2. Use additions and subtractions to show the transactions' effects on the elements of the equation. **Do not determine new totals for the items of the equation after each transaction**. Next to each change in equity, state whether the change was caused by an investment, a revenue, an expense, or a withdrawal. Determine the final total for each item and verify that the equation is in balance.

3. Prepare an income statement, a statement of changes in equity, and a balance sheet using the formats provided.

Analysis Component: Littlechild Enterprises' assets are financed 76% by debt. What does this mean? As part of your answer, include an explanation of how the 76% was calculated.

Problem 1-8A Analyzing transactions LO5,7 eXcel

CHECK FIGURE: Accounts payable balance, November 30, 2017 = $27,000
Larry Power, Capital balance, November 30, 2017 = $69,100

Larry Power started a new business in the name of Power Electrical on October 1, 2017. During October, a number of activities occurred and the following totals resulted at October 31, 2017 (shown in accounting equation format):

		Assets								=	Liabilities	+	Equity
Cash	+	Accounts Receivable	+	Office Supplies	+	Office Equip.	+	Electrical Equip.	=		Accounts Payable	+	Larry Power, Capital
$30,000	+	$7,000	+	$1,900	+	$28,000	+	$14,000	=		$18,000	+	$62,900

During November, the following occurred:

Nov.	1	Rented office space and paid cash for the month's rent of $7,200.
	3	Purchased electrical equipment for $18,000 from an electrician who was going out of business, by using $10,000 in personal funds and agreeing to pay the balance in 30 days.
	5	Purchased office supplies by paying $1,800 cash.
Nov.	6	Completed electrical work and immediately collected $2,000 for doing the work.
	8	Purchased $5,200 of office equipment on credit.
	15	Completed electrical work on credit in the amount of $6,000.
	16	Interviewed and hired a part-time electrician who will be paid $5,300 each month. He will begin work in three weeks.
	18	Purchased $1,000 of office supplies on credit.
	20	Paid for the office equipment purchased on November 8.
	24	Billed a client $4,800 for electrical work; the balance is due in 30 days.
	28	Received $6,000 for the work completed on November 15.
	30	Paid the office assistant's salary of $4,400.
	30	Paid the monthly utility bills of $3,600.
	30	Power withdrew $1,400 from the business for personal use.

Required Use additions and subtractions to show the effects of each November activity on the items in the equation. **Do not determine new totals for the items of the equation after each transaction**. Next to each change in equity, state whether the change was caused by an investment, a revenue, an expense, or a withdrawal. Determine the final total for each item and verify that the equation is in balance.

Analysis Component: Revenue is not recorded on November 28. Explain, using your understanding of GAAP.

Problem 1-9A **Preparing financial statements** LO8

CHECK FIGURES: Loss = $2,400; Total assets = $96,100

Required Using your answer to Problem 1-8A, prepare an income statement, a statement of changes in equity, and a balance sheet.

Analysis Component: Assets are financed by debt and equity. Profit is a component of equity. Therefore, profit helps to finance assets. Explain how/if profit helped to finance assets for Power Electrical for the month ended November 30, 2017.

Problem 1-10A **Identifying the effects of transactions on the financial statements** LO7,8

Identify how each of the following transactions affects the company's financial statements. For the balance sheet, identify how each transaction affects total assets, total liabilities, and equity. For the income statement, identify how each transaction affects profit. If there is an increase, place a "+" in the column or columns. If there is a decrease, place a "−" in the column or columns. If there is both an increase and a decrease, place a "+/−" in the column or columns. The line for the first transaction is completed as an example.

	Transaction	Total Assets	Total Liabilities	Equity	Profit
		Balance Sheet			**Income Statement**
1	Owner invests cash	+		+	
2	Sell services for cash				
3	Acquire services on credit				
4	Pay wages with cash				
5	Owner withdraws cash				
6	Borrow cash with note payable				
7	Sell services on credit				
8	Buy office equipment for cash				
9	Collect receivable from (7)				
10	Buy asset with note payable				

Alternate Problems

Problem 1-1B **Identifying type of business organization** LO2

a. Refer to Appendix III at the end of the book. Determine if WestJet Airlines is a sole proprietorship, partnership, or corporation.

b. Refer to Appendix III at the end of the book. Determine if Danier Leather is a sole proprietorship, partnership, or corporation.

Problem 1-2B **Understanding assets** LO6

You are the accountant at Global Consulting. The marketing manager is excited about the success of their new marketing campaign. She boasts, "We spent $1 million on marketing in 2016 and we have already seen an increase in sales of 5% this year!" When you show her the financial statements, she exclaims, "You have made a big mistake! I want to see $1 million recorded under assets for our investment in marketing!"

Required Write an e-mail to the marketing manager explaining whether money spent on marketing should be recorded as an asset on the balance sheet. Be sure to explain your reasoning based on the definition of an asset.

Problem 1-3B **Financial statements: analysis of statement of changes in equity** LO6

CHECK FIGURE: 2016 Loss = $31,000

Dublin Window Cleaners began operations on January 1, 2016. The owner invested $400,000 during the first year and made no withdrawals.

During 2017, the business reported profit of $192,000, owner withdrawals of $104,000, and zero owner investments.

In 2018, Dublin Window Cleaners earned profit of $366,000. The owner withdrew $218,000 during 2018 and made no investments. Owner's capital at December 31, 2018, was $605,000.

Required Calculate the profit or loss for the year 2016.

Problem 1-4B **Financial statements** LO6

CHECK FIGURE: Wes Gandalf, Capital, Dec. 31, 2017 = $192,000

On January 1, 2017, Fireworks Fantasia entered its third year of operations. On December 31, 2017, Wes Gandalf, the owner, finalized the company's records that showed the following items.

Accounts payable	$ 58,000	Office equipment	$ 14,000
Accounts receivable	14,000	Office supplies	3,000
Advertising expense	9,000	Office supplies expense	3,600
Building	81,000	Rent revenue	66,000
Cash	8,000	Tools	18,000
Revenue	140,000	Utilities expense	25,100
Fireworks supplies	49,000	Wages expense	92,000
Fireworks supplies expense	77,500	Wes Gandalf, capital, December 31, 2013	175,200
Land	63,000	Wes Gandalf, withdrawals	12,000

Hint: *The ending capital balance for one period is the beginning capital balance for the next period. The owner made investments of $30,000 during the year ended December 31, 2017.*

Required Prepare an income statement and statement of changes in equity for the year ended December 31, 2017, and a December 31, 2017, balance sheet, similar to Exhibits 1.8, 1.9, and 1.10.

Analysis Component: Analyze the balance sheet and calculate what percentage of the assets at December 31, 2017, were financed by (a) debt and (b) equity.

Problem 1-5B Calculating and interpreting profit and preparing a balance sheet LO6,7,8

CHECK FIGURES: 1. Total assets 2016 = $279,000; Total assets 2017 = $936,000

The accounting records of Carmen Creek Gourmet Meats show the following assets and liabilities as of the end of 2017 and 2016:

	December 31	
	2017	2016
Cash	$ 20,000	$ 28,000
Accounts receivable	60,000	50,000
Office supplies	25,000	20,000
Office equipment	120,000	120,000
Machinery	61,000	61,000
Land	130,000	
Building	520,000	
Accounts payable	30,000	10,000
Notes payable	520,000	

During 2017, Carmen Munch, the owner, purchased a small office building and moved the business from rented quarters to the new building. The building and the land it occupies cost $650,000. The business paid $130,000 in cash and a note payable was signed for the balance. Munch had to invest an additional $50,000 to enable it to pay the $130,000. The business earned a profit during 2017, which enabled Munch to withdraw $2,000 per month from the business for personal use.

Required
1. Prepare balance sheets for the business as of the end of 2016 and the end of 2017.

2. Prepare a calculation to show how much profit was earned by the business during 2017.

Analysis Component: Assets increased from $279,000 at December 31, 2016, to $936,000 at December 31, 2017. Using numbers wherever possible, explain how these assets were financed.

Problem 1-6B Missing information LO7 e**X**cel

The following financial statement information is known about five unrelated companies:

	Company V	Company W	Company X	Company Y	Company Z
December 31, 2016:					
Assets	$165,000	$70,000	$121,500	$82,500	$124,000
Liabilities	30,000	50,000	58,500	50,000	?
December 31, 2017:					
Assets	192,000	90,000	136,500	?	160,000
Liabilities	26,000	?	55,500	72,000	52,000
During 2017:					
Owner investments	60,000	10,000	?	38,100	40,000
Profit (loss)	?	30,000	16,500	(46,000)	32,000
Owner withdrawals	4,500	2,000	-0-	18,000	6,000

Required

1. Answer the following questions about Company V:
    a. What was the equity on December 31, 2016?
    b. What was the equity on December 31, 2017?
    c. What was the profit (loss) for 2017?

2. Answer the following questions about Company W:
    a. What was the equity on December 31, 2016?
    b. What was the equity on December 31, 2017?
    c. What was the amount of liabilities owed on December 31, 2017?

3. Calculate the amount of owner investments in Company X made during 2017.

4. Calculate the amount of assets owned by Company Y on December 31, 2017.

5. Calculate the amount of liabilities owed by Company Z on December 31, 2016.

Problem 1-7B Analyzing transactions and preparing financial statements LO6,7,8 e**X**cel

CHECK FIGURES: 2. Cash balance, December 31, 2017 = $43,800
3. Profit = $5,700; Total assets = $324,200

Lily Zhang started a new business on January 1, 2017, called Zhang Consulting. She develops financial investment plans for young adults. During the business's first year of operations, the following activities occurred:

a. Zhang invested $120,000 cash and office equipment valued at $10,000 in the business.

b. Purchased a small building for $240,000 to be used as an office. Paid $50,000 in cash and signed a note payable promising to pay the balance over several years.

c. Purchased $18,000 of office equipment for cash.

d. Purchased $4,000 of office supplies and $6,400 of office equipment on credit.

e. Paid a local online newspaper $4,500 for an announcement that the office had opened.

f. Completed a financial plan on credit and billed the client $6,000 for the service.

g. Designed a financial plan for another client and collected an $8,000 cash fee.

h. Zhang withdrew $5,500 cash from the company bank account to pay personal expenses.

i. Zhang signed a $20,000 contract for the office to be painted in February 2018. A deposit of $6,000 will be paid on January 15, 2018.

j. Received $4,000 from the client described in (f).

k. Paid for the equipment purchased in (d).

l. Paid $3,800 cash for the administrative assistant's wages.

Required

1. Create a table like the one presented in Exhibit 1.15, using the following headings for the columns: Cash; Accounts Receivable; Office Supplies; Office Equipment; Building; Accounts Payable; Notes Payable; and Lily Zhang, Capital. Leave space for an Explanation of Equity Transaction column to the right of the Capital column. Identify revenues and expenses by name in the Explanation column.

2. Use additions and subtractions to show the effects of the above transactions on the elements of the equation. **Do not determine new totals for the items of the equation after each**

transaction. Next to each change in equity, state whether the change was caused by an investment, a revenue, an expense, or a withdrawal. Determine the final total for each item and verify that the equation is in balance.

3. Prepare an income statement, a statement of changes in equity, and a balance sheet for 2017 using the formats provided.

Zhang Consulting
Income Statement
For Year Ended December 31, 2017

Revenues:
  Consulting services revenue ....
Operating expenses:
  Wages expense ....
  Advertising expense...
    Total operating expenses ....
Profit..

Zhang Consulting
Statement of Changes in Equity
For Year Ended December 31, 2017

Lily Zhang, capital, January 1 ....
Add: Investments by owner..
    Profit ....
    Total ....
Less: Withdrawals by owner...
Lily Zhang, capital, December 31 ....

ZhangConsulting
Balance Sheet
December 31, 2017

Assets	Liabilities
Cash	Accounts payable ....
Accounts receivable...................	Notes payable ....
Office supplies..........................	Total liabilities ....
Office equipment	
Building....................................	**Equity**
	Lily Zhang, capital ....
Total assets.............................	Total liabilities and equity.........

Analysis Component: Zhang's assets are financed 60% by debt. What does this mean? As part of your answer, include an explanation of how the 60% was calculated.

Problem 1-8B Analyzing transactions LO5,7 eXcel

CHECK FIGURE: Cash balance, July 31 = $20,000

Beyond Music provides DJ services for events such as high school dances, weddings, and corporate events. Michael Cantu started the business on June 1, 2017. The June activities resulted in totals at June 30, 2017, as follows (illustrated in accounting equation format):

Assets											=	Liabilities	+	Equity
Cash	+	Accounts Receivable	+	Office Supplies	+	Event Equip.	+	Sound System Equip.		=		Accounts Payable	+	Michael Cantu, Capital
$12,000	+	$4,600	+	$1,560	+	$9,600	+	$24,000		=		$6,200	+	$45,560

During July, the following occurred:

July	1	Cantu invested $20,000 cash in the business.
	1	Rented office space and paid the month's rent of $1,000.
	1	Purchased sound system equipment for $8,000 by paying $3,000 in cash and agreeing to pay the balance in 30 days.
	6	Purchased office supplies by paying $1,000 cash.
	8	Provided DJ services for three weddings and immediately collected $4,400 in total for completing the services.
	10	Purchased $7,600 of projectors and screens on credit.
	15	Completed DJ services for a customer on credit in the amount of $4,800.
	17	Purchased $3,840 of office supplies on credit.
	23	Paid for the event equipment purchased on July 10.
	25	Billed a large corporate customer $6,000 for DJ services and $4,000 for the rental of event equipment; the balance is due in 30 days.
	28	Received $4,800 for the work completed on July 15.
	31	Paid DJ wages of $4,500.
	31	Paid the monthly utility bills of $1,700.
	31	Cantu withdrew $2,400 cash from the business to pay personal expenses.

Required Use additions and subtractions to show the effects of each July transaction on the items in the equation. **Do not determine new totals for the items of the equation after each transaction**. Next to each change in equity, state whether the change was caused by an investment, a revenue, an expense, or a withdrawal. Determine the final total for each item and verify that the equation is in balance.

Analysis Component: Identify which GAAP guides your treatment of the July 15 transaction. Explain your answer.

Problem 1-9B Preparing financial statements LO8

CHECK FIGURES: Profit = $12,000; Total assets = $90,200

Required Using your answer to Problem 1-8B, prepare an income statement, a statement of changes in equity, and a balance sheet.

Analysis Component: Assets are financed by debt and equity. Owner investment is a component of equity. Therefore, owner investment helps to finance assets. Explain how/if owner investment helped to finance assets for Beyond Music for the month ended July 31, 2017.

Problem 1-10B Identifying the effects of transactions on the financial statements LO7,8

You are to identify how each of the following transactions affects the company's financial statements. For the balance sheet, you are to identify how each transaction affects total assets, total liabilities, and equity. For the income statement, you are to identify how each transaction affects profit. If there is an increase, place a "+" in the column or columns. If there is a decrease, place a "−" in the column or columns. If there is both an increase and a decrease, place "+/−" in the column or columns. The line for the first transaction is completed as an example.

	Transaction	Total Assets	Total Liabilities	Equity	Profit
			Balance Sheet		Income Statement
1	Owner invests cash	+		+	
2	Pay wages with cash				
3	Acquire services on credit				
4	Buy store equipment for cash				
5	Borrow cash with note payable				
6	Sell services for cash				
7	Sell services on credit				
8	Pay rent with cash				
9	Owner withdraws cash				
10	Collect receivable from (7)				

Analytical and Review Problems

A & R Problem 1-1

CHECK FIGURE: Total assets = $89,775

Jack Tasker opened his Auto Repair Shop in November 2017. The balance sheet at November 30, 2017, prepared by an inexperienced part-time bookkeeper, is shown below.

Required Prepare a correct balance sheet.

Tasker Auto Repair Shop
Balance Sheet
November 30, 2017

Assets		Liabilities and Equity	
Cash	$ 6,300	Parts and supplies	$14,175
Accounts payable............................	34,650	Accounts receivable.........................	47,250
Equipment	22,050	Mortgage payable............................	28,350
Jack Tasker, capital	26,775		
Total income.................................	$89,775	Total equities................................	$89,775

A & R Problem 1-2

CHECK FIGURES: Profit = $5,880; Total liabilities and equity = $17,430

Susan Huang began the practice of law October 1, 2017, with an initial investment of $10,500 in cash. She made no withdrawals during the month. After completing the first month of practice, the financial statements were prepared by Ryan Player, the secretary/bookkeeper Ms. Huang had hired. Ms. Huang almost burst out laughing when she saw them. She had completed a course in legal accounting in law school and knew the statements prepared by Player left much to be desired. Consequently, she asked you to revise the statements. The Player version is presented as follows:

Susan Huang, Lawyer Balance Sheet October 31, 2017			
Assets		**Liabilities and Equity**	
Cash	$ 3,780	Susan Huang, capital	$10,500
Furniture..	2,100		
Supplies expense.............................	420		
Accounts payable.............................	1,050		
Rent expense....................................	2,100		
Supplies...	1,050		
	$10,500		$10,500

Susan Huang, Lawyer Income Statement For Month Ended October 31, 2017			
Revenues:			
Legal revenue.	$11,550		
Accounts receivable	2,100	$13,650	
Expenses:			
Salaries expense	$ 2,940		
Telephone expense.	210		
Law library	8,400	11,550	
Profit.		$ 2,100	

Required Prepare the corrected financial statements for Susan Huang.

A & R Problem 1-3

For each of the following activities, identify the effect on each component of the income statement and balance sheet. The first one has been done as an example for you.

1. $14,000 of services were provided to clients on credit today.

	Income Statement		Balance Sheet		
	Revenues	**Expenses**	**Assets**	**Liabilities**	**Equity**
1.	⬆$14,000		⬆$14,000		⬆$14,000

2. $5,000 cash was collected for services performed on credit last month.
3. $25,000 cash was borrowed from the bank.
4. $500 of advertising was done in the local newspaper today on account.
5. $500 was paid regarding the advertising in (4) above.
6. The owner invested an additional $10,000 cash into the business.
7. The owner withdrew $5,000 of cash from the business.
8. The owner took $200 worth of office supplies home for personal use.
9. A new computer was purchased for $2,000 cash.
10. A one-year insurance policy costing $12,000 was purchased today.
11. Purchased $45 of fuel for the van; paid cash.
12. Collected $900 from a client for work performed today.

Ethics Challenge

EC 1-1

Sue Santos is a new entry-level accountant for a snowboard manufacturer. At the end of the fiscal period, Santos is advised by a supervisor to include as revenue for the period any orders that have been submitted online, but have not yet been shipped. Santos is also advised to include as revenue any orders where payment has already been received but where shipment is still pending.

Required

1. Identify relevant accounting principles that Santos should be aware of in view of the supervisor's instructions.
2. What are the ethical factors in this situation?
3. Would you recommend that Santos follow the supervisor's directives?
4. What alternatives might be available to Santos if she decides not to follow the supervisor's directions?

Focus on Financial Statements

FFS 1-1   e**X**cel

CHECK FIGURES: 3. Cash, June 30, 2017 = $15,000; Total assets, June 30, 2017 = $23,000; Cash, July 31, 2017 = $12,500; Total assets, July 31, 2017 = $23,800

Glenrose Servicing began operations on June 1, 2017. The transactions for the first two months follow:

	2017		
June	1	The owner, Diane Towbell, invested $20,000 cash and office equipment with a value of $6,000.
	5	Glenrose Servicing performed $3,000 of services for a client on account.
	7	Paid rent for June in the amount of $1,500.
	9	Collected $1,000 from the customer of June 5.
	15	Paid $5,000 of mid-month wages to part-time employees.
	17	Provided $2,000 of services to a client and collected the cash immediately.
	29	Received the $300 June utilities bill. It will be paid in July.
	30	Paid $1,500 in wages to part-time employees.
July	5	Did work for a customer on account; $3,500.
	8	Collected $2,000 from credit customers.
	9	Paid $1,500 rent for July.
	12	Purchased $1,800 of additional office equipment on account.
	14	Paid $1,000 of the amount owing regarding July 12.
	15	Paid mid-month wages to part-time staff; $2,500.
	17	Performed services for a customer and immediately collected $4,800.
	25	Paid $300 in utilities for the month of July plus the balance owing from June.
	31	Paid $1,700 in wages to part-time employees.
	31	The owner withdrew cash of $2,000 for personal use.

Required

1. Create two tables like the one in Exhibit 1.15 for each of June and July using the following headings for the columns: Cash; Accounts Receivable; Office Equipment; Accounts Payable; Diane Towbell, Capital; and Explanation of Equity Transaction.

2. Use additions and subtractions to show the effects of the above transactions on the elements of the equation for each of June and July.

3. Prepare an income statement and statement of changes in equity for each of the months ended June 30, and July 31, 2017. Also prepare a balance sheet at June 30, 2017, and July 31, 2017.

Analysis Component: Answer each of the following questions:

1. Assets increased by $800 from June 30, 2017, to July 31, 2017. How was this increase financed?

2. Which financial statement reports on a company's

   a. performance?

   b. financial position?

   Explain what is meant by each of these terms.

3. Explain how Glenrose Servicing's July income statement, statement of changes in equity, and balance sheet are linked.

FFS 1-2

Part A:

1. Refer to Appendix III at the end of the textbook for the December 31, 2014, balance sheet for **WestJet Airlines Ltd.,** a Canadian airline based in Calgary, Alberta. What types of assets does WestJet have?

2. To what level of significance are the dollar amounts rounded on the financial statements?

3. Prove the accounting equation for WestJet at December 31, 2014.

4. Assume that the personal home of one of the owners of WestJet (a shareholder) is valued at over $2,000,000. Should it be included as an asset on the balance sheet for WestJet? Why or why not?

5. Identify a potential internal user who would be interested in WestJet's statements and explain his or her interest.

Part B:

6. Refer to Appendix III at the end of the textbook for the June 28, 2014, balance sheet for **Danier Leather Inc.,** a Canadian specialty-clothing designer, manufacturer, and retailer based in Toronto, Ontario. Identify the following for Danier at June 28, 2014:

   a. Total assets

   b. Total net assets

   Prove the accounting equation for Danier at June 28, 2014.

7. Notice that the balance sheet provides data for two years. Why do you think information has been presented for both June 28, 2013, and June 28, 2014?

8. Identify a potential external user who would be interested in Danier's statements and explain his or her interest.

Critical Thinking Mini Case

You have worked with XYZ Consulting as the marketing manager for a number of years. Each of your salespeople must submit a monthly report detailing money they spent while conducting business on behalf of XYZ Consulting. Each item on the monthly report must be coded as to the effect on assets, liabilities, and equity. As marketing manager, one of your duties is to review the monthly reports. One salesperson's report for September shows the following:

Date	Description of Transaction	Amount of Transaction	Effect on Assets	Effect on Liabilities	Effect on Equity
Aug. 28	Delivered market strategy report for a key customer	$150,000	Increased cash	No effect	Increased revenue
Sept. 10	Purchased new desk for office to be paid in October	$1,500	No effect	Increased accounts payable	Increased office expense
Sept. 2–30	Took clients for lunch and paid cash	$680	Decreased cash		Increased owner investments
Oct. 5	Paid for September cell phone usage	$130	Decreased cash		Increased expenses

Required Using the elements of the critical thinking model described on the inside front cover, respond, focussing on the following key areas:

1. What problems are identified in the September report?
2. What is the goal of the monthly report and what is the purpose of your review?
3. What assumptions have been made or principles need to be considered in presenting the transactions?
4. What are the key facts and how do we rely on the facts to identify errors in the report?
5. How will you address the issues you have found with the salesperson?

Analyzing and Recording Transactions

A Look Back

Chapter 1 defined accounting and introduced financial statements. We described forms of organizations and identified users and uses of accounting. We defined the accounting equation and applied it to transaction analysis.

A Look at This Chapter

This chapter focuses on the accounting process. We describe transactions and source documents, and we explain the analysis and recording of transactions. The accounting equation, T-account, general ledger, trial balance, and debits and credits are key tools in the accounting process.

© Jonathan Hayward/The Canadian Press

LEARNING OBJECTIVES

LO1 Explain the accounting cycle.

LO2 Describe an account, its use, and its relationship to the ledger.

LO3 Define debits and credits and explain their role in double-entry accounting.

LO4 Describe a chart of accounts and its relationship to the ledger.

LO5 Analyze the impact of transactions on accounts, record transactions in a journal, and post entries to a ledger.

LO6 Prepare and explain the use of a trial balance.

ACCOUNTING IN ACTION

Alexandre Bilodeau is the first athlete to win back-to-back Olympic gold medals in any freestyle skiing discipline. Alexandre dominated the men's Moguls event in freestyle skiing in both the Vancouver 2010 and Sochi 2014 Olympic games. His commitment and thirst for success motivated Bilodeau to push himself to the next level in his sport, breaking down previously established barriers. Because the conditions are constantly changing, Alexandre needed to be incredibly adaptable and maintain a high degree of precision, skiing 11.5 metres per second while landing impressive jumps with rock-solid stability. In Sochi, conditions were especially challenging on the slushy Rosa Khutor Extreme Park course in the medal round.

The athlete faced a huge setback in his pursuit of gold at the 2006 Turin Olympics when a landing error put him in 11th place. He later said, "It was a reality check for me ... I did a perfect downhill sprint but a single landing error in the final jump cost me three points." But he learned determination and perseverance were the keys to success. "I promised myself to give it everything and then to have no regrets. And how do you avoid regrets? You do what you have to do. You don't skip training one day just because you don't feel like it. You don't make excuses. That's an attitude I now carry with me in everything I do."

Right after Sochi, Alexandre announced he was leaving the competitive sport to study accounting at Concordia University. From the age of 12, Alexandre has fond memories of accompanying his father, a tax accountant at KPMG, on visits to clients. He plans to keep his options open in the field of accounting. "Many opportunities present themselves to me, but I want to prove myself ... Accounting is so vast, it's a launch pad that can lead to so many things." For career options as a professional accountant, visit your provincial CPA recruiting website.

In business the customer, political, technological and social environments are constantly changing. Accountants and business professionals need to be prepared to navigate through challenging and often unfamiliar situations. The best leaders will maintain rock-solid stability while responding quickly to changes impacting the organization. How will you make a difference in your future career?

Sources: https://www.cpacanada.ca/en/connecting-and-news/cpa-magazine/articles/2014/June/bumps-spins-and-spectacular-wins; accessed September 2014. http://www.thestar.com/sports/sochi2014/skiing/2014/02/10/sochi_olympics_all_four_canadians_advance_to_mens_moguls_final.html; accessed May 2015. http://espn.go.com/olympics/winter/2014/freestyleskiing/story/_/id/10432528/2014-winter-olympics-canada-alex-bilodeau-repeats-gold-medalist-men-moguls, accessed May 2015. http://olympic.ca/team-canada/alexandre-bilodeau, accessed May 2015.

Video Link: http://nsb.com/speakers/alexandre-bilodeau/

CRITICAL THINKING CHALLENGE   What can we take away from Alexandre Bilodeau's determination in the face of challenges?

CHAPTER PREVIEW

The accounting process identifies business transactions and events, analyzes and records their effects, and summarizes and presents information in reports and financial statements. These reports and statements are used for making investing, lending, and other business decisions. The steps in the accounting process that focus on *analyzing and recording* transactions and events are shown in Exhibit 2.1.

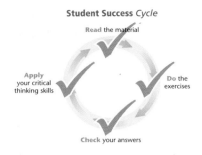

Student Success *Cycle*

Read the material

Apply
your critical
thinking skills

Do the
exercises

Check your answers

Business transactions and events are the starting points. Relying on source documents, the transactions and events are analyzed using the accounting equation to understand how they affect company performance and financial position. These effects are recorded in accounting records, informally referred to as the *accounting books,* or simply the *books.* Additional steps such as posting and then preparing a trial balance help summarize and classify the effects of transactions and events. Ultimately, the accounting process provides information in useful reports or financial statements to decision makers. Student success in mastering this cycle requires commitment to read the material, do the exercises, check the appropriate answers, and apply critical thinking skills in analyzing conclusions.

The Accounting Cycle

LO1 Explain the accounting cycle.

The **accounting cycle** refers to the series of steps required to prepare a set of financial statements for users. These steps are referred to as a cycle because they are repeated each time financial statements are prepared for that company, also known as a reporting period. Exhibit 2.1 illustrates the required steps in

EXHIBIT 2.1

Accounting Cycle

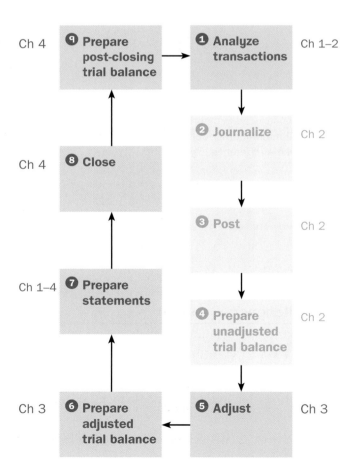

Ch 4   **9 Prepare post-closing trial balance** → **1 Analyze transactions**   Ch 1–2

2 Journalize   Ch 2

Ch 4   **8 Close**

3 Post   Ch 2

Ch 1–4   **7 Prepare statements**

4 Prepare unadjusted trial balance   Ch 2

Ch 3   **6 Prepare adjusted trial balance** ← **5 Adjust**   Ch 3

the accounting cycle. Chapter 1 introduced transaction analysis, the first step in the accounting cycle. Chapter 2 will focus on the next three steps of the accounting cycle. Step 7, the preparation of financial statements, was introduced in Chapter 1 and is reinforced in Chapters 2 through 4.

Accounts

LO2   Describe an account, its use, and its relationship to the ledger.

This section explains the importance of an account to accounting and business. We also describe several crucial elements of an accounting system, including ledgers, T-accounts, debits and credits, double-entry accounting, and the chart of accounts.

The Account

An **account** is a detailed record of increases and decreases in a specific asset, liability, or equity item. Information is taken from accounts, analyzed, summarized, and presented in useful reports and financial statements for users. Separate accounts[1] are kept for each type of asset, liability, and equity item. Exhibit 2.2 shows examples of the different types of accounts used by Organico.

EXHIBIT 2.2

Types of Accounts for Organico

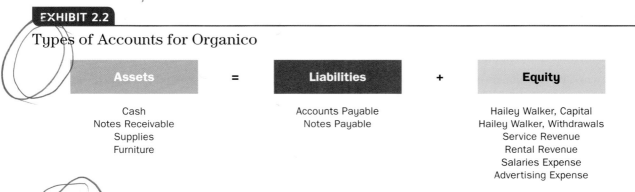

Assets	=	Liabilities	+	Equity
Cash		Accounts Payable		Hailey Walker, Capital
Notes Receivable		Notes Payable		Hailey Walker, Withdrawals
Supplies				Service Revenue
Furniture				Rental Revenue
				Salaries Expense
				Advertising Expense

A **ledger** is the term used to describe a record containing all individual accounts used by a business. A ledger is typically maintained electronically and summarizes the final balances in each account after being entered in the journal. Each company will have its own unique set of accounts to suit its type of operation. The following section introduces accounts that are most commonly used by businesses today.

Asset Accounts

Assets are properties or economic resources held by a business with three key attributes:

1. The transaction to acquire the asset has occurred.

2. The company owns/has title to the asset.

3. A future benefit exists for the company as it is used in operations.[2]

Assets have value and are used in the operations of the business to create revenue. For example, airplanes are assets held by **WestJet** for the purpose of creating revenue in current and future periods. A separate account is maintained for each asset category.

Cash increases and decreases are recorded in a separate Cash account. Examples are coins, currency, cheques, money orders, and chequing account balances. Each bank account used by the company

---

1   As an example of an account, Exhibit 2.5 shows the Cash account as one of several asset accounts used by Organico.

2   IFRS 2014 "Framework," para. 4.44.

will have a separate account number. *Receivables* are amounts that the business is expecting to receive or collect in the future. Types of receivables include:

- **Accounts receivable**, which are created when services are performed for or goods are sold to customers in return for a commitment from the customer to pay in the future, instead of settling in cash today. These transactions are said to be on credit or *on account*. Accounts receivable are *increased* as services are performed or goods are sold on credit and *decreased* by customer payments.

- **Notes receivable** (or **promissory notes**), which are a formal contract signed by the customer or another party that owes a specific sum of money to the company. The contract provides details regarding the total dollar value of the commitment, when the payment is due, and any interest required to be paid.

Prepaid expenses occur when a company pays in advance for a service or goods for which the benefit extends beyond the current accounting period. Examples include Office Supplies, Store Supplies, Prepaid Rent, and Prepaid Insurance. As these assets are used up, the costs of the used assets become expenses. This account supports the *matching principle* introduced in Chapter 1. Because the benefits of these goods/services are used in future periods, they should be matched to the revenue in future periods. A prepaid cost can be initially recorded as an expense *if* it is used up before the end of the period.

Equipment includes assets such as vehicles, machinery, computers, printers, desks, chairs, display cases, and cash registers. These assets are used in the operations of a business for more than one accounting period.

Buildings are assets owned by an organization that can provide space for a store, an office, a warehouse, or a factory. The benefits of buildings purchased by the company generally extends many years into the future.

Land owned by a business is shown as an asset. The cost of land is separated from the cost of buildings located on the land to provide more useful information in financial statements.

Liability Accounts

Liabilities are obligations of the business that have two key attributes:

1. That are a present obligation as a result of a past event
2. Where the company has an outstanding obligation to pay via a transfer assets or provision of services in the future[3]

An organization often has several different liabilities, each of which is represented by a separate account that shows amounts owed to each creditor. The more common liability accounts are described here.

Payables are promises by a business to pay later for an asset or service already received. Types of payables include:

- **Accounts payable**, which occur with the purchase of merchandise, supplies, equipment, or services made with a commitment to pay later

- **Notes payable**, which occur when an organization formally recognizes a promise to pay by signing a contract referred to as a promissory note

Unearned revenues result when customers pay in advance for products or services. Because cash from these transactions is received before revenues are earned, the seller considers them unearned, as they do not meet the requirements of the revenue recognition principle introduced in Chapter 1. Unearned revenue is a liability because a service or product is *owed* to a customer. It will be earned when the service or product is delivered in the future. Examples of unearned revenue include magazine subscriptions

---

3   IFRS 2014, "Framework," para. 4.46.

collected in advance by a publisher, sales of gift certificates by stores, airline tickets sold in advance, and rent collected in advance by a landlord.

> WestJet Airlines Ltd. reported *advance ticket sales* of $551,022,000 on December 31, 2013.
>
> See Appendix III.

Other liabilities include wages payable, taxes payable, and interest payable. Each of these is often recorded in a separate liability account. If they are not large in amount, two or more of them may be added and reported as a single amount on the balance sheet.

> The liabilities section of WestJet Airlines Ltd.'s balance sheet at December 31, 2013, included accounts payable and accrued liabilities of $543,167,000.
>
> See Appendix III.

Equity Accounts

We described in the previous chapter four types of transactions that affect equity: (1) investments by the owner, (2) withdrawals by the owner, (3) revenues, and (4) expenses. In Chapter 1, we entered all equity transactions in a single column under the owner's name as copied in Exhibit 2.3. When we later prepared the income statement and the statement of changes in equity, we had to review the items in that column to classify them properly in financial statements.

A preferred approach is to use separate accounts, as illustrated under the Equity heading in Exhibit 2.2.

Owner Capital records owner investments. The capital account is identified by including the owner's name. The owner's capital account includes transactions in addition to owner investments, as discussed in the following two paragraphs.

Owner withdrawals are recorded in an account with the name of the owner and the word *Withdrawals*. This account is also sometimes called the owner's *Personal* account or *Drawing* account.

Revenues and expenses incurred for a period must be known to decision makers. Businesses use a variety of accounts to report revenues earned and expenses incurred on the income statement. Examples of revenue accounts are Sales, Commissions, Consulting Revenue, Rent Revenue, Subscription Revenue, and Interest Income. WestJet uses the simple term *Revenue* to report its airline revenue and breaks down its revenue into two revenue categories "Guest" and "Other." WestJet reported $3.4 billion in guest revenue and $324.6 million in other revenue in fiscal 2013. Examples of expense accounts include Advertising Expense, Store Supplies Expense, Office Salaries Expense, Office Supplies Expense, Rent Expense, Utilities Expense, and Insurance Expense.

EXHIBIT 2.3

Equity Transactions as Analyzed in Chapter 1

Equity	Explanation
Hailey Walker, Capital	
$10,000	Investment by Owner
$10,000	
$10,000	
+ 2,200	Food Services Revenue
$12,200	
– 1,000	Rent Expense
$11,200	
– 700	Salaries Expense
$10,500	
+ 1,600	Food Services Revenue
+ 300	Teaching Revenue
$12,400	
$12,400	
$12,400	
– 600	Withdrawal by Owner
$11,800	

Important Tip: Turn to Appendix IV to find detailed information relating to accounts used within the book. It will help you tremendously to study this Appendix to familiarize yourself with common account names and the categories of accounts they fall under. For example, terminology for several types of expense accounts are listed. The accounts listed will be needed to solve some of the exercises and problems in this book.[4]

CHECKPOINT

1. Explain the accounting cycle.
2. Classify the following accounts as either assets, liabilities, or equity: (1) Prepaid Rent, (2) Rent Expense, (3) Unearned Rent, (4) Rent Revenue, (5) Buildings, (6) Owner Capital, (7) Wages Payable, (8) Wages Expense, (9) Office Supplies, and (10) Owner Withdrawals.
3. What is the difference between the accounts Rent Earned, Rent Revenue, and Earned Rent?

Do Quick Study question: QS 2-1

T-Accounts

A **T-account** is a helpful learning tool that represents an account in the ledger. It shows the effects of individual transactions on specific accounts. The T-account is so named because it looks like the letter T. It is shown in Exhibit 2.4.

The format of a T-account includes (1) the account title on top, (2) a left or debit side, and (3) a right or credit side. Debits and credits are explained in the next section. A T-account provides one side for recording increases in the item and the other side for decreases. As an example, the T-account for Organico's Cash account after recording the transactions in Chapter 1 is in Exhibit 2.5.

EXHIBIT 2.4	EXHIBIT 2.5
The T-Account	Calculating the Balance of a T-Account

Account Title

(Left side)	(Right side)
Debit	*Credit*

Cash

Investment by owner	10,000	2,500	Purchase of supplies
Received from providing		1,000	Payment of rent
Food services	2,200	700	Payment of salary
Collection of account		900	Payment of account payable
Receivable	1,900	600	Withdrawal by owner
Total increases	14,100	5,700	Total decreases
Less decreases	−5,700		
Balance	8,400		

T-accounts are used throughout this text to help illustrate debits and credits and to solve accounting problems. *This form of account is a learning tool and is typically not used in actual accounting systems. However, many professional accountants often find T-accounts useful for analytical purposes.*

---

[4] Different companies can use account titles different from those listed in Appendix III. For example, a company might use *Interest Revenue* instead of *Interest Earned*, or *Subscription Fees Revenue* or *Subscription Fees Earned* instead of *Earned Subscription Fees*, or *Rental Expense* instead of *Rent Expense*. It is only important that an account title describes the item it represents. We must use our good judgment when reading financial statements since titles can differ even within the same industry.

Balance of an Account

An **account balance** is the difference between the increases and decreases recorded in an account. To determine the balance, we:

1. Calculate the total increases shown on one side (including the beginning balance)
2. Calculate the total decreases shown on the other side
3. Subtract the sum of the decreases from the sum of the increases, and
4. Calculate the account balance.

The total increases in Organico's Cash account are $14,100, the total decreases are $5,700, and the account balance is $8,400. The T-account in Exhibit 2.5 shows how we calculate the $8,400 balance:

Debits and Credits

LO3 Define debits and credits and explain their role in double-entry accounting.

The left side of a T-account is always called the **debit** side, often abbreviated Dr. The right side is always called the **credit** side, abbreviated Cr.[5] We enter amounts on the left side of an account to *debit* the account. We enter amounts on the right side of the T-account to *credit* the account. The difference between total debits and total credits for an account is the account balance. When the sum of debits exceeds the sum of credits, the account has a *debit balance* as is demonstrated with the following example:

Office Supplies	
100	60
300	200
Balance 140	

Total debits = 100 + 300 = 400
Total credits = 60 + 200 = $260
Balance = 400 − 260 = $140 debit balance

A T-account has a *credit balance* when the sum of credits exceeds the sum of debits, as is illustrated next:

Accounts Payable	
350	400
500	600
	150 Balance

Total debits = 350 + 500 = 850
Total credits = 400 + 600 = 1,000
total credits; credits are greater than debits, so the
Balance = 850 − 1,000 = $150 credit balance.

When the sum of debits equals the sum of credits, the account has a zero balance. This dual method of recording transactions as debits and credits is an essential feature of *double-entry accounting*, and is the topic of the next section.

Double-Entry Accounting

Double-entry accounting means every transaction affects and is recorded in at least two accounts. *For the accounting records to be accurate, every time a transaction is recorded the total amount debited must equal the total amount credited.* Therefore, the sum of the debits recorded must equal the sum of the credits for each economic event captured in the accounting records. As well, the sum of debit account balances in the ledger must equal the sum of credit account balances. The only reason that the sum of debit balances would not equal the sum of credit balances is if an error had

---

5 These abbreviations are remnants of 18th-century English recordkeeping practices in which the terms *Debitor* and *Creditor* were used instead of *debit* and *credit*. The abbreviations use the first and last letters of these terms where **Dr** resulted from **D**ebito**r**, and **Cr** from **C**redito**r**, just as we still do for *Saint* (St.) and *Doctor* (Dr.).

occurred. Double-entry accounting helps to prevent errors by ensuring that debits and credits for each transaction are equal.

$$\text{Debits} = \text{Credits}$$

The system for recording debits and credits follows from the accounting equation in Exhibit 2.6.

EXHIBIT 2.6
_____

Accounting Equation

Assets	=	**Liabilities**	+	**Equity**

Assets are on the left side of this equation. Liabilities and equity are on the right side. Like any mathematical equation, increases or decreases on one side have equal effects on the other side. For example, the net increase in assets must be accompanied by an identical net increase in the liabilities and equity side. Some transactions affect only one side of the equation. This means that two or more accounts on one side are affected, but their net effect on this one side is zero.

The debit and credit effects for asset, liability, and equity accounts are captured in Exhibit 2.7.

EXHIBIT 2.7
_____

Debit and Credit Effects for Accounts

Assets	=	Liabilities	+	Equity
Debit for increases Credit for decreases		Debit for decreases Credit for increases		Debit for decreases Credit for increases
+ −		− +		− +

Debits are always on the left and credits are always on the right.

Important Tip: Ensure you know the following rules as illustrated in Exhibit 2.7 before reading Chapter 3. For a helpful learning tool, review the following video by Colin Dodds, an educational music video enthusiast.

Video Link: https://youtu.be/7EuxfW76BWU

Three important rules for recording transactions in a double-entry accounting system follow from Exhibit 2.7.

1. Increases in assets are debited to asset accounts. Decreases in assets are credited to asset accounts.

2. Increases in liabilities are credited to liability accounts. Decreases in liabilities are debited to liability accounts.

3. Increases in equity are credited to equity accounts. Decreases in equity are debited to equity accounts.

CAUTION: Do not assume the terms *debit* and *credit* mean increase or decrease. For asset accounts debit means increase and credit means decrease. When liabilities and equity are increased the related account is credited and when they are decreased the related account is debited.

EXHIBIT 2.8

Debit and Credit Effects for Accounts

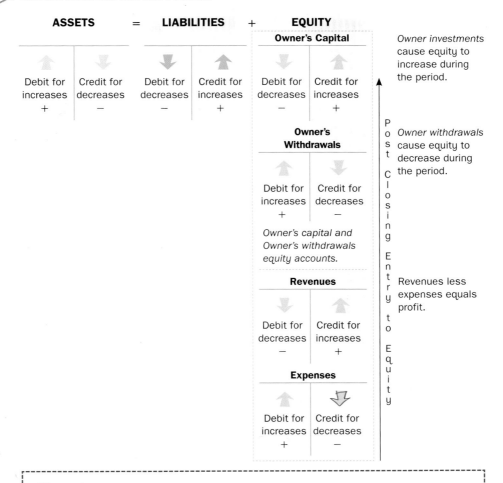

Profit: Only adjusts owner's capital after financial statement preparation to prepare owner's capital for next period.

We explained in Chapter 1 how equity increases with owner investments and revenues, and decreases with expenses and owner withdrawals. Please note that revenues and expenses impact equity through the profit (loss) recognized on the income statement. The equity adjustment of recording the profit (loss) to the owner's capital account is not made until after the financial statements have been prepared. The closing process is covered in Chapter 4 (refer to Exhibit 4.5 outlining the recording and posting of closing entries). We can therefore expand the accounting equation and debit and credit effects as shown in Exhibit 2.8 and summarize them in Exhibit 2.9.

Important Tip: Profit (loss) is booked to the Owner's Capital account only after financial statements have been prepared, during the closing process discussed in Chapter 4. It is added to equity in the statement of owner's equity, as is shown at the end of chapter Demonstration Problem featuring The Cutlery.

EXHIBIT 2.9		EXHIBIT 2.10	

The Debit and Credit Summary

Debit and Credit Summary	
Debits Record	**Credits Record**
Assets	Liabilities
Expenses/Losses	Revenues/Profit
Withdrawals	Owner's Capital ⇒ Investments
Debits Decrease:	**Credits Decrease:**
Existing Liabilities	Existing Assets

Normal Account Balances

Normal Account Balances	
Debit	**Credit**
Assets	Liabilities
Withdrawals	Owner's Capital*
Expenses	Revenue

* Used to record[6]: owner investments profit closing entry after f/s preparation

Exhibit 2.10 highlights the *normal balance* of each type of account. The **normal balance** refers to the debit or credit side when *increases* are recorded and in most cases where the balance in the account should rest. For example, the normal balance for an asset account would be a debit because a debit balance indicates that the company has something that will provide a future benefit. The normal balance for a revenue account would be a credit because revenues are increased by credits and result in an increase in equity.

> **Important Tip:** The following video highlights a "Hand Game," presenting a quick way to remember your debit and credits:
>
> Video Link: https://www.youtube.com/watch?v=onq8AfjxjRo
>
> Thanks to Leanne Vig, MBA, CGA, Accounting Instructor, Red Deer College for sharing this helpful learning tool.

Increases in owner's capital or revenues *increase* equity. Increases in owner's withdrawals or expenses *decrease* equity. These important relations are reflected in the following four additional rules:

4. Investments in the company made by the owner are credited to owner's capital because they increase equity.
5. Revenues are credited to revenue accounts because they increase equity, as they increase profit.
6. Expenses are debited to expense accounts because they decrease equity, as they decrease profit.
7. Withdrawals made by the owner are debited to owner's withdrawals because they decrease equity.

Our understanding of these diagrams and rules is crucial to analyzing and recording transactions. This also helps us to prepare and analyze financial statements.[7]

---

6 The Owner's Capital account is also used to record end of period profit (loss); however, entries are not made to the capital account until the financial statements are prepared. Refer to the closing process for a proprietorship covered in Chapter 4, Exhibit 4.5.

7 We can use good judgment to our advantage in applying double-entry accounting. For example, revenues and expenses often (but not always) accumulate in a growing business. This means they increase and rarely decrease over the course of an accounting period. Accordingly, we should be alert to unexpected decreases in these accounts (debit revenues or credit expenses) as a sign of potential errors.

Chart of Accounts

LO4 Describe a chart of accounts and its relationship to the ledger.

Recall that the collection of all accounts in a company's accounting information system is called a *ledger*. The number of accounts needed in the ledger is affected by a company's size and diversity of operations. A small company may have as few as 20 accounts, while a large company may need several thousand.

The **chart of accounts** is a list of all accounts used in the ledger by a company. The chart includes an identification number assigned to each account. The chart of accounts in Appendix IV of the text uses the following numbering system for its accounts:

101–199	→	Asset accounts
201–299	→	Liability accounts
301–399	→	Owner capital and withdrawals accounts
401–499	→	Revenue accounts
501–599[8]	→	Cost of sales expense accounts
601–699	→	Operating expense accounts

The numbers provide a three-digit code that is useful in recordkeeping. In this case, the first digit assigned to asset accounts is 1, while the first digit assigned to liability accounts is 2, and so on. The first digit of an account's number also shows whether the account appears on the balance sheet or the income. The second and subsequent digits may also relate to the accounts' categories. The numerical basis of a chart of accounts is a fundamental component of a computerized accounting system. A partial chart of accounts for Organico follows.

ORGANICO

Account Number	Account Name	Account Number	Account Name
101	Cash	301	Hailey Walker, Capital
106	Accounts Receivable	302	Hailey Walker, Withdrawals
125	Supplies	403	Food Services Revenue
128	Prepaid Insurance	406	Teaching Revenue
167	Equipment	622	Salaries Expense
201	Accounts Payable	641	Rent Expense
236	Unearned Teaching Revenue	690	Utilities Expense
240	Notes Payable		

CHECKPOINT

4. What is the relationship of an account to the ledger and chart of accounts?
5. What is the normal balance for assets, liabilities, revenue, expenses, withdrawals, and capital accounts?

Do Quick Study questions: QS 2-2, QS 2-3, QS 2-4, QS 2-5

---

8 Organico does not use accounts 501–599. These accounts are used by merchandisers (such as Danier Leather in Appendix II), a topic discussed in Chapter 5.

DECISION INSIGHT

TWC Enterprises Limited (Formerly Clublink Enterprises Limited) is engaged in golf club, resort, rail, and tourism operations, and is Canada's largest owner and operator of golf clubs with 45 locations distributed in Ontario, Quebec, and Florida. Its income statement for the year ended December 31, 2013, showed total revenues of $213,711,000. On the December 31, 2012, balance sheet, there were total assets of $658,679,000, total liabilities of $465,386,000, and total equity of $193,293,000. Although the details of TWC's chart of accounts can't be seen on its financial statements, it likely has hundreds of accounts to track its wide range of transactions.

SOURCE: http://www.twcenterprises.ca/pdf/2013%20Annual%20Report.pdf, accessed September 2, 2014.

Recording and Posting Transactions

LO5 Analyze the impact of transactions on accounts, record transactions in a journal, and post entries to a ledger.

In this section, we analyze transactions and record their effects directly in T-accounts to help you understand the double-entry accounting system. This process is illustrated using examples from Organico in the next section.

The *first step* in the accounting cycle is identifying a business transaction as was highlighted in the Chapter 1 discussion of transaction analysis.

The *second step* involves analyzing the effect each transaction has on specific asset, liability, and equity accounts., as a subset of the accounting equation.

The *third* step is to assess which accounts are debited and which accounts are credited, identifying the appropriate dollar value impact.

The *fourth step* is to record the journal entry in proper form.

The fifth step is to **post**, or transfer, entries from the journal to the appropriate accounts.

The *sixth* step is to determine a big picture assessment of the effect of each transaction on the accounting equation as was covered in Chapter 1.

This section describes both journalizing and posting of transactions. *Step Seven* of the accounting cycle, preparing a *trial balance*, is explained later in the chapter. Exhibit 2.1 outlines the accounting cycle. The first four steps of the accounting cycle are illustrated in Exhibit 2.11.

EXHIBIT 2.11

First Four Steps of the Accounting Cycle

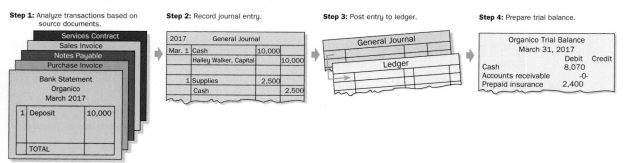

Journal Entry Analysis

A journal is a record where journal entries are posted in chronological order. Recording all journal entries in a journal helps to prevent errors and enables us to identify mistakes effectively. A journal gives us a complete record of each transaction entered in the accounting information system. A **journal entry** refers to an individual transaction that has been entered in the journal, and provides information regarding the dated the transaction is entered, which accounts are debited, which accounts are credited, and the corresponding transaction amounts. The process of recording transactions in a journal is called **journalizing**. The **general journal** is flexible in that it can be used to record any economic transaction not captured in a special journal, and is typically used in practice to record non-routine transactions. Special journals are used to capture journal entries relating to similar types of transactions. Examples of special journals include sales journal, cash receipts journal, cash disbursements journal, purchases journal, and the payroll journal.

A journal entry includes the following information about each transaction:

1. Date of transaction
2. Titles of affected accounts with corresponding account number
3. Dollar amount of each debit and credit
4. Explanation of transaction

Exhibit 2.12 shows how the first three transactions of Organico are recorded chronologically using a general journal. Although businesses use computerized systems, this textbook will demonstrate the processes of journalizing and posting using a manual system to ensure you have a strong foundation in accounting processes. Computerized journals and ledgers all operate on the same basic principles and processes as manual systems.

The third entry in Exhibit 2.12 uses four accounts. There are debits to the two assets purchased, Supplies and Equipment. There are also credits to the two sources of payment, Accounts Payable and Notes Payable. A transaction affecting two accounts is called a **simple journal entry**. A transaction affecting three or more accounts is called a **compound journal entry**.

ORGANICO

| EXHIBIT 2.12 |

Partial General Journal for Organico

General Journal					Page 1
Date	Account Titles and Explanation	PR	Debit		Credit
2017					
Mar. 1	Cash		10,000		
	Hailey Walker, Capital				10,000
	Investment by owner..				
1	Supplies		2,500		
	Cash				2,500
	Purchased store supplies for cash.				
1	Supplies		1,100		
	Equipment		6,000		
	Accounts Payable				1,100
	Notes Payable...				6,000
	Purchased supplies and equipment on credit.				

Recording Journal Entries

> **Important Tip:** Ensure total debits equal total credits; in other words, the journal entry balances before moving on to the next transaction.

The **posting reference (PR) column** is left blank when a transaction is initially recorded. Individual account numbers are later entered into the PR column when entries are posted to the ledger.

Computerized accounting software programs include error-checking routines that ensure that debits equal credits for each entry. Shortcuts often allow record keepers to enter account numbers instead of names, and to enter account names and numbers with pull-down menus.

Posting Journal Entries

To ensure that the ledger is up to date, entries are posted as soon as possible. This might be daily, weekly, or monthly. Electronic journal entries entered in computerized accounting software are posted each time a journal entry is recorded. All entries must be posted to the ledger by the end of a reporting period. Updating account balances in a timely manner to reflect current values is especially important when financial statements are prepared. The ledger is the final destination for individual transactions; as such, it is referred to as the *book of final entry*.

When posting manual entries to the ledger, the debits in journal entries are copied into ledger accounts as debits, and credits are copied into the ledger as credits. To demonstrate the posting process, Exhibit 2.13 lists six steps to post each debit and credit from a journal entry.

EXHIBIT 2.13

Posting an Entry to the Ledger

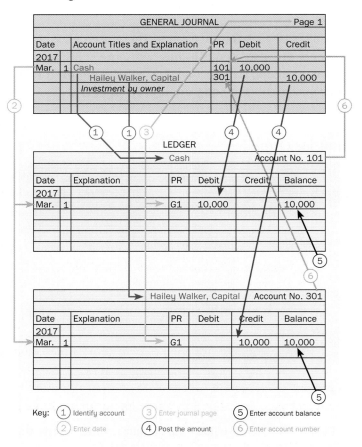

Posting occurs after debits and credits for each transaction are entered into a journal. This process leaves a helpful trail that can be followed in checking for accuracy. T-accounts are a useful tool to demonstrate the posting of journal entries to the ledger accounts and determining the impact of a transaction on the account balance.

For each journal entry, the usual process is to post debit(s) and then credit(s).

SIX-STEP PROCESS TO POST A MANUAL JOURNAL ENTRY

① Identify the ledger account that was debited in the journal entry.

② Enter the date of the journal entry in this ledger account.

③ Enter the source of the debit in the PR column, both the journal and page. The letter G shows it came from the general journal.[9]

④ Enter the amount debited from the journal entry into the Debit column of the ledger account.

⑤ Calculate and enter the account's new balance in the Balance column.

⑥ Enter the ledger account number in the PR column of the journal entry.

Repeat the six steps for credit amounts and Credit columns. Notice that posting does not create new information; posting simply transfers (or copies) information from the general journal to the appropriate account in the ledger.

Step six in the posting process for both debit and credit amounts of an entry inserts the account number in the journal's PR column. This creates a cross-reference between the ledger and the journal entry for tracing an amount from one record to another.

T-ACCOUNTS

T-accounts are used to demonstrate the impact of posting the transactions to the general ledger accounts. Refer to Exhibit 2.4 for an explanation of T-accounts.

Remember that in a double-entry accounting system we always have a minimum of two accounts included in each journal entry posted and we need to ensure that total debits equal total credits.

COMPUTERIZED SYSTEMS

Computerized systems require no added effort to post journal entries to the ledger. These systems automatically transfer debit and credit entries from the journal to the ledger database. Journal entries are posted directly to ledger accounts. Many systems have controls built into the software that test the reasonableness of a journal entry and the account balance when recorded. For example, a payroll program might alert a preparer to hourly wage rates that are greater than $100.

FINANCIAL STATEMENT IMPACT OF TRANSACTION

It is helpful to assess overall what the big picture impact is to the accounting equation after posting the transactions to T-accounts. This process serves as a double-check that the entry we recorded is keeping the accounting equation in balance. We need to determine which elements of the accounting equation are increasing and which are decreasing. For example, if Assets increase, then either a corresponding asset decreased or either liabilities or owner's equity must have increased. To illustrate, when if a company purchases new supplies (increasing, they either pay cash (resulting in a

---

9 Other journals are identified by their own letters. We discuss other journals later in the book.

decrease to assets) or incur a liability for future payment, referred to as accounts payable (increasing a liability).

$$\text{Assets} = \text{Liabilities} + \text{Owner's Equity}$$

CHECKPOINT

6. Assume Maria Sanchez, the owner of a new business called La Casa de Cafe, invested $15,000 cash and equipment with a market value of $23,000. Assume that La Casa de Cafe also took responsibility for an $18,000 note payable issued to finance the purchase of equipment. Prepare the journal entry to record Sanchez's investment.
7. Explain what a compound journal entry is.
8. Why are posting reference numbers entered in the journal when entries are posted to accounts?

Accounting Transactions in Action

We return to the activities of Organico to show how debit and credit rules and double-entry accounting are useful in analyzing and processing transactions. We analyze Organico's transactions in six steps.

- *Step one* analyzes a transaction and its source document(s).
- *Step two* applies double-entry accounting to identify the effect of a transaction on account balances.
- *Step three* analyzes the journal entry required to record the transaction.
- *Step four* records the journal entry.
- *Step five* uses T-accounts to post the transaction to ledger accounts and identify the effect of a transaction on account balances.
- *Step six* determines the financial statement impact of the transaction on Asset, Liability and Equity.

We should study each transaction thoroughly before proceeding to the next transaction. The first 11 activities are familiar to us from Chapter 1. We expand our analysis of these items and consider four new transactions (numbered 12 through 15) of Organico.

1. Investment by owner.

Transaction. Hailey Walker invested $10,000 in Organico on March 1, 2017.

Analysis. Assets increase as business receives cash. Equity increases due to owner investment.

Journal Entry Analysis. **Assets increased**, debit cash $10,000. **Equity increased**, credit Hailey Walker, Capital account for $10,000.

Journal Entry. Debit the Cash asset account for $10,000. Credit the Hailey Walker, Capital account in equity for $10,000.

Mar. 1	Cash	10,000	
	Hailey Walker, Capital ...		10,000
	Investment by owner.		

Post to Ledger.

	Cash	101
(1)	10,000	

	Hailey Walker, Capital	301
	10,000	(1)

Financial Statement Impact.
A = L + E[10]
↑   ↑

---

[10] The effect of each transaction on the accounting equation is repeated here from Chapter 1 to help you transition to debits and credits.

2. Purchase supplies for cash.

Transaction. March 1, Organico purchases supplies by paying $2,500 cash.

Analysis. **Assets increase** as supplies are brought in. **Assets decrease** as cash is spent. This changes the composition of assets, but does not change the total amount of assets.

Journal Entry Analysis. Assets increased, debit the Supplies asset account for $2,500. Assets decreased, credit the Cash asset account for $2,500.

Journal Entry.

Mar. 1	Supplies............................	2,500	
	Cash		2,500
	Purchased store supplies for cash.		

Financial Statement Impact.
$A = L + E$
↑↓

Post to Ledger.

Supplies 125

(1)	2,500	

Cash 301

10,000	2,500	(2)

3. Purchase equipment and supplies on credit.

Transaction. March 4, Organico purchases $1,100 of supplies and $6,000 of equipment on credit. Organico signs a promissory note, agreeing to pay for the $6,000 of equipment at a future date.

Analysis. **Assets increase** as equipment and supplies are brought into the company for use. **Liabilities increase** as the company purchases on a short-term credit arrangement for supplies and a longer-term credit arrangement for the equipment.

Journal Entry Analysis. Assets increased for equipment and supplies, debit Supplies for $1,100 and debit Equipment for $6,000. Liabilities increase; credit Accounts Payable for $1,100 and credit Notes Payable for $6,000.

Journal Entry.

March 4	Supplies......................................	1,100	
	Equipment	6,000	
	Accounts Payable		1,100
	Notes Payable......................		6,000
	Purchased supplies and equipment on credit.		

Financial Statement Impact.
$A = L + E$
↑   ↑

Post to Ledger.

Supplies 125

(2)	2,500	
(3)	1,100	

Equipment 167

(3)	6,000	

Accounts Payable 201

	1,100	(3)

Notes Payable 240

	6,000	(3)

4. Services rendered for cash.

Transaction. On March 10, Organico sets up the truck outside a concert facility before a sold-out venue and sells $2,200 worth of burritos for cash.

Analysis. **Assets increase** as cash is collected. **Equity increases** from earned Revenue.

Journal Entry.

Mar. 10	Cash	2,200	
	Food Services Revenue .		2,200
	Food truck sales for cash.		

Financial Statement Impact.
$A = L + E$
↑   ↑

Journal Entry Analysis. Assets increase; debit the Cash asset account for $2,200. Equity increases; credit the Food Services Revenue account for $2,200.

Post to Ledger.

	Cash		125
(1)	10,000	2,500	(2)
(4)	2,200		

	Food Services Revenue		403
		2,200	(4)

5. Payment of expense in cash.

Transaction. On March 10, Organico pays $1,000 cash for March rent.

Analysis. **Assets decrease** as payment for rent is made out of cash. **Equity decreases** due to Expense incurred.

Journal Entry Analysis. Equity decreases, debit the Rent Expense account for $1,000 (this decreases equity). Assets decrease; credit the Cash asset account for $1,000.

Journal Entry.

Mar. 10	Rent Expense......................	1,000	
	Cash		1,000
	Payment of March rent.		

Financial Statement Impact.
$A = L + E$
↓   ↓

Post to Ledger.

	Rent Expense		641
(5)	1,000		

	Cash		101
(1)	10,000	2,500	(2)
(4)	2,200	1,000	(5)

6. Payment of expense in cash.

Transaction. On March 10, Organico pays $700 cash for employee's salary for the pay period ending on March 14.

Analysis. **Assets decrease** to due cash payment. **Equity decreases** due to Expense incurred.

Journal Entry Analysis. Equity decreases due to expense incurred, debit the Salaries Expense account for $700. Assets decrease; credit the Cash asset account for $700.

Journal Entry.

Mar. 10	Salaries Expense	700	
	Cash		700
	Payment of employee salaries.		

Financial Statement Impact.
$A = L + E$
↓   ↓

Post to Ledger.

	Salaries Expense		622
(6)	700		

	Cash		101
(1)	10,000	2,500	(2)
(4)	2,200	1,000	(5)
		700	(6)

7. Service contract signed for April.

Event. On March 11, the accounting club at the local university and Hailey Walker sign a $2,700 contract that requires Organico to provide food for a group of graduating students at a CPA recruitment event. Organico has agreed to attend the event to be held in April.

Analysis. There has been no economic exchange between two parties (the services have not been provided and Organico did not receive any assets); therefore, this has no effect on the accounting equation.

8. Services and rental revenues rendered on credit.

Transaction. On March 17, Organico provided catering for a corporate event for $1,600 and taught a fresh Mexican cooking class for $300. The customer is billed $1,900 for the services and Organico expects to collect this money in the near future.

Analysis. **Assets increase** as customer is billed for services provided. **Equity increases** due to earned Revenue.

Journal Entry Analysis. Assets increase; debit the Accounts Receivable asset account for $1,900. Equity increases; credit two revenue accounts: Food Services Revenue for $1,600 (this increases equity) and Teaching Revenue for $300 (this increases equity).

Journal Entry.

Mar. 1	Cash	1,900	
	Food Services Revenue		
	Teaching Revenue		1,600
	Customer billed for services provided		300

Post to Ledger.

Accounts Receivable   106

(8)	1,900	

Food Services Revenue   403

	2,200	(4)
	1,600	(8)

Teaching Revenue   406

	300	(8)

Financial Statement Impact.
A = L + E
↑   ↑

9. Receipt of cash on account.

Transaction. On March 27, an amount of $1,900 is received from the customer in Transaction 8.

Analysis. **Assets increase** as cash is received. **Assets decrease**, as customer obligation to pay is no longer outstanding. This changes the composition of assets, but does not change the total amount of assets.

Journal Entry Analysis. Debit the Cash asset account for $1,900. Credit the Accounts Receivable asset account for $1,900.

Journal Entry.

Mar. 27	Cash	1,900	
	Accounts Receivable.....		1,900
	Collection of cash from customer.		

Post to Ledger.

Cash   101

(1)	10,000	2,500	(2)
(4)	2,200	1,000	(5)
(9)	1,900	700	(6)

Accounts Receivable   106

(8)	1,900	1,900	(9)

Financial Statement Impact.
A = L + E
↑↓

10. Partial payment of accounts payable.

Transaction. On March 27, Organico pays CanFood Supply $900 cash toward the account payable of $1,100 owed from the purchase of supplies in Transaction 3.

Analysis. **Assets decrease** as cash is paid. **Liabilities decrease** as $900 of the obligation is settled.

Journal Entry Analysis. Liabilities decrease; debit the Accounts Payable liability account for $900. Assets decrease; credit the Cash asset account for $900.

Journal Entry.

Mar. 27	Accounts Payable................	900	
	Cash		900
	Cash payment to supplier.		

Post to Ledger.

Accounts Payable   201

(10)	900	1,100	(3)

Financial Statement Impact.
A = L + E
↓   ↓

Cash			101
(1)	10,000	2,500	(2)
(4)	2,200	1,000	(5)
(9)	1,900	700	(6)
		900	(10)

11. Withdrawal of cash by owner.

Transaction. On March 28, Hailey Walker withdraws $600 from Organico for personal living expenses.

Analysis. **Equity decreases** as owner extracts equity from the business. **Assets decrease** as cash is withdrawn.

Journal Entry Analysis. Equity decreases; debit the Hailey Walker, withdrawals account for $600. Assets decrease, credit the Cash asset account for $600.

Journal Entry.

Mar. 28	Hailey Walker, Withdrawals	600	
	Cash		600
	Withdrawal of cash by owner.		

Financial Statement Impact.

A = L + E
↓   ↓

Post to Ledger.

Hailey Walker, withdrawals		302
(11)	600	

Cash			101
(1)	10,000	2,500	(2)
(4)	2,200	1,000	(5)
(9)	1,900	700	(6)
		900	(10)
		600	(11)

12. Receipt of cash for future services.

Transaction. On March 29, Organico enters into (signs) a contract with a local advertising agency to provide food for its April 7th Friday Family Fun Night social event. Organico receives $3,000 cash in advance of the event.

Analysis. **Assets increase** as cash is received. **Liabilities increase** as accepting the $3,000 cash obligates Organico to provide food services for the event next month, classified for accounting purposes as unearned revenue. No revenue is earned until services are provided.

Journal Entry Analysis. Assets increase debit the Cash asset account for $3,000. Liability incurred, credit Unearned Food Services Revenue this is a *liability* account for $3,000.

Journal Entry.

Mar. 29	Cash	3,000	
	Unearned Food Services Revenue......		3,000
	Collection of payment for future services.		

Financial Statement Impact.

A = L + E
↑   ↑

Post to Ledger.

Cash			101
(1)	10,000	2,500	(2)
(4)	2,200	1,000	(5)
(9)	1,900	700	(6)
(12)	3,000	900	(10)
		600	(11)

Unearned Food Services Revenue		236
	3,000	(12)

13. Payment of cash for future insurance coverage.

Journal Entry.

Transaction. On March 30, Organico pays $2,400 cash (premium) for a two-year insurance policy. Coverage begins on May 1.

Analysis. Assets increase as company benefits from having insurance coverage for the next two years. Assets decrease as cash is expended. This changes the composition of assets from cash to a "right" of insurance coverage. Expense will be incurred monthly as the benefit of the insurance coverage is utilized through the passage of time.

Journal Entry Analysis. Asset increases, debit the Prepaid Insurance asset account for $2,400. Asset decreases, credit the Cash asset account for $2,400.

Mar. 30	Prepaid Insurance	2,400	
	Cash		2,400
	Payment for insurance coverage.		

Financial Statement Impact.
A = L + E
↑↓

Post to Ledger.

Prepaid Insurance		128
(13)	2,400	

Cash			101
(1)	10,000	2,500	(2)
(4)	2,200	1,000	(5)
(9)	1,900	700	(6)
(12)	3,000	900	(10)
		600	(11)
		2,400	(13)

14. Payment of expense in cash.

Journal Entry.

Transaction. On March 31, Organico pays $230 cash for March Internet/phone connectivity/usage.

Analysis. **Assets decrease** as cash is expended. **Equity decreases** due to Expense incurred.

Journal Entry Analysis. Equity decreases, debit the Communications Expense account for $230 (this decreases equity). Asset decreases, credit the Cash asset account for $230.

Mar. 31	Communications Expense	230	
	Cash		230
	Payment of March Communications.		

Financial Statement Impact.
A = L + E
↓   ↓

Post to Ledger.

Communications Expense		690
(14)	230	

Cash			101
(1)	10,000	2,500	(2)
(4)	2,200	1,000	(5)
(9)	1,900	700	(6)
(12)	3,000	900	(10)
		600	(11)
		2,400	(13)
		230	(14)

15. Payment of expense in cash.

Journal Entry.

Transaction. On March 31, Organico pays $700 cash for employee's salary for the two-week pay period ending on March 28.

Analysis. **Assets decrease** as cash is expended. **Equity decreases** through Expenses incurred.

Journal Entry Analysis. Equity decreases, debit the Salaries Expense account for $700. Assets decrease; credit the Cash asset account for $700.

Mar. 31	Salaries Expense	700	
	Cash		700
	Payment of employee wages.		

Financial Statement Impact.
A = L + E
↓   ↓

Post to Ledger.

Salaries Expense		622
(6)	700	
(15)	700	

Cash			101
(1)	10,000	2,500	(2)
(4)	2,200	1,000	(5)
(9)	1,900	700	(6)
(12)	3,000	900	(10)
		600	(11)
		2,400	(13)
		230	(14)
		700	(15)

Accounting Equation Analysis

Exhibit 2.14 shows Organico's accounts in the ledger after all March transactions are recorded and the balances calculated. For emphasis, the accounts are grouped into three major columns representing the terms in the accounting equation: assets, liabilities, and equity.

DECISION MAKER
Answer—End of chapter

Accounting Clerk

You recently got a job as a part-time accounting clerk to earn money while you attend school. Today, your employer, the owner of the business, made some purchases and instructed you to debit Office Supplies and credit Accounts Payable for the entire amount. He tells you that the invoice is for a few office supplies but mainly for some items that he needed for personal use at home. Explain which GAAP is being violated, and the impact of this error on the financial statements of the business.

Exhibit 2.14 highlights three important points.

1. The totals for the three columns show that the accounting equation is in balance

Assets $20,070	=	Liabilities $9,200	+	Equity $10,870

2. The owner's investment is recorded in the capital account and the withdrawals, revenue, and expense accounts reflect the transactions that change equity. Their ending balances make up the statement of changes in equity.

3. The revenue and expense account balances are summarized and reported in the income statement.

CHECKPOINT

9. Does *debit* always mean increase and *credit* always mean decrease?
10. What kinds of transactions increase equity? What kinds decrease equity?
11. Why are most accounting systems called *double entry*?
12. Double-entry accounting requires that (select the best answer):
    a. All transactions that create debits to asset accounts must create credits to liability or equity accounts.
    b. A transaction that requires a debit to a liability account also requires a credit to an asset account.
    c. Every transaction must be recorded with total debits equal to total credits.

Do Quick Study questions: QS 2-6, QS 2-7, QS 2-8, QS 2-9, QS 2-10, QS 2-11, QS 2-12, QS 2-13, QS 2-14

EXHIBIT 2.14

Ledger for Organico at March 31, 2017

| Assets | | = | Liabilities | | + | Equity |

Cash   101

(1)	10,000	2,500	(2)
(4)	2,200	1,000	(5)
(9)	1,900	700	(6)
(12)	3,000	900	(10)
		600	(11)
		2,400	(13)
		230	(14)
		700	(15)
Balance	8,070		

Accounts Receivable   106

(8)	1,900	1,900	(9)
Balance	0		

Supplies   125

(2)	2,500	
(3)	1,100	
Balance	3,600	

Prepaid Insurance   128

(13)	2,400	
Balance	2,400	

Equipment   167

(3)	6,000	
Balance	6,000	

Accounts Payable   201

(10)	900	1,100	(3)
		200	Balance

Unearned Food Services Revenue   236

	3,000	(12)
	3,000	Balance

Notes Payable   240

	6,000	(3)
	6,000	Balance

Accounts in the white area reflect increases and decreases in equity. Their balances are reported on the income statement or the statement of changes in equity

Hailey Walker, Capital   301

	10,000	(1)
	10,000	Balance

Hailey Walker, Withdrawals   302

(11)	600	
Balance	600	

Food Services Revenue   403

	2,200	(4)
	1,600	(8)
	3,800	Balance

Teaching Revenue   406

	300	(8)
	300	Balance

Salaries Expense   622

(6)	700	
(15)	700	
Balance	1,400	

Rent Expense   641

(5)	1,000	
Balance	1,000	

Communications Expense   690

(14)	230	
Balance	230	

TOTALS: $\$20,070^1$ = $\$9,200^2$ + $\$10,870^3$

[1] $\$8,070 + \$0 + \$3,600 + \$2,400 + \$6,000 = \$20,070$
[2] $\$200 + \$3,000 + \$6,000 = \$9,200$
[3] $\$10,000 - \$600 + \$3,800 + \$300 - \$1,400 - \$1,000 - \$230 = \$10,870$

MID-CHAPTER DEMONSTRATION PROBLEM

Kara Morris founded her dream business, called Kara's Kiteboarding Adventures. The following transactions occurred during June 2017, her first month of operations.

    a. Kara invested $15,000 cash into the business on June 1.

    b. Kara's Kiteboarding paid $400 to cover insurance for the month of June.

    c. June 3, Kara's Kiteboarding purchased $12,000 worth of kiteboarding equipment on credit.

    d. June 6, the business rented additional kiteboarding equipment for $1,500 on account.

    e. June 9, the business provided lessons to a group of clients for $3,500 on account.

    f. June 14, the business collected $2,000 from its credit customers.

    g. The kiteboarding equipment purchased June 3, on credit was paid for June 28.

Required

1. Open the following T-accounts: Cash; Accounts Receivable; Equipment; Accounts Payable; Kara Morris, Capital; Teaching Revenue; Insurance Expense; Equipment Rental Expense.
2. Post the June entries directly into the T-accounts.

Analysis Component:

Using your answer in Part 2, prove that the accounting equation balances at the end of June.

SOLUTION

1 and 2.

Cash			
(a)	15,000	400	(d)
(f)	2,000	12,000	(g)
(Bal.)	4,600		

Accounts Receivable			
(e)	3,500	2,000	(f)
(Bal.)	1,500		

Equipment	
(b)	12,000

Accounts Payable			
(g)	12,000	12,000	(b)
		1,500	(c)
		1,500	(Bal.)

Kara Morris, Capital		
	15,000	(a)

Teaching Revenue		
	3,500	(e)

Insurance Expense	
(d)	400

Equipment Rental Expense	
(c)	1,500

Analysis Component:

Total assets   = Cash 4,600 + Accounts Receivable 1,500 + Equipment 12,000 = 18,100
Total liabilities = Accounts Payable 1,500
Total equity   = Kara Morris, Capital 15,000 + Teaching Revenue 3,500 – Insurance Expense 400 – Equipment Rental Expense 1,500 = 16,600

Assets 18,100 = Liabilities 1,500 + Equity 16,600
18,100   = 18,100

Ledgers

As highlighted previously, T-accounts are a simple and direct learning tool to show how the accounting process works. They allow us to omit less relevant details and concentrate on calculating the balance in a specific account. Once journal entries are recorded in the appropriate journal, transaction details need to be posted to the appropriate ledger. Ledgers contain financial statement activity for each specific account. A **general ledger** summarizes each financial statement account, providing a total balance in each account used in the organization's chart of accounts. Detailed information on account activity is required to be maintained in subsidiary ledgers; the control account in the general ledger contains the total balance for each account. The accounts receivable subsidiary ledger for example, maintains specific information regarding each customer's account history, including sales invoice details and information regarding customer cash payments. Exhibit 2.15 provides an example of the cash control account detail in the general ledger for Organico.

EXHIBIT 2.15

Cash Control Account in General Ledger

	Cash					Account No. 101
Date		Explanation	PR	Debit	Credit	Balance
2017						
Mar.	1		G1	10,000		10,000
	1		G1		2,500	7,500
	10		G1	2,200		9,700

The T-account was derived from the ledger account format and it too has a column for debits and a column for credits. Look at the imaginary T-account superimposed over Exhibit 2.15. The ledger account is different from a T-account because it includes a transaction's date and explanation and has a third column with the balance of the account after each entry is posted. This means that the amount on the last line in this column is the account's current balance. For example, Organico's Cash account in Exhibit 2.15 is debited on March 1 for the $10,000 investment by Hailey Walker. The account then shows a $10,000 debit balance. The account is also credited on March 1 for $2,500, and its new $7,500 balance is shown in the third column. The Cash account is debited for $2,200 on March 10, and its balance increases to a $9,700 debit.

ABNORMAL BALANCE

Unusual transactions can sometimes give an abnormal balance to an account. An *abnormal balance* refers to a balance on the side where decreases are recorded. For example, a customer might mistakenly overpay a bill. This gives that customer's account receivable an abnormal credit balance.[11] It is helpful to be alert for abnormal balances as they may be as a result of an error in recording a journal entry.

ZERO BALANCE

A zero balance for an account is usually shown by writing zeros or a dash in the Balance column. This practice avoids confusion between a zero balance and one omitted in error.

Trial Balance

LO6 Prepare and explain the use of a trial balance.

Double-entry accounting records every transaction with equal debits and credits. An error exists if the sum of debit entries in the ledger does not equal the sum of credit entries. The sum of debit account balances must always equal the sum of credit account balances.

Step Four of the accounting cycle shown in Exhibit 2.1 requires the preparation of a trial balance to check whether debit and credit account balances are equal. A **trial balance** is a list of accounts and their

---

11 Assume a customer overpaid an account, causing an abnormal balance. To highlight this, brackets can be used as illustrated below or the value could be shown in red.

	Accounts Receivable			Account No. 106		
Date		Explanation	PR	Debit	Credit	Balance
2017						
May	1		G1	100		100
	15		G6		125	(25)

EXHIBIT 2.16

Trial Balance

	Organico **Trial Balance** **March 31, 2017**		
Acct. No.	**Account**	**Debit**	**Credit**
101	Cash	$ 8,070	
106	Accounts receivable..	-0-	
125	Supplies...	3,600	
128	Prepaid insurance	2,400	
167	Equipment..	6,000	
201	Accounts payable...		$ 200
236	Unearned food services revenue		3,000
240	Notes payable		6,000
301	Hailey Walker, capital		10,000
302	Hailey Walker, withdrawals..	600	
403	Food Services revenue		3,800
406	Teaching revenue		300
622	Salaries expense	1,400	
641	Rent expense...	1,000	
690	Communications expense	230	
	Totals..	$23,300	$23,300

balances at a point in time. Account balances are reported in the debit or credit column of the trial balance. Exhibit 2.16 shows the trial balance for Organico after the entries described earlier in the chapter are posted to the ledger.

Another use of the trial balance is as an internal report for preparing financial statements. Preparing statements is easier when we can take account balances from a trial balance instead of searching the ledger. The preparation of financial statements using a trial balance is illustrated in the End-of-Chapter Demonstration Problem. We expand on this process in Chapter 3.

Preparing a Trial Balance

Preparing a trial balance involves five steps:

1. Identify each account balance from the ledger.
2. List each account and its balance (in the same order as the Chart of Accounts). Debit balances are entered in the Debit column and credit balances in the Credit column.[12]
3. Calculate the total of debit balances.
4. Calculate the total of credit balances.
5. Verify that total debit balances equal total credit balances.

Notice that the total debit balance equals the total credit balance for the trial balance in Exhibit 2.16. If these two totals were not equal, we would know that one or more errors exist. Equality of these two totals does *not* guarantee the absence of errors.

---

12 If an account has a zero balance, it can be listed in the trial balance with a zero in the column for its normal balance.

Using a Trial Balance

We know that one or more errors exist when a trial balance does not *balance* (when its columns are not equal). When one or more errors exist, they often arise from one of the following steps in the accounting process:

1. Preparing journal entries
2. Posting entries to the ledger
3. Calculating account balances
4. Copying account balances to the trial balance
5. Totalling the trial balance columns

When a trial balance does balance, the accounts are likely free of the kinds of errors that create unequal debits and credits. Yet errors can still exist. One example is when a debit or credit of a correct amount is made to a wrong account. This can occur when either journalizing or posting. The error would produce incorrect balances in two accounts but the trial balance would balance. Another error is to record equal debits and credits of an incorrect amount. This error produces incorrect balances in two accounts but again the debits and credits are equal. We give these examples to show that when a trial balance does balance, it does not prove that all journal entries are recorded and posted correctly.

In a computerized accounting system, the trial balance would *always* balance. Accounting software is such that unbalanced entries would not be accepted by the system. However, errors as described in the last paragraph can still exist in a computerized system.

Searching for Errors

When performing accounting manually, if the trial balance does not balance, the error (or errors) must be found and corrected before financial statements are prepared. To search for the error, we check the journalizing, posting, and trial balance preparation process in *reverse order*. Otherwise, we would need to look at every transaction until the error was found. The steps involved are:

1. Verify that the trial balance columns are correctly added. If this fails to show the error, then
2. Verify that account balances are accurately copied from the ledger.
3. Determine if a debit or credit balance is mistakenly listed in the trial balance as a credit or debit. Look for this when the difference between total debits and total credits in the trial balance equals twice the amount of the incorrect account balance.
4. Recalculate each account balance. If the error remains, then
5. Verify that each journal entry is properly posted to ledger accounts.
6. Verify that the original journal entry has equal debits and credits.

One frequent error is called a **transposition error**, in which two digits are switched or transposed within a number (e.g., 619 instead of 691). Another type of error, a **slide**,[13] occurs when adding or delet-

---

[13] To find a slide error, follow steps 1 and 2 for a transposition error. The quotient resulting from Step Two identifies the correct value (the incorrect value +/− the correct zeros).

ing a zero (or zeros) in a value (e.g., 32 instead of 320). If transposition or a slide is the only error, then the difference between the totals of the trial balance columns will be *evenly divisible by 9*. For example, to find a transposition error:

1. Subtract total debits in the trial balance from total credits.

    Based on the transposition given above, the difference between total debits and credits is $72 ($691 − $619)

2. Divide the difference by 9.

    $72 ÷ 9 = 8

3. The quotient equals the difference between the two transposed numbers.

    8 is the difference between 9 and 1 in both 91 of 691 and 19 of 619.

4. The number of digits in the quotient tells us the location of the transposition.

    The quotient of 8 is only one digit, so the transposition can be found by checking the first digit from the right in each number.[14]

Formatting Conventions

Dollar signs are *not* used in journals and ledgers. They *do* appear in financial statements and other reports, including trial balances, to identify the kind of currency being used. This book follows the usual practice of putting a dollar sign beside the first amount in each column of numbers and the first amount appearing after a ruled line that indicates that an addition or subtraction has been performed. The financial statements in Exhibit 1.16 demonstrate how dollar signs are used in this book. Different companies use various conventions for dollar signs.

When amounts are entered manually in a formal journal, ledger, or trial balance, commas are not needed to indicate thousands, millions, and so forth. Also, decimal points are not needed to separate dollars and cents. If an amount consists of even dollars without cents, a convenient shortcut uses a dash in the cents column instead of two zeros. However, commas and decimal points are used in financial statements and other reports. An exception is when this detail is not important to users.

It is common for companies to round amounts to the nearest dollar, and to an even higher level for certain accounts. WestJet is typical of many companies in that it rounds its financial statement amounts to the nearest thousand dollars.

CHECKPOINT

13. If a $4,000 debit to Equipment in a journal entry is incorrectly posted as a $4,000 credit to the Equipment account in the ledger, what is the effect of this error on the trial balance column totals, assuming no other errors?

14. When are dollar signs typically used in accounting reports?

Do Quick Study questions: QS 2-15, QS 2-16, QS 2-17, QS 2-18

CRITICAL THINKING CHALLENGE

Refer to the Critical Thinking Challenge questions at the beginning of the chapter. Compare your answers to those suggested on Connect.

---

14 Consider another example where a transposition error involves posting $961 instead of the correct $691. The difference in these numbers is $270, and its quotient is $30 ($270/9). Because the quotient has two digits, it tells us to check the second digits from the right for a transposition of two numbers that have a difference of 3.

IFRS AND ASPE—THE DIFFERENCES

Difference	International Financial Reporting Standards (IFRS)	Accounting Standards for Private Enterprises (ASPE)
Financial statement elements	• The level of account detail for expenses must allow the income statement to show the nature and/or function of expenses incurred for the purpose of providing relevant information to financial statement users.* The nature vs. function of an expense is discussed in greater detail in Chapter 5.	• No minimum level of account detail is prescribed for expenses under ASPE.

*IFRS 2014, IAS 1, para. 99–105.

A Look Ahead

Chapter 3 extends our focus on processing information. We explain the importance of adjusting accounts and the procedures in preparing financial statements.

For further study on some topics of relevance to this chapter, please see the following Extend Your Knowledge supplements:

EYK 2-1   Chapter 2 Corporate Supplement

EYK 2-2   How Banks Account for Cash

EYK 2-3   Preparing Financial Statements

EYK 2-4   Recording and Posting Transactions

EYK 2-5   Case: Journalizing Based on Source Documents, Posting, and Preparing a Trial Balance

Summary

LO1 Explain the accounting cycle. The accounting cycle includes the steps in preparing financial statements for users that are repeated each reporting period.

LO2 Describe an account, its use, and its relationship to the ledger. An account is a detailed record of increases and decreases in a specific asset, liability, or equity item. Information is taken from accounts, analyzed, summarized, and presented in useful reports and financial statements for users.

LO3 Define debits and credits and explain their role in double-entry accounting. Debit refers to left, and credit refers to right. The following table summarizes debit and credit effects by account type:

	Assets =	Liabilities +		Equity		
			Owner's Capital	Owner's Withdrawals	Revenues	Expenses
Increases	Debits	Credits	Credits	Debits	Credits	Debits
Decreases	Credits	Debits	Debits	Credits	Debits	Credits

Double-entry accounting means that every transaction affects at least two accounts. The total amount debited must equal the total amount credited for each transaction. The system for recording debits and credits follows from the accounting equation. The debit side is the normal balance for assets, owner's withdrawals, and expenses, and the credit side is the normal balance for liabilities, owner's capital, and revenues.

LO4 Describe a chart of accounts and its relationship to the ledger. A ledger is a record that contains all accounts used by a company. This is what is referred to as *the books*. The chart of accounts is a listing of all accounts and usually includes an identification number that is assigned to each account.

LO5 Analyze the impact of transactions on accounts, record entries in a journal, and post entries to a ledger. We analyze transactions using the concepts of double-entry accounting. This analysis is performed by determining a transaction's effects on accounts. We record transactions in a journal to give a record of their effects. Each entry in a journal is posted to the accounts in the ledger. This provides information in accounts that are used to produce financial statements. General ledger accounts are widely used and include columns for debits, credits, and the account balance after each entry.

LO6 Prepare and explain the use of a trial balance.
A trial balance is a list of accounts in the ledger showing their debit and credit balances in separate columns. The trial balance is a convenient summary of the ledger's contents and is useful in preparing financial statements. It reveals errors of the kind that produce unequal debit and credit account balances.

Guidance Answer to DECISION MAKER

Accounting Clerk

The business entity principle is being violated because it requires that the owner's personal expenses be recorded separately from those of his business. By debiting the entire amount to Office Supplies, assets will be overstated on the balance sheet. By crediting Accounts Payable for the whole amount, liabilities will also be overstated. At the end of the accounting period when the amount of supplies used is recorded, Office Supplies Expense will be overstated on the income statement, causing profit to be understated. When profit is too low, equity is also understated.

Guidance Answers to CHECKPOINT

1. The accounting cycle represents the steps followed each reporting period for the purpose of preparing financial statements.

2. Assets   Liabilities   Equity
   1, 5, 9   3, 7   2, 4, 6, 8, 10

3. The difference between the three accounts is in the name only; they are variations of a revenue account for rent.

4. An account is a record in the ledger where increases and decreases in a specific asset, liability, or equity item are recorded and stored. A ledger is a collection of all accounts used by a business. A chart of accounts is a numerical list of the accounts in the ledger. The numbers represent whether the account is an asset, liability, or type of equity.

5. The normal balance for assets, expenses, and withdrawals is a debit balance. The normal balance for revenue, liabilities, and capital accounts is a credit balance.

6. The entry is:

Cash	15,000	
Equipment	23,000	
Notes Payable		18,000
Maria Sanchez, Capital		20,000

7. A compound journal entry is one that affects three or more accounts.

8. Posting reference numbers are entered in the journal when posting to the ledger as a control over the posting process. They provide a cross-reference that allows the bookkeeper or auditor to trace debits and credits from journals to ledgers and vice versa.

9. No. Debit and credit both can mean increase or decrease. The particular meaning depends on the type of account.

10. Equity is increased by revenues and owner's investments in the company. Equity is decreased by expenses and owner's withdrawals.

11. The name *double-entry* is used because all transactions affect and are recorded in at least two accounts. There must be at least one debit in one account and at least one credit in another.

12. c

13. This error, if uncorrected, will cause the trial balance's debit column total to be understated by $8,000.

14. Dollar signs are used in financial statements and other reports to identify the kind of currency being used in the reports. At a minimum, they are placed beside the first and last numbers in each column. Some companies place dollar signs beside any amount that appears after a ruled line to indicate that an addition or subtraction has taken place.

DEMONSTRATION PROBLEM

This Demonstration Problem is based on the same facts as the Demonstration Problem at the end of Chapter 1 except for two additional items: (b) August 1 and (k) August 18. The following activities occurred during the first month of Joanne Cardinal's new haircutting business called The Cutlery:

a. On August 1, Cardinal put $16,000 cash into a chequing account in the name of The Cutlery. She also invested $10,000 of equipment that she already owned.

b. On August 1, Cardinal paid $2,400 for six months of insurance effective immediately.

c. On August 2, she paid $2,000 cash for furniture for the shop.

d. On August 3, she paid $3,200 cash to rent space in a strip mall for August.

e. On August 4, she furnished the shop by installing the old equipment and some new equipment that she bought on credit for $21,000. This amount is to be repaid in three equal payments at the end of August, September, and October.

f. On August 5, The Cutlery opened for business. Cash receipts from haircutting services provided in the first week and a half of business (ended August 15) were $1,100.

g. On August 15, Cardinal provided haircutting services on account for $750.

h. On August 17, Cardinal received a $750 cheque in the mail for services previously rendered on account.

i. On August 17, Cardinal paid $250 to an assistant for working during the grand opening.

j. On August 18, Cardinal interviewed a job applicant. The applicant was successful in getting the position and will receive $750 per week for part-time work starting in September.

k. On August 18, a regular customer paid $500 for services to be provided over the next three months.

l. Cash receipts from haircutting services provided during the second half of August were $1,950.

m. On August 31, Cardinal paid an instalment on the account payable created in (e) above.

n. On August 31, the August hydro bill for $450 was received. It will be paid on September 14.

o. On August 31, she withdrew $500 cash for her personal use.

Required

1. Prepare general journal entries for the preceding transactions.

2. Open the following accounts: Cash, 101; Accounts Receivable, 106; Prepaid Insurance, 128; Furniture, 161; Store Equipment, 165; Accounts Payable, 201; Unearned Haircutting Services Revenue, 236; Joanne Cardinal, Capital, 301; Joanne Cardinal, Withdrawals, 302; Haircutting Services Revenue, 403; Wages Expense, 623; Rent Expense, 640; and Hydro Expense, 690.

3. Post the journal entries to the ledger accounts.

4. Prepare a trial balance as of August 31, 2017.

5. Prepare a income statement and a statement of changes in equity for the month ended August 31, 2017, and a balance sheet at August 31, 2017.

Analysis Component:

Refer to The Cutlery's August 31, 2017, financial statements. What do each of *equity* and *liabilities* represent?

Planning the Solution

- Analyze each activity to determine if it is a transaction.
- For each transaction, identify the accounts affected and the amount of each effect.
- Use the debit and credit rules to prepare a journal entry for each transaction.
- Post each debit and each credit in the journal entries to the appropriate ledger accounts and cross-reference each amount in the Posting Reference columns in the journal and account.
- Calculate each account balance and list the accounts with their balances on a trial balance.
- Verify that the total debits in the trial balance equal total credits.
- Prepare an income statement, statement of changes in equity, and balance sheet using the information in the trial balance.
- Prepare an answer to each part of the *analysis component* question.

Solution

1. General journal entries:

	General Journal				Page G1
Date	**Account Titles and Explanations**	**PR**	**Debit**		**Credit**
2017					
Aug. 1	Cash..	101	16,000		
	Store Equipment..	165	10,000		
	Joane Cardinal, Capital	301			26,000
	Owner's initial investment.				
1	Prepaid Insurance	128	2,400		
	Cash	101			2,400
	Purchased six months of insurance.				
2	Furniture	161	2,000		
	Cash	101			2,000
	Purchased furniture for cash.				
3	Rent Expense	640	3,200		
	Cash	101			3,200
	Paid rent for August.				
4	Store Equipment..	165	21,000		
	Accounts Payable..	201			21,000
	Purchased additional equipment on credit.				
15	Cash..	101	1,100		
	Haircutting Services Revenue	403			1,100
	Cash receipts from 10 days of operations.				

Continued

General Journal				Page G1	
Date	Account Titles and Explanations	PR	Debit	Credit	
15	Accounts Receivable	106	750		
	Haircutting Services Revenue	403		750	
	To record revenue for services provided on account.				
17	Cash..	101	750		
	Accounts Receivable...................................	106		750	
	To record cash received as payment on account.				
17	Wages Expense	623	250		
	Cash	101		250	
	Paid wages to assistant.				
18	No entry required since there has been no economic exchange.				
18	Cash..	101	500		
	Unearned Haircutting Services Revenue	236		500	
	To record payment in advance.				
31	Cash..	101	1,950		
	Haircutting Services Revenue	403		1,950	
	Cash receipts from second half of August.				
31	Accounts Payable	201	7,000		
	Cash	101		7,000	
	Paid an installment on accounts payable.				
31	Hydro Expense	690	450		
	Accounts Payable.......................................	201		450	
	August hydro to be paid by Sept. 14.				
31	Joane Cardinal, Withdrawals	302	500		
	Cash	101		500	
	Owner withdrew cash from the business.				

2. & 3. Accounts in the ledger:

	Cash				Account No. 101
Date	Explanation	PR	Debit	Credit	Balance
2017					
Aug. 1		G1	16,000		16,000
1		G1		2,400	13,600
2		G1		2,000	11,600
3		G1		3,200	8,400
15		G1	1,100		9,500
17		G1	750		10,250
17		G1		250	10,000
18		G1	500		10,500
31		G1	1,950		12,450
31		G1		7,000	5,450
31		G1		500	4,950

Accounts Receivable					Account No. 106
Date	Explanation	PR	Debit	Credit	Balance
2017					
Aug. 15		G1	750		750
17		G1		750	-0-

Prepaid Insurance					Account No. 128
Date	Explanation	PR	Debit	Credit	Balance
2017					
Aug. 1		G1	2,400		2,400

Furniture					Account No. 161
Date	Explanation	PR	Debit	Credit	Balance
2017					
Aug. 2		G1	2,000		2,000

Store Equipment					Account No. 165
Date	Explanation	PR	Debit	Credit	Balance
2017					
Aug. 1		G1	10,000		10,000
4		G1	21,000		31,000

Accounts Payable					Account No. 201
Date	Explanation	PR	Debit	Credit	Balance
2017					
Aug. 4		G1		21,000	21,000
31		G1	7,000		14,000
31		G1		450	14,450

Note: The T-account has been superimposed on each general ledger account for illustrative purposes only. It emphasizes that using T-accounts will produce identical balances to the balance column ledger account but in a shortened form. This shortened form is what makes the T-account a convenient tool.

2. & 3.

Unearned Haircutting Services Revenue					Account No. 236
Date	Explanation	PR	Debit	Credit	Balance
2017					
Aug. 18		G1		500	500

		Joanne Cardinal, Capital			Account No. 301	
Date		**Explanation**	**PR**	**Debit**	**Credit**	**Balance**
2017						
Aug.	1		G1		26,000	26,000

		Joanne Cardinal, Withdrawals			Account No. 302	
Date		**Explanation**	**PR**	**Debit**	**Credit**	**Balance**
2017						
Aug.	31		G1	500		500

		Haircutting Services Revenue			Account No. 403	
Date		**Explanation**	**PR**	**Debit**	**Credit**	**Balance**
2017						
Aug.	15		G1		1,100	1,100
	15		G1		750	1,850
	31		G1		1,950	3,800

		Wages Expense			Account No. 623	
Date		**Explanation**	**PR**	**Debit**	**Credit**	**Balance**
2017						
Aug.	17		G1	250		250

		Rent Expense			Account No. 640	
Date		**Explanation**	**PR**	**Debit**	**Credit**	**Balance**
2017						
Aug.	3		G1	3,200		3,200

		Hydro Expense			Account No. 690	
Date		**Explanation**	**PR**	**Debit**	**Credit**	**Balance**
2017						
Aug.	31		G1	450		450

4.

5.

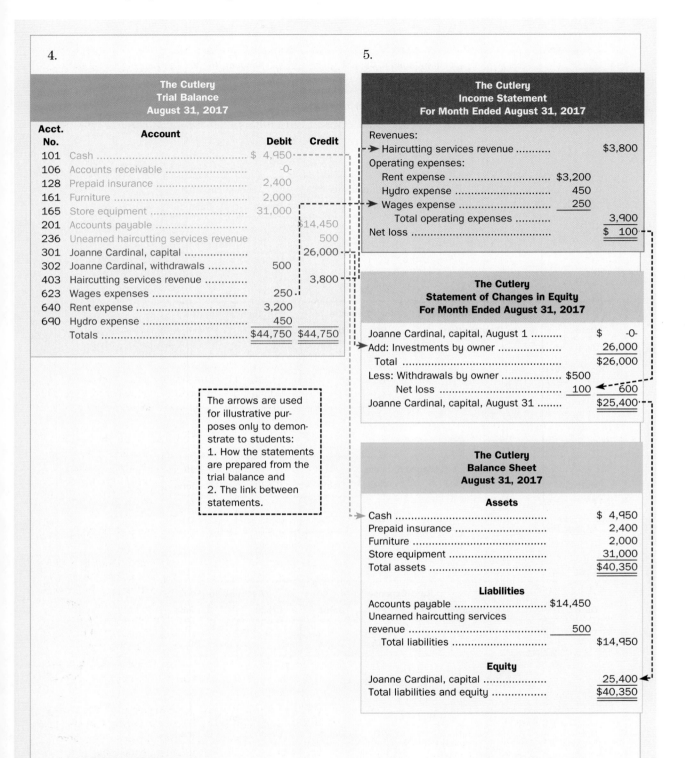

Analysis Component:

Equity represents how much of the total assets are owned (or financed) by the owner of the business. In the case of The Cutlery, the owner, Joanne Cardinal, owns $25,400 of the total

$40,350 in assets or 63% ($25,400/$40,350 × 100% = 62.949% or 63%). Most of her equity in the business is a result of her $26,000 investment at start-up. The original $26,000 investment was decreased during the month by a $100 loss and a $500 withdrawal by the owner.

Liabilities represent how much of the total assets have been financed by debt. In the case of The Cutlery, $14,950 or 37% of the total assets are financed by liabilities ($14,950/$40,350 × 100% = 37.051% or 37%).

Glossary

Account A record within an accounting system in which the increases and decreases in a specific asset, liability, or equity are recorded and stored.

Account balance The total for a specific account. It is calculated by determining the difference between the increases (including the beginning balance) and decreases recorded in an account over a period.

Accounting cycle The steps repeated each reporting period for the purpose of preparing financial statements for users.

Accounts payable Obligations that arise when the company promises to pay a supplier/service provider in the future for purchases of merchandise, supplies, or equipment.

Accounts receivable An asset representing the amount owed to the company from their customers. *Accounts receivable* are created when services are performed for or goods are sold to customers in return for promises to pay in the future. These transactions are said to be *on credit* or *on account*. Accounts receivable are *increased* by services performed or goods sold on credit and *decreased* by customer payments.

Chart of accounts A list of all accounts used by a company; includes the identification number assigned to each account.

Compound journal entry A journal entry that affects at least three accounts.

Credit An entry that decreases asset, expense, and owner's withdrawals accounts or increases liability, owner's capital, and revenue accounts; recorded on the right side of a T-account.

Debit An entry that increases asset, expense, and owner's withdrawals accounts or decreases liability, owner's capital, and revenue accounts; recorded on the left side of a T-account.

Double-entry accounting An accounting system where every transaction affects and is recorded in at least two accounts; the sum of the debits for all entries must equal the sum of the credits for all entries.

General journal The most flexible type of journal; typically used to record non-recurring transactions.

General ledger A complete summary of each financial statement account, providing a total balance in each account used in the organization's chart of accounts. T-Accounts are often utilized for learning purposes to represent the individual general ledger accounts.

Journal A record where transactions are recorded before they are recorded in accounts; transaction amounts are posted from the journal to the ledger; special journals are used to group recurring transactions of a similar nature.

Journal entry An individual transaction that has been entered in the journal. It includes information regarding the dated the transaction is entered, which accounts are debited, which accounts are credited and the corresponding transaction amounts.

Journalizing Recording transactions in a journal.

Ledger A record containing all accounts used by a business.

Normal balance The debit or credit side on which a specific account increases. For example, assets increase with debits, therefore the normal balance for an asset is a debit. Revenues increase with credits; therefore, a credit is the normal balance for a revenue account. Liabilities and Equity have a default credit balance; expense accounts have a default debit balance.

Notes payable Obligations that arise when an organization formally recognizes a promise to pay by signing a promissory note.

Notes receivable Unconditional written promises to pay a definite sum of money on demand or on a defined future date(s); also called *promissory notes*. They represent an asset, signalling a future benefit on a company's balance sheet.

Post(ing) Transfer(ring) journal entry information to ledger accounts.

Posting reference (PR) column A column in *journals* where individual account numbers are entered when entries are posted to the ledger. A column in *ledgers* where journal page numbers are entered when entries are posted.

Prepaid Expenses An asset account containing payments made for assets that are not to be used until later. For example, an annual insurance policy that is paid for upfront provides a benefit of protection for the next 12 months.

Promissory notes Unconditional written promises to pay a definite sum of money on demand or on a defined future date(s); also called *notes receivable*.

Simple journal entry A journal entry that impacts only two accounts.

Slide An error that results from adding or deleting a zero (or zeros) in a value.

T-account A simple characterization of an account form used as a helpful tool in showing the effects of transactions on specific accounts.

Transposition error Error due to two digits being switched or transposed within a number.

Trial balance A list of accounts and their balances at a point in time; the total debit balances should equal the total credit balances.

Unearned revenues Liabilities created when customers pay in advance for products or services; created when cash is received before revenues are earned. Revenue is earned and the liability is relieved when the products or services are delivered/provided in the future.

Concept Review Questions

1. You are an accounting manager training a co-op student at the **Lululemon** head office. Explain to the student the fundamental steps in the accounting process. Why is the accounting cycle important for Lululemon?

2. What is the difference between an accounts receivable and a notes receivable?

3. Review the **Danier Leather** balance sheet for fiscal year-end June 28, 2014, in Appendix III. Identify four different asset accounts and three different liability accounts.

4. Ted says, "This debit and credit stuff is easy! Debits increase an account and credits decrease an account!" You do not agree with Ted. Give three examples of accounts where a debit decreases an account and a credit increases an account.

5. Review the WestJet balance sheet for fiscal year-end December 31, 2014, in Appendix III. Identify three accounts on the balance sheet that would carry debit balances and three accounts on the balance sheet that would carry credit balances.

6. Explain the concept of Accounts Receivable and Revenue. What are the differences between these two accounts in terms of (1) type of account (2) normal balance and (3) the financial statement the

account is recorded on, and (4) the time period each balance represents?

7. Explain the concept of owner's withdrawals and expenses and give an example of each. What are the differences between these two accounts in terms of (1) type of account, (2) normal balance, and (3) the financial statement the account is recorded on?

8. Are debits or credits listed first in general journal entries? Are the debits or the credits indented?

9. Should a transaction be recorded first in a journal or the ledger? Why?

10. Julia says, "I heard that companies use software to do their accounting. Why do we need to learn how to draw T-accounts and prepare trial balances manually?" Explain why knowing the basics of accounting is important.

11. Nicholas wants to save time by not preparing a trial balance. What are the risks of skipping this step?

12. Examine the financial statements shown in Chapter 1. What three things must be included in the title? Where are dollar signs used? Why are some numbers indented? Do indentations represent debits and credits?

Quick Study

QS 2-1 Identifying accounts LO2

Identify the account as an asset, liability, or equity by entering the letter of the account type beside the account name. If the item is an equity account, indicate the type of equity account.

A = Asset   OE = Owner's Capital (Equity)   R = Revenues (Equity)
L = Liability   W = Owner's Withdrawals (Equity)   E = Expenses (Equity)

_A_ 1. Buildings

_E_ 2. Building Repair Expense

_E_ 3. Wages Expense

_L_ 4. Wages Payable

_A_ 5. Notes Receivable

_L_ 6. Notes Payable

_A_ 7. Prepaid Advertising

_E_ 8. Advertising Expense

_L_ 9. Advertising Payable

_L_ 10. Unearned Advertising

_R_ 11. Advertising Revenue

_R_ 12. Interest Income (R)

_E_ 13. Interest Expense

_L_ 14. Interest Payable

_R_ 15. Subscription Revenue

_L_ 16. Unearned Subscription Revenue

_A_ 17. Prepaid Subscription Fees

_A_ 18. Supplies

_E_ 19. Supplies Expense

_R_ 20. Rent Revenue

_L_ 21. Unearned Rent Revenue

_A_ 22. Prepaid Rent

_L_ 23. Rent Payable

_R_ 24. Service Revenue

_W_ 25. Jessica Vuong, Withdrawals

_OE_ 26. Jessica Vuong, Capital

_E_ 27. Salaries Expense

_L_ 28. Salaries Payable

_A_ 29. Furniture

_A_ 30. Equipment

QS 2-2 Identifying normal balance as a debit or credit LO3

Indicate whether the normal balance of each of the following accounts is a debit or a credit:

a. Equipment D

b. Land D

c. Amrit Sandhu, Withdrawals D

d. Rent Expense D

e. Interest Income D C

f. Prepaid Rent D

g. Accounts Receivable D

h. Office Supplies D

i. Notes Receivable D

j. Notes Payable C

k. Amrit Sandhu, Capital C

l. Rent Revenue C

m. Rent Payable C

n. Interest Expense D

o. Interest Payable C

QS 2-3 Analyzing debit or credit by account LO3

Identify whether a debit or credit entry would be made to record the indicated change in each of the following accounts:

a. To increase Notes Payable C

b. To decrease Accounts Receivable C

c. To increase Owner, Capital C

d. To decrease Unearned Revenue D

e. To decrease Prepaid Insurance C

f. To decrease Cash C

g. To increase Utilities Expense D

h. To increase Revenue C

i. To increase Store Equipment D

j. To increase Owner, Withdrawals D

k. To decrease Rent Payable D

l. To decrease Prepaid Rent C

m. To increase Supplies D

n. To increase Supplies Expense D

o. To decrease Accounts Payable D

QS 2-4 Linking credit or debit with normal balance LO3

Indicate whether a debit or credit is necessary to _decrease_ the normal balance of each of the following accounts:

a. Buildings

b. Interest Income

c. Bob Norton, Withdrawals

d. Bob Norton, Capital

e. Prepaid Insurance

f. Interest Payable

g. Accounts Receivable   j. Repair Services Revenue   m. Salaries Payable

h. Salaries Expense   k. Interest Expense   n. Furniture

i. Office Supplies   l. Unearned Revenue   o. Interest Receivable

QS 2-5 Developing a chart of accounts LO4

Using the chart of accounts numbering system, develop a chart of accounts that assigns an account number to each of the following accounts:

a. Buildings	f. Interest Payable	k. Interest Expense
b. Interest Revenue	g. Accounts Receivable	l. Unearned Revenue
c. Matthew Lee, Withdrawals	h. Salaries Expense	m. Salaries Payable
d. Matthew Lee, Capital	i. Office Supplies	n. Furniture
e. Prepaid Insurance	j. Repair Services Revenue	o. Interest Receivable

QS 2-6 Analyze the impact of transactions on accounts LO5

Douglas Malone started CityBnB, which is a bed and breakfast in Vancouver. CityBnB offers accommodations and breakfast to travelers exploring the city. The following are the transactions for the month of August.

    a. On August 1, purchased an IKEA bed for $400 cash.

    b. On August 7, discussed the prices of staying at CityBnB with a customer over the phone.

    c. On August 13, rented a room to a family and billed them $600 on credit.

    d. On August 14, purchased and used cleaning services for $300 on credit.

    e. On August 31, invested $25,000 cash into the business.

Required

For each transaction, complete the **analysis** and determine the journal entry analysis. Use the template below. The first transaction has been completed for you.

a.	**Analysis**	Assets increase. Assets decrease.
	Journal entry analysis	Debit the furniture account for $400.
		Credit the cash account for $400.
		Continue...

QS 2-7 Preparing general journal entries LO5

Using the information and analysis prepared in QS 2-6, prepare the journal entries for the month of August. Use the following template. Ensure to include the **date**, the account descriptions, the **debit and credit amount** and a **description of the journal entry**. The first transaction has been completed for you.

	Date	Account Titles and Explanation		Debit	Credit
a.	Aug. 1	Furniture..		400	
		Cash			400
		To record purchase of furniture			
		Continue...			

QS 2-8 Posting entries to T-accounts LO5

CityBnB's records showed the following beginning balances on July 31, 2017. Using the information provided and the analysis completed in QS 2-6 and QS 2-7, complete the following:

1. Post the journal entries to the general ledger using T-accounts. Include the date of each transaction next to your posting.

2. Calculate the balance in each T-account.

3. Prove the accounting equation (Assets = Liabilities + Equity).

Cash			Accounts Receivable			Furniture		
Jul 31	25,000		Jul 31	1,500		Jul 31	5,000	

Accounts Payable			Douglas Malone, Capital			Revenue		
	500	Jul 31		28,000	Jul 31		4,500	Jul 31

Cleaning Expense		
Jul 31	1,500	

QS 2-9 Analyzing and recording journal entries LO5

Bell's company had the following transactions in the month of May.

May	2	Dee Bell transferred her personal car valued at $8,000 into the business.
	10	Did $4,000 of work for a customer on account.
	12	Collected $10,000 from a customer for work to be done in July 2017.
	15	Paid wages of $6,000.
	16	Collected $4,000 from the customer of May 10.
	22	Paid $3,000 of the outstanding accounts payable.

Required

For each transaction, **(1) complete the analysis,** (2) determine the journal entry analysis and (3) record the journal entry. Use the template below. The first transaction on May 2 has been completed for you.

May 2	**Analysis**	Assets increase. Equity increases.			
	Journal entry analysis	Debit the Car account for $8,000. Credit the Dee Bell, Capital account for $8,000.			
	Journal Entry				
	Date	Account Titles and Explanation		Debit	Credit
	May 2	Car		8,000	
		Dee Bell, Capital			8,000
		To record investment by owner.			
May 10		**Continue...**			

QS 2-10 Posting entries to T-accounts LO5

Dee Bell Company's records showed the following April 30, 2017, account balances:

Cash	
Apr 30 15,000	

Accounts Receivable	
Apr 30 3,200	

Car	

Accounts Payable	
	6,000 Apr 30

Unearned Revenue	
	1,800 Apr 30

Dee Bell, Capital	
	8,900 Apr 30

Revenue	
	3,000 Apr 30

Wages Expense	
Apr 30 1,500	

Required

1. Using the chart of accounts numbering system, assign an account number to each account.

2. Using the information provided and the analysis performed in QS 2-9, post the May transactions into the general ledger using T-accounts.

3. Calculate the May 31 balance in each T-account and prove the accounting equation.

QS 2-11 Calculating account balances LO5

Calculate the account balance for each of the following:

Accounts Receivable	
1,000	650
400	920
920	1,500
3,000	

Accounts Payable	
250	250
900	1,800
650	1,400
	650

Service Revenue	
	13,000
	2,500
	810
	3,500

Utilities Expense	
610	
520	
390	
275	

Cash	
3,900	2,400
17,800	3,900
14,500	21,800
340	

Notes Payable	
4,000	50,000
8,000	

QS 2-12 Preparing journal entries LO3,5

Prepare journal entries for the following transactions that occurred during 2017:

May	1	Purchased equipment on account; $500.
	2	Paid for the equipment purchased on May 1.
	3	Purchased supplies for cash; $100.
	4	Paid wages to employees; $2,000.
	5	Performed services for a client and collected cash; $750.
	6	Did work for a customer on credit; $2,500.
	7	Collected the amount owing from the customer of May 6.

QS 2-13 Preparing journal entries LO3,5

Prepare journal entries for the following transactions that occurred during January 2017:

January 3	Stan Adams opened a landscaping business by investing $60,000 cash and equipment having a $40,000 fair value.
4	Purchased office supplies on credit for $340.
6	Received $5,200 for providing landscaping services to a customer.
15	Paid $200 regarding the office supplies purchase of January 4.
16	Purchased $700 of office supplies on account.
30	Paid the balance owing regarding the office supplies purchase of January 4.

QS 2-14 Posting entries in T-accounts LO5

a. Set up the following general ledger accounts (use the balance column format as illustrated in Exhibit 2.12: Cash (101), Office Supplies (124), Equipment (163), Accounts Payable (201), Stan Adams, Capital (301), and Landscaping Services Revenue (403).

b. Post the journal entries from QS 2-13 to the general ledger accounts and enter the balance after each posting.

QS 2-15 Preparing a trial balance LO6

Using the account information shown below, prepare a trial balance at January 31, 2017.

Vahn Landscaping
General Ledger

Cash	101		Equipment	163		Unearned Revenue	233		Brea Vahn, Capital	301
5,000	6,000		9,000				2,000			14,000
2,000	4,000									
3,000	1,000									
8,000										

Brea Vahn, Withdrawals	302		Revenue	401		Rent Expense 640			Utilities Expense	690
1,000				3,000		6,000			4,000	
				8,000						

QS 2-16 Identifying a posting error LO3,5,6

A trial balance has total debits of $21,000 and total credits of $25,500. Which one of the following errors would create this imbalance? Explain.

a. A $4,500 debit to Salaries Expense in a journal entry was incorrectly posted to the ledger as a $4,500 credit, leaving the Salaries Expense account with a $750 debit balance.

b. A $2,250 credit to Teaching Revenue in a journal entry was incorrectly posted to the ledger as a $2,250 debit, leaving the Teaching Revenue account with a $6,300 credit balance.

c. A $2,250 debit to Rent Expense in a journal entry was incorrectly posted to the ledger as a $2,250 credit, leaving the Rent Expense account with a $3,000 debit balance.

QS 2-17 Identifying a transposition error LO6

Identify the transposition error in the following trial balance, assuming this is the only error.

Acct. No.	Account	Debit	Credit
	Be Fabulous Flowers **Trial Balance** **September 30, 2017**		
101	Cash	$ 9,800	
165	Equipment	10,350	
201	Accounts payable		$ 750
301	Tracy Rumanko, Capital		3,800
403	Consulting revenue		17,000
640	Rent expense	4,100	
	Totals	$24,250	$21,550

QS 2-18 Identifying a slide error LO6

Identify the slide error in the following trial balance, assuming this is the only error.

	Debit	Credit
Body Boot Camp **Trial Balance** **April 30, 2017**		
Cash	$330	
Supplies	38	
Notes payable		$ 25
Michelle Jackson, capital		100
Revenue		378
Wages expense	360	
Totals	$728	$503

Exercises

Exercise 2-1 Classifying accounts LO2,3

The following accounts are from Yoojin Chang's interior design company, Big Apple Design. For each account, complete the following. The first one has been completed for you as an example.

(1) The **basic account** category (asset, liability, owner's capital, drawings, revenue or expense)

(2) The financial statement the account is recorded on (Income Statement, Statement of Changes in Equity or Balance Sheet).

(3) The normal balance (debit or credit).

(4) The effect of a debit to the account (increase or decrease).

(5) The effect of a credit (increase or decrease).

a. Cash
b. Supplies
c. Accounts payable
d. Yoojin Chang, Capital Account
e. Yoojin Chang, Withdrawals

f. Design Revenue
g. Salaries Expense
h. Accounts Receivable
i. Notes Payable
j. Prepaid Insurance

	(1) Basic Account	**(2) Financial Statement**	**(3) Normal Balance**	**(4) Effect of a Debit**	**(5) Effect of a Credit**
a. Cash	Asset	Balance Sheet	Debit	Increase	Decrease

Exercise 2-2 Analyzing transactions LO3,5

Christina Reis is a photographer who owns Lola Lemon Photography. This is the first month of operations. The following are the transactions for the month of September.

a. On September 1, Reis invested $15,000 cash into her new business.

b. On September 12, purchased $2,000 of equipment (cameras) on credit.

c. On September 13, purchased $500 of equipment (lighting), paying cash.

d. On September 18, photographed an engagement session for $1,000; collected cash.

e. On September 21, photographed a family session for $700 on credit.

f. On September 26, paid $1,000 regarding (b).

g. On September 29, collected $300 regarding (e).

Required For each transaction, complete the **analysis** and determine the journal entry analysis. Use the template below. The first transaction has been completed for you.

a.	**Analysis**	Assets increase. Equity increases.
	Journal entry analysis	Debit the cash account for $15,000.
		Credit the Christina Reis, Capital account in equity for $15,000
		Continue...

Exercise 2-3 Journalizing general journal entries LO5

Using the analysis prepared in Exercise 2-2, prepare the journal entries for the month of September. Use the following template. Ensure to include the **date**, the account descriptions, the **debit and credit amount** and a **description of the journal entry**. The first transaction has been completed for you.

	Date	Account Titles and Explanation	Debit	Credit
a.	Sept. 1	Cash	15,000	
		Christina Reis, Capital		15,000
		Investment by owner.		
		Continue...		

Exercise 2-4 Posting entries to T-accounts LO5

Using the information provided in Exercise 2-2 and the analysis prepared in Exercise 2-3 complete the following:

1. Post the journal entries to the general ledger using T-accounts. Include the letter of each transaction next to your posting.

2. Calculate the balance in each T-account.

3. Prove the accounting equation (Assets = Liabilities + Equity).

Cash	101

Accounts Receivable	106

Equipment	161

Accounts Payable	201

Christina Reis, Capital	301

Revenue	403

Exercise 2-5 Analyzing transactions LO3,5

William Curtis is a personal finance expert and owns "Much Money" Consulting. This is his first month of operations and William has hired you to do his accounting. The following transactions are for the month of October.

    a. On October 2, William Curtis invested $32,600 cash into his business.

    b. On October 4, purchased $925 of office supplies for cash.

    c. On October 6, purchased $13,600 of office equipment on credit.

    d. On October 10, received $3,000 cash as revenue for being a guest on the TV show *CityTalk*.

    e. On October 12, paid for the office equipment purchased in transaction (c).

    f. On October 16, billed a customer $5,400 for delivering a corporate workshop on smart investing.

    g. On October 18, paid October's rent for the downtown office with $3,500 cash.

    h. On October 26, collected cash for all of the account receivable created in transaction (f).

    i. On October 31, withdrew $5,000 cash from the business for a trip to Hawaii.

Required For each transaction, **(1) complete the analysis**, (2) determine the journal entry analysis and (3) record the journal entry. Use the template below. Transaction a. has been completed for you.

a.	**Analysis**	Assets increase. Equity increases.			
	Journal entry analysis	Debit the Cash account for $32,600. Credit the William Curtis, Capital account for $32,600.			
	Journal Entry				
	Date	**Account Titles and Explanation**		**Debit**	**Credit**
	Oct. 2	Cash		32,600	
		William Curtis, Capital			32,600
		Investment by owner.			
b.		Continue			

Exercise 2-6 Posting transactions to the general ledger LO3,5

Use the information given and the analysis completed in Exercise 2-5.

Required

1. Set up the following general ledger accounts using T-accounts: Cash; Accounts Receivable; Office Supplies; Office Equipment; Accounts Payable; William Curtis, Capital; William Curtis, Withdrawals; Revenue; and Rent Expense.

2. Post the journal entries from Exercise 2-5 into the T-accounts. Include the letter of the transaction next to your posting.

3. Determine the balance of each account.

Exercise 2-7 Analyzing and journalizing revenue transactions LO3,5

Examine the following transactions and identify those that created revenues for TI Servicing, a sole proprietorship owned by Todd Iver. Prepare general journal entries to record those transactions and explain why the other transactions did not create revenues.

    a. Invested $76,500 cash in the business.

    b. Provided $2,700 of services on credit.

    c. Received $3,150 cash for services provided to a client.

    d. Received $18,300 from a client in payment for services to be provided next year.

    e. Received $9,000 from a client in partial payment of an account receivable.

    f. Borrowed $300,000 from the bank by signing a promissory note.

Exercise 2-8 Analyzing and journalizing expense transactions LO3,5

Myra Sharma owns and operates a yoga studio, Green Yoga. Examine the following transactions and identify those that created expenses for Green Yoga. Prepare journal entries to record those transactions and explain why the other transactions did not create expenses.

    a. Paid $14,100 cash for office supplies purchased 30 days previously.

    b. Paid the $1,125 salary of the receptionist.

    c. Paid $45,000 cash for yoga studio equipment.

    d. Paid utility bill with $930 cash.

    e. Withdrew $5,000 from the business account for personal use.

Exercise 2-9 Journalizing, posting, preparing a trial balance, and financial statements LO3,5,6

CHECK FIGURES: 4. Total debits = $19,000; 5. Total assets = $15,250

Manny Gill is an entrepreneur who started West Secure, a business that provides a number of security guard services. West Secure incurred the following transactions during July 2017, its first month of operations:

July	1	The owner, Manny Gill, invested $5,000 cash.
	10	Purchased $2,500 worth of security equipment on credit.
	12	Performed security services for a sold-out concert and received $10,000 cash from the client.
	14	Paid for expenses; $3,500.
	15	Completed security services for a graduation event and sent the client a bill for $1,500.
	31	The owner withdrew $250 cash for personal use.

Required

1. Set up the following general ledger accounts using either the T-account format or the balance column format: Cash, 101; Accounts Receivable, 106; Equipment, 150; Accounts Payable, 201; Manny Gill, Capital, 301; Manny Gill, Withdrawals, 302; Revenue, 401; Expenses, 501.

2. Record the journal entries for the month of July.

3. Post the July journal entries into your general ledger accounts. Include the date next to each number posted. Determine the balances.

4. Prepare a trial balance using the balances in your general ledger accounts.

	Wild West Secure Trial Balance July 31, 2017		
Acct. No.	**Account Title**	**Debit**	**Credit**

5. Prepare an income statement, statement of changes in equity, and balance sheet based on your trial balance.

Wild West Secure Income Statement For Month Ended July 31, 2017		
Revenue		
Expenses		
Profit		

Wild West Secure Statement of Changes in Equity For Month Ended July 31, 2017	
Manny Gill, capital, July 1	
Add: Investments by owner	
Profit	
Total	
Less: Withdrawals by owner	
Manny Gill, capital, July 31	

Wild West Secure Balance Sheet July 31, 2017			
Assets		**Liabilities**	
Cash		Accounts payable	
Accounts receivable			
Equipment		**Equity**	
		Manny Gill, capital	
		Total liabilities and equity	
Total assets			

Analysis Component: Assets are financed by debt and equity transactions, a concept reinforced by the accounting equation: $A = L + E$. Since accounts receivable are an asset, are they financed by debt and/or equity? Explain.

Exercise 2-10 Chart of accounts LO4

You have been given the following guide regarding the chart of accounts for Paquette Advisors:

100–199	Assets	400–499	Revenues
200–299	Liabilities	500–599	Expenses
300–399	Equity		

Required Using the account information from Exercise 2-11, develop a chart of accounts for Paquette Advisors.

Exercise 2-11 Journalizing, posting, preparing a trial balance, and financial statements LO3,5,6

CHECK FIGURES: 4. Profit = $21,700; 6. Total assets = $35,400

After its first month of operations, Paquette Advisors showed the following account balances in its general ledger accounts (T-accounts) as at January 31, 2017.

Cash	Accounts Receivable	Office Equipment
15,000	3,800	22,500

Accounts Payable	Unearned Revenue	Aaron Paquette, Capital
8,000	2,600	9,500

Aaron Paquette, Withdrawals	Consulting Revenues	Salaries Expense
2,000	41,700	10,000

Rent Expense	Utilities Expense
7,500	1,000

During February, the following transactions occurred:

Feb.	1	Performed work for a client and received cash of $8,500.
	5	Paid $5,000 regarding outstanding accounts payable.
	10	Received cash of $3,600 for work to be done in March.
	12	Called FasCo Rentals to book the use of some equipment next month. The $400 rental fee will be paid in full when the equipment is returned.
	17	The owner withdrew cash of $3,000 for personal use.
	28	Paid salaries of $10,000.

Required

1. Record the journal entries for the month of February.

2. Post the journal entries to the general ledger (T-accounts above). Include the date next to each posting.

3. Prepare a trial balance based on the balances in your T-accounts.

4. Prepare an income statement for the two months ended February 28, 2017.

5. Prepare a statement of changes in equity for the two months ended February 28, 2017.

6. Prepare the balance sheet as at February 28, 2017.

Analysis Component: Paquette Advisors shows Unearned Revenue on its February 28, 2017, balance sheet. Explain what Unearned Revenue is. As part of your answer, be sure to address why Unearned Revenue is reported as a liability.

Exercise 2-12 Analyzing transactions from T-accounts LO3,5

Prepare journal entries for each of the seven transactions posted to the following T-accounts. Provide a short description of each transaction. The first description is done as an example.

(a)   *The owner invested cash, an automobile, and equipment in the business.*

Cash			
(a)	7,000	3,600	(b)
(e)	2,500	600	(c)
		2,400	(f)
		700	(g)

Office Supplies		
(c)	600	
(d)	200	

Prepaid Insurance		
(b)	3,600	

Equipment		
(a)	5,600	
(d)	9,400	

Automobiles		
(a)	11,000	

Accounts Payable			
(f)	2,400	9,600	(d)

Jerry Steiner, Capital		
	23,600	(a)

Delivery Services Revenue		
	2,500	(e)

Gas and Oil Expense		
(g)	700	

Exercise 2-13 General journal entries LO3,5

TLC Laser Eye Centres showed the following selected activities during the month of April 2017. Record the journal entries for the following transactions.

April	5	Performed surgery on a customer today and collected $4,600 cash.
	8	Purchased surgical supplies on credit; $19,000.
	15	Paid salaries; $41,000.
	20	Paid for the surgical supplies purchased on April 8.
	21	Contacted a client's lawyer today regarding a complaint about the surgery. The client is planning to sue for $100,000.
	22	Performed six surgeries today, all on credit; $3,800 each.
	29	Collected from four of the credit customers of April 22.
	30	Paid the April utilities bill today; $1,800.

Exercise 2-14 Posting from the general journal to the general ledger LO5

CHECK FIGURE: b. Jan. 31, 2017, Cash balance = $3,600

Sato Inspection Services is in its second month of operations. You have been given the following journal entries regarding its January 2017 transactions.

Required

a. Set up the following accounts (use the balance column format) entering the opening balances brought forward from the end of last month, December 31, 2016: Cash (101) $850; Accounts Receivable (106) $300; Equipment (167) $1,500; Accounts Payable (201) $325; Toshi Sato, Capital (301) $2,325; Toshi Sato, Withdrawals (302) $300; Revenue (401) $1,800; and Salaries Expense (622) $1,500.

General Journal				Page 1
Date	Account Titles and Explanation	PR	Debit	Credit
2017				
Jan. 1	Cash..		3,500	
	Toshi Sato, Capital..			3,500
	Additional owner investment.			
12	Accounts Receivable		9,000	
	Revenue..			9,000
	Performed work for a customer on account.			
20	Equipment..		12,000	
	Accounts Payable			10,000
	Cash			2,000
	Purchased equipment by paying cash and the balance on credit.			
31	Cash..		5,000	
	Accounts Receivable			5,000
	Collected cash from credit customer.			
31	Salaries Expense		3,000	
	Cash			3,000
	Paid month-end salaries.			
31	Toshi Sato, Withdrawals		750	
	Cash			750
	Toshi Sato withdrew cash for personal use.			

Analysis Component: The accounting cycle requires that transactions be journalized in the general journal and then posted in the general ledger. This seems to indicate that we are recording the same information in two different places. Why can't we eliminate journalizing or posting?

Exercise 2-15 Preparing journal entries LO3,5

Prepare journal entries to record the following August 2017 transactions of a new business called The Pixel Shop.

Aug.	1	Joseph Eetok, the owner, invested $20,000 cash and photography equipment with a fair value of $42,000.
	1	Rented a studio, paying $12,000 for the next three months in advance.
	5	Purchased office supplies for $1,800 cash.
	20	Received $9,200 in photography revenue.
	31	Paid $1,400 for August utilities.

Exercise 2-16 General ledger accounts and the trial balance LO3,5,6

CHECK FIGURE: Trial balance total debits = $71,200

Set up the following accounts (use the balance column format): Cash (101); Office Supplies (124); Prepaid Rent (131); Photography Equipment (167); Joseph Eetok, Capital (301); Photography Revenue (401); and Utilities Expense (690). Then, using your journal entries from Exercise 2-15, post to the general ledger (balance column format). Finally, prepare the August 31, 2017, trial balance.

Analysis Component: Joseph Eetok wanted to buy a building for his business and took the August 31, 2017, trial balance to his bank manager. Is the trial balance used for external reporting? Explain.

Exercise 2-17 T-accounts and the trial balance LO3,5,6

Follow the instructions in Exercise 2-16, but instead of using a balance column format for the accounts, use T-accounts. Include the date next to each posting.

Exercise 2-18 Preparing financial statements from a trial balance LO6

CHECK FIGURES: Loss = $19,000; Total assets = $93,300

Extreme Hockey trains top-level hockey players with on-ice and off-ice programs. Extreme Hockey aims to maximize every hockey player's full potential. The company showed the following trial balances for its first year just ended December 31, 2017:

Account Title	Debit	Credit
Cash	$ 18,000	
Accounts receivable	5,200	
Prepaid rent	13,000	
Machinery	57,100	
Accounts payable		$ 17,300
Notes payable		47,000
Ryan Roy, capital		50,000
Ryan Roy, withdrawals	2,000	
Training revenue..................................		18,000
Wages expense.....................................	29,000	
Rent expense	8,000	
Totals	$132,300	$132,300

Required Use the information provided to complete an income statement, statement of changes in equity, and balance sheet.

Analysis Component: If Extreme Hockey continues to experience losses, what alternatives are available to prevent assets from decreasing?

Exercise 2-19 Preparing financial statements from a trial balance LO6

CHECK FIGURES: Profit = $840; Total assets = $3,450

JenCo showed the following trial balance information (in alphabetical order) for its first month just ended March 31, 2017:

Account	Debit	Credit
Accounts payable..		$ 500
Accounts receivable.......................................	$1,950	
Cash	500	
Equipment...	700	
Interest expense	10	
Marie Jensen, capital		2,050
Marie Jensen, withdrawals...........................	1,500	
Notes payable		1,100
Prepaid insurance	300	
Salaries expense	800	
Service revenue		1,650
Unearned service revenue............................		460
Totals...	$5,760	$5,760

Required Use the information provided to complete an income statement, statement of changes in equity, and balance sheet.

Exercise 2-20 **Preparing financial statements from a trial balance** LO6

CHECK FIGURES: Loss = $27,000; Total assets = $237,000

Media Marketing Services has been operating for several years. It showed the following trial balance information (in alphabetical order) for the month just ended March 31, 2017:

Account	Debit	Credit
Accounts payable....................................		$ 46,000
Accounts receivable..............................	$ 3,000	
Building...	80,000	
Cash..	17,000	
Revenue...		126,000
Sam Smith, capital*.............................		122,000
Sam Smith, withdrawals	18,000	
Land	84,000	
Machinery	50,000	
Notes payable		114,000
Office supplies......................................	3,000	
Office supplies expense	7,000	
Wages expense.....................................	146,000	
Totals...	$408,000	$408,000

*The $122,000 balance includes $35,000 invested by the owner during March.

Required Using the information provided, prepare an income statement and a statement of changes in equity for the month ended March 31, 2017, and a balance sheet at March 31, 2017.

Exercise 2-21 **Effects of posting errors on the trial balance** LO3,5,6

Complete the following table by filling in the blanks. For each of the listed posting errors:

1. Enter in column (1) the amount of the difference that the error would create between the two trial balance columns (show a zero if the columns would balance).

2. Identify if there would be a difference between the two columns, and identify in column (2) the trial balance column that would be larger.

3. Identify the account(s) affected in column (3).

4. Identify the amount by which the account(s) is (are) under- or overstated in column (4).

   The answer for the first error is provided as an example.

	Description	(1) Difference Between Debit and Credit Columns	(2) Column With the Larger Total Stated	(3) Identify Account(s) Incorrectly Understated	(4) Amount That Account(s) Is (Are) Over- or Understated
a.	A $2,400 debit to Rent Expense was posted as a $1,590 debit.	$810	Credit	Rent Expense	Rent Expense is understated by $810
b.	A $42,000 debit to Machinery was posted as a debit to Accounts Payable.				
c.	A $4,950 credit to Services Revenue was posted as a $495 credit.				
d.	A $1,440 debit to Store Supplies was not posted at all.				
e.	A $2,250 debit to Prepaid Insurance was posted as a debit to Insurance Expense.				
f.	A $4,050 credit to Cash was posted twice as two credits to the Cash account.				
g.	A $9,900 debit to the owner's withdrawals account was debited to the owner's capital account.				

Exercise 2-22 Analyzing the trial balance LO3,5,6

During March, Salma Ahmad, the owner of Doan Cleaning Services, had trouble keeping her debits and credits equal. The following errors were noted:

    a. Ahmad did not post the entry to record $3,500 of services performed on account.

    b. In posting a $300 payment on account, debited Cash and credited Accounts Payable.

    c. In posting a cash payment, correctly debited Accounts Payable for $425 but incorrectly credited Cash for $245.

    d. In posting a cash receipt of $750, debited Cash but forgot to post the credit to Accounts Receivable.

    e. In posting the purchase of $1,000 of equipment on credit, debited Accounts Payable and credited Equipment.

Required For each of the errors described, indicate:

  1. Whether debits equal credits on the trial balance, and

  2. Which account(s) have incorrect balances.

Exercise 2-23 Transposition and slide errors on the trial balance LO6

Required Identify the single transposition or slide error in each of the following independent trial balances.

	Case A		Case B		Case C	
Cash	$ 120		$ 3,900		$ 59	
Accounts receivable	260		1,900		46	
Equipment	3,170		12,900		791	
Accounts payable		$ 190		$ 2,350		$ 72
Capital		1,100		16,150		229
Withdrawals	850		7,000		-0-	
Revenue		3,000		9,600		641
Wages expense	610		8,700		10	
Totals	$5,010	$4,290	$34,400	$28,100	$906	$942

Problems

Problem 2-1A **Analyzing transactions and recording journal entries** LO3,5

Tobias Eaden started a sole proprietorship named Sky High Ads. A customer's message can be displayed on an airplane banner across the city. The following are Sky High Ad's business activities during the month of November 2017:

Nov	1	Invested $200,000 cash and aircraft equipment with a $50,000 fair value in a new sole proprietorship named Sky High Ads.
	3	Purchased land and a small office building. The land was worth $400,000, and the building was worth $100,000. The purchase price was paid with $125,000 cash and a long-term note payable for the balance.
	7	Eaden transferred title of his personal airplane to the business. The airplane had a value of $200,000 and was to be used exclusively in the business.
	9	Purchased $5,000 of supplies on credit.
	13	Provided services to a customer for a marriage proposal and collected $16,000 on credit.
	17	Paid $3,000 wages to a pilot.
	21	Signed an advertising contract to commence in January. A deposit of $250 must be paid by December 15.
	23	Paid for half of the account payable from the November 9 transaction.
	27	Purchased $20,000 of new aircraft equipment by paying $15,000 cash and trading in old aircraft equipment with a recorded cost of $5,000.
	30	Withdrew $3,200 cash from the business for personal use.

Required For each transaction, (1) **complete the analysis**, (2) determine the journal entry analysis and (3) record the journal entry. Use the template below.

Nov 1	**Analysis**				
	Journal entry analysis				
	Journal Entry				
	Date	**Account Titles and Explanation**		**Debit**	**Credit**
Nov 3					

Problem 2-2A **Posting journal entries to T-accounts** LO5

CHECK FIGURE: 2. Cash balance, Nov. 30, 2017 = $51,300

Refer to the scenario described in Problem 2-1A.

Required

1. Set up the following general ledger accounts using T-accounts: Cash; Accounts Receivable; Supplies; Airplane; Aircraft Equipment; Building; Land; Accounts Payable; Long-Term Notes Payable; Tobias Eaden, Capital; Tobias Eaden, Withdrawals; Revenue; and Wages Expense.

2. Post the journal entries into the T-accounts. Identify the date next to each posting. Determine the balance in each account.

3. Prove the accounting equation.

Problem 2-3A **Preparing general journal entries** LO3,5

Bruce Ibach owns Biotech Fitness Centre, which showed the following selected transactions for the month ended May 31, 2017:

May	1	Purchased new equipment, paying cash of $14,000 and signing a 90-day note payable for the balance of $32,000.
	2	Purchased 12 months of insurance to begin May 2; paid $24,000.
	3	Completed a fitness contract for a group of clients today and received $6,000.
	4	Purchased office supplies on account; $3,750.
	6	Returned to the supplier $750 of defective office supplies purchased on May 4.
	10	Provided services to a client today on account; $11,500.
	15	Paid for the May 4 purchase less the return of May 6.
	20	Received payment from the client of May 10.
	25	Received cash of $2,500 from a client for work to be done in June.
	31	Paid month-end salaries of $47,000.
	31	Paid the May telephone bill today; $2,250.
	31	Received the May electrical bill today; $3,100. It will be paid on June 15.

Required Prepare journal entries for each of the above transactions.

Problem 2-4A **Preparing general journal entries** LO3,5

Abe Factor opened a new accounting practice called X-Factor Accounting and completed these activities during March 2017:

Mar.	1	Invested $50,000 in cash and office equipment that had a fair value of $12,000.
	1	Prepaid $9,000 cash for three months' rent for an office.
	3	Made credit purchases of used office equipment for $6,000 and office supplies for $1,200.
	5	Completed work for a client and immediately received $6,200 cash.
	9	Completed a $4,000 project for a client, who will pay within 30 days.
	11	Paid the account payable created on March 3.
	15	Paid $3,000 cash for the annual premium on an insurance policy.
	20	Received $1,500 as partial payment for the work completed on March 9.
	22	Placed an order with a supplier for $4,800 of supplies to be delivered April 7. They must be paid for within 15 days of being received.
	23	Completed work for another client for $2,850 on credit.
	27	Abe Factor withdrew $3,600 cash from the business to pay some personal expenses.
	30	Purchased $650 of additional office supplies on credit.
	31	Paid $860 for the month's utility bill.

Required Prepare journal entries to record the transactions.

Problem 2-5A Posting, preparing a trial balance LO4,5,6,

CHECK FIGURE: 3. Total Dr = $75,700

Required Using the journal entries prepared in Problem 2-4A, complete the following:

1. Set up the following accounts (use the balance column format or T-accounts): Cash (101); Accounts Receivable (106); Office Supplies (124); Prepaid Insurance (128); Prepaid Rent (131); Office Equipment (163); Accounts Payable (201); Abe Factor, Capital (301); Abe Factor, Withdrawals (302); Accounting Revenue (401); and Utilities Expense (690).

2. Post the entries to the accounts and enter the balance after each posting.

3. Prepare a trial balance as of the end of the month.

Problem 2-6A Preparing financial statements from a trial balance LO6

CHECK FIGURES: Profit = $12,190; Total assets = $71,240

Using the trial balance prepared for X-Factor Accounting in Part 3 of Problem 2-5A, prepare an income statement and statement of changes in equity for the month ended March 31, 2017, and a balance sheet at March 31, 2017.

Problem 2-7A Preparing and posting journal entries; preparing a trial balance LO3,4,5,6

CHECK FIGURE: 4. Total Dr = $168,280

Elizabeth Wong has strong problem-solving skills and loves to work with people. After becoming a Certified Human Resources Professional (CHRP) and working for several companies, she opened her own business, HR Solutions. She completed the following transactions during May 2017:

May	1	Invested $75,000 in cash and office equipment that had a fair value of $48,000 in the business.
	1	Prepaid $14,400 cash for three months' rent for an office.
	2	Made credit purchases of office equipment for $24,000 and office supplies for $4,800.
	6	Completed a report on hiring solutions for a client and collected $8,000 cash.
	9	Completed a $16,000 project implementing a training program for a client, who will pay within 30 days.
	10	Paid half of the account payable created on May 2.
	19	Paid $7,500 cash for the annual premium on an insurance policy.
	22	Received $12,800 as partial payment for the work completed on May 9.
	25	Developed a performance review process for another client for $5,280 on credit.
	25	Paid wages for May totalling $34,000.
	31	Withdrew $5,000 cash from the business to take a trip to Paris in June.
	31	Purchased $1,600 of additional office supplies on credit.
	31	Paid $1,400 for the month's utility bill.

Required

1. Prepare journal entries to record the transactions. Use page 1 for the journal.

2. Set up the following accounts (use the balance column format or T-accounts): Cash (101); Accounts Receivable (106); Office Supplies (124); Prepaid Insurance (128); Prepaid Rent (131); Office Equipment (163); Accounts Payable (201); Elizabeth Wong, Capital (301);

Elizabeth Wong, Withdrawals (302); Services Revenue (403); Wages Expense (623); and Utilities Expense (690).

3. Post the entries to the accounts and enter the balance after each posting.

4. Prepare a trial balance at May 31, 2017.

Analysis Component: Utilities Expense, Services Revenue, and Elizabeth Wong, Withdrawals are equity accounts. Explain why.

Problem 2-8A Preparing financial statements from a trial balance LO6

CHECK FIGURES: Loss = $6,120; Total assets = $127,880

Using the trial balance prepared for HR Solutions in Part 4 of Problem 2-7A, prepare an income statement and statement of changes in equity for the month ended May 31, 2017, and a balance sheet at May 31, 2017.

Problem 2-9A Preparing financial statements from a trial balance LO6

CHECK FIGURES: Profit = $4,580; Total assets = $68,800

	Hipster Optical Trial Balance May 31, 2017		
Acct. No.	Account Title	Debit	Credit
101	Cash	$18,500	
106	Accounts receivable	8,480	
124	Office supplies	6,400	
128	Prepaid insurance	9,820	
163	Office equipment	25,600	
201	Accounts payable		$ 1,600
230	Unearned service revenue		7,800
301	Peeta Black, capital		56,300
302	Peeta Black, withdrawals	1,480	
403	Services revenue		25,280
623	Wages expense	15,000	
640	Rent expense	4,300	
690	Utilities expense	1,400	
	Totals	$90,980	$90,980

Required Using the trial balance provided above, prepare an income statement and statement of changes in equity for the first month ended May 31, 2017, and a balance sheet at May 31, 2017.

Analysis Component: Prepare two different journal entries, including explanations, that might have created the May 31, 2017, balance in Utilities Expense of $1,400. Use May 31, 2017, as the date for your entries.

Problem 2-10A Journalizing, posting, preparing a trial balance LO3,4,5,6

CHECK FIGURE: 4. Total Dr = $658,740

Binbutti Engineering, a sole proprietorship, completed the following transactions during July 2017, the third month of operations:

July	1	Bishr Binbutti, the owner, invested $300,000 cash, office equipment with a value of $12,000, and $90,000 of drafting equipment in the business.
	2	Purchased land for an office. The land was worth $108,000, which was paid with $10,800 cash and a long-term note payable for $97,200.
	3	Purchased a portable building with $150,000 cash and moved it onto the land.
	5	Paid $12,000 cash for the premiums on two one-year insurance policies.
	7	Completed and delivered a set of plans for a client and collected $1,400 cash.
	9	Purchased additional drafting equipment for $45,000. Paid $21,000 cash and signed a long-term note payable for the $24,000 balance.
	10	Completed $4,000 of engineering services for a client. This amount is to be paid within 30 days.
	12	Purchased $4,500 of additional office equipment on credit.
	15	Completed engineering services for $7,000 on credit.
	16	Received a bill for rent on equipment that was used on a completed job. The $13,800 rent must be paid within 30 days.
	17	Collected $400 from the client of July 10.
	19	Paid $12,000 wages to the drafting assistants.
	22	Paid the account payable created on July 12.
	25	Paid $1,350 cash for some repairs to an item of drafting equipment.
	26	Binbutti withdrew $800 cash from the business for personal use.
	30	Paid $12,000 wages to the drafting assistants.
	31	Paid $6,000 cash for advertising in the local newspaper during July.

Required

1. Prepare journal entries to record the transactions. Use page 1 for the journal.

2. Set up the following general ledger accounts (use the balance column format or T-accounts), entering the balances brought forward from June 30, 2017: Cash (101) $26,000; Accounts Receivable (106) $3,000; Prepaid Insurance (128) $500; Office Equipment (163) $1,700; Drafting Equipment (167) $1,200; Building (173) $42,000; Land (183) $28,000; Accounts Payable (201) $1,740; Long-Term Notes Payable (251) $24,000; Bishr Binbutti, Capital (301) $54,000; Bishr Binbutti, Withdrawals (302) $1,000; Engineering Revenue (401) $29,600; Wages Expense (623) $4,000; Equipment Rental Expense (645) $1,000; Advertising Expense (655) $640; and Repairs Expense (684) $300.

3. Post the entries to the general ledger accounts and enter the balance after each posting.

4. Prepare a trial balance at July 31, 2017.

Problem 2-11A Preparing financial statements from a trial balance LO6

CHECK FIGURES: Loss = $9,090; Total assets = $605,850

Using the trial balance prepared for Binbutti Engineering in Part 4 of Problem 2-10A, prepare an income statement and statement of changes in equity for the three months ended July 31, 2017, and a balance sheet at July 31, 2017.

Problem 2-12A Journalizing, posting, preparing a trial balance and financial statements LO1,3,4,5,6

CHECK FIGURES: 4. Dr = $66,200 5. Profit = $11,350; Total assets = $16,050

Tayler Smith is a singer who has experienced international success in her career. On May 1, 2017, Tayler started her business, "Glitter and Gold Studio" where she teaches singing. The following activities occurred during July, the third month of operations:

July	1	Purchased supplies including sheet music on credit for $100.
	2	Collected $4,000 in advance for singing lessons to be delivered in August.
	3	Collected $2,000 for teaching singing lessons in July.
	4	Paid $3,000 to rent her music studio for the month of July.
	5	Paid $500 for supplies purchased on account last month.
	15	Tayler Smith withdrew cash of $500 to do some personal shopping on the weekend.
	20	Paid her assistant wages of $1,300.
	31	Purchased new microphone equipment on credit for $300.

Required

1. Prepare journal entries to record the July transactions.

2. Set up the following general ledger accounts using T-accounts, entering the balances brought forward from June 30, 2017: Cash (101) $6,000; Supplies (126) $950; Equipment (161) $8,000; Accounts Payable (201) $1,500; Unearned Teaching Revenue (233) $9,800; Tayler Smith, Capital (301) $3,000; Tayler Smith, Withdrawals (302) $13,000; Teaching Revenue (401) $46,000; Wages Expense (623) $26,350; and Rent Expense (640) $6,000.

3. Post the entries to the T-accounts; calculate the ending balance in each account.

4. Prepare a trial balance at July 31, 2017.

5. Use the trial balance to prepare an income statement and statement of changes in equity for the three months ended July 31, 2017, as well as a balance sheet at July 31, 2017.

Problem 2-13A Preparing financial statements from a trial balance LO6

CHECK FIGURES: Loss = $2,000; Total assets = $393,300

	Feline Pet Care		
	Trial Balance		
	July 31, 2017		
Acct. No.	**Account Title**	**Debit**	**Credit**
101	Cash	$ 23,000	
106	Accounts receivable	11,600	
128	Prepaid insurance	12,500	
163	Equipment	18,200	
173	Building	192,000	
183	Land	136,000	
201	Accounts payable		$ 15,540
230	Unearned revenue		92,000
301	Betty Lark, capital		292,760
302	Betty Lark, withdrawals	5,000	
401	Revenue		117,000
623	Wages expense	58,000	
645	Equipment rental expense	34,000	
655	Advertising expense	9,200	
684	Pet food expense	17,800	
	Totals	$517,300	$517,300

Required Using the trial balance provided above, prepare an income statement and statement of changes in equity for the first year ended July 31, 2017, and a balance sheet at July 31, 2017.

Analysis Component: Prepare two different journal entries, including explanations, that might have created the July 31, 2017, balance in Revenue of $117,000. Use July 31, 2017, as the date for your entries.

Problem 2-14A Analyzing trial balance errors LO3,5,6

CHECK FIGURE: Total Dr = $118,400

Wilm Schmidt, the owner of Wilm's Window Washing Services, had difficulty getting the debits to equal credits on the January 31, 2017, trial balance.

Wilm's Window Washing Services Trial Balance January 31, 2017		
	Debit	**Credit**
Cash	$ 11,600	
Accounts receivable	9,240	
Prepaid insurance	2,400	
Equipment	24,000	
Accounts payable		$ 5,400
Wilm Schmidt, capital		45,000
Wilm Schmidt, withdrawals	8,960	
Service revenues		60,400
Salaries expense	32,000	
Insurance expense	5,200	
Maintenance expense	13,000	
Utilities expense	5,200	
Totals	$111,600	$110,800

The following errors were discovered:

   a. Schmidt did not post a $4,000 purchase of equipment on credit.

   b. In posting a $1,400 collection from a credit customer, Schmidt debited Accounts Receivable and credited Cash.

   c. In posting a cash receipt, Schmidt correctly debited Cash for $2,660 but incorrectly credited Accounts Receivable for $6,260.

   d. In posting a $4,400 payment on account, Schmidt debited Accounts Payable but forgot to post the credit to Cash.

   e. In posting the entry for services of $3,600 performed for a customer on credit, Schmidt debited Accounts Receivable but credited Maintenance Expense.

Required Prepare a corrected trial balance.

Alternate Problems

Problem 2-1B Analyzing and recording journal entries LO3,5

Peeters Consulting completed these transactions during June 2017:

June	2	Trevor Peeters, the sole proprietor, invested $46,000 cash and office equipment with a $24,000 fair value in the business.
	4	Purchased land and a small office building. The land was worth $268,000 and the building was worth $66,000. The purchase price was paid with $30,000 cash and a long-term note payable for $304,000.
	8	Transferred title of his personal automobile to the business. The automobile had a value of $7,000 and was to be used exclusively in the business.
	10	Purchased $600 of office supplies on credit.
	14	Completed $2,400 of services for a client. This amount is to be paid within 30 days.
	18	Paid $1,800 salary to an assistant.
	22	Paid the account payable from the transaction on June 10.
	24	Purchased $4,000 of new office equipment by paying $2,400 cash and trading in old equipment with a recorded cost of $1,600.
	28	Received $1,000 payment on the receivable created from the transaction on June 14th.
	30	Withdrew $1,050 cash from the business for personal use.

Required For each transaction, (1) **complete the analysis**, (2) determine the journal entry analysis and (3) record the journal entry. Use the template below.

June 2	Analysis	
	Journal entry analysis	
	Journal Entry	
	Date	Account Titles and Explanation	Debit	Credit
June 4				

Problem 2-2B Posting general journal entries LO5

CHECK FIGURE: 2. Cash balance June 30, 2017 = $11,150

Using the information in Problem 2-1B, complete the following:

Required
1. Set up the following general ledger accounts using T-accounts: Cash; Accounts Receivable; Office Supplies; Vehicle; Office Equipment; Building; Land; Accounts Payable; Long-Term Notes Payable; Trevor Peeters, Capital; Trevor Peeters, Withdrawals; Revenue; and Salaries Expense.

2. Post the journal entries into the T-accounts. Identify the date next to each posting. Determine the balance in each account.

3. Prove the accounting equation.

Problem 2-3B **Preparing general journal entries** LO3,5

Airdrie Advertising showed the following selected transactions for the month ended March 31, 2017:

Mar. 1   Purchased a new portable building, paying cash of $75,000 and signing a five-year note payable for the balance of $300,000.

1   Purchased six months of insurance to begin March 1; paid $5,700.

2   Made a hotel reservation by phone regarding a business meeting to be held on March 28. The full payment of $240 will be required upon arrival at the hotel.

4   Purchased cleaning supplies on account; $450.

15   Paid for the March 4 purchase.

19   Performed advertising work for a client today on account; $35,000.

20   Collected cash of $8,000 from a customer. The advertising work will be done in April.

28   Registered at the hotel booked on March 2 and paid the bill. Attended the out-of-town business meeting and returned to the office the next day.

29   Provided advertising services to the local botanical garden society; collected $5,000.

30   Paid month-end salaries of $25,600.

30   Received the March telephone bill today; $1,300. It will be paid April 14.

30   Collected half of the amount owed by the customer of March 19.

Required Prepare journal entries for each of the above transactions.

Problem 2-4B **Preparing general journal entries** LO3,5

Susan Hurley, Public Accountant, completed these activities during September 2017, the first month of operations:

Sept. 1   Began a public accounting practice by investing $20,000 in cash and office equipment having a $9,200 fair value.

1   Prepaid two months' rent in advance on suitable office space, $5,600.

2   Purchased on credit used office equipment, $3,800, and office supplies, $1,380.

4   Completed accounting work for a client and immediately received payment of $2,900 cash.

8   Completed accounting work on credit for Frontier Bank, $5,080.

10   Paid for the items purchased on credit on September 2.

14   Paid the annual $3,300 premium on an insurance policy.

15   Paid $1,250 to attend an all-day seminar on September 20 regarding ethical accounting practices.

18   Received payment in full from Frontier Bank for the work completed on September 8.

20   Attended the seminar paid for on September 15.

24   Completed accounting work on credit for Travis Realty, $5,000.

28   Withdrew $2,500 cash from the practice to pay personal expenses.

29   Purchased additional office supplies on credit, $450.

30   Paid the September utility bills, $1,750.

Required Prepare journal entries to record the transactions.

Problem 2-5B **Posting, preparing a trial balance** LO4,6

CHECK FIGURE: 3. Total Dr = $42,630

Required Using the general journal entries prepared in Problem 2-4B, complete the following:

1. Set up the following accounts (use the balance column format or T-accounts): Cash (101); Accounts Receivable (106); Office Supplies (124); Prepaid Insurance (128); Prepaid Rent (131); Office Equipment (163); Accounts Payable (201); Susan Hurley, Capital (301); Susan Hurley, Withdrawals (302); Accounting Revenue (401); Professional Development Expense (680); and Utilities Expense (690).

2. Post the entries to the general ledger accounts and enter the balance after each posting.

3. Prepare a trial balance as of September 30, 2017.

Problem 2-6B **Preparing financial statements from a trial balance** LO6

CHECK FIGURES: Profit = $9,980; Total assets = $37,130

Using the trial balance prepared in Part 3 of Problem 2-5B, prepare an income statement and statement of changes in equity for the month ended September 30, 2017, and a balance sheet at September 30, 2017.

Problem 2-7B **Preparing and posting general journal entries; preparing a trial balance** LO3,4,5,6

CHECK FIGURE: 4. Total Dr = $96,300

WiCom Servicing completed these transactions during November 2017, its first month of operations:

Nov.	1	Tait Unger, the owner, invested $62,000 cash and office equipment that had a fair value of $19,000 in the business.
	2	Prepaid $21,000 cash for three months' rent for an office.
	4	Made credit purchases of used office equipment for $9,000 and office supplies for $1,650.
	8	Completed work for a client and immediately received $5,200 cash.
	12	Completed a $4,800 project for a client, who will pay within 30 days.
	13	Paid the account payable created on November 4.
	19	Paid $3,750 cash as the annual premium on an insurance policy.
	22	Received $2,000 as partial payment for the work completed on November 12.
	24	Completed work for another client for $3,600 on credit.
	28	Withdrew $5,300 from the business for personal use.
	29	Purchased $1,700 of additional office supplies on credit.
	30	Paid $19,000 in wages.
	30	Paid $1,650 for the month's utility bill.

Required

1. Prepare journal entries to record the transactions. Use general journal page 1.

2. Set up the following general ledger accounts (use the balance column format or T-accounts): Cash (101); Accounts Receivable (106); Office Supplies (124); Prepaid Insurance (128); Prepaid Rent (131); Office Equipment (163); Accounts Payable (201); Tait Unger, Capital (301); Tait Unger, Withdrawals (302); Service Revenue (401); Wages Expense (680); and Utilities Expense (690).

3. Post the entries to the general ledger accounts, and enter the balance after each posting.

4. Prepare a trial balance at November 30, 2017.

Analysis Component: Is the November 29 purchase of office supplies recorded as a debit to an asset or an expense account? Explain.

Problem 2-8B **Preparing financial statements from a trial balance** LO6

CHECK FIGURES: Loss = $7,050; Total assets = $70,350

Using the trial balance prepared in Part 4 of Problem 2-7B, prepare an income statement and statement of changes in equity for the month ended November 30, 2017, and a balance sheet at November 30, 2017.

Problem 2-9B **Preparing financial statements from a trial balance** LO6

CHECK FIGURES: Loss = $3,120; Total assets = $135,680

	Rush Innovations Trial Balance November 30, 2017		
Acct. No.	**Account Title**	**Debit**	**Credit**
101	Cash	$ 23,480	
106	Accounts receivable	7,000	
124	Office supplies	5,800	
128	Prepaid insurance	10,400	
131	Prepaid rent	21,000	
163	Office equipment	68,000	
201	Accounts payable		$ 3,400
301	Jay Rush, capital		146,000
302	Jay Rush, withdrawals	10,600	
401	Service Revenue		15,800
680	Wages expense	16,000	
690	Utilities expense	2,920	
	Totals	$165,200	$165,200

Required Use the trial balance provided above to prepare an income statement and statement of changes in equity for the first month ended November 30, 2017, and a balance sheet at November 30, 2017.

Analysis Component: Prepare two journal entries, including explanations: one that would have caused Accounts Receivable to increase, and one that would have caused it to decrease. Use November 30, 2017, as the date for your entries.

Problem 2-10B **Journalizing, posting, preparing a trial balance** LO3,4,5,6

CHECK FIGURE: 4. Total Dr = $271,500

At the beginning of June 2017, Brett Wilson created a moving company called Frog Box Company. The company had the following transactions during July, its second month of operations:

July	1	Purchased office equipment for $9,000 and a truck for $56,000 by signing a long-term note payable.
	2	Purchased land for an office. The land was worth $124,000, which was paid with $40,800 cash and a long-term note payable for the balance.
	3	Purchased a used portable building with $21,000 cash and moved it onto the land.
	5	Paid $9,600 cash for the premiums on two one-year insurance policies.
	9	Provided services to a client and collected $3,200 cash.
	12	Purchased additional office equipment for $6,500. Paid $700 cash and signed a long-term note payable for the balance.
	15	Completed $3,750 of services for a client. This amount is due within 30 days.
	20	Completed another hauling job for $9,200 on credit.
	21	Received a bill for rent on a specialized hauling truck that was used to complete the job done on July 20. The $1,300 rent must be paid within 30 days.
	22	Collected $5,000 from the client described in the transaction on July 20.
	23	Paid $1,600 wages to an assistant.
	24	Paid the account payable created in the transaction of July 21.
	25	Paid $1,425 cash for some repairs to the truck.
	26	Wilson withdrew $3,875 in cash from the business for personal use.
	27	Paid $1,600 wages to an assistant.
	28	Paid $800 cash for advertising in the local newspaper during July.
	29	Received $1,400 from a client for services to be performed in August.

Required

1. Prepare journal entries to record the transactions. Use page 1 for the journal.

2. Set up the following general ledger accounts (use the balance column format or T-accounts), entering the balances brought forward from June 30, 2017: Cash (101) $75,000; Accounts Receivable (106) $950; Prepaid Insurance (128) $275; Trucks (153) $20,800; Office Equipment (163) $1,200; Building (173) $-0-; Land (183) $-0-; Accounts Payable (201) $725; Unearned Revenue (233) $-0-; Long-Term Notes Payable (251) $7,000; Brett Wilson, Capital (301) $83,825; Brett Wilson, Withdrawals (302) $600; Revenue (401) $8,400; Wages Expense (623) $780; Truck Rental Expense (645) $230; Advertising Expense (655) $75; and Repairs Expense (684) $40.

3. Post the entries to the general ledger accounts and enter the balance after each posting.

4. Prepare a trial balance as of the end of the month.

Problem 2-11B Preparing financial statements from a trial balance LO6

CHECK FIGURES: Profit = $16,700; Total assets = $259,175

Using the trial balance prepared in Part 4 of Problem 2-10B, prepare an income statement and statement of changes in equity for the two months ended July 31, 2017, and a balance sheet at July 31, 2017.

Problem 2-12B Journalizing, posting, preparing a trial balance and financial statements LO1,3,4,5,6

CHECK FIGURES: 4. Dr = $137,000 5. Profit = $3,750; Total assets = $86,750

Ike Petrov started a tour company, Tour-Along, on October 1, 2017. The following activities occurred during November, the second month of operations:

Nov.	1	Paid $10,000 regarding purchases made on account during October.
	2	Purchased a $34,000 photocopier, paying $6,000 cash and signing a note payable for the balance.
	3	Purchased office supplies for cash; $800.
	4	Signed a $200,000 contract with RBC to arrange travel for its employees beginning January 1, 2015.
	14	Paid wages of $6,000.
	20	Collected $14,000 for clients travelling in November.
	25	Ike Petrov withdrew $2,000 cash for personal use.
	30	Paid interest on the notes payable; $150.

Required

1. Prepare journal entries to record the November transactions.

2. Set up the following T-accounts, entering the balances brought forward from October 31, 2017: Cash (101) $26,000; Office Supplies (124) $900; Office Equipment (163) $36,000; Accounts Payable (201) $43,000; Notes Payable (205) $20,000; Ike Petrov, Capital (301) $8,000; Ike Petrov, Withdrawals (302) $4,000; Travel Revenue (401) $34,000; Wages Expense (623) $38,000; and Interest Expense (633) $100.

3. Post the entries to the T-accounts; calculate the ending balance in each account.

4. Prepare a trial balance at November 30, 2017.

5. Use the trial balance to prepare an income statement and statement of changes in equity for the two months ended November 30, 2017, as well as a balance sheet at November 30, 2017.

Analysis Component: Part 2 of the *Required* states that the account Ike Petrov, Capital had a balance of $8,000 at October 31, 2017. Explain what this balance represents.

Problem 2-13B **Preparing financial statements from a trial balance** LO6

CHECK FIGURES: Loss = $33,680; Total assets = $120,670

	Lincoln Landscaping		
	Trial Balance		
	July 31, 2017		
Acct. No.	**Account Title**	**Debit**	**Credit**
101	Cash	$ 23,720	
106	Accounts receivable	18,600	
128	Prepaid insurance	13,750	
167	Equipment	64,600	
201	Accounts payable		$ 37,500
233	Unearned revenue		2,800
251	Long-term notes payable		58,000
301	Brielle Lincoln, capital		65,000
302	Brielle Lincoln, withdrawals	8,950	
401	Revenue		29,100
623	Wages expense	59,000	
645	Rental expense	1,100	
655	Advertising expense	1,750	
684	Repairs expense	930	
	Totals	$192,400	$192,400

Required Using the trial balance provided above, prepare an income statement and a statement of changes in equity for the first three months ended July 31, 2017, and a balance sheet at July 31, 2017.

Analysis Component: Analyze the balance sheet and calculate what percentage of the assets is financed by (a) debt and (b) equity.

Problem 2-14B **Analyzing trial balance errors** LO3,5,6

CHECK FIGURE: Total Dr = $49,860

On January 1, 2017, Paula Fernandes started a new business called Wicked Dance. Near the end of the year, she hired a new bookkeeper without checking references or requesting an academic transcript. As a result, a number of mistakes have been made in preparing the following trial balance:

	Wicked Dance		
	Trial Balance		
	December 31, 2017		
		Debit	**Credit**
Cash		$ 5,500	
Accounts receivable			$ 7,900
Office supplies		2,650	
Office equipment		20,500	
Accounts payable			9,465
Paula Fernandes, Capital		16,745	
Services revenue			22,350
Wages expense			6,000
Rent expense			4,800
Advertising expense			1,250
Totals		$45,395	$52,340

Paula's analysis of the situation has uncovered these errors:

a. The sum of the debits in the Cash account is $37,175 and the sum of the credits is $30,540.

b. A $275 payment from a credit customer was posted to Cash but was not posted to Accounts Receivable.

c. A credit purchase of office supplies for $400 was not posted at all.

d. A transposition error occurred in copying the balance of the Services Revenue account to the trial balance. The correct amount was $23,250.

Other errors were made in placing account balances in the wrong trial balance columns and in taking the totals of the columns.

Required Prepare a corrected trial balance.

Analytical and Review Problems

A & R Problem 2-1

Carlos Young started an engineering firm called Young Engineering. He began operations in March 2017 and completed seven transactions, including his initial investment of $17,000 cash. After these transactions, the ledger included the following accounts with their normal balances:

Cash	$26,660
Office Supplies	660
Prepaid Insurance	3,200
Office Equipment	16,500
Accounts Payable	16,500
Carlos Young, Capital	17,000
Carlos Young, Withdrawals	3,740
Engineering Revenue	24,000
Rent Expense	6,740

Required

Preparation Component: Prepare a trial balance for the business.

Analysis Component: Analyze the accounts and balances and prepare narratives that describe each of the seven most likely transactions and their amounts.

A & R Problem 2-2

Designer Drycleaning showed the following information for its first and second months just ended, March and April of 2017:

Account Title	April 30, 2017	March 31, 2017
Cash	7,000	3,000
Cleaning supplies	3,500	900
Prepaid rent	12,000	16,000
Equipment	76,000	30,000
Accounts payable	700	500
Notes payable	40,000	15,000
Christopher Dior Fresh, capital*	?	?

*Christopher Dior made a $10,000 investment during March and had withdrawals of $1,000 in March and $25,100 in April.

Required Use the information provided to complete a statement of changes in equity and a balance sheet for each of March and April 2017. *NOTE: Prepare the statements on a comparative*[15] *basis similar to the statements for Danier Leather and WestJet in Appendix III at the end of the textbook.*

Analysis Component:

    a. Liabilities increased by $25,200 from March 31, 2017, to April 30, 2017. Review the balance sheet and identify why liabilities increased.

    b. Equity increased by $34,400 during March and by $23,400 during April, yet profit was much higher in April. Explain.

Ethics Challenge

EC 2-1

You are a cashier at a retail convenience store. When you were hired, the owner explained to you the policy of immediately ringing up each sale. Recently, lunch hour traffic has increased dramatically and the manager asks you to take customers' cash and make change without ringing up sales to avoid delays. The manager says she will add up cash and ring up sales equal to the cash amount after lunch. She says that in this way the register will always be accurate when the owner arrives at 3:00 p.m.

Required

1. Identify the advantages and disadvantages of the manager's suggestion.
2. Identify the ethical dilemma and evaluate at least two courses of action you might consider and why.

---

15 Preparing statements on a *comparative basis* means to have numbers for at least two periods side by side. This kind of presentation provides decision makers with something meaningful against which the current period can be compared.

Focus on Financial Statements

FFS 2-1

Travis McAllister operates a surveying company. For the first few months of the company's life (through April), the accounting records were maintained by an outside bookkeeping service. According to those records, McAllister's equity balance was $75,000 as of April 30. To save on expenses, McAllister decided to keep the records himself. He managed to record May's transactions properly, but was a bit rusty when the time came to prepare the financial statements. His first versions of the balance sheet and income statement follow. McAllister is bothered that the company apparently operated at a loss during the month, even though he was very busy.

McAllister Surveying Income Statement For Month Ended May 31, 2017		
Revenue:		
Investments by owner		$ 3,000
Unearned surveying fees		6,000
Total revenues		$ 9,000
Operating expenses:		
Rent expense	$3,100	
Telephone expense	600	
Surveying equipment	5,400	
Advertising expense	3,200	
Utilities expense	300	
Insurance expense	900	
Withdrawals by owner	6,000	
Total operating expenses		19,500
Profit (loss)		$(10,500)

McAllister Surveying Balance Sheet May 31, 2017				
Assets		**Liabilities**	
Cash	$ 3,900	Accounts payable	$ 2,400
Accounts receivable	2,700	Surveying fees earned	18,000
Prepaid insurance	1,800	Short-term notes payable	48,000
Prepaid rent	4,200	Total liabilities	$ 68,400
Office supplies	300		
Buildings	81,000	**Equity**	
Land	36,000	Travis McAllister, capital	64,500
Salaries expense	3,000		
Total assets	$132,900	Total liabilities and equity	$132,900

Required Using the information contained in the original financial statements, prepare revised statements, including a statement of changes in equity, for the month of May.

Analysis Component: The owner, Travis McAllister, made a withdrawal during May. Withdrawals cause equity to decrease. Why would the owner intentionally cause equity to decrease by making a withdrawal?

FFS 2-2

1. Refer to **WestJet's** income statement in Appendix III at the end of the textbook.

    a. Total *Guest revenues* for 2014 were $3,599,157 (thousand).

    (i) Prepare two possible journal entries that might have been recorded to create this result.

    (ii) What effect do revenues have on the balance sheet?

    (iii) What assurances do we have that the revenues appearing on the income statement are for the year 2014? *Hint:* Which GAAP?

    b. Total *Finance costs* for 2014 were $51,838 (thousand).

    (i) Prepare a possible journal entry that might have recorded the interest expense.

    (ii) Do expenses affect the balance sheet? Explain.

2. Refer to **WestJet's** balance sheet in Appendix III at the end of the textbook. Find the line showing *Advance ticket sales* of $575,781 (thousand).

    a. Explain what you think the account *Advance ticket sales* represents.

    b. Prepare the journal entry that might have recorded this account balance.

Critical Thinking Mini Case

Prairie Insurance sells life insurance, disability insurance, vehicle insurance, crop insurance, and home-owners' insurance. You are employed by Prairie Insurance and have been promoted to sales division manager for the Western Canadian division. You will be supervising approximately 25 salespeople, along with five administrative assistants at various locations. The salespeople travel extensively and submit expense reports along with sales information monthly. A sample expense report for September shows:

Prairie Insurance—Western Canadian Division Sales Report: John Bishop Month Ended September 30, 2017	
Sales revenue*	$56,000
Expenses**	34,000

*Sales invoices attached
**Receipts attached

The former manager was dismissed because division results have been deteriorating. The consolidated sales report for the past three months shows the following:

Prairie Insurance—Western Canadian Division Sales Report Month Ended			
	September 30, 2017	August 31, 2017	July 31, 2017
Sales revenue..	$680,000	$510,000	$440,000
Expenses..	544,000	382,500	321,200
Profit...	$136,000	$127,500	$118,800

You learn that the company has one revenue account called Sales Revenue and one expense account called Expenses. You proceed to prepare a brief memo to the company's accountant requesting information that is needed to help you analyze the situation.

Required

Using the elements of critical thinking described on the inside front cover, respond to the following:

1. What are the main problem you need to address in your memo to the company's accountant?

2. What are your goals as division manager in addressing your main concerns?

3. What principles need to be considered in order to improve the reporting at Prairie Insurance?

4. What are the key facts you need to consider in improving the reporting at Prairie Insurance?

5. What will you do about your concerns to improve the reporting at Prairie Insurance?

Cumulative Comprehension Problem: Echo Systems

(This comprehensive problem starts in this chapter and continues in Chapters 3, 4, and 5. Because of its length, this problem is most easily solved if you use the Working Papers[16] that accompany this text.)

On October 1, 2017, Mary Graham organized a computer service company called Echo Systems. Echo is organized as a sole proprietorship and will provide consulting services, computer system installations, and custom program development. Graham has adopted the calendar year for reporting, and expects to prepare the company's first set of financial statements as of December 31, 2017. The initial chart of accounts for the accounting system includes these items:

Account Number	Account Name	Account Number	Account Name
101	Cash	301	Mary Graham, Capital
106	Accounts Receivable	302	Mary Graham, Withdrawals
126	Computer Supplies	403	Computer Services Revenue
128	Prepaid Insurance	623	Wages Expense
131	Prepaid Rent	655	Advertising Expense
163	Office Equipment	676	Mileage Expense
167	Computer Equipment	684	Repairs Expense, Computer
201	Accounts Payable	699	Charitable Donations Expense

PART A:

CHECK FIGURES: 4. Total Dr = $159,4505. Profit = $8,920; Total assets = $145,720

Required

1. Set up balance column accounts based on the chart of accounts provided.

2. Prepare journal entries to record each of the following October transactions.

3. Post the October entries.

4. Prepare a trial balance at October 31, 2017.

5. Prepare an income statement and a statement of changes in equity for the month ended October 31, 2017, as well as a balance sheet at October 31, 2017.

---

16 If students have not purchased the Working Paper package, the Working Papers for the Serial Problem are available on Connect.

Oct. 1 Graham invested $90,000 cash, a $36,000 computer system, and $18,000 of office equipment in the business.

2 Paid rent in advance of $9,000.

3 Purchased computer supplies on credit for $2,640 from Abbott Office Products.

5 Paid $4,320 cash for one year's premium on a property and liability insurance policy.

6 Billed Capital Leasing $6,600 for installing a new computer.

8 Paid for the computer supplies purchased from Abbott Office Products.

10 Hired Carly Smith as a part-time assistant for $200 per day, as needed.

12 Billed Capital Leasing another $2,400 for computer services rendered.

15 Received $6,600 from Capital Leasing on its account.

17 Paid $1,410 to repair computer equipment damaged when moving into the new office.

20 Paid $3,720 for an advertisement in the local newspaper.

22 Received $2,400 from Capital Leasing on its account.

28 Billed Decker Company $6,450 for services.

31 Paid Carly Smith for seven days' work.

31 Withdrew $7,200 cash from the business for personal use.

Part B:

CHECK FIGURES: 8. Total Dr = $184,950 9. Profit = $27,920; Total assets = $161,120

Required

6. Prepare journal entries to record each of the following November transactions.

7. Post the November entries.

8. Prepare a trial balance at November 30, 2017.

9. Prepare an income statement and a statement of changes in equity for the two months ended November 30, 2017, as well as a balance sheet at November 30, 2017.

Nov. 1 Reimbursed Graham's business automobile expense for 1,000 kilometres at $1.00 per kilometre.

2 Received $9,300 cash from Elite Corporation for computer services rendered.

5 Purchased $1,920 of computer supplies for cash from Abbott Office Products.

8 Billed Fostek Co. $8,700 for computer services rendered.

13 Notified by Alamo Engineering Co. that Echo's bid of $7,500 for an upcoming project was accepted.

18 Received $3,750 from Decker Company against the bill dated October 28.

22 Donated $1,500 to the United Way in the company's name.

24 Completed work for Alamo Engineering Co. and sent a bill for $7,500.

25 Sent another bill to Decker Company for the past due amount of $2,700.

28 Reimbursed Graham's business automobile expense for 1,200 kilometres at $1.00 per kilometre.

30 Paid Carly Smith for 14 days' work.

30 Withdrew $3,600 cash from the business for personal use.

Adjusting Accounts for Financial Statements

A Look Back

Chapter 2 explained the analysis and recording of transactions. We showed how to apply and interpret company accounts, T-accounts, double-entry accounting, ledgers, postings, and trial balances.

A Look at This Chapter

This chapter explains the timing of reports and the need to adjust accounts. Adjusting accounts is important for recognizing revenues and expenses in the proper period. We describe the adjusted trial balance and how it is used to prepare financial statements.

Used with permission from Frogbox.

LEARNING OBJECTIVES

LO1 Describe the purpose of adjusting accounts at the end of a period.

LO2 Explain how the timeliness, matching, and revenue recognition principles affect the adjusting process.

LO3 Explain accrual accounting and cash basis accounting and how accrual accounting adds to the usefulness of financial statements.

LO4 Prepare and explain adjusting entries for prepaid expenses, depreciation, unearned revenues, accrued expenses, and accrued revenues.

LO5   Explain how accounting adjustments link to financial statements.

LO6   Explain and prepare an adjusted trial balance.

LO7   Prepare financial statements from an adjusted trial balance.

*Appendix 3A

LO8   Explain and prepare correcting entries.

*Appendix 3B

LO9   Identify and explain an alternative in recording prepaid assets and unearned revenues.

An asterisk (*) identifies appendix material.

"Being Green Is the New Sexy"

Doug Burgoyne founded Vancouver-based Frogbox Inc. in 2008 to pursue his goal of filling a niche in the $5 billion residential moving market by creating an eco-friendly alternative to cardboard moving boxes. The company's mission is to "minimize the stress of moving on (their) customers and on the earth." The business plan? To drop off green, reusable boxes to your current home or office and pick them up empty at your new place. It's convenient and affordable as well as appealing to the go-green mindset. Cardboard boxes can be used twice, on average, while a plastic Frogbox can be cleaned and reused about 400 times before needing to be recycled. Frogbox doesn't stop there. In addition to providing recycled packing paper and other eco-friendly moving supplies, its delivery trucks are equipped with software that maps routes to efficiently schedule deliveries and pickups, reducing mileage and, thereby, greenhouse gas emissions.

Frogbox's appearance on the popular CBC television show *Dragons' Den* attracted significant attention from prospective North American franchisees. Doug convinced Jim Treliving and Brett Wilson to invest $200,000 in return for a 13% equity stake in the company.

Frogbox seems to have all its bases covered. In addition to managing the business from an accounting perspective, it has also consciously taken steps to be socially responsible—Frogbox donates 1 percent of its gross revenues to frog-habitat restoration projects, including the Vancouver Aquarium's Oregon Spotted Frog Recovery and BC Frogwatch programs. "We want to run the company in every way we can with the lowest environmental footprint . . . we believe that we can be a successful business and do what is right for the environment—both at the same time."

Doug categorized a great company as one that has three main attributes: "happy customers, happy employees and a positive bottom line." He believed that "as an entrepreneur it's critical to have proper accounting data to drive strategic decisions in the business. Without proper accounting it's not possible to fully understand the impact of the decisions a business makes." In 2014, Doug passed away due to cancer and his "entrepreneurial energy" was greatly missed. His wife Celeste has since jumped into the business and began to manage it hands on, having left her position as VP of Global Store Operations at Lululemon Athletica Inc.

During its first nine years in operation, the business has grown across Canada to 17 locations and has pursued an international expansion strategy, successfully establishing itself in the U.S. market with locations in Seattle, Washington; Boise, Idaho; and Minneapolis, Minnesota. In the future, Frogbox is focussed on continued growth in leaps and bounds!

Sources: www.frogbox.com; http://www.vancouversun.com/business/smallbusiness/Vancouver+Frogbox+makes+smooth+transition+after/10998693/story.html#__federated=1; http://www.makeitbusiness.com/frogbox-on-the-path-to-greatness, accessed 08/2014

Video Links: Frogbox Dragon's Den Episode: http://www.cbc.ca/dragonsden/pitches/frogbox
          Frogbox Dragon's Den Update: http://www.cbc.ca/player/Shows/Shows/Dragons'+Den/Web+Exclusives/Where+Are+They+Now%3F/ID/2120672219/

2014 Update: http://www.vancouversun.com/business/smallbusiness/Vancouver+Frogbox+makes+smooth+transition+after/10998693/story.html#__federated=1

| CRITICAL THINKING CHALLENGE | Assuming you are promoted to a VP of finance role at Frogbox Inc., how might you inflate earnings to create a better image with potential investors? Explain how GAAP would be violated by this strategy. |

CHAPTER PREVIEW

Financial statements reflect revenues when earned and expenses when incurred. This is known as *accrual basis accounting*. Accrual basis accounting is achieved by following the steps of the accounting cycle. We described the first four of these steps in Chapter 2.

An important part of the accounting cycle is the adjustment of account balances. The adjusted account balances are what is reported in the financial statements that are prepared according to generally accepted accounting principles. Adjustment of accounts is necessary so that financial statements at the

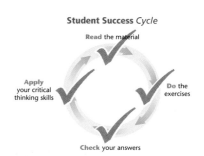

Student Success *Cycle*

Read the material

Apply your critical thinking skills

Do the exercises

Check your answers

end of a reporting period reflect the effects of all transactions. This chapter emphasizes Steps 5 and 6 of the accounting cycle as highlighted in Exhibit 3.1. Preparation of financial statements, Step 7 of the accounting cycle, is reinforced in this chapter, with an emphasis on how *adjusting entries* impact the financial statements. Companies like **Frogbox Inc.**, in the chapter opening vignette, use adjusting entries to ensure their financial statements are fairly stated. To illustrate the adjusting process, we continue with the example of Organico used in previous chapters.

Purpose of Adjusting

LO1 Describe the purpose of adjusting accounts at the end of a period.

The usual process during an accounting period is to record *external transactions*. **External transactions** are exchanges between two parties; these were the focus of Chapters 1 and 2. After external transactions are recorded, several accounts in the ledger need adjustment for their balances to appear in financial statements. This need arises because *internal transactions* remain unrecorded. **Internal transactions** represent exchanges within an organization that affect the accounting equation and are the focus of this chapter.

An example is the cost of certain assets that expire or are used up as time passes. The Prepaid Insurance account of Organico is one of these. Organico's trial balance (Exhibit 3.2) shows Prepaid Insurance with a balance of $2,400. This amount is the premium for two years of insurance protection beginning on March 1, 2017. By March 31, 2017, because one month's coverage is used up, the $2,400 is no longer the correct account balance for Prepaid Insurance. The Prepaid Insurance account balance must be reduced by one month's cost, or $100 ($2,400/24 months). The income statement must report this $100 cost as insurance expense for March.

EXHIBIT 3.1

Steps in the Accounting Cycle Introduced in Chapter 3

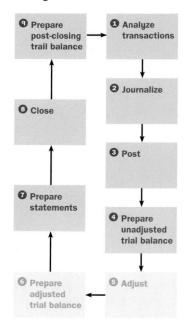

① Prepare post-closing trail balance

❶ Analyze transactions

❷ Journalize

❽ Close

❸ Post

❼ Prepare statements

❹ Prepare unadjusted trial balance

❻ Prepare adjusted trial balance

❺ Adjust

EXHIBIT 3.2

Trial Balance

Organico Trial Balance March 31, 2017		
	Debit	**Credit**
Cash	$ 8,070	
Accounts receivable	-0-	
Prepaid insurance	2,400	
Supplies	3,600	
Equipment	6,000	
Accounts payable		$ 200
Unearned food services revenue		3,000
Notes payable		6,000
Hailey Walker, capital		10,000
Hailey Walker, withdrawals	600	
Food services revenue		3,800
Teaching revenue		300
Rent expense	1,000	
Salaries expense	1,400	
Utilities expense	230	
Totals	$23,300	$23,300

Another example is the $3,600 balance in Supplies. Part of this balance includes the cost of supplies that were used in March. The cost of the supplies used must be reported as an expense in March. The balances of both the Prepaid Insurance and Supplies accounts must be *adjusted* before they are reported on the March 31 balance sheet.

Another adjustment necessary for Organico relates to one month's usage of equipment. The balances of the Unearned Food Services Revenue, Food Services Revenue, and Salaries Expense accounts often also need adjusting before they appear on the statements. We explain *why* this adjusting process is carried out in the next section.

GAAP and the Adjusting Process

LO2 Explain how the timeliness, matching, and revenue recognition principles affect the adjusting process.

The adjusting process is based on three generally accepted accounting principles: the timeliness principle, the revenue recognition principle, and the matching principle. In this section, we explain how GAAP principles contribute to the usefulness of financial statements.

The Accounting Period

The adjusting process is often linked to timeliness of information. Information must reach decision makers frequently and promptly; therefore, accounting systems need to prepare periodic reports at regular intervals. This results in an accounting process impacted by the timeliness principle.[1] The **timeliness**

---

1   IFRS 2014, IAS 1, para. 36; "Framework," para. QC29.

principle assumes that an organization's activities can be divided into specific time periods such as a month, a three-month quarter, or a year, as illustrated in Exhibit 3.3. It requires that statements be presented at least annually.

EXHIBIT 3.3

Accounting Periods—For Year-End Adjusting Entries TIMING IS EVERYTHING!

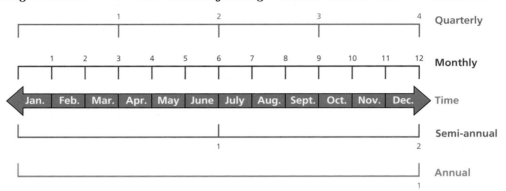

Time periods covered by statements are called **accounting periods** (or **reporting periods**). Reports covering a one-year period are known as *annual financial statements*. Recall that a company can adopt a *fiscal year* based on the *calendar year* or its *natural business year*. Many organizations also prepare **interim financial reports** covering one, three (quarterly), or six (semi-annual) months of activity.

The annual reporting period is not always a calendar year ending on December 31. An organization can adopt a fiscal year consisting of any 12 consecutive months. It is also acceptable to adopt an annual reporting period of 52 weeks. For example, **Gap**'s fiscal year consistently ends the final week of January or the first week of February each year.

Companies with little seasonal variation in sales often choose the calendar year as their fiscal year. For example, **Facebook, Inc.** uses calendar-year reporting. However, the financial statements of **The Kellogg Company** (the company that controls characters such as Tony the Tiger, Snap! Crackle! Pop! and the Keebler Elf) reflect a fiscal year that ends on the Saturday nearest December 31. Companies experiencing seasonal variations in sales often choose a natural business year-end, which is when sales activities are at their lowest level for the year. The natural business year for retailers such as **Walmart**, **Target**, and **Macy's** usually ends around January 31, after the holiday season. **Danier Leather Inc.** opted for a floating year-end that falls on the last Saturday in June each year. Likely this it is because summer is Danier's slowest sales season.

Recognizing Revenues and Expenses

Because it is critical for external users to understand how the company performed financially compared to previous years, accounting standard-setting bodies developed a set of principles to clarify the appropriate level of revenue and expense to report. Two main generally accepted accounting principles are used in the adjusting process: the *matching principle* and the *revenue recognition principle*. The **matching principle** aims to report or *match* expenses in the same accounting period as the revenues they helped to earn.[2] For example, assume that as part of an upcoming catering event Organico is to supply a customized menu and event plan to a corporate customer in May. Hailey agreed on a price of $500 with her customer for the menu/event plan. In the process of earning this $500 in revenue, Organico will use $150 of office supplies purchased and paid for in April. The $150 of office supplies used in May is an expense that will be reported on the May income statement even though the supplies were purchased and paid for in April. The $150 of office supplies used in May must be *matched* against the $500 of May revenues in accordance with the matching principle. Financial statements will reflect accurate information about the profit actually earned during the period only if expenses are properly matched against the revenues they helped to create.

To illustrate *revenue recognition*, we will look at two situations. First, assume that in May, Organico teaches a healthy cooking class for a fee of $500 to a Foodie club at a local college and collects the cash from the students immediately. The $500 of revenue is earned in May and is reported on the May income statement in accordance with the revenue recognition principle. Second, assume that Organico collected $1,000 cash in May for work to be done in June. The $1,000 of revenue will be earned in June and will therefore be reported on the June income statement; the $1,000 will *not* be reported as revenue in May because it has not yet been earned. A major goal of the adjusting process is to have revenue *recognized* (reported) in the time period when it is *earned* regardless of when the cash is actually received. This concept is the foundation on which the *accrual basis of accounting* was developed.

Accrual Basis Compared to Cash Basis

LO3   Explain accrual accounting and cash basis accounting and how accrual accounting adds to the usefulness of financial statements.

Accrual basis accounting is founded on the revenue recognition principle, where revenues and expenses are *recognized* or recorded when earned or incurred regardless of when cash is received or paid. The word *accrual* and its root word *accrue* mean *to accumulate* or *to add*. So accrual basis accounting means that revenues and expenses must be *added* or *matched* to the *time period* in which they actually happened; when cash was received or paid is irrelevant to the recording of revenues and expenses. Accrual basis accounting, then, is based on the three GAAP of *revenue recognition, matching*, and *timeliness*.

In contrast, **cash basis accounting** recognizes revenues and expenses when *cash* is received or paid. Cash basis accounting for the income statement, balance sheet, and statement of changes in equity is *not* consistent with generally accepted accounting principles. It is commonly held that accrual basis accounting provides a better indication of business performance than information about current cash receipts and payments. Accrual basis accounting also increases the comparability of financial statements from one period to another. Yet information about cash flows is also useful. This is why companies also include a cash flow statement, discussed in Chapter 16.

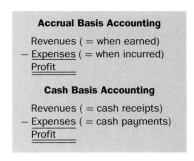

Accrual Basis Accounting

Revenues (= when earned)
− Expenses (= when incurred)
Profit

Cash Basis Accounting

Revenues (= cash receipts)
− Expenses (= cash payments)
Profit

Important Tip: The cash basis of accounting is not an acceptable method for use in financial reporting. IFRS and Canadian ASPE Standards require companies to use the accrual basis of accounting. CRA also requires companies to adopt the accrual basis of accounting.

---

2   IFRS 2014, IAS 18, para. 19; "Framework," para. 4.50.

Chris Brown Tweets "The Vancouver Show is a FAKE"

Chronico Music Group is a Canadian concert organizer based in Vancouver, BC. At a pre-awards party for the 2011 MTV Music Awards in Hollywood, CA, a couple of talent buyers from BC's Chronico Music Group were approached by a man claiming to be an agent representing the hip-hop and R&B star Chris Brown. After checking a few of the agent's references, Chronico wrote a cheque in the name of Chris Brown's manager—Tina Davis—as a deposit to schedule a concert at the Pacific Coliseum in Vancouver on November 10, 2011. After issuing a press release to announce the venue, Chronico was notified by Davis that they must have been misrepresented by the agent, as Vancouver wasn't on the tour. The questionable agent set up a fake bank account in the name of Tina Davis. Chronico lost its deposit and was shaken over the experience. How would this fraudulent event have impacted Chronico's 2011 Income Statement? In the future, how could Chronico prevent this from happening?

SOURCES: *The Globe and Mail,* September 28, 2011; http://news.nationalpost.com/arts/vancouver-chris-brown-show-revealed-as-fraud-cancelled#__federated=1; http://blogs.vancouversun.com/2011/09/27/chris-browns-vancouver-concert-cancelled-due-to-fraud/.

1. Describe a company's annual reporting period.
2. Why do companies prepare interim financial statements?
3. What accounting principles most directly lead to the adjusting process?
4. Is cash basis accounting consistent with generally accepted accounting principles?

Do Quick Study questions: QS 3-1, QS 3-2, QS 3-3

Adjusting Accounts

The process of adjusting accounts is similar to our process of analyzing and recording transactions in Chapter 2. We must analyze each account balance and the transactions that affect it to determine any needed adjustments. An **adjusting entry** is recorded at the *end* of the accounting period to bring an asset or liability account balance to its proper amount. This entry also updates the related expense or revenue account and is necessary to prepare the financial statements. Adjustments are journalized in the general journal and then posted to accounts in the ledger—this is the same process described in Chapter 2 for routine transactions. This next section demonstrates how to handle common adjusting entries and their relationship to the adjusted trial balance and period-end financial statements.

Framework for Adjustments

LO4 Prepare and explain adjusting entries for prepaid expenses, depreciation, unearned revenues, accrued expenses, and accrued revenues.

Exhibit 3.4 identifies the five main adjustments, each of which is detailed in the following sections. As you navigate through each example, pay close attention to the logic behind which accounts are debited/credited and why the adjusting entry is required at period end. Each entry requires consideration of the timing of cash receipt or payment in comparison to when the revenue is earned or the matched expense has been incurred.

EXHIBIT 3.4

Framework For Adjustments

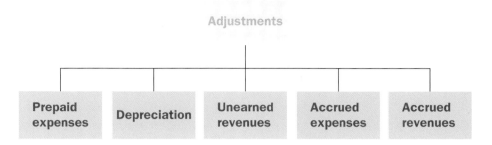

Adjusting Prepaid Expenses

Prepaid expenses[3] refer to costs *paid for* in advance of receiving their benefits. Don't be fooled by the name, *prepaid expenses are assets.* As these assets are used, their costs become expenses. Three common prepaid expenses are insurance, rent payments made in advance, and supplies purchased for use in the business. When the payment is initially made, it is important for businesses to capture these costs as assets—labelled as prepaid expenses. In general, the benefits of prepaid expenses are utilized within a year, thus they are classified as current assets. The adjusting entry comes into effect at period-end when these assets have been depleted through direct usage or usage due to the passing of time.

EXHIBIT 3.5

Adjusting for Prepaid Expenses

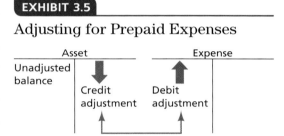

Adjusting entries for prepaids involve increasing (debiting) expenses and decreasing (crediting) prepaid assets as shown in Exhibit 3.5.

PREPAID INSURANCE

We illustrate prepaid insurance using Organico's payment of $2,400 for two years of insurance protection beginning on March 1, 2017. The following entry records the purchase of the insurance:

Mar.	1	Prepaid Insurance..	2,400	
		Cash..		2,400
		To record purchase of insurance for 24 months.		

By March 31, one month's insurance coverage is used, causing a portion of the asset Prepaid Insurance to become an expense. This expense is $100 ($2,400 × 1/24). Our adjusting entry to record this expense and reduce the asset is:

Adjustment (a)

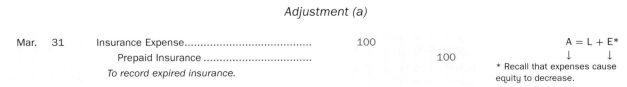

Mar.	31	Insurance Expense..	100	
		Prepaid Insurance		100
		To record expired insurance.		

$A = L + E^*$
↓   ↓
* Recall that expenses cause equity to decrease.

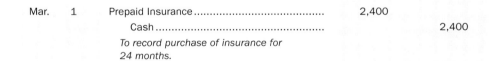

---

3 Prepaids are also called *deferrals* because the recognition of the expense or revenue on the income statement is *deferred* to a future accounting period.

Posting this adjusting entry affects the accounts shown in Exhibit 3.6:

EXHIBIT 3.6

Insurance Accounts After Adjusting for Prepaids

Prepaid Insurance				Insurance Expense	
Mar. 1	2,400	100	Mar. 31	Mar. 31	100
Balance	2,300				

After posting, the $100 balance in Insurance Expense and the $2,300 balance in Prepaid Insurance are ready for reporting in the financial statements. If the adjustment is *not* made at March 31, then (a) expenses are *understated* by $100 and profit is *overstated* by $100 for the March income statement, and (b) both Prepaid Insurance and equity are overstated by $100 in the March 31 balance sheet.

An **understated account** is too low. For example, if Revenue has a balance of $100 and it is understated by $20, the correct balance is $120. An **overstated account** is too high. For example, if Equipment has a balance of $450 and it is overstated by $40, the correct balance is $410.

SUPPLIES

Organico purchased $3,600 of supplies in March and used some of them during this month. Daily usage of supplies is not generally recorded for accounting purposes because of the difficulty of tracking each miscellaneous item used (each piece of paper, pen, pencil etc). When we report account balances in financial statements at the end of a month, making only one adjusting entry at that time can reduce recordkeeping costs. This entry needs to record the total cost of all supplies used in the month.

The cost of supplies used during March must be determined to recognized supplies expense. Organico calculates ("takes inventory of") the remaining unused supplies. The cost of the remaining supplies is then deducted from the cost of the purchased supplies (plus any supplies left over from the prior month) to calculate the amount used for March. Organico has **$2,550** of supplies remaining out of the **$3,600** ($2,500 + $1,100) purchased in March. The $1,050 difference between these two amounts is the cost of the supplies used. This amount is March's Supplies Expense. Our adjusting entry to record this expense and reduce the Supplies asset account is:

Adjustment (b)

A = L + E	Mar.	31	Supplies Expense	1,050	
↓			Supplies..		1,050
↓			*To record supplies used.*		

Posting this adjusting entry affects the accounts shown in Exhibit 3.7:

EXHIBIT 3.7

Supplies Ledger Accounts After Adjusting for Prepaids

Supplies				Supplies Expense	
Mar. 1	2,500	1,050	Mar. 31	Mar. 31	1,050
1	1,100				
Balance	2,550				

The balance of the Supplies account is $2,550 after posting and equals the cost of remaining unused supplies. If the adjustment is *not* made at March 31, then (a) expenses are understated by $1,050 and profit is overstated by $1,050 for the March income statement, and (b) both Supplies and equity are overstated by $1,050 in the March 31 balance sheet.

OTHER PREPAID EXPENSES

There are other prepaid expenses (including Prepaid Rent), which are accounted for in exactly the same manner as Insurance and Supplies above. We should also note that some prepaid expenses are both paid for and fully used up within a single accounting period. One example is when a company pays monthly rent on the first day of each month. The payment creates a prepaid expense on the first day of each month that fully expires by the end of the month. In these special cases, we can record the cash paid with a debit to the expense account instead of an asset account.

DECISION MAKER
Answer—End of chapter

Investor

A small publishing company signed a well-known athlete to write a book. The company paid the athlete $500,000 today and will pay future book royalties. A note to the company's financial statements indicates "prepaid expenses include $500,000 in author signing fees to be matched against future expected sales." Is this accounting for the signing bonus acceptable? How might it affect your analysis as an investor in the publishing company?

CHECKPOINT

5. If the entry to adjust Prepaid Insurance was not recorded, what effect would this have on each of the three components of the accounting equation (Assets, Liabilities, and Equities)?

Do Quick Study questions: QS 3-4, QS 3-5, QS 3-6

Adjusting for Depreciation[4]

Property, plant, and equipment (PPE) are assets owned and controlled by the business as a result of past transactions and used within the business to produce and sell products and services. PPE also includes **intangible assets** (such as patents). Both of these asset groups are expected to provide benefits for more than one accounting period. Examples of property, plant, and equipment assets are land, buildings, machines, vehicles, and furniture. Because these assets (except for land) wear out or decline in usefulness as they are used, an expense must be recorded to match the cost of the asset over the time the asset helped earn revenues. **Depreciation** is the process of calculating expense from matching (or allocating) the cost of plant and equipment assets over their expected useful lives. Businesses that have significant dollars invested in plant and equipment can have large amounts of depreciation appearing on the income statement. For example, **Air Canada** reported buildings and equipment at a value of $5,073,000 with $500 million of corresponding depreciation in its December 31, 2013, financial statements. **WestJet**, on its December 31,

---

4   Prior to 2011, the term **amortization** was used instead of *depreciation*. IFRS use the terminology *depreciation* for plant and equipment (IFRS 2014, IAS 16, para. 43). *Amortization* will continue to be used for intangible assets (IFRS 2014, IAS 38, para. 97). *Intangible assets include items such as copyrights, patents, and trademarks* and are introduced in Chapter 4. *Amortization* for intangible assets is discussed in more detail in Chapter 9.

2013 statements, reported its property, plant, and equipment at a value of $2,487,734 with depreciation expense of $191,794,000.

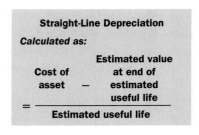

Organico uses equipment in earning revenue. This equipment's cost must be depreciated to match the cost of the equipment over the time that the equipment helps earn revenue. Recall that Organico purchased its food truck for $6,000 on March 1. Hailey Walker expects the equipment to have a useful life (benefit period) of two years. Hailey expects to sell the truck for about $1,200 at the end of two years. This means that the *net cost* expected to expire over the estimated useful life is $4,800 (= $6,000 − $1,200).

There are several methods that we can use to allocate this $4,800 net cost to expense. Organico uses *straight-line depreciation.*[5] The **straight-line depreciation method** allocates equal amounts of an asset's net cost over its estimated useful life. When the $4,800 net cost is divided by the asset's useful life of 24 months (2 years × 12 months per year), we get an average monthly cost of $200 ($4,800/24). Our adjusting entry to record monthly depreciation expense is:

Calculation:

$$= \frac{\$6,000 - \$1,200}{24 \text{ months}} = \underline{\$200} \text{ per month}$$

Adjustment (c)

A = L + E		Mar.	31	Depreciation Expense, Equipment............................	200	
↓	↓			Accumulated Depreciation, Equipment...............		200
				To record monthly depreciation on equipment		

Posting this adjusting entry affects the accounts shown in Exhibit 3.8:

EXHIBIT 3.8

Accounts After Depreciation Adjustments

Equipment				Accumulated Depreciation, Equipment			Depreciation Expense, Equipment		
Mar. 1	6,000				200	Mar. 31	Mar. 31	200	
Bal.	6,000								

Accumulated depreciation is recorded in a *contra asset account.* A **contra account** is an account that is linked with another account and has an opposite normal balance to its counterpart. It is reported at the net amount, after subtracting the contra account from the normal account balance. On Organico's balance sheet, the balance in the contra asset account, *Accumulated Depreciation, Equipment,* will be subtracted from the Equipment account balance as shown in Exhibit 3.10. The cost of an asset less its accumulated depreciation is the net **book value of an asset**. The **market value of an asset** is the amount it can be sold for. It is important to note that market value and book values do not agree because book values are based on historical costs less residual and depreciation will not match perfectly with swings in the current market values.

After posting the adjustment, the *Equipment* account less its *Accumulated Depreciation, Equipment* account equals the March 31 balance sheet amount for this asset. The balance in the Depreciation Expense,

---

5 We investigate the different types of *depreciation* methods in Chapter 9. We briefly describe the straight-line method here to help you understand the adjusting process.

Equipment account is the expense reported in the March income statement. If the adjustment is *not* made at March 31, then (1) expenses are understated by $200 and profit is overstated by $200 for the March income statement, and (2) both assets and equity are overstated by $200 in the March 31 balance sheet.

The use of the contra asset account Accumulated Depreciation allows balance sheet readers to know both the cost of assets and the total amount of depreciation charged to expense to date. The title of the contra account to the Equipment asset account is *Accumulated* Depreciation. This means that the account includes *total* depreciation expense for all prior periods when the assets were being used. Organico's Equipment and Accumulated Depreciation, Equipment accounts would appear on May 31, 2017, as shown in Exhibit 3.10, after the three monthly adjusting entries detailed in Exhibit 3.9.

EXHIBIT 3.9

Accounts After Three Months of Depreciation Adjustments

Equipment			Accumulated Depreciation, Equipment		
Mar. 1	6,000			200	Mar. 31
				200	Apr. 30
				200	May 31
Total	6,000			600	Total

EXHIBIT 3.10

Accumulated Depreciation Contra Account in the Balance Sheet

Assets		
Cash..		$ ____
Equipment	**$6,000**	
Less: Accumulated depreciation	600	**5,400**
Total assets		$ ____

CHECKPOINT

6. If the year-end adjusting entry to record depreciation expense were not recorded, what effect would this have on each component of the accounting equation?

7. Explain what a contra account is.

Do Quick Study questions: QS 3-7, QS 3-8

DECISION MAKER
Answer—End of chapter

Small Business Owner

You are preparing to make an offer to purchase a small family-run restaurant. The manager gives you a copy of her depreciation schedule for the restaurant's building and equipment. It shows costs of $75,000 and accumulated depreciation of $55,000. This leaves a net total for building and equipment of $20,000. Is this information valuable in deciding on a purchase offer for the restaurant?

Adjusting Unearned Revenues

Unearned revenues refer to cash received in advance of providing products and services. Unearned revenues, also known as *deferred revenues*, are a *liability*. When cash is accepted, an obligation to provide products and services is also accepted. As products and services are provided, the amount of unearned revenues becomes *earned* revenues. Adjusting entries for unearned revenues involve increasing (crediting) revenues and decreasing (debiting) unearned revenues as shown in Exhibit 3.11. These adjustments reflect economic events (including passage of time) that impact unearned revenues.

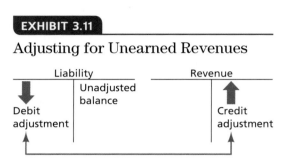

EXHIBIT 3.11

Adjusting for Unearned Revenues

We see an example of unearned revenues in **Telus'** 2013 annual report. Telus reports unearned revenue of $729 million on its balance sheet that includes customer deposits and amounts received related to services to be provided in the future. Another example is WestJet, which reports advance (unearned) ticket sales at December 31, 2013, of $551 million.

Organico also has unearned revenues. On March 26, Organico agreed to cater a series of Tuesday night ski/snowboard instructor training events over the next two months for a local ski hill called Mount Mundy. When the contract was signed, the ski hill paid Organico $3,000 for the series. The entry to record the cash received in advance is:

Mar.	26	Cash	3,000	
		Unearned Food Services Revenue		3,000
		Received advance payment for future		
		ski/snowboard catering services for		
		Mount Mundy.		

This advance payment increases cash and creates an obligation to provide catering services over the next two months. As time passes, Organico will earn this payment. No external transactions are linked with this earnings process. By March 31, Organico provided food services in the amount of $250 for the first "Train the Trainer" event. The revenue recognition principle requires that $250 of unearned revenue is reported as food services revenue on the March income statement. The adjusting entry to reduce the liability account and recognize earned revenue is:

Adjustment (d)

A = L + E*
  ↓ ↑

* Recall that revenues cause equity to increase.

Mar.	31	Unearned Food Services Revenue	250	
		Food Services Revenue		250
		To record the earned portion of revenue received		
		in advance		

The accounts look as shown in Exhibit 3.12 after posting the adjusting entry.

EXHIBIT 3.12

Unearned Revenue and Revenue Accounts After Adjustments

Unearned Food Services Revenue			
Mar. 31	**250**	3,000	Mar. 26
		2,750	Balance

Food Services Revenue		
	2,200	Mar. 10
	1,600	15
	250	31
	4,050	Total

The adjusting entry transfers $250 out of Unearned Food Services Revenue (a liability account) to a revenue account. If the adjustment is *not* made, then (a) revenue and profit are understated by $250 in the March income statement, and (b) Unearned Food Services Revenue is overstated and equity understated by $250 on the March 31 balance sheet.

CHECKPOINT

8. AltaCo credited Unearned Revenue for $20,000 received on November 3, 2017, for work to be done just prior to year-end. The work was completed as scheduled. If Unearned Revenue is not adjusted at year-end to reflect the completion of the work, which GAAP will be violated and why?

9. Describe how unearned revenue arises. Give an example.

Do Quick Study questions: QS 3-9, QS 3-10

Adjusting Accrued Expenses

Accrued expenses refer to costs incurred in a period that are both unpaid and unrecorded prior to adjustment. Generally they relate to expenses incurred for services provided or products received for which the company has yet to be billed. For example, **Telus Corporation** reported $1,735 million of accounts payable and accrued liabilities on its December 31, 2013, balance sheet. Accrued expenses are part of expenses and reported on the income statement. Adjusting entries for recording accrued expenses involve increasing (debiting) expenses and recording the required accounts payable, crediting liabilities as shown in Exhibit 3.13.

Common examples of accrued expenses are interest, salaries, rent, and taxes. We use interest and salaries to show how to adjust accounts for accrued expenses.

EXHIBIT 3.13

Adjusting for Accrued Expenses

Expense	Liability
Debit adjustment	Credit adjustment

ACCRUED INTEREST EXPENSE

It is common for companies to have accrued interest expense on notes payable, certain accounts payable and other debt at the end of an accounting period. Interest expense is incurred with the passage of time. Unless interest is paid on the last day of an accounting period, we need to adjust accounts for interest expense incurred but not yet paid.

Interest of $35 has accrued on Organico's $6,000, 7%, six-month note payable for the month of March.[6] The journal entry is:

Adjustment (e)

A = L + E	Mar.	31	Interest Expense..	35	
↑ ↓			Interest Payable..		35
			To record accrued interest.		

After the adjusting entry is posted, the expense and liability accounts appear as shown in Exhibit 3.14.

EXHIBIT 3.14

Notes Payable and Interest Accounts After Accrual Adjustments

Notes Payable			Interest Payable			Interest Expense		
	6,000	Mar. 1	Mar. 31	35			35	Mar. 31

This means that $35 of interest expense is reported on the income statement and that $35 interest payable is reported on the balance sheet. Notice that the Notes Payable account is *not* affected by recording interest. If the interest adjustment is not made, then (a) Interest Expense is understated and profit overstated by $35 in the March income statement, and (b) Interest Payable is understated and equity overstated by $35 on the March 31 balance sheet.

> Interest = Principal of the note × Annual interest rate × Time expressed years OR $i = Prt$
>
> Where the term of the note is in days,
>
> $$\text{Interest} = \text{Principal} \times \text{Rate} \times \frac{\text{Exact days}}{365}.$$

The $6,000 principal and total interest of $210 ($6,000 × 7% × 6/12 = $210) will be paid six months from March 1, the date the note was issued.[7]

ACCRUED SALARIES EXPENSE

Organico's only employee earns $70 per day or $350 for a five-day workweek beginning on Monday and ending on Friday. This employee gets paid every two weeks on Friday. On the 14th and the 28th of March, the wages are paid, recorded in the journal, and posted to the ledger. The *unadjusted* Salaries Expense and Cash paid for salaries appear as shown in Exhibit 3.15.

EXHIBIT 3.15

Salary and Cash Accounts Before Adjusting

Cash			Salaries Expense		
700	Mar. 14		Mar. 14	700	
700	28		28	**700**	

---

6 Interest on the $6,000, 7%, six-month note payable was calculated using the above formula

Therefore $6,000 × 7% × $\frac{1}{12}$ = $35.

Interest is discussed in greater detail in Chapter 9.

7 When the note payable and accrued interest are paid to the lender on September 1, six months after the date of issue on March 1, the entry would be (assuming interest expense of $35 per month has accrued):

Sept.	1	Notes Payable..	6,000	
		Interest Payable	210	
		Cash..		6,210
		To record payment of note payable and accrued interest.		

The calendar in Exhibit 3.16 shows one working day after the March 28 payday (March 31). This means that the employee earns one day's salary by the close of business on Monday, March 31. While this salary expense is incurred, it is not yet paid or recorded by the company. The period-end adjusting entry to account for accrued salaries is:

Adjustment (f)

Mar. 31	Salaries Expense..	70		A = L + E
	Salaries Payable...		70	↑ ↓
	To record one day's accrued salary; 1 × $70.			

EXHIBIT 3.16

Salary Accrual Period and Paydays

March						
Sun	Mon	Tue	Wed	Thu	Fri	Sat
			1	2	3	4
5	6	7	8	9	10	11
12	13	14	15	16	17	18
19	20	21	22	23	24	25
26	27	28	29	30	31	

April						
Sun	Mon	Tue	Wed	Thu	Fri	Sat
						1
2	3	4	5	6	7	8
9	10	11	12	13	14	15
16	17	18	19	20	21	22
23	24	25	26	27	28	29
30						

Salary expense incurred ———┘   Payday   Payday

After the adjusting entry is posted, the expense and liability accounts appear as shown in Exhibit 3.17.

EXHIBIT 3.17

Salary Accounts After Accrual Adjustments

Salaries Expense			**Salaries Payable**	
Mar. 14	700		70	**Mar. 31**
28	700			
31	**70**			
Total	1,470			

This means that $1,470 of salaries expense is reported on the income statement and that $70 in salaries payable (liability) is reported in the balance sheet. If the adjustment is *not* made, then (1) Salaries Expense is understated and net profit overstated by $70 in the March income statement, and (2) Salaries Payable is understated and equity overstated by $70 on the March 31 balance sheet.

The accrued salaries are paid on the first payday of the next biweekly period, which occurs on Friday, April 11. The entry includes the added salaries expense for the nine days worked in April:

Apr. 11	Salaries Payable..	70		
	Salaries Expense	630		
	Cash...		700	
	Paid two weeks' salary including one day			
	accrued in March (1 day at $70; 9 days			
	at $70 = $630).			

CHECKPOINT

10. In error, the May utility bill for $6,900 was not included in the May 31 adjusting entries. What effect would this error have on the components of the accounting equation?

11. What is an accrued expense? Give an example.

12. Digitalworld.com, an internet-based music store, records $1,000 of accrued salaries on December 31. Five days later on January 5 (the next payday), salaries of $7,000 are paid. What is the January 5 entry?

Do Quick Study questions: QS 3-11, QS 3-12, QS 3-13

DECISION MAKER Answer—End of chapter

Financial Officer

At year-end, the president instructs you, the financial officer, not to record accrued expenses until next year because they will not be paid until then. The president also directs you to record in the current-year sales a recent purchase order from a customer that requires merchandise to be delivered two weeks after the year-end. Your company would report profit instead of a loss if you carried out these instructions. What will you do?

Adjusting Accrued Revenues

When products and services are delivered, we expect to receive payment for them. **Accrued revenues** refer to revenues earned in a period that are both unrecorded and not yet received in cash (or other assets). Accrued revenues are part of revenues and must be reported on the income statement. The adjusting entries increase (debit) assets and increase (credit) revenues as shown in Exhibit 3.18.

EXHIBIT 3.18

Adjusting for Accrued Revenues

Common examples of accrued revenues are fees for services and products, interest income, and rent revenue. We use service fees and interest income to show how to adjust accounts for accrued revenues.

ACCRUED SERVICES REVENUE

Accrued revenue is revenue that is earned but not yet recorded because either the customer has not paid for them or the seller has not yet billed the customer. Organico provides us with an example of accrued revenue. In the second week of March, Organico agrees to provide daily lunch catering services at 11:00 am to a local builder on a residential building project for a fixed fee of $2,700 per month to feed the staff for the period from March 11 to April 10, or 30 days of service. The client agrees to pay $2,700 cash to Organico on April 10, 2017, when the catering service period is complete.

At March 31, 2017, 20 days of catering services are already provided to the client. Since the contracted services are not yet entirely provided, the client is not yet billed nor has Organico recorded the services already provided. Organico has earned $1,800 (= $2,700 × 20/30). The *revenue recognition principle* requires that we report the $1,800 on the March income statement because it is earned in March. The balance sheet also must report that this client owes Organico $1,800. The adjusting entry to account for accrued teaching services revenue is:

Adjustment (g)

Mar. 31	Accounts Receivable	1,800		A = L + E	
	Food Services Revenue..		1,800	↑	↑
	To record 20 days' accrued revenue.				

After the adjusting entry is posted, the affected accounts look as shown in Exhibit 3.19.

EXHIBIT 3.19

Receivable and Revenue Accounts After Accrual Adjustments

Accounts Receivable				Food Services Revenue	
Mar. 15	1,900	1,900	Mar. 25	2,200	Mar. 10
31	1,800			1,600	15
Balance	1,800			250	31
				1,800	31
				5,850	Total

Accounts receivable are reported on the balance sheet at $1,800, and $5,850 of revenues are reported on the income statement. If the adjustment is *not* made, then (1) both Food Services Revenue and profit are understated by $1,800 in the March income statement, and (2) both Accounts Receivable and equity are understated by $1,800 on the March 31 balance sheet.

When the catering fee is received from the builder on April 10, Organico makes the following entry to remove the accrued asset (accounts receivable) and recognize the added 10 days of revenue earned in April:

Apr. 10	Cash	2,700	
	Accounts Receivable		1,800
	Food Services Revenue		900
	Received cash for accrued asset and earned		
	teaching revenue; $900 = $2,700 × 10/30		

ACCRUED INTEREST INCOME

In addition to the accrued interest expense we described earlier, interest can yield accrued revenue when a company is owed money (or other assets) by a debtor. If a company is holding notes or accounts receivable that produce interest income, we must adjust the accounts to record any earned and yet uncollected interest income. The adjusting entry is recorded as a debit to Interest Receivable (asset) and a credit to Interest Income (equity). The approach to calculate interest income is the same as was discussed previously to calculate interest payable on a note.

 **CHECKPOINT**

13. An adjusting entry to record $6,000 of accrued interest income was omitted due to an oversight. What effect would this error have on the components of the accounting equation?

Do Quick Study question: QS 3-14

Adjustments and Financial Statements

LO5   Explain how accounting adjustments link to financial statements.

Exhibit 3.20 lists the five major types of transactions requiring adjustment. Understanding this exhibit is important to understanding the adjusting process and its link to financial statements. Remember that each adjusting entry affects both income statement accounts and balance sheet accounts.

EXHIBIT 3.20

Summary of Adjustments and Financial Statement Impact

Type	Before Adjusting		Adjusting Entry		
	Balance Sheet Account	Income Statement Account			
Prepaid Expense	Asset & equity overstated	Expense understated	Dr Expense.............. XX Cr Asset............... XX		where XX = how much of the prepaid was used during the period
Depreciation/ Amortization	Asset & equity overstated	Expense understated	Dr Expense.............. XX Cr Contra Asset XX		where XX = how much of the asset's cost was matched as an expense to the period
Unearned Revenues	Liability overstated; equity understated	Revenue understated	Dr Liability............... XX Cr Revenue XX		where XX = how much of the liability was earned during the period
Accrued Expenses	Liability understated; equity overstated	Expense understated	Dr Expense.............. XX Cr Liability............ XX		where XX = the amount of the unpaid and unrecorded expense for the period
Accrued Revenues	Asset & equity understated	Revenue understated	Dr Asset.................. XX Cr Revenue XX		where XX = the amount of the uncollected and unrecorded revenue for the period

Important Tip: *Note that adjusting entries related to the framework in Exhibit 3.20 never affect cash.*[8] In the case of prepaid assets and unearned revenues, cash has already been correctly recorded; it is the prepaid asset and unearned revenues account balances that need to be *fixed* or adjusted. In the case of accrued revenues and expenses, cash will be received or paid in the future and is not to be accounted for until that time; it is the revenue or expense account balance that needs to be fixed or adjusted. Depreciation is a non-cash transaction and therefore does not affect cash.

A common error made by students learning to prepare adjusting entries is either to debit or to credit cash.

Exhibit 3.21 summarizes the adjusting entries of Organico on March 31. The posting of adjusting entries to individual ledger accounts was shown when we described the transactions above and is not repeated here. Adjusting entries are often set apart from other journal entries with the caption *Adjusting Entries*, as shown in Exhibit 3.21.

CHECKPOINT

14. Explain how adjusting entries are linked to the components of the accounting equation.

Do Quick Study questions: QS 3-15, QS 3-16, QS 3-17

---

[8]   Adjusting entries related to bank reconciliations affect cash but these adjustments are excluded from the framework in Exhibit 3.20 and will be discussed in Chapter 7.

EXHIBIT 3.21

Journalizing Adjusting Entries of Organico

GENERAL JOURNAL					Page 2
Date	**Account Titles and Explanations**	**PR**	**Debit**	**Credit**	
2017	Adjusting Entries				
Mar. 31	Insurance Expense		100		
	Prepaid Insurance..			100	
	To record expired insurance; $2,400/24.				
31	Supplies Expense...		1,050		
	Supplies			1,050	
	To record supplies used; $3,600 − $2,550.				
31	Depreciation Expense, Equipment		200		
	Accumulated Depreciation, Equipment			200	
	To record monthly depreciation on equipment; $6,000 − $1,200 = $4,800/24.				
31	Unearned Food Services Revenue...		250		
	Food Services Revenue...			250	
	To record earned revenue received in advance.				
31	Interest Expense		35		
	Interest Payable..			35	
	To record one month of accrued interest.				
31	Salaries Expense		70		
	Salaries Payable			70	
	To record one day's accrued salary; 1 × $70.				
31	Accounts Receivable..		1,800		
	Food Services Revenue...			1,800	
	To record 20 days of accrued revenue; $2,700 × 20/30.				

MID-CHAPTER DEMONSTRATION PROBLEM

The owner of a landscape company prepares *annual* financial statements.

Part A

Prepare the appropriate adjusting entries for July 31, 2017, based on the following information available at the end of July.

a. An annual insurance policy amounting to $1,200 was purchased on May 1, 2017. The Prepaid Insurance account was debited and Cash credited on the same date.

b. The landscape company's lawn tractor was purchased for $3,200 in 2015. The salvage value of the lawn tractor at the end of its four-year useful life is estimated to be $800. Calculate the annual depreciation for the year ended July 31, 2017, and record the corresponding adjusting journal entry.

c. On April 1, 2017, a customer paid for a six-month lawn service plan to begin June 1, 2017. The journal entry credited the Unearned Service Revenue account when the $3,000 payment was received. The monthly fee is $500.

d. The last weekly salary of $1,400 was paid to employees on Friday, July 25. Employees are paid based on a five-day workweek. Salaries for July 28, 29, 30, and 31 have accrued.

e. Service fees of $1,800 were earned by July 31 but not recorded.

Part B

Refer to (d) above. Prepare the entry to pay the salaries on Friday, August 1.

Analysis Component:

Assume a business was to falsify its earnings by understating them for tax purposes. Omitting which of the adjustments in Part A would accomplish this? What are the repercussions for doing so?

Solution

Part A

a. July 31	Insurance Expense..	300	
	Prepaid Insurance		300
	To record insurance for May, June, and July;		
	calculated as: $1,200/12 = $100 × 3 = $300.		
b. 31	Depreciation Expense, Lawn Tractor	600	
	Accumulated Depreciation, Lawn Tractor		600
	Annual depreciation, calculated as		
	$3,200 − $800 = $2,400/4 years = $600/year.		
c. 31	Unearned Service Fees	1,000	
	Service Fee Revenue...		1,000
	To record service fees earned for June and July;		
	calculated as $500 × 2 = $1,000.		
d. 31	Salaries Expense..	1,120	
	Salaries Payable..		1,120
	To record salaries for the last two days of July,		
	calculated as $1,400/5 = $280/day ×		
	4 days = $1,120.		
e. 31	Accounts Receivable	1,800	
	Service Fee Revenue...		1,800
	To record accrued service revenue for July.		

Part B

Aug. 1	Salaries Payable..	1,120	
	Salaries Expense..	280	
	Cash...		1,400
	To record payment of weekly salaries;		
	where salaries expense is calculated as		
	$1,400/5 = $280/day × 1 day = $280.		

Analysis Component:

Omitting adjustments (c) and (e) would cause revenues to be understated; hence, profit would also be understated. CRA could audit the company's reported taxable earnings and fine the company with interest penalties for not recording earnings correctly.

Adjusted Trial Balance

LO6 Explain and prepare an adjusted trial balance.

An **unadjusted trial balance** is a listing of accounts and balances prepared *before* adjustments are recorded. An **adjusted trial balance** is a list of accounts and balances prepared *after* adjusting entries are recorded and posted to the ledger. Exhibit 3.22 shows the unadjusted and adjusted trial balances for Organico at March 31, 2017, using an electronic spreadsheet. Electronic spreadsheet software such as Excel allows us to compile and adjust the relevant numbers efficiently.

EXHIBIT 3.22

Unadjusted and Adjusted Trial Balance for Organico

	Organico Trial Balances.xls						

Home Insert Page Layout Formulas Data Review View

P18   fx

	A	B	C	D	E	F	G
1		Organico					
2		Trial Balances					
3		March 31, 2017					
4		Unadjusted				Adjusted	
5		Trial Balance		Adjustments		Trial Balance	
6		Dr.	Cr.	Dr.	Cr.	Dr.	Cr.
7	Cash	$ 8,070				$ 8,070	
8	Accounts receivable			(g) $1,800		1,800	
9	Supplies	3,600			(b) $1,050	2,550	
10	Prepaid insurance	2,400			(a) 100	2,300	
11	Equipment	6,000				6,000	
12	Accumulated depreciation, equipment				(c) 200		$ 200
13	Accounts payable		$ 200				200
14	Interest payable				(e) 35		35
15	Salaries payable				(f) 350		350
16	Unearned food services revenue		3,000	(d) 250			2,750
17	Notes payable		6,000				6,000
18	Hailey Walker, capital		10,000				10,000
19	Hailey Walker, withdrawals	600				600	
20	Food services revenue		3,800		(d) 250 / (g) 1,800		5,850
21	Teaching revenue		300				300
22	Depreciation expense, equipment			(c) 200		200	
23	Salaries expense	1,260		(f) 350		1,610	
24	Interest expense			(e) 35		35	
25	Insurance expense			(a) 100		100	
26	Rent expense	1,000				1,000	
27	Supplies expense			(b) 1,050		1,050	
28	Utilities expense	230				230	
29	**Totals**	$23,300	$23,300	$3,505	$3,505	$25,545	$25,545

In Exhibit 3.22, notice several new accounts arising from the adjusting entries. The listing of accounts is also slightly changed to match the order listed in the Chart of Accounts in Appendix IV at the end of the book.

Preparing Financial Statements

LO7 Prepare financial statements from an adjusted trial balance.

We prepare financial statements directly from information in the *adjusted* trial balance. An adjusted trial balance includes all balances appearing in financial statements. We know that a trial balance summarizes information in the ledger by listing accounts and their balances. This summary is easier to work from than the entire ledger when preparing financial statements.

Exhibit 3.23 shows how Organico's revenue and expense balances are transferred from the adjusted trial balance to (1) the income statement, and (2) the statement of changes in equity. Note how we use the profit as reported on the income statement and the end-of-year balance in the withdrawals account to prepare the statement of changes in equity.

> **Important Tip:** Notice how the balance in the capital account in Exhibit 3.23 cannot be used as the opening capital balance in the statement of changes in equity. You always need to deduct owner investments made during the year from the *balance* in the Capital account to determine the owner's capital account balance at the beginning of the period.

Exhibit 3.23 also shows how Organico's asset and liability balances on the adjusted trial balance are transferred to the balance sheet. The ending equity is determined on the statement of changes in equity and transferred to the balance sheet. There are different formats for the balance sheet. The **account form balance sheet**, which has been demonstrated previously, lists assets on the left and liabilities and equity on the right side of the balance sheet. Its name comes from its link to the accounting equation, *Assets = Liabilities + Equity*. The balance sheet in Exhibit 1.16 is in account form. The **report form balance sheet** lists items vertically, as shown in Exhibit 3.23. Both forms are widely used and are considered equally helpful to users. For consistency, we will use the report form in the preparation of financial statements from this point forward.

We usually prepare financial statements in the order shown: income statement, statement of changes in equity, and balance sheet. This order makes sense since the balance sheet uses information from the statement of changes in equity, which in turn uses information from the income statement.

 **CHECKPOINT**

15. Jordan Air Company has the following information in its unadjusted and adjusted trial balances:

	Unadjusted		Adjusted	
	Debit	Credit	Debit	Credit
Prepaid insurance	$6,200		$5,900	
Salaries payable		$ -0-		$1,400

What are the adjusting entries that Jordan Air likely recorded?

16. What types of accounts are taken from the adjusted trial balance to prepare an income statement?

17. In preparing financial statements from an adjusted trial balance, what statement is usually prepared first? second? third? Explain why.

Do Quick Study question: QS 3-18

EXHIBIT 3.23

Preparing the Income Statement, Statement of Changes in Equity, and Balance Sheet From the Adjusted Trial Balance

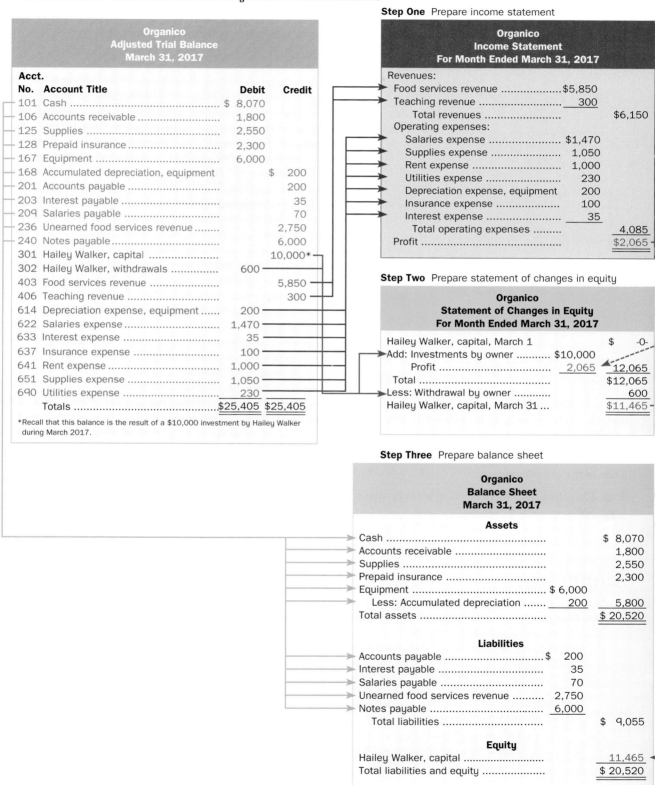

Step One Prepare income statement

Organico
Adjusted Trial Balance
March 31, 2017

Acct. No.	Account Title	Debit	Credit
101	Cash	$ 8,070	
106	Accounts receivable	1,800	
125	Supplies	2,550	
128	Prepaid insurance	2,300	
167	Equipment	6,000	
168	Accumulated depreciation, equipment		$ 200
201	Accounts payable		200
203	Interest payable		35
209	Salaries payable		70
236	Unearned food services revenue		2,750
240	Notes payable		6,000
301	Hailey Walker, capital		10,000*
302	Hailey Walker, withdrawals	600	
403	Food services revenue		5,850
406	Teaching revenue		300
614	Depreciation expense, equipment	200	
622	Salaries expense	1,470	
633	Interest expense	35	
637	Insurance expense	100	
641	Rent expense	1,000	
651	Supplies expense	1,050	
690	Utilities expense	230	
	Totals	$25,405	$25,405

*Recall that this balance is the result of a $10,000 investment by Hailey Walker during March 2017.

Organico
Income Statement
For Month Ended March 31, 2017

Revenues:		
Food services revenue	$5,850	
Teaching revenue	300	
Total revenues		$6,150
Operating expenses:		
Salaries expense	$1,470	
Supplies expense	1,050	
Rent expense	1,000	
Utilities expense	230	
Depreciation expense, equipment	200	
Insurance expense	100	
Interest expense	35	
Total operating expenses		4,085
Profit		$2,065

Step Two Prepare statement of changes in equity

Organico
Statement of Changes in Equity
For Month Ended March 31, 2017

Hailey Walker, capital, March 1		$ -0-
Add: Investments by owner	$10,000	
Profit	2,065	12,065
Total		$12,065
Less: Withdrawal by owner		600
Hailey Walker, capital, March 31		$11,465

Step Three Prepare balance sheet

Organico
Balance Sheet
March 31, 2017

Assets

Cash		$ 8,070
Accounts receivable		1,800
Supplies		2,550
Prepaid insurance		2,300
Equipment	$ 6,000	
Less: Accumulated depreciation	200	5,800
Total assets		$ 20,520

Liabilities

Accounts payable	$ 200	
Interest payable	35	
Salaries payable	70	
Unearned food services revenue	2,750	
Notes payable	6,000	
Total liabilities		$ 9,055

Equity

Hailey Walker, capital		11,465
Total liabilities and equity		$ 20,520

CRITICAL THINKING CHALLENGE

Refer to the Critical Thinking Challenge questions at the beginning of the chapter. Compare your answers to those suggested on Connect.

IFRS AND ASPE—THE DIFFERENCES

Difference	International Financial Reporting Standards (IFRS)	Accounting Standards for Private Enterprises (ASPE)
Recording adjusting entries	• IFRS require that financial statements be presented at least annually*; therefore, adjustments would be prepared at least annually. However, for publicly listed companies, Securities Commissions' Law requires publicly listed companies to present quarterly financial statements, which, in turn, would require that adjusting entries be prepared at least quarterly.	• Unlike IFRS, ASPE does not explicitly require that financial statements be presented at least annually although it is implied given that financial statements must be presented in a timely manner** and items must be presented consistently from period to period.*** Financial statements are prepared at least annually for tax purposes and, for example, to meet any banking requirements.
	• Both public and private enterprises may prepare adjusting entries more frequently, such as monthly, to enhance the accuracy of information required for decision making.	
Depreciation vs. amortization	• IFRS uses the term *depreciation***** (although it uses *amortization* for intangible assets).*****	• ASPE uses the term *amortization*.******

*IFRS 2014, IAS 1 Para. 36.
**ASPE, Accounting Standards, Section 1000.17(b).
***ASPE, Accounting Standards, Section 1000.19–20.
****IFRS 2014, IAS 16 Para. 6.
*****IFRS 2014, IAS 38 Para. 8.
******ASPE, Accounting Standards, Section 3061.16.

A Look Ahead

Chapter 4 highlights the completion of the accounting cycle. We explain the important final steps in the accounting process. These include closing procedures, the post-closing trial balance, and reversing entries.

For further study on some topics of relevance to this chapter, please see the following Extend Your Knowledge supplements:

EYK 3-1 Using the Trial Balance as a Framework for Adjustments
EYK 3-2 Subsequent Payment/Collection of Accruals

Summary

LO1 Describe the purpose of adjusting accounts at the end of a period. After routine daily transactions are recorded, several accounts need adjusting for their balances to be correct, as several transactions relating to revenues/expenses are triggered simply due to the passage of time. The purpose of adjusting accounts at the end of a period is to recognize unrecorded revenues and expenses.

LO2 Explain how the timeliness, matching, and revenue recognition principles affect the

adjusting process. The value of information is often linked to its timeliness. Accounting systems deliver timely financial information by preparing periodic reports at regular intervals such as each month, every three-month quarter, or, at minimum, once a year. Adjustments are made so that revenues and expenses are recognized as they occur and matched to the proper period.

LO3 Explain accrual accounting and cash basis accounting and how accrual accounting adds to

the usefulness of financial statements. Accrual accounting recognizes revenue when earned and expenses when incurred, not necessarily when cash inflows and outflows occur. The accrual basis of accounting requires adjusting entries to be posted at the end of the period to reflect the economic reality of the company's true financial position. Cash basis accounting recognizes revenues when cash is received and expenses when cash is paid; it is not in accordance with IFRS or ASPE standards.

LO4 Prepare and explain adjusting entries for prepaid expenses, depreciation, unearned revenues, accrued expenses, and accrued revenues. Prepaid expenses, an asset, refer to items paid for in advance of receiving their benefits. As this asset is used, its cost becomes an expense.

Dr. Expense xx
    Cr. Prepaid xx
To adjust prepaid for amount used.

Depreciation is the expense created by spreading the cost of plant and equipment assets over the periods these assets are used. Accumulated Depreciation, a contra asset account, is credited to track the total amount of the plant and equipment asset used.

Dr. Depreciation Expense xx
    Cr. Accumulated Depreciation xx
To adjust for depreciation.

Unearned revenues, a liability, refer to cash received in advance of providing products and services. As products and services are provided, the amount of unearned revenues becomes earned revenues.

Dr. Unearned Revenue xx
    Cr. Revenue xx
To adjust for unearned revenue that is earned.

Accrued expenses are costs incurred in a period that are unpaid by the company and have not yet been recorded.

Dr. Expense xx
    Cr. Liability...................................... xx
To adjust for unrecorded and unpaid expenses.

Accrued revenues are revenues earned in a period and not yet collected from the customer/client.

Dr. Receivable....................................... xx
    Cr. Revenue xx
To adjust for unrecorded revenues not yet collected.

LO5 Explain how accounting adjustments link to financial statements. Accounting adjustments bring an asset or liability account balance to its correct amount and update related expense or revenue accounts. Every adjusting entry affects one or more income statement *and* balance sheet accounts. An adjusting entry never affects cash. Adjustments are necessary for transactions that extend over more than one period. Exhibit 3.20 summarizes financial statement links by type of adjustment.

LO6 Explain and prepare an adjusted trial balance. An adjusted trial balance is a list of accounts and balances prepared after adjusting entries are recorded and posted to the ledger. Financial statements are often prepared from the adjusted trial balance.

LO7 Prepare financial statements from an adjusted trial balance. We can prepare financial statements directly from the adjusted trial balance that includes all account balances. Revenue and expense balances are transferred to the income statement and statement of changes in equity. Asset, liability, and equity balances are transferred to the balance sheet. We usually prepare statements in the following order: income statement, statement of changes in equity, and balance sheet (statement of financial position).

Guidance Answer to DECISION MAKER

Investor

Prepaid expenses are items paid for in advance of receiving their benefits. They are assets and are expensed as they are used up. The publishing company's treatment of the signing bonus is acceptable provided future book sales can at least match the $500,000 expense. As an investor, you are concerned about the risk of future book sales. The more uncertain future book sales are, the more likely your analysis is to treat the $500,000, or a portion of it, as an expense in the current accounting period, not a prepaid expense (an asset on the balance sheet).

Small Business Owner

We know that depreciation is a process of cost allocation, not asset valuation. Knowing the depreciation schedule of the restaurant is not especially useful in your estimation of what the restaurant's building and equipment are currently worth, as they do not reflect current market values. Your assessment of the age, quality, and usefulness of the building and equipment is much more important. Also, you would use the current market values of similar assets as a benchmark in estimating the value of this restaurant's building and equipment.

Financial Officer

Omitting accrued expenses and recognizing revenue early can mislead financial statement users and lead to fraudulent financial reporting. One action is to request a second meeting with the president so you can explain that accruing expenses when incurred and recognizing revenue when earned are requirements that need to be followed due to both the revenue recognition and matching principles. If the president persists, you might discuss the situation with legal counsel and any auditors involved. Your ethical action might cost you this job, but the potential pitfalls for falsification of statements, reputation and personal integrity loss, and other costs are too great.

Guidance Answers to CHECKPOINT

1. An annual reporting (or accounting) period covers one year and refers to the preparation of annual financial statements. The annual reporting period can follow the calendar year or a fiscal year. The fiscal year can follow the business's natural business year.

2. Interim (less than one year) financial statements are prepared to provide decision makers with information frequently and promptly.

3. The revenue recognition principle, the timeliness principle, and the matching principle lead most directly to the adjusting process.

4. No. Cash basis accounting is not consistent with generally accepted accounting principles.

5. If Prepaid Insurance is not adjusted, assets and equity will be overstated.

6. If the adjusting entry to record depreciation were not recorded, assets and equity would be overstated.

7. A contra account is an account that is subtracted from the balance of a related account. Use of a contra account often provides more complete information than simply reporting a net amount.

8. The revenue recognition principle will be violated because revenues earned have not been recognized. The matching principle will also be violated because revenues earned will not be assigned to the correct accounting period—the period in which the expenses related to the revenues were incurred.

9. Unearned revenue arises when cash is (or other assets are) received from a customer before the services and products are delivered to the customer. Magazine subscription receipts in advance are one example.

10. The omission of the $6,900 interest expense accrual will cause liabilities to be understated by $6,900 and equity to be overstated by $6,900.

11. An accrued expense refers to costs incurred in a period that are both unpaid and unrecorded prior to adjusting entries. One example is salaries earned by employees but not yet paid at the end of a period.

12. The January 5 entry to settle the accrued salaries and pay for added salaries is:

Jan. 5	Salaries Payable	1,000	
	Salaries Expense	6,000	
	Cash		7,000
	Paid salary including		
	accrual from December.		

13. The omission of an adjusting entry to record $6,000 of accrued interest would cause assets and equity to be understated by $6,000 each.

14. The various adjusting entries are linked to the accounting equation as follows: (a) adjustment to account for prepaid assets and the recording of depreciation cause assets and equity to decrease; (b) adjustment of

unearned amounts causes liabilities to decrease and equity to increase; (c) accrual of revenues causes assets and equity to increase; and (d) accrual of expenses causes liabilities to increase and equity to decrease.

15. The probable adjusting entries of Jordan Air are:

Insurance Expense	300	
Prepaid Insurance		300
To record insurance expired.		

Salaries Expense	1,400	
Salaries Payable		1,400
To record accrued salaries.		

16. Revenue accounts and expense accounts.

17. The income statement is usually prepared first, followed by the statement of changes in equity because profit (loss) from the income statement flows into the statement of changes in equity. The balance sheet is then prepared since the ending capital balance from the statement of changes in equity flows into the equity section of the balance sheet. This is illustrated in Exhibit 3.23.

DEMONSTRATION PROBLEM

The following information continues with The Cutlery, featured in the Chapter 1 and 2 Demonstration Problems. After the first month of business, The Cutlery's August 31, 2017, unadjusted trial balance appeared as follows:

The Cutlery Trial Balance August 31, 2017		
Account	**Debit**	**Credit**
Cash	$ 4,950	
Accounts receivable	-0-	
Prepaid insurance	2,400	
Furniture	2,000	
Store equipment	31,000	
Accounts payable		$14,450
Unearned haircutting services revenue		500
Joanne Cardinal, capital		26,000
Joanne Cardinal, withdrawals	500	
Haircutting services revenue		3,800
Wages expense	250	
Rent expense	3,200	
Hydro expense	450	
Totals	$44,750	$44,750

The following additional information is available for the *month* just ended:

a. Depreciation of $100 per month will be taken on the furniture.

b. It is estimated that the store equipment will have a $1,000 value at the end of its estimated five-year (or 60-month) useful life. Joanne Cardinal will record a full month of depreciation for August.

c. It was determined that the balance in unearned haircutting services revenue at August 31 should be $420.

d. The prepaid insurance represents six months of insurance beginning August 1.

e. On August 31, The Cutlery provided $130 of services to a client who will pay in September.

f. On August 31, Joanne Cardinal received the business's August cell phone bill totalling $50. It will be paid in September.

Required

1. Prepare the adjusting entries needed on August 31, 2017, to record the previously unrecorded items.

2. Prepare T-accounts for accounts affected by the adjusting entries. Post the adjusting entries to the T-accounts.

3. Prepare an adjusted trial balance.

4. Prepare an income statement, a statement of changes in equity, and a balance sheet.

Analysis Component:

Calculate the net effect of the adjusting entries on the balance sheet. Is profit positively or negatively affected by these adjusting entries overall? Could the opposite effect be achieved? If so, how?

Planning the Solution

- Analyze the information for each situation to determine which accounts need to be updated with an adjustment.

- Calculate the dollar amount of each adjustment and prepare the necessary journal entries.

- Show the amount entered by each adjustment in the designated accounts and determine the adjusted balance.

- Determine each entry's effect on profit for the year and on total assets, total liabilities, and equity at the end of the year.

- Using the adjusted balances, prepare an adjusted trial balance.

- Using the adjusted trial balance, prepare the income statement, statement of changes in equity, and balance sheet.

- Analyze the adjusting entries and calculate the effect on each component of the accounting equation.

Solution

1. Adjusting journal entries.

a.	Aug. 31	Depreciation Expense, Furniture...............................	100	
		Accumulated Depreciation, Furniture....................		100
		To record depreciation expense for the month of August for the furniture.		

b.	31	Depreciation Expense, Store Equipment	500	
		Accumulated Depreciation,		
		Store Equipment		500
		To record depreciation expense for the month;		
		($31,000 − $1,000)/60 months = $500/month.		

c.	31	Unearned Haircutting Services Revenue	80	
		Haircutting Services Revenue		80
		To recognize haircutting services revenue		
		earned; $500 − $420 = $80.		

d.	31	Insurance Expense...	400	
		Prepaid Insurance		400
		To adjust for the expired portion of prepaid		
		insurance; $2,400/6 months = $400/month.		

e.	31	Accounts Receivable	130	
		Haircutting Services Revenue		130
		To record revenue earned.		

f.	31	Phone Expense...	50	
		Accounts Payable		50
		To record August cell phone bill.		

2.

Accounts Receivable

| (e) | 130 | |

Prepaid Insurance

| Balance | 2,400 | 400 | (d) |
| Balance | 2,000 | | |

Accumulated Depreciation, Furniture

| | | 100 | (a) |

Accumulated Depreciation, Store Equipment

| | | 500 | (b) |

Accounts Payable

		14,450	Balance
		50	(f)
		14,500	Balance

Unearned Haircutting Services Revenue

| (c) | 80 | 500 | Balance |
| | | 420 | Balance |

Haircutting Services Revenue

		3,800	Balance
		80	(c)
		130	(e)
		4,010	Balance

Depreciation Expense, Furniture

| (a) | 100 | |

Depreciation Expense, Store Equipment

| (b) | 500 | |

Insurance Expense

| (d) | 400 | |

Phone Expense

| (f) | 50 | |

3.

The Cutlery
Adjusted Trial Balance
August 31, 2017

Account	Debit	Credit
Cash	$ 4,950	
Accounts receivable	130	
Prepaid insurance	2,000	
Furniture	2,000	
Accumulated depreciation, furniture		$ 100
Store equipment	31,000	
Accumulated depreciation, store equipment		500
Accounts payable		14,500
Unearned haircutting services revenue		420
Joanne Cardinal, capital		26,000
Joanne Cardinal, withdrawals	500	
Haircutting services revenue		4,010
Depreciation expense, furniture	100	
Depreciation expense, store equipment	500	
Wages expense	250	
Insurance expense	400	
Rent expense	3,200	
Hydro expense	450	
Phone expense	50	
Totals	$45,530	$45,530

4.

The Cutlery
Income Statement
For Month Ended August 31, 2017

Revenues:		
Haircutting services revenue		$4,010
Operating expenses:		
Rent expense	$3,200	
Depreciation expense, store equipment...	500	
Hydro expense	450	
Insurance expense	400	
Wages expense	250	
Depreciation expense, furniture	100	
Phone expense	50	
Total operating expenses		4,950
Loss		$ 940

The Cutlery
Statement of Changes in Equity
For Month Ended August 31, 2017

Joanne Cardinal, capital,		
August 1		$ -0-
Add: Investments by owner		26,000
Total		$26,000
Less: Withdrawals by owner	$500	
Loss	940	1,440
Joanne Cardinal, capital,		
August 31		$24,560

The Cutlery
Balance Sheet
August 31, 2017

Assets		
Cash		$ 4,950
Accounts receivable		130
Prepaid insurance		2,000
Furniture	$ 2,000	
Less: Accumulated depreciation	100	1,900
Store equipment	$31,000	
Less: Accumulated depreciation	500	30,500
Total assets		$39,480
Liabilities		
Accounts payable	$14,500	
Unearned haircutting services revenue	420	
Total liabilities		$14,920
Equity		
Joanne Cardinal, capital		24,560
Total liabilities and equity		$39,480

Reminder: The loss on the income statement flows into the statement of changes in equity. The August 31 balance in capital on the statement of changes in equity is reported on the balance sheet.

Analysis Component:

The net effect of the adjustments on assets, liabilities, and equity is detailed below.

Entry	a.	b.	c.	d.	e.	f.	Net effect
Assets	$100 ↓	$500 ↓	No effect	$400 ↓	$130 ↑	No effect	$870 ↓
Liabilities	No effect	No effect	$80 ↓	No effect	No effect	$50 ↑	$ 30 ↓
Equity	$100 ↓	$500 ↓	$80 ↑	$400 ↓	$130 ↑	$50 ↓	$840 ↓

Equity decreased by $840 as a result of the adjusting entries. All of the adjustments that affected equity were income statement items (revenues or expenses); therefore profit was negatively affected by the adjusting entries (a net decrease in income of $840).

The opposite effect could have been achieved if accrued revenues (Dr Receivables and Cr Revenues) plus the adjustment of unearned amounts (Dr Unearned Revenues and Cr Revenues) were greater than the adjustment for prepaid assets (Dr Expense and Cr Prepaid) plus depreciation (Dr Depreciation Expense and Cr Accumulated Depreciation) and accrued expenses (Dr Expense and Cr Payable).

APPENDIX 3A

Correcting Errors

Correcting entries, as the term implies, account for the correction of errors, and are not to be confused with adjusting entries.

If an error in a journal entry is discovered before the error is posted, it can be corrected in a manual system by drawing a line through the incorrect information. The correct information is written above it to create a record of change for the auditor. Many computerized systems allow the operator to replace the incorrect information directly.

When an error in a journal entry is *not* discovered until after it is posted, the usual practice is to correct the error by creating *another* journal entry.[9] This *correcting entry* removes the amount from the wrong account and records it to the correct account. For example, suppose we recorded a purchase of office supplies with an incorrect debit to Office Equipment as follows:

Oct.	14	Office Equipment...	1,600	
		Cash...		1,600
		To record the purchase of office supplies.		

Once posted, the Office Supplies account balance is understated by $1,600 and the Office Equipment account balance is overstated by the same amount. When we discover the error three days later, a correcting entry is made using either one or two entries as shown below:

	17	Office Supplies...	1,600	
		Office Equipment		1,600
		To correct the entry of October 14 that incorrectly debited Office Equipment instead of Office Supplies.		

OR

	17	Cash 1,600		
		Office Equipment		1,600
		To reverse the incorrect entry.		

	17	Office Supplies...	1,600	
		Cash...		1,600
		To journalize the purchase of office supplies correctly.		

---

9 For tracking purposes, correcting entries must be referenced to the incorrect entry and any calculations are to be documented.

In the approach to the left, the credit removes the error and the debit correctly records supplies. Alternatively, the two entries on the right could be used: the first entry reverses the incorrect entry *entirely*, and the second entry records the transaction, as it should have been. Both methods achieve the same final results.

Computerized systems often use similar correcting entries. The exact procedure depends on the system used and management policy. Yet nearly all systems include controls to show when and where a correction is made.

CHECKPOINT

18. On March 14, Accounts Receivable was debited for $4,100 and Service Revenue was credited for $4,100. At the end of the month, it was discovered that the March 14 entry should have been credited to Rent Revenue. What correcting entry is required?

Do Quick Study questions: *QS 3-19, *QS 3-20

An Alternative in Recording Prepaid Assets and Unearned Revenues

LO9 Identify and explain an alternative in recording prepaid assets and unearned revenues.

This section explains an alternative in recording prepaid expenses and unearned revenues.

Recording Prepaid Expenses in Expense Accounts

We explained that prepaid expenses are assets when they are purchased and are recorded with debits to asset accounts. Adjusting entries transfer the used amounts to expense accounts at the end of an accounting period.

There is an acceptable alternative practice of recording *all* prepaid expenses with debits to expense accounts. If any prepaid assets remain unused at the end of an accounting period, then adjusting entries transfer the unused portions from expense accounts to asset accounts. The financial statements are identical under either procedure, but the adjusting entries are different.

To illustrate, let's look at Organico's cash payment for 24 months of insurance coverage beginning on March 1. Organico recorded that payment with a debit to an asset account, but alternatively it could have been recorded as a debit to an expense account. Exhibit 3B.1 shows the two approaches.

EXHIBIT 3B.1

Initial Entry for Prepaid Expenses for Two Approaches

		Payment Recorded As an Asset	Payment Recorded As an Expense
Mar. 1	Prepaid Insurance	2,400	
	Cash	2,400	
1	Insurance Expense		2,400
	Cash		2,400

On March 31, insurance protection for one month is used up. This means $100 ($2,400/24) is the expense for March. Exhibit 3B.2 shows that the adjusting entry depends on how the original payment is recorded:

EXHIBIT 3B.2

Adjusting Entry for Prepaid Expenses for Two Approaches

		Payment Recorded As an Asset		Payment Recorded As an Expense	
Mar. 31	Insurance Expense	100			
	Prepaid Insurance..		100		
31	Prepaid Insurance			2,300	
	Insurance Expense				2,300

When these entries are posted, we can see in Exhibit 3B.3 that these two approaches give identical adjusted account balances at March 31.

EXHIBIT 3B.3

Account Balances Under Two Approaches for Recording Prepaid Expenses

Payment Recorded as Asset			
Prepaid Insurance			
Mar. 1	2,400	100	Mar. 31
Balance	2,300		

Insurance Expense			
Mar. 31	100		

Payment Recorded as Expense			
Prepaid Insurance			
Mar. 31	2,300		

Insurance Expense			
Mar. 1	2,400	2,300	Mar. 31
Balance	100		

Recording Unearned Revenues in Revenue Accounts

Unearned revenues are liabilities requiring delivery of products and services and are recorded as credits to liability accounts when cash and other assets are received. Adjusting entries at the end of an accounting period transfer to revenue accounts the earned portion of unearned revenues.

An acceptable alternative is to record *all* unearned revenues with credits to revenue accounts. If any revenues are unearned at the end of an accounting period, then adjusting entries transfer the unearned portions from revenue accounts to unearned revenue accounts. While the adjusting entries are different for these two approaches, the financial statements are identical.

To illustrate, let's look at Organico's March 26 receipt of $3,000 for catering food services covering the period for the Mount Mundy ski hill. Organico recorded this transaction with a credit to a liability account. The alternative, shown in Exhibit 3B.4, is to record it with a credit to a revenue account as follows:

EXHIBIT 3B.4

Initial Entry for Unearned Revenues for Two Approaches

		Receipt Recorded As a Liability		Receipt Recorded As Revenue	
Mar. 26	Cash	3,000			
	Unearned Food Services Revenue..................		3,000		
26	Cash			3,000	
	Food Services Revenue.................................				3,000

By the end of the accounting period (March 31), Organico earns $250 of this revenue. This means that $250 of the liability is satisfied. Depending on how the initial receipt is recorded, Exhibit 3B.5 shows the adjusting entry:

EXHIBIT 3B.5

Adjusting Entry for Unearned Revenues for Two Approaches

		Receipt Recorded As a Liability	Receipt Recorded As Revenue
Mar. 31	Unearned Food Services Revenue.........................	250	
	Food Services Revenue................................		250
31	Food Services Revenue.......................................		2,750
	Unearned Food Services Revenue.................		2,750

After adjusting entries are posted, the two approaches give identical adjusted account balances at March 31 as shown in Exhibit 3B.6.

EXHIBIT 3B.6

Account Balances Under Two Approaches for Recording Unearned Revenues

Receipt Recorded as Liability					Receipt Recorded as Revenue			
Unearned Food Services Revenue					**Unearned Food Services Revenue**			
Mar. 31	250	3,000	Mar. 26				2,750	Mar. 31
		2,750	Balance					
Food Services Revenue					**Food Services Revenue**			
					Mar. 31	2,750	3,000	Mar. 26
		250	Mar. 31				250	Balance

CHECKPOINT

19. Miller Company records cash receipts of unearned revenues and cash payments of prepaid expenses in balance sheet accounts. Bud Company records these items in income statement accounts. Explain any difference in the financial statements of these two companies from their different ways of recording prepaid assets.

Do Quick Study question: *QS 3-21

Summary of Appendix 3A and Appendix 3B

LO8 Explain and prepare correcting entries. A correcting entry is required when an error in a journal entry is not discovered until after it has been posted. The correcting entry can be done in one of two ways: the incorrect portion of the entry can be corrected, or the entire incorrect entry can be

reversed and the correct entry recorded; both methods accomplish the same result.

LO9 Identify and explain an alternative in recording prepaid assets and unearned revenues. It is acceptable to charge all prepaid expenses to expense accounts when they are purchased. When this is done, adjusting entries must transfer any unexpired amounts from expense accounts to asset accounts. It is also acceptable to credit

all unearned revenues to revenue accounts when cash is received. In this case the adjusting entries must transfer any unearned amounts from revenue accounts to unearned revenue accounts.

Guidance Answers to CHECKPOINT

18. The correcting entry can be done in one of two ways:

31	Service Revenue...........................	4,100	
	Rent Revenue........................		4,100
	To correct the March 14 entry.		

OR

31	Service Revenue...........................	4,100	
	Accounts Receivable..............		4,100
	To reverse the incorrect March 14 entry.		
31	Accounts Receivable....................	4,100	
	Rent Revenue........................		4,100
	To enter the correct entry for March 14.		

19. When adjusting entries are correctly prepared, the financial statements of these companies will be identical under both approaches.

Glossary

Account form balance sheet A balance sheet that lists assets on the left and liabilities and equity on the right side of the balance sheet.

Accounting periods Time frames covered by financial statements and other reports; also called *reporting periods*.

Accrual basis accounting The approach to preparing financial statements that uses the adjusting process to recognize revenues when earned and expenses when incurred, not when cash is paid or received; the required approach for generally accepted accounting principles.

Accrued expenses Costs incurred in a period that are unpaid and unrecorded; adjusting entries for recording accrued expenses involve increasing (debiting) expenses and increasing (crediting) liabilities.

Accrued revenues Revenues earned in a period that are both unrecorded and not yet received in cash (or other assets); adjusting entries for recording accrued revenues involve increasing (debiting) assets and increasing (crediting) revenues.

Adjusted trial balance A listing of accounts and balances prepared after adjustments are recorded and posted to the ledger.

Adjusting entry A journal entry at the end of an accounting period to bring an asset or liability account balance to its proper amount while also updating the related expense or revenue account.

Amortization The expense created by allocating the cost of intangible assets to the periods in which they are used; represents the expense of using these assets.

Book value of an asset The cost of the asset less its accumulated depreciation. It represents the reported value of the asset on the balance sheet.

Cash basis accounting Revenues are recognized when cash is received, and expenses are recorded when cash is paid. This method ignores the matching principle and revenue recognition principle and is not acceptable under GAAP.

Contra account An account linked with another account and having an opposite normal balance; reported as a subtraction from the other account's balance, at the net amount. Example: Accumulated Depreciation Equipment is the contra account for the Equipment account.

Correcting entries Accounting entries made in order to correct errors.

Depreciation The expense created by allocating the cost of plant and equipment to the periods in which they are used; represents the expense of using the associated assets.

External transactions Exchanges between the entity and some other person or organization.

Intangible assets Long-lived assets that have no physical substance, but provide a right to produce or use a product or process.

Interim financial reports Financial reports covering less than one year; usually based on one-, three- or six-month periods. Publicly listed companies report financial statements every three months, also referred to as quarterly.

Internal transactions Exchanges within an organization that can also affect the accounting equation.

Market value of an asset Amount an asset can be sold for today. Market value is not tied to the book value of an asset.

Matching principle The GAAP principle that requires expenses to be recorded in the same period as the associated revenues are recognized.

Overstated account An account that is listed at an amount that is higher than the correct balance.

Prepaid expenses Items that are paid for in advance of receiving their benefits. These are assets.

Property, plant, and equipment (PPE) Tangible long-lived assets used to produce goods or services.

Report form balance sheet A balance sheet that lists items vertically with assets above the liabilities and equity.

Reporting periods See *accounting periods*.

Straight-line depreciation method Allocates equal amounts of an asset's cost to depreciation expense during its useful life.

Timeliness principle A broad principle that assumes that an organization's activities can be divided into specific time periods such as in months, quarters, or years.

Unadjusted trial balance A listing of accounts and balances prepared before adjustments are recorded and posted to the ledger.

Understated account An account that is listed at an amount lower than the correct balance.

Unearned revenues Liabilities created when customers pay in advance for products or services; created when cash is received before revenues are earned; satisfied by delivering the products or services in the future.

Concept Review Questions

1. What is the difference between the cash basis and accrual basis of accounting? Why is the accrual basis of accounting preferred over the cash basis?

2. Your friend is a graphic designer who started his own business. He asks you "How do I record revenue and expenses correctly?" Explain when to record revenue and expenses based on the accrual basis of accounting. Give one example for revenue and one example for expenses to show your point.

3. Hannah is preparing an income statement for homework. She identifies revenues as service revenue, rent revenue, and unearned revenue. She identifies expenses as advertising expense, prepaid expense and rent expense. Check Hannah's work and explain any errors.

4. In your personal life, when do you need to prepay for products or services? Why do you think companies want you to prepay instead of paying later?

5. After reviewing the financial statements, the marketing department will finalize its decision on launching a new advertising campaign and the human resources department will finalize how many employees to hire. The accounting department is very busy and has decided not to post the year-end adjusting entries. What are the potential consequences of not posting adjusting entries?

6. What contra account is used when recording and reporting the effects of depreciation? Why is it used?

7. What is an accrued revenue? Give an example.

8. Review the consolidated balance sheet of Danier Leather in Appendix III. Identify an asset account that requires adjustment before annual financial statements can be prepared. What would be the effect on the income statement if this asset account were not adjusted?

9. Review the income statement of WestJet in Appendix III. How much depreciation was recorded in the adjusting entry for depreciation at the end of 2014? What types of assets would WestJet need to depreciate?

*10. If a company initially records prepaid expenses with debits to expense accounts, what type of account is debited in the adjusting entries for prepaid expenses?

Quick Study

QS 3-1 GAAP and adjusting entries LO2

For each of the following, identify the primary GAAP that has been violated and explain why.

1. Delta Company prepared its first set of financial statements for the three years ended July 31, 2017.

Timeliness

An asterisk (*) identifies assignment material based on Appendix 3A or Appendix 3B.

2. Warren Consulting purchased $9,800 of supplies on September 30, 2017, and debited Office Supplies Expense. Warren's year-end is September 30.   *Matching Principle*

3. On May 3, 2017, Nikos Car Wash collected $3,000 in advance from a new limousine company to begin operating June 1, 2017. Nikos credited a revenue account for the $3,000.   *Rev Rec*

4. On November 15, 2017, Scooter Town rented equipment for $1,500. Scooter Town is not recording the transaction until it pays (payment is required 15 days from the rental date).   *Matching principle*

QS 3-2 Accrual accounting LO3

Based on the accrual basis of accounting, determine when the following independent companies should recognize revenue.

1. **Starbucks** sells you a $25 gift card for your friend's birthday in February. Your friend spends the gift card on coffee and baked goods in March.   *once the gift card is used*

2. You paid your university tuition in September for the Fall semester that runs from September to December.   *once you receive full semester education*

QS 3-3 Accrual and cash accounting LO3

In its first year of operations, Harris Construction earned $39,000 in revenues and received $33,000 cash from customers. The company incurred expenses of $22,500, but had not paid for $2,250 of them at year-end. In addition, Harris prepaid $3,750 for expenses that would be incurred the next year.

1. Calculate the first year's profit under the cash basis.

2. Calculate the first year's profit under the accrual basis.

3. What is the difference?

QS 3-4 Preparing adjusting entries (annual)—prepaid expense LO4

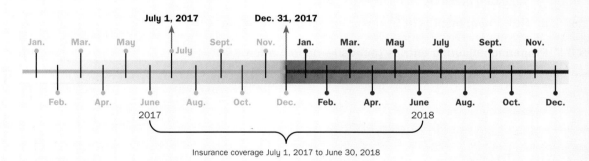

Insurance coverage July 1, 2017 to June 30, 2018

Stud Muffin Bakery prepares financial statements on an annual basis and has a December 31, 2017 year-end. On July 1, 2017, the bakery purchased a one-year insurance policy for $12,000 cash. The insurance policy covers July 1, 2017 to June 30, 2018.

    a. How much does the insurance policy cost per month?

    b. How many months are between July 1, 2017 and December 31, 2017?

    c. Record the journal entry on July 1, 2017.

    d. In order to prepare the annual financial statements, record the adjusting journal entry on December 31, 2017.

QS 3-5 Preparing adjusting entries (annual)—supplies LO4

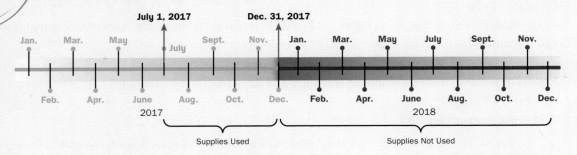

Organic Market, a grocery store, purchased supplies for $12,000 cash on July 1, 2017. As of December 31, 2017, $7,000 had been used and $5,000 of supplies had not been used. Organic Market prepares financial statements on an annual basis and has a December 31 year-end.

    a. Record the journal entry on July 1, 2017.

    b. In order to prepare the annual financial statements, record the adjusting journal entry to reflect the amount of supplies used as of December 31, 2017.

    c. On January 1, 2018, how much supplies does Organic Market have? 5,000

QS 3-6 Preparing adjusting entries (annual)—prepaid expense LO4

Kiss the Chef Co., a cooking school, purchased a two-year insurance policy on April 1, 2017, paying cash of $7,680. Its year-end is December 31.

    a. Record the journal entry on April 1, 2017.

    b. How many months are between April 1, 2017 and December 31, 2017? Record the adjusting entry on December 31, 2017.

    c. How many months are between January 1, 2018 and December 31, 2018? Record the adjusting entry on December 31, 2018.

    d. How many months of the insurance policy are left in 2019?

QS 3-7 Preparing adjusting entries (annual)—depreciation LO4

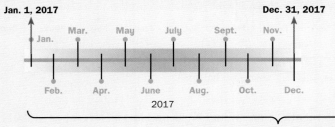

On January 1, 2017, Taco Taqueria, a Mexican restaurant, purchased equipment for $12,000 cash. Taco Taqueria estimates that the equipment will last five years (useful life). The restaurant expects to sell the equipment for $2,000 at the end of five years. Taco Taqueria prepares financial statements on an annual basis and has a December 31 year-end.

    a. Record the journal entry on January 1, 2017.

    b. What is the formula to calculate straight-line depreciation?

c. Using the straight-line depreciation method, calculate the annual depreciation for 2017 (Jan. 1 to Dec. 31 2017).

d. In order to prepare the annual financial statements, record the adjusting journal entry for depreciation on December 31, 2017.

QS 3-8 Preparing adjusting entries (annual)—depreciation expense LO4

Gold Co. purchased a vehicle on March 1, 2017, for cash of $32,000. It will be used by the president for business purposes for four years and then sold for an estimated amount of $8,000. Gold Co.'s year-end is December 31.

a. Record the journal entry on March 1, 2017.

b. Using the straight-line depreciation method, calculate the depreciation expense for March 1, 2017 to December 31, 2017.

c. To prepare the 2017 annual financial statements, record the adjusting entry for December, 31, 2017.

d. Using the straight-line depreciation method, calculate the depreciation expense for January 1, 2018 to December 31, 2018.

e. To prepare the 2018 annual financial statements, record the adjusting entry for December, 31, 2018.

QS 3-9 Preparing adjusting entries (annual)—unearned revenue LO4

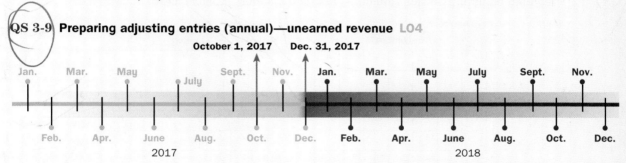

Club 17X Fitness prepares financial statements on an annual basis and has a December 31 year-end. On October 1, 2017, Club 17X sells a one-year prepaid gym membership for $300 cash.

a. Record the journal entry on October 1, 2017.

b. How much is the gym membership per month?

c. How many months have passed between October 1, 2017 and December 31, 2017?

d. In order to prepare the annual financial statements, record the adjusting journal entry on December 31, 2017.

QS 3-10 Preparing adjusting entries (annual)—unearned revenue LO4

On November 1, 2017, Race Car Repairs collected $12,000 from a customer for services to be provided in the future. On December 31, 2017, Race Car Repairs' year-end, it was determined that $3,000 of the services had not been provided (unearned).

a. Record the journal entry on November 1, 2017.

b. How much revenue was earned as of December, 31, 2017?

c. To prepare the 2017 annual financial statements, record the adjusting entry for December, 31, 2017.

QS 3-11 Preparing adjusting entries (annual)—accrued interest expense LO4

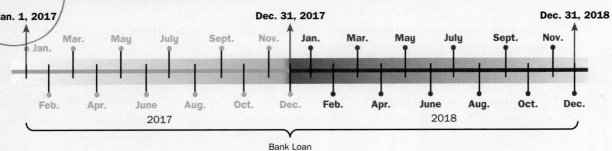

Bank Loan

Rise and Shine Ice Cream prepares annual financial statements and has a December 31 year-end. As of March 1, 2017, Rise and Shine Ice Cream took out a bank loan for $12,000 with an interest rate of 8%. Interest is incurred on a monthly basis and needs to be paid on December 31, 2018.

    a. What is the formula to calculate interest expense?

    b. How many months of interest expense have been incurred at December 31, 2017?

    c. In order to prepare the annual financial statements, record the adjusting journal entry on December 31, 2017.

QS 3-12 Preparing adjusting entries (annual)—accrued salaries expense LO4

December 2017

			December			
Sun	Mon	Tue	Wed	Thu	Fri	Sat
					1	2
3	4	5	6	7	8	9
10	11	12	13	14	15	16
17	18	19	20	21	22	23
24	25	26	27	28	29	30
31						

Salary expense incurred

January 2018

			January			
Sun	Mon	Tue	Wed	Thu	Fri	Sat
	1	2	3	4	5	6
7	8	9	10	11	12	13
14	15	16	17	18	19	20
21	22	23	24	25	26	27
28	29	30	31			

Payday

Yara Clothing (Yara), a retail store at the mall, hires a number of employees to work 7 days a week. Yara's owes its employee wages for the period of December 31, 2017 to January 13, 2018 (14 days) for $5,600. The wages owed are equal each day and the employees will be paid on January 15, 2018. Yara prepares annual financial statements and has a December 31 year-end.

    a. How much does Yara owe its employees per day?

    b. How many days are between December 31, 2017 and December 31, 2017?

    c. In order to prepare the annual financial statements, record the adjusting journal entry on December 31, 2017.

    d. Record the payment of wages on January 15, 2018.

QS 3-13 Preparing adjusting entries (annual)—accrued expenses LO4

On December 31, 2017, Beautiful Brows Salon received the business cell phone bill for December (Dec. 1 to Dec. 31) usage of $2,000. It must be paid by January 15, 2018.

a. To prepare the 2017 annual financial statements, record the adjusting entry on December 31, 2017.

b. Record the payment of the cell phone bill on January 15, 2018.

QS 3-14 Preparing adjusting entries (monthly)—accrued revenues LO4

TigrSoft provided $17,000 of services to customers in the month of March 2017. On March 31, 2017, TigrSoft has not yet billed or collected payment for the $17,000. On April 16, $12,000 of these were collected.

a. Using the accrual basis of accounting, explain whether TigrSoft earned revenue of $17,000 as of March 31, 2017.

b. Record the adjusting journal entry on March 31, 2017.

c. Record the journal entry on April 16, 2017.

QS 3-15 Preparing adjusting entries LO4

Stark Company records prepayments of expenses in asset accounts and receipts of unearned revenues in liability accounts. Using the list of accounts provided, identify the debit and credit entry required for each of the annual adjustments described in (a) through (e). The first one is done as an example.

1. Cash
2. Prepaid Advertising
3. Advertising Payable
4. Advertising Expense
5. Accounts Receivable
6. Equipment Expense
7. Depreciation Expense
8. Accumulated Depreciation—Equipment
9. Equipment
10. Services Revenue
11. Unearned Services Revenue

	Debits	Credits
Example: Accrual of uncollected and unrecorded services revenue.	5	10
a. Accrual of unpaid and unrecorded advertising that was used by Stark Company.	___	___
b. Adjustment of Unearned Services Revenue to recognize earned revenue.	___	___
c. Recorded revenue for work completed this accounting period; the cash will be received in the next period.	___	___
d. The cost of Equipment was matched to the time periods benefited.	___	___
e. Adjustment of Prepaid Advertising to recognize the portion used.	___	___

QS 3-16 Recording and analyzing adjusting entries LO4,5

Adjusting entries affect one balance sheet account and one income statement account. For the entries listed below, identify the account to be debited and the account to be credited. Indicate which of the two accounts is the income statement account and which is the balance sheet account.

a. Entry to record annual depreciation expense.
b. Entry to show wages earned by employees but not yet paid.
c. Entry to show revenue earned that was previously received as cash in advance.
d. Entry to show expiration of prepaid insurance.
e. Entry to show revenue earned but not yet billed.

QS 3-17 Linking adjustments to financial statements LO5

For each type of adjustment in (a) through (e), indicate the effect on profit (overstated or understated) if the adjustment is not recorded.

	If adjustment is not recorded:			
Type of Adjustment	Profit will be overstated, under-stated, or no effect	Assets will be overstated, under-stated, or no effect	Liabilities will be over-stated, understated, or no effect	Equity will be over-stated, understated, or no effect
a. Prepaid Expenses				
b. Depreciation				
c. Unearned Revenues				
d. Accrued Expenses				
e. Accrued Revenues				

QS 3-18 Interpreting adjusting entries LO4,6

The following information has been taken from Out Loud Comedy Club's unadjusted and adjusted trial balances at October 31, 2017.

	Unadjusted		Adjusted	
	Debit	Credit	Debit	Credit
Prepaid insurance	$3,100		$2,350	
Interest payable...........................		$ -0-		$750
Insurance expense	-0-		750	
Interest expense	-0-		750	

Given this trial balance information, prepare the adjusting journal entries.

*QS 3-19 Correcting entries LO8

The following entry was recorded on November 14.

Nov.	14	Salaries Expense...	14,800	
		Cash		14,800
		To record supplies expense.		

At month-end, it was discovered that *Supplies Expense* should have been debited on November 14 instead of *Salaries Expense*. Prepare the correcting entry required on November 30.

*QS 3-20 Correcting entries LO8

The following entry was recorded on January 10.

Jan.	10	Office Furniture..	25,000	
		Accounts Payable		25,000
		To record purchase of computer equipment by borrowing from the bank.		

At month-end, it was discovered that on January 10, computer equipment was purchased for $25,000 by borrowing from the bank. Prepare the correcting entry required on January 31.

An asterisk (*) identifies assignment material based on Appendix 3A or Appendix 3B.

*QS 3-21 Recording prepaids and unearned amounts as expenses and revenues LO9

Foster Company initially records prepaid and unearned items in income statement accounts. Given Foster Company's practices, what is the appropriate adjusting entry for each of the following at November 30, 2017, the end of the company's first accounting period?

    a. There are unpaid salaries of $3,000.

    b. Unused office supplies of $800 were counted at year-end. There was no beginning balance in office supplies.

    c. Earned but unbilled consulting revenue of $2,300 was discovered.

    d. It was determined that there was unearned revenue of $4,200.

Exercises

Exercise 3-1 **Recognizing revenue** LO3

The following are independent situations. Based on the accrual basis of accounting, explain when the companies should recognize revenue.

    a. You order a leather jacket from **Aritzia** online. You submit your credit card information, submit the order and receive the shipment in 14 days.

    b. Telus Communications sends your cell phone bill for the month of March. Your bill shows the invoice date as March 31, 2017 and the payment is due April 15, 2017.

    c. The **Toronto Transit Commission** (TTC) sells monthly bus passes. The September bus passes can be purchased in August. The bus pass then provides access to the TTC in September.

Exercise 3-2 **Identifying adjusting entries** LO4

For each entry (1) to (12) below, enter the letter of the explanation that describes it in the blank space to the left. You can use some letters more than once.

    a. To record depreciation expense.

    b. To record an accrued expense.

    c. To record the use of a prepaid expense.

    d. To record accrued revenue.

    e. To record the earning of previously unearned revenue.

    f. Not an adjusting entry.

___ 1.	Depreciation Expense.................	3,000		___ 7.	Insurance Expense......................	6,000	
	Accumulated Depreciation........		3,000		Prepaid Insurance....................		6,000
___ 2.	Unearned Professional Revenue...	2,000		___ 8.	Salaries Payable.........................	1,500	
	Professional Revenue..............		2,000		Cash		1,500
___ 3.	Rent Expense	1,000		___ 9.	Cash	6,500	
	Prepaid Rent...........................		1,000		Unearned Professional Revenue..		6,500
___ 4.	Interest Expense........................	4,000		___10.	Cash	9,000	
	Interest Payable......................		4,000		Interest Receivable..................		9,000
___ 5.	Prepaid Rent.............................	3,500		___11.	Interest Receivable....................	7,000	
	Cash		3,500		Interest Income........................		7,000
___ 6.	Salaries Expense	5,000		___12.	Cash	8,000	
	Salaries Payable......................		5,000		Accounts Receivable................		8,000

An asterisk (*) identifies assignment material based on Appendix 3A or Appendix 3B.

Exercise 3-3 Preparing adjusting entries (annual)—prepaid expense LO4

Dr. Erica Chan, MD owns EC Health Clinic. She prepares annual financial statements and has a December 31, 2017 year-end.

  a. On October 1, 2017, Dr. Chan prepaid $8,000 for four months of rent.

  b. On November 1, 2017, Dr. Chan prepaid $480 to renew the clinic's magazine subscriptions. The subscription is for one year.

  c. On December 1, 2017, Dr. Chan pays $3,000 for supplies. At the end of the year, $2,000 of supplies had not been used.

Required For each transaction, record the initial journal entry and the adjusting entry required on December 31, 2017.

Exercise 3-4 Preparing adjusting entries (annual)—depreciation LO4

Mean Beans, a local coffee shop, has the following assets on January 1, 2017. Mean Beans prepares annual financial statements and has a December 31, 2017 year-end.

  a. On January 1, 2017, purchase equipment costing $15,000 with an estimated life of five years. Mean Beans will scrap the equipment after five years for $0.

  b. On July 1, 2017, purchase furniture (tables and chairs) costing $12,000 with an estimated life of ten years. Mean Beans estimates that it can sell the furniture for $2,000 after ten years.

  c. On January 1, 2015, Mean Beans had purchased a car costing $25,000 with an estimated life of eight years. Mean Beans estimates that it can sell the car for $5,000 after eight years.

Required

 1. For each transaction, calculate the annual depreciation expense and record the adjusting entry on December 31, 2017.

 2. For the car, determine the accumulated depreciation as of December 31, 2017.

 3. For the car, determine the carrying amount as of December 31, 2017.

Exercise 3-5 Preparing adjusting entries (annual)—unearned revenue LO4

Splish Splash Art is a centre that offers children's music and dance lessons. Splish Splash prepares annual financial statements and has a December 31, 2017, year-end.

  a. On September 1, Splish Spash Art collects $15,000 cash for dance lessons running from September 1, 2017 to December 31, 2017.

  b. On October 1, Splish Splash Art collects $5,000 cash ($2,500 per month) to rent its performance stage for the full month of December 2017 and January 2018.

  c. On October 1, 2017, Splish Splash Art collects $8,000 cash for four months of music lessons. The lessons run from October 1, 2017 to January 31, 2018.

Required For each transaction, record the **initial journal entry** and the **adjusting entry** required on December 31, 2017.

Exercise 3-6 Preparing adjusting entries (annual)—accrued expenses and revenue LO4

Jurassic Jumpers Co. (JJ Co.) offers bungee jumping for those looking for an extreme activity. JJ Co. prepares annual financial statements and has a December 31, 2017 year-end.

a. On April 1, 2017, JJ Co. took out a five-year, $500,000 bank loan with an interest rate of 3%. Interest expense is paid on the first day of each month.

b. On July 1, 2017, JJ Co. issued a two-year, $50,000 Note Receivable with an interest rate of 4%. Interest income will be collected on January 1 and July 1 of each year.

c. On December 15, 2017, JJ Co. took a university student club bungee jumping for $2,000. The student club was invoiced on January 1, 2018 and pays JJ Co. on January 15, 2018.

Required Record the adjusting journal entries at December 31, 2017.

Exercise 3-7 **Adjusting entries (annual)** LO4

On January 1, you started a tutoring business called Brain Worx and charge $30 an hour for tutoring. The following are your transactions for 2017.

a. On January 1, you purchased a computer from **Apple Inc.** for $1,500 cash. You estimate that your computer will last three years. After that time, you will give the computer to your sister as a gift.

b. On February 1, you paid $1,200 cash for one-year of insurance coverage.

c. On March 1, you purchased supplies including paper, pens, and notebooks for $650 cash at **Staples Canada Inc**. At the end of the year, you had $230 of supplies left.

d. On November 1, Charlotte, a student, pays cash for eight hours of tutoring per month, for November 2017, December 2017, and January 2018.

e. You tutor George four hours in December. However, George was away for Christmas and has promised to pay you January 2018.

f. On January 2, 2018, Telus Communications sends your December business cell phone bill for $65. The bill is due January 15, 2018.

Required

1. For transactions (a) to (d), record the initial journal entry during the year.

2. For transactions (a) to (f), record the adjusting entries on December 31, 2017.

Exercise 3-8 **Adjusting entries (annual)** LO4

Enviro Waste's year-end is December 31. The information in (a) to (e) is available at year-end for the preparation of adjusting entries:

a. Of the $18,500 balance in Unearned Revenue, $3,050 remains unearned.

b. The annual building depreciation is $14,600.

c. The Spare Parts Inventory account shows an unadjusted balance of $1,200. A physical count reveals a balance on hand of $980.

d. Unbilled and uncollected services provided to customers totalled $14,600.

e. The utility bill for the month of December was received but is unpaid; $2,100.

Required Prepare the required adjusting entries at December 31, 2017, for (a) to (e) and the subsequent cash entries required for (f) and (g).

f. The accrued revenues of $14,600 recorded in (d) were collected on January 4, 2018.

g. The $2,100 utility bill accrued in (e) was paid on January 14, 2018.

Exercise 3-9 Adjusting entries—different accounting periods LO4

Queen & Ace Games (Q&A Games) runs its business from January 1 to December 31 (year-end). On January 1, 2017, Q&A Games pays $12,000 for a one-year insurance policy that covers January 1, 2017 to December 31, 2017. Record the journal entries for the following:

1. Record the initial entry on January 1, 2017, when Q&A Games pays for the insurance policy.

2. The following are independent situations. Assume Q&A Games reports using the following accounting periods.

   a. **Monthly (1 month)**—Assume Q&A Games reports on a monthly basis. Record the adjusting journal entry on **January 30, 2017**.

   b. **Quarterly (3 months)**—Assume Q&A Games reports on a quarterly basis. Record the adjusting journal entry on **March 30, 2017**.

   c. **Semi-annual (6 months)**—Assume Q&A Games reports on a semi-annual basis. Record the adjusting journal entry on **June 30, 2017**.

   d. **Annual (12 months)**—Assume Q&A Games reports on an annual basis. Record the adjusting journal entry on **December 31, 2017**.

Exercise 3-10 Adjusting entries (monthly) LO4

After winning the TV show competition, *Star Chef*, Adriana started a cooking school, Adriana's Apron. Adriana's Apron prepares monthly financial statements. The following are the transactions for the month of September 2017.

   a. On January 1, 2017, Adriana took out a bank loan for $60,000 with an interest rate of 5%. Interest is payable on the first day of each following month.

   b. Students paid $30,000 in advance for cooking classes. At the end of the month, Adriana finished teaching $10,000 worth of cooking classes.

   c. During the month, Adriana purchased supplies for her cooking classes such as meats and cheese for $5,000. At the end of the month, a physical count shows that $1,000 of supplies are left.

   d. On September 1, Adriana purchased a refrigerator costing $2,400. This equipment will be used for 5 years and then donated to the food bank.

   e. Adriana was hired to teach at a food festival. She taught the "Secrets to Italian Cooking" on September 30 and sent the festival organizers an invoice for $9,350. The invoice was paid in full on October 15, 2017.

   f. Adriana will pay salaries of $3,360 for two weeks (14 days) on October 7, 2017. At the end of the month, nine days of salaries are unpaid and unrecorded.

Required

For transactions (a) to (f), help Adriana prepare the adjusting entries on September 30, 2017.

Exercise 3-11 Unearned and accrued revenues LO4

Landmark Properties owns and operates an apartment building and prepares annual financial statements based on a March 31 fiscal year-end.

Required Journalize the adjusting entry for each of (a) and (b) and the subsequent entry required in (c).

   a. The tenants of one of the apartments paid five months' rent in advance on November 1, 2016. The monthly rental is $2,200 per month. The journal entry credited the Unearned Rent account when the payment was received. No other entry had been recorded prior to March 31, 2017. Give the adjusting journal entry that should be recorded on March 31, 2017.

b. On January 1, 2017, the tenants of another apartment moved in and paid the first month's rent. The $2,650 payment was recorded with a credit to the Rent Revenue account. However, the tenants have not paid the rent for February or March. They have agreed to pay it as soon as possible. Give the adjusting journal entry that should be recorded on March 31, 2017.

c. On April 22, 2017, the tenants described in (b) paid $7,950 rent for February, March, and April. Give the journal entry to record the cash collection.

Exercise 3-12 **Identifying adjusting entries** LO4

Selected information in T-account format is presented below. Journalize the most likely adjustments that caused the balances to change.

a. Accounts Receivable

Unadjusted Bal. Dec. 31/17	8,000
Adjusted Bal. Dec. 31/17	9,800

b. Prepaid Rent

Unadjusted Bal. Dec. 31/17	32,000
Adjusted Bal. Dec. 31/17	26,400

c. Accumulated Depreciation, Machinery

	9,200 Unadjusted Bal. Dec. 31/17
	12,600 Adjusted Bal. Dec. 31/17

d. Unearned Revenue

	6,100 Unadjusted Bal. Dec. 31/17
	1,500 Adjusted Bal. Dec. 31/17

e. Salaries Expense

Unadjusted Bal. Dec. 31/17	62,000
Adjusted Bal. Dec. 31/17	65,000

Exercise 3-13 **Missing data in supplies expense calculations** LO4,5

Determine the missing amounts in each of these four independent situations:

	a	b	c	d
Supplies on hand, January 1	$ 300	$ 900	$ 2,600	?
Supplies purchased during the year	2,900	3,100	?	$78,800
Supplies on hand, December 31	1,000	?	3,300	9,100
Supplies expense for the year	?	850	26,000	86,000

Exercise 3-14 **Adjusting and subsequent cash entries for accrued expenses** LO4

IKEO is a store with trendy and affordable furniture. IKEO has five part-time employees, each of whom earns $280 per day. They are normally paid on Fridays for work completed on Monday through Friday of the same week. They were all paid in full on Friday, December 26, 2017. The next week, all five of the employees worked only four days because New Year's Day was an unpaid holiday. Show the adjusting entry that would be recorded on Wednesday, December 31, 2017, IKEO's year-end, and the journal entry that would be made to record paying the employees' wages on Friday, January 2, 2018.

Exercise 3-15   Adjustments and subsequent cash entries for accrued expenses   LO4

The following three situations require adjusting journal entries to prepare financial statements as of April 30, 2017. For each situation, present the adjusting entry and the entry that would be made to record the payment of the accrued liability during May 2017.

a. The company has a $460,000 note payable that requires 0.3% interest to be paid each month on the 20th of the month. The interest was last paid on April 20 and the next payment is due on May 20.

b. The total weekly salaries expense for all employees is $14,500. This amount is paid at the end of the day on Friday of each week with five working days. April 30 falls on a Wednesday this year, which means that the employees had worked three days since the last payday. The next payday is May 2.

c. On April 1, the company retained a lawyer at a flat monthly fee of $4,500. This amount is payable on the 12th of the following month.

Exercise 3-16   Identifying the effects of adjusting entries   LO4,5   eXcel

Following are two income statements for Javelin Company for the month ended December 31, 2017. Column B was prepared before any adjusting entries were recorded and column D includes the effects of adjusting entries. The company records cash receipts and disbursements related to unearned and prepaid items in balance sheet accounts. Analyze the statements and prepare the adjusting entries that must have been recorded. (Note: Of the $12,000 increase in *Revenue*, 30% represents additional revenue but not billed. The other 70% was earned by performing services that the customers had paid for in advance.)

	A	B	C	D
		Javelin Company		
		Income Statements		
		For Month Ended December 31, 2017		
		Before		**After**
		Adjustments	**Adjustments**	**Adjustments**
6	Revenues:			
7	Service revenue	$ 48,000		$ 60,000
8	Commissions revenue	85,000		85,000
9	Total revenues	$133,000		$145,000
10	Operating expenses:			
11	Depreciation expense, computers	$ -0-		$ 3,000
12	Depreciation expense, office furniture	-0-		3,500
13	Salaries expense	25,000		29,900
14	Insurance expense	-0-		2,600
15	Rent expense	9,000		9,000
16	Office supplies expense	-0-		960
17	Advertising expense	6,000		6,000
18	Utilities expense	2,500		2,640
19	Total operating expenses	$ 42,500		$ 57,600
20	**Profit**	$ 90,500		$ 87,400

Javelin Company Income Statements.xls — Home | Insert | Page Layout | Formulas | Data | Review | View — P18 fx

Analysis Component: Identify and explain which GAAP requires that adjusting entries be recorded. By how much would revenues, expenses, and profit be overstated/understated if adjustments were *not* recorded at December 31, 2017, for Javelin Company?

Exercise 3-17 Adjusting entries LO4,6 eXcel

CHECK FIGURE: Adjusted trial balance, debits = $511,500

	Nuna Music Trial Balances.xls						

Home   Insert   Page Layout   Formulas   Data   Review   View

P18   fx

Nuna Music
Trial Balances
February 28, 2017

		Unadjusted Trial Balance		Adjustments		Adjusted Trial Balance	
		Dr.	Cr.	Dr.	Cr.	Dr.	Cr.
7	Cash	$ 14,000					
8	Accounts receivable	32,000					
9	Prepaid insurance	16,800					
10	Equipment	102,000					
11	Accumulated depreciation, equipment		$ 23,000				
12	Accounts payable		19,000				
13	Abraham Nuna, capital		213,000				
14	Abraham Nuna, withdrawals	102,000					
15	Revenues		214,000				
16	Depreciation expense, equipment	-0-					
17	Salaries expense	187,700					
18	Insurance expense	14,500					
19	**Totals**	$ 469,000	$ 469,000				

Additional information:

   a. Annual depreciation of the equipment; $11,500.

   b. $12,000 of the Prepaid Insurance balance has expired.

   c. Unbilled and unrecorded revenues at year-end totalled $31,000.

Required Referring to Exhibit 3.22, use the information provided to complete the columns.

Exercise 3-18 Preparing financial statements LO7

CHECK FIGURES: Profit = 19,300; Total assets = $149,300

Using the completed adjusted trial balance columns from Exercise 3-17, prepare an income statement, a statement of changes in equity, and a balance sheet for the year ended February 28, 2017. Assume that the owner made no investments during the year.

Analysis Component: Which GAAP requires the preparation of financial statements?

*Exercise 3-19 **Journalizing correcting entries** LO8

For each of the following incorrect entries, journalize the appropriate correcting entry(ies).

a. The purchase of office supplies on credit for $1,800 was recorded as:

Office Supplies...	1,800	
Cash		1,800

b. A credit customer paid her account in full: $4,500. This was recorded as:

Cash..	4,500	
Revenue...		4,500

c. The owner withdrew cash of $1,500. This was recorded as:

Salaries Expense.....................................	1,500	
Cash		1,500

d. Work was performed for a customer today and cash of $750 was received. This was recorded as:

Cash..	750	
Accounts Receivable		750

Analysis Component: If the error in (b) is not corrected, what is the effect on the income statement and balance sheet?

*Exercise 3-20 **Entering adjustments for prepaid items recorded in expense and revenue accounts** LO9

Classic Customs began operations on December 1, 2017. In setting up the bookkeeping procedures, the company decided to debit expense accounts when the company prepays its expenses and to credit revenue accounts when customers pay for services in advance. Prepare journal entries for items (a) through (c) and adjusting entries as of December 31, 2017, for items (d) through (f):

   a. Supplies were purchased on December 1 for $8,000.

   b. The company prepaid insurance premiums of $3,200 on December 2.

   c. On December 15, the company received an advance payment of $16,100 from one customer for remodelling work.

   d. By counting the supplies on December 31, Classic Customs determined that $1,450 was on hand.

   e. An analysis of the insurance policies in effect on December 31 showed that $800 of insurance coverage had expired.

   f. As of December 31, it was determined that $8,500 of the amount received in advance on December 15 had been earned.

An asterisk (*) identifies assignment material based on Appendix 3A or Appendix 3B.

*Exercise 3-21 **Alternative procedures for revenues received in advance** LO9

Pavillion Company experienced the following events and transactions during July:

July	1	Received $4,000 in advance of performing work for Andrew Renking.
	6	Received $16,800 in advance of performing work for Matt Swarbuck.
	12	Completed the job for Andrew Renking.
	18	Received $15,000 in advance of performing work for Drew Sayer.
	27	Completed the job for Matt Swarbuck.
	31	The job for Drew Sayer has not been started.

  a. Give journal entries (including any adjusting entry as of the end of the month) to record these items using the procedure of initially crediting the Unearned Revenue account when a payment is received from a customer in advance of performing services.

  b. Give journal entries (including any adjusting entry as of the end of the month) to record these items using the procedure of initially crediting the Revenue account when a payment is received from a customer in advance of performing services.

  c. Under each method, determine the amount of earned revenue that should be reported on the income statement for July and the amount of unearned revenue that should appear on the balance sheet as of July 31.

Problems

Problem 3-1A **Preparing adjusting entries (monthly)—prepaid expenses** LO4

Impala Window Washing Services prepares adjustments monthly and shows the following selected accounts on its December 31, 2017, unadjusted trial balance:

Account	Debit	Credit
Prepaid insurance	$ 3,600	
Prepaid office rent	21,000	
Prepaid subscriptions	1,260	
Prepaid equipment rental	25,200	

Required Prepare the required monthly adjusting entries at December 31, 2017, based on the following additional information:

  a. The remaining balance in Prepaid Insurance was for a six-month insurance policy purchased for $7,200 and in effect on September 1, 2017.

  b. $4,800 of the balance in Prepaid Office Rent had not been used as at December 31, 2017.

  c. $1,100 of the balance in Prepaid Subscriptions had been used as at December 31, 2017.

  d. The company paid $32,400 on April 1, 2017, to rent equipment for a three-year period beginning April 1, 2017.

Analysis Component: If the above adjustments were not recorded, identify the types of accounts that would be affected and if they would be over- or understated.

An asterisk (*) identifies assignment material based on Appendix 3A or Appendix 3B.

Problem 3-2A Preparing adjusting entries (annual)—depreciation expense LO4

Details regarding Leroux Steel's purchases of plant and equipment items during 2017 follow:

Date of Purchase	Plant and Equipment Item	Cost	Estimated Useful Life	Estimated Sales Value at End of Estimated Useful Life
a. Jan. 1	Machine A	$102,000	5 years	$ -0-
b. Apr. 1	Machine B	61,000	4 years	3,400
c. Nov. 1	Machine C	30,500	2 years	2,900

Required Prepare the annual adjusting entry at December 31, 2017, Leroux's year-end, for each plant and equipment item.

Analysis Component: What is the purpose of recording depreciation? If depreciation is not recorded, how would the income statement be affected?

Problem 3-3A Preparing adjusting entries (monthly)—unearned revenues LO4

Outdoor's Best pre-sells yard maintenance packages for the gardening season. During October, the company collects cash from clients for Christmas trees to be delivered in December. Snow removal services are also provided. Outdoor's Best prepares adjusting entries monthly. The following selected accounts appear on the November 30, 2017, unadjusted trial balance:

Account	Debit	Credit
Unearned lawn services............................		$102,000
Unearned garden services		36,400
Unearned snow removal services		11,800
Unearned Christmas tree sales		21,200

Required Prepare the monthly adjusting journal entries at November 30, 2017, using the following additional information.

a. $86,000 of the Unearned Lawn Services account represents payments received from customers for the 2018 season. The remainder represents fall lawn services actually performed during November 2017.

b. $31,950 of the Unearned Garden Services account had been earned by November 30, 2017.

c. $9,200 of the Unearned Snow Removal Services account remained unearned at November 30, 2017.

d. Outdoor's arranges with its customers to deliver trees from December 5 to December 20. As a result, the Unearned Christmas Tree Sales account will be earned in total by December 20.

Analysis Component: If the Unearned Lawn Services of $102,000 had been recorded as a revenue when received instead of as a liability, what would the effect have been on the November 30, 2017, financial statements assuming no adjustment was made on November 30, 2017?

Problem 3-4A **Preparing adjusting (monthly) and subsequent cash entries—accrued expenses** LO4

Mannix Resources prepares adjusting entries monthly. In reviewing the accounts on March 31, Mannix Resources discovered the following:

a. Interest of $1,050 had accrued on the note payable as at March 31. It is to be paid on April 2.

b. Unpaid and unrecorded salaries at March 31 totalled $32,850. The $32,850 plus salaries of $21,900 for the first four days of April were paid on April 4.

c. The March telephone bill for $440 is unpaid and unrecorded at March 31. It is to be paid on April 15.

d. Mannix normally pays rent in three-month installments. At March 31, rent of $4,200 per month had not been paid for February, March, or April. Rent of $4,200 was correctly accrued at the end of February. The balance owing plus rent for May, June, and July was paid on April 26.

e. Mannix pays commissions to the technicians at the rate of 4% of services performed. During March, total services performed were $410,000. Commissions are unrecorded and unpaid at March 31. Commissions are paid on the 15th of the following month.

Required Using the information provided above, prepare the monthly adjusting journal entries at March 31 along with the appropriate subsequent cash entries.

Problem 3-5A **Preparing adjusting and subsequent cash entries (annual)—accrued revenues** LO4

In reviewing the accounts on March 31 for the year just ended, DigiTech discovered the following:

a. DigiTech owns the building that it occupies. Part of the building is rented to E-Quip Company for $4,150 per month. E-Quip had not paid the March rent as at March 31. On April 3, DigiTech collected the rent accrued on March 31.

b. Services performed but unrecorded at March 31 totalled $8,400. This amount was collected on April 7.

c. Interest for the month of March had accrued on a note receivable in the amount of $640. The interest accrued on March 31 was collected on April 1.

d. On February 1, DigiTech signed a $34,500 six-month contract to perform services for a client. DigiTech has been providing the services but as of March 31 no cash had been received. On April 2, DigiTech collected the revenue accrued on March 31.

Required Using the information provided above, prepare the annual adjusting journal entries at March 31 along with the appropriate subsequent cash entries.

Problem 3-6A **Adjusting entries (annual); adjusted trial balance** LO4,6 e**X**cel

CHECK FIGURE: 2. Adjusted Trial Balance debits = $572,520

PacRim Careers provides training to individuals who pay tuition directly to the business. The business also offers extension training to groups in off-site locations. Additional information available at the December 31, 2017, year-end follows:

a. An analysis of the company's policies shows that $1,250 of insurance coverage has expired.

b. An inventory shows that teaching supplies costing $450 are on hand at the end of the year.

c. The estimated annual depreciation on the equipment is $8,000.

d. The estimated annual depreciation on the professional library is $4,500.

e. The school offers off-campus services for specific employers. On November 1, the company agreed to do a special six-month course for a client. The contract calls for a monthly fee of $950, and the client paid the first five months' revenue in advance. When the cash was received, the Unearned Extension Revenue account was credited.

	PacRim Careers Trial Balances.xls						
	A	B	C	D	E	F	G
1		**PacRim Careers**					
2		Trial Balances					
3		December 31, 2017					
4		Unadjusted				Adjusted	
5		Trial Balance		Adjustments		Trial Balance	
6	**Account**	Dr.	Cr.	Dr.	Cr.	Dr.	Cr.
7	Cash	$ 18,000					
8	Accounts receivable	-0-					
9	Teaching supplies	6,500					
10	Prepaid insurance	1,400					
11	Prepaid rent	7,200					
12	Professional library	60,000					
13	Accumulated depreciation, professional library		$ 18,000				
14	Equipment	96,000					
15	Accumulated depreciation, equipment		32,000				
16	Accounts payable		2,500				
17	Salaries payable		-0-				
18	Unearned extension revenue		6,300				
19	Karoo Ashevak, capital		229,000				
20	Karoo Ashevak, withdrawals	92,000					
21	Tuition revenue		196,000				
22	Extension revenue		72,500				
23	Depreciation expense, equipment	-0-					
24	Depreciation expense, professional library	-0-					
25	Salaries expense	206,000					
26	Insurance expense	-0-					
27	Rent expense	44,000					
28	Teaching supplies expense	-0-					
29	Advertising expense	14,000					
30	Utilities expense	11,200					
31	**Totals**	$ 556,300	$ 556,300				

f. On October 15, the school agreed to teach a four-month class for an individual for $1,200 tuition per month payable at the end of the class. The services to date have been provided as agreed, but no payment has been received.

g. The school's two employees are paid weekly. As of the end of the year, three days' wages have accrued at the rate of $120 per day for each employee.

h. The balance in the Prepaid Rent account represents the rent for three months: December, January, and February.

Required

1. Prepare the necessary annual adjusting journal entries at December 31, 2017, based on (a) to (h) above.

Analysis Component:

2. Refer to the format presented in Exhibit 3.22 and complete the adjusted trial balance using the information in (a) through (h) above.

3. If the adjustments were *not* recorded, calculate the over- or understatement of income.

4. Is it ethical to ignore adjusting entries?

Problem 3-7A Adjusting entries (monthly) LO4

Wedona Energy Consultants prepares adjusting entries monthly. Based on an analysis of the unadjusted trial balance at January 31, 2017, the following information was available for the preparation of the January 31, 2017, month-end adjusting entries:

a. Equipment purchased on November 1 of this accounting period for $21,600 is estimated to have a useful life of three years. After three years of use, it is expected that the equipment will be scrapped due to technological obsolescence.

b. Of the $11,400 balance in Unearned Consulting Revenue, $8,700 had been earned.

c. The Prepaid Rent account showed a balance of $13,500. This was paid on January 1 of this accounting period and represents six months of rent commencing on the same date.

d. Accrued wages at January 31 totalled $18,500.

e. One month of interest had accrued at the rate of 4% per year on a $42,000 note payable.

f. Unrecorded and uncollected consulting revenue at month-end were $6,150.

g. A $3,510 insurance policy was purchased on April 1 of the current accounting period and debited to the Prepaid Insurance account. Coverage began April 1 for 18 months.

h. The monthly depreciation on the office furniture was $625.

i. Repair revenues accrued at month-end totalled $3,400.

j. The Store Supplies account had a balance of $800 at the beginning of January. During January, $1,780 of supplies were purchased and debited to the Store Supplies account. At month-end, a count of the supplies revealed a balance of $650.

Required Prepare adjusting journal entries for the month ended January 31, 2017, based on the above.

Problem 3-8A Adjusting (annual) and subsequent cash journal entries LO4

The following information concerns the adjusting entries to be recorded on November 30, 2017, for RaiLink's year just ended.

a. The Office Supplies account started the year with a $4,800 balance. During 2017, the company purchased supplies at a cost of $24,800, which was added to the Office Supplies account. The inventory of supplies on hand at November 30 had a cost of $6,300.

b. An analysis of the company's insurance policies provided these facts:

Policy	Date of Purchase	Years of Coverage	Total Cost
1	March 1, 2016	2	$ 5,760
2	March 1, 2017	3	22,320
3	July 1, 2017	1	3,780

The total premium for each policy was paid in full at the purchase date, and the Prepaid Insurance account was debited for the full cost. *Appropriate adjusting entries have been made to November 30, 2016.*

c. The company has 15 employees who earn a total of $4,800 in salaries for every working day. They are paid each Monday for their work in the five-day workweek ending on the preceding Friday. November 30, 2017, falls on a Sunday, and all 15 employees worked November 24 to 28 inclusive. They will be paid salaries for five full days on Monday, December 1, 2017.

d. The company purchased a building on July 1, 2017. The building cost $306,000 and is expected to have a $25,000 residual value at the end of its predicted 30-year life.

e. Because the company is not large enough to occupy the entire building, it arranged to rent some space to a tenant at $3,100 per month, starting on October 1, 2017. The rent was paid on time on October 1, and the amount received was credited to the Rent Revenue account. However, the tenant has not paid the November rent. The company has worked out an agreement with the tenant, who has promised to pay both November's and December's rent in full on December 15.

f. On October 1, the company also rented space to another tenant for $3,650 per month. The tenant paid five months' rent in advance on that date. The payment was recorded with a credit to the Unearned Rent account.

Required

1. Use the information to prepare the annual adjusting entries as of November 30, 2017.

2. Prepare journal entries to record the subsequent cash transactions in December 2017 described in parts (c) and (e).

Problem 3-9A Adjusting entries (annual) LO4

Rainmaker Environmental Consultants is just finishing its second year of operations. The company's unadjusted trial balance at October 31, 2017, follows:

Rainmaker prepares adjustments each October 31. The following additional information is available on October 31, 2017.

a. It was determined that $12,000 of the unearned consulting revenue had not yet been earned.

b. It was discovered that $14,000 of the balance in the Consulting Revenue account was for services to be performed in November.

c. The balance in the Prepaid Rent account represents three months of rent beginning September 1, 2017.

d. Accrued wages at October 31 totalled $6,800.

e. The office furniture was purchased on March 1, 2016, and has an estimated useful life of two years. After two years of use, it is expected that the furniture will be worthless.

f. Accrued consulting revenue at year-end totalled $4,200.

	Rainmaker Environmental Consultants Unadjusted Trial Balance October 31, 2017		
Acct. No.	**Account**	**Debit**	**Credit**
101	Cash	$ 26,000	
106	Accounts receivable...	61,000	
109	Interest receivable..	-0-	
111	Notes receivable	50,000	
126	Supplies..	5,300	
128	Prepaid insurance	3,400	
131	Prepaid rent...	27,000	
161	Office furniture..	84,000	
162	Accumulated depreciation, office furniture..		$ 28,000
201	Accounts payable..		18,000
210	Wages payable		-0-
233	Unearned consulting revenue		26,000
301	Jeff Moore, capital		223,000
302	Jeff Moore, withdrawals..	28,000	
401	Consulting revenue..		232,020
409	Interest income...		480
601	Depreciation expense, office furniture	-0-	
622	Wages expense..	192,000	
637	Insurance expense	-0-	
640	Rent expense...	44,000	
650	Supplies expense...	6,800	
	Totals..	$527,500	$527,500

g. Interest of $85 had accrued on the note receivable for the month of October.

h. The balance in the Prepaid Insurance account represents the remaining balance of a two-year policy purchased on April 1, 2016.

i. A count of the supplies on October 31 revealed a balance remaining of $620.

Required Prepare the annual adjusting journal entries for October 31, 2017, based on the above.

Problem 3-10A Posting, adjusted trial balance, and preparing financial statements LO6,7

CHECK FIGURES: 3. Adjusted trial balance, debits = $580,585 4. Loss = $79,895

Required Using the information in Problem 3-9A, complete the following:

1. Set up balance column accounts for Rainmaker Environmental Consultants and enter the balances listed in the unadjusted trial balance.

2. Post the adjusting entries prepared in Problem 3-9A to the accounts.

3. Prepare an adjusted trial balance.

4. Use the adjusted trial balance to prepare an income statement, a statement of changes in equity, and a balance sheet. Assume that the owner, Jeff Moore, made no owner investments during the year.

Analysis Component: Assume that total revenues and expenses reported for the year ended October 31, 2016, were $189,000 and $157,600, respectively. Compare the business's financial performance for the years ended October 31, 2016 and 2017.

Note

For Part 1, your instructor may ask you to set up T-accounts instead of balance column accounts. The solution is available in both formats.

Problem 3-11A Adjusting entries (monthly) LO4

Arrow Hospitality prepares adjustments monthly and showed the following at September 30, 2017:

	Arrow Hospitality Trial Balances.xls						
	Home Insert Page Layout Formulas Data Review View						
	P18	*fx*					
	A	B	C	D	E	F	G
1		Arrow Hospitality					
2		Trial Balances					
3		September 30, 2017					
4		Unadjusted				Adjusted	
5		Trial Balance		Adjustments		Trial Balance	
6	**Account**	**Dr.**	**Cr.**	**Dr.**	**Cr.**	**Dr.**	**Cr.**
7	Cash	$ 6,000					
8	Accounts receivable	11,200					
9	Repair supplies	2,200					
10	Prepaid rent	14,000					
11	Office furniture	26,000					
12	Accounts payable		$ 8,000				
13	Notes payable		21,600				
14	Eli Arrow, capital		67,758				
15	Eli Arrow, withdrawals	5,000					
16	Hospitality revenues		128,000				
17	Salaries expense	144,000					
18	Wages expense	16,958					
19	**Totals**	$ 225,358	$ 225,358				

Additional information available for the month ended September 30, 2017:

   a. Interest of $162 had accrued on the notes payable for the month of September.

   b. The office furniture was acquired on September 1, 2017, and has an estimated four-year life. The furniture will be sold for about $2,000 at the end of its four-year life.

   c. A count of the Repair Supplies revealed a balance on hand of $700.

   d. A review of the Prepaid Rent account showed that $10,000 had been used during September.

   e. Accrued wages of $2,800 had not been recorded at month-end.

   f. The September Internet bill for $100 had been received and must be paid by October 14.

   g. Accrued revenues of $6,200 were not recorded at September 30.

Required Prepare adjusting entries for the month ended September 30, 2017, for each of (a) through (g) above.

Problem 3-12A Preparation of financial statements LO6,7 e**X**cel

CHECK FIGURES: 1. Adjustments columns = $21,262; Adjusted trial balance columns = $235,120;
2. Loss = $41,820

Required

1. Using the format presented in Problem 3-11A, complete the adjusted trial balance by including the adjusting entries prepared in Problem 3-11A.

2. Prepare an income statement, a statement of changes in equity and a balance sheet based on the adjusted trial balance completed in Part 1. Assume that the owner, Eli Arrow, made an investment during September of $3,600.

Analysis Component: Assume that total assets reported at August 31, 2017, were $76,900. Determine what total liabilities and equity were on that date and comment on the change in the financial position from August to September.

Problem 3-13A Preparing financial statements from the adjusted trial balance LO7

CHECK FIGURES: a. Profit = $84,925; c. Total assets = $264,500

This alphabetized adjusted trial balance is for GalaVu Entertainment as of its December 31, 2017, year-end:

	Debit	Credit
Accounts payable...		$ 44,000
Accounts receivable...	$ 18,700	
Accumulated depreciation, automobiles............		69,000
Accumulated depreciation, equipment...............		20,500
Advertising expense	9,000	
Automobiles..	140,000	
Cash	11,000	
Depreciation expense, automobiles	13,200	
Depreciation expense, equipment.....................	4,100	
Equipment	65,000	
Revenue..		240,000
Interest income...		150
Interest expense	3,500	
Interest payable...		75
Interest receivable...	300	
John Conroe, capital..		23,000
John Conroe, withdrawals	19,000	
Land	35,000	
Long-term notes payable		115,000
Notes receivable (due in 90 days)	80,000	
Office supplies...	4,000	
Office supplies expense	13,000	
Repairs expense, automobiles	8,400	
Salaries expense	76,225	
Salaries payable		5,500
Unearned revenue		11,000
Wages expense..	27,800	
Totals..	$528,225	$528,225

Required Use the information in the trial balance to prepare:

    a. The income statement for the year ended December 31, 2017.

    b. The statement of changes in equity for the year ended December 31, 2017, assuming that the owner made additional investments of $15,000 during the year.

    c. The balance sheet as of December 31, 2017.

Analysis Component: The owner, John Conroe, is very pleased with the change in the business's financial position. Specifically, he noted that his equity increased. "My banker told me that as long as equity is increasing, my business is doing great." Comment.

Problem 3-14A Journalizing, posting, adjusted trial balance, adjusting entries (monthly), financial statements LO4,5,6,7

CHECK FIGURES: 3. Cash balance, Aug. 31, 2017 = $4,600; 4. Dr = $19,100; 6. Dr = $19,524; 7. Profit = $1,376

On August 1, 2017, Delanie Tugut began a tour company in the Northwest Territories called Tugut Arctic Tours. The following occurred during the first month of operations:

Aug.	1	Purchased office furniture on account; $5,200.
	1	Delanie Tugut invested $7,000 cash into her new business.
	2	Collected $3,900 in advance for a three-week guided caribou hunt beginning the last week of August.
	3	Paid $6,000 for six months' rent for office space effective August 1.
	4	Received $3,000 for a four-day northern lights viewing tour just completed.
	7	Paid $1,500 for hotel expenses regarding the August 4 tour.
	15	Delanie withdrew cash of $500 for personal use.
	22	Met with a Japanese tour guide to discuss a $150,000 tour contract.
	31	Paid wages of $1,300.

Required

1. Prepare general journal entries to record the August transactions.

2. Set up the following T-accounts: Cash (101); Prepaid Rent (131); Office Furniture (161); Accumulated Depreciation, Office Furniture (162); Accounts Payable (201); Unearned Revenue (233); Delanie Tugut, Capital (301); Delanie Tugut, Withdrawals (302); Revenue (401); Depreciation Expense, Office Furniture (602); Wages Expense (623); Rent Expense (640); Telephone Expense (688); and Hotel Expenses (696).

3. Post the entries to the accounts; calculate the ending balance in each account.

4. Prepare an unadjusted trial balance at August 31, 2017.

5. Use the following information to prepare and post adjusting entries on August 31:

    a. The office furniture has an estimated life of four years and a $208 residual value.

    b. Two-thirds of the August 2 advance has been earned.

    c. One month of the Prepaid Rent has been used.

    d. The August telephone bill was not received as of August 31 but amounted to $320.

6. Prepare an adjusted trial balance.

7. Prepare an income statement, a statement of changes in equity, and a balance sheet.

Analysis Component: When a company shows revenue on its income statement, does this mean that cash equal to revenues was received during the period in which the revenues were reported?

*Problem 3-15A Correcting entries LO8

The accountant for Karma Counselling Services found several errors in reviewing the unadjusted trial balance on September 30. You are to prepare correcting entries based on the following information:

    a. The Counselling Revenue account included an entry debiting cash for $7,000 that should have been debited to Accounts Receivable.

    b. Utilities Expense was debited $1,680 that should have been recorded as Telephone Expense.

    c. The Office Supplies account shows a credit of $2,800 regarding the use of Cleaning Supplies.

    d. A transaction involving $19,600 of service revenue performed on account was incorrectly recorded as a debit to Accounts Payable and a credit to Unearned Service Revenue.

    e. Equipment was incorrectly debited for $1,200 with a corresponding credit to Accounts Payable regarding supplies that were sold to a neighbouring store on credit.

Required Journalize the correcting entries required on September 30.

Analysis Component: The error in (b) shows that an incorrect expense account was debited. Since the net effect on the financial statements is nil after recording the correction, is it necessary to prepare a correcting entry for this type of error?

***Problem 3-16A Recording prepaid expenses and unearned revenues LO9 **

CHECK FIGURE: Adjusted trial balance, debits = $136,400

Willis Consulting follows the approach of recording prepaid expenses as expenses and unearned revenues as revenues. Willis's unadjusted trial balance for the year ended March 31, 2017, follows.

			Willis Consulting Trial Balances.xls			
	Home Insert Page Layout Formulas Data Review View					
	P18	fx				
	A	B	C	D	E	F	G
1		**Willis Consulting**					
2		**Trial Balances**					
3		**March 31, 2017**					
4		**Unadjusted**				**Adjusted**	
5		**Trial Balance**		**Adjustments**		**Trial Balance**	
6	**Account**	**Dr.**	**Cr.**	**Dr.**	**Cr.**	**Dr.**	**Cr.**
7	Cash	$ 32,000					
8	Accounts receivable	63,000					
9	Prepaid rent	-0-					
10	Prepaid insurance	-0-					
11	Accounts payable		$ 16,000				
12	Unearned consulting revenue		-0-				
13	Bruce Willis, capital		38,400				
14	Consulting revenue		82,000				
15	Rent expense	38,990					
16	Insurance expense	2,410					
17	**Totals**	$ 136,400	$ 136,400				

An asterisk (*) identifies assignment material based on Appendix 3A or Appendix 3B.

Additional information:

a. A review of the Consulting Revenue account showed that $6,400 of the balance has not yet been earned.

b. The balance in the Rent Expense account was paid on January 15, 2017, and represents seven months of rent beginning February 1, 2017.

c. It was determined that $1,900 of the balance in the Insurance Expense account was used by March 31, 2017.

Required Refer to Exhibit 3.22 and use the information provided to complete the columns above.

*Problem 3-17A Recording prepaid expenses and unearned revenues LO4,9

The following events occurred for a company during the last two months of its fiscal year ended December 31, 2017:

Nov.	1	Paid $4,500 for future newspaper advertising.
	1	Paid $7,800 for insurance through October 31 of the following year.
	30	Received $6,600 for future services to be provided to a customer.
Dec.	1	Paid $5,850 for the services of a consultant, to be received over the next three months.
	15	Received $12,100 for future services to be provided to a customer.
	31	Of the advertising paid for on November 1, $1,780 worth had not yet been published by the newspaper.
	31	Part of the insurance paid for on November 1 had expired.
	31	Services worth $1,650 had not yet been provided to the customer who paid on November 30.
	31	One-third of the consulting services paid for on December 1 had been received.
	31	The company had performed $2,750 of the services that the customer had paid for on December 15.

Required

1. Prepare the November and December entries for the above activities under the approach that records prepaid expenses as assets and records unearned revenues as liabilities. Also, prepare adjusting entries at the end of the year.

2. Prepare the November and December entries under the approach that records prepaid expenses as expenses and records unearned revenues as revenues. Also, prepare adjusting entries at the end of the year.

Analysis Component: Explain why the alternative sets of entries in requirements 1 and 2 do not result in different financial statement amounts.

Alternate Problems

Problem 3-1B Preparing adjusting entries (annual)—prepaid expenses LO4

Domino's Cleaning Services is gathering information for its year-end, April 30, 2017. Selected accounts on the April 30, 2017, unadjusted trial balance are reproduced below:

Account	Debit	Credit
Prepaid equipment rental..........................	$24,750	
Prepaid warehouse rental	7,800	
Prepaid insurance	8,160	
Cleaning supplies....................................	3,100	

An asterisk (*) identifies assignment material based on Appendix 3A or Appendix 3B.

Required Prepare the required annual adjusting entries at April 30, 2017, based on the following additional information:

    a. The balance in the Prepaid Equipment Rental account is for 18 months of equipment rental that began December 1, 2016.

    b. $6,000 of the balance in the Prepaid Warehouse Rental account had been used as of April 30, 2017.

    c. The balance in the Prepaid Insurance account represents six months of insurance effective February 1, 2017.

    d. A count of the cleaning supplies revealed that $2,400 had been used.

Analysis Component: Which GAAP require the recording of adjusting entries and why?

Problem 3-2B **Preparing adjusting entries (monthly)—depreciation expense** LO4

Zebra Consulting prepares adjusting entries and financial statements monthly. Details regarding Zebra Consulting's plant and equipment items follow:

	Date of Purchase	Plant and Equipment Item	Cost	Estimated Useful Life	Estimated Sales Value at End of Estimated Useful Life
a.	Dec. 1, 2016	Furniture	$ 27,000	3 years	$ -0-
b.	Mar. 1, 2017	Equipment	171,600	10 years	24,000
c.	Nov. 1, 2017	Building	491,000	15 years	140,000

Required Prepare the monthly adjusting entry to record depreciation for each plant and equipment item at November 30, 2017.

Analysis Component: What is the purpose of recording depreciation? If depreciation is not recorded, how would each of the components of the accounting equation be affected?

Problem 3-3B **Preparing adjusting entries (annual)—unearned revenues** LO4

Blackfeather Tours sells scuba diving and kayaking excursions, along with a number of unique sightseeing packages. The company requires a 50% payment from the customer at the time of booking. The following selected accounts appear on Blackfeather's January 31, 2017, year-end unadjusted trial balance:

Account	Debit	Credit
Unearned heli-tour revenue		$ 38,000
Unearned tour package revenue		652,000
Unearned scuba diving revenue		290,000
Unearned kayaking tour revenue		116,000

Required Prepare the annual adjusting journal entries at January 31, 2017, using the following additional information:

    a. Blackfeather Tours has custom helicopter packages in which groups are flown in and out of island retreats. The balance in this unearned account is for a group scheduled for early March 2017.

    b. Three-quarters of the Unearned Tour Package Revenue account had been earned by January 31, 2017.

    c. $72,000 of the Unearned Scuba Diving Revenue account remained unearned at January 31, 2017.

d. $15,500 of the Unearned Kayaking Tour Revenue account represents payments received from customers for February and March 2017. The balance in the account is for tours provided in January 2017.

Analysis Component: Using your understanding of GAAP, explain how and why unearned revenues are adjusted at the end of the accounting period.

Problem 3-4B Preparing adjusting (annual) and subsequent cash entries—accrued expenses LO4

In reviewing the accounts on September 30, 2017, for the year just ended, Geek Designers discovered the following:

a. Interest of $1,500 had accrued on the bank loan as at September 30. It is to be paid on October 2.

b. Accrued wages at September 30 totalled $80,500. On October 3, the first biweekly payday of October, $115,000 was paid to employees representing the seven days accrued on September 30 plus the first three working days in October.

c. The September cell phone bill for $215 was unpaid and unrecorded at September 30. It will be paid on October 5.

d. On September 30, $1,150 of cable charges were accrued regarding the past two months of usage that were not recorded or paid. This amount was paid on October 2.

e. $1,140 of property taxes covering September were accrued on September 30. This amount was paid on October 15.

Required Using the information provided above, prepare the annual adjusting journal entries at September 30 along with the appropriate subsequent cash entries.

Problem 3-5B Preparing adjusting (monthly) and subsequent cash entries—accrued revenues LO4

WonderWeb prepares adjusting entries monthly. In reviewing the accounts on March 31, 2017, Wonder-Web discovered the following:

a. Interest of $450, representing 25 days in March, had accrued on the note receivable as of March 31. The accrual of $450 plus an additional five days in April was collected on April 5.

b. Accrued consulting revenue totalling $5,600 was not recorded on March 31. This amount was collected on April 6.

c. Web design work totalling $8,750 was completed on March 31 but not recorded. This amount was collected on April 13.

d. WonderWeb rents the basement of its building to a student. The student has not paid the March rent of $950 as at March 31. On April 27, the March rent plus the rent for April was collected.

Required Using the information provided above, prepare the March 31 month-end adjusting journal entries along with the appropriate subsequent cash entries.

Problem 3-6B Adjusting entries (monthly); adjusted trial balance LO4,6   *eXcel*

CHECK FIGURE: 2. Adjusted Trial Balance, debits = $588,570

Fawcett Institute provides one-on-one training to individuals who pay tuition directly to the business and also offers extension training to groups in off-site locations. Fawcett prepares adjusting entries monthly. Additional information available on December 31, 2017:

a. An analysis of the company's policies shows that $31,000 of insurance coverage has expired.

b. An inventory shows that teaching supplies costing $13,400 are on hand at the end of the month.

c. The estimated monthly depreciation on the equipment is $650.

d. The estimated monthly depreciation on the professional library is $320.

e. The school offers off-campus services for specific operators. On December 1, the company agreed to do a special four-month course for a client. The contract calls for a $5,400 monthly fee, and the client paid the first two months' revenue in advance. When the cash was received, the Unearned Extension Revenue account was credited.

f. On December 15, the school agreed to teach a four-month class to an individual for $1,600 tuition per month payable at the end of the class. The services have been provided as agreed, and no payment has been received.

g. The school's only employee is paid weekly. As of the end of the month, wages of $1,200 have accrued.

h. The balance in the Prepaid Rent account represents the rent for December, January, February, and March.

Fawcett Institute Trial Balance.xls

Home Insert Page Layout Formulas Data Review View

P18   *fx*

Fawcett Institute
Trial Balance
December 31, 2017

Account	Unadjusted Trial Balance Dr.	Cr.	Adjustments Dr.	Cr.	Adjusted Trial Balance Dr.	Cr.
Cash	$ 25,000					
Accounts receivable	-0-					
Teaching supplies	107,200					
Prepaid insurance	36,000					
Prepaid rent	11,600					
Professional library	20,000					
Accumulated depreciation, professional library		$ 3,000				
Equipment	141,400					
Accumulated depreciation, equipment		32,000				
Accounts payable		24,400				
Salaries payable		-0-				
Unearned extension revenue		55,200				
Jay Fawcett, capital		62,000				
Jay Fawcett, withdrawals	40,000					
Tuition revenue		285,000				
Extension revenue		124,000				
Depreciation expense, equipment	-0-					
Depreciation expense, professional library	-0-					
Salaries expense	143,600					
Insurance expense	-0-					
Rent expense	-0-					
Teaching supplies expense	-0-					
Advertising expense	36,000					
Utilities expense	24,800					
Totals	**$ 585,600**	**$ 585,600**				

Required

1. Prepare the necessary December 31, 2017, month-end adjusting journal entries based on (a) through (h) above.

Analysis Component:

2. Refer to the format presented in Exhibit 3.22 and prepare an adjusted trial balance using the information in (a) through (h) above.

3. If the adjustments were *not* recorded, calculate the over- or understatement of income.

4. Is it ethical to ignore adjusting entries?

Problem 3-7B Adjusting entries (annual) LO4

Kazz Industries' year-end is May 31. Based on an analysis of the unadjusted trial balance at May 31, 2017, the following information was available:

    a. Machinery costing $65,500 was acquired on September 1 of this accounting period. It is estimated to have a useful life of six years. The machinery is estimated to have a $7,000 value at the end of its six-year life.

    b. It was determined that $6,000 of completed work was included in the $9,200 Unearned Revenue account balance at year-end.

    c. The Prepaid Insurance account showed a balance of $23,040. This was paid and takes effect on March 1 of this accounting period and represents a two-year policy.

    d. Accrued salaries at year-end were $17,300.

    e. $2,160 of interest had accrued on the $144,000 note payable.

    f. Accrued revenues at year-end totalled $16,800.

    g. $11,340 worth of advertising was prepaid on January 1 of the current accounting period and debited to the Prepaid Advertising account. This covered four months of advertising beginning on the same date.

    h. The annual depreciation on the office equipment was $4,100.

    i. Interest income accrued at year-end totalled $620.

    j. The Office Supplies account had a balance of $4,000 at the beginning of the accounting period. During the year, $27,500 of supplies were purchased and debited to the Office Supplies account. At year-end, a count of the supplies revealed that $29,400 had been used.

Required Prepare adjusting journal entries for the year ended May 31, 2017, based on the above.

Problem 3-8B Identifying adjusting (monthly) and subsequent cash journal entries LO4

Valor Ventures prepares adjusting entries monthly. The following information concerns the adjusting entries that need to be recorded on October 31, 2017, for the month just ended.

    a. The Office Supplies account had a $1,000 balance on October 1. During October, the company purchased supplies at a cost of $9,100, which was added to the Office Supplies account. The inventory of supplies on hand at October 31 had a cost of $600.

    b. An analysis of the company's insurance policies provided these facts:

Policy	Date of Purchase	Years of Coverage	Total Cost
1	April 1, 2016	2	$ 8,400
2	April 1, 2017	3	6,660
3	August 1, 2017	1	1,500

The total premium for each policy was paid in full at the purchase date, and the Prepaid Insurance account was debited for the full cost. *Appropriate adjusting entries have been made to September 30, 2017.*

   c. The company has 10 employees who earn a total of $3,250 for every working day. They are paid each Monday for their work in the five-day workweek ending on the preceding Friday. October 31, 2017, falls on a Friday, and all 10 employees worked the five days that week. They will be paid salaries for five full days on Monday, November 3, 2017.

   d. The company purchased a building on August 1, 2015. The building cost $250,000, and is expected to have a $40,000 residual value at the end of its predicted 25-year life.

   e. Because the company is not large enough to occupy the entire building, it arranged to rent some space to a tenant at $2,600 per month, starting on September 1, 2017. The rent was paid on time on September 1, and the amount received was credited to the Rent Revenue account. However, the tenant has not paid the October rent. The company has worked out an agreement with the tenant, who has promised to pay both October's and November's rent in full on November 15.

   f. On October 1, the company also rented space to another tenant for $2,350 per month. The tenant paid five months' rent in advance on that date. The payment was recorded with a credit to the Unearned Rent account.

Required

 1. Use the information to prepare the October 31, 2017, month-end adjusting entries.

 2. Prepare journal entries to record the subsequent cash transactions described in items (c) and (e).

Problem 3-9B Adjusting journal entries (monthly) LO4

Ben Hallmark, the owner of Hallmark Surveying Services, has been in business for two years. The unadjusted trial balance at December 31, regarding the month just ended, follows:

The following additional information is available on December 31, 2017:

   a. Depreciation on the equipment for the month was $430.

   b. $9,600 of the balance in Unearned Surveying Revenue is unearned at December 31.

   c. The balance in Prepaid Rent is for six months of rent beginning December 1.

   d. Accrued wages at month-end were $12,400.

   e. December's interest in the amount of $120 had accrued on the notes payable.

   f. Accrued surveying revenue at month-end totalled $21,800.

   g. The balance in Prepaid Advertising covers four months of advertising beginning December 15.

   h. A count of the supplies on December 31 showed $1,320 had been used.

   i. The December electricity bill for $2,340 was received on December 31. It is unrecorded and unpaid.

Required Prepare adjusting journal entries for the month ended December 31, 2017, based on the above.

Analysis Component: Explain the differences between *Accumulated Depreciation* and *Depreciation Expense*.

	Hallmark Surveying Services Unadjusted Trial Balance December 31, 2017		
Acct. No.	**Account**	**Debit**	**Credit**
101	Cash	$ 15,600	
106	Accounts receivable	29,200	
126	Supplies	1,640	
128	Prepaid advertising	1,280	
131	Prepaid rent	17,880	
167	Surveying equipment	58,000	
168	Accumulated depreciation, surveying equipment		$ 7,348
201	Accounts payable		13,800
203	Interest payable		-0-
210	Wages payable		-0-
233	Unearned surveying revenue		14,800
251	Notes payable		36,000
301	Ben Hallmark, capital		28,652
302	Ben Hallmark, withdrawals	24,300	
401	Surveying revenue		170,948
601	Depreciation expense, surveying equipment	-0-	
622	Salaries expense	56,000	
623	Wages expense	39,726	
633	Interest expense	-0-	
637	Insurance expense	6,000	
640	Rent expense	-0-	
650	Supplies expense	2,958	
655	Advertising expense	-0-	
671	Gas and oil expense	6,564	
684	Repairs expense	12,400	
690	Utilities expense	-0-	
	Totals	$271,548	$271,548

Problem 3-10B Posting, adjusted trial balance, and preparing financial statements LO6,7

CHECK FIGURES: 3. Adjusted trial balance, debits = $308,638; 4. Profit = $54,550

Required Using the information in Problem 3-9B, complete the following:

1. Set up balance column accounts for Hallmark Surveying Services and enter the balances listed in the unadjusted trial balance.
2. Post the adjusting entries prepared in Problem 3-9B to the balance column accounts.
3. Prepare an adjusted trial balance.
4. Use the adjusted trial balance to prepare an income statement, a statement of changes in equity, and a balance sheet. Assume that the owner, Ben Hallmark, made owner investments of $4,000 during the month.

Analysis Component: At December 31, 2017, how much of the business's assets are financed by the owner? by debt? Assuming total assets at the end of the previous month totalled $84,200, did equity financing increase or decrease during December? Generally speaking, is this a favourable or unfavourable change?

Note:

For Part 1, your instructor may ask you to set up T-accounts instead of balance column accounts. The solution is available in both formats.

Problem 3-11B Adjusting entries (annual) LO4

B52 Skate Training prepares adjustments annually and showed the following on its June 30, 2017, year-end:

	B52 Skate Training Unadjusted Trial Balance.xls						
	Home Insert Page Layout Formulas Data Review View						
	P18 *fx*						
	A	B	C	D	E	F	G
1	**B52 Skate Training**						
2	**Unadjusted Trial Balance**						
3	**June 30, 2017**						
4		Unadjusted				Adjusted	
5		Trial Balance		Adjustments		Trial Balance	
6	**Account**	**Dr.**	**Cr.**	**Dr.**	**Cr.**	**Dr.**	**Cr.**
7	Cash	$ 112,000					
8	Accounts receivable	28,000					
9	Repair supplies	2,800					
10	Prepaid arena rental	182,000					
11	Skate equipment	428,000					
12	Accumulated depreciation,						
	skate equipment		$ 164,000				
13	Accounts payable		5,400				
14	Unearned training revenue		19,600				
15	Notes payable		160,000				
16	Ben Gibson, capital		451,400				
17	Ben Gibson, withdrawals	72,000					
18	Training revenue		550,000				
19	Salaries expense	350,000					
20	Arena rental expense	168,000					
21	Other expenses	7,600					
22	**Totals**	$1,350,400	$1,350,400				

Additional information available at year-end:

   a. The Prepaid Arena Rental of $182,000 was paid on February 1, 2017. It represents seven months of rent on the arena.

   b. A count of the Repair Supplies at year-end revealed that $1,900 had been used.

   c. Annual depreciation of the skate equipment was $82,000.

   d. A review of the Unearned Training Revenue account at year-end showed that included in the balance was $12,600 that had not yet been earned.

   e. Accrued salaries of $58,000 had not been recorded at year-end.

   f. Interest of $1,800 had accrued regarding the Notes Payable.

   g. On June 5, 2017, cash of $92,000 was received for 2017/2018 training sessions (lessons begin in October). This amount is included in the Training Revenue balance.

Required Prepare the annual adjusting entries on June 30, 2017, for each of (a) through (g) above.

Problem 3-12B Preparing financial statements LO6,7

CHECK FIGURES: 1. Adjustments columns = $372,700; Adjusted trial balance columns = $1,492,200
2. Loss = $334,300

Required

1. Using the format presented in Problem 3-11B, complete the adjusted trial balance by including the adjusting entries prepared in Problem 3-11B.

2. Prepare an income statement, a statement of changes in equity, and a balance sheet based on the adjusted trial balance completed in Part 1. Assume that the owner, Ben Gibson, made an investment during the year of $20,000.

Analysis Component: Assume that total liabilities reported at June 30, 2016, were $90,000. Determine what equity and total assets were on that date and comment on the change in the financial position from 2016 to 2017.

Problem 3-13B Preparing financial statements from the adjusted trial balance (month-end) LO7

CHECK FIGURES: 1. Loss = $80,900; 3. Total assets = $273,925

This alphabetized adjusted trial balance is for Mad Catz Courier as of its December 31, 2017, month-end:

	Debit	Credit
Accounts payable...		$ 37,000
Accounts receivable...	$ 25,000	
Accumulated depreciation, equipment...............		95,000
Accumulated depreciation, trucks		24,000
Advertising expense	9,800	
Cash	14,000	
Delivery revenue		190,000
Depreciation expense, equipment.....................	23,000	
Depreciation expense, trucks	12,000	
Equipment	130,000	
Interest income...		250
Interest expense	650	
Interest payable..		325
Interest receivable..	125	
Land	60,000	
Long-term notes payable		100,000
Madison Catz, capital		152,500
Madison Catz, withdrawals...............................	5,000	
Notes receivable (due in 90 days)....................	100,000	
Office supplies..	1,800	
Office supplies expense	5,400	
Repairs expense	17,300	
Salaries expense	41,000	
Salaries payable		15,000
Trucks	62,000	
Unearned delivery revenue...............................		55,000
Wages expense...	162,000	
Totals...	$669,075	$669,075

Required Use the information in the trial balance to prepare:

1. The income statement for the month ended December 31, 2017.

2. The statement of changes in equity for the month ended December 31, 2017, assuming the owner invested $127,000 during December.

3. The balance sheet as of December 31, 2017.

Problem 3-14B Journalizing, posting, adjusted trial balance, adjusting entries (monthly), financial statements (quarterly) LO4,5,6,7

CHECK FIGURES: 3. Cash balance, July 31, 2017 = $3,400; 4. Dr = $45,820; 6. Dr = $50,100; 7. Profit = $7,550

On July 1, 2017, Melanie Thornhill began her third month of operating an electronics repair shop called MT Repairs out of her dad's garage. The following occurred during the third month of operations:

July	1	Collected $3,600 as a deposit for work to be done at the local college in the fall.
	1	Melanie Thornhill withdrew $4,000 cash for personal expenses.
	2	Paid $2,200 for repair supplies purchased on account last month.
	3	Did work for a client and immediately collected $1,400.
	4	Performed services for a customer and collected $3,600.
	7	Hired a new technician to start next week on a casual basis at $400 per day.
	15	Melanie withdrew cash of $1,000 for personal use.
	22	Purchased repair supplies for cash; $1,600.
	31	Paid wages of $2,800.

Required

1. Prepare general journal entries to record the July transactions.

2. Set up the following T-accounts with June 30 adjusted balances: Cash (101), $6,400; Repair Supplies (131), $3,000; Tools (161), $16,800; Accumulated Depreciation, Tools (162), $560; Accounts Payable (201), $3,200; Unearned Revenue (233), $700; Melanie Thornhill, Capital (301) $?; Melanie Thornhill, Withdrawals (302), $0; Revenue (401), $25,800; Depreciation Expense, Tools (602), $560; Wages Expense (623), $1,960; Rent Expense (640), $8,000; and Repair Supplies Expense (696), $2,700.

3. Post the entries to the accounts; calculate the ending balance in each account.

4. Prepare an unadjusted trial balance at July 31, 2017.

5. Use the following information to prepare and post adjusting entries for the month of July:

   a. The tools have an estimated life of five years with no residual value.

   b. One-quarter of the repair supplies balance remained on hand at July 31.

   c. Accrued the July rent expense of $4,000; it will be paid in August.

   d. $3,800 of the unearned revenues remained unearned as at July 31.

6. Prepare an adjusted trial balance.

7. Prepare an income statement and a statement of changes in equity for the three months ended July 31, 2017, and a July 31, 2017, balance sheet.

Analysis Component: When a company shows expenses on its income statement, does this mean that cash equal to the expenses was paid during the period in which the expenses were reported?

*Problem 3-15B Correcting entries L08

As the accountant for Jasper's Telemarketing Services, you discovered the following errors in the May 31 unadjusted trial balance that require correction:

 a. Advertising Expense was debited and Accounts Receivable was credited on May 17 for $16,200 of repairs paid for by Jasper's.

 b. On May 18, Computer Equipment was debited and Accounts Payable was credited, each for $8,100 regarding the purchase of office furniture in exchange for a promissory note.

 c. On May 28, Cash was debited and Telemarketing Revenue was credited for $15,000 cash received in advance from a client.

 d. The Telephone Expense account included $6,300 of delivery expense.

 e. The Telemarketing Revenue account was credited for $1,200 of interest income.

Required Journalize the correcting entries required on May 31.

Analysis Component: The error in (e) shows that an incorrect revenue account was credited. Since the net effect on the financial statements is nil after recording the correction, is it necessary to prepare a correcting entry for this type of error?

*Problem 3-16B Recording prepaid expenses and unearned revenues L09 e**X**cel

CHECK FIGURE: Adjusted trial balance, debits = $110,850

Rainbow Janitorial Services follows the approach of recording prepaid expenses as expenses and unearned revenues as revenues. Rainbow's unadjusted trial balance for the year ended October 31, 2017, follows.

	Rainbow Janitorial Services Trial Balances.xls						
	Home Insert Page Layout Formulas Data Review View						
	P18 fx						
	A	B	C	D	E	F	G
1	**Rainbow Janitorial Services**						
2	Trial Balances						
3	October 31, 2017						
4		Unadjusted				Adjusted	
5		Trial Balance		Adjustments		Trial Balance	
6	**Account**	Dr.	Cr.	Dr.	Cr.	Dr.	Cr.
7	Cash	$ 3,500					
8	Accounts receivable	7,200					
9	Prepaid advertising	-0-					
10	Cleaning supplies	-0-					
11	Equipment	29,000					
12	Accumulated depreciation, equipment		$ 3,200				
13	Unearned window washing revenue		-0-				
14	Unearned office cleaning revenue		-0-				
15	William Nahanee, capital		9,150				
16	Window washing fees revenue		23,800				
17	Office cleaning fees revenue		71,500				
18	Advertising expense	2,900					
19	Salaries expense	56,900					
20	Depreciation expense, equipment	-0-					
21	Cleaning supplies expense	8,150					
22	**Totals**	$ 107,650	$ 107,650				

An asterisk (*) identifies assignment material based on Appendix 3A or Appendix 3B.

Additional information:

    a. On October 31, a physical count revealed cleaning supplies on hand of $6,150.

    b. Annual depreciation on the equipment is $3,200.

    c. It was determined that $6,900 of the balance in Office Cleaning Revenue had not yet been earned as of October 31.

    d. A review of the Window Washing Revenue account showed that only $21,400 had been earned as of October 31.

    e. $1,500 of the total recorded in the Advertising Expense account had not yet been used.

Required Refer to Exhibit 3.22 and use the information provided to complete the columns above.

*Problem 3-17B Recording prepaid expenses and unearned revenues LO4,9

The following occurred for a company during the last two months of its fiscal year ended May 31, 2017:

Apr.	1	Paid $7,200 for future consulting services.
	1	Paid $1,920 for insurance through March 31 of the following year.
	30	Received $7,500 for future services to be provided to a customer.
May	1	Paid $1,200 for future newspaper advertising.
	23	Received $9,200 for future services to be provided to a customer.
	31	Of the consulting services paid for on April 1, $5,000 worth had been received.
	31	Part of the insurance paid for on April 1 had expired.
	31	Services worth $7,200 had not yet been provided to the customer who paid on April 30.
	31	Of the advertising paid for on May 1, $340 worth had not been published yet.
	31	The company had performed $9,000 of the services that the customer had paid for on May 23.

Required

1. Prepare entries for April and May under the approach that records prepaid expenses and unearned revenues in balance sheet accounts. Also, prepare adjusting entries at the end of the year.

2. Prepare entries for April and May under the approach that records prepaid expenses and unearned revenues in income statement accounts. Also, prepare adjusting entries at the end of the year.

Analysis Component: Explain why the alternative sets of entries in requirements 1 and 2 do not result in different financial statement amounts.

Analytical and Review Problem

A & R Problem 3-1

The Salaries Payable account of James Bay Company Limited appears below:

Salaries Payable			
		22,520	Bal. Jan. 1, 2017
Entries during 2017	398,120	388,400	Entries during 2017

An asterisk (*) identifies assignment material based on Appendix 3A or Appendix 3B.

225

The company records the salary expense and related liability at the end of each week and pays the employees on the last Friday of the month.

Required

1. What was the salary expense for 2017?

2. How much was paid to employees in 2017 for work done in 2016?

3. How much was paid to employees in 2017 for work done in 2017?

4. How much will be paid to employees in 2018 for work done in 2017?

Ethics Challenge

EC 3-1

Jackie Houston is a new accountant for Seitzer Company. She is learning on the job from Bob Welch, who has already worked several years for Seitzer. Jackie and Bob are preparing the year-end adjusting entries. Jackie has calculated that depreciation expense for the fiscal year should be recorded as:

Depreciation Expense, Equipment............	123,546	
Accum. Dep., Equipment		123,546

Bob is rechecking the numbers and says that he agrees with her computation. However, he says that the credit entry should be made directly to the Equipment account. He argues that while accumulated depreciation is taught in the classroom, "It is easier to ignore the contra account and just credit the Equipment account directly for the annual depreciation. Besides, the balance sheet shows the same amount for total assets under both methods."

Required

1. How should depreciation be recorded? Do you support Jackie or Bob?

2. Evaluate the strengths and weaknesses of Bob's reasons for preferring his method.

3. Indicate whether the situation faced by Jackie is an ethical problem.

Focus on Financial Statements

FFS 3-1 e**X**cel

You have been given the following information for RPE Consulting for the year ended July 31, 2017.

	RPE Consulting Trial Balances.xls						
Home Insert Page Layout Formulas Data Review View							
P18	fx						
	A	B	C	D	E	F	G
1	RPE Consulting						
2	Trial Balances						
3	July 31, 2017						
4		Unadjusted				Adjusted	
5		Trial Balance		Adjustments		Trial Balance	
6	Account	Dr.	Cr.	Dr.	Cr.	Dr.	Cr.
7	Accounts payable		$ 9,300				$ 10,200
8	Accounts receivable	$ 12,000				$ 22,460	
9	Accumulated depreciation, office equipment		12,000				18,000
10	Advertising expense	13,800				14,700	
11	Cash	27,000				27,000	
12	Consulting revenue		156,000				168,160
13	Depreciation expense, office equipment	-0-				6,000	
14	Insurance expense	-0-				2,440	
15	Interest expense	1,400				2,200	
16	Interest payable		-0-				800
17	Notes payable		44,000				44,000
18	Office equipment	92,000				92,000	
19	Office supplies	18,000				3,000	
20	Office supplies expense	-0-				15,000	
21	Prepaid insurance	7,320				4,880	
22	Ray Edds, capital		28,420				28,420
23	Ray Edds, withdrawals	10,000				10,000	
24	Rent expense	13,200				13,200	
25	Salaries expense	71,000				77,600	
26	Salaries payable		-0-				6,600
27	Unearned consulting revenue		16,000				14,300
28	**Totals**	$ 265,720	$ 265,720			$ 290,480	$ 290,480

Required

1. Prepare the company's income statement, statement of changes in equity, and balance sheet. Assume that the owner, Ray Edds, invested $20,000 during the year ended July 31, 2017.

Analysis Component:

2. Analyze the unadjusted and adjusted trial balances and identify the adjustments that must have been made by inserting them in the two middle columns. Label each entry with a letter.

3. If the adjustments had not been recorded, identify the net overstatement/understatement of each component of the accounting equation.

FFS 3-2

Part 1

Refer to WestJet's income statement in Appendix III at the end of the textbook.

a. Prepare two possible adjusting entries that would have caused 2014 Guest revenues to increase.

b. Prepare two possible adjusting entries that would have caused 2014 Aircraft leasing expenses to increase.

Part 2

Refer to WestJet's balance sheet in Appendix III at the end of the textbook.

c. Prepare a possible adjusting entry that could have caused the December 31, 2014, balance in Prepaid expenses, deposits and other to decrease.

d. Prepare a possible adjusting entry that could have caused the December 31, 2014, balance in Accounts payable and accrued liabilities to increase.

Critical Thinking Mini Case

It's a week before **Scotiabank**'s October 31, 2017, year-end. You are the personnel director and are reviewing some financial information regarding the March 1, 2015, purchase of office furniture for the Western Region offices totalling $700,000 ($300,000 was paid in cash and the balance was financed over four years at 4% annual interest with annual principal payments of $100,000). The useful life of the furniture was estimated to be five years with a projected resale value at that time of $20,000. Insurance was purchased on the furniture at a cost of $8,000 annually, payable each March 1. You leave the office for the day wondering what needs to be considered regarding these items in preparation for year-end.

Required

1. Identify the relevant facts.

2. Describe what principles need to be considered.

3. Outline the goal of financial reporting.

4. Recommend an appropriate accounting policy and describe the impact to the year-end financial statements.

Cumulative Comprehension Problem: Echo Systems

(This comprehensive problem was introduced in Chapter 2 and continues in Chapters 4 and 5. If the Chapter 2 segment has not been completed, the assignment can begin at this point. You need to use the facts presented in Chapter 2. Because of its length, this problem is most easily solved if you use the Working Papers[10] that accompany this book.)

---

[10] If students have not purchased the Working Papers package, the Working Papers for the Serial Problem are available on Connect.

After the success of its first two months, Mary Graham has decided to continue operating Echo Systems. (The transactions that occurred in these months are described in Chapter 2.) Before proceeding in December, Graham adds these new accounts to the chart of accounts for the ledger:

Account	No.
Accumulated Depreciation, Office Equipment	164
Accumulated Depreciation, Computer Equipment	168
Wages Payable	210
Unearned Computer Services Revenue	236
Depreciation Expense, Office Equipment	612
Depreciation Expense, Computer Equipment	613
Insurance Expense	637
Rent Expense	640
Computer Supplies Expense	652

Required

1. Prepare journal entries to record each of the following transactions for Echo Systems. Post the entries to the accounts in the ledger.

Dec.	3	Paid $2,100 to the Lakeshore Mall for the company's share of mall advertising costs.
	3	Paid $1,200 to repair the company's computer.
	4	Received $7,500 from Alamo Engineering Co. for the receivable from the prior month.
	10	Paid Carly Smith for six days' work at the rate of $200 per day.
	14	Notified by Alamo Engineering Co. that Echo's bid of $12,000 on a proposed project was accepted. Alamo paid an advance of $3,000.
	17	Purchased $2,310 of computer supplies on credit from Abbott Office Products.
	18	Sent a reminder to Fostek Co. to pay the fee for services originally recorded on November 8.
	20	Completed a project for Elite Corporation and received $11,250 cash.
	24–28	Took the week off for the holidays.
	31	Received $5,700 from Fostek Co. on its receivable.
	31	Reimbursed Mary Graham's business automobile expenses of 600 kilometres at $1.00 per kilometre.
	31	Graham withdrew $3,600 cash from the business.

2. Prepare adjusting entries to record the following additional information collected on December 31, 2017. Post the entries to the accounts in the ledger.

   a. The December 31 inventory of computer supplies was $1,440.

   b. Three months have passed since the annual insurance premium was paid.

   c. As of the end of the year, Carly Smith has not been paid for four days of work at the rate of $200 per day.

   d. The computer is expected to have a four-year life with no residual value.

   e. The office equipment is expected to have a three-year life with no residual value.

   f. Prepaid rent for three of the four months has expired.

3. Prepare an adjusted trial balance as of December 31, 2017.

4. Prepare an income statement and statement of changes in equity for the three months ended December 31, 2017.

5. Prepare a balance sheet as of December 31, 2017.

Completing the Accounting Cycle and Classifying Accounts

A Look Back

Chapter 3 explained the timing of reports. We described why adjusting accounts is key for recognizing revenues and expenses in the proper period. We prepared an adjusted trial balance and used it to prepare financial statements.

A Look at This Chapter

This chapter emphasizes the final steps in the accounting process and reviews the entire accounting cycle. We explain the closing process, including accounting procedures and the use of a post-closing trial balance. We show how a work sheet aids in preparing financial statements.

Supplied by Cupcakes.

LEARNING OBJECTIVES

LO1   Describe and prepare a work sheet and explain its usefulness.

LO2   Describe the closing process and explain why temporary accounts are closed each period.

LO3   Prepare closing entries.

LO4   Explain and prepare a post-closing trial balance.

LO5   Complete the steps in the accounting cycle.

LO6   Explain and prepare a classified balance sheet.

LO7   Calculate the current ratio and debt to equity ratios, and describe what they reveal about a company's financial condition.

*Appendix 4A

LO8   Prepare reversing entries and explain their purpose.

Sweet Dreams

Heather White and Lori Joyce met when they were just 15 years old working in retail in Victoria, BC, and often dreamed of the day when they would start a business together. After high school they parted ways, but kept in touch and reconnected in 2001 when they found themselves working together selling an industrial product in New York City (NYC). They were working at Ground Zero a week after the terrorist attack on the World Trade Center, witnessing the massive cleanup efforts, including the somber retrieval of bodies from the wreckage. According to Lori, at that time "the hustle and bustle of the City was gone, the City was eerie and silent, people slowed down and were kind, opening doors for each other." To get a break from the intensity, Lori brought Heather to her favourite bakery in the city, Magnolia, which was located in the heart of NYC. Over delicious cupcakes, Heather dreamed up their next initiative, a trendy cupcake shop.

Three months later the friends were jogging in Vancouver's popular West End on Denman Street when Lori had an epiphany as they came upon an empty shop that appeared to be the perfect location for the bakery they had imagined that afternoon in NYC. Heather and Lori saw this as the perfect time in their lives to take action and pursue their dream of running their own company. They wanted their company to be "fresh, fun and a reminder of simpler and innocent times." Without any previous experience in food services or baking, in April 2002 the dynamic duo took a leap of faith and co-founded their first urban bakery—Cupcakes.

Focussing on maximizing each other's strengths and building the brand reputation of their business, Heather and Lori have had an incredible 12 years. Today with an impressive 11 locations in Victoria and the Greater Vancouver Area, these West Coast women have recently opened up their first location outside British Columbia in the heart of downtown Toronto. They meet customer demand through maximizing usage of their bakeries with a focus on wholesome fresh ingredients, and a commitment to quality, and by presenting themselves as a "sweet escape" from the everyday.

Their fresh approach to business and willingness to share their experiences has been highlighted by their own reality series on W, We TV and the Oprah Network (OWN)—which has sold to 95 countries worldwide—called *The Cupcake Girls*. Throughout the episodes they openly expose their business experiences via behind-the-scenes views of the challenges of executing their strategy with time constraints and real-world mishaps. Lori recently embraced a philosophy from the Canadian owner of Boston Pizza and Dragon's Den Investor—Jim Treliving. In his book *Decisions* he advises people to "make decisions about work with their heart, decisions about money with their head and decisions about people with their gut."

Understanding the importance of paying attention to a balance of customer needs and profitability, they have found that in order for business to be successful, "Financials need to be organized and relevant—it is essential that they are up to date and current to make appropriate decisions." It is important to be able to read

(Continued)

an income statement and a balance sheet." Lori encourages future business leaders: "Once you understand the language of accounting it is less intimidating, and you can leverage that and turn it into power. Knowledge is power. Reading monthly P&L's put us in control of the business. For any business decision first the numbers have to make sense, then go beyond the numbers, as many other variables need to be considered—even factors such as culture of the location, luck and timing can drive the success of a store."

Today Heather and Lori have proven creativity and an acute business sense can be successfully combined. They maintain a strong reputation as two of BC's top entrepreneurs and are role models for future entrepreneurs, actively sharing their experiences at speaking events. Their advice to future entrepreneurs: "If you trust your gut and you trust you're disciplined to put in the required effort to make your business succeed, take the leap. Trust your gut instinct! You can't be risk averse to be an entrepreneur."

Source: http://cupcakesonline.com
Inteview with Lori Joyce, dated November, 2014.

Video Link: Find Season 1 of The Cupcake Girls at: https://www.youtube.com/playlist?list=PLesO1cn-vYHeDy7Nr19XlDV4fCyBfZpgr

CRITICAL THINKING CHALLENGE

What type of external users might Cupcakes have for its financial statements? If your job was to review bank loan applications for a bank, what financial statement information would you examine (and why) if Heather and Lori submitted a loan application to open a new bakery to supply their stores?

CHAPTER PREVIEW

Many of the important steps leading to financial statements were explained in earlier chapters. We described how transactions and events are analyzed, journalized, and posted. This chapter begins with an introduction to the work sheet, which is a useful tool for these final steps and in preparing financial statements. Steps 8 and 9 of the accounting cycle are now demonstrated (Exhibit 4.1). Steps 8 and 9 (see Exhibit 4.1) involving the closing process that prepares revenue, expense, and withdrawal accounts for the next reporting period and updates the capital account. It also explains how accounts are classified on a balance sheet to increase their usefulness to decision makers. These tools for managing data are the kind White and Joyce of Cupcakes (in the chapter opening vignette) use to improve decision making.

Completing the Accounting Cycle

Work Sheet

- Benefits of a work sheet
- Use of a work sheet

Closing Process

- Temporary and permanent accounts
- Closing entries
- Post-closing trial balance

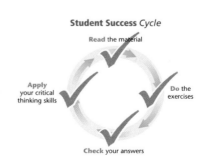

Student Success *Cycle*

Read the material

Do the exercises

Check your answers

Apply your critical thinking skills

Accounting Cycle

- Definition of accounting cycle
- Review of accounting cycle

Classified Balance Sheet

- Classification structure
- Classification categories

Work Sheet as a Tool

LO1 Describe and prepare a work sheet and explain its usefulness.

When compiling the financial statements, accountants prepare several reports and informal documents to help them understand, summarize, and evaluate the numbers presented. These informal documents, called **working papers**, are important tools for accountants to ensure the financial statements are appropriately presented. The **work sheet** is an *optional* working paper that can simplify the accountant's efforts in preparing financial statements. It is an internal document that is not generally distributed to decision makers. The work sheet gathers information about the accounts, the needed adjustments, and the financial statements. When it is finished, the work sheet contains information that is recorded in the journal and then presented in the statements.

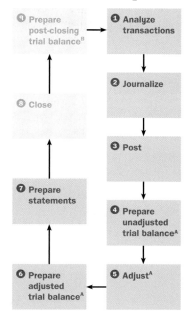

EXHIBIT 4.1

Steps in the Accounting Cycle Introduced in Chapter 4

ᴬSteps 4, 5, and 6 can be done on a *work sheet.*
ᴮ*Reversing entries* are optional and, if prepared, are done between Steps 9 and 1. Reversing entries are covered in Appendix 4A.

Benefits of a Work Sheet (Spreadsheet)

Computerized accounting systems prepare financial statements without the need for a work sheet. Yet there are several potential benefits to using a manual or electronic work sheet:

1. It is useful in preparing interim (monthly or quarterly) financial statements when journalizing and posting adjusting entries are postponed until the year-end.
2. It captures the entire accounting process, linking economic transactions to their effects in financial statements.
3. Auditors of financial statements often use a work sheet for planning and organizing the audit. It can also be used to reflect any additional adjustments necessary as a result of the audit.
4. It helps preparers to avoid errors when working with a lot of information in accounting systems involving many accounts and adjustments.

EXHIBIT 4.2

Preparing the Work Sheet at the End of the Accounting Period

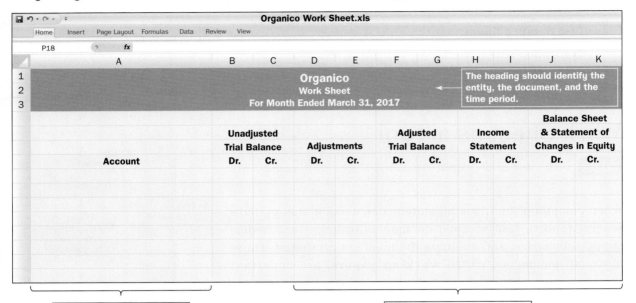

The work sheet can be prepared manually or with a computer spreadsheet program.

The work sheet collects and summarizes the information used to prepare adjusting entries, financial statements, and closing entries.

DECISION INSIGHT

Benefits of Spreadsheets to Produce Work Sheets

Electronic work sheets using spreadsheet software such as Excel make it easy to change numbers, assess the impact of alternative strategies, and prepare financial statements quickly and at less cost. This can also increase the time available for analysis and interpretation. Several of the end-of-chapter exercises and problems include the symbol shown here, which means that an Excel template is available to help in the preparation of a solution. **eXcel**

Using a Work Sheet

Exhibit 4.2 shows a blank work sheet. Notice that it has five sets of double columns for the:

1. Unadjusted trial balance.
2. Adjustments.
3. Adjusted trial balance.
4. Income statement.
5. Balance sheet and statement of changes in equity.

The purpose of double columns is to accommodate both debits and credits. Because the statement of changes in equity includes only a few items, they are simply listed with the balance sheet items.

The work sheet can be completed by following five steps.

ENTER UNADJUSTED TRIAL BALANCE

Step 1 requires us to list the number and title of each account from the ledger along with the account's unadjusted debit or credit balance as shown in Exhibit 4.3.[1] We use the financial information of Organico to demonstrate the function of the work sheet.

ENTER ADJUSTMENTS

Step 2 begins with the entry of adjustments in the adjustments columns. The adjustments shown in Exhibit 4.3 are the same as those discussed in Chapter 3. They are as follows:

   a. Expiration of $100 of prepaid insurance.

   b. Used $1,050 of supplies.

   c. Depreciation on equipment of $200.

   d. Earned $250 of revenue received in advance.

   e. Accrued interest of $35 on the note payable.

   f. Accrued $70 of salaries owed to an employee.

   g. Accrued $1,800 of revenue owed by a customer.

To help you correctly match the debit and credit of each adjusting entry, notice that an identifying letter is used for each adjustment. In entering adjustments, we sometimes find additional accounts that need to be inserted on the work sheet. Additional accounts are inserted below the initial list. ***After entering adjustments on a work sheet, we still must enter adjusting entries in the journal and post them to the ledger.***

PREPARE ADJUSTED TRIAL BALANCE

Step 3 prepares the adjusted trial balance by combining the adjustments with the unadjusted balances for each account. As an example, in Exhibit 4.3, the Supplies account has a $3,600 debit balance in the Unadjusted Trial Balance columns. This $3,600 debit is combined with the $1,050 credit in the Adjustments columns to give Supplies a $2,550 debit in the Adjusted Trial Balance columns. The totals of the Adjusted Trial Balance columns confirm the equality of debits and credits.

EXTEND ADJUSTED TRIAL BALANCE AMOUNTS TO FINANCIAL STATEMENT COLUMNS

Step 4 involves sorting adjusted amounts to their proper financial statement columns. Expense items go to the Income Statement Debit column, and revenues to the Income Statement Credit column. Assets and withdrawals go to the Balance Sheet and Statement of Changes in Equity Debit column. Liabilities and owner's capital go to the Balance Sheet and Statement of Changes in Equity Credit column. At this point it is essential that you know your account titles and to which financial statement each account belongs. These concepts were covered in Chapter 1. Each statement column is totalled. Notice in Exhibit 4.3 that for this step the debits do not equal the credits (explained in Step 5).

---

1 In practice, accounts with a zero balance that are likely to require an adjusting entry would also be listed.

EXHIBIT 4.3

Work Sheet

NOTE: The steps for completing a work sheet are colour coded and correspond to the described steps.

Organico Work Sheet.xls

Home Insert Page Layout Formulas Data Review View

P18   fx

Organico
Work Sheet
For Month Ended March 31, 2017

		Account	Unadjusted Trial Balance Dr.	Cr.	Adjustments Dr.	Cr.	Adjusted Trial Balance Dr.	Cr.	Income Statement Dr.	Cr.	Balance Sheet & Statement of Changes in Equity Dr.	Cr.
8	101	Cash	8,070				8,070				8,070	
9	125	Supplies	3,600			b) 1,050	2,550				2,550	
10	128	Prepaid insurance	2,400			a) 100	2,300				2,300	
11	167	Equipment	6,000				6,000				6,000	
12	168	Accumulated depreciation, equipment				c) 200		200				200
13	201	Accounts payable		200				200				200
14	236	Unearned food services revenue		3,000	d) 250			2,750				2,750
15	240	Notes payable		6,000				6,000				6,000
16	301	Hailey Walker, capital		10,000				10,000				10,000
17	302	Hailey Walker, withdrawals	600				600				600	
18						d) 250						
19	403	Food services revenue		3,800		g) 1,800		5,850		5,850		
20	406	Teaching revenue		300				300		300		
21	622	Salaries expense	1,400		f) 70		1,470		1,470			
22	641	Rent expense	1,000				1,000		1,000			
23	690	Utilities expense	230				230		230			
24		Totals	23,300	23,300								
25	637	Insurance expense			a) 100		100		100			
26	651	Supplies expense			b) 1,050		1,050		1,050			
27	614	Depreciation expense, equipment			c) 200		200		200			
28	209	Salaries payable				f) 70		70				70
29	633	Interest expense			e) 35		35		35			
30	203	Interest payable				e) 35		35				35
31	106	Accounts receivable			g) 1,800		1,800				1,800	
32		Totals			3,505	3,505	25,405	25,405	4,085	6,150	21,320	19,255
33		Profit							2,065			2,065
34		Totals							6,150	6,150	21,320	21,320

③

1. When entering the unadjusted trial balances, include all accounts that have balances or that are expected to have balances after adjustments.

2. Adjustments may create the need for additional accounts. Add new accounts to the existing list as required.

Add two new lines for the profit (or loss) and the totals.

These two columns must show equal totals.

Enter the drafts of the adjusting entries and find the total debits and credits.

These two columns must show equal totals.

Sum the unadjusted trial balance accounts with the adjustments, and enter them in the adjusted trial balance.

These two columns must show equal totals.

Extend revenues and expenses from the adjusted trial balance columns to these columns.

The totals are not equal because the debit and the credit balances in the revenue and expense accounts are not equal.

4. Extend assets, liabilities, and the owner's capital and withdrawals from the adjusted trial balance columns to these columns.

The totals are not equal because the profit component of equity is missing.

5. Enter the profit amount as the difference between the debits and the credits in the income statement columns.

Also enter the profit amount in the credit column to include in equity the change caused by net income.

ENTER PROFIT (OR LOSS) AND BALANCE THE FINANCIAL STATEMENT COLUMNS

Step 5 calculates the difference between the Debit and Credit totals of the Income Statement columns to determine the profit or loss. If the Credit total exceeds the Debit total, there is a profit. If the Debit total exceeds the Credit total, there is a loss. In Exhibit 4.3, Organico's work sheet shows the Credit total to exceed the Debit total, resulting in profit of $2,065. The difference is added to the *Income Statement* and *Balance Sheet & Statement of Changes in Equity* columns for balancing. In the case of Organico where a profit of $2,065 has been calculated, the $2,065 is listed as a *debit* in the Income Statement columns. It is also listed in the Balance Sheet & Statement of Changes in Equity columns, but as a *credit*.

The *new totals* are entered for both sets of columns, showing that the Income Statement columns and Balance Sheet & Statement of Changes in Equity columns now *balance*. If they do not balance, an error has occurred in the completion of the work sheet.[2] The term *profit* (or *loss*) is listed in the Account column to label the $2,065. Adding profit to the last Credit column implies that it is to be added to owner's capital. If a loss occurs, it is listed in the last Debit column, implying that it is to be subtracted from owner's capital.

PREPARE FINANCIAL STATEMENTS USING A WORK SHEET

In *Step 6* the completed work sheet is used to prepare the financial statements. It is important to note that a work sheet is not a substitute for financial statements, it was a tool to help us prepare the financial statements.

Calculate the ending balance of owner's capital, as it does not appear in the last two columns as a single amount.

> Owner's capital = Owner's capital account balance + profit (or minus loss) − Withdrawals account balance

The opening capital balance for the period used for the Statement of Changes in Equity can be calculated by subtracting any owner investments made during the period from the owner's capital account balance, as shown in the last credit column on the work sheet. Exhibit 4.4 shows the statements for Organico as prepared from the work sheet.[3]

DECISION MAKER

Answer—End of chapter

Analyzing Results

You make a printout of the electronic work sheet used to prepare financial statements. There is no depreciation adjustment, yet you own a large amount of equipment. Does the absence of a depreciation adjustment concern you?

---

2 If the columns balance, an error(s) could still be present. For example, the columns would still balance if Accounts Payable were listed as a credit, but in the Income Statement columns. Profit would be incorrect, but the columns would still balance.

3 Notice that the $21,320 balance of the last two columns in the work sheet in Exhibit 4.3 does not agree with the balance of $20,520 on the balance sheet; there is a difference of $800 (= $21,320 − $20,520). *This is not an error!* Notice that accumulated depreciation of $200 is subtracted on the balance sheet to arrive at total assets; it is *added* in the last Credit column on the work sheet. Also, withdrawals of $600 are *subtracted* on the statement of changes in equity to arrive at ending capital; on the work sheet, they are *added* in the last Debit column. These two items account for the difference of $800 (= $200 + $600).

EXHIBIT 4.4

Step 6—Prepare Financial Statements Using a Work Sheet

Organico
Income Statement
For Month Ended March 31, 2017

Revenues:		
Food Services revenue	$5,850	
Teaching revenue	300	
Total revenues		$6,150
Operating expenses:		
Salaries expense	$1,470	
Supplies expense	1,050	
Rent expense	1,000	
Utilities expense	230	
Depreciation expense, equipment	200	
Insurance expense	100	
Interest expense	35	
Total operating expenses		4,085
Profit		$2,065

Organico
Statement of Changes in Equity
For Month Ended March 31, 2017

Hailey Walker, capital, March 1		$ -0-
Add: Investments by owner	$10,000	
Profit	2,065	12,065
Total		$12,065
Less: Withdrawals by owner		600
Hailey Walker, capital, March 31		$11,465

Organico
Balance Sheet
March 31, 2017

Assets		
Cash		$ 8,070
Accounts receivable		1,800
Supplies		2,550
Prepaid insurance		2,300
Equipment	$ 6,000	
Less: Accumulated depreciation	200	5,800
Total assets		$20,520
Liabilities		
Accounts payable	$ 200	
Interest payable	35	
Salaries payable	70	
Unearned food services revenue	2,750	
Notes payable	6,000	
Total liabilities		$ 9,055
Equity		
Hailey Walker, capital		11,465
Total liabilities and equity		$20,520

1. Where do we get the amounts entered in the Unadjusted Trial Balance columns of a work sheet?

2. What are the advantages of using a work sheet to prepare adjusting entries?

3. What are the benefits of a work sheet?

Do Quick Study questions: QS 4-1, QS 4-2, QS 4-3, QS 4-4

Closing Process

LO2 Describe the closing process and explain why temporary accounts are closed each period.

The **closing process** is an important step of the accounting cycle that is performed at the end of an accounting period after financial statements are prepared. It prepares accounts for recording the transactions of the next period. Accounting software automatically performs this step; however, it is important for us to understand the process.

An income statement aims to report revenues earned and expenses incurred during one accounting period. We know that the profit (or loss) from the income statement is shown on the statement of changes in equity, along with withdrawals, to show the change caused to the owner's capital account during one period. Because revenues, expenses, and withdrawals are a part of equity, their balances need to be transferred to the owner's capital account at the end of the period. This transfer of account balances is accomplished by using **closing entries**.

Therefore, closing entries are a necessary step because we want the:

1. Revenue, expense, and withdrawals accounts to begin with zero balances to measure the results from the period just ending.

2. Owner's capital account to reflect:
   a. Increases from profit (or decreases from losses), and
   b. Decreases from withdrawals from the period just ending.

In the closing process, we must:

1. Identify accounts for closing,

2. Record and post the closing entries, and

3. Prepare the post-closing trial balance.

Identify Accounts for Closing—Temporary and Permanent Accounts

Temporary (or nominal) accounts accumulate data related to one accounting period. They include all income statement accounts, withdrawals accounts, and the *Income Summary account*. They are temporary because the accounts are opened at the beginning of a period, used to record transactions for that period, and then closed at the end of the period by transferring their balances to the owner's capital account. They are *temporary* because the accounts describe transactions or changes that have occurred rather than the financial position that exists at the end of the period.

> **Important Tip:** Only temporary accounts are closed, resulting in a reset to zero for the next accounting period. Permanent account balances carry into the next accounting period.

Temporary Accounts	Permanent Accounts
Revenues	Assets
Expenses	Liabilities
Withdrawals	Owner's Capital
Income Summary	

Permanent (or real) accounts report on transactions related to one or more future accounting periods. They carry their ending balances into the next period, and include all balance sheet accounts. *Asset, liability, and owner's capital accounts are not closed* as long as a company continues to own the assets, owe the liabilities, and have equity. They are permanent because they reflect the existing financial position.

Recording and Posting Closing Entries

LO3 Prepare closing entries.

Recording and posting closing entries transfers the end-of-period balances in the revenue, expense, and withdrawals to the permanent owner's capital account.

To close revenue and expense accounts, we transfer their balances first to an account called *Income Summary*. **Income Summary** is a temporary account that contains a credit for the sum of all revenues and a debit for the sum of all expenses. Its balance equals profit or loss, and is transferred to the owner's capital account. Next, we transfer the withdrawals account balance to the owner's capital account. After these closing entries are posted, the revenue, expense, income summary, and withdrawals accounts have zero balances. These accounts are then said to be closed or cleared. The four-step closing process is illustrated in Exhibit 4.5.

EXHIBIT 4.5

Closing Process for a Proprietorship

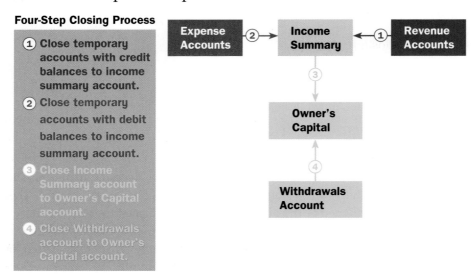

Four-Step Closing Process

1. Close temporary accounts with credit balances to income summary account.
2. Close temporary accounts with debit balances to income summary account.
3. Close Income Summary account to Owner's Capital account.
4. Close Withdrawals account to Owner's Capital account.

EXHIBIT 4.6

Adjusted Trial Balance

Organico Adjusted Trial Balance March 31, 2017	Debit	Credit
Cash..	$ 8,070	
Accounts receivable	1,800	
Supplies	2,550	
Prepaid insurance..	2,300	
Equipment..	6,000	
Accumulated depreciation, equipment.....................................		$ 200
Accounts payable		200
Interest payable		35
Notes payable...		6,000
Salaries payable..		70
Unearned food services revenue...		2,750
Hailey Walker, capital...		10,000
Hailey Walker, withdrawals	600	
Food services revenue		5,850
Teaching revenue...		300
Depreciation expense, equipment..	200	
Salaries expense...	1,470	
Interest expense...	35	
Insurance expense..	100	
Rent expense	1,000	
Supplies expense	1,050	
Utilities expense..	230	
Totals	$25,405	$25,405

Organico's adjusted trial balance on March 31, 2017, is shown in Exhibit 4.6. Exhibit 4.7 shows the four closing entries necessary to close Organico's revenue, expense, income summary, and withdrawals accounts. We explain each of these four entries.

ENTRY 1: CLOSE TEMPORARY ACCOUNTS WITH CREDIT BALANCES
TO INCOME SUMMARY

The first closing entry in Exhibit 4.7 transfers credit balances in revenue accounts to the Income Summary account. We get accounts with credit balances to zero by debiting them as shown in Exhibit 4.8. This prepares each account to record new revenues for the next period. The Income Summary account is created and used only for the closing process. The $6,150 total credit balance in Income Summary equals the total revenues for the year.

ENTRY 2: CLOSE TEMPORARY ACCOUNTS WITH DEBIT BALANCES
TO INCOME SUMMARY

The second closing entry in Exhibit 4.7 transfers debit balances in expense accounts to the Income Summary account. We get the debit balances in the expense accounts to zero by crediting them as

EXHIBIT 4.7			

Closing Entries for Organico

Entry 1:	**Close temporary accounts with credit balances to Income Summary**		
Mar. 31	Food Services Revenue	5,850	
	Teaching Revenue..	300	
	Income Summary.................................		6,150
	To close the revenue accounts.		
Entry 2:	**Close temporary accounts with debit balances to Income Summary**		
31	Income Summary	4,085	
	Depreciation Expense, Equipment		200
	Salaries Expense		1,470
	Interest Expense.................................		35
	Insurance Expense..............................		100
	Rent Expense		1,000
	Supplies Expense		1,050
	Utilities Expense		230
	To close expense accounts.		
Entry 3:	**Close Income Summary to owner's capital**		
31	Income Summary	2,065	
	Hailey Walker, Capital		2,065
	To close the Income Summary account.		
Entry 4:	**Close withdrawals account to owner's capital**		
31	Hailey Walker, Capital	600	
	Hailey Walker, Withdrawals...................		600
	To close the withdrawals account.		

shown in Exhibit 4.8. This prepares each account for expense entries for the next period. The entry makes the balance of income summary equal to March's profit of $2,065. All debit and credit balances related to expense and revenue accounts have now been collected in the Income Summary account.

ENTRY 3: CLOSE INCOME SUMMARY TO OWNER'S CAPITAL

The third closing entry in Exhibit 4.7 transfers the balance of the Income Summary account to the owner's capital account. As illustrated in Exhibit 4.8, the Income Summary account has a zero balance after posting this entry. It continues to have a zero balance until the closing process occurs at the end of the next period. The owner's capital account has now been increased by the amount of profit. Since we know that the normal balance of owner's capital is a credit, increases to owner's capital from profit are credits.

ENTRY 4: CLOSE WITHDRAWALS ACCOUNT TO OWNER'S CAPITAL

The fourth closing entry in Exhibit 4.7 transfers any debit balance in the withdrawals account to the owner's capital account (withdrawals *is not* closed to the Income Summary account). This entry gives

EXHIBIT 4.8

Closing Entries of Organico

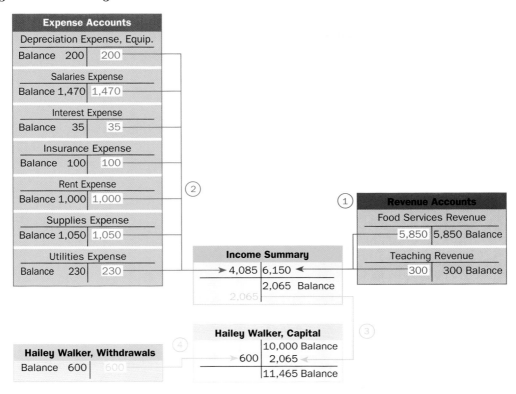

the withdrawals account a zero balance, and the account is ready to accumulate next period's payments to the owner. As illustrated in Exhibit 4.8, this entry reduces the Hailey Walker, Capital account balance to $11,465, the amount reported on the balance sheet.

SOURCES OF CLOSING ENTRY INFORMATION

We can identify the accounts that need to be closed and the amounts in the closing entries by looking to individual revenue, expense, and withdrawals accounts in the ledger.[4] If we prepare an adjusted trial balance after the adjusting process, the information for closing entries is available on the trial balance as illustrated in Exhibit 4.6.

Exhibit 4.9 highlights the posting of closing entries of Exhibit 4.7 in the ledger accounts for Organico. Notice that all of the temporary accounts (revenues, expenses, and withdrawals) have a zero balance. The closing process transferred the balances of the temporary accounts to the Hailey Walker, Capital account. The capital account balance of $11,465 includes owner investment of $10,000 and profit of $2,065, less withdrawals of $600.

---

4   When accounting software is in use, closing entries are done automatically.

CHECKPOINT

4. What are the four major closing entries?

5. Why are revenue and expense accounts called temporary? Are there other temporary accounts?

Do Quick Study questions: QS 4-5, QS 4-6, QS 4-7, QS 4-8

EXHIBIT 4.9	

Ledger After the Closing Process for Organico

Ledger				
Asset Accounts				

Cash			101
Mar. 1	10,000	2,500	Mar. 1
10	2,200	2,400	1
25	1,900	1,000	10
26	3,000	700	14
		900	25
		600	26
		230	26
		700	28
Bal.	8,070		

Accounts Receivable		106	
Mar. 15	1,900	1,900	Mar. 25
31	1,800		
Bal.	1,800		

Supplies		125	
Mar. 1	2,500	1,050	Mar. 31
1	1,100		
Bal.	2,550		

Prepaid Insurance		128	
Mar. 1	2,400	100	Mar. 31
Bal.	2,300		

Equipment		167
Mar. 1	6,000	
Bal.	6,000	

Accumulated Depreciation, Equipment		168
	200	Mar. 31
	200	Bal.

Liability and Equity Accounts				

Accounts Payable		201	
Mar. 25	900	1,100	Mar. 1
		200	Bal.

Interest Payable	203	
	35	Mar. 31
	35	Bal.

Salaries Payable	209	
	70	Mar. 31
	70	Bal.

Unearned Teaching Revenue		236	
Mar. 31	250	3,000	Mar. 26
		2,750	Bal.

Notes Payable	240	
	6,000	Mar. 1
	6,000	Bal.

Hailey Walker, Capital			301
Mar. 31	600	10,000	Mar. 1
		2,065	31
		11,465	Bal.

Hailey Walker, Withdrawals			302
Mar. 26	600	600	Mar. 31
Bal.	-0-		

EXHIBIT 4.9 (continued)

Ledger After the Closing Process for Organico

Revenues and Expense Accounts (including Income Summary)

Food Services Revenue			403
Mar. 31	5,850	2,200	Mar. 10
		1,600	15
		250	31
		1,800	31
		-0-	Bal.

Salaries Expense			622
Mar. 14	700	1,470	Mar. 31
28	700		
31	70		
Bal.	-0-		

Rent Expense			641
Mar. 10	1,000	1,000	Mar. 31
Bal.	-0-		

Income Summary			901
Mar. 31	4,085	6,150	Mar. 31
31	2,065	2,065	Bal.
		-0-	Bal.

Teaching Revenue			406
Mar. 31	300	300	Mar. 15
		-0-	Bal.

Interest Expense			633
Mar. 31	35	35	Mar. 31
Bal.	-0-		

Supplies Expense			651
Mar. 31	1,050	1,050	Mar. 31
Bal.	-0-		

Depreciation Expense, Equipment			614
Mar. 31	200	200	Mar. 31
Bal.	-0-		

Insurance Expense			637
Mar. 31	100	100	Mar. 31
Bal.	-0-		

Utilities Expense			690
Mar. 26	230	230	Mar. 31
Bal.	-0-		

Preparing a Post-Closing Trial Balance

LO4   Explain and prepare a post-closing trial balance.

A **post-closing trial balance** is a list of permanent accounts and their balances from the ledger after all closing entries are journalized and posted. It is a list of balances for accounts not closed. These accounts are a company's assets, liabilities, and equity at the end of a period. They are identical to those in the balance sheet. The aim of a post-closing trial balance is to verify that (1) total debits equal total credits for permanent accounts, and (2) all temporary accounts have zero balances.

Organico's post-closing trial balance is shown in Exhibit 4.10 and is the last step in the accounting process. The post-closing trial balance in Exhibit 4.10 was created by listing the account balances found in Exhibit 4.9. Like the trial balance, the post-closing trial balance does not prove that all transactions are recorded or that the ledger is correct.

CLOSING ENTRIES AFTER PERIOD-END DATE

We are not usually able to make closing entries on the last day of each period. This is because information about certain transactions that require *adjusting* is not always available until several days or even weeks later. Because some adjusting entries are recorded later, closing entries are recorded later, but both are dated as of the last day of the period. Financial statements therefore reflect what is known on the date they are prepared instead of what was known as of the last day of the period.

| EXHIBIT 4.10 | |

Post-Closing Trial Balance

Organico Post-Closing Trial Balance March 31, 2017		
	Debit	**Credit**
Cash..	$ 8,070	
Accounts receivable	1,800	
Supplies	2,550	
Prepaid insurance..	2,300	
Equipment..	6,000	
Accumulated depreciation, equipment...........................		$ 200
Accounts payable		200
Interest payable		35
Salaries payable...		70
Unearned food services revenue.....................................		2,750
Notes payable..		6,000
Hailey Walker, capital..		11,465
Totals	$20,720	$20,720

One example is a company that receives a utility bill on February 4 for costs incurred for the month of January. In preparing the January financial statements, the company's accountant identifies the utility bill as a required accrual and records the expense and the payable as of January 31. The January income statement then reflects expenses incurred in January and the January 31 balance sheet includes the payable, even though the amounts are not actually known on January 31.

CHECKPOINT

6. What accounts are listed on the post-closing trial balance?

Do Quick Study question: QS 4-9

Completing the Accounting Cycle

LO5   Complete the steps in the accounting cycle.

We have now completed the steps in the accounting cycle that have been the focus in this and the previous chapters. Let's now briefly summarize these steps in Exhibit 4.11 to emphasize their importance in providing users with information for decision making.

CHECKPOINT

7. What steps in the accounting cycle are optional?

Do Quick Study question: QS 4-10

The closing process just demonstrated using account information for Organico was a case where revenues were greater than expenses, thus creating profit. The closing process is applied in an identical manner when a loss occurs, as illustrated in the following Mid-Chapter Demonstration Problem.

EXHIBIT 4.11

Summary of Steps in the Accounting Cycle

1. Analyze transactions	Analyze transactions in preparation for journalizing.
2. Journalize	Record debits and credits with explanations in a journal.
3. Post	Transfer debits and credits from journal entries to the ledger accounts.
4. Unadjusted trial balance^A	Summarize ledger accounts and amounts.
5. Adjust^A	Record adjustments to bring account balances up to date; journalize and post adjusting entries to the accounts.
6. Adjusted trial balance^A	Summarize adjusted ledger accounts and amounts.
7. Prepare statements	Use adjusted trial balance to prepare: income statement, statement of changes in equity, balance sheet, and statement of cash flows (details of preparing the statement of cash flows are in Chapter 16).
8. Close	Journalize and post entries to close temporary accounts (revenue, expense, and withdrawals) and update the owner's capital account.
9. Post-closing trial balance^B	Test clerical accuracy of adjusting and closing steps.

^A Steps 4, 5, and 6 can be done on a work sheet.
^B *Reversing entries* are optional and, if prepared, are done between Steps 9 and 1. Reversing entries are covered in Appendix 4A.

MID-CHAPTER DEMONSTRATION PROBLEM

Using the account information in the following adjusted trial balance for Melodies's Piano School:
1. Prepare the closing entries for December 31, 2017.
2. Post the closing entries.
3. Prepare the post-closing trial balance at December 31, 2017.

Analysis Component:

Rather than closing temporary accounts, it would be more efficient to record all transactions affecting temporary accounts (revenues, expenses, and owner withdrawals) directly into capital. Explain why this would be problematic.

Melodie's Piano School Adjusted Trial Balance December 31, 2017		
	Debit	**Credit**
Cash	$ 7,000	
Accounts receivable	3,000	
Piano	31,000	
Accumulated depreciation, piano		$27,000
Salaries payable		700
Melodie Martin, capital		17,200
Melodie Martin, withdrawals	2,300	
Teaching revenue		38,000
Salaries expense	30,000	
Depreciation expense, piano	5,000	
Utilities expense	4,600	
Totals	$82,900	$82,900

Planning the Solution

1. Journalize the four closing entries.
2. Post the closing entries.
3. Prepare the post-closing trial balance.
4. Prepare a response to the analysis question.

Solution

Part 1

Entry 1:	Close the revenue account:		
Dec. 31	Teaching Revenue..	38,000	
	Income Summary..		38,000
	To close the revenue account.		

Entry 2:	Close the expense accounts:		
31	Income Summary	39,600	
	Salaries Expense		30,000
	Depreciation Expense, Piano.............................		5,000
	Utilities Expense		4,600
	To close the expense accounts.		

Entry 3:	Close Income Summary to owner's capital:		
31	Melodie Martin, Capital...	1,600	
	Income Summary..		1,600
	To close the loss in the Income Summary account to capital.		

Entry 4:	Close withdrawals account to owner's capital:		
31	Melodie Martin, Capital...	2,300	
	Melodie Martin, Withdrawals..............................		2,300
	To close the withdrawals account.		

Part 2

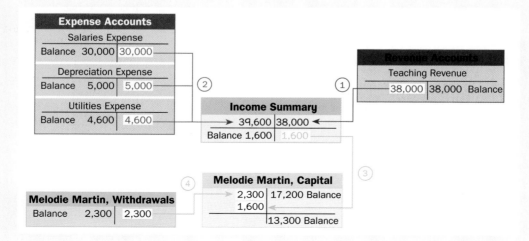

Part 3

Melodie's Piano School Post-Closing Trial Balance December 31, 2017	Debit	Credit
Cash...	$ 7,000	
Accounts receivable	3,000	
Piano	31,000	
Accumulated depreciation, piano		$27,000
Salaries payable..		700
Melodie Martin, capital		13,300
Totals	$41,000	$41,000

Analysis Component:

It might be more efficient to record all transactions affecting temporary accounts directly in capital, but the result would be that the information needed by decision makers regarding the business's performance would be *hidden* within the capital account balance. The purpose of using temporary accounts is to have revenues and expenses appear on the income statement to detail the business's performance for the period. The resulting profit or loss is then combined with owner withdrawals and owner investments as part of capital to show the business's equity position at a specific point in time.

Classified Balance Sheet

LO6 Explain and prepare a classified balance sheet.

Our discussion to this point has been limited to unclassified financial statements. An **unclassified balance sheet** is one in which items are broadly grouped into assets, liabilities, and equity. One example is Organico's balance sheet in Exhibit 4.4. A **classified balance sheet** organizes assets and liabilities into important subgroups to provide users with more useful information for making decisions. One example is information to differentiate liabilities that are due in the near future from those not due within the next fiscal year. Information in this case helps financial statement users assess a company's ability to meet liabilities when they come due.

Classification Scheme

There is no required layout for a classified balance sheet.[5] Yet a classified balance sheet often contains common groupings, including those shown in Exhibit 4.12:

EXHIBIT 4.12

Sections of a Classified Balance Sheet

Assets	Liabilities and Equity
Current Assets	Current Liabilities
Non-current Investments*	Non-current Liabilities
Property, Plant, and Equipment*	Equity
Intangible Assets*	
*Noncurrent assets	

---

5   IFRS 2014, IAS 1, Presentation of Financial Statements, para. 57.

One of the more important classifications is the separation between current and noncurrent items for both assets and liabilities. Current items are those that are expected to come due within the longer of one year or the company's normal *operating cycle*. An **operating cycle** is the average length of time between (1) paying employees who perform services and receiving cash from customers (for a service company) or (2) paying for merchandise and receiving cash from customers (for a company that sells goods).[6]

Exhibit 4.13 shows the steps of an operating cycle for both service and merchandising companies.

EXHIBIT 4.13

Operating Cycles for a Service Company and a Merchandising Company

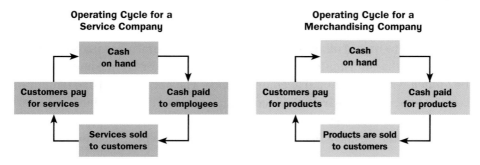

Most operating cycles are less than one year. This means that most companies use a one-year period in deciding which assets and liabilities are current. Yet there are companies with an operating cycle that is longer than one year. One example is a company that routinely allows customers to take more than one year to pay for purchases. Another example is a producer of distilled beverages and other products that require aging for several years. These companies use their operating cycle in deciding which balance sheet items are current.[7]

In most cases, companies present their balance sheet items with current assets before long-term assets, and current liabilities before non-current liabilities. This highlights to users assets that are most easily converted to cash, and liabilities that are shortly coming due. Items in the current group are usually listed in the order of how quickly they could be converted to or paid in cash, which is referred to as a company's liquidity.

Classification Example

The balance sheet for Elite Boardshop is shown in Exhibit 4.14. It shows the most commonly used groupings. Its assets are classified into (1) current assets, (2) equity investments, (3) property, plant, and equipment, and (4) intangible assets. Its liabilities are classified as either current or non-current. Not all companies use the same categories of assets and liabilities on their balance sheets. For example, **TransCanada PipeLines Limited's** December 31, 2014, balance sheet lists six asset classes: current assets; property, plant, and equipment; equity investments, goodwill; regulatory assets; and intangible and other assets.

---

6   IFRS 2014, IAS 1, Presentation of Financial Statements, para. 68.

7   In these uncommon situations, companies provide supplemental information about their current assets and liabilities to allow users to compare them with other companies.

EXHIBIT 4.14

A Classified Balance Sheet

Elite Boardshop Balance Sheet* January 31, 2017			
Assets			
Current assets:			
Cash		$ 6,500	
Short-term investments		2,100	
Accounts receivable		4,400	
Merchandise inventory		29,000	
Prepaid expenses.......................................		2,400	
Total current assets			$ 44,400
Non-current investments:			
Notes receivable, due March 31, 2019.........		$ 18,000	
Land not currently used in operations...........		48,000	
Total investments.......................................			66,000
Property, plant, and equipment:			
Land		$ 73,200	
Buildings...	$170,000		
Less: Accumulated depreciation................	45,000	125,000	
Store equipment	$ 33,200		
Less: Accumulated depreciation...............	8,000	25,200	
Total property, plant, and equipment			223,400
Intangible assets:			
Trademark			10,000
Total assets			$343,800
Liabilities			
Current liabilities:			
Accounts payable.......................................		$ 15,300	
Wages payable		3,200	
Notes payable		3,000	
Current portion of non-current liabilities		7,500	
Total current liabilities		$ 29,000	
Non-current liabilities:			
Notes payable (less current portion).............		150,000	
Total liabilities			$179,000
Equity			
Nolan Jacobsen, capital...............................			164,800
Total liabilities and equity.............................			$343,800

*The classified balance sheet is labelled "Balance Sheet"; it is *not* labelled "Classified Balance Sheet," a common error made by students.

Classification Groups

CURRENT ASSETS

Assets classified under the **current assets** category include all assets such as cash and other resources that are expected to be sold, collected, or used within the longer of *one year of the company's balance*

EXHIBIT 4.15

EXHIBIT 4.15

Example Presentation: Current Assets—Apple Inc. as at September 28, 2013

Apple Inc. Consolidated Balance Sheets	
Current assets (in millions of United States dollars)	
Cash and equivalents..	$14,259
Short-term marketable securities	26,287
Accounts receivable, less allowance of $99...........................	13,102
Inventories	1,764
Deferred tax assets...	3,453
Vendor non-trade receivables..	7,539
Other current assets	6,882
Total current assets	$73,286

sheet date or the company's operating cycle.[8] Examples are cash, short-term investments, accounts receivable, notes receivable, goods for sale to customers (called *merchandise inventory* or *inventory*), and prepaid expenses. Notes receivable expected to be collected after a year or operating cycle would be classified under noncurrent assets. As of September 28, 2013, **Apple Inc.**'s current assets were reported as shown in Exhibit 4.15.

Short-term marketable securities is the terminology used to describe the company's equity or debt investments for which an active trading market exists and those that management intends to sell in the next fiscal year. Deferred tax assets relates to a future benefit the company can utilize to reduce future taxes. Vendor non-trade receivables is a result of Apple's selling raw materials to its manufacturing subcontractors which assemble either subcomponents or final products for which Apple expects to collect in the future. Other current assets include items such as the company's prepaid expenses and are usually small compared to other assets, and are often combined and shown as a single item. It is likely that other current assets in Exhibit 4.15 include items such as prepaid insurance, prepaid rent, office supplies, and store supplies.

NON-CURRENT INVESTMENTS

Non-current investments include all investments management intends to hold to maturity. The distinction between current and non-current classification is determined largely by management's strategic intent to keep the instrument to maturity. Examples of non-current investments in debt instruments include bonds, loans outstanding, and non-current notes receivable. Non-current equity investments generally relate to significant equity ownership in another company usually held for strategic purposes. Non-current investments also can include land that is not being used in operations.

PROPERTY, PLANT, AND EQUIPMENT (PPE)

Property, plant, and equipment (PPE) are tangible assets of which the company has legal ownership as a result of a past business transaction and can use for more than one accounting period to produce or sell products and services.[9] Examples of PPE include machinery, vehicles, computer hardware, buildings, and land. All PPE items are expected to be used in the business to carry out its operations and are not intended to be sold.

---

8 IFRS 2014, IAS 1, para. 66.
9 IFRS 2014, IAS 16, para. 6–7.

INTANGIBLE ASSETS

Intangible assets are resources that lack physical form 'and have benefits that flow to the company for more than one accounting period.,[10] result from a past transaction, for which the company has the legal right, and are expected to provide future benefits. These intangibles add value to the company and are used to produce or sell products and services. Examples include patents, trademarks, copyrights, and franchise rights. Their value comes from the privileges or rights granted to or held by the owner. Apple Inc. lists intangible assets at September 28, 2013, as shown in Exhibit 4.16.

EXHIBIT 4.16

Example Presentation: Intangible Assets—Apple Inc., as at September 28, 2013

(presented in US Dollars) Apple Inc. (in millions)	
Intangible assets..	$4,224

CURRENT LIABILITIES

Current liabilities are obligations due to be paid or settled within the longer of one year of the company's balance sheet date or its normal operating cycle. They are usually settled by paying out current assets. Current liabilities include accounts payable, notes payable, wages payable, taxes payable, interest payable, and unearned revenues. Any portion of a non-current liability due to be paid within the longer of one year or the operating cycle is classified as a current liability. Exhibit 4.14 shows how the current portion of long-term liabilities is usually reported. Unearned revenues are current liabilities when they will be settled by delivering products or services within the longer of the year or the operating cycle. While practice varies, current liabilities are often reported in the order of those that are due to be settled first.

NON-CURRENT LIABILITIES

Non-current liabilities are obligations due beyond the longer of one year or the company's normal operating cycle. Common non-current liabilities include notes payable, mortgages payable, bonds payable, and lease obligations. If a portion of a non-current liability is due to be paid within the year immediately following the balance sheet date, it must be separated and shown as a current liability on the balance sheet. For example, assume the Long-Term Notes Payable account at December 31, 2017, shows a balance of $150,000. We know that $25,000 of this amount will be paid during 2018. On the December 31, 2017, balance sheet, the $25,000 current portion is disclosed as a current liability and the balance of $125,000 ($150,000 − $25,000) is listed as a non-current liability as follows:

Liabilities	
Current liabilities:	
Current portion of long-term notes payable	$ 25,000
Non-current liabilities:	
Long-term notes payable (less current portion)	125,000

EQUITY

Equity is the owner's claim on the assets of a company. In a sole proprietorship, it is reported in the equity section with an owner's capital account. The equity sections of a partnership and corporation are discussed in detail in later chapters.

---

10   IFRS 2014, IAS 38, para. 8–12. Intangible assets are subject to *amortization* in a way similar to how plant and equipment are depreciated. *Amortization* is discussed in Chapter 9.

CHECKPOINT

8. Identify which of the following assets are classified as (1) current assets, (2) property, plant, and equipment, or (3) intangible assets: (a) land used in operations; (b) office supplies; (c) receivables from customers due in 10 months; (d) insurance protection for the next nine months; (e) trucks used to provide services to customers; or (f) trademarks used in advertising the company's services.
9. Name two examples of assets classified as non-current investments on the balance sheet.
10. Explain an operating cycle for a service company, and identify its importance to the classified balance sheet.

Do Quick Study questions: QS 4-11, QS 4-12, QS 4-13

Financial Statement Analysis
Current Ratio

LO7 Calculate the current ratio and debt to equity ratios, and describe what they reveal about a company's financial condition.

Financial statements are important tools for helping decision makers to determine a company's ability to pay its debts in the near future.

The **current ratio** is one important measure used to evaluate a company's ability to pay its short-term obligations. The *ability to pay* day-to-day obligations (current liabilities) with existing *liquid assets* is commonly referred to as **liquidity**. **Liquid assets** are those that can easily be converted to cash or used to pay for services or obligations. Cash is the most liquid asset. The current ratio is useful for decision making and is a widely used tool in making decisions like whether or not to lend money to a company or allow a customer to buy on credit. The current ratio is calculated as current assets divided by current liabilities, as shown in Exhibit 4.17.

EXHIBIT 4.17

Current Ratio

$$\text{Current ratio} = \frac{\text{Current assets}}{\text{Current liabilities}}$$

Using information from the financial statements of **Brick Brewing Co. Limited** (Brick Brewing), we calculate and compare its current ratios at January 31, 2014, and January 31, 2013 (rounded to two decimal places):

January 31, 2014	**January 31, 2013**
$\dfrac{13,618,419}{9,301,928} = 1.46$	$\dfrac{9,497,340}{10,272,571} = 0.92$

Brick Brewing's current ratio at January 31, 2014, can also be expressed as 1.46:1, meaning that there are $1.46 of current assets available to cover each $1.00 of current debt. This tells us that Brick Brewing is in a good position to pay its day-to-day obligations. On January 31, 2013, Brick's ratio was a low 0.92:1, indicating that in the previous year the company did not have sufficient liquid assets to cover its current obligations. Although it varies between industries, generally speaking, a healthy (favourable) current ratio falls between

1.5 and 2.0. When the current ratio is less than this, a company could face challenges in paying for its current obligations. A current ratio greater than 2:1 may signal that an excess of current assets exists. More information would be needed to understand why management is holding on to liquid assets instead of using funds to grow the business. Excessive current assets could represent an inefficient use of assets.

Quick Ratio

The quick ratio is a simple modification from the current ratio, and is a more robust measure of liquidity. The current ratio includes under-the-numerator-only assets that are easily converted into cash, including cash and marketable securities, short-term investments, and receivables. It measures the dollar value of liquid assets available to settle current liabilities. It excludes items such as inventory and prepaid assets to focus on assets that more easily convert to cash. A quick ratio of greater than one is important.

EXHIBIT 4.18

Quick Ratio

$$\text{Quick Ratio} = \frac{\text{Cash} + \text{Equivalents} + \text{Marketable Securities} + \text{Accounts Receivable}}{\text{Current Liabilities}}$$

 **DECISION INSIGHT**

Mountains of Cash

According to Business Insider Inc., companies are still "building up their balance sheets with mountains of cash" since the recent US financial crisis of 2008. The article states that according "to Moody the combined cash of Apple, Microsoft, **Google, Verizon,** and **Pfizer** climbed to $404 billion" by December 2013, which is "in excess of some of Asia's most cash-laden nations including South Korea, with foreign exchange reserves of $226 billion, Hong Kong ($311 billion), Singapore ($270 billion) and India ($268 billion)."[11]

Debt to Equity Ratio

The debt to equity ratio is another calculation that is important for understanding financial statements as it indicates the risk position of a company. Debt financing can be costly for companies, as interest is required to be paid to the bank in conjunction with principal repayments. Investors and external users typically like to assess debt to equity to determine the riskiness of the company in relation to the risk of default on its outstanding loans, as too high of a debt load can lead to bankruptcy. It is important to determine what is normal for the industry when assessing debt to equity ratios as some industries will naturally have higher debt loads such as airlines, which need to finance new aircraft. Automotive manufacturers, food services establishments, and accommodations establishments have higher ratios. The high-tech sector, including computer and electronic manufacturing, typically has lower debt to equity ratios. A lower number is more favourable, the higher the number, the higher the risk associated with the potential for bankruptcy. Refer to Statistics Canada's debt to equity ratio by industry at http://www.statcan.gc.ca for more information on industry trends.

EXHIBIT 4.19

Debt to Equity Ratio

$$\text{Debt to Equity Ratio} = \frac{\text{Total Debt}}{\text{Total Equity}}$$

---

11   http://www.businessinsider.com/global-cash-reserves-companies-nations-2014-4, (accessed September 2014).

We return to the financial statements of Brick Brewing Co. Limited (Brick Brewing), to calculate and compare its debt to equity ratios at January 31, 2014, and January 31, 2013 (rounded to two decimal places):

2014	2013
$= \dfrac{13,856,029}{32,513,225} = 0.43$	$= \dfrac{16,677,936}{28,960,554} = 0.58$

The 2014 decrease in the debt to equity over 2013 signals a favorable change. In 2014 Brick Brewing Co. lowered its debt and increased its ownership interest (equity).

 **CHECKPOINT**

> **11.** If a company misclassifies a portion of liabilities as non-current when they are current how does this affect its current ratio?
>
> **Do Quick Study questions: QS 4-14, QS 4-15, QS 4-16**

 DECISION MAKER   Answer—End of chapter

Analyst

You are analyzing the financial condition of a company to assess its ability to meet upcoming loan payments. You calculate its current ratio as 1.2. You also find that a major portion of accounts receivable is due from one client who has not made any payments in the past 12 months. Removing this receivable from current assets lowers the current ratio to 0.7. What do you conclude?

CRITICAL THINKING CHALLENGE

Refer to the Critical Thinking Challenge questions at the beginning of the chapter. Compare your answers to those suggested on Connect.

IFRS AND ASPE—THE DIFFERENCES

Difference	International Financial Reporting Standards (IFRS)	Accounting Standards for Private Enterprises (ASPE)
Depreciation vs. amortization	• IFRS use the term *depreciation** (although they use *amortization* for intangible assets**)	• ASPE use the term *amortization****

* IFRS 2014, IAS 16, para. 6.
**IFRS 2014, IAS 38, para. 8.
***ASPE, Accounting Standards, Section 3061.16.

A Look Ahead

Chapter 5 looks at accounting for merchandising activities. We describe the sale and purchase of merchandise and their implications for preparing and analyzing financial statements.

For further study on some topics of relevance to this chapter, please see the following Extend Your Knowledge supplements:

EYK 4-1 Work Sheet Demonstration
EYK 4-2 Corporate Supplement
EYK 4-3 Summary of Business Activities
EYK 4-4 Examples of Classified Balance Sheets

Summary

LO1 Describe and prepare a work sheet and explain its usefulness. A work sheet is optional and can be a useful tool when preparing and analyzing financial statements. It is helpful at the end of a period for preparing adjusting entries, an adjusted trial balance, and financial statements. A work sheet often contains five pairs of columns for an unadjusted trial balance, the adjustments, an adjusted trial balance, an income statement, and the balance sheet and statement of changes in equity.

LO2 Describe the closing process and explain why temporary accounts are closed each period. The closing process is the final step of the accounting cycle; it closes temporary accounts at the end of each accounting period: (1) to update the owner's capital account for revenue, expense, and withdrawals transactions recorded for the period; and (2) to prepare revenue, expense, and withdrawals accounts for the next reporting period by giving them zero balances.

LO3 Prepare closing entries. Closing entries involve four steps: (1) close credit balances in revenue accounts to Income Summary, (2) close debit balances in expense accounts to Income Summary, (3) close Income Summary to Owner's Capital, and (4) close the Withdrawals account to Owner's Capital.

LO4 Explain and prepare a post-closing trial balance. A post-closing trial balance is a list of permanent accounts and their balances after all closing entries are journalized and posted. Permanent accounts are asset, liability, and equity accounts. The purpose of a post-closing trial balance is to verify that (1) total debits equal total credits for permanent accounts and (2) all temporary accounts have zero balances.

LO5 Complete the steps in the accounting cycle. The accounting cycle consists of nine steps: (1) analyze transactions, (2) journalize, (3) post, (4) prepare unadjusted trial balance, (5) adjust, (6) prepare adjusted trial balance, (7) prepare statements, (8) close, and (9) prepare post-closing trial balance. If a work sheet is prepared, it covers Steps 4 to 6. Reversing entries are an optional step that is done between Steps 9 and 1.

LO6 Explain and prepare a classified balance sheet. Classified balance sheets usually report four groups of assets: current assets; non-current investments; property, plant, and equipment; and intangible assets. Also, they include at least two groups of liabilities: current and non-current. The equity section on the balance sheet for a proprietorship reports the capital account balance.

LO7 Calculate the current ratio and debt to equity ratios, and describe what they reveal about a company's financial condition. A company's current ratio is defined as current assets divided by current liabilities. We use it to evaluate a company's ability to pay its current liabilities out of current assets. A company's debt to equity ratio is calculated as total debt divided by total equity and is used to determine whether the company is at higher risk of bankruptcy.

Guidance Answer to DECISION MAKER

Analyzing Results

Yes, you are concerned about the absence of a depreciation adjustment. Equipment does lose value as it is used in the business, and financial statements must recognize this occurrence. Its absence suggests an error or a misrepresentation (there is also the possibility that equipment is fully utilized and should have been completely depreciated or that it was scrapped).

Analyst

A current ratio of 1.2 suggests that current assets are sufficient to cover current liabilities, but it implies a minimal buffer in case of errors in measuring current assets or current liabilities. Removing the past due receivable reduces the current ratio to 0.7. Your assessment is that the company will have some difficulty meeting its loan payments.

Guidance Answers to CHECKPOINT

1. Amounts in the Unadjusted Trial Balance columns are taken from account balances in the ledger.

2. A work sheet offers the advantage of listing on one page all of the necessary information to make adjusting entries.

3. A work sheet can help in (a) preparing interim financial statements, (b) linking transactions and events to their effects in financial statements, (c) showing adjustments for audit purposes, (d) avoiding errors, and (e) showing effects of proposed or "what-if" transactions.

4. The four major closing entries consist of closing (1) credit balances in revenue accounts to Income Summary, (2) debit balances in expense accounts to Income Summary, (3) Income Summary to Owner's Capital, and (4) Withdrawals account to Owner's Capital.

5. Revenue and expense accounts are called temporary because they are opened and closed every reporting period. The Income Summary and owner's withdrawals accounts are also temporary accounts.

6. Permanent accounts are listed on the post-closing trial balance. These accounts are the asset, liability, and equity accounts.

7. Making reversing entries is an optional step in the accounting cycle. Also, a work sheet is an optional tool for completing Steps 4 to 6.

8. Current assets: b, c, d. Property, plant, and equipment: a, e. Intangible assets: f.

9. Notes receivable, land not currently used in business operations.

10. An operating cycle for a service company is the average time between (1) paying employees who do the services and (2) receiving cash from customers. Knowing the operating cycle allows current versus long-term assets and liabilities to be disclosed appropriately on the balance sheet.

11. Since the current ratio is defined as current assets divided by current liabilities, then ignoring a portion of current liabilities (1) decreases the reported amount of current liabilities and (2) increases the current ratio because current assets are now divided by a smaller number.

DEMONSTRATION PROBLEM

The partial adjusted trial balance for The Cutlery shows the following account balances as at December 31, 2017.

			Debit	Credit
_____	101	Cash	$ 15,000	
_____	106	Accounts receivable	22,665	
_____	124	Spare parts supplies	5,800	
_____	128	Prepaid insurance	8,700	
_____	141	Notes receivableA	36,900	
_____	163	Office equipment	12,510	
_____	164	Accumulated depreciation, office equipment		$ 2,825
_____	173	Building	129,000	
_____	174	Accumulated depreciation, building		33,000
_____	183	Land	55,000	
_____	191	Patent	11,500	
_____	193	Franchise	26,000	
_____	201	Accounts payable		16,500
_____	209	Salaries payable		26,300
_____	230	Unearned revenue		7,600
_____	251	Long-term notes payableB		142,000
_____	301	Joanne Cardinal, capitalC		104,000
_____	302	Joanne Cardinal, withdrawals	72,000	

AThe note receivable is due to be collected May 1, 2019.
B$22,000 of the December 31, 2017, balance in notes payable will be paid during 2018.
CJoanne Cardinal, the owner, invested $5,000 during the accounting period.

Required

Using the information provided above for The Cutlery,

1. Prepare a classified balance sheet at December 31, 2017. For simplicity, The Cutlery lists accounts on the balance sheet in account order.

2. Prepare a statement of changes in equity for the year ended December 31, 2017.

Analysis Component:

Has Joanne Cardinal, the owner of The Cutlery, financed growth by reinvesting profits? Explain.

Planning the Solution

1. Prepare a classified balance sheet by first listing all of the classification headings under assets and liabilities. Then, sort the accounts by listing them under the appropriate heading. *Hint: Place an X in the column provided to the left of the account number column on the adjusted trial balance as you transfer account information from the adjusted trial balance to the balance sheet. This process will help you determine whether all of the appropriate accounts have been transferred to the balance sheet.*

2. Prepare a statement of changes in equity. *Hint: Revenue and expense information has not been provided from which to calculate profit or loss. However, you will be able to determine what the profit or loss was by taking into consideration the balance sheet prepared in Step 1 and the other elements of equity that have been provided.*

3. Review the information and prepare an answer to the analysis component question.

Solution

1. Prepare a classified balance sheet.

The Cutlery			
Balance Sheet			
December 31, 2017			
Assets			
Current assets:			
Cash		$ 15,000	
Accounts receivable		22,665	
Spare parts supplies		5,800	
Prepaid insurance		8,700	
Total current assets			$ 52,165
Non-current investments:			
Notes receivable			36,900
Property, plant, and equipment:			
Land		$ 55,000	
Building	$129,000		
Less: Accumulated depreciation	33,000	96,000	
Office equipment	$ 12,510		
Less: Accumulated depreciation	2,825	9,685	
Total property, plant, and equipment			160,685

(continued)

(continued)

Intangible assets:

Patent..	$ 11,500	
Franchise	26,000	
Total intangible assets		37,500
Total assets..		$287,250

Liabilities

Current liabilities:

Accounts payable..	$ 16,500		
Salaries payable...	26,300		
Unearned revenue...	7,600		
Current portion of long-term notes payable	22,000		
Total current liabilities		$ 72,400	

Non-current liabilities:

Long-term notes payable (less current portion)		120,000	
Total liabilities...			$192,400

Equity

Joanne Cardinal, capital...		94,850
Total liabilities and equity...		$287,250

2. Prepare a statement of changes in equity.

The Cutlery **Statement of Changes in Equity** **For Year Ended December 31, 2017**		
Joanne Cardinal, capital December 31, 2016		$ 99,000[1]
Add: Profit...	$62,850[3]	
Investment by owner	5,000	67,850[4]
Total...		$166,850[2]
Less: Withdrawals by owner		72,000
Joanne Cardinal, capital, December 31, 2017		$ 94,850

[1]Adjusted capital balance on December 31, 2017 = $104,000; $104,000 − $5,000 owner investment during 2017 = $99,000 capital balance on December 31, 2016.
[2]$94,850 post-closing balance per December 31, 2017, balance sheet + $72,000 owner withdrawals = $166,850
[3]$166,850 − $5,000 − $99,000 = $62,850
[4]$62,850 + $5,000 = $67,850

3. Keiko Nakasu is not reinvesting profits. This is evident from the amount of his withdrawals, $72,000, which represents 115% of the profit earned ($72,000/$62,850 × 100% = 115%). Reinvesting profits occurs when assets are retained by the business for the purpose of growth of the business rather than being taken out through withdrawals, which depletes assets.

Reversing Entries

Reversing Entries

LO8 Prepare reversing entries and explain their purpose.

Reversing entries are optional entries used to simplify recordkeeping. They are prepared on the first day of the new accounting period. Reversing entries are prepared for those adjusting entries that created accrued assets and liabilities (such as interest receivable and salaries payable).

Exhibit 4A.1 shows how reversing entries work for Organico. The top of the exhibit shows the adjusting entry recorded by Organico on March 31, 2017, for earned but unpaid salary. The entry recorded one day's salary to increase March's total salary expense to $1,470. The entry also recognized a liability of $70. The expense is reported on March's income statement and the expense account is closed. As a result, the ledger on April 1, 2017, reflects a $70 liability and a zero balance in the Salaries Expense account. At this point, April 1, the company would make the choice to use reversing entries or not.

Accounting *Without* Reversing Entries

The path down the left side of Exhibit 4A.1 is described in Chapter 3. That is, when the next payday occurs on April 1, we record payment with a compound entry that debits both the expense and liability accounts. Posting that entry creates a $630 balance in the expense account and reduces the liability account balance to zero because the debt has been settled.

The disadvantage of this approach is the complex entry required on April 1. Paying the accrued liability means that this entry differs from the routine entries made on all other paydays. To construct the proper entry on April 1, we must recall the effect of the adjusting entry. Reversing entries overcome this disadvantage.

Accounting *With* Reversing Entries

The right side of Exhibit 4A.1 shows how a reversing entry on April 1 overcomes the disadvantage of the complex April 11 entry. The reversing entry is the exact opposite of the adjusting entry recorded on March 31. The Salaries Payable liability is debited for $70, meaning that this account now has a zero balance after the entry is posted. Technically, the Salaries Payable account now understates the liability, but this is not a problem since financial statements are not prepared before the liability is settled on April 11. The credit to the Salaries Expense account is unusual because it gives the account an *abnormal credit balance.*

Because of the reversing entry, the April 11 entry to record payment is simple. This entry debits the Salaries Expense account for the full $700 paid. It is the same as all other entries made to record 10 days' salary for the employee.

EXHIBIT 4A.1

Reversing Entries for Accrued Expenses

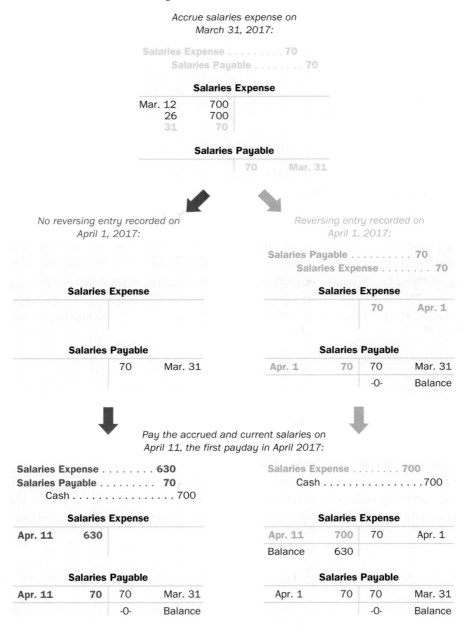

After the payment entry is posted, the expense and liability accounts have exactly the same balances whether reversing entry is made or not.

CHECKPOINT

12. How are financial statements affected by a decision to make reversing entries?

Do Quick Study question: QS 4-17

Summary of Appendix 4A

LO8 **Prepare reversing entries and explain their purpose.** Reversing entries are an optional step. They are applied to accrued assets and liabilities. The purpose of reversing entries is to simplify subsequent journal entries. Financial statements are unaffected by the choice to use reversing entries or not.

Guidance Answers to CHECKPOINT

12. Financial statements are unchanged by the choice of using reversing entries or not.

Glossary

Classified balance sheet A balance sheet that presents the assets and liabilities in relevant subgroups.

Closing entries Journal entries recorded at the end of each accounting period that transfer the end-of-period balances in revenue, expense, and withdrawals accounts to the permanent owner's capital account in order to prepare for the upcoming period and update the owner's capital account for the period just finished.

Closing process A step at the end of the accounting period that prepares accounts for recording the transactions of the next period.

Current assets Cash or other assets that are expected to be sold, collected, or used within the longer of one year or the company's operating cycle.

Current liabilities Obligations due to be paid or settled within the longer of one year or the operating cycle.

Current ratio A ratio that is used to evaluate a company's ability to pay its short-term obligations, calculated by dividing current assets by current liabilities.

Equity The owner's claim on the assets of a company.

Income Summary A temporary account used only in the closing process to which the balances of revenue and expense accounts are transferred; its balance equals profit or loss and is transferred to the owner's capital account.

Intangible assets Long-lived assets that lack physical form and are used to produce or sell products or services.

Liquid assets Assets that can easily be converted to cash or used to pay for services or obligations; cash is the most liquid asset.

Liquidity The ability to pay day-to-day obligations (current liabilities) with existing liquid assets.

Non-current investments Assets not used in day-to-day operating activities that are held for more than one year or the operating cycle, such as a non-current note receivable.

Non-current liabilities Obligations that are not due to be paid within the longer of one year or the operating cycle.

Nominal accounts See *temporary accounts*.

Operating cycle For a business, the average time between paying cash for employee salaries or merchandise and receiving cash from customers.

Permanent accounts Accounts that are used to report on activities related to one or more future accounting periods; their balances are carried into the next period, and include all balance sheet accounts; permanent account balances are not closed as long as the company continues to own the assets, owe the liabilities, and have equity; also called *real accounts*.

Post-closing trial balance A list of permanent accounts and their balances from the ledger after all closing entries are journalized and posted; a list of balances for all accounts not closed.

PPE See *property, plant, and equipment*.

Property, plant, and equipment (PPE) Long-lived tangible assets used to produce or sell products and services; abbreviated *PPE*.

Real accounts See *permanent accounts*.

Reversing entries Optional entries recorded at the beginning of a new period that prepare the accounts for simplified journal entries subsequent to accrual adjusting entries.

Temporary accounts Accounts that are used to describe revenues, expenses, and owner's withdrawals for one accounting period; they are closed at the end of the reporting period; also called *nominal accounts*.

Unclassified balance sheet A balance sheet that broadly groups the assets, liabilities, and equity.

Working papers Internal documents that are used to assist the preparers in doing the analyses and organizing the information for reports to be presented to internal and external decision makers.

Work sheet A 10-column spreadsheet used to draft a company's unadjusted trial balance, adjusting entries, adjusted trial balance, and financial statements; an optional step in the accounting process.

Concept Review Questions

1. What tasks are performed with the work sheet?

2. What two purposes are accomplished by recording closing entries?

3. What are the four closing entries?

4. Daniel is having trouble determining whether withdrawals, the owner's capital, interest income and prepaid insurance are temporary or permanent accounts. Explain to him the difference between a temporary and a permanent account in accounting and classify the accounts into each category.

5. Alexis believes that temporary account information is deleted through the closing entries. Do you agree or disagree? Explain. What is the relationship between temporary and permanent accounts?

6. Describe the similarities and differences between adjusting and closing entries.

7. What is the purpose of the Income Summary account? How is it different from the Income Statement?

8. Explain whether an error has occurred if a post-closing trial balance includes a Depreciation Expense, Building account.

9. Refer to **Danier's** income statement in Appendix III at the end of the book. What journal entry was recorded as of June 28, 2014, to close the revenue account?

10. What is a company's operating cycle?

11. Why is a classified balance sheet more useful to financial statement users than a non-classified balance sheet?

12. What classes of assets and liabilities are shown on a typical classified balance sheet?

13. What are the characteristics of property, plant, and equipment?

14. Refer to the December 31, 2014, balance sheet for **WestJet** in Appendix III at the end of the book. What amount of WestJet's long-term debt is coming due before December 31, 2015?

*15. How do reversing entries simplify a company's accounting efforts?

*16. If a company had accrued unpaid salaries expense of $500 at the end of a fiscal year, what reversing entry could be made? When would it be made?

Quick Study

QS 4-1 Applying a work sheet LO1

In preparing a work sheet, indicate the financial statement debit column to which a normal balance of each of the following accounts should be extended. Use *IS* for the Income Statement Debit column and *BS* for the Balance Sheet or Statement of Changes in Equity Debit column.

1. Equipment

2. Owner, withdrawals

3. Insurance expense

4. Prepaid insurance

5. Accounts receivable

6. Depreciation expense, equipment

QS 4-2 Completing a work sheet LO1

Enter the following unadjusted trial balance and adjustment information onto a work sheet. Complete the work sheet.

An asterisk (*) identifies assignment material based on Appendix 4A.

	Trial Balance.xls				
Home Insert Page Layout Formulas Data Review View					
P18	fx				
	A	B	C	D	E
1	Trial Balance				
2					
3		Unadjusted			
4		Trial Balance		Adjustments	
5	Account	Dr.	Cr.	Dr.	Cr.
6	Cash	15			
7	Accounts receivable	22			
8	Supplies	25			8
9	Ed Wolt, capital		40		
10	Ed Wolt, withdrawals	12			
11	Service revenue		48		
12	Supplies expense	14		8	
13	**Totals**	88	88	8	8

QS 4-3 Work sheet information LO1

The following information is from the work sheet for Pursley Company as of December 31, 2017. Using this information, determine the amount that should be reported for Alice Pursley, Capital on the December 31, 2017, balance sheet.

	Income Statement		Balance Sheet and Statement of Changes in Equity	
	Debit	Credit	Debit	Credit
Cash...			7,000	
Alice Pursley, capital.......................				50,000
Alice Pursley, withdrawals			32,000	
Totals	125,000	184,000		

QS 4-4 Interpreting a work sheet LO1

The following information is from the work sheet for Hascal Company as of December 31, 2017. Using this information, determine the amount for Sam Hascal, Capital that should be reported on the December 31, 2017, balance sheet.

	Income Statement		Balance Sheet and Statement of Changes in Equity	
	Debit	Credit	Debit	Credit
Cash...			4,500	
Sam Hascal, capital........................				165,000
Sam Hascal, withdrawals			32,000	
Totals	115,000	74,000		

QS 4-5 Classifying temporary and permanent accounts LO2

You are the accountant at Stephos Greek Taverna. After completing the December 31, 2017 financial statements, you need to post the closing entries to prepare for the 2018 year. Start the process by completing the following table.

Required

(1) Identify whether the following accounts are temporary or permanent with an "✓" and

(2) Determine what financial statement(s) each account is recorded on (Income statement, Balance Sheet or Statement of Changes in Equity). Note that some accounts may be recorded on more than one financial statement. *anything in the B/S doesn't close*

Account	(1) Temporary?	(1) Permanent?	(2) Financial Statement?
a. Accounts Payable		✓	BS
b. Insurance Expense	✓		IS
c. Delivery Vehicle			BS
d. Interest Income	✓	✓	IS
e. Unearned Revenue		✓	BS
f. Accumulated Depreciation		✓	BS
g. Stephos Petridis, Capital		✓	E.E / BS
h. Depreciation Expense	✓		IS
i. Stephos Petridis, Withdrawals	✓		EE
j. Wages Payable		✓	BS
k. Prepaid Insurance		✓	BS
l. Utility Expense	✓		IS
m. Building		✓	BS
n. Supplies Expense	✓		I.S

QS 4-6 Effects of closing entries LO2,3

Jontil Co. began the current period with a $14,000 balance in the Peter Jontil, Capital account. At the end of the period, the company's adjusted account balances include the following temporary accounts with normal balances:

Service revenue	$35,000	Interest income	$3,500
Salaries expense	19,000	Peter Jontil, withdrawals	6,000
Depreciation expense	4,000	Utilities expense	2,300

a. After closing the revenue and expense accounts, what will be the balance of the Income Summary account?

b. After all of the closing entries are journalized and posted, what will be the balance of the Peter Jontil, Capital account?

QS 4-7 Closing entries LO3

Pure Plant Beauty is a sole proprietorship that has a developed a new line of skin care and makeup that uses natural and organic ingredients. The company showed the following adjusted account balances on April 30, 2017. Prepare and post the closing entries.

Assets	Liabilities	Capital
250	30	200

Withdrawals	Revenue	Expenses
20	100	60

Income Summary

QS 4-8 Closing entries LO3

Warden Repairs showed the following adjusted account balances on October 31, 2017. Prepare and post the closing entries.

Assets	Liabilities	Capital
250	110	200

Withdrawals	Revenue	Expenses
20	100	140

Income Summary

QS 4-9 Post-closing trial balance LO4

SilverStar Automotive showed the following account balances at October 31, 2017, after posting the closing entries. Prepare the post-closing trial balance.

	Cash			Accounts Receivable			Unearned Revenue	
Bal.	40		Bal.	20			10	Bal.

	Capital			Withdrawals			Revenues	
	5	40		5	5		23	23
		15						
		50	Bal.	Bal.	-0-		-0-	Bal.

	Expenses	
	8	8
Bal.	-0-	

QS 4-10 Explaining the accounting cycle LO5

List the following steps of the accounting cycle in the proper order:

    a. Preparing the unadjusted trial balance.

    b. Preparing the post-closing trial balance.

    c. Journalizing and posting adjusting entries.

    d. Journalizing and posting closing entries.

    e. Preparing the financial statements.

    f. Journalizing transactions.

    g. Posting the transaction entries.

    h. Completing the work sheet.

QS 4-11 Classifying balance sheet items L06

The following are categories on a classified balance sheet:

    a. Current assets   **d.** Intangible assets

    b. Non-current investments   **e.** Current liabilities

    c. Property, plant, and equipment   **f.** Non-current liabilities

For each of the following items, select the letter that identifies the balance sheet category in which the item should appear.

    _____ **1.** Store equipment

    _____ **2.** Wages payable

    _____ **3.** Cash

    _____ **4.** Notes payable (due in three years)

    _____ **5.** Land not currently used in business operations

    _____ **6.** Accounts receivable

    _____ **7.** Trademarks

QS 4-12 Balance sheet classifications L06

In the blank space beside each numbered balance sheet item, enter the letter of its balance sheet classification. If the item should not appear on the balance sheet, enter an _h_ in the blank.

    a. Current assets   **e.** Current liabilities

    b. Non-current investments   **f.** Non-current liabilities

    c. Property, plant, and equipment   **g.** Equity

    d. Intangible assets   **h.** Does not appear on balance sheet

    _H_ **1.** Depreciation expense, trucks   _A_ **12.** Cash

    _G_ **2.** Lee Hale, capital   _C_ **13.** Building

    _A_ **3.** Interest receivable   _d_ **14.** Brand name

    _G_ **4.** Lee Hale, withdrawals   _C_ **15.** Office equipment

    _C_ **5.** Automobiles   _C_ **16.** Land (used in operations)

    _F_ **6.** Notes payable (due in three years)   _H_ **17.** Repairs expense

    _P_ **7.** Accounts payable   _A_ **18.** Prepaid property taxes

    _A_ **8.** Prepaid insurance   _e_ **19.** Notes payable (due in

    _b_ **9.** Land not currently used in   two months)

        business operations   _b_ **20.** Notes receivable (due in

    _e_ **10.** Unearned services revenue   two years)

    _C_ **11.** Accumulated depreciation, trucks

QS 4-13 **Classifying liabilities** LO6

Use the following March 31, 2017, year-end adjusted balances to prepare Jardine Servicing's liabilities section on its March 31, 2017, classified balance sheet.

Accounts payable	$ 14,000
Unearned revenue	26,000
Notes payable, due February 1, 2018	45,000
Mortgage payable*	115,000

*$56,000 of this amount will be paid by March 31, 2018.

QS 4-14 **Calculating current ratio** LO7

Calculate Tucker Company's current ratio, given the following information about its assets and liabilities (round to two decimal places) and compare it to the industry average current ratio of 2.2.

Accounts receivable	$15,000	Long-term notes payable*	$20,000
Accounts payable	10,000	Office supplies	1,800
Buildings	42,000	Prepaid insurance	2,500
Cash	6,000	Unearned services revenue	4,000

*Due in three years.

QS 4-15 **Calculating quick ratio** LO7

Using the information in QS 4-14, calculate Tucker Company's quick ratio (round to two decimal places).

QS 4-16 **Calculating debt to equity ratio** LO7

The following is selected financial information from **WestJet**'s Balance Sheet as at December, 31, 2014 and 2013. Calculate the debt to equity ratio for 2014 and 2013 (round to two decimal places). Comment on the change.

(Numbers in thousands)	2014	2013
Current liabilities	1,338,301	1,406,460
Non-current liabilities	1,530,630	1,147,163
Shareholders' Equity	1,777,502	1,589,840

*QS 4-17 **Reversing entries** LO8

On December 31, 2017, Ace Management Co. prepared an adjusting entry to accrue $9,800 of earned but unrecorded rent revenue. On January 20, 2018, Ace received rent payments in the amount of $15,500. Assuming Ace uses reversing entries, prepare the 2018 entries pertaining to the rent transactions.

Exercises

Exercise 4-1 **Extending adjusted account balances on a work sheet** LO1

These accounts are from the Adjusted Trial Balance columns in a company's 10-column work sheet. In the blank space beside each account, write the letter of the appropriate financial statement column to which a normal account balance should be extended.

An asterisk (*) identifies assignment material based on Appendix 4A.

a. Debit column for the income statement.

b. Credit column for the income statement.

c. Debit column for the balance sheet and statement of changes in equity.

d. Credit column for the balance sheet and statement of changes in equity.

_____ 1. Roberta Jefferson, withdrawals	_____ 9. Cash
_____ 2. Interest income	_____ 10. Office supplies
_____ 3. Accumulated depreciation, machinery	_____ 11. Roberta Jefferson, capital
_____ 4. Service revenue	_____ 12. Wages payable
_____ 5. Accounts receivable	_____ 13. Machinery
_____ 6. Rent expense	_____ 14. Insurance expense
_____ 7. Depreciation expense, machinery	_____ 15. Interest expense
_____ 8. Accounts payable	_____ 16. Interest receivable

Exercise 4-2 Extending accounts in the work sheet LO1 eXcel

CHECK FIGURE: Loss = $8,150

The Adjusted Trial Balance columns of a 10-column work sheet for Webber Co. follow. Complete the work sheet by extending the account balances into the appropriate financial statement columns and by entering the amount of profit or loss for the reporting period.

Webber Co. Work Sheet.xls

Home   Insert   Page Layout   Formulas   Data   Review   View

P18   fx

Webber Co.
Work Sheet
December 31, 2017

	Account	Adjusted Trial Balance Debit	Credit
101	Cash	$ 21,000	
106	Accounts receivable	8,200	
153	Trucks	48,000	
154	Accumulated depreciation, trucks		$ 31,250
193	Franchise	6,500	
201	Accounts payable		13,000
209	Salaries payable		14,600
233	Unearned revenue		2,450
301	Bo Webber, capital		37,750
302	Bo Webber, withdrawals	7,200	
401	Plumbing revenue		31,600
611	Depreciation expense, trucks	12,100	
622	Salaries expense	17,800	
640	Rent expense	6,000	
677	Miscellaneous expense	3,850	
	Totals	**$ 130,650**	**$ 130,650**

Exercise 4-3 Preparing a work sheet LO1

CHECK FIGURE: 3. Adjusted trial balance columns = $358,200

The December 31, 2017, unadjusted trial balance for Musical Sensations after its second year of operations follows:

	Musical Sensations Work Sheet.xls	
Home Insert Page Layout Formulas Data Review View		
P18 ⌐ *fx*		
A	**B**	**C**

	Account	Unadjusted Trial Balance Debit	Credit
1	**Musical Sensations**		
2	**Work Sheet**		
3	**December 31, 2017**		
4		**Unadjusted**	
5		**Trial Balance**	
6	**Account**	**Debit**	**Credit**
7	Cash	$ 7,500	
8	Accounts receivable	14,200	
9	Office supplies	790	
10	Musical equipment	125,000	
11	Accumulated depreciation, musical equipment		$ 21,600
12	Accounts payable		4,200
13	Unearned performance revenue		12,400
14	Jim Daley, capital		154,300
15	Jim Daley, withdrawals	52,000	
16	Performance revenue		138,000
17	Salaries expense	86,000	
18	Travelling expense	45,010	
19	**Totals**	**$ 330,500**	**$ 330,500**

Required
1. Enter the unadjusted trial balance onto a work sheet.
2. Using the following additional information, enter the adjustments into the work sheet:
   a. A review of the Unearned Performance Revenue account revealed a balance remaining of $9,225.
   b. Annual depreciation on the musical equipment is $21,600.
   c. Accrued salaries at December 31 totalled $6,100. — Salaries payable
   d. It was determined that $650 of the balance in the Office Supplies account had been used.
3. Complete the work sheet.
4. Calculate the balance in the capital account as it would appear on the December 31, 2017, balance sheet.

Exercise 4-4 **Work sheet interpretation and closing entries** LO1,3

Below are excerpts from the work sheets of two businesses as at March 31, 2017. Those rows that calculate totals are at the bottom of the last two sets of columns.

Required Do the following for each business:

1. Identify the profit or loss for the year ended March 31, 2017.

2. Prepare the entry to close the Income Summary account to capital.

3. Calculate the post-closing balance in capital at March 31, 2017.

a.

Income Statement		Balance Sheet and Statement of Changes in Equity	
Debit	Credit	Debit	Credit
263,700	300,500	357,300	320,500
36,800			36,800
300,500	300,500	357,300	357,300

*The adjusted balances in withdrawals and capital were $17,000 and $63,000, respectively.

b.

Income Statement		Balance Sheet and Statement of Changes in Equity	
Debit	Credit	Debit	Credit
540,000	480,000	945,000	1,005,000
	60,000	60,000	
540,000	540,000	1,005,000	1,005,000

*The adjusted balances in withdrawals and capital were $0 and $114,000, respectively.

Exercise 4-5 **Completing the income statement columns and preparing closing entries** LO1,3

These partially completed Income Statement columns from a 10-column work sheet are for the Winston Sail'em Boat Rental Company for the year ended December 31, 2017. Use the information to determine the amount that should be entered on the profit line of the work sheet. In addition, prepare closing entries for the company. The owner's name is Carl Winston, and the preclosing balance of the withdrawals account is $18,000.

	Debit	Credit
Rent revenue		99,000
Salaries expense	35,300	
Insurance expense	4,400	
Dock rental expense....................................	12,000	
Boat supplies expense	6,220	
Depreciation expense, boats...........................	21,500	_____
Totals...		
Profit..	_____	_____
Totals...		

Exercise 4-6 **Preparing closing entries and the post-closing trial balance** LO2,3,4

CHECK FIGURE: Post-closing trial balance columns = $51,300

The adjusted trial balance at April 30, 2017, for Willard Co. follows.

		Debit	Credit
101	Cash	$ 3,600	
106	Accounts receivable..	8,500	
153	Trucks	26,000	
154	Accumulated depreciation, trucks		$ 8,250
193	Franchise...	13,200	
201	Accounts payable..		9,600
209	Salaries payable		3,200
233	Unearned revenue		1,300
301	Sid Willard, capital		29,100
302	Sid Willard, withdrawals	9,600	
401	Plumbing revenue..		42,050
611	Depreciation expense, trucks	4,900	
622	Salaries expense	17,800	
640	Rent expense...	3,000	
677	Advertising expense	6,900	
901	Income summary		
	Totals...	$93,500	$93,500

Required

1. Prepare the four closing entries.

2. Prepare a post-closing trial balance.

Exercise 4-7 **Closing entries** LO2,3

Following is the adjusted trial balance, with accounts in alphabetical order, for TRN Magazine as at January 31, 2017:

	Debit	Credit
Accounts receivable..	$ 21,000	
Accumulated depreciation, equipment..............		$ 12,000
Cash	8,500	
Depreciation expense, equipment.....................	1,500	
Equipment	19,000	
Interest income...		450
Rent expense...	17,500	
Salaries expense	61,000	
Subscription revenues		71,000
Trish Norris, capital		45,450
Trish Norris, withdrawals...................................	19,400	
Unearned subscription revenue		19,000
Totals...	$147,900	$147,900

Required Prepare the closing entries.

Exercise 4-8 **Closing entries** LO2,3

Improv Club (IC) features entertaining improvisational theatre performances. The theatre features a range of shows and talented performers. IC prepares financial statements on an annual basis. The following year-end accounts as of December 31, 2017 are listed in alphabetical order and have normal balances.

Accumulated depreciation, equipment...................	$ 13,000		Prepaid insurance...............................	$ 6,500
Cash	40,000		Rent expense	61,000
Depreciation expense, equipment.........................	4,000		Salaries expense.................................	42,000
Equipment	46,000		Supplies	4,000
Insurance expense	3,000		Supplies expense	8,600
Nick Stilz, capital	110,100		Ticket revenue....................................	131,000
Nick Stilz, withdrawals	43,000		Unearned revenue	4,000

Required

1. Prepare an adjusted trial balance as at December 31, 2017. Will Nick Stilz's capital account of $110,100 appear on the balance sheet as at December 31, 2017? Explain.

2. Prepare the closing entries for the company.

3. What is the ending balance of Nick Stilz's capital account as at December 31, 2017?

Exercise 4-9 Preparing and posting closing entries LO2,3

CHECK FIGURE: Post-closing balance, Marcy Jones, Capital = $91,000

Set up the following general ledger accounts using T-accounts for Jones's Consulting with the balances provided. Prepare closing entries at December 31, 2017, and post them to the T-accounts.

Assets		Liabilities			Marcy Jones, Capital	
Dec. 31 142,000			51,000 Dec. 31			71,800 Dec. 31

Rent Expense		Marcy Jones, Withdrawals		Salaries Expense	
Dec. 31 9,100		Dec. 31 38,000		Dec. 31 27,000	

Income Summary		Insurance Expense		Services Revenue	
		Dec. 31 1,500			103,000 Dec. 31

Depreciation Expense	
Dec. 31 8,200	

Exercise 4-10 Post-closing trial balance LO4

Required Using your answer from Exercise 4-9, prepare a post-closing trial balance.

Exercise 4-11 Post-closing trial balance LO2,3,4

Jozef's Roofing Services showed the following post-closing trial balance after the posting of the closing entries on June 30, 2017:

	Debit	Credit
Cash	$ 21,000	
Accounts receivable	36,000	
Equipment	59,500	
Accumulated depreciation, equipment		$ 12,000
Trucks	138,000	
Accumulated depreciation, trucks		66,000
Accounts payable		19,200
Jozef Jones, capital		216,200
Jozef Jones, withdrawals	59,900	
Interest income		1,150
Other expenses	150	
Totals	$314,550	$314,550

Required

1. Identify the error(s) in the post-closing trial balance.

2. What entry is required to correct the error(s)?

3. Calculate the correct balance at June 30, 2017, for Jozef Jones, Capital.

Exercise 4-12 **Post-closing trial balance** LO2,3,4

CHECK FIGURE: b. = $200,150

The March 31, 2017, adjusted trial balance for Amusement Park Repair is shown below with accounts in alphabetical order.

		Debit	Credit
_____	Accounts payable..		$ 31,000
_____	Accounts receivable...	$ 48,000	
_____	Accumulated depreciation, equipment.........................		9,000
_____	Accumulated depreciation, truck................................		21,000
_____	Cash	14,400	
_____	Depreciation expense	3,800	
_____	Equipment...	19,000	
_____	Franchise...	21,000	
_____	Gas and oil expense..	7,500	
_____	Interest expense	450	
_____	Interest payable...		750
_____	Land not currently used in business operations............	148,000	
_____	Long-term notes payable[1]..		35,000
_____	Notes payable, due February 1, 2018		7,000
_____	Notes receivable[2]...	6,000	
_____	Intangible asset...	7,000	
_____	Prepaid rent..	14,000	
_____	Rent expense..	51,000	
_____	Repair revenue..		266,000
_____	Repair supplies	13,100	
_____	Repair supplies expense..	29,000	
_____	Truck	26,000	
_____	Unearned repair revenue..		12,600
_____	Vic Sopik, capital		74,900
_____	Vic Sopik, withdrawals	49,000	
	Totals...	$457,250	$457,250

[1]$5,000 of the long-term note payable is due during the year ended March 31, 2018.
[2]$2,000 of the notes receivable will be collected by March 31, 2018.

Required

Preparation Component:

    a. Place an X in the space provided beside each *account balance* that would *not* appear on the post-closing trial balance.

    b. Calculate the post-closing balance in the owner's capital.

Analysis Component: Explain why the account balances identified in part (a) would not appear on the post-closing trial balance.

Exercise 4-13 **Classified balance sheet** LO6

CHECK FIGURE: i. = $286,500

Using the information in Exercise 4-12, calculate each of the following:

    a. Current assets

    b. Property, plant, and equipment

    c. Intangible assets

    d. Non-current investments

    e. Total assets

    f. Current liabilities

    g. Non-current liabilities

    h. Total liabilities

    i. Total liabilities and equity

Exercise 4-14 Preparing a classified balance sheet L06   e**X**cel

Sunshine Sushi, a Japanese restaurant, has the following adjusted trial balance with accounts listed in alphabetical order. Using the template provided, prepare a classified balance sheet for the year-ended December 31, 2017. For the bank loan, $50,000 is due in 2018. For Notes receivable, $30,000 will be collected in 2018.

Account Title	Debit	Credit
Accounts payable..		$30,000
Accumulated depreciation, equipment...............		80,000
Accumulated depreciation, furniture.................		37,500
Bank loan		400,000
Cash	$100,000	
Equipment	300,000	
Operating expenses	30,000	
Furniture..	100,000	
Merchandise inventory	25,000	
Natsuki Miyakawa, capital		27,500
Natsuki Miyakawa, withdrawal.........................	5,000	
Notes receivable	85,000	
Revenue		50,000
Wages payable		20,000
Total...	$645,000	$645,000

Sunshine Sushi Balance Sheet December 31, 2017			
Assets			
Current assets:			
Total current assets			
Non-current investments:			
Property, plant, and equipment:			
Total assets			
Liabilities			
Current liabilities:			
Total current liabilities			
Non-current liabilities:			
Total liabilities			
Equity			
Total liabilities and equity			

Exercise 4-15 **Preparing a classified balance sheet** LO6

CHECK FIGURE: Total assets = $122,150

A partial alphabetized list of adjusted account balances for Dover Pacific Tours as at November 30, 2017, is shown (all accounts have normal balances). Pat Dover, the owner, uses the following account classification system:

101–149	Current assets		190–199	Non-current investments
150–169	Property, plant, and equipment		201–249	Current liabilities
170–189	Intangible assets		250–299	Non-current liabilities

Acct. No.	Account Title	Adjusted Account Balance
201	Accounts payable...	$41,000
106	Accounts receivable...	19,000
155	Accumulated depreciation, office furniture	4,100
153	Accumulated depreciation, vehicles	15,800
101	Cash	7,200
172	Copyright..	9,000
240	Notes payable	14,000
270	Notes payable[1]	21,600
195	Notes receivable[2]..	20,500
154	Office furniture..	6,500
110	Prepaid insurance	4,600
112	Prepaid rent..	9,000
205	Salaries payable	12,100
118	Supplies...	2,250
206	Unearned touring revenue	23,000
152	Vehicles	64,000

[1]$10,000 of this note payable is to be paid by November 30, 2018.
[2]$7,500 of the notes receivable is to be collected by November 30, 2018.

Required Prepare a classified balance sheet.

Exercise 4-16 **Preparing a classified balance sheet** LO6

CHECK FIGURE: Total assets = $444,700

Use the following adjusted trial balance of Hanson Trucking Company to prepare a classified balance sheet as of December 31, 2017.

Account Title	Debit	Credit
Cash	$ 13,000	
Accounts receivable...	29,600	
Office supplies...	3,100	
Trucks	170,000	
Accumulated depreciation, trucks		$ 46,000
Land	275,000	
Accounts payable..		31,000
Interest payable..		400
Long-term notes payable (due in 4 years)		152,000
Stanley Hanson, capital....................................		206,200
Stanley Hanson, withdrawals	19,000	
Trucking revenue		168,000
Depreciation expense, trucks	22,500	
Salaries expense	58,000	
Office supplies expense	6,500	
Repairs expense, trucks	6,900	
Total...	$603,600	$603,600

Exercise 4-17 **Comprehensive accounting cycle** LO2,3,4,5,6

CHECK FIGURES: c. Total debits = $38,000; e. Total debits = $40,000; f. Profit = $3,400;
Total assets = $18,000; h. Total debits = $30,000

After five years of operations, Svenson's Tutoring Clinic showed the following post-closing balances at December 31, 2016.

Cash	Accounts Receivable	Prepaid Rent	Office Equipment
2,000	5,000	3,000	20,000

Accumulated Depreciation, Office Equipment	Unearned Revenue	Leda Svenson, Capital	Leda Svenson, Withdrawals
10,000	2,900	17,100	-0-

Tutoring Revenue	Rent Expense	Depreciation Expense	Advertising Expense
-0-	-0-	-0-	-0-

Required

Analysis Component:

a. Explain why Leda Svenson, Withdrawals, Tutoring Revenue, Rent Expense, Depreciation Expense, and Advertising Expense have zero balances.

Preparation Component:

b. Journalize and post the following transactions that occurred during 2017.

Jan 15	Provided $8,000 of tutoring services on account.
Feb. 20	Paid $2,000 for advertising that appeared in today's newspaper.
Jul. 7	Collected $9,000 from credit customers.
Dec. 10	The owner withdrew $3,000 cash for personal use.

c. Prepare an unadjusted trial balance as at December 31, 2017.

d. Journalize and post the adjusting entries on December 31, 2017, based on the following additional information:

– Annual depreciation on the office equipment is $2,000.

– $2,400 of the balance in unearned revenue has been earned.

– The entire balance in prepaid rent has expired.

e. Prepare an adjusted trial balance at December 31, 2017.

f. Prepare an income statement, statement of changes in equity, and classified balance sheet.

g. Journalize and post the closing entries.

h. Prepare a post-closing trial balance.

Exercise 4-18 Complete Accounting cycle (monthly) LO2,3,5,6

Emily Lee grew up in Vancouver and loves to be a tourist in her own city. In order to make money to pay for university, she opened a walking tour company, Very Vancouver. The following are transactions for the month of May 2017, the first month of operations.

May 2	Emily moved $5,500 from her personal bank account to a business bank account at TD Bank. She also invested a laptop worth $900 into the business.
May 3	Purchased supplies, including a microphone, and brochures for $600 cash.
May 4	Purchased a printer for $360 on account.
May 5	Purchased a one-year insurance policy for $2,400 cash.
May 6	Emily withdrew $200 for a Mother's Day gift.
May 8	Interviewed and hired one employee to assist with leading tours.
May 10	Emily launched a social media campaign of Very Vancouver on Facebook. As a result, she received $1,920 of cash for future tour bookings.
May 15	Led three tours of Stanley Park and received $600 cash.
May 25	Led four tours of Granville Island for $1,000. The customers on this tour had prepaid on May 10.

The following information is known at May 31, 2017.

- The laptop has an estimated life of three years.
- The printer has an estimated life of three years.
- There are $200 of supplies that are not used.
- A portion of the insurance policy has expired.
- Wages of $500 were unpaid and unrecorded.

Required

1. Prepare journal entries for the May transactions.
2. Post the journal entries to the general ledger accounts using T-accounts.
3. Prepare and post all required adjusting entries to the T-accounts.
4. Prepare an income statement, statement of changes in equity, and classified balance sheet.
5. Prepare the journal entries for the closing entries and post them to the T-accounts.
6. Prepare a post-closing trial balance.

Exercise 4-19 Calculating the current ratio LO7

Calculate (to two decimal places) the current ratio in each of the following cases and indicate whether it is *Favourable* (F) or *Unfavourable* (U) (assuming that the current ratio for the industry is an average of 1.1):

	Case 1	Case 2	Case 3	Case 4
Current Assets	$78,000	$104,000	$44,000	$84,500
Current Liabilities	31,000	75,000	48,000	80,600

Exercise 4-20 Calculating the current ratio and quick ratio LO7

The following is selected simplified information from **Second Cup Ltd.**'s Balance Sheet as at December 28, 2013, and December 29, 2012. You, business analyst at Second Cup, have been asked to calculate the current ratio and the quick ratio (round to two decimal places). Provide your manager with comments on the ratios and the change from 2012 to 2013.

(Numbers in thousands)	2013	2012
Cash	$ 6,501	$ 3,880
Accounts receivable	4,368	4,616
Notes receivable (current)	220	265
Inventories	123	137
Prepaid expenses and other (current) assets	190	695
Current liabilities	11,061	10,649
Total liabilities	31,376	31,980
Shareholders' equity	45,964	56,700
Source: Second Cup 2013 Annual Report		

Exercise 4-21 Calculating the debt to equity ratio LO7

Refer to the information in Exercise 4-20. You, business analyst at Second Cup Ltd. have been asked to calculate the debt to equity ratio (round to two decimal places). Provide your manager with comments on the ratio and the change from 2012 to 2013.

*Exercise 4-22 Reversing entries LO8

Breaker Corporation records prepaid assets and unearned revenues in balance sheet accounts. The following information was used to prepare adjusting entries for Breaker Corporation as of August 31, 2017, the end of the company's fiscal year:

    a. The company has earned $5,000 of unrecorded service revenue.

    b. The expired portion of prepaid insurance is $2,700.

    c. The earned portion of the Unearned Revenue account balance is $1,900.

    d. Depreciation expense for the office equipment is $2,300.

    e. Employees have earned but have not been paid salaries of $2,400.

Required Prepare the appropriate reversing entries that would simplify the bookkeeping effort for recording subsequent cash transactions related to these adjustments.

*Exercise 4-23 Reversing entries LO8

The following conditions existed for Maxit Co. on October 31, 2017, the end of its fiscal year:

    a. Maxit rents a building for $3,200 per month. By a prearrangement, the company delayed paying October's rent until November 5. On this date, the company paid the rent for both October and November.

    b. Maxit rents space in a building it owns to a tenant for $750 per month. By prearrangement, the tenant delayed paying the October rent until November 8. On this date, the tenant paid the rent for both October and November.

Required

  1. Prepare the adjusting entries that Maxit should record for these situations as of October 31.

  2. Assuming that Maxit does not use reversing entries, prepare journal entries to record Maxit's payment of rent on November 5 and the collection of rent on November 8 from Maxit's tenant.

An asterisk (*) identifies assignment material based on Appendix 4A.

3. Assuming that Maxit does use reversing entries, prepare those entries and the journal entries to record Maxit's payment of rent on November 5 and the collection of rent on November 8 from Maxit's tenant.

Problems

Problem 4-1A **Completing a work sheet** L01   e**X**cel

CHECK FIGURE: 3. Adjusted trial balance columns = $646,265

The March 31, 2017, unadjusted trial balance for Silva Rentals after its first year of operations is shown below:

🖫 🕤 ▾ 🕑 ▾) ≑		**Nanimahoo Rentals Trial Balance.xls**		
	Home	Insert Page Layout Formulas Data Review View		
	P18	⤵ fx		
	A		B	C
1		**Silva Rentals**		
2		**Unadjusted Trial Balance**		
3		**March 31, 2017**		
4			**Unadjusted**	
5			**Trial Balance**	
6	**No.**	**Account**	**Dr.**	**Cr.**
7	101	Cash	$ 7,000	
8	110	Rent receivable	31,000	
9	124	Office supplies	2,250	
10	141	Notes receivable, due 2020	46,000	
11	161	Furniture	16,000	
12	173	Building	216,000	
13	183	Land	41,000	
14	191	Patent	9,600	
15	201	Accounts payable		$ 13,750
16	252	Long-term note payable		175,000
17	301	Stephen Silva, capital		90,250
18	302	Stephen Silva, withdrawals	92,000	
19	406	Rent revenue		328,800
20	620	Office salaries expense	52,000	
21	633	Interest expense	5,250	
22	655	Advertising expense	14,600	
23	673	Janitorial expense	41,000	
24	690	Utilities expense	34,100	
25		**Totals**	**$ 607,800**	**$ 607,800**

Required

1. Enter the unadjusted trial balance onto a work sheet.

2. Using the following additional information, enter the adjustments into the work sheet (the Chart of Accounts at the back of the textbook may be useful when additional accounts are required):

   a. It was determined that the balance in the Rent Receivable account at March 31 should be $36,000.

   b. A count of the office supplies showed $1,830 of the balance had been used.

c. Annual depreciation on the building is $25,000 and $3,500 on the furniture.

d. The two part-time office staff members each get paid $1,600 biweekly. The last biweekly pay period ended Friday, March 21. At March 31, six days' salary had accrued.

e. A review of the balance in Advertising Expense showed that $2,400 was for advertisements to appear in the April issue of *Canadian Business* magazine.

f. Accrued utilities at March 31 totalled $2,620.

g. March interest of $425 on the long-term note payable is unrecorded and unpaid as of March 31.

3. Complete the work sheet.

Problem 4-2A Completing a work sheet LO1 eXcel

CHECK FIGURE: 3. Adjusted trial balance columns = $67,380

The June 30, 2017, unadjusted trial balance for Trenton Consulting after its first year of operations follows:

		Trenton Consulting Trial Balance.xls	
	Home Insert Page Layout Formulas Data Review View		
	P18	fx	
	A	B	C
1	**Trenton Consulting**		
2	**Unadjusted Trial Balance**		
3	**June 30, 2017**		
4		**Unadjusted**	
5		**Trial Balance**	
6	**Account**	**Dr.**	**Cr.**
7	Cash	680	
8	Accounts receivable	2,900	
9	Prepaid rent	3,660	
10	Equipment	9,600	
11	Accounts payable		1,730
12	Toni Trenton, capital		26,650
13	Toni Trenton, withdrawals	6,880	
14	Consulting revenue		30,200
15	Wages expense	24,920	
16	Insurance expense	1,620	
17	Rent expense	8,320	
18	**Totals**	58,580	58,580

Required

1. Enter the unadjusted trial balance onto a work sheet.

2. Using the following additional information, enter the adjustments onto the work sheet:

   a. Annual depreciation on the equipment is $1,500.

   b. The balance in the Prepaid Rent account is for six months of rent commencing March 1, 2017.

   c. Unpaid and unrecorded wages at June 30 totalled $3,200.

   d. Accrued revenues at June 30 totalled $4,100.

3. Complete the work sheet.

4. Calculate the balance in the capital account as it would appear on the June 30, 2017, balance sheet.

Analysis Component: What effect does a loss have on the accounting equation?

Problem 4-3A Work sheet, journal entries, and financial statements LO1,6 e**X**cel

CHECK FIGURES: 1. Adjusted trial balance columns = $447,890; 3. Profit = $64,130; Total assets = $130,300

This unadjusted trial balance is for Challenger Construction at the end of its fiscal year, September 30, 2017. The beginning balance of the owner's capital account was $46,000 and the owner invested another $25,000 cash in the company during the year.

		Challenger Construction Trial Balance.xls		
	Home Insert Page Layout Formulas Data Review View			
	P18	fx		
	A		B	C
1	**Challenger Construction**			
2	**Unadjusted Trial Balance**			
3	**September 30, 2017**			
4			**Unadjusted**	
5			**Trial Balance**	
6	**No.**	**Account**	**Dr.**	**Cr.**
7	101	Cash	$ 22,000	
8	126	Supplies	17,200	
9	128	Prepaid insurance	9,600	
10	149	Land not currently used in operations	50,000	
11	167	Equipment	106,000	
12	168	Accumulated depreciation, Equipment		$ 40,500
13	191	Copyright	6,000	
14	201	Accounts payable		8,100
15	203	Interest payable		-0-
16	210	Wages payable		-0-
17	251	Long-term notes payable		50,000
18	301	Chris Challenger, capital		71,000
19	302	Chris Challenger, withdrawals	68,000	
20	401	Construction revenue		255,620
21	612	Depreciation expense, equipment	-0-	
22	623	Wages expense	96,000	
23	633	Interest expense	1,200	
24	637	Insurance expense	-0-	
25	640	Rent expense	26,400	
26	652	Supplies expense	-0-	
27	683	Business taxes expense	10,000	
28	684	Repairs expense	5,020	
29	690	Utilities expense	7,800	
30		**Totals**	**$ 425,220**	**$ 425,220**

Required

1. Prepare a 10-column work sheet for fiscal 2017, starting with the unadjusted trial balance and including these additional facts:

   a. The inventory of supplies at the end of the year had a cost of $3,200.

   b. The cost of expired insurance for the year is $8,400.

c. Annual depreciation of the equipment is $17,600.

d. The September utilities expense was not included in the trial balance because the bill arrived after it was prepared. Its $750 amount needs to be recorded.

e. The company's employees have earned $4,200 of accrued wages.

f. The interest expense of $120 for September has not yet been paid or recorded.

2. Use the work sheet to prepare the adjusting and closing entries.

3. Prepare an income statement, a statement of changes in equity, and a classified balance sheet. $16,000 of the long-term note payable is to be paid by September 30, 2018.

Analysis Component: Analyze the following potential errors and describe how each would affect the 10-column work sheet. Explain whether the error is likely to be discovered in completing the work sheet and, if not, the effect of the error on the financial statements.

a. The adjustment to record used supplies was credited to Supplies for $3,200 and debited the same amount to Supplies Expense.

b. When completing the adjusted trial balance in the work sheet, the $22,000 cash balance was incorrectly entered in the Credit column.

Problem 4-4A Closing entries LO2,3,4

CHECK FIGURE: 2. Post-closing trial balance = $122,000

MY Autobody's adjusted trial balance on December 31, 2017, appears in the work sheet as follows:

No.	Account	Debit	Credit
101	Cash	$ 28,000	
124	Shop supplies	1,800	
128	Prepaid insurance	4,200	
167	Equipment	88,000	
168	Accumulated depreciation, equipment		$ 7,500
201	Accounts payable		19,000
210	Wages payable		8,860
301	Mike Yang, capital		140,000
302	Mike Yang, withdrawals	36,000	
401	Repair revenue		157,630
612	Depreciation expense, equipment	8,500	
623	Wages expense	104,500	
637	Insurance expense	1,900	
640	Rent expense	52,350	
650	Office supplies expense	4,800	
690	Utilities expense	2,940	
	Totals	$332,990	$332,990

Required

1. Prepare closing entries.

2. Prepare the post-closing trial balance at December 31, 2017.

Problem 4-5A Financial statements LO6

CHECK FIGURES: Loss = $17,360; Total assets = $114,500

Using the information from Problem 4-4A, prepare an income statement and a statement of changes in equity for the year ended December 31, 2017, and a classified balance sheet at December 31, 2017. There were no investments by the owner during the year.

Analysis Component: MY Autobody experienced a loss during 2017. If you were one of the business's creditors, should this loss cause you to be concerned about being paid in 2018?

Problem 4-6A Closing entries LO2,3

The adjusted trial balance for Lloyd Construction as of December 31, 2017, follows:

No.	Account	Debit	Credit
101	Cash	$ 16,000	
104	Current investments	21,000	
126	Supplies	7,600	
149	Notes receivable	42,000	
167	Equipment	78,000	
168	Accumulated depreciation, equipment		$ 38,000
173	Building	260,000	
174	Accumulated depreciation, building		141,000
183	Land	86,000	
193	Franchise	31,000	
201	Accounts payable		17,000
203	Interest payable		130
233	Unearned professional revenue		27,000
251	Long-term notes payable		132,000
301	Sig Lloyd, capital		92,000
302	Sig Lloyd, withdrawals	3,000	
401	Professional revenue		206,480
406	Rent revenue		26,000
606	Depreciation expense, building	20,000	
612	Depreciation expense, equipment	8,000	
623	Wages expense	64,000	
633	Interest expense	610	
637	Insurance expense	18,000	
652	Supplies expense	12,800	
688	Telephone expense	4,400	
690	Utilities expense	7,200	
	Totals	$679,610	$679,610

An analysis of other information reveals that Lloyd Construction is required to make a $45,000 payment on the long-term notes payable during 2018. The notes receivable are due May 1, 2016. Also, Sig Lloyd invested $75,000 cash early in 2017.

Required Prepare the closing entries made at the end of the year.

Problem 4-7A Financial statements LO6

CHECK FIGURES: Profit = $97,470; Total assets = $362,600

Using the adjusted trial balance in Problem 4-6A, prepare the income statement and statement of changes in equity for the year ended December 31, 2017, and the classified balance sheet at December 31, 2017.

Analysis Component: Why must liabilities be separated on the balance sheet between *current* and *non-current*? What effect would it have had on Lloyd's balance sheet if the long-term note was not separated?

Problem 4-8A Adjusting entries and closing entries LO2,3,5

Adventure Elements provides outdoor activities including ropes courses, rock climbing, and zip-lining. The company offers a unique experience for team building activities, camps for youth and anyone seeking outdoor adventure.

No.	Account	Debit	Credit
201	Accounts payable and accrued liabilities...........................		$ 2,300
103	Accounts receivable	$ 5,100	
168	Accumulated depreciation, equipment		5,900
300	Becky Brenner, capital...		34,700
301	Becky Brenner, withdrawals	31,200	
101	Cash..	9,600	
194	Copyright	6,500	
167	Equipment...	22,000	
633	Insurance expense..	1,875	
623	Interest expense	120	
141	Notes receivable, due January 1, 2020	10,000	
233	Long-term notes payable		19,000
610	Rent expense	7,500	
402	Revenues..		61,015
126	Supplies..	270	
637	Supplies expense..	1,800	
652	Telephone expense	2,000	
203	Unearned revenues		10,600
688	Utilities expense	2,150	
612	Wages expense	33,400	
	Totals..	$133,515	$133,515

You are the accounting manager. Your staff submitted the following trial balance for the year ended March 31, 2017. In your review, you discover the following additional information that has not been included in the trial balance.

a. On April 2, you received the telephone bill for the month of March for $300.

b. On March 31, Adventure Element took a university student club zip-lining. An invoice had been sent to the student club for $2,000 due April 30.

c. On March 31, the company held a teen's camp for $1,500. All tickets had been prepaid two weeks in advance.

d. The equipment has an estimated useful life of 20 years. If you need to create a new account, use account number 606.

Required

1. Prepare the missing adjusting entries for transactions a–d.

2. Prepare an adjusted trial balance.

3. Based on your adjusted trial balance, prepare the closing entries.

Problem 4-9A **Financial statements** L06

CHECK FIGURES: Profit = $14,270; Total assets = $48,470

Based on the adjusted trial balance prepared in Problem 4-8A, prepare an income statement and a statement of changes in equity for the year ended March 31, 2017, and a classified balance sheet at March 31, 2017. The owner made an additional investment during the year of $15,000. A $6,500 payment on the long-term notes payable will be made during the year ended March 31, 2018.

Analysis Component: Why might Adventure Elements be tempted to report the notes receivable as a current asset on the March 31, 2017, balance sheet?

Problem 4-10A **Analyzing closing entries** L02,3,4

CHECK FIGURE: 1. Profit = $60,800

The following closing entries were prepared for Apex Architectural Designs regarding its year just ended June 30, 2017:

2017				
June	30	Design Revenue..	136,000	
		Income Summary		136,000
		To close the revenue account.		
	30	Income Summary..	75,200	
		Depreciation Expense, Office Equipment..............		1,750
		Depreciation Expense, Office Furniture.................		950
		Insurance Expense		1,200
		Interest Expense		350
		Supplies Expense...		2,150
		Telephone Expense..		1,600
		Utilities Expense		2,700
		Salaries Expense..		64,500
		To close expense accounts.		
June	30	Income Summary..	60,800	
		Noel Apex, Capital		60,800
		To close Income Summary to capital.		
	30	Noel Apex, Capital...	35,000	
		Noel Apex, Withdrawals......................................		35,000
		To close withdrawals to capital.		

Required

1. Prepare an income statement based on the information provided.

2. Calculate the post-closing balance in the capital account at June 30, 2017, given that the adjusted balance on June 30, 2016, was $86,000.

Problem 4-11A Preparing financial statements LO6

CHECK FIGURES: Loss = $63,420; Total assets = $231,720

The adjusted trial balance for Impressions Dance School has been provided for the year ended September 30, 2017. The new bookkeeper alphabetized the accounts.

Account	Debit	Credit
Accounts payable		$ 22,680
Accounts receivable	$ 13,500	
Accumulated depreciation, automobiles......................		39,360
Accumulated depreciation, building		164,000
Alisha Bjorn, capital		168,960
Alisha Bjorn, withdrawals...	10,000	
Automobiles	71,000	
Building	236,000	
Cash..	11,600	
Copyright	6,900	
Depreciation expense, automobiles...........................	7,100	
Depreciation expense, building	28,400	
Dance lesson revenue...		154,680
Gas, oil, and repairs expense	29,600	
Land...	32,900	
Land for future expansion...	50,000	
Notes payable*		90,000
Brand name	8,800	
Rent revenue...		21,000
Salaries expense	174,000	
Store supplies	4,380	
Unearned revenue..		23,500
Totals	$684,180	$684,180

*The notes payable plus interest are due in 18 months.

Required Prepare an income statement and a statement of changes in equity for the year ended September 30, 2017, plus a September 30, 2017, classified balance sheet. The owner made no investments during the year.

Analysis Component: Alisha wants to buy a new car for the business. As her bank manager, what do you advise?

Problem 4-12A Preparing a classified balance sheet LO6,7

CHECK FIGURES: 1. Capital = $520,775; 2. Total assets = $895,400

An alphabetical list of the adjusted trial balance accounts for North Country Rentals after its first year of operations ending March 31, 2017, is shown below:

Account	Adjusted Account Balance*
Accounts payable	$ 9,100
Accumulated depreciation, building	25,000
Accumulated depreciation, furniture	3,500
Advertising expense	16,200
Building	591,000
Cash	17,000
Depreciation expense, building	25,000
Depreciation expense, furniture	3,500
Furniture	42,800
Interest expense	10,260
Interest payable	900
Janitorial expense	41,000
Land	110,000
Long-term notes payable	362,000
Notes receivable, due 2020	143,000
Office salaries expense	126,625
Office supplies	700
Office supplies expense	6,100
Brand name	3,000
Prepaid advertising	400
Rent revenue	398,400
Rent receivable	16,000
Salaries payable	2,625
Utilities expense	36,720
Wyett North, capital	415,780
Wyett North, withdrawals	28,000

*Assume all accounts have a normal balance.

Required

1. Calculate the capital balance as it would appear on the March 31, 2017, balance sheet.

2. Prepare a classified balance sheet. Assume that $215,000 of the Long-Term Notes Payable will be paid during the year ended March 31, 2018. Also, $55,000 of the notes receivable will be collected by March 31, 2018.

3. Calculate the current ratio and the debt to equity ratio (round to two decimal places).

Analysis Component: North Country shows an adjusted balance in the *Long-Term Notes Payable* account of $362,000 at March 31, 2017. Review the balance sheet just prepared and make a reasonable assumption about what the $362,000 was most logically used for by North Country. Explain whether or not this is generally considered a good use of borrowed funds and why.

Problem 4-13A **Performing the steps in the accounting cycle** LO2,3,4,5,6

CHECK FIGURES: 4. Loss = $1,070; Total assets = $102,100; 6. Post-closing trial balance = $104,150

On June 1, 2017, Sam Near created a new travel agency called Tours-For-Less. These activities occurred during the company's first month:

June	1	Near created the new company by investing $40,000 cash, $5,000 of furniture, and computer equipment worth $60,000.
	2	The company rented furnished office space by paying $3,200 rent for the first month.
	3	The company purchased $2,400 of office supplies for cash.
	10	The company paid $7,200 for the premium on a one-year insurance policy.
	14	The owner's assistant was paid $3,600 for two weeks' salary.
	24	The company collected $13,600 of commissions from airlines on tickets obtained for customers.
	28	The assistant was paid another $3,600 for two weeks' salary.
	29	The company paid the month's $3,500 phone bill.
	30	The company repaired its computer for $700 on account.
	30	The owner withdrew $2,850 cash from the business for personal use.

The company's chart of accounts included these accounts:

101	Cash		302	Sam Near, Withdrawals
106	Accounts Receivable		405	Commissions Revenue
124	Office Supplies		610	Depreciation Expense, Furniture
128	Prepaid Insurance		612	Depreciation Expense, Computer Equipment
160	Furniture		622	Salaries Expense
161	Accumulated Depreciation, Furniture		637	Insurance Expense
167	Computer Equipment		640	Rent Expense
168	Accumulated Depreciation, Computer Equipment		650	Office Supplies Expense
201	Accounts Payable		684	Repairs Expense
209	Salaries Payable		688	Telephone Expense
301	Sam Near, Capital		901	Income Summary

Required

1. Set up each of the listed accounts. *Note: Your instructor will tell you to use either the balance column format or T-accounts.*

2. Prepare journal entries to record the transactions for June and post them to the accounts.

3. Use the following information to journalize and post the adjustments for the month:

   a. Two-thirds of one month's insurance coverage was consumed.

   b. There were $1,600 of office supplies on hand at the end of the month.

   c. Depreciation on the computer equipment was estimated to be $1,650 and $400 on the furniture.

   d. The assistant had earned $320 of unpaid and unrecorded salary.

   e. The company had earned $3,500 of commissions that had not yet been billed.

4. Prepare an income statement, a statement of changes in equity, and a classified balance sheet.

5. Prepare journal entries to close the temporary accounts and post them to the accounts.

6. Prepare a post-closing trial balance.

Problem 4-14A **Calculating current, quick, and debt to equity ratios** LO7

You are the accountant at **Indigo**. Refer to Appendix III for Indigo's Consolidated Balance Sheets as at March 29, 2014. Your manager has assigned you the following tasks.

    a. Calculate the current ratio, quick ratio, and debt to equity ratios for 2013 and 2014. Round your answer to two decimal places.

    b. Comment on the ratios, the change between 2013 and 2014, and what additional information you would want to know to get a better picture of Indigo's financial performance.

*Problem 4-15A **Adjusting, reversing, and subsequent cash entries** LO8

The unadjusted trial balance for Lewis Fitness Centre as of December 31, 2017, follows:

Account	Debit	Credit
Cash	$ 22,000	
Accounts receivable	-0-	
Supplies	9,000	
Equipment	300,000	
Accumulated depreciation, equipment		$ 30,000
Interest payable		-0-
Salaries payable		-0-
Unearned membership revenue		48,000
Notes payable		100,000
Bev Lewis, capital		116,500
Bev Lewis, withdrawals	60,000	
Membership revenue		180,000
Depreciation expense, equipment	-0-	
Salaries expense	76,000	
Interest expense	7,500	
Supplies expense	-0-	
Totals	$474,500	$474,500

Information necessary to prepare adjusting entries is as follows:

    a. As of December 31, employees have earned $1,600 of unpaid and unrecorded wages. The next payday is January 4, and the total wages to be paid will be $2,400.

    b. The cost of supplies on hand at December 31 is $3,600.

    c. The note payable requires an interest payment to be made every three months. The amount of unrecorded accrued interest at December 31 is $2,500, and the next payment is due on January 15. This payment will be $3,000.

    d. An analysis of the unearned membership revenue shows that $32,000 remains unearned at December 31.

    e. In addition to the membership revenue included in the revenue account, the company has earned another $24,000 in revenue that will be collected on January 21. The company is also expected to collect $14,000 on the same day for new revenue during January.

    f. Depreciation expense for the year is $30,000.

An asterisk (*) identifies assignment material based on Appendix 4A.

Required

1. Prepare adjusting journal entries.

2. Prepare journal entries to reverse the effects of the adjusting entries that involve accruals.

3. Prepare journal entries to record the cash payments and collections that are described for January.

Alternate Problems

Problem 4-1B **Completing a work sheet** LO1   e**X**cel

CHECK FIGURE: 3. Adjusted trial balance columns = $99,307

The July 31, 2017, unadjusted trial balance for Daimler Tours after its first month of operations is shown below:

			Daimler Tours Trial Balance.xls	
			Home Insert Page Layout Formulas Data Review View	
			P18 ◯ fx	

	A		B	C
1		**Daimler Tours**		
2		**Unadjusted Trial Balance**		
3		**July 31, 2017**		
4			**Unadjusted**	
5			**Trial Balance**	
6	**No.**	**Account**	**Dr.**	**Cr.**
7	101	Cash	$ 9,100	
8	106	Accounts receivable	18,700	
9	111	Notes receivable, due Feb. 2018	16,000	
10	128	Prepaid insurance	5,100	
11	161	Furniture	6,750	
12	201	Accounts payable		$ 6,925
13	230	Unearned tour revenue		12,430
14	301	Jan Rider, capital		60,975
15	302	Jan Rider, withdrawals	-0-	
16	403	Tour revenue		16,700
17	623	Wages expense	41,380	
18		**Totals**	$ 97,030	$ 97,030

Required

1. Enter the unadjusted trial balance onto a work sheet.

2. Using the following additional information, enter the adjustments into the work sheet (the Chart of Accounts at the back of the textbook may be useful when additional accounts are required):

   a. Interest of $40 had accrued on the note receivable by month-end.

   b. The July utility bill for $175 was received in the mail on July 31. It is unpaid and unrecorded.

   c. Depreciation on the furniture for the month of July is $210.

   d. The balance in Prepaid Insurance is from a six-month policy that went into effect on July 1, 2017.

e. The company has two part-time employees, each of whom gets paid $315 every Friday for a five-day part-time workweek. July 31 falls on a Tuesday, therefore two days of accrued wages need to be recorded.

f. At July 31, it was determined that $4,900 of the balance in Unearned Tour Revenue was not yet earned.

g. Accrued tour revenue of $1,600 was unrecorded and uncollected at July 31.

3. Complete the work sheet.

Problem 4-2B **Completing a work sheet—profit** L01 e**X**cel

CHECK FIGURE: 3. Adjusted trial balance columns = $83,310

The December 31, 2017, unadjusted trial balance for Tucker Photographers after the first month of operations is shown below:

	Tucker Photographers Trial Balance.xls		
Home Insert Page Layout Formulas Data Review View			
P18	fx		
	A	B	C
1	**Tucker Photographers**		
2	**Unadjusted Trial Balance**		
3	**December 31, 2017**		
4		**Unadjusted**	
5		**Trial Balance**	
6	**Account**	**Dr.**	**Cr.**
7	Cash	$ 9,100	
8	Accounts receivable	13,000	
9	Prepaid equipment rental	3,860	
10	Automobile	49,000	
11	Accumulated depreciation, automobile		$ -0-
12	Accounts payable		1,920
13	Unearned revenue		5,740
14	Jim Tucker, capital		65,700
15	Jim Tucker, withdrawals	2,600	
16	Service revenue		8,400
17	Depreciation expense, automobile	-0-	
18	Equipment rental expense	4,200	
19	**Totals**	$ 81,760	$ 81,760

Required
1. Enter the unadjusted trial balance onto a work sheet.
2. Using the following additional information, enter the adjustments into the work sheet.
   a. It was determined that $2,000 of the balance in the Prepaid Equipment Rental account had been used during December.
   b. Depreciation on the automobile for the month of December was $610.
   c. Accrued utilities expense of $940 was unrecorded at December 31.
   d. $460 of the Unearned Revenue account had been earned by December 31.

3. Complete the work sheet.

4. Calculate the balance in the capital account as it would appear on the December 31, 2017, balance sheet.

Analysis Component: What effect does a profit have on the balance sheet?

Problem 4-3B **Work sheet, journal entries, financial statements** LO1,6   e**X**cel

CHECK FIGURES: 1. Adjusted trial balance columns = $174,085; 3. Loss = $3,835; Total assets = $71,150

Presented below is the unadjusted trial balance of Webster Demolition Company as of June 30, 2017, the end of its fiscal year. The owner invested $17,500 cash in the company during the year.

		Webster Demolition Company Trial Balance.xls		
		Home Insert Page Layout Formulas Data Review View		
		P18 fx		
		A	B	C
1		**Webster Demolition Company**		
2		**Unadjusted Trial Balance**		
3		**June 30, 2017**		
4			**Unadjusted**	
5			**Trial Balance**	
6	**No.**	**Account**	**Dr.**	**Cr.**
7	101	Cash	$ 4,500	
8	126	Supplies	8,200	
9	128	Prepaid insurance	7,300	
10	167	Equipment	72,000	
11	168	Accumulated depreciation, equipment		$ 5,000
12	201	Accounts payable		9,100
13	203	Interest payable		-0-
14	210	Wages payable		-0-
15	251	Long-term notes payable		45,000
16	301	Rusty Webster, capital		21,400
17	302	Rusty Webster, withdrawals	2,100	
18	401	Demolition revenue		83,300
19	612	Depreciation expense, equipment	-0-	
20	623	Wages expense	27,400	
21	633	Interest expense	1,100	
22	637	Insurance expense	-0-	
23	640	Rent expense	24,400	
24	652	Supplies expense	-0-	
25	683	Business tax expense	4,200	
26	684	Repairs expense	4,200	
27	690	Utilities expense	8,400	
28		**Totals**	$ 163,800	$ 163,800

Required

Preparation Component:

1. Prepare a 10-column work sheet for 2017, starting with the unadjusted trial balance and including these additional facts:

   a. The inventory of supplies at the end of the year had a cost of $6,800.

   b. The cost of expired insurance for the year is $5,750.

c. Annual depreciation on the equipment is $8,700.

d. The June utilities expense of $375 was not included in the trial balance because the bill arrived after it was prepared. The $375 amount owed needs to be recorded.

e. The company's employees have earned $1,100 of accrued wages.

f. Interest of $110 for June has not yet been paid or recorded. In addition, the company is required to make a $2,000 payment on the note on August 30, 2017.

2. Use the work sheet to journalize the adjusting and closing entries.

3. Prepare an income statement, a statement of changes in equity, and a classified balance sheet.

Analysis Component: Analyze the following independent errors and describe how each would affect the 10-column work sheet. Explain whether the error is likely to be discovered in completing the work sheet and, if not, the effect of the error on the financial statements.

a. The adjustment for consumption of the insurance coverage credited the Prepaid Insurance account for $5,750 and debited the same amount to the Insurance Expense account.

b. When completing the adjusted trial balance in the work sheet, the $4,200 Repairs Expense account balance was extended to the Debit column for the balance sheet.

Problem 4-4B Closing entries LO2,3,4

CHECK FIGURE: 2. Post-closing trial balance = $86,800

Dillan's Tailoring Services' adjusted trial balance on December 31, 2017, appears as follows:

No.	Account	Debit	Credit
101	Cash	$ 15,500	
125	Store supplies	6,500	
128	Prepaid insurance	3,800	
167	Equipment	61,000	
168	Accumulated depreciation, equipment		$ 19,700
201	Accounts payable		39,400
210	Wages payable		6,400
301	Vy Dillan, capital		23,300
302	Vy Dillan, withdrawals	32,000	
401	Sewing revenue		109,920
612	Depreciation expense, equipment	5,400	
623	Wages expense	61,200	
637	Insurance expense	2,200	
640	Rent expense	4,800	
651	Store supplies expense	2,600	
690	Utilities expense	3,720	
	Totals	$198,720	$198,720

Required

1. Prepare closing entries.

2. Prepare a post-closing trial balance.

Problem 4-5B **Financial statements** LO6

CHECK FIGURES: Profit = $30,000; Total assets = $67,100

Using the information from Problem 4-4B, prepare an income statement and a statement of changes in equity for the year ended December 31, 2017, and a classified balance sheet at December 31, 2017. The owner made no investments during the year.

Analysis Component: Dillan's Tailoring Services experienced a profit during 2017. If you were one of the business's creditors, would you conclude that because of this profit Dillan's Tailoring will pay its obligations in 2018?

Problem 4-6B **Closing entries** LO2,3

The adjusted trial balance for Warren's Photo Studio as of December 31, 2017, follows:

No.	Account	Debit	Credit
101	Cash	$ 4,100	
104	Current investments	6,800	
126	Supplies	2,250	
149	Notes receivable, due May 1, 2019	41,000	
167	Equipment	27,000	
168	Accumulated depreciation, equipment		$ 14,600
173	Building	69,400	
174	Accumulated depreciation, building		58,000
183	Land	47,000	
193	Franchise	8,900	
201	Accounts payable		5,000
203	Unearned professional revenue		1,300
233	Long-term notes payable		64,000
251	Warren Jones, capital		31,000
301	Warren Jones, withdrawals	1,500	
302	Photography revenue		86,342
401	Interest income		240
605	Depreciation expense, building	4,000	
606	Depreciation expense, equipment	3,000	
612	Wages expense	34,000	
623	Interest expense	2,400	
633	Insurance expense	2,850	
637	Supplies expense	1,800	
652	Telephone expense	842	
688	Utilities expense	3,640	
	Totals	$260,482	$260,482

An analysis of other information reveals that Warren's Photo Studio is required to make a $25,000 payment on the long-term notes payable during 2018. Also, Warren Jones invested $15,000 cash early in the year.

Required Prepare the closing entries made at the end of the year.

Problem 4-7B **Financial statements** LO6

CHECK FIGURES: Profit = $34,050; Total assets = $133,850

Using the adjusted trial balance in Problem 4-6B, prepare the income statement, statement of changes in equity, and classified balance sheet.

Analysis Component: Why must liabilities be separated on the balance sheet between *current* and *non-current*? What effect would it have had on Warren's balance sheet if the non-current notes were not separated?

Problem 4-8B **Adjusting entries and Closing entries** LO2,3,5

Bullseye Market Research Company (BMRC) specializes in conducting focus groups for businesses launching a new product. BMRC analyzes customer likes and dislikes to ensure new products will be successful.

No.	Account	Debit	Credit
201	Accounts payable..		$ 100
108	Accounts receivable	2,000	
168	Accumulated depreciation, equipment		7,250
184	Accumulated depreciation, office furniture		3,100
101	Cash..	$ 1,500	
302	Consulting revenue		44,000
194	Copyright	4,200	
251	Dan Eagle, capital..		24,715
301	Dan Eagle, withdrawals	3,500	
606	Depreciation expense, office furniture	700	
167	Equipment...	16,000	
633	Insurance expense	600	
401	Interest income...		70
623	Interest expense..	30	
233	Long-term notes payable		4,000
145	Notes receivable	5,000	
183	Office furniture	5,100	
104	Short-term investments	4,000	
126	Supplies..	750	
637	Supplies expense...	2,150	
652	Telephone expense	470	
203	Unearned consulting revenue.....................................		3,375
688	Utilities expense	3,230	
612	Wages expense	37,380	
	Totals..	$86,610	$86,610

You are the accounting manager. Your staff submitted the above trial balance for December 31, 2017. In your review, you discover the following additional information that has not been included in the trial balance.

a. The equipment has an estimated useful life of 16 years. If you need to create a new account, use account number 604.

b. Employees were paid $3,100 for ten days of work. This payroll included 2 days of payroll in December that were not recorded at year-end. If you need to add an account, use account number 202.

   c. On December 31, BMRC completed a focus group for a client on handbags. An invoice was sent to the company for $5,000 due January 31, 2018.

   d. On December 31, the company completed a market research report for a client. The client had prepaid $3,000 for this service in November.

Required

  1. Prepare the missing adjusting entries for transactions a-d.

  2. Prepare an adjusted trial balance.

  3. Based on your adjusted trial balance, prepare the closing entries.

Problem 4-9B   Financial statements   LO6

CHECK FIGURES: Profit = $5,890; Total assets = $32,200

Using the information in Problem 4-8B, prepare an income statement and a statement of changes in equity for the year ended December 31, 2017, and a classified balance sheet at December 31, 2017. The owner made no additional investments during the year. A $2,500 payment on the long-term notes payable will be made during 2018. Also, $1,500 of the notes receivable will be collected by December 31, 2018.

Analysis Component: Bullseye Market Research Company's equity increased by $2,390 during 2017. What effect does an increase in equity have on the other major components of the balance sheet?

Problem 4-10B   Analyzing closing entries   LO2,3,4

CHECK FIGURE: 1. Total operating expenses = $177,290

The following closing entries were prepared for Greenway Gardening Services regarding the year ended October 31, 2017:

2017				
Oct.	31	Service Revenue	136,000	
		Income Summary		136,000
		To close the revenue account.		
	31	Income Summary...	177,290	
		Depreciation Expense,		
		Gardening Equipment		9,950
		Depreciation Expense, Vehicles		10,600
		Insurance Expense		6,900
		Interest Expense		340
		Supplies Expense..		24,800
		Telephone Expense...		1,700
		Utilities Expense		1,800
		Fuel Expense		9,200
		Wages Expense..		112,000
		To close expense accounts.		
Oct.	31	Grant Greenway, Capital..	41,290	
		Income Summary		41,290
		To close the Income Summary to capital.		
	31	Grant Greenway, Capital..	10,000	
		Grant Greenway, Withdrawals..............................		10,000
		To close withdrawals to capital.		

Required

1. Prepare an income statement based on the information provided.

2. Calculate the post-closing balance in the capital account at October 31, 2017, given that the adjusted balance on October 31, 2016, was $76,000.

Problem 4-11B **Preparing financial statements** LO6

CHECK FIGURES: Profit = $35,680; Total assets = $136,580

Required Using the adjusted trial balance below, for FairQuest Drill Servicing for the year ended August 31, 2017, prepare an income statement, statement of changes in equity, and classified balance sheet. The owner made a $50,000 investment into the business during the year. The investment in Nova shares is expected to be held for the long term.

No.	Account	Debit	Credit
101	Cash	$ 7,500	
106	Accounts receivable	16,000	
109	Interest receivable	280	
124	Office supplies	1,700	
141	Investment in Nova shares	35,000	
161	Furniture	81,000	
162	Accumulated depreciation, furniture		$ 21,400
193	Franchise	16,500	
201	Accounts payable		4,300
205	Notes payable, due in 7 months		3,200
230	Unearned servicing revenue		5,000
251	Long-term notes payable*		31,000
301	Jade Fairquest, capital		61,400
302	Jade Fairquest, withdrawals	4,000	
403	Drill servicing revenue		171,080
409	Interest income		2,600
601	Depreciation expense, furniture	2,060	
623	Wages expense	116,000	
637	Insurance expense	16,680	
688	Telephone expense	2,800	
690	Utilities expense	460	
	Totals	$299,980	$299,980

*An $18,000 payment will be made on the long-term notes payable during the year ended August 31, 2018.

Analysis Component: Why might FairQuest Drill Servicing be tempted to report the investment in Nova shares as a current asset on the August 31, 2017, balance sheet?

Problem 4-12B **Preparing a classified balance sheet** LO6,7

CHECK FIGURES: 1. Capital = $84,484; 2. Total assets = $133,100

An alphabetical list of the adjusted trial balance accounts at July 31, 2017, for Delta Tours after its first month of operations is shown below:

Account	Adjusted Account Balance*
Accounts payable	$ 27,000
Accounts receivable	21,300
Accumulated depreciation, furniture	700
Cash	25,300
Depreciation expense, furniture	700
Furniture	29,000
Insurance expense	5,250
Interest receivable	100
Interest income	700
Jan Delta, capital	95,434
Jan Delta, withdrawals	10,700
Notes receivable (due in 6 months)	56,000
Prepaid insurance	2,100
Tour revenue	146,000
Unearned tour revenue	19,600
Utility expense	1,300
Wages expense	139,700
Wages payable	2,016

*Assume all accounts have a normal balance.

Required
1. Calculate the capital balance as it would appear on the July 31, 2017, balance sheet.
2. Prepare a classified balance sheet.
3. Calculate the current ratio and the debt to equity ratio (round to two decimal places).

Problem 4-13B **Performing the steps in the accounting cycle** LO2,3,4,5,6

CHECK FIGURES: 4. Profit = $5,140; Total assets = $604,000; 6. Post-closing trial balance = $606,400

On July 1, 2017, Amy Young created a new self-storage business called Young Co. These events occurred during the company's first month:

July	1	Young invested $40,000 cash and land and buildings worth $320,000 and $240,000, respectively.
	2	Rented equipment by paying $3,600 rent for the first month.
	5	Purchased $4,600 of office supplies for cash.
	10	Paid $10,800 for the premium on a one-year insurance policy effective today.
	14	Paid an employee $1,800 for two weeks' salary.
	24	Collected $17,600 of storage revenue from customers.
	28	Paid another $1,800 for two weeks' salary.
	29	Paid the month's $600 phone bill.
	30	Repaired leaking roof for $1,700 on account.
	31	Young withdrew $3,200 cash from the business for personal use.

The company's chart of accounts included these accounts:

101	Cash		302	Amy Young, Withdrawals
106	Accounts Receivable		401	Storage Revenue
124	Office Supplies		606	Depreciation Expense, Buildings
128	Prepaid Insurance		622	Salaries Expense
170	Land		637	Insurance Expense
173	Buildings		640	Equipment Rental Expense
174	Accumulated Depreciation, Buildings		650	Office Supplies Expense
201	Accounts Payable		684	Repairs Expense
209	Salaries Payable		688	Telephone Expense
301	Amy Young, Capital		901	Income Summary

Required

1. Set up each of the listed accounts. *Note: Your instructor will tell you to use either the balance column format or T-accounts.*

2. Prepare journal entries to record the transactions for July and post them to the accounts. Record prepaid and unearned items in balance sheet accounts.

3. Use the following information to journalize and post the adjustments for the month:

    a. Two-thirds of one month's insurance coverage was used.

    b. There were $3,100 of office supplies on hand at the end of the month.

    c. Depreciation on the buildings was estimated to be $2,400 per month.

    d. The employee had earned $360 of unpaid and unrecorded salary.

    e. The company had earned $1,900 of storage revenue that had not yet been billed.

4. Prepare an income statement, a statement of changes in equity, and a classified balance sheet.

5. Prepare journal entries to close the temporary accounts and post them to the accounts.

6. Prepare a post-closing trial balance.

Problem 4-14B Calculating current ratios and debt to equity ratios LO7

You are the accountant at Danier. Refer to Appendix III for Danier's Consolidated Balance Sheets as at June 28, 2014. Your manager has asked you to do the following:

   a. Calculate the current ratio, quick ratio, and debt to equity ratios for 2013 and 2014 (round to two decimal places).

   b. Comment on the ratios, the change between 2013 and 2014 and what additional information you would want to know to get a better picture of Danier's financial performance.

*Problem 4-15B Adjusting, reversing, and subsequent cash entries LO8

IBS Company's unadjusted trial balance on December 31, 2017, the end of its annual accounting period, is as follows:

Account	Debit	Credit
Cash	$ 73,725	
Note receivable	37,500	
Office supplies	4,200	
Land	45,000	
Unearned service revenue		$ 18,000
Note payable		90,000
Jean Boat, capital		37,500
Jean Boat, withdrawals	60,000	
Service revenue		267,000
Interest income		2,550
Rent revenue		12,375
Salaries expense	193,500	
Insurance expense	4,950	
Interest expense	8,550	
Totals	$427,425	$427,425

An asterisk (*) identifies assignment material based on Appendix 4A.

Information necessary to prepare adjusting entries is as follows:

   a. Employees, who are paid $7,500 every two weeks, have earned $5,250 since the last payment. The next payment of $7,500 will be on January 4.

   b. IBS rents office space to a tenant who has paid only $450 of the $1,125 rent for December. On January 12, the tenant will pay the remainder along with the rent for January.

   c. An inventory of office supplies discloses $675 of unused supplies.

   d. Premiums for insurance against injuries to employees are paid monthly. The $450 premium for December will be paid January 12.

   e. IBS owes $90,000 on a note payable that requires quarterly payments of accrued interest. The quarterly payments of $2,700 each are made on the 15th of January, April, July, and October.

   f. An analysis of IBS's service contracts with customers shows that $6,300 of the amount customers have prepaid remains unearned.

   g. IBS has a $37,500 note receivable on which interest of $175 has accrued. On January 22, the note and the total accrued interest of $575 will be repaid to IBS.

   h. IBS has earned but not recorded revenue for $8,250 for services provided to a customer who will pay for the work on January 24. At that time, the customer will also pay $3,100 for services IBS will perform in early January.

Required

1. Prepare adjusting journal entries.

2. Prepare reversing entries.

3. Prepare journal entries to record the January 2018 cash receipts and cash payments identified in the above information.

Analytical and Review Problems

A & R Problem 4-1   e**X**cel

The owner of Dynamo Stores has come to you for assistance because his bookkeeper has just moved to another city. The following is the only information his bookkeeper left him.

1. Balance sheets as of December 31, 2017 and 2018.

2. The owner withdrew $105,000 in 2018 for his personal use.

3. The business incurred total expenses of $168,000 for 2018, of which $126,000 was for wages and $42,000 was for advertising.

	2018	2017
Assets...................................	$168,000	$210,000
Liabilities...............................	$ 42,000	$ 63,000
Capital	126,000	147,000
	$168,000	$210,000

Required

1. Calculate the profit and total revenue for 2018.

2. Prepare closing entries for 2018.

A & R Problem 4-2   e**X**cel

The partially completed work sheet for the current fiscal year of Sandy's Delivery Service appears below:

	Sandy's Delivery Service Work Sheet.xls

Home   Insert   Page Layout   Formulas   Data   Review   View

P18   fx

	A	B	C	D	E	F	G	H	I	J	K
1		**Sandy's Delivery Service**									
2		**Work Sheet**									
3		**For the Year Ended December 31, 2017**									
4										**Balance Sheet**	
5		**Unadjusted**				**Adjusted**		**Income**		**& Statement of**	
6		**Trial Balance**		**Adjustments**		**Trial Balance**		**Statement**		**Changes in Equity**	
7	**Account**	**Dr.**	**Cr.**	**Dr.**	**Cr.**	**Dr.**	**Cr.**	**Dr.**	**Cr.**	**Dr.**	**Cr.**
8	Cash	10,650									
9	Accounts receivable	7,000				9,000					
10	Supplies	4,200								1,600	
11	Prepaid insurance	2,400									
12	Prepaid rent	1,800									
13	Delivery trucks	40,000				40,000					
14	Accounts payable		3,130				3,130				
15	Unearned delivery revenue		4,500								2,000
16	Sandra Berlasty, capital		50,000								
17	Sandra Berlasty, withdrawals	3,000									
18	Delivery service revenue		18,500								
19	Advertising expense	600									
20	Gas and oil expense	680									
21	Salaries expense	5,600									
22	Utilities expense	200									
23	**Totals**	76,130	76,130								
24	Insurance expense					800					
25	Rent expense					900					
26	Supplies expense										
27	Dep. expense, delivery trucks										
28	Accumulated dep., delivery trucks										2,000
29	Salaries payable										400
30	Profit										

Required

1. Complete the work sheet.

2. Journalize the adjusting and closing entries (omit narratives).

Ethics Challenge

EC 4-1

On January 20, 2017, Jennifer Nelson, the staff accountant for Newby Enterprises, is feeling pressure to complete the preparation of the annual financial statements. The president of the company has said he needs up-to-date financial statements to share with several bankers on January 21 at a dinner meeting that has been called to discuss the possibility of Newby's obtaining loan financing for a special building project. Jennifer knows that she won't be able to gather all the needed information in the next 24 hours to prepare the entire set of adjusting entries that must be posted before the financial statements will accurately portray the company's performance and financial position for the fiscal period just ended

December 31, 2016. Jennifer ultimately decides to estimate several expense accruals at the last minute. When deciding on estimates for the expenses, Jennifer uses low estimates as she doesn't want to make the financial statements look worse than they possibly are in reality. Jennifer finishes the financial statements before the deadline and gives them to the president without mentioning that several accounts could be only estimated as to their balance on December 31, 2016.

Required

1. List several courses of action that Jennifer could have taken instead of the one on which she ultimately decided.

2. If you had been in Jennifer's situation, what would you have done? Briefly justify your response.

Focus on Financial Statements

FFS 4-1

CHECK FIGURES: 1. Profit = $70,575; Total assets = $95,850; 3. Post-closing trial balance = $121,350

Sarda Electrical Servicing began operations two years ago. Its adjusted account balances at December 31, 2017, are listed alphabetically below. The owner, Nymeth Sarda, made a $20,000 investment early in the year just ended December 31, 2017.

Required

1. Prepare an income statement, statement of changes in equity, and classified balance sheet based on the information provided.

2. Prepare the closing entries.

3. Prepare the post-closing trial balance.

Account	Account Balance*
Accounts payable	$ 21,000
Accounts receivable	10,500
Accumulated depreciation, tools	4,500
Accumulated depreciation, truck	21,000
Cash	5,000
Copyright	5,100
Depreciation expense, tools	2,250
Depreciation expense, truck	3,600
Electrical revenue	126,600
Electrical supplies	19,000
Insurance expense	1,275
Interest expense	900
Notes receivable**	12,000
Nymeth Sarda, capital	27,825
Nymeth Sarda, withdrawals	61,500
Notes payable, due August 31, 2019	27,000
Notes payable, due June 1, 2018	2,550
Prepaid insurance	1,050
Prepaid rent	7,200
Rent expense	21,000
Salaries expense	27,000
Salaries payable	3,150
Tools	21,000
Truck	40,500
Unearned electrical revenue	5,250

*Assume all account balances are normal.
**$2,000 of the note is due September 15, 2018.

Analysis Component: Cupcakes owners Lori and Heather, featured in the chapter opening vignette, have financed a significant portion of their growth by reinvesting profits. Is Nymeth Sarda, the owner of Sarda Electrical Servicing, following a similar practice? Explain.

FFS 4-2

Cineplex Inc. is Canada's largest film exhibition operator with theatres in ten provinces. An excerpt from its comparative balance sheet at December 31, 2014, shows the following assets and liabilities, in alphabetical order:

(thousands of dollars)	2014	2013
Accounts payable and accrued expenses	$159,152	$157,333
Cash and cash equivalents	34,367	44,140
Deferred revenue (unearned revenue)	149,644	136,373
Dividends payable to be paid in 2015	7,877	7,552
Income taxes payable	9,735	2,656
Intangible assets	109,746	113,601
Inventories	7,978	7,234
Long-term debt	229,754	217,151
Other current liabilities	9,522	15,180
Other non-current assets	852,229	859,562
Other non-current liabilities	311,883	306,861
Prepaid expenses and other current assets	8,102	6,838
Property, equipment and leaseholds	495,532	459,112
Trade and other receivables	101,462	100,891

Required

Part 1

   a. Calculate total current assets at December 31, 2014, and December 31, 2013.

   b. Calculate total current liabilities at December 31, 2014, and December 31, 2013.

Part 2

   c. Calculate the current ratio for December 31, 2014 and December 31, 2013 (round to two decimal places).

   d. Explain the meaning of Cineplex's current ratio results calculated in part (c). Also indicate whether the change in the ratio was favourable or unfavourable.

Critical Thinking Mini Case

The owner of Delton Property Rentals, Teal Delton, has requested an emergency meeting with you, a representative from the bank. "Our accountant has been on leave for the past several months and her replacement has resigned suddenly. I'm told we can't pay our employees this month and your bank won't lend us any money. I don't understand. We have lots of assets that can be used to pay expenses, as you can see from our balance sheet."

Delton Property Rentals Balance Sheet March 31		
	2017	**2016**
Assets	$2,850,000	$750,000
Liabilities	2,780,000	240,000
Equity	70,000	510,000

You explain to Mr. Delton that you will need to obtain some additional information. He faxes you the following:

Delton Property Rentals Post-Closing Trial Balance March 31		
	2017	**2016**
Accounts payable	$ 340,000	$ 7,000
Accounts receivable	75,000	215,000
Accumulated depreciation, buildings	165,000	150,000
Accumulated depreciation, equipment	35,000	30,000
Buildings	2,112,000	430,000
Cash	15,000	40,000
Equipment	45,000	45,000
Land	675,000	150,000
Notes payable*	2,440,000	204,000
Notes receivable, due Nov. 30, 2021	120,000	-0-
Supplies	8,000	50,000
Teal Delton, capital**	70,000	510,000
Unearned revenue	-0-	29,000

*$200,000 principal is due annually each February 1.
**No withdrawals were made during 2016 or 2017.

Required Using the elements of critical thinking described on the inside front cover, outline how you will respond to Teal Delton.

Cumulative Comprehension Problem: Echo Systems

CHECK FIGURE: 2. Total credits in post-closing trial balance = $155,720

(The first two segments of this comprehensive problem were in Chapters 2 and 3, and the final segment is presented in Chapter 5. If the Chapter 2 and 3 segments have not been completed, the assignment can begin at this point. It is recommended that you use the Working Papers[12] that accompany this book because they reflect the account balances that resulted from posting the entries required in Chapters 2 and 3.)

The transactions of Echo Systems for October through December 2017 have been recorded in the problem segments in Chapters 2 and 3, as well as the year-end adjusting entries. Prior to closing the temporary accounts for 2017, the accounting system is modified to include the Income Summary account, which is given the number 901.

Required

1. Record and post the appropriate closing entries.
2. Prepare a post-closing trial balance.

---

12 If students have not purchased the Working Papers package, the Working Papers for the serial problem are available on Connect.

Accounting for Merchandising Activities

A Look Back

Chapters 3 and 4 focused on the final steps of the accounting process. We explained the importance of proper revenue and expense recognition, and described the adjusting and closing processes. We also prepared financial statements.

A Look at This Chapter

This chapter emphasizes merchandising activities. We explain how reporting merchandising activities differs from reporting service activities. We also analyze and record merchandise purchases and sales transactions, and explain the adjustments and financial statement presentation for merchandisers.

© eye35.pix/Alamy

LEARNING OBJECTIVES

LO1 Describe merchandising, and identify and explain the important income statement and balance sheet components for a merchandising company.

LO2 Describe both perpetual and periodic inventory systems.

LO3 Analyze and record transactions for merchandise purchases and sales using a perpetual system.

LO4 Prepare adjustments for a merchandising company.

LO5 Define, prepare, and analyze merchandising income statements.

LO6 Calculate gross margin and markup on inventory cost.

*Appendix 5A

LO7 Record and compare merchandising transactions using both periodic and perpetual inventory systems.

*Appendix 5B

LO8 Explain and record Provincial Sales Tax (PST), Goods and Services Tax (GST), and Harmonized Sales Tax (HST).

Sustainable Gear for Outdoor Enthusiasts

Mountain Equipment Co-op, more commonly referred to as MEC, is Canada's leading retailer of outdoor merchandise including clothing and gear for self-propelled sports like cycling, hiking, paddling, and climbing. MEC was founded in 1971 in Vancouver by six individuals interested in providing mountain climbers with reasonably priced, quality wilderness gear in Canada. MEC is a members-only cooperative and before you can buy or rent from MEC, you have to purchase a $5 membership that is good for your lifetime. This investment in the store hasn't put people off, and in fact, the idea of membership is obviously appealing to many: Membership at the end of 2014 stood at approximately 4.32 million, and sales for the year totalled $336 million. In 2015, in addition to its online store at http://www.mec.ca, MEC has 18 outlets in six provinces, and will be opening stores in Kelowna, BC, and North York, ON, in 2016.

MEC carries a huge variety of merchandise inventory and, to minimize its ecological impact, it promotes sustainable products. This means in part that MEC-brand contract manufacturing centres are required to follow MEC's Social Compliance Program designed to improve the human condition in factories. Also, to the greatest extent possible, the components of MEC's products are organic (cotton), recycled (polyester), and PVC-free.

Clearly, implementing the many facets of MEC's philosophy in such a massive business is no simple task. But MEC seeks simplicity wherever it can be found, and inventory management is one such area. MEC's public affair's manager Tim Southam says, "Continually balancing supply against demand is the crux of MEC's inventory management practices. A perpetual inventory system allows us to replenish stock in a timely manner to best meet the needs of our members. It also enables us to respond quickly to discrepancies and gives us a high level of control over our inventory. At any given time—in real time—we are able to access the current inventory levels in our stores and our distribution centre." A perpetual inventory system updates inventory records continually each time an item is purchased from a supplier or sold to a customer, resulting in up-to-date inventory records.

MEC celebrates its 45th year of operation in 2016. As a member of *1% for the Planet* and through its community grants program, MEC is widely recognized for its commitment to sustainable outdoor recreation and environmental initiatives. In 2014, MEC made more than $3 million in community investments in support of outdoor recreation in Canada. MEC has raised the bar in terms of how a business can meet social and environmental goals and make millions at the same time.

Source: http://www.mec.ca

Video Link: https://www.youtube.com/watch?v=XwHdLwHen4U

CRITICAL THINKING CHALLENGE Why would MEC choose a perpetual inventory system over a periodic inventory system? Is the periodic inventory system acceptable under GAAP?

CHAPTER PREVIEW

Our emphasis in previous chapters was on the accounting and reporting activities of companies providing services. Chapter 5 emphasizes merchandising, a major part of modern business. Consumers expect a wealth of products, discount prices, inventory on demand, and high quality. This chapter introduces us to the business and accounting practices used by companies engaged in merchandising activities. These companies buy products and then resell them to customers. We show how financial statements capture merchandising transactions. The new financial statement elements created by merchandising transactions are demonstrated using fictitious information from MEC, the company introduced in the chapter opening vignette. We also analyze and record merchandise purchases and sales, and explain adjusting entries and the closing process for merchandising companies. An understanding of these important topics is what MEC in the opening article knows is critical to ensure continued success.

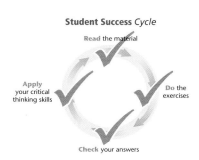

Student Success *Cycle*

Merchandising Activities

LO1 Describe merchandising, and identify and explain the important income statement and balance sheet components for a merchandising company.

A merchandising company's activities are different from those of a service company. A **merchandiser** earns profit by buying and selling merchandise. **Merchandise** consists of products that a company acquires for the purpose of reselling them to customers. The cost of these goods is an expense presented on the income statement as **cost of goods sold (COGS)**.[1]

Merchandisers are often identified as either *wholesalers* or *retailers*. A **wholesaler** is a company that buys products from manufacturers or other wholesalers and sells them to retailers or other wholesalers. Wholesalers include companies such as General Mills Inc., Webber Natural Pharmaceuticals Inc., **Western Family Foods**, and **Westfair Foods**. A **retailer** is an *intermediary* that buys products from manufacturers or wholesalers and sells them to consumers. Examples of retailers include **Roots Canada**, **Lululemon Athletica Inc.**, **Amazon.ca**, **Canadian Tire**, and **The Gap**. Some retailers, such as **Bell Canada**, sell a combination of products and services.

Reporting Financial Performance

Profit to a merchandiser results when revenue from selling merchandise exceeds both the cost of merchandise sold to customers and the cost of other operating expenses for the period (see Exhibit 5.1). The usual accounting term for revenues from selling merchandise is *sales*. **Net sales** refers to the result of subtracting *sales discounts*[2] and *sales returns and allowances* from total or gross sales. The term used for the cost of merchandise sold to customers is an expense called *cost of goods sold*.[3] A merchandiser's other expenses are often called *operating expenses*.

---

1 *Cost of goods sold* is also commonly called **cost of sales**.

2 *Sales discounts* and *sales returns and allowances* are discussed in more detail later in this chapter.

3 When preparing the income statement using the "function of expense" method per IFRS 2014, IAS 1, para. 103, cost of goods sold must be shown separately from other expenses.

EXHIBIT 5.1

Calculating Profit for Both a Service Company and a Merchandising Company

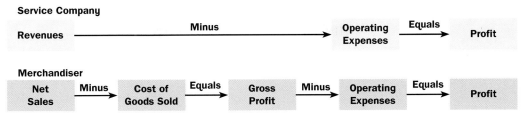

Service Company

Revenues —— Minus ——→ Operating Expenses —— Equals ——→ Profit

Merchandiser

Net Sales — Minus → Cost of Goods Sold — Equals → Gross Profit — Minus → Operating Expenses — Equals → Profit

EXHIBIT 5.2

Summarized Income Statement Information for a Merchandiser

MEC Summarized Income Statement Information For Year Ended December 31, 2017	
Net sales	$314,700
Cost of goods sold	230,400
Gross profit from sales	$ 84,300
Total operating expenses and other revenues and expenses	68,960
Profit	$ 15,340

Note: The above income statement of MEC is prepared for illustrative purposes only. The figures used are not representative of MEC's true financial position.

The summarized illustrative income statement information for MEC in Exhibit 5.2 shows us how net sales, gross profit, and profit are related. This statement shows that MEC sold products to customers for $314,700. MEC acquired these goods at a cost of $230,400. This yields an $84,300 gross profit. **Gross profit**, also called **gross margin**, equals net sales less cost of goods sold. Changes in gross profit often greatly impact a merchandiser's operations since gross profit must cover all other expenses and yield a return for the owner. MEC, for instance, used gross profit to cover $68,960 of operating and other revenues and expenses. This left $15,340 in profit for the year 2017.

Reporting Financial Position

A merchandising company's balance sheet includes an item not on the balance sheet of a service company. This item is a current asset called *merchandise inventory*. **Merchandise inventory**, or **inventory**, refers to products a company owns for the purpose of selling to customers. Exhibit 5.3 shows an example of what a classified balance sheet would look like for a retailer like MEC; note that merchandise inventory is presented at $21,000. The cost of this asset includes the cost incurred to buy the goods, ship them to the store, and otherwise get them ready for sale. Although companies usually hold inventories of other items such as supplies, *most companies simply refer to merchandise inventory as inventory*. We will use both terms in reference to merchandise inventory.

EXHIBIT 5.3

Classified Balance Sheet for a Merchandiser

MEC Balance Sheet December 31, 2017			
Assets			
Current assets:			
Cash		$ 8,200	
Accounts receivable		11,200	
Merchandise inventory		21,000	
Prepaid expenses...		1,100	
Total current assets			$41,500
Plant and equipment:			
Office equipment	$ 4,200		
Less: Accumulated depreciation........................	1,400	$ 2,800	
Store equipment	$30,000		
Less: Accumulated depreciation........................	6,000	24,000	
Total plant and equipment			26,800
Total assets			$68,300
Liabilities			
Current liabilities:			
Accounts payable..		$16,000	
Salaries payable		800	
Total liabilities			$16,800
Equity			
David Wingate*, capital....................................			51,500
Total liabilities and equity...................................			$68,300
*For ease of illustrative purposes it will be assumed that the owner is David Wingate, one of the six original founders of MEC.			

Note: The above balance sheet of MEC is prepared for illustrative purposes only. The figures used are not representative of MEC's true financial position.

Operating Cycle

A merchandising company's operating cycle[4] begins with the purchase of merchandise and ends with the collection of cash from the sale of merchandise.

Exhibit 5.4 graphically shows an operating cycle for a merchandiser with (1) cash sales and (2) credit sales. Credit sales delay the receipt of cash until the account receivable balance is paid by the customer. Company assets tied up in the form of inventory or receivables are not enhancing the company's value, but are a required part of business. Merchandise inventory is not productive (earning profit) until it is sold and any outstanding receivables are collected. Supply chain management (SCM) is a field that attempts to maximize value from the sourcing of the product to final delivery to the customer. A shorter operating cycle is desirable so that the resulting cash from the sale of inventory can be used in the business to earn profit. The length of an operating cycle differs across the types of businesses.

Car manufacturers such as **BMW AG, Honda Motor Co. Inc.,** and **Ford Motor Company** typically have a longer operating cycle, as they need to purchase materials and manufacture the vehicle, ship the vehicle to a dealership, and sell it to the end consumer. Department stores such as **Hudson's Bay Company**

---

4 IFRS 2014, IAS 1, para. 68.

EXHIBIT 5.4

Operating Cycle of a Merchandiser

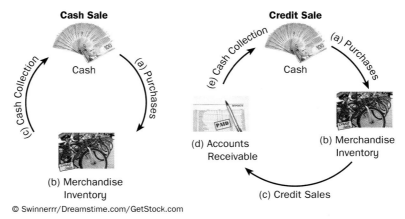

© Swinnerrr/Dreamstime.com/GetStock.com

commonly have operating cycles of three to five months, but operating cycles for grocery merchants such as **Superstore** and **Marketplace IGA** usually range from one to two months. Obsolescence is a concern for inventory that is subject to expiry or rapid technological advancement; as such, these companies attempt to minimize inventories held at their warehouse and aim to find the right balance to meet customer demands.

Inventory Systems

Exhibit 5.5 shows that a company's merchandise available for sale is a combination of what it begins with (beginning inventory) and what it purchases (net cost of purchases). The merchandise available is either sold (cost of goods sold) or kept for future sales (ending inventory).

There are two types of inventory accounting systems used to collect information about cost of goods sold and cost of inventory on hand: perpetual and periodic. Both inventory systems are permitted under both IFRS and ASPE; therefore, companies have a choice and must disclose their policy to account for inventory in their financial statement notes. We now describe these two inventory accounting options in more detail.

EXHIBIT 5.5

Merchandising Cost Flow

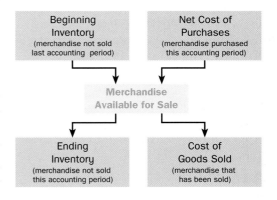

PERPETUAL INVENTORY SYSTEM

LO2 Describe both perpetual and periodic inventory systems.

A **perpetual inventory system** provides an up-to-date record of the amount of inventory on hand. Have you noticed at some retail stores it is possible for the store to determine through a quick computer search whether the specific product you are looking for is available at another location? This is because they are using a perpetual inventory system that updates the inventory records continually each time a purchase or sale of inventory is made. When a purchase is made under a perpetual inventory system, the inventory account is debited for the cost of each purchase and a corresponding accounts payable account is credited, as items are received from the supplier.

Purchase of Inventory

Dr. Inventory.. xxx
    Cr. Accounts Payable........................ xxx
Purchased merchandise on credit

Important Tip: When a sale occurs in a perpetual inventory system, two key journal entries are booked. First, the sale to the customer is recorded, with a debit to accounts receivable and a credit to sales. Second, the item is immediately removed from the Inventory account and the cost of the inventory is recorded on the income statement as a Cost of Goods Sold (COGS).

---

1) Sales transaction:

Dr. Accounts Receivable xxx
    Cr. Sales xxx
Sold merchandise on credit

2) Perpetual inventory adjustment:

Dr. Inventory.. xxx
    Cr. Cost of Goods Sold. xxx
Record the cost of the sale of merchandise
and the reduction of inventory

With a perpetual system, we can find out the cost of merchandise on hand at any time by looking at the balance of the inventory account. The company can also determine the up-to-date dollar amount of cost of goods sold by looking up the balance in the Cost of Goods Sold account. A detailed illustration of the perpetual inventory system is demonstrated using a fictitious example from MEC later in the chapter.

Before advancements in IT infrastructures, a perpetual system was often limited to businesses making a small number of daily sales, such as automobile dealers and major appliance stores. Today, with widespread use of computerized data management software, the use of a perpetual system has dramatically grown to include merchandisers with high-volume sales, such as **Walmart**, Canadian Tire, **Superstore**, **Staples**, **The Gap**, and **London Drugs**. Because perpetual inventory systems give users more timely information and are widely used in practice, our discussion in this chapter emphasizes a perpetual system.

Merchandise Inventory (MI)		
Beginning MI 10	LESS	
PLUS	COGS	COGS
Purchases 50	55---→55	
EQUALS		
Ending MI 5		

Under a perpetual system, the MI account is updated continually for purchases and goods sold. The balance in MI and COGS is always up to date.

PERIODIC INVENTORY SYSTEM

A **periodic inventory system** requires updating the inventory account only at the *end of a period* to reflect the quantity and cost of both goods on hand and goods sold. It does not require continual updating of the inventory account.

Important Tip: A periodic inventory system records the cost of all new inventory in a temporary expense account called Purchases.

Purchase of Inventory

Dr. Purchases.. xxx
    Cr. Accounts Payable........................ xxx
Purchased merchandise on credit

Important Tip: Under the perpetual method only one journal entry is booked at the time of sale, debiting A/R and crediting Sales. No adjustment to inventory or COGS is made.

When merchandise is sold, revenue is recorded but the cost of the merchandise sold is *not* recorded as a cost at this time.

Sales transaction:

Dr. Accounts Receivable   xxx
    Cr. Sales   xxx
Sold merchandise on credit

Merchandise Inventory (MI)	
Beginning MI 10	
PLUS	
Purchases	
Purchases 50	
LESS	
Ending MI (per a physical count)	
5	
EQUALS	
COGS	
55	

Under a periodic system, the MI account is updated when a physical count is performed. COGS is calculated once ending MI is known.

DETERMINING ENDING INVENTORY AND COST OF GOODS SOLD

When financial statements are prepared, the company takes a *physical count of inventory* by counting the quantities of merchandise on hand. The accuracy of the inventory count is critical because it determines both the dollar value of the asset "Inventory" on the balance sheet at period end, as well as the "Cost of Goods Sold" on the income statement. Cost of merchandise on hand is determined by relating the quantities on hand to records showing each item's original cost. This cost of merchandise on hand is used to calculate cost of goods sold as shown to the right. The Merchandise Inventory account and Cost of Goods Sold is then updated to reflect end of period balances through booking a closing entry to reflect the amount from the physical count of inventory.[5]

Historically, periodic systems were used by companies such as hardware, drug, grocery, and department stores that sold large quantities of low-value items. Before computers and scanners, it was not feasible for accounting systems to track small items such as nails, pencils, paper clips, soap, and apples through inventory and into customers' hands. The next section highlights accounting for merchandising transactions using the perpetual inventory method. *We provide a comparison of recording of merchandising transactions using both periodic and perpetual inventory systems in Appendix 5A.*

DECISION INSIGHT

Loblaw Companies Limited Converts from Periodic to Perpetual

Loblaw Companies Limited began a process of converting its corporate-owned grocery stores from a periodic inventory system to a perpetual inventory system that was completed in 2014. The improved information is a result of an upgrade to its IT infrastructure, enabling the stores to integrate costing information more effectively for items held in inventory.

SOURCES: http://www.newswire.ca/en/story/1390772/loblaw-companies-limited-reports-a-65-1-increase-in-adjusted-operating-income-2-for-the-second-quarter-of-2014-1, accessed October 12, 2014; http://www.loblaw.ca/files/4.%20Investor%20Centre/Financial%20Reports/2014/Annual/AIF-English.pdf, accessed June 26, 2015; *Loblaw Companies Limited 2014 Annual Report* http://www.loblaw.ca/files/4.%20Investor%20Centre/Financial%20Reports/2015/Annual/655210_Eng_LR_v001_h33m0e.pdf.

CHECKPOINT

    1. Describe what a company's cost of goods sold is and where the value comes from.
    2. What is gross profit for a merchandising company?
    3. Explain why use of the perpetual inventory system has grown dramatically.

Do Quick Study questions: QS 5-1, QS 5-2, QS 5-3, QS 5-4

---

5   Refer to the Appendix 5A section on Closing Entries for a detailed illustration demonstrating the closing entry adjustments.

Accounting for Merchandise Transactions— Perpetual Inventory System

LO3   Analyze and record transactions for merchandise purchases and sales using a perpetual system.

Recording merchandise transactions involves issues regarding the purchase and sale of merchandise inventory. In this first section, we will examine purchase transactions and associated items. Then, in the next section, transactions related to sales will be examined.

Accounting for Merchandise Purchases—Perpetual Inventory System

With a perpetual inventory system, the cost of merchandise bought for resale is recorded in the Merchandise Inventory account. MEC records a $1,200 credit purchase of merchandise on November 2 with this entry:

Nov.	2	Merchandise Inventory.................................	1,200	
		Accounts Payable		1,200
		Purchased merchandise on credit.		

The invoice for this merchandise is shown in Exhibit 5.6. The buyer usually receives the original, while the seller keeps a copy. This single source document serves as the purchase invoice of MEC (buyer) and the sales invoice for Trex (seller). The costs that can be included in inventory include all costs incurred in acquiring the goods and bringing them to the purchaser's warehouse and any costs incurred to get them ready for sale to the final customer. Specifically, we can include in merchandise inventory all purchase costs, shipping fees, duties, and any other costs necessary to get the products ready for sale.

Important Tip: To calculate the total cost of merchandise inventory purchases, we must adjust the invoice cost as follows:

(1)   Subtract the cost of any returns and allowances for unsatisfactory items received from a supplier;

(2)   Subtract discounts given to a purchaser by a supplier for early payment; and

(3)   Add required freight costs if paid by the purchaser.

This section explains these items in more detail.

ACCOUNTING FOR SALES TAXES IN THE ACQUISITION OF INVENTORY

In Canada, sales taxes include **Provincial Sales Tax** (PST), **Goods and Services Tax** (GST) and the **Harmonized Sales Tax** (HST). HST is a combination of PST and GST that has been adopted by several provinces in Canada.

In most provinces, inventory acquired by a merchandising business with the purpose of resale to an end consumer is excluded from PST. Merchandisers can apply for a PST exemption certificate /tax exemption number, which is to be provided to vendors so they are not charged PST on purchases of goods solely for resale. In Canada it is intended for PST to be paid only by the final consumer.[6] As a result, PST is *not included* in the cost of acquiring inventory.

---

6   An example exemption certificate for BC can be found at http://www.sbr.gov.bc.ca/documents_library/forms/0490FILL.pdf

In Saskatchewan the Vendor License issued by the Ministry of Finance provides exemption on goods purchased for resale: http://finance.gov.sk.ca/forms/FI-1213ApplicationforVendorsLicence-ConsumerRegistration.pdf.

GST and HST paid on the acquisition of goods is *recoverable* from collections of GST and HST from the end customer, and therefore is also *not included* in the cost of inventory.

Appendix 5B provides a high-level overview of accounting for sales taxes in Canada under both perpetual and periodic inventory systems. Additional information relating to accounting for sales tax is provided in Chapter 10.

PURCHASE RETURNS AND ALLOWANCES

Purchase returns are merchandise received by a purchaser and subsequently returned to the supplier. Reasons for returns can vary. The merchandise received may have been the wrong colour or size. A *purchase allowance* is a reduction in the cost of defective merchandise received by a purchaser from a supplier. Purchasers will often keep defective merchandise that is still saleable if the supplier grants an acceptable reduction in the price, providing a sufficient allowance. For example, assume that the merchandise received by the purchaser was furniture scratched during shipment. The purchaser may decide to keep the furniture and pay to repair the furniture if the supplier provides a discount on the original price.

EXHIBIT 5.6

Invoice

The purchaser informs the supplier of any returns and allowances. This is often through written communication, initiated by the purchaser to inform the supplier of a debit made to the supplier's account, including the reason for a return or allowance. This communication can be in a formal document called a debit memo.

To illustrate how a buyer accounts for an allowance, we assume that the Roadster mountain bike purchased by MEC on November 2 was discovered to be defective when received on November 5. The November 5 entry by MEC for the purchase allowance is:

Nov.	5	Accounts Payable	300	
		Merchandise Inventory		300
		Purchase allowance re debit memo		
		dated November 5.		

The entry reduces the Merchandise Inventory account to reflect the allowance. The Accounts Payable account is debited to reduce the liability to the supplier, hence the term *debit memo*.

If this had been a return, then the recorded cost[7] of the defective merchandise would be entered. If there is a refund of cash, then the Cash account is debited for $300 instead of Accounts Payable.

TRADE DISCOUNTS—PROVIDED FOR VOLUME PURCHASES

When a manufacturer or wholesaler prepares a catalogue of items that it has for sale, each item is usually given a **list price**, also called a **catalogue price**. Often the intended selling price equals list price minus a given percentage called a **trade discount**. The amount of trade discount usually depends on the quantities purchased and on whether a buyer is a wholesaler, retailer, or final consumer. For example, a wholesaler buying 50,000 pens might be granted a 35% trade discount, while a retailer purchasing 500 pens might be granted a 5% trade discount.

Trade discounts are commonly used by manufacturers and wholesalers to change selling prices without republishing their catalogues. When a seller wants to change selling prices, it can notify its customers merely by sending them a new table of trade discounts that they can apply to catalogue prices.

Because a list price is not intended to reflect the actual selling price of merchandise, a buyer records the net amount of list price minus the expected trade discount rather than accounting separately for the discount. For example, on November 2, MEC purchased clothing for resale from The North Place that was listed at $2,000 in the catalogue. Since MEC receives a 40% trade discount, the company records the transaction at $1,200 [= $2,000 − (40% × $2,000)].

Nov.2	Merchandise Inventory..................................	1,200	
	Accounts Payable		1,200
	Purchase of inventory from The North Place.		

PURCHASE DISCOUNTS—PROVIDED FOR EARLY PAYMENT

The purchase of goods on credit requires a clear statement of the *credit terms* to avoid misunderstanding. **Credit terms** are a listing of the amounts and timing of payments between a buyer (customer) and seller (supplier). In some industries, purchasers expect terms requiring full or "net" payment within 10 days after the end of a month in which purchases occur. These credit terms are entered on sales invoices or tickets as "n/10 EOM." The **EOM** refers to "end of month." In other industries, invoices are due and payable 30 calendar days after the invoice date. These credit terms are entered as "n/30," meaning "net amount due in 30 days." The 30-day period is called the **credit period**. Credit terms may include a **cash discount**. A buyer views a cash discount as a **purchase discount**. If cash discounts for early payment exist, they are described in the credit terms on an invoice. Referring to point 5 in Exhibit 5.6, notice that MEC's November 2 credit purchase was on terms of 2/10, n/30. This should be read "there is a 2% discount if paid within 10 days; the net balance is due within 30 days." The seller allows MEC to deduct 2% of the invoice amount from the payment if it is paid within 10 days; of the invoice date. Sellers do this to encourage early payment, improving their operating cycle as described previously. The 10 days are the **discount period**, the period in which the reduced payment can be made. Exhibit 5.7 explains these credit terms.

---

7 Recorded cost is the cost reported in a Merchandise Inventory account minus any discounts.

EXHIBIT 5.7

Credit Terms Illustration—2/10, n/30

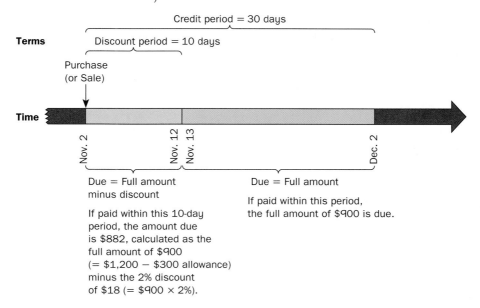

When MEC takes advantage of the discount and pays the amount due on November 12, the entry to record payment is:

Nov.	12	Accounts Payable	900	
		Merchandise Inventory		18
		Cash		882
		Paid for the purchase of November 2		
		less the allowance of November 5 and		
		the discount; $1,200 − $300 = $900;		
		2% × $900 = $18; $900 − $18 = $882.		

> **Important Tip:** Notice that this entry shows that when goods are returned within the discount period, a buyer will take the discount only on the remaining balance of the invoice.

MEC's Merchandise Inventory account now reflects the net cost of merchandise purchased. Its Accounts Payable account also shows the debt to be satisfied.

Merchandise Inventory				Accounts Payable			
Nov. 2	1,200	300	Nov. 5	Nov. 5	300	1,200	Nov. 2
		18	Nov. 12	Nov. 12	900		
Balance	882					-0-	Balance

MANAGING DISCOUNTS

A buyer's failure to pay within a discount period is often quite expensive. If MEC does not pay within the 10-day discount period, it delays the payment by 20 more days. This delay costs MEC an added 2%. Most buyers try to take advantage of purchase discounts. For MEC's terms of 2/10, n/30, missing the 2%

discount for an additional 20 days is equal to an annual interest rate of 36.5%, calculated as (365 days ÷ 20 days × 2%).

Most companies set up a system to pay invoices with favourable discounts within the discount period. Careful cash management means that no invoice is paid until the last day of a discount period. Computerized systems achieve this goal by using a code that identifies the last date in the discount period. When that date occurs, the system automatically identifies accounts to be paid.[8]

DECISION MAKER

Answer—End of chapter

Accounts Payable Manager

You are the new accounts payable manager for a merchandising company that purchases its merchandise on credit. You are trained for your new job by the outgoing employee. You are to oversee payment of payables to maintain the company's credit standing with suppliers and to take advantage of favourable cash discounts. The outgoing employee explains that the computer system is programmed to prepare cheques for amounts net of favourable cash discounts, and cheques are dated the last day of the discount period. You are told that cheques are not mailed until five days later, however. "It's simple," this employee explains. "Our company gets free use of cash for an extra five days, and our department looks better. When a supplier complains, we blame the computer system and the mail room." Your first invoice arrives with a 10-day discount period for a $10,000 purchase. This transaction occurs on April 9 with credit terms of 2/10, n/30. Do you mail the $9,800 cheque on April 19 or April 24?

TRANSFER OF OWNERSHIP

The point where ownership of merchandise inventory transfers from the buyer to the seller must be identified on the invoice because it determines who pays transportation costs and other incidental costs of transit such as insurance. The party responsible for paying shipping costs is also responsible for insuring the merchandise during transport. The point of transfer is called the **FOB** point, where FOB stands for *free on board* or *freight on board.*

Exhibit 5.8 identifies two alternative points of transfer. *FOB shipping point,* also called *FOB factory,* means the buyer accepts ownership at the seller's place of business. The buyer is then responsible for paying shipping costs and bears the risk of damage or loss when goods are in transit. The seller records the revenue as soon as the items leave their warehouse. The goods are part of the buyer's inventory when they are in transit since ownership has transferred to the buyer.

FOB destination means ownership of the goods transfers to the buyer at the buyer's place of business. The seller is responsible for paying shipping charges and bears the risk of damage or loss in transit. The seller does not record revenue from this sale until the goods arrive at the destination because this transaction is not complete before that point.

There are situations when the party not responsible for shipping costs pays the carrier/transportation agency. In these cases, the party paying these costs either bills the party responsible or, more commonly, adjusts its account payable or receivable with the other party.

---

8 Companies that automatically take advantage of favourable discounts use the *net method* to record merchandise purchases as opposed to using the gross invoice amount when debiting Merchandise Inventory and crediting Accounts Payable (as illustrated in the textbook; known as the *gross method*). Under the net method, both Merchandise Inventory and Accounts Payable are debited/credited for the gross purchase amount *less* the discount. If payment is not made within the discount period, the payment would debit Accounts Payable for the net amount originally recorded, debit *Discounts Lost* for the amount of the lost discount, and credit Cash for the gross amount of the invoice. The gross method more strictly adheres to the revenue recognition principle than the net method, hence its inclusion in the textbook.

EXHIBIT 5.8

Identifying Transfer of Ownership

FOB Shipping Point   Carrier   FOB Destination
(Buyer Pays Transportation)   (Seller Pays Transportation)

	Ownership transfers when goods:	Transportation costs paid by:
FOB Shipping Point	Leave the seller's warehouse	**Buyer**
FOB Destination	Arrive at buyer's warehouse	**Seller**

DreamPictures/Shannon Faulk/Blend Images, © Alamy Images and
© Sean Pavone/Alamy

TRANSPORTATION COSTS

Shipping costs on purchases are called **transportation-in** or **freight-in** costs. MEC's $1,200 purchase on November 2 is on terms of FOB destination. This means that MEC is not responsible for paying transportation costs.

A different situation arises when a company is responsible for paying transportation costs. The cost principle requires these transportation costs to be included as part of the cost of merchandise inventory. This means that a separate entry is necessary when they are not listed on the invoice. For example, MEC's entry to record a $75 freight charge to an independent carrier for merchandise purchased FOB shipping point is:

Nov.	2	Merchandise Inventory	75	
		Cash		75
		Paid freight charges on purchased merchandise.		

> **Important Note:** The cost of shipping goods to customers is different from transportation-in costs. **Transportation-out** or **freight-out** costs for the shipping of goods to customers are debited to the *Delivery Expense* account when the seller is responsible for these costs, and are reported as a *selling expense* in the income statement.

 **CHECKPOINT**

    4. Locate the sample invoice in Exhibit 5.6. When the merchandise inventory is shipped by Trex to MEC, identify at what point ownership of the product transfers to MEC.

    5. How long are the credit and discount periods when credit terms are 2/10, n/60?

    6. Identify which of the following items are subtracted from the list amount when calculating purchase price: (a) freight-in, (b) trade discount, (c) purchase discount, (d) purchase return and/or allowance.

Do Quick Study questions: QS 5-5, QS 5-6, QS 5-7, QS 5-8

Net Cost of Merchandise Purchases Calculation—Perpetual

Merchandise Inventory		
Dec. 31, 2016, balance................. 19,000		
Reflects entries to record **purchases of merchandise** during 2017 235,800	Reflects entries to record **purchase discounts** during 2017	Net Cost of Purchases during 2017 = $232,400
	4,200	
	Reflects entries to record **purchase returns and**	
Reflects **transportation-in** costs incurred during 2017............. 2,300	1,500 ....**allowances** during 2017	

RECORDING PURCHASES INFORMATION

We have explained how purchase returns and allowances, purchase discounts, and transportation-in are included in calculating the total cost of merchandise inventory. An example presentation of MEC's 2017 net cost of merchandise purchases is summarized in Exhibit 5.9 and is presented for illustrative purposes only.

Accounting for Merchandise Sales—Perpetual Inventory System

Merchandising companies also must account for sales, sales discounts, sales returns and allowances, and cost of goods sold. A merchandising company such as MEC reports these items in an income statement, as shown in Exhibit 5.10.

Gross Profit Section of Income Statement

MEC Calculation of Gross Profit For Year Ended December 31, 2017		
Sales..		$321,000
Less: Sales discounts..	$4,300	
Sales returns and allowances	2,000	6,300
Net sales		$314,700
Cost of goods sold		230,400
Gross profit from sales		$ 84,300

Note: The above calculation for MEC was prepared for illustrative purposes only. The figures used are not representative of MEC's true financial position.

This section explains how information in this calculation is derived from transactions involving sales, sales discounts, and sales returns and allowances.

SALES TRANSACTIONS

Accounting for a sales transaction for a seller of merchandise involves capturing information about two related parts:

1. Receiving revenue in the form of an asset from a customer, and

2. Recognizing the cost of merchandise sold to a customer.

As an example, MEC sold $2,400 of merchandise on credit on November 3. The revenue part of this transaction is recorded as:

Nov.	3	Accounts Receivable	2,400	
		Sales		2,400
		Sold merchandise on credit.		

This entry reflects an increase in MEC's assets in the form of an account receivable. It also shows the revenue from the credit sale. If the sale is for cash, the debit is to Cash instead of Accounts Receivable.

The expense or cost of the merchandise sold by MEC on November 3 is $1,600. We explain in Chapter 6 how the cost of this merchandise is calculated. The entry to record the cost part of this sales transaction (under a perpetual inventory system) is:

Nov.	3	Cost of Goods Sold.......................................	1,600	
		Merchandise Inventory		1,600
		To record the cost of Nov. 3 sale		
		and reduce inventory.		

This entry records the cost of the merchandise sold as an expense and reduces the Merchandise Inventory account to reflect the remaining balance of inventory on hand.

SALES DISCOUNTS

When sellers offer credit terms that include a cash discount, the cash discount is referred to as a **sales discount**. Sales discounts can encourage prompt payments to customers for early payment, improve cash flow, and also reduce future efforts and costs of billing customers.

A seller does not know whether a customer will pay within the discount period and take advantage of a cash discount at the time of a credit sale, so a sales discount is usually not recorded until a customer pays within the discount period. As an example, MEC completed a credit sale for $1,000 on November 12, subject to terms of 2/10, n/60 (the cost of the inventory sold was $600). The entry to record this sale is:

Nov.	12	Accounts Receivable	1,000	
		Sales		1,000
		Sold merchandise under terms of 2/10, n/60.		
	12	Cost of Goods Sold.......................................	600	
		Merchandise Inventory		600
		To record the cost of the Nov. 12 sale		
		and reduce inventory.		

This entry records the receivable and the revenue as if the full amount will be paid by the customer.

The customer has two options. One option is to wait 60 days until January 11 and pay the full $1,000. In this case, MEC records the payment as:

Jan.	11	Cash..	1,000	
		Accounts Receivable		1,000
		Received payment for November 12 sale.		

The customer's second option is to pay $980 within a 10-day period that runs through November 22. If the customer pays on or before November 22, MEC records the payment as:

Nov.	22	Cash...	980	
		Sales Discounts	20	
		Accounts Receivable		1,000
		Received payment for November 12 sale		
		less the discount; $1,000 × 2% = $20.		

Sales discounts are recorded in a *contra revenue* account called Sales Discounts. This is so management can monitor sales discounts to assess their effectiveness and cost. The Sales Discounts account is deducted from the Sales account when calculating a company's net sales (refer to Exhibit 5.10). While information about sales discounts is useful internally, it is seldom reported on income statements distributed to external users.

SALES RETURNS AND ALLOWANCES

Sales returns refer to merchandise that customers return to the seller after a sale. Customers return merchandise for a variety of reasons, such as having received an incorrect item or one of poor quality. Many companies allow customers to return merchandise for a full refund. *Sales allowances* refer to reductions in the selling price of merchandise sold to customers. This can occur with damaged merchandise that a customer is willing to purchase if the selling price is decreased. **Sales returns and allowances** involve dissatisfied customers and the possibility of lost future sales. To monitor these problems, managers need detailed information, so many accounting systems record returns and allowances in a separate contra revenue account.

Recall MEC's sale of merchandise on November 3. As already recorded, the merchandise is sold for $2,400 and cost $1,600, but what if the customer returns part of the merchandise on November 6, when returned items sell for $800 and cost $600? The revenue part of this transaction must reflect the decrease in sales from the customer's return:

Nov.	6	Sales Returns and Allowances........................	800	
		Accounts Receivable		800
		Customer returned merchandise.		

MEC can record this return with a debit to the Sales account instead of Sales Returns and Allowances. This method provides the same net sales, but does not provide information needed by managers to monitor returns and allowances. By using the Sales Returns and Allowances contra account, this information is available. Published income statements usually omit this detail and show only net sales.

If the merchandise returned to MEC is not defective and can be resold to another customer, then MEC returns these goods to its inventory. The entry necessary to restore the cost of these goods to the Merchandise Inventory account is:

Nov.	6	Merchandise Inventory...................................	600	
		Cost of Goods Sold..............................		600
		Returned goods to inventory.		

If the merchandise returned is defective, however, the seller may discard the returned items. In this case, the cost of returned merchandise is not restored to the Merchandise Inventory account. Instead, most companies leave the cost of defective merchandise in the Cost of Goods Sold account.[9]

Another possibility is that $800 of the merchandise sold by MEC on November 3 is defective but the customer decides to keep it because MEC grants the customer a price reduction of $500. The only entry that MEC must make in this case is one to reflect the decrease in revenue:

Nov.	6	Sales Returns and Allowances........................	500	
		Accounts Receivable		500
		To record sales allowance.		

Some companies require the seller to prepare a **credit memo** to confirm a customer's return or allowance. A credit memo informs a customer of a credit to his or her account receivable, hence the term *credit memo*.

The information in a credit memo is similar to that of a debit memo. The following table summarizes what debit and credit memos are and why they arise:

Inventory Adjustment for Purchaser (Debit Memo)	Vendor Sales Adjustment (Credit Memo)

• Document prepared by the purchaser to "debit" or reduce the purchaser's account payable and "credit" the inventory account.
 	
Why is a debit memo issued?
• To reduce the purchaser's account payable because of:
  1. Return of unsatisfactory goods
  2. Allowance
  3. Error
	• Document prepared by the seller to "credit" or reduce the customer's account receivable and "debit" sales returns and allowances.
	
	Why is a credit memo issued?
	• To reduce the seller's account receivable because of:
	  1. Return of unsatisfactory goods
	  2. Allowance
	  3. Error

CHECKPOINT

7. Why are sales discounts and sales returns and allowances recorded in contra revenue accounts instead of directly in the Sales account?

8. Under what conditions are two entries necessary to record a sales return?

9. When merchandise is sold on credit and the seller notifies the buyer of a price reduction, does the seller send a credit memo or a debit memo?

Do Quick Study questions: QS 5-9, QS 5-10, QS 5-11, QS 5-12

---

[9] When managers want to monitor the cost of defective merchandise, a more informative method is to remove the cost from Cost of Goods Sold and charge it to a *Loss from Defective Merchandise* account.

MID-CHAPTER DEMONSTRATION PROBLEM

Thorsten Company, a trendy clothing retailer, had the following transactions in March:

March	2	Purchased merchandise from Sabine Company under the following terms: $1,800 invoice price, 2/15, n/60, FOB factory. (The cost of the merchandise to Sabine Company was $990.)
	3	Paid UBS Shipping $125 for shipping charges on the purchase of March 2.
	4	Returned to Sabine Company unacceptable merchandise that had an invoice price of $300 (and a cost to Sabine of $165). Sabine returned the merchandise to inventory.
	17	Sent a cheque to Sabine Company for the March 2 purchase, net of the discount and the returned merchandise.

Required

Assuming both Thorsten and Sabine use a perpetual inventory system:

   a. Present the journal entries Thorsten Company should record for these transactions.

   b. Present the journal entries Sabine Company should record for these transactions.

Analysis Component:

Who should be insuring the merchandise during shipping: Thorsten or Sabine? Explain.

Solution

a.

Thorsten Company (the buyer)

March 2	Merchandise Inventory	1,800	
	Accounts Payable—Sabine Company		1,800
	Purchased merchandise on credit.		
3	Merchandise Inventory	125	
	Cash		125
	Paid shipping charges on purchased merchandise		
4	Accounts Payable— Sabine Company	300	
	Merchandise Inventory		300
	Returned unacceptable merchandise.		
17	Accounts Payable—Sabine Company	1,500	
	Merchandise Inventory		30
	Cash		1,470
	Paid balance within the discount period and took a 2% discount.		

b.

Sabine Company (the seller)

March 2	Accounts Receivable—Thorsten Company	1,800	
	Sales		1,800
	Sold merchandise under terms 2/15, n/60.		
	Cost of Goods Sold	990	
	Merchandise Inventory		990
	Recorded cost of sales.		
	No entry		
4	Sales Returns and Allowances	300	
	Accounts Receivable—Thorsten Company		300
	Customer returned merchandise.		
	Merchandise Inventory	165	
	Cost of Goods Sold		165
	Merchandise returned to inventory.		
17	Cash	1,470	
	Sales Discounts	30	
	Accounts Receivable—Thorsten Company		1,500
	Received payment for March 2 sale less the return and discount.		

Analysis Component:

Thorsten should be insuring the merchandise during shipping because the terms *FOB factory* transfers ownership to Thorsten Company the moment the merchandise leaves Sabine Company.

MERCHANDISING INVENTORY JOURNAL ENTRIES SUMMARY—PERPETUAL			
PURCHASES		**SALES**	
Transaction	**Journal Entry**	**Transaction**	**Journal Entry**

Purchase inventory on credit	Merchandise Inventory xxx
	    Accounts Payable xxx
		Sell inventory on credit	**Revenue on sale of goods:**
			Accounts Receivable................... xxx
			    Sales xxx
			Recording transfer of inventory and COGS on sale:
			Cost of Goods Sold xxx
			    Merchandise Inventory xxx

Return unacceptable merchandise to supplier	Accounts Payable............... xx
	    Merchandise Inventory xx
		Merchandise returned by customer	**Adjustment to customer's account for return of goods:**
			Sales Returns and Allowances xxx
			    Accounts Receivable xxx
			If items are returned in a salable condition need to reinstate inventory:
			Merchandise Inventory xxx
			    Cost of Goods Sold................. xxx

Purchase allowances provided by supplier for defective merchandise[1]	**If supplier provides a discount on the defective goods and the goods are kept for resale:**
	Accounts Payable............... xx
	    Merchandise Inventory xx
		Sales allowances provided to customer[2]	**If customer keeps defective product and an allowance is provided:**
			Sales Returns and Allowances xx
			    Accounts Receivables xx

Pay freight/shipping charges (FOB Shipping Point)	Merchandise Inventory xx
	    Cash xx
		Pay shipping charges (FOB Destination)	Delivery expense........................ xxx
			    Cash..................................... xxx

Pay supplier within discount period	Accounts Payable............... xxx
	    Merchandise Inventory* ... xx
	Cash** xxx
	
	*discount = % discount*AP balance
	**cash paid = AP balance − discount
		Receive balance from customer within discount period	Cash## xxx
			Sales Discounts#...................... xx
			    Accounts Receivable xxx
			
			#discount = % discount*AR balance
			##cash received = AR balance − discount

Pay supplier after discount period	Accounts Payable............... xxx
	    Cash............................. xxx
		Receive balance from customer after discount period	Cash xxx
			    Accounts Receivable xxx

[1] Note: The same journal entry is booked as a return of goods if vendor provides a discount on the goods, except adjustment to A/P is for a lesser amount.

[2] Note: The same journal entry as a return of goods is booked if customer is provided a discount on the goods, except adjustment to A/P is for a lesser amount.

Additional Merchandising Issues—Perpetual Inventory System

This section identifies and explains how merchandising activities affect other accounting processes. We address preparing adjusting entries, and relationships between important accounts.

Adjusting Entries

LO4 Prepare adjustments for a merchandising company.

Most adjusting entries are the same for merchandising companies and service companies and involve prepaid expenses, unearned revenues, depreciation, accrued expenses, and accrued revenues.

A merchandising company using a perpetual inventory system needs one additional adjustment to update the Merchandise Inventory account for any losses of merchandise referred to as **shrinkage**. Merchandising companies can lose merchandise in several ways, including theft by employees and customers, accounting errors such as input errors or inventory counting errors, and damage.

Perpetual inventory systems track all goods as they move into and out of the company; however, they do not capture inventory losses due to shrinkage. Since inventory is a high dollar–value item for a merchandising company, nearly all retailers perform a regular detailed count of their inventory. Some companies will perform regular cycle counts of portions of their inventory (daily, weekly or monthly) and others will choose to do one thorough detailed count once a year. Shrinkage is calculated by comparing the recorded quantities of inventory in the accounting system with quantities recorded during the physical inventory count. Most companies record any necessary adjustment due to shrinkage by charging it to Cost of Goods Sold, assuming that shrinkage is not abnormally large.

As an example, consider a situation where MEC's Merchandise Inventory account at the end of 2017 had an unadjusted balance of $21,250, but a physical count of inventory revealed only $21,000 of inventory on hand. The adjusting entry to record this $250 shrinkage is:

Dec. 31	Cost of Goods Sold..	250	
	Merchandise Inventory		250
	To adjust for $250 shrinkage determined by physical count of inventory.		

DECISION INSIGHT

A 2012 Canadian Retail Consumer Security Survey performed by PwC revealed the following facts about Canadian retailers:

- It is estimated that Canadian retailers are losing over $4 billion per year due to shrinkage, which is approximately $10.8 million per shopping day or approximately $115 per Canadian citizen.

- Items most commonly impacted (in order) are alcohol, ladies apparel, and cosmetics and fragrances.

- Internal theft was up from 19% in the 2008 study to 33.4% in 2012, signalling a need for strengthened internal loss prevention policies and procedures, and investment in resources to aid in reducing such occurrences.

- 88% of employees who had engaged in theft were charged criminally and 94% were dismissed with cause; 65% of customers engaging in theft were charged criminally.

- 76% of respondents perform either annual or semiannual inventory counts; only 6% of respondents did not perform regular inventory counts.

- The most common loss prevention controls implemented by retail stores include alarm systems, closed-circuit TV/DVR recording systems, armored car deposit/pick-ups/merchandise alarms, exception reporting systems, and safes.

SOURCE: www.pwc.com/ca/retailsecuritysurvey

CHECKPOINT

10. When a merchandising company uses a perpetual inventory system, why is it often necessary to adjust the Merchandise Inventory balance with an adjusting entry?

Do Quick Study question: QS 5-13

Summary of Merchandising Cost Flows

The Merchandise Inventory account balance at the end of one period is the amount of beginning inventory in the next period.

To summarize the effects of merchandising transactions on the Merchandise Inventory and Cost of Goods Sold accounts, MEC's merchandising activities during 2017 are illustrated in Exhibit 5.11. Most amounts in these T-accounts are summary representations of several entries during the year 2017. Notice that the Cost of Goods Sold balance of $230,400 is the amount reported in the income statement information in Exhibit 5.2. The Merchandise Inventory balance of $21,000 is the amount reported as a current asset on the balance sheet in Exhibit 5.3. These amounts also appear on MEC's adjusted trial balance in Exhibits 5.12 and 5.18.

EXHIBIT 5.11

T-Account Summary of MEC's Merchandising Activities for 2017 (for illustrative purposes only)

Adjusted Trial Balance for a Merchandising Company—Perpetual Inventory System

When using a perpetual system, adjusting entries are similar for merchandising companies and service companies.

The year-end adjustments required for MEC include the following entries:

a. Expiration of $600 of prepaid insurance.
b. Use of $1,200 of store supplies.
c. Use of $1,800 of office supplies.
d. Depreciation of the store equipment for $3,000.
e. Depreciation of the office equipment for $700.
f. Accrual of $300 of unpaid office salaries and $500 of unpaid store salaries.
g. Physical count of merchandise inventory revealed $21,000 on hand.

Accounts unique to a merchandiser are bolded in the adjusted trial balance in Exhibit 5.12 and include Sales, Sales Discounts, Sales Returns and Allowances, and Cost of Goods Sold.

The accounts unique to a merchandiser are highlighted below.

EXHIBIT 5.12

Adjusted Trial Balance

MEC Adjusted Trial Balance December 31, 2017	Debit	Credit	
Cash	$ 8,200		
Accounts receivable	11,200		
Merchandise inventory	21,000		
Office supplies	550		
Store supplies	250		
Prepaid insurance	300		
Office equipment	4,200		
Accumulated depreciation, office equipment		$ 1,400	
Store equipment	30,000		
Accumulated depreciation, store equipment		6,000	
Accounts payable		16,000	
Salaries payable		800	
David Wingate, capital		40,160	
David Wingate, withdrawals	4,000		Notice the temporary accounts unique to a merchandiser high-lighted on the left. These accounts will need to be closed to income summary using a similar process to that illustrated in Chapter 4.
Rent revenue		2,800	
Sales		**321,000**	
Sales returns and allowances	**2,000**		
Sales discounts	**4,300**		
Cost of goods sold	**230,400**		
Depreciation expense, store equipment	3,000		
Depreciation expense, office equipment	700		
Office salaries expense	25,300		
Sales salaries expense	18,500		
Interest expense	360		
Insurance expense	600		
Rent expense, office space	900		
Rent expense, selling space	8,100		
Office supplies expense	1,800		
Store supplies expense	1,200		
Advertising expense	11,300		
Totals	$388,160	$388,160	

From Periodic to Perpetual to Virtual Inventory Systems

"Traditional models . . . are going away," according to Keyur Patel, a KPMG partner. Web businesses are changing the way inventory is managed and accounted for. Rather than risk having too little or too much in inventory along with all of the related costs, e-businesses are turning to the manufacturers to package and ship products direct to consumers. The result is that these merchants maintain no inventory balances. Instead, they take customer orders and transmit that information directly to the respective manufacturer, who fulfills the distribution obligation to the customer. Therefore, for these merchants, discussion of an inventory costing system has become redundant.

SOURCE: http://www.planetit.com.

Income Statement Formats—Perpetual Inventory System

LO5 Define, prepare, and analyze merchandising income statements.

Companies have flexibility as to what format can be used for the presentation of financial statements. As a result, there will be many different formats in practice. However, there are minimum classification requirements regarding how expenses are to be shown on the income statement. The first part of this section looks at formulating a draft income statement through the preparation of a work sheet. The second part of this section describes the classification requirements for expenses and illustrates three presentation formats using MEC's data.

Expense Classification Requirements

Expenses are to be shown on an income statement for companies reporting under IFRS standards based on either their *nature* or their *function*.[10] In previous chapters, expenses were listed on the income statement based on their *nature*. The **nature of an expense** is determined by the type of expense, which is organized based on the basic characteristics of reported expenses. For example, when expenses are identified on the income statement as depreciation, rent, property tax, and salaries, the nature of each expense is being identified.

The **function of an expense** describes the grouping of expenses based on their purpose or what they relate to. For example, an income statement that shows cost of goods sold, *selling expenses*, and *general and administrative expenses* has grouped expenses by their function. When expenses are grouped by function, additional information must be *disclosed* to show the nature of expenses within each group.[11]

ASPE standards provide the opportunity for flexibility in presenting expenses on the income statement. The **full disclosure principle** is the generally accepted accounting principle that requires financial statements to report all relevant information about the operations and financial position of the entity. Information that is relevant but not included in the body of the statements is provided in **notes to financial statements** such as those for **WestJet** in Appendix III of the text book.

---

10 IFRS 2014, IAS 1, para. 99–105.

11 IFRS 2014, IAS 1, para. 104. Although students at the introductory level should understand the concept of disclosure, the actual preparation of notes is left to a more advanced accounting course.

Multiple-Step Income Statement

There are two general types of multiple-step income statements: the *classified, multiple-step* and the multiple-step format. Both formats can be used in either a perpetual or periodic inventory system.

CLASSIFIED, MULTIPLE-STEP FORMAT (FOR INTERNAL REPORTING)

Exhibit 5.13 shows a **classified, multiple-step income statement** using data generated for illustrative purposes only for MEC. This format is useful for internal reporting because of the detail it includes, such as the calculation of net sales. The difference between net sales and cost of goods sold is MEC's gross profit.

Exhibit 5.13 shows operating expenses, a broad function or category. Operating expenses are divided into two additional functions: *selling expenses* and *general and administrative expenses*. **Selling expenses** include the expenses of promoting sales through displaying and advertising merchandise, making sales, and delivering goods to customers. In Exhibit 5.13, the selling expenses are disclosed within the body of the statement by providing detailed information on the nature of expenses, including sales salaries, advertising, rent expense allocated to selling, depreciation on the store equipment, and

EXHIBIT 5.13

Classified, Multiple-Step Income Statement—Perpetual Inventory System

MEC Income Statement For Year Ended December 31, 2017			
Sales...			$321,000
Less: Sales discounts		$ 4,300	
Sales returns and allowances......................		2,000	6,300
Net sales...			$314,700
Cost of goods sold			230,400
Gross profit from sales			$ 84,300
Operating expenses:			
Selling expenses:			
Sales salaries expense	$18,500		
Advertising expense..	11,300		
Rent expense, selling space	8,100		
Depreciation expense, store equipment.............	3,000		
Store supplies expense	1,200		
Total selling expenses......................................		$42,100	
General and administrative expenses:			
Office salaries expense...................................	$25,300		
Office supplies expense	1,800		
Rent expense, office space	900		
Depreciation expense, office equipment.............	700		
Insurance expense...	600		
Total general and administrative expenses.........		29,300	
Total operating expenses			71,400
Profit from operations			$ 12,900
Other revenues and expenses:			
Rent revenue		$ 2,800	
Interest expense..		360	2,440
Profit			$ 15,340

Note: Rent revenue is added
Interest expense is subtracted
to get total *Other revenues and expenses.*

store supplies. **General and administrative expenses** support the overall operations of a company and include expenses related to accounting, human resource management, and financial management. In Exhibit 5.13, the general and administrative expenses section provides detail on the nature of these expenses by including office salaries, office supplies, rent expense allocated to the general and administrative category, depreciation on the office equipment, and insurance expense.

Notice that an expense may be divided between categories when it contributes to more than one activity. For example, Exhibit 5.13 shows that MEC allocates rent expense of $9,000 for its store building between two categories: $8,100 is a selling expense, while $900 is listed as a general and administrative expense based on relative rental values.[12]

Revenues and expenses that are *not* part of normal operating activities are reported under the functional heading *Other revenues and expenses* of the income statement. MEC's main operating activity is merchandising; therefore, rent revenue—not a merchandising activity—is added under *Other revenues and expenses*. Another example, interest expense, arises because of a financing (or borrowing) activity and not because of MEC's merchandising (or operating) activities. It is subtracted under *Other revenues and expenses* as highlighted in Exhibit 5.13. Other examples of *Other revenues and expenses* include dividend income and gains and losses on the sale of property, plant, and equipment assets.

MULTIPLE-STEP FORMAT (FOR EXTERNAL REPORTING)

Exhibit 5.14 shows a multiple-step income statement format that can be used in external reports. In comparison to Exhibit 5.13, a multiple-step statement leaves out the detailed calculation of net sales. The functional categories of *selling expenses* and *general and administrative expenses* are not included on a multiple-step income statement; operating expenses are listed by nature only on a multiple-step income statement.

EXHIBIT 5.14

Multiple-Step Income Statement—Perpetual Inventory System

MEC Income Statement For Year Ended December 31, 2017		
Net sales...		$314,700
Cost of goods sold..		230,400
Gross profit from sales..		$ 84,300
Operating expenses:		
Salaries expense	$43,800	
Advertising expense...	11,300	
Rent expense	9,000	
Depreciation expense.......................................	3,700	
Supplies expense	3,000	
Insurance expense...	600	
Total operating expenses		71,400
Profit from operations...		$ 12,900
Other revenues and expenses:		
Rent revenue...	$ 2,800	
Interest expense..	360	2,440
Profit..		$ 15,340

---

[12] These expenses can be recorded in a single ledger account or in two separate accounts. If they are recorded in one account, we allocate its balance between the two expenses when preparing statements.

Single-Step Income Statement

A **single-step income statement** is another format for external reporting. It shows items based on their function only and is shown in Exhibit 5.15 for MEC. This simple format includes cost of goods sold as an operating expense and shows only one subtotal for total expenses. Because operating expenses are highly summarized on a single-step income statement, additional information regarding the nature of expenses included in each function must be disclosed in the notes to the financial statements.

Single-Step Income Statement—Perpetual Inventory System

MEC Income Statement For Year Ended December 31, 2017		
Revenues:		
Net sales	$314,700	
Rent revenue	2,800	
Total revenues		$317,500
Expenses:		
Cost of goods sold	$230,400	
Selling expenses	42,100	
General and administrative expense	29,300	
Interest expense	360	
Total expenses		302,160
Profit		$ 15,340

Companies can use formats that combine features of both the single- and multiple-step statements for external reporting. As long as income statement items are shown sensibly and minimum requirements are satisfied, management can choose the presentation format.

CHECKPOINT

11. What income statement format shows detailed calculations for net sales? What format gives no subtotals except total expenses?

Do Quick Study question: QS 5-14

Financial Statement Analysis Tools for Inventory

LO6 Calculate gross margin and markup on inventory cost.

Gross Profit Margin

Gross profit margin, also called gross margin or gross profit ratio, is an important ratio, as it identifies the percentage of sales dollars left over after covering cost of goods sold. Competitors pay close attention to gross margins, as a company with higher margins is either able to achieve better pricing on its inventory or is able to convince customers to pay a premium for its product. Companies compare their margins achieved in the current year to prior years to assess their performance from one year to the next. Industry benchmarks, competitor performance, and historical margins achieved are all helpful tools in determining whether the gross margins achieved are reasonable. A merchandising company needs sufficient gross profit to cover operating expenses or it will not be able to remain competitive.

The **gross profit margin ratio** is defined as shown in Exhibit 5.16. The higher the gross profit margin, the better the company is at achieving a combination of good pricing on its products and managing its costs of inventory.

EXHIBIT 5.16

Gross Profit Margin

$$\text{Gross Profit Margin} = \frac{\text{Net Sales} - \text{Cost of Goods Sold}}{\text{Net Sales}}$$

Exhibit 5.17 shows the gross profit ratios of MEC based on fictitious data for the years 2015, 2016, and 2017.

EXHIBIT 5.17

MEC's Gross Profit Ratio

	2017	2016	2015
Units sold	214,000	160,000	100,000
Gross profit from sales	$84,300	$69,440	$46,400
Net sales	$314,700	$248,000	$160,000
Gross profit ratio	26.8%	28.0%	29.0%

This ratio represents the gross profit in each dollar of sales. For example, Exhibit 5.17 shows that MEC's gross profit ratio in 2015 was 29.0%. This means that each $1 of sales yielded 29¢ in gross profit to cover all other expenses. Exhibit 5.17 shows that MEC's gross profit ratio decreased from 2015 to 2017, reflecting an unfavourable trend. How is this possible given that net sales and gross profit in dollars are both increasing? If net sales are increasing but at a slower rate than the increase in cost of goods sold, gross profit on sales will grow but at a decreasing rate.[13] Success for companies such as MEC depends on a gross profit that adequately covers operating expenses.

---

13   A more detailed analysis of the information in Exhibit 5.17 shows that net sales are increasing but at a slower rate than the increases in cost of goods sold. This has caused gross profit to shrink as a percentage of sales (an unfavourable trend). This conclusion is supported by the following:

	2017	% Change	2016	% Change	2015
Units sold	214,000	33.8	160,000	60.0	100,000
Net sales	$314,700	26.9	$248,000	55.0	$160,000
COGS	230,400	29.0	178,560	57.2	113,600
Gross profit from sales	$ 84,300	21.4	$ 69,440	49.7	$ 46,400
Gross profit ratio	26.8%	−4.3	28.0%	−3.4	29.0%

Exhibit 5.18 highlights a snapshot of gross margins of several Canadian and US public companies. Notice the differences in gross margins achieved by the different companies. **Loblaw Companies Ltd.** is largely a grocery chain; its margins are lower than a retail chain like **Lululemon Athletica Inc.** and **Apple Inc. Costco Wholesale Corporation** has relatively low gross margins at 13%; however, its sales for fiscal 2014 reached in excess of $112.6 billion, with profit of $2.06 billion compared to Loblaw Companies Limited with sales of over 32 billion and profit of $630 million for the year ended December 28, 2013. In order to get a snapshot of overall company performance, you would also need to look at net profit margins, which is calculated by dividing profit by net revenue to assess overall profitability, as gross margin ignores all operating expenses.

EXHIBIT 5.18

Gross Margin Snapshot by Company

	Year End	GM%	Prior Year	GM%	Change
Lululemon Athletica Inc.	2-Feb-14	53%	3-Feb-14	56%	−3%
Canadian Tire Corporation Limited	28-Dec-13	32%	29-Dec-12	31%	1%
Loblaw Companies Limited	28-Dec-13	24%	29-Dec-12	23%	0%
Costco Wholesale Corporation	31-Aug-14	13%	1-Sep-13	13%	0%
Apple Inc.	28-Sep-13	38%	29-Sep-12	44%	−6%
Amazon.com Inc.	31-Dec-13	27%	31-Dec-12	25%	2%
Rogers Communications Inc.	31-Dec-13	71%	31-Dec-12	71%	0%
Telus Corporation	31-Dec-13	56%	31-Dec-12	56%	1%

Source: Company annual reports.

MARKUP ON INVENTORY COST

A **markup percentage** is the average increase in selling price of a product over the cost. If your product cost is $10 and your retail-selling price is $15, your markup is $5, or 5/10 = 50%. A company that has a set markup percentage can determine selling price for a specific item through the formula presented below in Exhibit 5.19.

$$\text{Selling Price} = \text{Cost} \times (1 + \text{Markup \%}) = 10 \times (1 + 0.50) = \$15$$

In some industries the selling price is set by the manufacturer to achieve standardized pricing. It can be helpful for businesses to calculate their markup percentage to determine the profitability of the different products they sell. For example, consider you work for **Best Buy Canada** as a Sales Director for the Apple product line. You have been asked to determine how much each iPad mini sale contributes to gross profit. The selling price set by Apple is $319. Assume **Apple Inc.** charges **Best Buy** $269 for each iPad mini it purchases. What is the markup percentage on the product?

$$\text{Markup Percentage} = \frac{\text{Selling Price} - \text{Cost}}{\text{Cost}} = \frac{319 - 259}{259} = 18.6\%$$

Target gross margin is a fixed percentage markup that is concerned with gross margin achieved on a specific product based on the final selling price. If you know that your cost is $10 and you know you must achieve a gross margin of 50%, the required selling price can be calculated using the following formula:

$$\text{Selling Price} = \frac{\text{Cost}}{(1 - \text{Target Margin percentage})} = \frac{10}{(1 - 0.50)} = \$20$$

Consider an example where **Lululemon Athletica** Inc. acquires a new line of men's athletic running jackets and wants to ensure the pricing that is set will contribute equivalently to the bottom line as the company's other product mix. Lululemon has established a target product gross margin percentage of 55%. The manufacturing cost of the jackets is determined to be $45. At what price should the company sell the product? Selling price is $100 calculated as $45 ÷ (1 – 0.55).

When setting pricing, it is also important to pay attention to customer demand, competitor pricing, and potential substitute products. Many marketers perform detailed market research to ensure the pricing they set finds the optimum balance between company profitability and ability to attract customers to a given product.

 **CHECKPOINT**

12. Surf's Up Merchandising shows gross profit ratios of 39%, 39.5%, and 41% for 2016, 2017, and 2018 respectively. Assuming that all other factors have remained constant, does this reflect a favourable (good) or unfavourable (bad) trend?

Do Quick Study questions: QS 5-15, QS 5-16, QS 5-17, QS 5-18, QS 5-19

CRITICAL THINKING CHALLENGE

Refer to the Critical Thinking Challenge questions at the beginning of the chapter. Compare your answers to those suggested on Connect.

IFRS AND ASPE—THE DIFFERENCES

Difference	International Financial Reporting Standards (IFRS)	Accounting Standards for Private Enterprises (ASPE)
Expense classification	• Must be classified by nature or by function	• Can be classified in way most useful for the company

A Look Ahead

Chapter 6 extends our analysis of merchandising activities and focuses on the valuation of inventory. Topics include the items in inventory, costs assigned, costing methods used, and inventory estimation techniques.

For further study on some topics of relevance to this chapter, please see the following Extend Your Knowledge Supplements:

EYK 5-1 PST/GST Comprehensive Exercises

EYK 5-2 Comprehensive Merchandising Problems—Perpetual

Summary

LO1 Describe merchandising, and identify and explain the important income statement and balance sheet components for a merchandising company. Operations of merchandising companies involve buying products and reselling them. A merchandiser's costs on an income statement include an amount for cost of goods sold. Gross profit, or gross margin, equals net sales minus cost of goods sold. The current assets section of the balance sheet includes merchandise inventory, which refers to the products a merchandiser sells and has on hand at the balance sheet date.

LO2 Describe both perpetual and periodic inventory systems. A perpetual inventory system continuously tracks the cost of goods on hand and the cost of goods sold. A periodic system accumulates the cost of goods *purchased* during the period and does not compute the amount of inventory on hand or the cost of goods sold until the end of a period.

LO3 Analyze and record transactions for merchandise purchases and sales using a perpetual system. For a perpetual inventory system, purchases net of volume purchase discounts are added (debited) to the Merchandise Inventory account. Purchase discounts and purchase returns and allowances are subtracted from (credited to) Merchandise Inventory, and transportation-in costs are added (debited) to Merchandise Inventory. A merchandiser records sales at list price less any volume purchase discounts. The cost of items sold is transferred from Merchandise Inventory to Cost of Goods Sold. Refunds or credits given to customers for unsatisfactory merchandise are recorded (debited) in Sales Returns and Allowances, a contra account to Sales. If merchandise is returned and restored to inventory, the cost of this merchandise is removed from Cost of Goods Sold and transferred back to Merchandise Inventory.

When cash discounts from the sales price are offered and customers pay within the discount period, the seller records (debits) discounts in Sales Discounts, a contra account to Sales. Debit and credit memos are documents sent between buyers and sellers to communicate that the sender is either debiting or crediting an account of the recipient.

LO4 Prepare adjustments for a merchandising company. With a perpetual inventory system, it is often necessary to make an adjustment for inventory shrinkage. This is calculated by comparing a physical count of inventory with the Merchandise Inventory account balance. Shrinkage is normally charged to Cost of Goods Sold.

LO5 Define, prepare, and analyze merchandising income statements. Multiple-step income statements show items by both function and nature. Classified multiple-step income statements are usually limited to internal use and show the calculation of net sales, and report expenses by function—such as selling and general and administrative—supported by a list of expenses by nature. The format of income statements published for external parties is flexible and includes the multiple-step or single-step format. The single-step format shows expenses by function with supporting note disclosure about the nature of the expenses.

LO6 Calculate gross margin and markup on inventory cost. The gross profit ratio is calculated as gross profit divided by net sales. It is an indicator of a company's profitability before deducting operating expenses. A gross profit ratio must be large enough to cover operating expenses and give an adequate profit. Markup on inventory cost is used by retailers to determine how much to set the selling price of inventory items when a specific gross margin percentage is targeted.

Guidance Answer to DECISION MAKER

Accounts Payable Manager

Your decision is whether to comply with prior policy or create a new policy not to abuse discounts offered by suppliers. Your first step should be to meet with your superior to find out if the automatic late payment policy is the actual policy and, if so, its rationale. It is possible that the prior employee was reprimanded because of this behaviour. If it is the policy to pay late, then you must apply your own sense of right and wrong.

One point of view is that the late payment policy is unethical. A deliberate plan to make late payments means that the company lies when it pretends to make purchases within the credit terms. There is the potential that your company could lose its ability to get future credit.

Another view is that the late payment policy is acceptable. There may exist markets in which attempts to take discounts through late payments are accepted as a continued phase of price negotiation. Also, your company's suppliers can respond by billing your company for the discounts not accepted because of late payments. This is a dubious viewpoint, especially given the old employee's proposal to cover up late payments as computer or mail problems, and given that some suppliers have previously complained.

Guidance Answers to CHECKPOINT

1. Cost of goods sold is the total cost of merchandise sold to customers during a period. In a perpetual inventory system the cost of goods sold amount is determined from the cost of inventory each time a sale is made. In a periodic system total cost of goods sold is calculated (Beginning Inventory + Purchases − Ending Inventory = COGS).

2. Gross profit is the difference between net sales and cost of goods sold.

3. Widespread use of computing and related technology has dramatically increased use of the perpetual inventory system in practice.

4. The invoice indicates that the shipping terms are FOB destination, which means that Trex maintains ownership until the merchandise inventory reaches MEC. Trex must therefore bear the freight costs and is responsible for insuring the merchandise inventory during transport.

5. Under credit terms of 2/10, n/60, the credit period is 60 days and the discount period is 10 days.

6. *b*

7. Recording sales discounts and sales returns and allowances separately from sales gives useful information to managers for internal monitoring and decision making.

8. When a customer returns merchandise and the seller restores the merchandise to inventory, two entries are necessary. One entry records the decrease in revenue and credits the customer's account. The second entry debits inventory and reduces cost of goods sold.

9. There will be a credit memo showing the *credit* to the seller's account receivable.

10. Merchandise Inventory balance may need adjusting to reflect shrinkage.

11. Classified, multiple-step income statement. Single-step income statement.

12. All other factors remaining constant, this reflects a favourable trend because Surf's Up is showing an increase in gross profit per $1 of net sales over time (from 39¢ of gross profit per $1 of net sales in 2016 to 41¢ of gross profit per $1 of net sales in 2018). This indicates that Surf's Up is generating more gross profit to cover operating expenses, which appears to be favourable.

DEMONSTRATION PROBLEM

Use the following adjusted trial balance and additional information to complete the requirements:

Paddle Boards Inc. Adjusted Trial Balance December 31, 2017		
Cash	$ 19,300	
Merchandise inventory	50,000	
Store supplies	1,000	
Equipment	44,600	
Accumulated depreciation, equipment		$ 16,500
Accounts payable		8,000
Salaries payable		1,000
Dee Rizzo, capital		69,000
Dee Rizzo, withdrawals	8,000	
Interest income		300
Sales		325,000
Sales discounts	6,000	
Sales returns and allowances	5,000	
Cost of goods sold	148,000	
Depreciation expense, store equipment	4,000	
Depreciation expense, office equipment	1,500	
Sales salaries expense	28,000	
Office salaries expense	32,000	
Insurance expense	12,000	
Rent expense (70% is store, 30% is office)	24,000	
Store supplies expense	6,000	
Advertising expense	30,400	
Totals	$419,800	$419,800

Paddle Boards Inc. showed the following additional information regarding merchandising activities for 2017:

Invoice cost of merchandise purchases	$140,000
Purchase discounts	3,500
Purchase returns and allowances	2,600
Transportation-in	4,000

Required

1. Use the additional information to calculate the total cost of merchandise purchases.
2. Prepare a 2017 classified, multiple-step income statement for internal use similar to Exhibit 5.13.
3. Present a single-step income statement for 2017 similar to the one in Exhibit 5.15.

Analysis Component:

Calculate the gross profit ratio for Paddle Boards Inc. and compare to the gross profit margin presented for Canadian Tire Corp in Exhibit 5.18. Round calculations to two decimal places. Can you compare the gross profit ratios for these two companies? Explain.

Planning the Solution

- Calculate the total cost of merchandise purchases.
- Calculate net sales. Subtract cost of goods sold from net sales to get gross profit. Then, classify the operating expenses as selling expenses and general and administrative expenses.

- To prepare the single-step income statement, begin with the net sales and interest income. Then, subtract the cost of goods sold and operating expenses.

- The first closing entry debits all temporary accounts with credit balances and opens the Income Summary account. The second closing entry credits all temporary accounts with debit balances. The third entry closes the Income Summary account to the owner's capital account, and the fourth closing entry closes the withdrawals account to the capital account.

- Prepare an answer to the analysis component.

Solution

1.

Invoice cost of merchandise purchases....................	$140,000
Less: Purchase discounts	3,500
Purchase returns and allowances	2,600
Add: Transportation-in	4,000
Total cost of merchandise purchases	$137,900

2. Classified, multiple-step income statement

Paddle Boards Inc.
Income Statement
For Year Ended December 31, 2017

Sales...			$325,000
Less: Sales discounts..		$ 6,000	
Sales returns and allowances........................		5,000	11,000
Net sales..			$314,000
Cost of goods sold..			148,000
Gross profit from sales			$166,000
Operating expenses:			
Selling expenses:			
Advertising expense	$30,400		
Sales salaries expense......................................	28,000		
Rent expense, selling space	16,800		
Store supplies expense	6,000		
Depreciation expense, store equipment..............	4,000		
Total selling expenses		$85,200	
General and administrative expenses:			
Office salaries expense	$32,000		
Insurance expense	12,000		
Rent expense, office space...............................	7,200		
Depreciation expense, office equipment	1,500		
Total general and administrative expenses..........		52,700	
Total operating expenses			137,900
Income from operations			$ 28,100
Other revenues and expenses:			
Interest income			300
Profit...			$ 28,400

3. Single-step income statement

Paddle Boards Inc.		
Income Statement		
For Year Ended December 31, 2017		
Revenues:		
Net sales		$314,000
Interest income		300
Total revenues		$314,300
Expenses:		
Cost of goods sold	$148,000	
Selling expenses	85,200	
General and administrative expense	52,700	
Total expenses		285,900
Profit		$ 28,400

Analysis Component:

The gross profit ratio for Paddle Boards Inc. is 52.87% ($166,000/$314,000 × 100%) and 32% for **Canadian Tire Corporation** Limited for the year ended December 28, 2013, as shown in Exhibit 5.18. You can expect deviations in the company's gross margins because Canadian Tire has a more diversified product base and Paddle Boards Inc. sells one main niche product that is currently a fitness and recreation trend—paddle boards.

APPENDIX 5A

Periodic and Perpetual Inventory Systems Compared

Accounting Comparisons

LO7 Record and compare merchandising transactions using both periodic and perpetual inventory systems.

Recall that under a perpetual system, the Merchandise Inventory account is updated after each purchase and each sale. The Cost of Goods Sold account is also updated after each sale so that during the period the account balance reflects the period's total cost of goods sold to date. At the end of the period, a physical count of the merchandise inventory is performed to adjust Merchandise Inventory and Cost of Goods Sold.

Under a periodic inventory system, the Merchandise Inventory account is updated only once each accounting period. This update occurs at the *end* of the period based on a physical count of the merchandise inventory. During the next period, the Merchandise Inventory balance remains unchanged. It reflects the beginning inventory balance until it is updated again at the end of the period. In a periodic inventory system, cost of goods sold is *not* recorded as each sale occurs. Instead, the total cost of goods sold during the period is calculated at the end of the period.

Recording Merchandise Transactions

Under a perpetual system, each purchase, purchase return and allowance, purchase discount, and transportation-in transaction is recorded in the Merchandise Inventory account. Under a periodic system, a separate temporary account is set up for each of these items. At the end of a period, each of these temporary accounts is closed and the Merchandise Inventory account is updated. To illustrate the differences, we use parallel columns to show journal entries for the most common transactions using both periodic and perpetual inventory systems (we drop explanations for simplicity).

PURCHASES

MEC purchases merchandise for $1,200 on credit with terms of 2/10, n/30, and records this purchase as:

Periodic			Perpetual		
Purchases...	1,200		Merchandise Inventory......................	1,200	
Accounts Payable		1,200	Accounts Payable		1,200

The periodic system debits all merchandise purchases to an expense account called *Purchases*.

PURCHASE RETURNS AND ALLOWANCES

MEC returns merchandise because of defects. If the recorded cost[14] of the defective merchandise is $300, MEC records the return with this entry:

Periodic		
Accounts Payable	300	
Purchase Returns and		
Allowances		300

Perpetual		
Accounts Payable	300	
Merchandise Inventory................		300

This entry is the same if MEC is granted a price reduction (allowance) instead of returning the merchandise. In the periodic system, the entry credits a contra expense account called **Purchase Returns and Allowances** that accumulates the cost of all returns and allowances transactions during a period. Because Purchase Returns and Allowances is a contra expense account related to the Purchases account, it is subtracted from Purchases when determining net purchases as shown in Exhibit 5A.1.

EXHIBIT 5A.1

Calculation of Net Purchases and Cost of Goods Purchased Under a Periodic Inventory System

Purchases..		$235,800
Less: Purchase discounts...	$4,200	
Purchase returns and allowances..	1,500	5,700
Net purchases..		$230,100
Add: Transportation-in		2,300
Cost of goods purchased		$232,400

PURCHASE DISCOUNT

When MEC pays the supplier for the previous purchase within the discount period, the required payment is $882 (= $1,200 − $300 = $900 × 98% = $882) and is recorded as:

Periodic		
Accounts Payable	900	
Purchase Discounts		18
Cash..		882

Perpetual		
Accounts Payable	900	
Merchandise Inventory................		18
Cash..		882

The periodic system credits a contra expense account called *Purchase Discounts* that accumulates discounts taken on purchase transactions during the period. Purchase Discounts, like Purchase Returns and Allowances, is subtracted from the Purchases account balance as shown in Exhibit 5A.1. If payment is delayed until after the discount period expires, the entry under both the periodic and perpetual methods is to debit Accounts Payable and credit Cash for $900 each.

TRANSPORTATION-IN

MEC paid a $75 freight charge to haul merchandise to its store. In the periodic system, this cost is charged to an expense account known as *Transportation-In*. Transportation-in is included as part of the $232,400 total cost of merchandise purchased as shown in Exhibit 5A.1.

---

14 Recorded cost is the cost recorded in the account after any discounts.

Periodic		
Transportation-In..............................	75	
Cash..		75

Perpetual		
Merchandise Inventory.....................	75	
Cash..		75

SALES

MEC sold $2,400 of merchandise on credit and MEC's cost of this merchandise is $1,600:

Under the periodic system, the cost of goods sold is *not* recorded at the time of sale. We later show how the periodic system calculates total cost of goods sold at the end of a period.

Periodic		
Accounts Receivable	2,400	
Sales...		2,400

Perpetual		
Accounts Receivable	2,400	
Sales...		2,400
Cost of Goods Sold.........................	1,600	
Merchandise Inventory................		1,600

SALES RETURNS

A customer returns part of the merchandise from the previous transaction, where returned items sell for $800 and cost $600. MEC restores the merchandise to inventory and records the return as:

Periodic		
Sales Returns and Allowances..........	800	
Accounts Receivable		800

Perpetual		
Sales Returns and Allowances..........	800	
Accounts Receivable		800
Merchandise Inventory.....................	600	
Cost of Goods Sold.....................		600

The periodic system records only the revenue reduction.

CHECKPOINT

13. Identify those accounts included in a periodic system that are not included in a perpetual system.

14. The perpetual system has a Cost of Goods Sold account. Explain why the periodic system does not have a Cost of Goods Sold account.

Do Quick Study questions: *QS 5-20, *QS 5-21

Adjusting Entries

The adjusting entries recorded under a periodic and a perpetual inventory system are identical except for the treatment of merchandise inventory. Under a perpetual inventory system, recall that the adjusting entry shown below was recorded to reflect shrinkage of $250 (the difference between the $21,250 unadjusted balance in Merchandise Inventory and the $21,000 physical count). Under a periodic inventory system, there is no corresponding adjustment to update the $19,000 unadjusted balance in Merchandise Inventory. Instead, we use closing entries to update the Merchandise Inventory account. We show the closing entry approach to update Merchandise Inventory in the next section.

Periodic
No entry

Perpetual		
Cost of Goods Sold.........................	250	
Merchandise Inventory................		250

MERCHANDISING INVENTORY JOURNAL ENTRIES SUMMARY—PERIODIC			
(Key differences to perpetual inventory are indicated in purple)			
PURCHASES		SALES	
Transaction	Journal Entry	Transaction	Journal Entry

Purchase inventory on credit	Purchases xxx
	   Accounts Payable xxx
		Sell inventory on credit[1]	**Revenue on sale of goods:**
			Accounts Receivable.................. xxx
			   Sales xxx
			No adjustment to inventory

Return unacceptable merchandise to supplier	Accounts Payable............... xx
	   Purchase Returns and
	   Allowances xx
		Merchandise returned by customer	**Adjustment to customer's account for return of goods:**
			Sales Returns and Allowances xxx
			   Accounts Receivable xxx
			No adjustment to inventory

Purchase allowances provided by supplier for defective merchandise[2]	If supplier provides a discount on the defective goods and the goods are kept for resale:
	Accounts Payable............... xx
	   Purchase Returns and
	   Allowances xx
		Sales allowances provided to customer[3]	**If customer keeps defective product and an allowance is provided:**
			Sales Returns and Allowances xx
			   Accounts Receivables xx

Pay freight/shipping charges (FOB Shipping Point)	Transportation In................ xx
	   Cash............................. xx
		Pay shipping charges (FOB Destination)	Delivery expense........................ xxx
			   Cash...................................... xxx

Pay supplier within discount period	Accounts Payable............... xx
	   Purchase Discounts* xxx
	   Cash** xxx
	*discount = % discount*AP balance
	**cash paid = AP balance − discount
		Receive balance from customer within discount period	Cash## xxx
			Sales Discounts#....................... xx
			   Accounts Receivable xxx
			#discount = % discount*AR balance
			##cash received = AR balance − discount

Pay supplier after discount period	Accounts Payable............... xxx
	   Cash............................. xxx
		Receive balance from customer after discount period	Cash xxx
			   Accounts Receivable xxx

[1]Note: Under periodic inventory systems, the Inventory account is not adjusted for the sales of inventory; instead, an adjusting entry is recorded at the end of the period based on a physical inventory count of the goods on hand.

[2]Note: The same journal entry is booked as a return of goods if vendor provides a discount on the goods, except adjustment to A/P is for a lesser amount.

[3] Note: The same journal entry as a return of goods is booked if customer is provided a discount on the goods, except adjustment to A/P is for a lesser amount.

An Income Statement for a Merchandising Company—Periodic Inventory

Exhibit 5A.2 presents an income statement for a merchandising company that uses the periodic inventory system. Recall that cost of goods sold is calculated as:

Beginning merchandise inventory	$ 19,000
Plus: Net cost of purchases......................................	232,400
Less: Ending merchandise inventory	21,000
Equals: Cost of goods sold.......................................	$230,400

The adjustments in the financial statements presented below reflect the following:

a. Expiration of $600 of prepaid insurance.
b. Use of $1,200 of store supplies.
c. Use of $1,800 of office supplies.
d. Depreciation of the store equipment for $3,000.
e. Depreciation of the office equipment for $700.
f. Accrual of $300 of unpaid office salaries and $500 of unpaid store salaries.

Once the adjusted amounts are extended into the financial statement columns, the accountant uses the information to develop the company's financial statements.

The classified, multiple-step income statement under a periodic inventory system is shown in Exhibit 5A.2.

EXHIBIT 5A.2

Classified, Multiple-Step Income Statement—Periodic

MEC
Income Statement
For Year Ended December 31, 2017

Sales			$321,000
Less: Sales discounts		$ 4,300	
Sales returns and allowances		2,000	6,300
Net sales			$314,700
Cost of goods sold			
Merchandise inventory, Dec. 31, 2016		$ 19,000	
Purchases	$235,800		
Less: Purchase returns and allowances	$1,500		
Purchase discounts	4,200	5,700	
Net purchases		$230,100	
Add: Transportation-in		2,300	
Cost of goods purchased		232,400	
Goods available for sale		$251,400	
Less: Merchandise inventory, Dec. 31, 2017		21,000	
Cost of goods sold			230,400
Gross profit from sales			$ 84,300
Operating expenses:			
Selling expenses:			
Sales salaries expense	$ 18,500		
Advertising expense	11,300		
Rent expense, selling space	8,100		
Depreciation expense, store equipment	3,000		
Store supplies expense	1,200		
Total selling expenses		$ 42,100	
General and administrative expenses			
Office salaries expense	$ 25,300		
Office supplies expense	1,800		
Rent expense, office space	900		
Depreciation expense, office equipment	700		
Insurance expense	600		
Total general and administrative expense		29,300	
Total operating expenses			71,400
Income from operations			$ 12,900
Other revenues and expenses:			
Rent revenue		$ 2,800	
Interest expense		360	2,440
Profit			$ 15,340

Credited to Income Summary in the first closing entry:

Merchandise Inventory (ending balance)	$ 21,000
Purchase Discounts...	4,200
Purchase Returns and Allowances	1,500

Debited to Income Summary in the second closing entry:

Merchandise Inventory (beginning balance)...........	(19,000)
Purchases	(235,800)
Transportation-in	(2,300)
Net effect on Income Summary	$(230,400)

This $230,400 effect on Income Summary is the cost of goods sold amount. This figure is confirmed as follows:

Beginning inventory		$ 19,000
Purchases.................................	$235,800	
Less: Purchase discounts............	4,200	
Less: Purchase returns and allowances.................................	1,500	
Add: Transportation-in	2,300	
Net cost of goods purchased.......		232,400
Cost of goods available for sale...		$251,400
Less: Ending inventory................		21,000
Cost of goods sold		$230,400

The periodic system transfers cost of goods sold to the Income Summary account but does not use a Cost of Goods Sold account. Exhibit 5A.3 shows the relation between inventory, purchases, and cost of goods sold across periods.

The periodic system does not measure shrinkage. Instead, it calculates cost of goods available for sale, subtracts the cost of ending inventory, and defines the difference as cost of goods sold, which includes shrinkage.

EXHIBIT 5A.3

Merchandising Cost Flows Across Periods

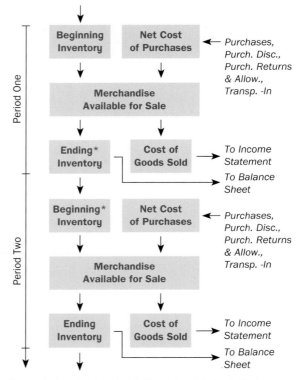

*One period's ending inventory is the next period's beginning inventory.

CHECKPOINT

15. Why does the Merchandise Inventory account on the periodic unadjusted trial balance differ from the Merchandise Inventory balance on the perpetual unadjusted trial balance?

16. What account is used in a perpetual inventory system but not in a periodic system?

17. How is cost of goods sold calculated under a periodic inventory accounting system?

Do Quick Study questions: *QS 5-22, *QS 5-23

Sales Tax

LO8 Explain and record Provincial Sales Tax (PST), Goods and Services Tax (GST), and Harmonized Sales Tax.

This section looks at the additional issue of recording sales tax. Most provinces and the federal government require retailers to collect sales tax from customers and to send these taxes periodically to the appropriate agency.

Provincial Sales Tax

Provincial Sales Tax (PST) is a tax applied on sales to the final consumers of products and/or services. In Canada, provinces with PST charge PST on the acquisition of inventory items purchased for resale. Under this circumstance, the *non-recoverable PST* cost becomes *included* in the cost of inventory.

All provinces except Alberta (and the territories) require retailers to collect PST from their customers and to remit this tax periodically to the appropriate provincial authority. It should be noted that not all sales are subject to PST.[15] PST collected is credited to a separate account, as shown in the following example where JC Sales sells merchandise on January 5 costing $600 for $900 on account (assuming PST of 7%).

As well as being collected, PST may be *paid* on items purchased for use or on non-current assets acquired. In these cases, the PST paid is part of the expense or asset cost associated with the purchase.

Goods and Services Tax

The **Goods and Services Tax (GST)** is a 5%[16] tax on almost all goods and services provided in Canada. GST applies to most property and services in Alberta, British Columbia, Manitoba, Northwest Territories, Nunavut, Quebec, Saskatchewan, and Yukon. GST is a federal tax on the end consumer. However, unlike the PST, businesses pay GST up front when they purchase goods but generally receive a full credit or refund for all GST paid. GST can be *recovered* from collections of GST from the end customer; therefore, it is *not included* in the cost of inventory.

Businesses with taxable supplies production at a cost of $30,000 or more are required to register their business with CRA and submit a GST return. Ultimately, only the final consumer pays this tax. This is because businesses collect GST on sales, but since they receive full credit for GST paid on purchases; they remit only the difference to the appropriate federal authority. Customers are not charged any GST on zero-rated goods and services and GST-exempt products. Zero-rated goods and services sold to customers enable the supplier to claim input tax credits to recover the GST paid on products purchased and used within the business, even though they did not charge customers GST. GST-exempt products sold to customers do not allow suppliers to claim input credits on goods or services acquired to supply the exempt product. Refer to Exhibit 5B.1 for a combined summary of Zero-Rated and Exempt products for GST and HST.

---

15 A detailed discussion of the liabilities created by PST and GST is found in Chapter 10.

16 Effective since January 1, 2008.

Summary of Zero-Rated and Exempt Products for GST/HST

GST/HST Zero-Rated Goods and Services	GST/HST Exempt Products
Basic groceries (milk, bread, vegetables)	Music lessons
Prescription drugs and dispensing fees	Educational services that lead to certificate or diploma
Fishery products	Childcare services
Agricultural products (grain, wool)	Most services provided by financial institutions
Exports to foreign countries	Medical devices
Issuing insurance policies	
For a full list of zero-rated goods and services refer to: www.cra-arc.gc.ca/E/pub/gm/4-3/4-3-e.html	For a full list of GST-exempt products refer to: www.cra-arc.gc.ca/tx/bsnss/tpcs/gst-tps/gnrl/txbl/xmptgds-eng.html

Harmonized Sales Tax

The **Harmonized Sales Tax (HST)** is a combined GST and PST rate applied to taxable supplies. At the time of writing, New Brunswick, Nova Scotia, Newfoundland and Labrador, Prince Edward Island, and Ontario apply HST in lieu of PST and GST. HST can be *recovered* from collections of HST from the end customer, therefore it is *not included* in the cost of inventory. In most cases, HST applies to the same property and services as GST.

Jan.	3	Merchandise Inventory...............................	600	
		GST Receivable[17,18].......................................	30	
		Accounts Payable		630
		To record the purchase of merchandise on account; $600 × 5% = $30 GST.		
Jan.	5	Accounts Receivable	1,117	
		Sales..		900
		PST Payable		72
		GST Payable.......................................		45
		To record the sale of merchandise on account; $900 × 8% = $72 PST; $900 × 5% = $45 GST; $900 + $72 + $45 = $1,017.		
	5	Cost of Goods Sold.......................................	600	
		Merchandise Inventory		600
		To record the cost of sales.		

PST and GST are accounted for under both perpetual and periodic inventory systems. To illustrate, assume JC Sales, a merchandiser located in Manitoba, purchases $600 of merchandise inventory on January 3 with terms n/10. These items are then sold for $900 on January 5 with terms of n/15. JC Sales records these transactions as follows:[17]

PST and GST are calculated as a percentage of the selling price. It should also be noted that while GST is a 5% federal tax, and thus is uniform in all of the provinces, PST is a provincial tax and differs in percentage from province to province. The detailed rates for each province are provided in Exhibit 5B.2.

To continue the example, assume the January 3 purchase is paid on January 13 and the sale of January 5 is collected on January 20. Assuming no other purchases and sales during the month, the

---

17   Assume that all amounts here and in related end-of-chapter materials are before PST and GST.

18   Some businesses will debit GST Payable instead of GST Receivable because they use only one account for GST. In such a case, when the account has a credit balance, cash must be paid to the Receiver General for Canada. When the account has a debit balance, a refund is applied for.

EXHIBIT 5B.2

Sales Tax Rates, effective January 1, 2016

	PST Rate	GST Rate	HST Rate*
Regions with GST Only			
Alberta	-0-	5%	—
Northwest Territories	-0-	5%	—
Nunavut	-0-	5%	—
Yukon	-0-	5%	—
Regions with GST and PST			
British Columbia	7%	5%	—
Manitoba	8%	5%	—
Quebec	9.975%	5%	—
Saskatchewan	5%	5%	—
Regions with HST			
New Brunswick	—	—	13%
Newfoundland and Labrador**	—	—	15%
Nova Scotia	—	—	15%
Ontario..	—	—	13%
Prince Edward Island	—	—	14%

*A Harmonized Sales Tax (HST) is applied in place of PST and GST. HST is the combination of the PST with the GST for a total sales tax. For example, for both New Brunswick and Ontario the PST rate of 8% is combined with the GST of 5%, resulting in an overall HST of 13%.
**The Newfoundland 2015 budget announced that the rate increases from 13% to 15%, effective January 1, 2016.

January sales taxes are paid to the appropriate government bodies on February 28. The entries to record these transactions are:

Jan.	13	Accounts Payable		630	
		Cash...			630
		To record payment of January 3 purchase.			
	20	Cash...		1,008	
		Accounts Receivable			1,008
		To record collection of January 5 sale.			
Feb.	28	PST Payable..		63	
		Cash...			63
		To record payment of PST to provincial government authority.			
	28	GST Payable		45	
		Cash...			15
		GST Receivable...................................			30
		To record payment of GST to Receiver General for Canada.			

Examples demonstrating PST/GST for each region in Canada can be found online in Extend Your Knowledge 5-1, along with reinforcement exercises.

CHECKPOINT

18. What is the difference between PST, GST, and HST?

Do Quick Study questions: *QS 5-24, *QS 5-25, *QS 5-26, *QS 5-27

Summary of Appendix 5A and Appendix 5B

**LO7 Record and compare merchandising trans-
actions using both periodic and perpetual
inventory systems.** Transactions involving
the sale and purchase of merchandise are recorded and analyzed under both inventory
systems. Adjusting and closing entries for both
inventory systems are also illustrated and
explained.

**LO8 Explain and record Provincial Sales Tax
(PST), Goods and Services Tax (GST), and
Harmonized Sales Tax.** PST is a tax applied on
sales to final consumers that varies in percent between provinces. GST is a 5% tax collected on
most sales but full credit is received for GST paid
by a GST registrant (business). Harmonized Sales
Tax (HST) is a combined GST and PST rate applied to taxable supplies.

Guidance Answers to CHECKPOINT

13. The beginning Merchandise Inventory balance is included on the periodic unadjusted
trial balance and not the perpetual along
with Purchases, Purchase Discounts,
Purchase Returns and Allowances, and
Transportation-In.

14. Cost of Goods Sold is calculated under the
periodic system using the account balances
of Merchandise Inventory (beginning inventory balance), Purchases, Purchase Discounts, Purchase Returns and Allowances,
Transportation-In, and subtracting the ending
inventory amount determined through a
physical count.

15. The Merchandise Inventory account on the
periodic unadjusted trial balance represents
the balance at the beginning of the period.
The Merchandise Inventory account on the
perpetual unadjusted trial balance has been

adjusted regularly during the accounting period for all transactions affecting inventory,
such as purchases, returns, discounts,
transportation-in, and cost of sales, and
therefore represents the balance at the
end of the period.

16. Cost of Goods Sold.

17. Under a periodic inventory system, the cost
of goods sold is determined at the end of an
accounting period by adding the net cost of
goods purchased to the beginning inventory
and subtracting the ending inventory.

18. PST is Provincial Sales Tax and varies across
Canada. GST is the Goods and Services Tax
of 5% that is constant across Canada. HST
is Harmonized Sales Tax that is a combination of the Provincial Sales Tax applicable
in the jurisdictions and the 5% Goods and
Services Tax.

Glossary

Cash discount A reduction in the price of merchandise
that is granted by a seller to a purchaser in exchange
for the purchaser paying within a specified period of
time called the *discount period*.

Catalogue price See *list price*.

Classified, multiple-step income statement An income
statement format that shows intermediate totals between sales and profit and detailed computations of
net sales and cost of goods sold and is used primarily
for internal reporting.

Cost of goods sold (COGS) The cost of merchandise
sold to customers during a period; also commonly
referred to as *cost of sales*.

Cost of sales See *cost of goods sold*.

Credit memo A notification that the sender has entered a
credit in the recipient's account maintained by the sender.

Credit period The time period that can pass before a
customer's payment is due.

Credit terms The description of the amounts and timing
of payments that a buyer agrees to make in the future.

Debit memo A notification that the sender has entered
a debit in the recipient's account maintained by the
sender.

Discount period The time period in which a cash discount is available and a reduced payment can be made
by the buyer.

EOM The abbreviation for *end of month*, used to describe credit terms for some transactions.

FOB The abbreviation for *free on board/freight on
board*, the designated point at which ownership of
goods passes to the buyer; *FOB shipping point* (or factory) means that the buyer pays the shipping costs and

accepts ownership of the goods at the seller's place of business; *FOB destination* means that the seller pays the shipping costs and the ownership of the goods transfers to the buyer at the buyer's place of business.

Freight-in See *transportation-in.*

Freight-out See *transportation-out.*

Full disclosure principle The generally accepted accounting principle that requires financial statements to report all relevant information about the operations and financial position of the entity; disclosure of items not contained in the body of financial statements is often accomplished by providing notes to financial statements such as those for WestJet in Appendix III of the text.

Function of an expense A method of classifying or grouping expenses based on their purpose or what the expenses relate to, such as cost of goods sold, selling expenses, and general and administrative expenses; this method must also provide additional information to show the nature of expenses within each group.

General and administrative expenses Expenses that support the overall operations of a business and include the expenses of activities such as providing accounting services, human resource management, and financial management.

Goods and Services Tax (GST) A federal tax on almost all goods and services provided in Canada.

Gross margin The difference between net sales and the cost of goods sold; also called *gross profit.*

Gross margin ratio See *gross profit ratio.*

Gross profit The difference between net sales and the cost of goods sold; also called *gross margin.*

Gross profit margin ratio Gross profit from sales (net sales minus cost of goods sold) divided by net sales; also called *gross margin ratio.*

Harmonized Sales Tax (HST) A combined GST and PST rate applied to taxable goods and services.

Inventory See *merchandise inventory.*

List price The catalogue price of an item before any trade discount is deducted.

Markup percentage The average increase in selling price of a product over the unit cost.

Merchandise Products, also called *goods,* that a company acquires for the purpose of reselling them to customers.

Merchandise inventory Products that a company owns for the purpose of selling them to customers. Also called *inventory.*

Merchandiser Earns profit by buying and selling merchandise.

Nature of an expense A method of classifying an expense based on its basic characteristics or what it is.

For example, when expenses are identified on the income statement as depreciation, rent, property tax, and salaries, the nature of the expense is being identified.

Net sales Calculated as gross sales less sales discounts and sales returns and allowances.

Notes to financial statements An integral part of financial statements that provides relevant information about the operations and financial position of the entity in addition to that contained in the financial statements; providing notes complies with the full disclosure principle; for an example, see the notes for WestJet in Appendix III of the text.

Periodic inventory system A method of accounting that records the cost of inventory purchased but does not track the quantity on hand or sold to customers; the records are updated at the end of each period to reflect the results of physical counts of the items on hand.

Perpetual inventory system A method of accounting that maintains continuous records of the cost of inventory on hand and the cost of goods sold.

Provincial Sales Tax (PST) A tax applied on sales to the final consumers of products and/or services.

Purchase discount A term used by a purchaser to describe a cash discount granted to the purchaser for paying within the discount period.

Purchase Returns and Allowances A contra expense account used when a periodic inventory system is in place in which purchase returns and/or purchase allowances are recorded.

Retailer An intermediary that buys products from manufacturers or wholesalers and sells them to consumers.

Sales discount A term used by a seller to describe a cash discount granted to customers for paying within the discount period.

Sales returns and allowances A contra revenue account in which sales returns and/or sales allowances are recorded.

Selling expenses The expenses of promoting sales by displaying and advertising the merchandise, making sales, and delivering goods to customers.

Shrinkage Inventory losses that occur as a result of theft or deterioration.

Single-step income statement An income statement format that includes cost of goods sold as an operating expense and shows only one subtotal for total expenses.

Trade discount A reduction below a list or catalogue price that may vary in amount for wholesalers, retailers, and final consumers.

Transportation-in The cost to the purchaser to transport merchandise purchased to the purchaser; transportation-in is part of Cost of Goods Sold.

Transportation-out The cost to the seller to transport merchandise sold to the customer; transportation-out is a selling expense.

Wholesaler A company that buys products from manufacturers or other wholesalers and sells them to retailers or other wholesalers.

Concept Review Questions

1. Refer to the income statement for WestJet in Appendix III. Is WestJet a merchandiser?

2. Refer to the income statement for **Danier** in Appendix III. Is a detailed calculation of the cost of goods sold presented?

3. In comparing the accounts of a merchandising company with those of a service company, what additional accounts would the merchandising company be likely to use, assuming it employs a perpetual inventory system?

4. What items appear in the financial statements of merchandising companies but not in the statements of service companies?

5. You are studying for your accounting exam with Mason and he says, "If a company has positive gross profit, then the company also has positive profit." Explain to Mason whether you agree or disagree with him and why.

6. Distinguish between volume purchase discounts (trade discounts) and early payment discounts (cash discounts). Is the amount of a trade discount on purchased merchandise recorded in the accounts?

7. The manager exclaims, "Why do we have so many purchase returns?" The accountant asks, "Why does it matter if our suppliers offer unlimited returns?" Explain why the manager is concerned.

8. What is the difference between FOB shipping point and FOB destination? Draw a diagram to clearly illustrate your explanation. Explain the concept to another student using your diagram.

9. Danier needs to be skillful in negotiating purchase contracts with suppliers. What shipping terms should Danier negotiate to minimize its shipping costs?

10. Does the sender of a debit memo record a debit or a credit in the account of the recipient? Which does the recipient record?

11. What is the difference between a sales discount and a purchase discount?

12. Briefly explain why a company's manager would want the accounting system to record a customer's return of unsatisfactory goods in the Sales Returns and Allowances account instead of the Sales account. In addition, explain whether the information would be useful for external decision makers.

13. How does a company that uses a perpetual inventory system determine the amount of inventory shrinkage?

14. What is the difference between single-step and multiple-step income statement formats?

15. George believes that a 50% markup percentage is the same as a 50% target gross margin. Do you agree or disagree with George? Explain and provide a calculation to prove your point using a cost of $20 as an example.

Quick Study

QS 5-1 Components of income for a merchandiser LO1

Referring to the format presented in Exhibit 5.2, calculate gross profit and the profit or loss for each of the following.

	A	B	C	D	E
Net sales	$14,000	$102,000	$68,000	$540,000	$398,000
Cost of goods sold	8,000	64,000	31,000	320,000	215,000
Operating expenses	9,000	31,000	22,000	261,000	106,000

QS 5-2 Contrasting periodic and perpetual systems LO2

For each description below, identify the inventory system as either periodic or perpetual.

    a. Requires a physical count of inventory to determine the amount of inventory to report on the balance sheet. _Periodic_

    b. Records the cost of goods sold each time a sales transaction occurs. _Perpetual_

    c. Provides more timely information to managers. _Perpetual_

    d. Was traditionally used by companies such as drug and department stores that sold large quantities of low-valued items. _Perpetual_

    e. Requires an adjusting entry to record inventory shrinkage. _periodic / perpetual_ _mouse ate some_

QS 5-3 Perpetual and periodic inventory systems LO2

For each situation given, calculate cost of goods sold and identify if the information provided reflects a perpetual or periodic inventory system.

    a.

Merchandise Inventory			Cost of Goods Sold		
Beginning Inventory	150	?		?	?
Purchases	340				
Ending Inventory	60				

    b.

Merchandise Inventory*			Purchases		
Beginning Inventory	150				?
				340	

    *A physical inventory count at year-end showed a balance on hand of $60.

QS 5-4 Perpetual and periodic inventory systems LO2

For each situation given, calculate cost of goods sold and identify if the information provided reflects a perpetual or periodic inventory system.

    a. Merchandise Inventory shows a balance at January 1, 2017, of $170, the Purchases account has a balance of $700 at December 31, 2017, and a physical count of merchandise inventory on the same date reveals a balance of $120 on hand.

    b. Merchandise Inventory shows a $200 balance at January 1, 2017, purchases during the period of $1,000, and a balance of $75 at December 31, 2017, after the adjustment for shrinkage.

QS 5-5 Purchase discounts—perpetual LO3

You are the accounts payable clerk at Liszt Music. The manager asks you to pay an invoice from the supplier Schumann Co. The date of purchase and the date of the invoice is October 15, 2017, for $5,000 of Taylor Swift and Beyoncé Knowles sheet music. The payment terms are 3/15, n/30.

    a. What do the purchase terms mean?

    b. Calculate the discount amount available.

    c. If today is October 28, 2017, calculate the number of days from the date of purchase to the date of payment. Record the journal entry.

    d. If today is November 1, 2017, calculate the number of days from the date of purchase to the date of payment. Record the journal entry.

QS 5-6 Merchandise purchase transactions—perpetual LO3

Journalize each of the following transactions assuming a perpetual inventory system.

May	1	Purchased $1,200 of merchandise inventory; terms 1/10, n/30.
	14	Paid for the May 1 purchase.
	15	Purchased $3,000 of merchandise inventory; terms 2/15, n/30.
	30	Paid for the May 15 purchase, less the applicable discount.

QS 5-7 Merchandise purchase: allowance—perpetual LO3

Journalize each of the following transactions assuming a perpetual inventory system.

Aug.	2	Purchased $14,000 of merchandise inventory; terms 1/5, n/15.
	4	Received a credit memo from the supplier confirming a $1,500 allowance regarding the August 2 purchase.
	17	Paid for the August 2 purchase, less the allowance.

QS 5-8 Merchandise purchase: trade discount, return—perpetual LO3

Prepare journal entries to record each of the following transactions of a merchandising company. Show any supporting calculations. Assume a perpetual inventory system.

Mar.	5	Purchased 500 units of product with a list price of $5 per unit. The purchaser was granted a trade discount of 20% and the terms of the sale were 2/10, n/60.
	7	Returned 50 defective units from the March 5 purchase and received full credit.
	15	Paid the amount due resulting from the March 5 purchase, less the return on March 7 and applicable discount.

QS 5-9 Sale of merchandise: trade discount—perpetual LO3

As a co-op student, you are working as an accounts receivable clerk at Asian Foods. The controller asks you to record a customer payment from Liu and Li Co. The sales invoice is dated October 1, 2017 for $3,000 of tea and tapioca pearls. The payment terms are 4/20, n/60.

    a. Determine the beginning and end date of the discount period.

    b. Calculate the discount amount available.

    c. If today is October 20, record the journal entry.

    d. If today is October 23, record the journal entry.

QS 5-10 Sale of merchandise transactions—perpetual LO3

Journalize each of the following transactions assuming a perpetual inventory system.

Sept.	1	Sold merchandise to JenAir for $6,000 (cost of sales $4,200); terms 2/10, n/30.
	14	Collected the amount owing regarding the September 1 sale to JenAir.
	15	Sold merchandise costing $1,500 to Dennis Leval for $1,800; terms 2/10, n/30.
	25	Collected the amount owing from the September 15 sale to Dennis Leval, less the applicable discount.

QS 5-11 Sale of merchandise: allowance—perpetual LO3

Journalize each of the following transactions assuming a perpetual inventory system.

Oct.	15	Sold merchandise to Leslie Garth for $900 (cost of sales $600); terms 1/5, n/20.
	16	Issued a $100 credit memo to Leslie Garth regarding an allowance on the October 15 sale.
	25	Collected the amount owing regarding the October 15 sale to Leslie Garth, less the allowance granted on October 16.

QS 5-12 Sale of merchandise: return—perpetual LO3

Prepare journal entries to record each of the following transactions of a merchandising company. Show any supporting calculations. Assume a perpetual inventory system.

Apr. 1 Sold merchandise for $2,000, granting the customer terms of 2/10, EOM. The cost of the merchandise was $1,400.

4 The customer in the April 1 sale returned merchandise and received credit for $500. The merchandise, which had cost $350, was returned to inventory.

11 Received payment for the amount due resulting from the April 1 sale, less the return and applicable discount, on April 4.

QS 5-13 Shrinkage LO4

Beamer Company's unadjusted ledger on July 31, the end of the fiscal year, includes the following accounts, which have normal balances (assume a perpetual inventory system):

Merchandise inventory	$ 34,800
Joy Beamer, capital	115,300
Joy Beamer, withdrawals	4,000
Sales	157,200
Sales discounts	1,700
Sales returns and allowances	3,500
Cost of goods sold	102,000
Depreciation expense	7,300
Salaries expense	29,500
Miscellaneous expenses	2,000

A physical count of the inventory discloses that the cost of the merchandise on hand is $32,900. Prepare the entry to record this information and calculate gross profit.

QS 5-14 Classified multi-step vs. single-step income statements LO5

Use the following adjusted trial balance information for JetCo's December 31, 2017, year-end to prepare (a) a classified multi-step income statement, and (b) a single-step income statement.

Account	Debit	Credit
Advertising expense	$ 6	
Assets	120	
Cost of goods sold	60	
Interest income		$ 5
Liabilities		90
Lisa Jet, capital		31
Lisa Jet, withdrawals	8	
Office salaries expense	10	
Office supplies expense	3	
Sales		100
Sales discounts	4	
Sales salaries expense	15	

QS 5-15 Profitability LO1,3,5,6

Using a format similar to Exhibit 5.11, calculate net sales, gross profit from sales, and the gross profit ratio (round to two decimal places).

	a	b	c	d
Sales	$130,000	$512,000	$35,700	$245,700
Sales discounts	4,200	16,500	400	3,500
Sales returns and allowances	17,000	5,000	5,000	700
Cost of goods sold	76,600	326,700	21,300	125,900

QS 5-16 Gross profit ratio LO6

Willaby Company had net sales of $248,000 and cost of goods sold of $114,080. Calculate and interpret the gross profit ratio, assuming the gross profit ratio for the industry is an average of 53%.

QS 5-17 Markups LO6

Your parents own a grocery store and you need to determine the selling price of fruit. It costs $0.81/kg for non-organic bananas and $1.21/kg for organic bananas. You decide to sell the non-organic produce at a markup percentage of 55% and the organic produce at a markup percentage of 75%. Determine the selling price for non-organic and organic bananas. Round your answer to two decimal places.

QS 5-18 Markups LO6

Assume it costs a manufacturer $80 to produce a pair of sunglasses. The manufacturer sells the sunglasses to a fashion designer for $100. The fashion designer puts its brand name on the sunglasses and sells them to an optical retail stores for $160. The optical retail stores then sell the sunglasses to the end customers at $320.

Required

1. What is the markup percentage between the following:
   a. Manufacturer and the fashion designer?
   b. Fashion designer and the optical retail store?
   c. Optical retail store to the end customer?   300%
2. What is the total markup from the manufacturer to the end customer?

QS 5-19 Markups LO6

You work at a clothing store. Determine the selling price of jeans with a target gross margin of 40% and tops with a markup percentage of 40%. Assume that the jeans and tops both have a cost of $30.

*QS 5-20 Merchandise purchase transactions—periodic LO7

Using the information in QS 5-6 through QS 5-8, prepare journal entries to record each of the transactions of the merchandising companies assuming a periodic inventory system.

*QS 5-21 Sale of merchandise transactions—periodic LO7

Using the information in QS 5-10 through QS 5-12, prepare journal entries to record each of the transactions of the merchandising companies assuming a periodic inventory system.

An asterisk (*) identifies assignment material based on Appendix 5A or Appendix 5B.

*QS 5-22 Cost of goods sold—periodic LO7

Using the following information, calculate cost of goods sold for the year ended December 31, 2017.

Merchandise inventory (January 1, 2017)...	$ 40,000
Kay Bondar, capital..	102,000
Kay Bondar, withdrawals	65,000
Sales...	450,000
Sales returns and allowances...	27,000
Purchases..	180,000
Purchase discounts	1,400
Transportation-in..	14,000
Merchandise inventory (December 31, 2017)...	22,000
Salaries expense..	120,000
Depreciation expense...	31,000

*QS 5-23 Profitability—periodic LO5,6,7

Calculate net sales, cost of goods sold, gross profit, and the gross profit ratio (round to two decimal places) in each of the following situations.

	a	b	c	d
Sales...	$130,000	$512,000	$35,700	$245,700
Sales discounts.....................................	4,200	16,500	400	3,500
Merchandise inventory, Jan. 1, 2017	8,000	21,000	1,500	4,300
Purchases...	120,000	350,000	29,000	131,000
Purchase returns and allowances...........	4,000	14,000	750	3,100
Merchandise inventory, Dec. 1, 2017	7,500	22,000	900	4,100

*QS 5-24 Sales tax on purchases—perpetual LO3,8

On March 1, Dolomite Sales purchased $5,000 of merchandise on account. Record the entry on March 1 including 5% GST. Assume a perpetual inventory system.

*QS 5-25 Sales tax on sales—perpetual LO3,8

On March 17, Dolomite Sales sold merchandise on credit for $5,800 (cost of sales $5,000). Assuming 7% PST and 5% GST, record the entries on March 17. Assume a perpetual inventory system.

*QS 5-26 Sales tax on purchases—periodic LO7,8

On March 1, Dolomite Sales purchased $5,000 of merchandise on account. Record the entry on March 1 including 5% GST. Assume a periodic inventory system.

*QS 5-27 Sales tax on sales—periodic LO7,8

On March 17, Dolomite Sales sold merchandise on credit for $5,800 (cost of sales $5,000). Assuming 7% PST and 5% GST, record the entry on March 17. Assume a periodic inventory system.

An asterisk (*) identifies assignment material based on Appendix 5A or Appendix 5B.

Exercises

Exercise 5-1 Calculating income statement components LO1

Referring to Exhibit 5.2, calculate the missing amounts.

	a	b	c	d	e
Sales.............................	$210,000	$165,000	$75,000	$?	$?
Cost of goods sold	?	?	42,000	303,000	206,000
Gross profit from sales	109,000	?	?	?	76,000
Operating expenses.........	92,000	93,000	?	106,000	?
Profit (loss)	?	(31,000)	(5,500)	57,000	(28,000)

Exercise 5-2 Recording journal entries for merchandise purchase transactions—perpetual LO3

Journalize each of the following transactions assuming a perpetual inventory system.

Feb.	1	Purchased $17,000 of merchandise inventory; terms 1/10, n/30.
	5	Purchased for cash $8,200 of merchandise inventory.
	6	Purchased $22,000 of merchandise inventory; terms 2/15, n/45.
	9	Purchased $1,900 of office supplies; terms n/15.
	10	Contacted a major supplier to place an order for $200,000 of merchandise in exchange for a 30% trade discount to be shipped on April 1 FOB destination.
	11	Paid for the merchandise purchased on February 1.
	24	Paid for the office supplies purchased on February 9.
Mar.	23	Paid for the February 6 purchase.

Exercise 5-3 Recording journal entries for merchandise purchase transactions—perpetual LO3

Jaleh Mehr is the owner of the retail store 151 Jeans. She purchases jeans from a number of manufacturers to bring great style and fit to her customers. Prepare journal entries for March 2017 to record the following transactions. Assume a perpetual inventory system.

Mar.	2	Purchased jeans from Paige Denim under the following terms: $4,200 invoice price, 2/15, n/60, FOB shipping point.
	3	Paid $350 for shipping charges on the purchase of March 2.
	4	Returned to Paige Denim unacceptable merchandise that had an invoice price of $400.
	17	Sent a cheque to Paige Denim for the March 2 purchase, net of the returned merchandise and applicable discount.
	18	Purchased jeans from J Brand under the following terms: $9,600 invoice price, 2/10, n/30, FOB destination.
	21	After brief negotiations, received from J Brand a $2,100 allowance on the purchase of March 18.
	28	Sent a cheque to J Brand paying for the March 18 purchase, net of the discount and the allowance.

Exercise 5-4 Recording journal entries for merchandise sales transactions—perpetual LO3

Journalize each of the following transactions assuming a perpetual inventory system. You are not required to identify the account number in your journal entries.

Jan.	5	Sold merchandise to a customer for $6,800; terms 1/10, n/30 (cost of sales $4,080).
	7	Made a cash sale of $5,100 of merchandise to a customer today (cost of sales $3,060).
	8	Sold merchandise for $12,400; terms 1/10, n/30 (cost of sales $7,440).
	15	Collected the amount owing from the credit customer of January 5.
Feb.	4	The customer of January 8 paid the balance owing.

The company's chart of accounts include the following:

101	Cash
106	Accounts Receivable
119	Merchandise inventory
201	Accounts Payable
201	Sales
414	Sales returns and allowances
415	Sales discounts
500	Cost of goods sold

Exercise 5-5 Recording journal entries for merchandise sales transactions—perpetual LO3

Journalize each of the following transactions assuming a perpetual inventory system.

Feb.	1	Sold merchandise with a cost of $1,500 for $2,100; terms 2/10, n/30, FOB destination.
	2	Paid $225 to ship the merchandise sold on February 1.
	3	The customer of February 1 returned half of the amount purchased because it was the incorrect product; it was returned to inventory.
	4	Sold merchandise to a customer for $3,800 (cost of sales $2,280); terms 2/10, n/30, FOB destination.
	11	Collected the amount owing from the customer of February 1.
	23	Sold merchandise to a customer for cash of $1,200 (cost of sales $720).
	28	The customer of February 4 paid the amount owing.

Exercise 5-6 Recording merchandise transactions: purchase and sale discounts—perpetual LO3

Chad Funk is a hair stylist who opened a business selling hair products. He imports products from around the world and sells to salons in Canada.

Oct.	1	Purchased $1,400 of hair spray from Orbit Pro; terms 3/10, n/30, FOB shipping point. The appropriate party paid the shipping cost of $200.
	5	Sold shampoo costing $420 to Barber & Co. for a price of $600 with terms of 2/10, n/30, FOB shipping point. The appropriate party paid the shipping cost of $80.
	7	Returned $500 of inventory to Orbit Pro due to an error in the Oct. 1 order.
	10	Paid Orbit Pro for the purchase on October 1.
	14	Barber & Co. returned $100 of inventory from the sale on Oct. 5. The inventory had a cost of $70.
	22	Received the payment from Barber & Co. on the October 5 sale.
	23	Purchased $2,000 of hair conditioner from Keratin Hair; terms 2/10, n/30, FOB shipping point. The appropriate party paid the shipping cost of $300.
	25	Sold hair gel to Styling Room for an invoice price of $1,000, terms 2/10, n/30, FOB destination. The hair gel had a cost of $700. The appropriate party paid the shipping cost of $150.
	26	Paid for the purchase on October 23.
	31	Received the payment from Styling Room on the October 25 sale.

Required Record the journal entries for the month of October.

Exercise 5-7 Analyzing and recording merchandise transactions—perpetual LO3

On May 11, 2017, Wilson Purchasing purchased $25,000 of merchandise from Hostel Sales; terms 3/10, n/90, FOB Hostel Sales. The cost of the goods to Hostel was $20,000. Wilson paid $1,500 to Express Shipping Service for the delivery charges on the merchandise on May 11. On May 12, Wilson returned $4,000 of goods to Hostel Sales, which restored them to inventory. The returned goods had cost Hostel $3,200. On May 20, Wilson mailed a cheque to Hostel for the amount owed on that date. Hostel received and recorded the cheque on May 21.

Required

a. Present the journal entries that Wilson Purchasing should record for these transactions. Assume that Wilson uses a perpetual inventory system.

b. Present the journal entries that Hostel Sales should record for these transactions. Assume that Hostel uses a perpetual inventory system.

Analysis Component: Assume that the buyer, Wilson Purchasing, borrowed enough cash to pay the balance on the last day of the discount period at an annual interest rate of 4% and paid it back on the last day of the credit period. Calculate how much the buyer saved by following this strategy. *Use a 365-day year and round all calculations to the nearest whole cent.*

Exercise 5-8 Merchandising terms LO1,2,3

Insert the letter for each term in the blank space beside the definition that it most closely matches:

a. Early payment discount   **e.** FOB shipping point   **h.** Volume purchase discount

b. Credit period   **f.** Gross profit   **i.** Sales discount

c. Discount period   **g.** Merchandise inventory   **j.** Trade discount

d. FOB destination

_____ **1.** An agreement that ownership of goods is transferred at the buyer's place of business.

_____ **2.** The time period in which a cash discount is available.

_____ **3.** The difference between net sales and the cost of goods sold.

_____ **4.** A reduction in a receivable or payable that is granted if it is paid within the discount period.

_____ **5.** A purchaser's description of an early payment discount received from a supplier of goods.

_____ **6.** An agreement that ownership of goods is transferred at the seller's place of business.

_____ **7.** A reduction below a list or catalogue price that is negotiated in setting the selling price of goods.

_____ **8.** A seller's description of a cash discount granted to customers in return for early payment.

_____ **9.** The time period that can pass before a customer's payment is due.

_____ **10.** The goods that a company owns and expects to sell to its customers.

Exercise 5-9 Effects of merchandising activities on the accounts—perpetual LO3,4

The following amounts summarize Transeer Company's merchandising activities during 2017. Set up T-accounts for Merchandise Inventory and Cost of Goods Sold (see Exhibit 5.13). Then record the activities directly in the accounts and calculate the account balances.

Cost of merchandise sold to customers in sales transactions.............................	$180,000
Merchandise inventory balance, Dec. 31, 2016...	35,000
Invoice cost of merchandise purchases..	186,000
Shrinkage determined on Dec. 31, 2017..	31,000
Cost of transportation-in	1,900
Cost of merchandise returned by customers and restored to inventory................	2,200
Purchase discounts received	1,600
Purchase returns and allowances received...	4,100

Analysis Component: You are the inventory manager and have reviewed these numbers. Comment on the shrinkage.

Exercise 5-10 **Calculating expenses and cost of goods sold—perpetual** LO1,3,5,6

Westlawn Company discloses the following for the year ended May 31, 2017:

Sales	$495,000
Sales discounts	5,900
Sales returns	13,000
Gross profit from sales	124,000
Loss	28,000

Required Calculate (a) net sales, (b) total operating expenses, (c) cost of goods sold, and (d) gross profit ratio (round to two decimal places).

Analysis Component: Refer to your answer in part (d). Westlawn experienced a gross profit ratio for the year ended May 31, 2016, of 23%. Is the change in the ratio favourable or unfavourable?

Exercise 5-11 **Calculating income statement components** LO1,5

Referring to Exhibit 5.15, calculate the missing amounts (round to two decimal places).

	Company A		Company B	
	2017	**2016**	**2017**	**2016**
Sales	$256,000	$180,000	$?	$45,000
Sales discounts	2,560	?	1,100	500
Sales returns and allowances	?	16,000	5,500	?
Net sales	?	163,000	?	42,000
Cost of goods sold	153,600	?	57,000	?
Gross profit from sales	51,000	?	48,400	20,000
Selling expenses	17,920	19,000	25,000	?
Administrative expenses	25,600	?	29,700	9,000
Total operating expenses	?	46,000	?	?
Profit (loss)	?	14,400	?	2,000
Gross profit ratio	?	?	?	?

Analysis Component: Company A and Company B are in similar industries. Comment on their comparative performances.

Exercise 5-12 **Preparing an income statement—perpetual** LO5

CHECK FIGURE: a. Profit = $7,815

The following is account information listed in alphabetical order for Compu-Soft for the month ended November 30, 2017.

Required

Prepare a multiple-step income statement for the month ended November 30, 2017.

	Account	Adjusted Trial Balance	
		Debit	**Credit**
201	Accounts payable..		$ 750
106	Accounts receivable..	$ 1,200	
166	Accumulated depreciation, store equipment................		4,600
101	Cash...	2,100	
502	Cost of goods sold..	14,800	
612	Depreciation expense, store equipment......................	120	
301	Peter Delta, capital..		1,935
302	Peter Delta, withdrawals...	4,600	
406	Rent revenue...		2,500
413	Sales..		29,400
415	Sales discounts...	45	
414	Sales returns and allowances...................................	720	
165	Store equipment..	7,200	
690	Utilities expense..	2,100	
623	Wages expense...	6,300	
	Totals...	$39,185	$39,185

Analysis Component: Assume that for the month ended October 31, 2017, net sales were $32,000, cost of goods sold was $19,200, and income from operations was $8,000. Calculate and compare the company's gross profit ratios for October and November.

Exercise 5-13 Adjusting entries and income statement—perpetual L05   e**X**cel

CHECK FIGURES: a. Balance sheet columns = $64,200; b. Profit = $8,500

The following list of accounts is taken from the December 31, 2017, unadjusted trial balance of Perdu Sales, a business that is owned by Eldon Perdu.

	Debit	**Credit**
Cash	$ 8,000	
Merchandise inventory	9,800	
Prepaid selling expense..	8,000	
Store equipment	40,000	
Accumulated depreciation, store equipment...............................		$ 9,800
Accounts payable..		14,840
Salaries payable		-0-
Eldon Perdu, capital		25,360
Eldon Perdu, withdrawals..	3,600	
Sales		858,000
Sales returns and allowances	33,000	
Sales discounts	8,000	
Cost of goods sold..	431,000	
Sales salaries expense..	94,000	
Utilities expense, store..	12,600	
Other selling expenses	70,000	
Other administrative expenses	190,000	

Additional information:

Accrued sales salaries amount to $3,200. Prepaid selling expenses of $5,200 have expired. Depreciation for the period is $2,500.

Required Assuming a perpetual inventory system, complete the following:

   a. Journalize the adjusting journal entries.

   b. Prepare a classified multiple-step income statement for the year ended December 31, 2017.

Analysis Component: Assume that for the year ended December 31, 2016, net sales were $600,000; operating expenses were $344,000; and there was a loss of $14,000. Calculate and compare the company's gross profit ratios for 2016 and 2017.

Exercise 5-14 Markups—perpetual LO6

Kim works at a sports store and needs to determine the selling price for running shoes. The running shoes have a cost of $40. The manager asked Kim to price the running shoes with a 60% target gross margin. Kim has priced the running shoes with a 60% markup percentage.

Required

1. What selling price does the manager want?

2. What selling price has Kim calculated?

3. If there are 50 running shoes, how much will the store lose in sales if the price is not corrected?

*Exercise 5-15 Calculating cost of goods sold LO2,7

Refer to Exhibit 5A.2 and determine each of the missing numbers in the following situations:

	a	b	c
Purchases...	$92,000	$158,000	$120,000
Purchase discounts	4,000	?	2,600
Purchase returns and allowances..............................	3,000	6,000	4,400
Transportation-in...	?	14,000	16,000
Beginning inventory	5,000	?	34,000
Cost of goods purchased	89,400	156,000	?
Ending inventory..	4,400	30,000	?
Cost of goods sold	?	166,400	136,520

*Exercise 5-16 Calculating expenses and income LO2,7

Referring to Exhibit 5A.2, fill in the following blanks. Identify any losses by putting the amount in brackets.

	Company A		Company B	
	2017	2016	2017	2016
Sales..	$110,000	$178,000	$90,000	$?
Cost of goods sold:				
Merchandise inventory (beginning)	8,700	27,300	8,875	6,000
Net cost of merchandise purchases...	82,000	?	?	26,100
Merchandise inventory (ending).........	?	(22,000)	(8,920)	(9,875)
Cost of goods sold	82,300	106,000	?	?
Gross profit from sales	?	?	39,545	19,775
Operating expenses............................	26,000	54,000	27,000	?
Profit (loss)	1,700	18,000	?	6,275
Gross profit ratio	?	?	?	?

An asterisk (*) identifies assignment material based on Appendix 5A or Appendix 5B.

Analysis Component: Company A and Company B are in similar industries. Comment on their gross profit ratios.

*Exercise 5-17 Components of cost of goods sold LO1,2,7

Referring to Exhibit 5A.2, use the data provided to determine each of the missing numbers in the following situations:

	a	b	c
Invoice cost of merchandise purchases......................	$44,000	$21,000	$16,250
Purchase discounts	2,000	?	325
Purchase returns and allowances..............................	1,500	750	550
Cost of transportation-in	?	1,750	2,000
Merchandise inventory (beginning of period)..............	4,500	?	3,500
Net cost of merchandise purchases...........................	44,700	19,750	?
Merchandise inventory (end of period).......................	2,200	3,750	?
Cost of goods sold	?	20,800	17,065

*Exercise 5-18 Journal entries to contrast the periodic and perpetual systems—perpetual and periodic LO2,7

Journalize the following merchandising transactions for Scout Systems assuming (a) a periodic system, and (b) a perpetual system.

Nov.	1	Scout Systems purchases merchandise for $4,400 on credit with terms of 2/10, n/30.
	5	Scout Systems pays for the previous purchase.
	7	Scout Systems receives payment for returned defective merchandise of $500 that was purchased on November 1.
	10	Scout Systems pays $400 to transport merchandise to its store.
	13	Scout Systems sells merchandise for $6,500 on account. The cost of the merchandise was $4,200.
	16	A customer returns merchandise from the November 13 transaction. The returned item sold for $1,200 and cost $780. The item will be returned to inventory.

*Exercise 5-19 Recording journal entries for merchandise purchase transactions—periodic LO7

Using the information in Exercise 5-2, prepare journal entries to record the transactions assuming a periodic inventory system.

*Exercise 5-20 Recording journal entries for merchandise purchase transactions—periodic LO7

Using the information in Exercise 5-3, prepare journal entries to record the March transactions assuming a periodic inventory system.

*Exercise 5-21 Recording journal entries for merchandise sales transactions—periodic LO7

Using the information in Exercise 5-4, prepare journal entries to record the transactions assuming a periodic inventory system. You are not required to identify the account number in your journal entries.

The company's chart of accounts is below:

101	Cash	501	Purchases
106	Accounts Receivable	502	Purchases returns and allowances
119	Merchandise inventory	503	Purchases discounts
201	Accounts Payable	501	Purchases
201	Sales	501	Purchases
414	Sales returns and allowances	504	Transportation-in
415	Sales discounts	663	Delivery expense

An asterisk (*) identifies assignment material based on Appendix 5A or Appendix 5B.

*Exercise 5-22 Recording journal entries for merchandise sales transactions—periodic LO7

Using the information in Exercise 5-5, prepare journal entries to record the transactions assuming a periodic inventory system.

*Exercise 5-23 Analyzing and recording merchandise transactions and discounts—periodic LO7

Using the information in Exercise 5-6, and assuming instead a periodic inventory system, record the journal entries.

*Exercise 5-24 Analyzing and recording merchandise transactions and returns—periodic LO7

Using the information in Exercise 5-7:

   a. Present the journal entries that Wilson Purchasing should record for these transactions assuming a periodic inventory system.

   b. Present the journal entries that Hostel Sales should record for these transactions assuming a periodic inventory system.

*Exercise 5-25 Calculating expenses and cost of goods sold—periodic LO7

CHECK FIGURE: c. $16,900

Friar Company discloses the following information for the year ended October 31, 2017:

Sales	$355,000
Sales discounts	5,500
Sales returns	14,000
Merchandise inventory (beginning of period)	31,000
Invoice cost of merchandise purchases	178,000
Purchase discounts	3,600
Purchase returns and allowances	6,000
Cost of transportation-in	11,000
Gross profit from sales	142,000
Profit	65,000

Required Calculate (a) total operating expenses, (b) cost of goods sold, (c) merchandise inventory (end of period), and (d) gross profit ratio (round to two decimal places).

Analysis Component: Assuming that the gross profit ratio for the year ended October 31, 2016, was 47%, compare Friar Company's performance from 2016 to 2017.

*Exercise 5-26 Preparing an income statement—periodic LO7

CHECK FIGURE: c. Loss = $1,822

The following is John's Electronic's adjusted account information listed in alphabetical order for the month ended April 30, 2017. A physical count on April 30, 2017, revealed a merchandise inventory balance actually on hand of $2,460.

An asterisk (*) identifies assignment material based on Appendix 5A or Appendix 5B.

	Account	Debit	Credit
201	Accounts payable..		$ 2,118
154	Accumulated depreciation, trucks.....................................		15,600
101	Cash..	$ 1,600	
611	Depreciation expense, delivery trucks..............................	640	
633	Interest expense..	130	
301	John Yu, capital...		26,964
302	John Yu, withdrawals	9,200	
119	Merchandise inventory	5,700	
507	Purchase discounts...		28
506	Purchase returns and allowances		110
505	Purchases	16,140	
413	Sales..		33,700
414	Sales returns and allowances	1,740	
688	Telephone expense, office...	150	
689	Telephone expense, store..	340	
508	Transportation-in..	380	
153	Trucks..	29,600	
623	Wages expense, office...	4,900	
624	Wages expense, selling..	8,000	
	Totals..	$78,520	$78,520

Required

   a. Calculate net sales.

   b. Calculate cost of goods sold.

   c. Prepare a classified multiple-step income statement for the month ended April 30, 2017.

*Exercise 5-27 Sales taxes—perpetual LO3,8

Journalize each of the following transactions assuming a perpetual inventory system and PST at 8% along with 5% GST.

June	1	Purchased $2,000 of merchandise; terms 1/10, n/30.
	5	Sold $1,000 of merchandise for $1,400; terms n/15.

*Exercise 5-28 Sales taxes—periodic LO7,8

Journalize each of the transactions in Exercise 5-27 assuming a periodic inventory system and PST at 8% along with 5% GST.

Problems

Problem 5-1A Journal entries for merchandising activities—perpetual LO3

CHECK FIGURE: 2c. $5,960

Part 1

Prepare general journal entries to record the following perpetual system merchandising transactions of Belton Company. *Use a separate account for each receivable and payable; for example, record the sale on June 1 in Accounts Receivable—Avery & Wiest.*

An asterisk (*) identifies assignment material based on Appendix 5A or Appendix 5B.

June	1	Sold merchandise to Avery & Wiest for $9,500; terms 2/5, n/15, FOB destination (cost of sales $6,650).
	2	Purchased $4,900 of merchandise from Angolac Suppliers; terms 1/10, n/20, FOB shipping point.
	4	Purchased merchandise inventory from Bastille Sales for $11,400; terms 1/15, n/45, FOB Bastille Sales.
	5	Sold merchandise to Gelgar for $11,000; terms 2/5, n/15, FOB destination (cost of sales $7,700).
	6	Collected the amount owing from Avery & Wiest regarding the June 1 sale.
	12	Paid Angolac Suppliers for the June 2 purchase.
	20	Collected the amount owing from Gelgar regarding the June 5 sale.
	30	Paid Bastille Sales for the June 4 purchase.

Part 2

Based on the information provided above, calculate (a) net sales, (b) cost of goods sold, and (c) gross profit for the month ended June 30, 2017.

Problem 5-2A Journal entries for merchandising activities—perpetual LO3

Prepare general journal entries to record the following perpetual system merchandising transactions of Belton Company. *Use a separate account for each receivable and payable; for example, record the purchase July 1 in Accounts Payable—Jones Company.* Do the analysis component.

July	1	Purchased merchandise from Jones Company for $14,800 under credit terms of 1/15, n/30, FOB factory.
	2	Sold merchandise to Terra Co. for $2,600 under credit terms of 2/10, n/60, FOB shipping point. The merchandise had cost $1,950.
	3	Paid $450 for freight charges on the purchase of July 1.
	8	Sold merchandise that cost $3,825 for $5,100 cash.
	9	Purchased merchandise from Keene Co. for $9,100 under credit terms of 2/15, n/60, FOB destination.
	12	Received a $1,500 credit memo acknowledging the return of merchandise purchased on July 9.
	12	Received the balance due from Terra Co. for the credit sale dated July 2.
	13	Purchased office supplies from EastCo on credit, $960, n/30.
	16	Paid the balance due to Jones Company.
	19	Sold merchandise that cost $2,850 to Urban Co. for $3,800 under credit terms of 2/15, n/60, FOB shipping point.
	21	Issued a $300 credit memo to Urban Co. for an allowance on goods sold on July 19.
	22	Received a debit memo from Urban Co. for an error that overstated the total invoice by $200.
	29	Paid Keene Co. the balance due.
	30	Received the balance due from Urban Co. for the credit sale dated July 19.
	31	Sold merchandise that cost $7,500 to Terra Co. for $10,000 under credit terms of 2/10, n/60, FOB shipping point.

Analysis Component: As the senior purchaser for Belton Company, you are concerned that the purchase discounts you have negotiated are not being taken advantage of by the accounts payable department. Calculate the total dollar value impact to Belton Company of paying the July 9 purchase from Keene Co. after the discount period. Consider both the lost early payment discount and the cost of capital for the period after the discount period elapsed to the date Belton Company made the payment (assume a 6% interest rate; round calculations to four decimal places). Draft an email to the accounts payable department explaining the overall dollar value impact of paying the invoice after the discount period and how Belton Company can better take advantage of purchase discounts going forward.

Problem 5-3A Journal entries for merchandising activities—perpetual LO3

The Jewel Box purchases jewellery from around the world and sells to local retailers in Canada. Prepare general journal entries to record the following perpetual system merchandising transactions of The Jewel Box. *Use a separate account for each receivable and payable; for example, record the purchase on August 1 in Accounts Payable—Luu Company.*

Aug.	1	Purchased necklaces from Luu Company for $4,000 under credit terms of 1/10, n/30, FOB destination.
	4	At Luu Company's request, paid $350 for freight charges on the August 1 purchase, reducing the amount owed to Luu.
	5	Sold rings to Green Ruby for $3,800 under credit terms of 2/10, n/60, FOB destination. The merchandise had cost $2,470.
	8	Purchased bracelets from Jane Co. for $5,200 under credit terms of 1/10, n/45, FOB shipping point.
	9	Paid $325 shipping charges related to the August 5 sale to Green Ruby.
	10	Green Ruby returned the rings purchased from the August 5 sale that had cost $440 and been sold for $800. The merchandise was restored to inventory.
	12	After negotiations with Jane Co. concerning problems with the merchandise purchased on August 8, received a credit memo from Jane granting a price reduction of $400.
	15	Received balance due from Green Ruby for the August 5 sale.
	17	Purchased office equipment from WestCo on credit, $6,000, n/45.
	18	Paid the amount due Jane Co. for the August 8 purchase.
	19	Sold earrings to Chic Jewellery for $1,800 under credit terms of 1/10, n/30, FOB shipping point. The merchandise had cost $990.
	22	Chic Jewellery requested a price reduction on the August 19 sale because the merchandise did not meet specifications. Sent Chic Jewellery a credit memo for $300 to resolve the issue.
	29	Received Chic Jewellery's payment of the amount due from the August 19 purchase.
	30	Paid Luu Company the amount due from the August 1 purchase.

Problem 5-4A Adjusting entries and multi-step income statement—perpetual L05

CHECK FIGURES: 1. Income statement columns = $529,310; 2. Profit = $5,025

Information from the unadjusted trial balance of Jumbo's on December 31, 2017, the end of the annual accounting period, is as follows:

	Debit	Credit
Cash	$ 8,100	
Accounts receivable	22,665	
Merchandise inventory	34,600	
Store supplies	2,415	
Office supplies	775	
Prepaid insurance	3,255	
Equipment	74,490	
Accumulated depreciation, equipment		$ 13,655
Accounts payable		8,000
Salaries payable		-0-
Sally Fowler, capital		168,965
Sally Fowler, withdrawals	62,000	
Interest income		310
Sales		529,000
Sales returns and allowances	5,070	
Cost of goods sold	381,160	
Salaries expense	96,300	
Rent expense	29,100	
Supplies expense	-0-	
Depreciation expense, equipment	-0-	
Insurance expense	-0-	
Totals	$719,930	$719,930

Required

1. Record adjusting entries for the following information.

    a. A review of the store supplies on December 31, 2017, revealed a balance on hand of $2,000; a similar examination of the office supplies showed that $640 had been used.

    b. The balance in the Prepaid Insurance account was reviewed and it was determined that $255 was unused at December 31, 2017.

    c. The records show that the equipment was estimated to have a total estimated useful life of 10 years with a resale value at the end of its life of $14,490.

    d. Accrued salaries payable, $1,800.

    e. A count of the merchandise inventory revealed a balance on hand December 31, 2017, of $33,800.

2. Using adjusted trial balance numbers, prepare a multiple-step income statement showing the expenses in detail.

Analysis Component: Explain why Interest income is shown under Other revenues and expenses on the multiple-step income statement.

Problem 5-5A Income statement calculations and formats—perpetual LO5

CHECK FIGURE: 1. Income from operations = $55,000

The following amounts appeared on Davison Company's adjusted trial balance as of October 31, 2017, the end of its fiscal year:

	Debit	Credit
Merchandise inventory	$ 16,000	
Other assets	256,800	
Liabilities		$ 78,400
Brenda Davison, capital		203,280
Brenda Davison, withdrawals	65,000	
Interest income		1,120
Sales		424,000
Sales discounts	6,500	
Sales returns and allowances	28,000	
Cost of goods sold	169,300	
Sales salaries expense	52,000	
Rent expense, selling space	19,000	
Store supplies expense	5,000	
Advertising expense	29,400	
Office salaries expense	53,000	
Rent expense, office space	5,200	
Office supplies expense	1,600	
Totals	$706,800	$706,800

Required

1. Prepare a classified, multiple-step income statement for internal use (see Exhibit 5.13) that lists the company's net sales, cost of goods sold, and gross profit, as well as the components and amounts of selling expenses and general and administrative expenses.

2. Present a condensed single-step income statement (see Exhibit 5.15) that lists these costs: cost of goods sold, selling expenses, and general and administrative expenses.

Problem 5-6A Markups LO5

Leah Wells, a yoga instructor, started a company that sells athletic yoga clothing. You are Leah's marketing manager. Round your answers to two decimal places.

   a. After assessing the competitors, you determine that Leah needs to price her products with a markup percentage of 60%. The cost of her tank tops is $20 and her pullovers is $30. Determine the selling price for each of Leah's clothing items.

   b. Leah is ready to launch her yoga pants. You have determined that she should set her price 30% below her competitor's price of $100. Leah's cost to produce yoga pants is $40 per unit. Determine the markup percentage on Leah's yoga pants.

   c. Calculate the gross profit margin for tank tops, pullovers, and yoga pants.

   d. After a year, you determine that Leah should set a standard target margin percentage of 45% on all products. Determine the new prices for tank tops, pullovers, and yoga pants.

Problem 5-7A Income statements—perpetual LO5

CHECK FIGURE: 1. Income from operations = $13,590

The following amounts appeared on Plymouth Electronics' adjusted trial balance as of December 31, 2017.

	Debit	Credit
Merchandise inventory	$ 19,500	
Other assets	487,785	
Liabilities		$ 312,370
Celine Plymouth, capital		247,605
Celine Plymouth, withdrawals	67,000	
Sales		942,000
Sales discounts	14,580	
Sales returns and allowances	5,715	
Interest income		720
Cost of goods sold	719,000	
Sales salaries expense	79,200	
Office salaries expense	56,500	
Rent expense, selling space	33,000	
Rent expense, office space	3,000	
Store supplies expense	1,620	
Office supplies expense	735	
Depreciation expense, store equipment	8,910	
Depreciation expense, office equipment	2,760	
Insurance expense	3,390	
Totals	$1,502,695	$1,502,695

Required
1. Prepare a 2017 classified, multiple-step income statement for Plymouth Electronics, like Exhibit 5.13.
2. Prepare a single-step income statement, like Exhibit 5.15.

Analysis Component: The gross profit ratio for Plymouth Electronics' year ended December 31, 2016, was 32%. Calculate this ratio for the year ended December 31, 2017, and compare it to the prior year, commenting on whether the change was favourable or unfavourable.

Problem 5-8A **Income statements—perpetual** LO5

CHECK FIGURES: 1. Operating expenses = $141,800; Profit = $73,200

The following adjusted trial balance for Bell Servicing was prepared at the end of the fiscal year, December 31, 2017:

		Debit	Credit
101	Cash	$ 8,000	
119	Merchandise inventory	16,200	
125	Supplies	10,000	
128	Prepaid insurance	4,000	
165	Store equipment	51,000	
166	Accumulated depreciation, store equipment		$ 46,800
167	Office equipment	69,000	
168	Accumulated depreciation, office equipment		34,200
201	Accounts payable		16,000
301	Jonah Bell, capital		29,000
302	Jonah Bell, withdrawals	41,000	
413	Sales		291,800
415	Sales discounts	2,000	
505	Cost of goods sold	74,800	
612	Depreciation expense, store equipment	5,200	
613	Depreciation expense, office equipment	3,800	
622	Sales salaries expense	46,000	
623	Office salaries expense	32,000	
637	Insurance expense, store	2,000	
638	Insurance expense, office	1,600	
640	Rent expense, office space	13,000	
641	Rent expense, selling space	17,000	
651	Office supplies expense	1,200	
652	Store supplies expense	2,400	
655	Advertising expense	17,600	
	Totals	$417,800	$417,800

Required

1. Prepare a classified multiple-step income statement that would be used by the business's owner (like Exhibit 5.13).

2. Prepare a multiple-step income statement that would be used by external users (like Exhibit 5.14).

3. Prepare a single-step income statement that would be provided to decision makers outside the company (like Exhibit 5.15).

Analysis Component: If you were a decision maker external to Bell Servicing, which income statement format would you prefer and why, if you had a choice? Which income statement format(s) could you expect as an external user? Why?

*Problem 5-9A **Journal entries for merchandising activities—periodic** LO7

Using the information provided in Part 1 of Problem 5-1A, journalize each of the transactions assuming a periodic inventory system.

An asterisk (*) identifies assignment material based on Appendix 5A or Appendix 5B.

*Problem 5-10A Journal entries for merchandising transactions—periodic LO7

Prepare general journal entries to record the following periodic system merchandising transactions for Schafer Merchandising. *Use a separate account for each receivable and payable:*

Oct. 1 Purchased merchandise from Zeon Company on credit, terms 2/10, n/30, $15,800.
      2 Sold merchandise for cash, $2,100.
      7 Purchased merchandise on credit from Billings Co., terms 2/10, n/30, $11,600, FOB the seller's factory.
      7 Paid $450 cash for freight charges on the merchandise shipment of the previous transaction.
      8 Purchased delivery equipment from Finlay Supplies on credit, $24,000.
     12 Sold merchandise on credit to Comry Holdings, terms 2/15, 1/30, n/60, $5,800.
     13 Received a $1,500 credit memo for merchandise purchased on October 7 and returned for credit.
     13 Purchased office supplies on credit from Staples, $620, n/30.
     15 Sold merchandise on credit to Tom Willis, terms 2/10, 1/30, n/60, $4,650.
     15 Paid for the merchandise purchased on October 7.
     16 Received a credit memo for unsatisfactory office supplies purchased on October 13 and returned, $120.
     19 Issued a $420 credit memo to the customer who purchased merchandise on October 15 and returned a portion for credit.
     25 Received payment for the merchandise sold on October 15.
     29 The customer of October 12 paid for the purchase of that date.
     31 Paid for the merchandise purchased on October 1.

*Problem 5-11A Income statement calculations and formats—periodic LO7

CHECK FIGURES: 3. $34,300; 4. Loss from operations = $18,265; Loss = $18,115

The following amounts appeared on the Mendelstein Company's adjusted trial balance as of October 31, 2017, the end of its fiscal year:

	Debit	Credit
Merchandise inventory	$ 1,400	
Other assets	40,000	
Liabilities		$ 36,340
Joe Mendelstein, capital		37,375
Joe Mendelstein, withdrawals	3,000	
Interest income		150
Sales		96,400
Sales returns and allowances	7,500	
Sales discounts	1,125	
Purchases	43,500	
Purchase returns and allowances		2,150
Purchase discounts		900
Transportation-in	5,050	
Sales salaries expense	17,800	
Rent expense, selling space	9,200	
Store supplies expense	3,200	
Advertising expense	9,000	
Office salaries expense	22,000	
Rent expense, office space	7,600	
Office supplies expense	2,940	
Totals	$173,315	$173,315

A physical count shows that the cost of the ending inventory is $12,600.

An asterisk (*) identifies assignment material based on Appendix 5A or Appendix 5B.

Required

1. Calculate the company's net sales for the year.

2. Calculate the company's cost of goods purchased for the year.

3. Calculate the company's cost of goods sold for the year.

4. Present a multiple-step income statement that lists the company's net sales, cost of goods sold, and gross profit from sales.

5. Present a condensed single-step income statement that lists these expenses: cost of goods sold, selling expenses, and general and administrative expenses.

*Problem 5-12A **Classified, multi-step income statement—periodic** L05,6 **eXcel***

CHECK FIGURE: 1. Profit = $60,515

Information from the December 31, 2017, year-end, unadjusted trial balance of Woodstock Store is as follows:

	Debit	Credit
Cash	$ 3,500	
Merchandise inventory	31,400	
Store supplies	1,715	
Office supplies	645	
Prepaid insurance	3,960	
Store equipment	57,615	
Accumulated depreciation, store equipment		$ 6,750
Office equipment	13,100	
Accumulated depreciation, office equipment		6,550
Accounts payable		4,000
Zen Woodstock, capital		52,000
Zen Woodstock, withdrawals	31,500	
Rental revenue		14,600
Sales		501,520
Sales returns and allowances	2,915	
Sales discounts	5,190	
Purchases	331,315	
Purchase returns and allowances		2,140
Purchase discounts		4,725
Transportation-in	3,690	
Sales salaries expense	34,710	
Rent expense, selling space	24,000	
Advertising expense	6,400	
Store supplies expense	-0-	
Depreciation expense, store equipment	-0-	
Office salaries expense	27,630	
Rent expense, office space	13,000	
Office supplies expense	-0-	
Insurance expense	-0-	
Depreciation expense, office equipment	-0-	
Totals	$592,285	$592,285

_____

An asterisk (*) identifies assignment material based on Appendix 5A or Appendix 5B.

Additional Information

    a. The balance on January 1, 2017, in the Store Supplies account was $480. During the year, $1,235 of store supplies were purchased and debited to the Store Supplies account. A physical count on December 31, 2017, shows an ending balance of $180.

    b. The balance on January 1, 2017, in the Office Supplies account was $50. Office supplies of $595 were bought in 2017 and added to the Office Supplies account. An examination of the office supplies at year-end revealed that $590 had been used.

    c. The balance in the Prepaid Insurance account represents a policy purchased on September 1, 2017; it was valid for 12 months from that date.

    d. The store equipment was originally estimated to have a useful life of 12 years and a residual value of $3,615.

    e. When the office equipment was purchased, it was estimated that it would last four years and have no residual value.

    f. Ending merchandise inventory, $29,000.

Required

Analyze and determine the impact of the adjustments from (a) to (f) on the unadjusted trial balance numbers. Prepare a classified multi-step income statement, like Exhibit 5A.2 using your adjusted trial balance numbers.

*Problem 5-13A Sales taxes—perpetual LO3,7

Journalize each of the following transactions assuming a perpetual inventory system and PST at 8% along with 5% GST. *Note: Any available cash discount is taken only on the sale price before taxes.*

Aug.	1	Purchased $2,000 of merchandise for cash.
	2	Purchased $6,800 of merchandise; terms 2/10, n/30.
	5	Sold merchandise costing $3,600 for $5,200; terms 1/10, n/30.
	12	Paid for the merchandise purchased on August 2.
	15	Collected the amount owing from the customer of August 5.
	17	Purchased $6,000 of merchandise; terms n/15.
	19	Recorded $7,000 of cash sales (cost of sales $5,800).

*Problem 5-14A Sales taxes—periodic LO7,8

Journalize each of the transactions in Problem 5-13A assuming a periodic inventory system and PST at 7% along with 5% GST.

Alternate Problems

Problem 5-1B Journal entries for merchandising activities—perpetual LO3

CHECK FIGURE: 2c. = $21,280

Part 1

Prepare general journal entries to record the following perpetual system merchandising transactions of Lyryx Company. *Use a separate account for each receivable and payable; for example, record the sale on March 6 in Accounts Receivable—Tessier & Welsh.*

An asterisk (*) identifies assignment material based on Appendix 5A or Appendix 5B.

Mar.	5	Purchased $48,000 of merchandise from Delton Suppliers paying cash.
	6	Sold merchandise for $36,000 to Tessier & Welsh; terms 2/10, n/30, FOB destination (cost of sales $27,100).
	7	Purchased merchandise from Janz Company for $71,000; terms 1/10, n/45, FOB shipping point.
	8	Paid $1,540 shipping costs regarding the purchase of March 7.
	9	Sold merchandise for $46,000 to Parker Company; terms 2/10, n/30, FOB destination (cost of sales $32,900).
	10	Purchased $17,800 of merchandise from Delton Suppliers; terms 2/10, n/45, FOB destination.
	16	Collected the balance owing from Tessier & Welsh regarding the March 6 sale.
	17	Paid for the March 7 purchase from Janz Company.
	30	Paid for the March 10 purchase from Delton Suppliers.
	31	Collected the balance owing from Parker Company regarding the sale of March 9.

Part 2

Based on the information provided above, calculate (a) net sales, (b) cost of goods sold, and (c) gross profit for the month ended March 31, 2017.

Problem 5-2B Journal entries for merchandising activities—perpetual LO3

Prepare general journal entries to record the following perpetual system merchandising transactions of Lyryx Company. *Use a separate account for each receivable and payable; for example, record the purchase on May 2 in Accounts Payable—Mobley Co.*

May	2	Purchased merchandise from Mobley Co. for $18,000 under credit terms of 1/15, n/30, FOB factory.
	4	Sold merchandise to Cornerstone Co. for $3,400 under credit terms of 2/10, n/60, FOB shipping point. The merchandise had cost $2,100.
	4	Paid $750 for freight charges on the purchase of May 2.
	9	Sold merchandise that cost $3,600 for $5,200 cash.
	10	Purchased merchandise from Richter Co. for $7,300 under credit terms of 2/15, n/60, FOB destination.
	12	Received a $600 credit memo acknowledging the return of merchandise purchased on May 10.
	14	Received the balance due from Cornerstone Co. for the credit sale dated May 4.
	15	Sold for cash a piece of office equipment at its original cost, $1,200.
	17	Paid the balance due to Mobley Co.
	18	Purchased $1,750 of cleaning supplies from A & Z Suppliers; terms n/15.
	20	Sold merchandise that cost $2,700 to Harrill Co. for $3,900 under credit terms of 2/15, n/60, FOB shipping point.
	22	Issued a $500 credit memo to Harrill Co. for an allowance on goods sold on May 20.
	23	Received a debit memo from Harrill Co. for an error that overstated the total invoice by $150.
	25	Paid Richter Co. the balance due.
	31	Received the balance due from Harrill Co. for the credit sale dated May 20.
	31	Sold merchandise that cost $10,200 to Cornerstone Co. for $15,000 under credit terms of 2/10, n/60, FOB shipping point.

Analysis Component: You are working in Lyryx's accounts payable department and have been instructed to pay the Richter account on the last day of the discount period even though the money will have to be borrowed at 6% interest. Why would the company borrow to pay within the discount period? Show your calculations (round to two decimal places).

Problem 5-3B Journal entries for merchandising activities—perpetual LO3

Amuse Me Co. buys and sells new and used equipment for amusement parks, carnivals, parks, and zoos. Prepare general journal entries to record the following perpetual system merchandising transactions of Amuse Me Co.. *Use a separate account for each receivable and payable; for example, record the purchase on July 3 in Accounts Payable—CMP Corp.*

July	3	Purchased bumper cars from CMP Corp. for $32,000 under credit terms of 1/10, n/30, FOB destination.
	4	At CMP's request, paid $1,500 for freight charges on the July 3 purchase, reducing the amount owed to CMP.
	7	Sold cotton candy machines to West Coast Zoo for $21,000 under credit terms of 2/10, n/60, FOB destination. The merchandise had cost $17,500.
	10	Purchased snow cone machines from Cimarron Corporation for $29,300 under credit terms of 1/10, n/45, FOB shipping point.
	11	Paid $1,200 shipping charges related to the July 7 sale to West Coast Zoo.
	12	West Coast Zoo returned merchandise from the July 7 sale that had cost $2,500 and been sold for $3,500. The merchandise was restored to inventory.
	14	After negotiations with Cimarron Corporation concerning problems with the merchandise purchased on July 10, received a credit memo from Cimarron granting a price reduction of $4,100.
	17	Received balance due from West Coast Zoo. for the July 7 sale.
	18	Sold for cash a piece of vacant land for its original cost of $62,000.
	19	Purchased a used van for the business, $28,000; paid cash of $10,000 and borrowed the balance from the bank.
	20	Paid the amount due Cimarron Corporation for the July 10 purchase.
	21	Sold a climbing wall to Canadian National Exhibition for $18,000 under credit terms of 1/10, n/30, FOB shipping point. The merchandise had cost $13,100.
	24	Canadian National Exhibition requested a price reduction on the July 21 sale because the merchandise did not meet specifications. Sent Canadian National Exhibition a credit memo for $3,000 to resolve the issue.
	31	Received Canadian National Exhibition's payment of the amount due from the July 21 purchase.
	31	Paid CMP Corp. the amount due from the July 3 purchase.

Analysis Component: Regarding the July 24 transaction, what alternative is there to granting a credit memo? Be sure to identify and explain an advantage and disadvantage of the alternative.

Problem 5-4B Adjusting entries and income statements—perpetual LO5 e

CHECK FIGURES: 1. Income statement columns = $435,000; 2. Loss = $44,000

The following information is from the unadjusted trial balance for Journey's End Company prepared at October 31, 2017, the end of the fiscal year:

	Debit	Credit
Cash	$ 12,800	
Merchandise inventory	41,500	
Store supplies	16,700	
Prepaid insurance	5,700	
Store equipment	167,600	
Accumulated depreciation, store equipment		$ 60,000
Accounts payable		34,700
Dallas End, capital		172,100
Dallas End, withdrawals	12,000	
Sales		391,000
Sales discounts	3,500	
Sales returns and allowances	8,000	
Cost of goods sold	149,600	
Depreciation expense, store equipment	-0-	
Salaries expense	144,000	
Interest expense	800	
Insurance expense	-0-	
Rent expense	56,000	
Store supplies expense	-0-	
Advertising expense	39,600	
Totals	$657,800	$657,800

Rent and salaries expense are equally divided between the selling and administrative functions. Journey's End Company uses a perpetual inventory system.

Required

1. Record adjusting entries for the following information:

 a. Store supplies on hand at year-end amount to $6,600.

 b. The balance in the Prepaid Insurance account represents 12 months of insurance that was in effect starting November 1, 2016.

 c. The store equipment was purchased several years ago, when it was estimated to have a 20-year useful life and a resale value at the end of its life of $47,600.

 d. A physical count of the ending merchandise inventory shows $29,800 of goods on hand.

2. Using adjusted trial balance numbers, prepare a multiple-step income statement (see Exhibit 5.13).

Analysis Component: Explain why *Interest Expense* is shown under *Other revenues and expenses* on the multiple-step income statement.

Problem 5-5B Income statement calculations and formats—perpetual LO5

CHECK FIGURE: 1. Profit = $10,050

The following amounts appeared on Excel Company's adjusted trial balance as of May 31, 2017, the end of its fiscal year:

	Debit	Credit
Merchandise inventory	$ 21,000	
Other assets..	385,200	
Liabilities...		$ 105,000
Reena Excel, capital		339,150
Reena Excel, withdrawals......................................	48,000	
Sales		636,000
Sales discounts	9,750	
Sales returns and allowances	42,000	
Cost of goods sold...	296,000	
Sales salaries expense...	87,000	
Rent expense, selling space	30,000	
Store supplies expense	7,500	
Advertising expense	54,000	
Office salaries expense	79,500	
Rent expense, office space...................................	17,800	
Office supplies expense	2,400	
Totals...	$1,080,150	$1,080,150

Required

1. Present a classified multiple-step income statement for internal users (see Exhibit 5.13) that lists the company's net sales, cost of goods sold, and gross profit, as well as the components and amounts of selling expenses and general and administrative expenses.

2. Present a condensed single-step income statement (see Exhibit 5.15) that lists these costs: cost of goods sold, selling expenses, and general and administrative expenses.

Problem 5-6B Mark-ups LO5

Nikki designed a line of environmentally friendly handbags under the brand Nik & Mik. You are the marketing manager. Round all numbers to two decimal places.

    a. After assessing the competitors, Nikki needs to price her products with a markup percentage of 40%. The cost is $50 for the small handbags and $60 for the medium handbags. Determine the selling price for each type of handbag.

    b. Nik & Mik is ready to launch their large handbags. You determine that Nikki should set her price 25% below her competitor's price of $160. Nikki's cost to produce the large handbags is $70 per unit. Determine the markup percentage.

    c. Calculate the gross profit margin for small, medium, and large handbags.

    d. After a year of operations, you determine that Nikki should set a standard target gross margin percentage of 40% on all of Nikki's products. Determine the new prices for the small, medium, and large handbags.

Problem 5-7B Income statements—perpetual LO5

CHECK FIGURE: 1. Total operating expenses = $98,484

The following account information appeared on Ucore Sales' adjusted trial balance as of December 31, 2017. The accounts are listed in alphabetical order.

	Debit	Credit
Cost of goods sold	$129,964	
Depreciation expense, office equipment	690	
Depreciation expense, store equipment	3,204	
Insurance expense	1.240	
Liabilities		84,000
Lyle Ucore, capital		46,547
Lyle Ucore, withdrawals	20,500	
Merchandise inventory	3,400	
Other assets	102,952	
Rent expense (80% sales)	19,950	
Salaries expense (70% sales)	71,000	
Sales		226,500
Sales discounts	278	
Sales returns and allowances	1,469	
Supplies expense (35% sales)	2,400	
Totals	$357,047	$357,047

Required

  1. Prepare a classified, multiple-step income statement for Ucore Sales, like Exhibit 5.13.

  2. Prepare a single-step income statement, like Exhibit 5.15.

Analysis Component: The gross profit ratio for Ucore Sales' year ended December 31, 2016, was 28%. Calculate this ratio for the year ended December 31, 2017, and compare it to the prior year, commenting on whether the change was favourable or unfavourable (round to two decimal places).

Problem 5-8B Income statements—perpetual LO5

CHECK FIGURES: 1. Operating expenses = $134,050; 2. Loss = $1,650

The following adjusted trial balance information was taken from the end of the July 31, 2017, fiscal year for Brilliant Sales:

		Debit	Credit
101	Cash	$ 6,500	
119	Merchandise inventory	12,220	
125	Supplies	2,400	
128	Prepaid insurance	1,150	
165	Store equipment	29,400	
166	Accumulated depreciation, store equipment		$ 7,500
167	Office equipment	15,600	
168	Accumulated depreciation, office equipment		8,100
201	Accounts payable		6,400
301	Ty Brilliant, capital		107,920
302	Ty Brilliant, withdrawals	61,000	
413	Sales		395,400
415	Sales discounts	1,200	
505	Cost of goods sold	261,800	
612	Depreciation expense, store equipment	1,500	
613	Depreciation expense, office equipment	1,250	
622	Sales salaries expense	39,000	
623	Office salaries expense	32,000	
637	Insurance expense, store	4,100	
638	Insurance expense, office	2,800	
640	Rent expense, office space	13,100	
641	Rent expense, selling space	21,000	
651	Office supplies expense	2,600	
652	Store supplies expense	1,800	
655	Advertising expense	14,900	
	Totals	$525,320	$525,320

Brilliant Sales uses a perpetual inventory system.

Required

1. Prepare a classified multiple-step income statement for use by internal users (like Exhibit 5.13).

2. Prepare a multiple-step income statement for external users (like Exhibit 5.14).

3. Prepare a single-step income statement (like Exhibit 5.15).

*Problem 5-9B Journal entries for merchandising activities—periodic LO7

Using the information provided in Part 1 of Problem 5-1B, journalize each of the transactions assuming a periodic inventory system.

An asterisk (*) identifies assignment material based on Appendix 5A or Appendix 5B.

*Problem 5-10B Journal entries for merchandising transactions—periodic LO7

Prepare general journal entries to record the following periodic system transactions of Inter-Cap Merchandising. *Use a separate account for each receivable and payable.*

March	1	Purchased merchandise on credit from Zender Holdings, terms 1/10, n/15, $40,000.
	2	Sold merchandise for cash, $5,100.
	7	Purchased merchandise on credit from Red River Co., terms 2/10, n/30, $29,500, FOB the seller's factory.
	8	Incurred freight charges for $1,750 on credit to Dan's Shipping regarding the merchandise shipment of the previous transaction.
	12	Sold merchandise on credit to Bev Dole, terms 2/10, n/45, $26,000.
	13	Received a $1,000 credit memo for merchandise purchased on March 7 and returned for credit.
	14	Purchased furniture for the office on credit from Wilson Supplies, $3,200.
	15	Sold merchandise on credit to Ted Smith, terms 2/10, n/45, $24,000.
	16	Paid for the merchandise purchased on March 7.
	17	Issued a credit memo to the customer of March 15 granting an allowance of $2,000 due to damage during shipment.
	19	The supplier issued a credit memo for $1,500 regarding unsatisfactory furniture purchased on March 14 and returned.
	24	Received payment for the merchandise sold on March 15.
	27	The customer of March 12 paid for the purchase of that date.
	31	Paid for the merchandise purchased on March 1.

*Problem 5-11B Income statement calculations and formats—periodic LO7

CHECK FIGURES: 3. $119,150; 4. Income from operations = $16,300

The following amounts appeared on the Mullen Company's adjusted trial balance in alphabetical order as of November 30, 2017, the end of its fiscal year:

	Debit	Credit
Advertising expense	$ 3,000	
Interest expense	350	
Liabilities		$ 31,000
Merchandise inventory	5,600	
Mitsy Mullen, capital		113,800
Mitsy Mullen, withdrawals	10,000	
Other assets	144,650	
Purchase discounts		1,150
Purchase returns and allowances		4,050
Purchases	120,000	
Rent expense (75% selling)	38,000	
Salaries expense (60% selling)	62,000	
Sales		276,000
Sales discounts	2,350	
Sales returns and allowances	28,500	
Supplies expense (80% selling)	6,700	
Transportation-in	4,850	
Totals	$426,000	$426,000

A physical count shows that the cost of the ending inventory is $6,100.

An asterisk (*) identifies assignment material based on Appendix 5A or Appendix 5B.

Required

1. Calculate the company's net sales for the year.

2. Calculate the company's cost of goods purchased for the year.

3. Calculate the company's cost of goods sold for the year.

4. Present a multiple-step income statement (like Exhibit 5.16) that lists the company's net sales, cost of goods sold, and gross profit, as well as the components and amounts of selling expenses and general and administrative expenses.

5. Present a single-step income statement (like Exhibit 5.17) that lists these expenses: cost of goods sold, selling expenses, general and administrative expenses, and interest expense.

*Problem 5-12B   Classified, multi-step income statement—periodic L05   e**X**cel

CHECK FIGURE: 1. Loss = $28,630

Information from the March 31, 2017, year-end, unadjusted trial balance of The Online Store is as follows:

	Debit	Credit
Cash	$ 7,000	
Merchandise inventory	39,500	
Supplies	1,600	
Prepaid rent	19,200	
Store equipment	60,000	
Accumulated depreciation, store equipment		$ 14,000
Office equipment	23,000	
Accumulated depreciation, office equipment		6,500
Accounts payable		16,000
Lucy Baker, capital		134,600
Lucy Baker, withdrawals	34,000	
Sales		506,750
Sales returns and allowances	13,800	
Sales discounts	6,000	
Purchases	346,000	
Purchase returns and allowances		4,600
Purchase discounts		7,150
Transportation-in	16,000	
Salaries expense (60% selling, 40% office)	58,000	
Rent expense (80% selling space; 20% office space)	49,000	
Advertising expense	7,000	
Supplies expense (30% selling supplies; 70% office supplies)	9,500	
Depreciation expense, store equipment	-0-	
Depreciation expense, office equipment	-0-	
Totals	$689,600	$689,600

Additional Information

a. Supplies inventory at year-end, $920.

b. The balance in the Prepaid Rent account represents a six-month contract effective November 1, 2016.

c. Depreciation on the store equipment, $1,600.

An asterisk (*) identifies assignment material based on Appendix 5A or Appendix 5B.

d. The useful life and trade-in value of the office equipment were originally estimated to be seven years and $250, respectively.

e. Ending merchandise inventory, $19,200.

Required

Analyze and determine the impact of the adjustments from (a) to (e) on the unadjusted trial balance numbers. Prepare a classified multi-step income statement (like Exhibit 5A.2) using your adjusted trial balance numbers.

*Problem 5-13B Sales taxes—perpetual LO3,7,8

Journalize each of the following transactions assuming a perpetual inventory system and PST at 8% along with 5% GST. *Note: Any available cash discount is taken only on the sale price before taxes.*

Sept.	2	Recorded $9,000 of cash sales (cost of sales $6,200).
	3	Purchased $11,000 of merchandise inventory for cash.
	7	Purchased $6,500 of merchandise; terms 1/10, n/45.
	8	Sold merchandise costing $13,200 for $16,200; terms 2/10, n/30.
	17	Paid for the merchandise purchased on September 7.
	18	Collected the amount owing from the customer of September 8.

*Problem 5-14B Sales taxes—periodic LO6,7,8

Journalize each of the transactions in Problem 5-13B assuming a periodic inventory system and PST at 8% along with 5% GST.

Analytical and Review Problem

A & R Problem 5-1—perpetual

The following income statement was prepared by an office clerk hired for July. As the accounting supervisor, you recognize that it is incorrect and prepare a corrected multi-step income statement.

Demo Sales Income Statement For Month Ended July 31, 2017		
Sales		$562,140
Accounts receivable		37,000
Unearned sales		18,000
Net sales		$617,140
Operating expenses:		
Accumulated depreciation, equipment	$ 30,000	
Advertising expense	14,000	
Cost of goods sold	394,000	
Depreciation expense, equipment	3,000	
Insurance expense	2,500	
Interest expense	1,700	
Interest payable	250	
Jen Conway, withdrawals	14,000	
Office supplies	9,000	
Prepaid insurance	14,000	
Prepaid rent	25,000	
Rent expense	5,000	
Salaries payable	175,000	
Sales discounts	2,800	690,250
Loss		$ 73,110

An asterisk (*) identifies assignment material based on Appendix 5A or Appendix 5B.

384

Ethics Challenge

EC 5-1

Claire Phelps is a popular high school student who attends approximately four dances a year at her high school. Each dance requires a new dress and accessories that necessitate a financial outlay of $100 to $200 per event. Claire's parents inform her that she is on her own with respect to financing the dresses. After incurring a major hit to her savings for the first dance in her second year, Claire developed a different approach. She buys the dress on credit the week before the dance, wears it to the dance, and returns the dress the next week to the store for a full refund on her charge card.

Required

1. Comment on the ethics exhibited by Claire and possible consequences of her actions.
2. How does the store account for the dresses that Claire returns?

Focus on Financial Statements

FFS 5-1

CHECK FIGURES: Loss = $154; Total current assets = $430; Total assets = $562; Total current liabilities = $74

Colombia Textiles began operations several years ago. Its post-closing trial balance at December 31, 2017, is shown below (with accounts listed in alphabetical order):

Account	Account Balance[1] ($000s)
Accounts payable	17
Accounts receivable	106
Accumulated depreciation, office furniture	38
Accumulated depreciation, store fixtures	61
Brandy Colombia, capital[2]	308
Cash	48
Franchise	62
Merchandise inventory	236
Notes payable[3]	225
Notes receivable[4]	14
Office furniture	52
Office supplies	5
Prepaid rent	32
Store fixtures	106
Unearned revenue	12

[1]Assume all accounts have a normal balance.
[2]The owner, Brandy Colombia, made no investments during 2017.
[3]$180,000 of the note is due after December 31, 2018.
[4]$3,000 of the notes receivable will be collected during 2018.

Additional information: The following closing entries were recorded on December 31, 2017, for the year just ended.

2017				
Dec. 31	Sales		640	
	Interest Income..		2	
	Income Summary			642
	To close temporary credit balance accounts			
	to the Income Summary account.			
31	Income Summary..		796	
	Depreciation Expense, Office Furniture.................			13
	Depreciation Expense, Store Fixtures...................			6
	Cost of Goods Sold			459
	Delivery Expense..			21
	Interest Expense			4
	Office Salaries Expense......................................			63
	Office Supplies Expense			17
	Rent Expense, Office			21
	Rent Expense, Sales...			46
	Sales Discounts			7
	Sales Returns and Allowances............................			19
	Sales Salaries Expense			120
	To close temporary debit balance accounts			
	to the Income Summary account.			
31	Brandy Colombia, Capital		154	
	Income Summary			154
	To close the Income Summary account to Capital.			
31	Brandy Colombia, Capital		78	
	Brandy Colombia, Withdrawals			78
	To close Withdrawals to Capital.			

Required Using the information provided, prepare a single-step income statement, statement of changes in equity, and classified balance sheet.

Analysis Component: Refer to Danier Leather's June 28, 2014, balance sheet in Appendix III at the back of the textbook. Compare Danier's liabilities to those of Colombia Textiles. Ignoring the balance sheet dates, which company has the stronger balance sheet? *(A balance sheet is considered to be stronger the fewer liabilities it has as a percentage of total assets.)*

FFS 5-2

Required Answer the following questions.

 a. Based on a review of the income statement for Danier in Appendix III at the end of the textbook, determine if Danier sells products or services. Explain your answer.

 b. Based on a review of WestJet's income statement in Appendix III at the end of the textbook, determine if WestJet sells products or services. Explain your answer.

 c. The income statement for Danier shows a gross profit of $68,233 (thousand) for the year ended June 28, 2014. Explain what this gross profit represents.

 d. Did Danier have sufficient gross profit to cover operating expenses for the year ended June 28, 2014?

 e. Is the income statement format used by Danier a classified multi-step, a multi-step, or a single-step? (Compare the income statement for Danier to those in Exhibits 5.13, 5.14, and 5.15.

 f. Refer to the balance sheets for Danier and WestJet in Appendix III at the end of the textbook. Both balance sheets include Inventory. Explain how Inventory is unique for each of these companies.

Critical Thinking Mini Case

You have just graduated with a business diploma in management and have been hired as the inventory manager for a local sporting goods store. Your first task is to review and assess the following information:

	2017	2016
Cost of merchandise sold to customers in sales transactions	$480,000	$320,000
Merchandise inventory balance, beginning of year...	?	84,000
Invoice cost of merchandise purchases	510,000	240,000
Shrinkage determined at end of year..	2,500	14,000
Cost of transportation-in..	25,500	12,000
Cost of merchandise returned by customers and restored to inventory	115,000	22,400
Purchase discounts received..	5,100	2,400
Purchase returns and allowances received	2,550	1,200

Required Using the elements of critical thinking described on the inside front cover, comment.

Cumulative Comprehension Problem: Echo Systems

Echo Systems—perpetual or periodic

Note: Solutions are available for both perpetual and periodic.

(The first three segments of this comprehensive problem were presented in Chapters 2, 3, and 4. If those segments have not been completed, the assignment can begin at this point. However, you should use the Working Papers[19] that accompany this text because they reflect the account balances that resulted from posting the entries required in Chapters 2, 3, and 4.)

CHECK FIGURES: 4. Profit = $23,198; 6. Total current assets = $162,358; Total assets = $208,858

Earlier segments of this problem have described how Mary Graham created Echo Systems on October 1, 2017. The company has been successful, and its list of customers has started to grow. To accommodate the growth, the accounting system is ready to be modified to set up separate accounts for each customer. The following list of customers includes the account number used for each account and any balance as of the end of 2017. Graham decided to add a fourth digit with a decimal point to the 106 account number that had been used for the single Accounts Receivable account. This modification allows the existing chart of accounts to continue being used. The list also shows the balances that two customers owed as of December 31, 2017:

Customer Account	No.	Dec. 31 Balance
Alamo Engineering Co...	106.1	-0-
Buckman Services..	106.2	-0-
Capital Leasing	106.3	-0-
Decker Co..	106.4	$2,700
Elite Corporation	106.5	-0-
Fostek Co.	106.6	$3,000
Grandview Co...	106.7	-0-
Hacienda, Inc...	106.8	-0-
Images, Inc..	106.9	-0-

---

19 If students have not purchased the Working Papers package, the Working Papers for the Serial Problem are available on Connect.

In response to frequent requests from customers, Graham has decided to begin selling computer software. The company will extend credit terms of 1/10, n/30 to customers who purchase merchandise. No cash discount will be available on consulting revenue. The following additional accounts were added to the general ledger to allow the system to account for the company's new merchandising activities:

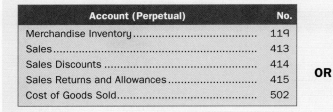

Account (Perpetual)	No.
Merchandise Inventory	119
Sales	413
Sales Discounts	414
Sales Returns and Allowances	415
Cost of Goods Sold	502

OR

Account (Periodic)	No.
Merchandise Inventory	119
Sales	413
Sales Discounts	414
Sales Returns and Allowances	415
Purchases	505
Purchase Returns and Allowances	506
Purchase Discounts	507
Transportation-In	508

Because the accounting system does not use reversing entries, all revenue and expense accounts have zero balances as of January 1, 2018.

Required

1. Prepare journal entries to record each of the following transactions for Echo Systems, assuming either a perpetual system or a periodic system.

2018

Jan. 4   Paid Carly Smith for five days at the rate of $200 per day, including one day in addition to the four unpaid days from the prior year.

5   Mary Graham invested an additional $48,000 cash in the business.

7   Purchased $11,200 of merchandise from Shephard Corp. with terms of 1/10, n/30, FOB shipping point.

9   Received $3,000 from Fostek Co. as final payment on its account.

11   Completed five-day project for Alamo Engineering Co. and billed them $9,000, which is the total price of $12,000 less the advance payment of $3,000.

13   Sold merchandise with a retail value of $8,400 and a cost of $6,720 to Elite Corporation with terms of 1/10, n/30, FOB shipping point.

15   Paid $1,400 for freight charges on the merchandise purchased on January 7.

16   Received $6,000 cash from Grandview Co. for computer services.

17   Paid Shephard Corp. for the purchase on January 7.

20   Elite Corporation returned $800 of defective merchandise from its purchase on January 13. The returned merchandise, which had a cost of $640, was scrapped.

22   Received the balance due from Elite Corporation.

24   Returned defective merchandise to Shephard Corp. and accepted credit against future purchases. Its cost, net of the discount, was $792.

26   Purchased $16,000 of merchandise from Shephard Corp. with terms of 1/10, n/30, FOB destination.

26   Sold merchandise with a cost of $9,280 for $11,600 on credit to Hacienda, Inc.

29   Received a $792 credit memo from Shephard Corp. concerning the merchandise returned on January 24.

31   Paid Carly Smith for 10 days' work at $200 per day.

Feb. 1   Paid $6,750 to the Lakeshore Mall for another three months' rent in advance.

3   Paid Shephard Corp. for the balance due.

5   Paid $1,600 to the local newspaper for advertising.

11   Received the balance due from Alamo Engineering Co. for revenue billed on January 11.

15   Mary Graham withdrew $9,600 cash for personal use.

23   Sold merchandise with a cost of $5,120 for $6,400 on credit to Grandview Co.; terms 1/10, n/30.

26   Paid Carly Smith for eight days' work at $200 per day.

27   Reimbursed Mary Graham's business automobile expenses for 600 kilometres at $1.00 per kilometre.

Mar.	8	Purchased $4,800 of computer supplies from Abbott Office Products on credit.
	9	Received the balance due from Grandview Co. for merchandise sold on February 23.
	11	Repaired the company's computer paying cash of $1,720.
	16	Received $8,520 cash from Images, Inc. for computing services.
	19	Paid the full amount due to Abbott Office Products, including amounts created on December 17 and March 8.
	24	Billed Capital Leasing for $11,800 of computing services.
	25	Sold merchandise with a cost of $2,004 for $3,600 on credit to Buckman Services.
	30	Sold merchandise with a cost of $2,200 for $4,440 on credit to Decker Company.
	31	Reimbursed Mary Graham's business automobile expenses for 400 kilometres at $1.00 per kilometre.

2. Post the journal entries to the accounts in the company's general ledger. (Use asset, liability, and equity accounts that start with balances as of December 31, 2017.)

3. Prepare a partial work sheet consisting of the first six columns showing the unadjusted trial balance, the March 31 adjustments described in (a) through (g) below, and the adjusted trial balance. *Do not prepare closing entries and do not journalize the adjusting entries or post them to the ledger.*

   a. The March 31 computer supplies on hand is $4,230.

   b. Three more months have passed since the company purchased the annual insurance policy at the cost of $4,320.

   c. Carly Smith has not been paid for seven days of work.

   d. Three months have passed since any prepaid rent cost has been transferred to expense. The monthly rent is $2,250.

   e. Depreciation on the computer for January through March is $2,250.

   f. Depreciation on the office equipment for January through March is $1,500.

   g. The March 31 inventory of merchandise is $1,960.

4. Prepare an interim single-step income statement for the three months ended March 31, 2018. List all expenses without differentiating between selling expenses and general and administrative expenses.

5. Prepare an interim statement of changes in equity for the three months ended March 31, 2018.

6. Prepare an interim classified balance sheet as of March 31, 2018.

Inventory Costing and Valuation

A Look Back

Chapter 5 focused on the final steps of the accounting process. We explained how reporting merchandising activities differs from reporting service activities. We also analyzed and recorded merchandise purchases and sales transactions, and explained the adjustments and financial statement presentation for merchandisers.

A Look at This Chapter

This chapter extends our analysis of merchandising activities, emphasizing concepts such as costing and valuation. Topics include the items in inventory, costs assigned, costing methods used, and inventory estimation techniques.

© Amazon.com

© Bloomberg/Getty Images

LEARNING OBJECTIVES

LO1 Identify the components and costs included in merchandise inventory.

LO2 Calculate cost of goods sold and merchandise inventory using specific identification, moving weighted average, and FIFO—perpetual.

LO3 Analyze the effects of the costing methods on financial reporting.

LO4 Calculate the lower of cost and net realizable value of inventory.

LO5 Analyze the effects of inventory errors on current and future financial statements—perpetual.

LO6 Apply both the gross profit and retail inventory methods to estimate inventory.

LO7 Assess inventory management using both inventory turnover and days' sales in inventory.

*Appendix 6A

LO8 Calculate cost of goods sold and merchandise inventory using FIFO—periodic, weighted average, and specific identification.

LO9 Analyze the effects of inventory errors on current and future financial statements—periodic.

Amazon.com: A Leader in Retail Innovation

Jeff Bezos, founder and CEO of Amazon.com, is known for his innovation and outside-the-box thinking when it comes to meeting customer needs and standing out from the competition. He is committed to having the largest selection of items and the best pricing, and is dedicated to providing engaged customer service. The company's many technological initiatives includes introducing new products and aligning with Amazon's mission to "be Earth's most customer-centric company where people can find and discover anything they want to buy online." These advances include products such as FireTV, Amazon Fire Phone, and Amazon Kindle Fire tablets. Amazon is demonstrating to customers that it is a one-stop shop for everything they can dream of. To showcase its new devices to consumers, this mega online retailer recently opened a brick-and-mortar store in New York City and began operating popup kiosks in other major cities.

Amazon acquired the robotics company Kiva Systems in March 2012 with the intent to improve warehouse efficiency and tighten delivery timelines for customers. Amazon workers used to walk many miles a day to fulfill customer orders with over 150 million inventory items to manage, and a 500,000 square foot warehouse (refer to the YouTube video below illustrating the warehouse functionality, "Inside One of Amazon's Busiest Days" presented by CNN).

With the new Kiva robots, all inventory is stored on "pods," which function similar to a portable shelf. Upon receipt of merchandise inventory, each item is scanned, assigned a location in inventory, and stored in their up to-date perpetual inventory records. At the time the customer executes an online purchase, the item's location is retrieved digitally by the Kiva robot and is used to direct the robot to the inventory item in the warehouse. Upon arriving at the appropriate pod storing the item, the robot connects itself to the shelf and delivers the shelf to human workers who pack the items in boxes and send them off for shipment. With the deployment of 10,000 robots in fiscal 2014, the workers are better able to focus their time and efforts on packing goods and expediting them to the customer. The YouTube video "High-Speed Robots Part 1: Meet BettyBot in 'Human Exclusion Zone' Warehouses-The Window-WIRED" demonstrates the way these Kiva robots navigate through a complex warehouse to bring the products to the packer for packing and shipping.

The company has expanded same-day delivery with "get it today" capabilities on over a million eligible items. Amazon Prime usage is expanding with customers benefiting from free two-day delivery and access to free movies, games, and TV episodes for an annual membership fee of $99. Amazon Prime Air is the company's latest R&D initiative that has developed drones called octocopters (depicted in the accompanying photo) to pick up products in small yellow buckets at Amazon's warehouse and deliver them to customers in as little as 30 minutes after purchase at Amazon.com.

Amazon is currently waiting for the Federal Aviation Administration to grant approval for the drones and develop regulations for unmanned aerial vehicles. In March 2015, Amazon was granted approval to test the drone delivery system in highly monitored conditions, and US Patent and Trademark office has published Amazon's patent application for the drone delivery system. In the meantime, Amazon continues to impress consumers with its incredible selection of online goods, competitive pricing, and quick delivery options. In its 2014 annual report, Amazon had $8.2 billion in inventory and discloses that it accounts for its inventory using the First-In First-Out Inventory Costing method, which assumes that inventory is sold in the order it is acquired, as is demonstrated later in this chapter.

Sources: http://www.amazon.com/b?node=8037720011; www.amazon.com; http://www.kivasystems.com/amazon-press/; Amazon.com 2013 annual report; Amazon.com 2014 annual report; http://www.cnn.com/2015/05/12/politics/amazon-patent-drone-delivery/

Video Links:

"Inside One of Amazon's Busiest Days," presented by CNN Money, demonstrates the inventory management required to fulfill a customer order before the Kiva robots. https://www.youtube.com/watch?v=Z2BsOnqVyqs

Kiva robots' assistance in warehouse management is presented in the following YouTube video 'High-Speed Robots Part 1: Meet BettyBot in "Human Exclusion Zone" Warehouses-The Window-WIRED' https://www.youtube.com/watch?v=8gy5tYVR-28

Amazon octocopter drones presented by Peter Mansbridge of CBC news in the following YouTube video: https://www.youtube.com/watch?v=8N87xtfp9JQ

Would Amazon have a merchandise turnover similar to **Lululemon Athletica's**? Explain why or why not. What does "inventory demand planning" refer to? What would the effect be of cost-saving strategies on the weighted average cost of inventory?

CHAPTER PREVIEW

In the previous chapter, we developed an understanding of how critical inventory management is to a merchandiser and gained an understanding of how both purchases and sales of merchandise are recorded in the accounting records and the related financial statement presentation. In this chapter, we extend our study and analysis of inventory by identifying the items that are included in the cost of inventory and we determine how purchase costs are applied to inventory. We will also consider the impact to financial statements when declines occur in the market values of inventory. We also explain methods used to assign costs to merchandise inventory and to cost of goods sold. The principles and methods we describe are used

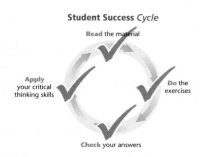

Student Success *Cycle*

Read the material

Apply your critical thinking skills

Do the exercises

Check your answers

in department stores, grocery stores, and many other merchandising companies that purchase products for resale. These principles and methods affect reported amounts of profit, assets, and equity. Understanding these fundamental concepts of inventory accounting increases our ability to analyze and interpret financial statements. As is the case for Amazon in the opening article, an understanding of these topics also helps in managing inventory.

A major goal in accounting for inventory is matching relevant costs against revenues. This is important in order to calculate profit appropriately.[1] We use the matching principle when accounting for inventory to decide how much of the cost of the goods available for sale is assigned to cost of goods sold, matching with current period sales and how much is carried forward as inventory, and matching against future sales. Management must make this decision and several others when accounting for inventory, including the following items:

- Items included in inventory and their costs
- Costing method (specific identification, moving weighted average, or FIFO)
- Inventory system (perpetual or periodic)
- Use of net realizable value or other estimates.

These selections affect the reported amounts for inventory, cost of goods sold, gross profit, profit, current assets, and other accounts. This chapter discusses all of these important issues and their reporting effects.

Inventory Items and Costs

Items in Merchandise Inventory

LO1 Identify the components and costs included in merchandise inventory.

Merchandise inventory includes all goods owned by a company and held for sale in the ordinary course of business[2]. This rule holds regardless of where goods are located at the time inventory is

---

1 IFRS 2014, IAS 2, para. 1.
2 IFRS 2014, IAS 2 para. 6 includes other items such as those in production to be later sold as inventory and materials or supplies used in the production process.

counted. Most inventory items are easy to identify when applying this rule, but certain items require special attention. These include goods in transit, goods on consignment, and goods damaged or obsolete.

GOODS IN TRANSIT

Do we include in inventory goods that are in transit from a supplier? Our answer depends on whether the rights and risks of ownership have passed from the supplier to the purchaser: whether the goods are FOB shipping point or FOB destination. If ownership has passed to the purchaser, they are included in the purchaser's inventory. Recall from Chapter 5 that items purchased FOB shipping point must be included in the purchaser's inventory from the point they leave the supplier's shipping docks. Items purchased FOB destination will be included in inventory until the time they reach the purchaser's receiving department. If it is not clear, it can be helpful to ask: if the goods were damaged in transit, which company's insurance policy would cover the loss? If the company's policy would cover the loss, it likely has title to the goods.

GOODS ON CONSIGNMENT

Goods on consignment are goods shipped by their owner, called the **consignor**, to another party called the **consignee**. A consignee is to sell goods for the owner without ever having legal title to the goods. Consigned goods are owned by the consignor and are reported in the consignor's inventory. The consignee acts as an agent to attempt to sell the item for the consignor. The consignee collects a commission on the sale when it finds a buyer for the item(s).

GOODS DAMAGED OR OBSOLETE

Damaged goods and obsolete (or expired) goods are not counted in inventory if they are not in a saleable condition. If these goods can be sold at a reduced price, they are included in inventory at their *net realizable value*. **Net realizable value (NRV)** is expected selling price minus the cost of making the sale. The period when damage or obsolescence (or deterioration) occurs is the period where the loss is reported. This is consistent with the GAAP relevance principle, as obsolete goods would result in overvalued inventory.

Costs of Merchandise Inventory

Costs included in merchandise inventory include all expenditures necessary, directly or indirectly, to bringing an item to a saleable condition and location.[3] This means the cost of an inventory item includes:

> **Purchase price**
>
> − Discounts provided by supplier (trade discounts/rebates)
> + Incidental costs necessary to put inventory in a place and condition for sale
> _____
> Cost of Inventory

Added or incidental costs can include import duties, transportation-in, storage, insurance, nonrecoverable taxes such as PST (see Appendix 5B), and handling and costs incurred in an aging process where the aging contributes to the value of the product produced (for example, aging of wine and cheese).

---

3 IFRS 2014, IAS 2, para. 10–22.

Accounting principles imply that incidental costs are assigned to every unit purchased. This is so that all inventory costs are properly matched against revenue in the period when inventory is sold. The **materiality principle**[4] states that an amount may not be ignored if its effect on the financial statements could impact the decisions of financial statement users. The *materiality principle* is relied on by some companies as the reason some incidental costs are not allocated to inventory. These companies argue either that incidental costs are immaterial or that the effort in assigning these costs to inventory outweighs the benefits. Such companies price inventory using invoice prices only. When this is done, the incidental costs are allocated to cost of goods sold in the period when they are incurred.

Physical Count of Merchandise Inventory

To help determine the dollar amount of inventory included on financial statements, units on hand need to be confirmed through a **physical count**. This often is performed as close as possible to the end of the fiscal year. Accuracy of inventory records at a company's fiscal year-end is important, as it is a significant current asset on a merchandising company's balance sheet.

The physical count is used to adjust the Merchandise Inventory account balance to the actual inventory on hand. In a perpetual inventory system inventory units can be different than the number of items recorded in the system due to errors, shrinkage, and obsolescence issues. A physical count enables companies to update their accounting records to reflect the true quantity of items available to be sold as inventory.

If the units counted in inventory are lower than the quantity in the accounting records, Cost of Goods Sold is debited and Merchandise Inventory is credited for the total value of inventory that was missing. If the inventory count identifies more inventory than the inventory records show, the entry is the opposite. Differences occur because of events including theft, loss, damage, and errors. If a periodic system is used, the inventory count is mandatory, as it determines how much merchandise inventory is on hand. Any differences automatically get booked to Cost of Goods Sold (Remember: under periodic: Beginning Inventory + Purchases − Ending Inventory = COGS).

EXHIBIT 6.1

Inventory Ticket

---

4 IFRS 2014, "Framework," para. QC 11.

When performing a physical count of inventory, *internal controls* should be followed to minimize errors. **Internal controls**, discussed in more detail in Chapter 7, are the policies and procedures used to protect assets, ensure reliable accounting, promote efficient operations, and urge adherence to company policies. To improve inventory management controls, some companies perform cycle counts, adopting an approach of regularly counting different sections of their inventory throughout the fiscal year. An important control is restricting movement of inventory during the count, which is critical to ensure the accuracy of the count. An example of an internal control technique is the use of pre-numbered inventory tickets, one for each product on hand, to reduce the risk of items being counted more than once or omitted. We show a typical inventory ticket in Exhibit 6.1. By multiplying the number of units counted for each product by its unit cost, we get the dollar amount for each product in inventory. The sum total of all products is the dollar amount reported for inventory on the balance sheet.

In lieu of inventory tickets, the merchandise inventory items of many businesses are labelled with UPC (Universal Product Code) bar codes. The UPC bar codes not only are used for the pricing and costing of sales, but also make physical counts easier, as items can be scanned using handheld scanners and can be tracked electronically.

DECISION INSIGHT

If you look at any grocery product, you will find a UPC bar code printed on the package. Universal Product Codes were created in 1973 to assist in the checkout and inventory process of grocery stores, and UPC bar codes have since spread to nearly every item in the retail world. The Uniform Code Council (UCC) is responsible for issuing the manufacturer's portion of the code. The manufacturer's UPC coordinator assigns the next digits as the item number. The retailer can then assign a price to each individual UPC code along with costing information. In this way, inventory and sales records can be updated instantly when the bar code is scanned.

CHECKPOINT

1. If SodaStream sells goods to Best Buy with terms FOB SodaStream's factory, does SodaStream or Best Buy report these goods in its inventory when they are in transit?
2. The Vancouver Art Gallery purchases a painting for $11,400. Additional costs in obtaining and offering the artwork for sale include $130 for transportation-in, $150 for import duties, $100 for insurance during shipment, $180 for advertising, $400 for framing, and $800 for sales salaries. For calculating inventory cost, what is assigned to the painting?

Do Quick Study questions: QS 6-1, QS 6-2, QS 6-3, QS 6-4

Assigning Costs to Inventory

LO2 Calculate cost of goods sold and merchandise inventory using specific identification, moving weighted average, and FIFO—perpetual.

One of the most important decisions in accounting for inventory is determining how the per-unit costs will be assigned to inventory items. When all units are purchased at the same unit cost, this process is simple, but when identical items are purchased at different costs, a question arises as to what amounts are recorded in cost of goods sold when sales occur and what dollar value should remain in inventory.

Important Tip: When using a perpetual inventory system, we must record inventory transactions both at the time of purchase as a debit to inventory and as sales occur, updating cost of goods sold and crediting inventory.

Recall that a periodic inventory system determines cost of goods sold and inventory amounts at the end of a period based on a physical count. How we assign these costs to inventory and cost of goods sold affects the reported amounts for both systems, as shown in Exhibit 6A.5.

Three methods are often used in assigning costs to inventory and cost of goods sold:

- First-in, first-out (FIFO)
- Moving weighted average
- Specific identification.

Each method assumes a particular pattern for how costs flow through inventory. All three methods are accepted under GAAP and are described in this section.[5] The last-in, first-out (LIFO) method is another way to assign costs to inventory and is popular in the United States, but it is not permitted under GAAP or the Canadian *Income Tax Act*.

If a business has inventory items that are alike and are interchangeable, either the FIFO or moving weighted average method may be used. A business is required to use the specific identification method for inventory items that are individually unique.[6] Examples of inventory where the specific identification method is appropriate include items such as custom furniture where each piece produced is different or cars at an automobile dealership, each with a unique serial number and unique options. Another example is custom jewellery where each item has a unique gem stone weight, cut, and quality, along with a unique gold carat value and weight. **Loblaw Companies Limited** and **Amazon** both chose to use weighted average cost as per their 2013 annual reports. **Lululemon Athletica Inc.** and **Procter & Gamble** use FIFO according to each company's 2014 annual reports. **Tiffany & Co.** discloses in its 2014 annual report that it uses specific item costing for certain diamond and gemstones and average costing for the remaining of its inventory.

Amazon.com Inc. discloses the following accounting policy over inventory in its December 31, 2013, annual report:

> Inventories, consisting of products available for sale, are primarily accounted for using the FIFO method, and are valued at the lower of cost or market value. This valuation requires us to make judgments, based on currently available information, about the likely method of disposition, such as through sales to individual customers, returns to product vendors, or liquidations, and expected recoverable values of each disposition category.
>
> We provide Fulfillment by Amazon services in connection with certain of our sellers' programs. Third-party sellers maintain ownership of their inventory, regardless of whether fulfillment is provided by us or the third-party sellers, and therefore these products are not included in our inventories.

---

5 Physical flow of goods depends on the type of product and the way it is used. Perishable goods such as fresh fruit demand that a business attempt to sell them in a first-in, first-out pattern. Other products such as canned food can often be sold in a random pattern.

6 IFRS 2014, IAS 2, para. 23–25.

Lululemon Athletica Inc. discloses the following significant accounting policy over inventory in its February 2, 2014 Annual Report:

> Inventories, consisting of finished goods and raw materials, are stated at the lower of cost and market value. Cost is determined using weighted-average costs. For finished goods, market is defined as net realizable value, and for raw materials, market is defined as replacement cost. Cost of inventories includes acquisition and production costs including raw material and labor, as applicable, and all costs incurred to deliver inventory, to the Company's distribution centers including freight, non-refundable taxes, duty and other landing costs.

Procter & Gamble Company discloses the following combination of costing methods it applies to different segments of its inventory in its June 30, 2014 Annual Report:

> Inventories are valued at the lower of cost or market value. Product-related inventories are primarily maintained on the first-in, first-out method. Minor amounts of product inventories, including certain cosmetics and commodities, are maintained on the last-in, first-out method. The cost of spare part inventories is maintained using the average-cost method.

Tiffany & Co. discloses its accounting policy for inventory in its January 31, 2014 annual report as follows:

> Inventories are valued at the lower of cost or market using the average cost method except for certain diamond and gemstone jewelry, which uses the specific identification method.

We use fictitious information from MEC, the sporting goods store introduced in the Chapter 5 chapter opening vignette, to illustrate the three methods. Among its many products, assume MEC carries one type of mountain bike. Its mountain bike ("unit") inventory at the beginning of August 2017 and its purchases during August are shown in Exhibit 6.2.

EXHIBIT 6.2

Cost of Goods Available for Sale

			Units		Cost Per Unit		Total Cost
Aug.	1	Beginning inventory	10	@	$ 91	=	$ 910
	3	Purchased...........................	15	@	$106	=	$1,590
	17	Purchased...........................	20	@	$115	=	$2,300
Total goods available for sale			45 Units available for sale				$4,800 Total cost of goods that were available for sale

MEC had two sales of mountain bikes to two different biking clubs in August, as shown in Exhibit 6.3. MEC ends August with 11 bikes in inventory (45 units available for sale less 34 units sold).

EXHIBIT 6.3

Retail Sales of Goods

			Units		Selling Price Per Unit		Total Sales
Aug.	14	Sales	20	@	$133	=	$2,660
	28	Sales	14	@	$150	=	$2,100
			34 Units				$4,760

In this section, we will determine how much of the cost of goods available for sale is to be assigned to cost of goods sold and to ending merchandise inventory using the three different cost flow assumptions.

We explained in the last chapter how use of a perpetual inventory system is increasing dramatically due to advances in accounting software, management information systems, and other related technology. Widespread use of electronic scanners, point-of-sale systems, and product bar codes further encourages its use having the ability to read bar codes and easily track movement of goods. The focus of the next section is assignment of costs to cost of goods sold and merchandise inventory in a perpetual system. The assignment of costs to inventory using a periodic system is discussed in Appendix 6A.

First-In, First-Out

The **first-in, first-out (FIFO)** method of assigning costs to inventory and to goods sold assumes that inventory items are sold in the order acquired. When sales occur, costs of the earliest units purchased are charged to cost of goods sold. This leaves the costs from the most recent purchases in inventory. Use of FIFO for MEC means the costs of mountain bikes are assigned to inventory and goods sold as shown in Exhibit 6.4.

EXHIBIT 6.4

FIFO Calculations—Perpetual

Transaction		Purchases			Sales (at cost)			Inventory Balance		
Transaction	Date	Units	Unit Cost	Total Cost	Units	Unit Cost	Cost of Goods Sold	Units	Unit Cost	Total Cost
Purchase	Aug. 1	Beginning inventory 10 @	$ 91 =	$ 910				10 @	$ 91 =	$ 910
Purchase	Aug. 3	15 @	$106 =	$1,590	① ②			10 @ 15 @	$ 91 = $106 =	$ 910 $1,590
Sale	Aug. 14				10 @ 10 @	$ 91 = $106 =	$ 910 $1,060	③ 5 @	$106 =	$ 530
Purchase	Aug. 17	20 @	$115 =	$2,300				5 @ 20 @	$106 = $115 =	$ 530 $2,300
Sale	Aug. 28				5 @ 9 @	$106 = $115 =	$ 530 $1,035	11 @	$115 =	$1,265
	Totals	45		$4,800	34		$3,535	11		$1,265

Cost of goods available for sale   =   Cost of goods sold   +   Ending inventory

① Under FIFO, units are assumed to be sold in the order acquired; therefore, of the 20 units sold on August 14, the first 10 units come from beginning inventory.

② The remaining 10 units sold on August 14 come from the next purchase, August 3.

③ All of the units from beginning inventory have been sold but 5 units remain from the August 3 purchase.

MEC's cost of goods sold on the income statement is $3,535 (= $910 + $1,060 + $530 + $1,035) and its ending inventory reported on the balance sheet is $1,265.

Moving Weighted Average

The **moving weighted average** inventory costing method under a perpetual inventory system requires calculating the average cost per unit of merchandise inventory at the time of each purchase. The average is calculated by dividing the cost of goods available for sale by the units on hand. Using the moving weighted average method for MEC means the costs of mountain bikes are assigned to inventory and goods sold as shown in Exhibit 6.5.

EXHIBIT 6.5

Moving Weighted Average Calculations—Perpetual

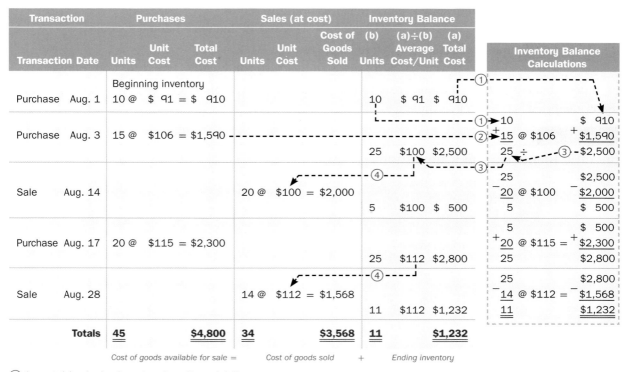

Transaction		Purchases			Sales (at cost)			Inventory Balance				Inventory Balance Calculations
Transaction	Date	Units	Unit Cost	Total Cost	Units	Unit Cost	Cost of Goods Sold	(b) Units	(a)÷(b) Average Cost/Unit	(a) Total Cost		
Purchase	Aug. 1	Beginning inventory 10 @ $ 91 = $ 910						10	$ 91	$ 910	①	
Purchase	Aug. 3	15 @ $106 = $1,590						10		$ 910 ① ►10		
								25	$100	$2,500	② +15 @ $106 +$1,590 25 ÷ ③ -$2,500
Sale	Aug. 14				20 @ $100 = $2,000						25 $2,500 ④ ¯20 @ $100 ¯$2,000
								5	$100	$ 500	5 $ 500
Purchase	Aug. 17	20 @ $115 = $2,300									5 $ 500 +20 @ $115 = +$2,300
								25	$112	$2,800	25 $2,800
Sale	Aug. 28				14 @ $112 = $1,568						25 $2,800 ④ ¯14 @ $112 = ¯$1,568
								11	$112	$1,232	11 $1,232
Totals		45		$4,800	34		$3,568	11		$1,232	

Cost of goods available for sale = Cost of goods sold + Ending inventory

① August 1 beginning inventory in units and dollars.

② August 1 beginning inventory is added to the purchase of August 3 to determine the total cost of the units in inventory on August 3.

③ The total cost of all units, at $2,500, is divided by the total number of units, 25 units, to get the average cost per unit of $100 on August 3.

④ The most current weighted average cost is assigned as the cost per unit sold.

Under the moving weighted average method (MWA) MEC's cost of goods sold reported on the income statement is $3,568 (= $2,000 + $1,568) and its ending inventory reported on the balance sheet is $1,232. Refer to Exhibit 6.7 for a comparison of the methods. The inventory balance is lower using the MWA method compared to FIFO in this example. Notice how the cost of goods sold is higher using the MWA compared to FIFO.

> **Important Tip:** The moving weighted average perpetual system often raises a rounding problem in the calculations because the currency figures are limited to two decimal places. The typical solution is to adjust or "plug" the inventory figure after calculating the cost of goods sold amount at the moving weighted average cost.

Specific Identification

The **specific identification** method applies best when each item sold and remaining in inventory can be directly identified with a unique identifier, as costs can then be tracked and assigned to each item sold. MEC's internal documents indicate the following details regarding purchases made in August:

August 1, 10 red MEC brand 16″ boys bikes were purchased at a cost of $91

August 3, 15 green MEC brand 16″ limited edition boys bikes were purchased at a cost of $106

August 17, 20 silver MEC brand 16″ anniversary edition boys bikes were purchased at a cost of $115

MEC's internal documents reveal the following items were sold during August:

August 14, 20 units were sold:	8 red MEC brand 16″ bikes
	12 green MEC brand 16″ limited edition boys bikes
August 28, 14 units were sold:	2 red MEC brand 16″ bikes
	12 silver anniversary edition MEC brand 16″ boys bikes.

Specific identification assigns costs to the goods sold and to ending inventory based on specific items identified, as shown in Exhibit 6.6.

EXHIBIT 6.6

Specific Identification Calculations—Perpetual

Date	Purchases			Sales (at cost)			Inventory Balance		
	Units	Unit Cost	Total Cost	Units	Unit Cost	Cost of Goods Sold	Units	Unit Cost	Total Cost
Aug. 1	Beginning inventory								
	10 @	$ 91	= $ 910				10 @	$ 91 =	$ 910
3	15 @	$106	= $1,590				10 @	$ 91 =	$ 910
							15 @	$106 =	$1,590
14				8 @	$ 91	= $ 728	2 @	$ 91 =	$ 182
				12 @	$106	= $1,272	3 @	$106 =	$ 318
							2 @	$ 91 =	$ 182
							3 @	$106 =	$ 318
17	20 @	$115	= $2,300				20 @	$115 =	$2,300
28				2 @	$ 91	= $ 182	3 @	$106 =	$ 318
				12 @	$115	= $1,380	8 @	$115 =	$ 920
Totals	45		$4,800	34		$3,562	11		$1,238

Cost of goods available for sale = Cost of goods sold + Ending inventory

① Of the 10 units from beginning inventory, 8 were specifically identified as the red MEC brand 16″ boys bike being sold.

② Of the 10 units from beginning inventory, 2 red MEC brand 16″ bikes remain in ending inventory.

③ Of the 15 units purchased on August 3, 12 green MEC brand 16″ bikes were specifically identified as being sold.

④ Of the 15 units purchased on August 3, 3 green MEC brand 16″ bikes remain in ending inventory.

When using specific identification, MEC's cost of goods sold reported on the income statement is $3,562 (= $728 + $1,272 + $182 + $1,380) and its ending inventory reported on the balance sheet is $1,238.

As mentioned previously, the specific identification method works best when each item of inventory is unique or different, as in an antique store, an art gallery, or a custom furniture manufacturer. For example, a car dealership would use specific identification because each car has a unique serial number, known as the vehicle identification number (VIN). In all cases where specific identification is used, each inventory item needs to be identified separately.

When inventory items are similar (such as bags of sugar, pallets of concrete blocks, or loaves of bread), specific units being purchased and sold cannot be easily traced; large quantities are often purchased at different times, possibly with different costs. When the cost is greater than the benefit of tracking the sale of individual units that are similar, one of the other methods may be better conceptually and more efficient to use.

Notice in Exhibit 6.7 that the total units and cost of the goods available for sale are the same regardless of the method used. What is different is the dollar amount assigned to the ending inventory and the cost of goods sold. In this example, the FIFO method would result in the higher gross profit and profit. FIFO also provided MEC a higher inventory value on the balance sheet. Once an inventory costing accounting policy is selected, companies are expected to consistently apply the same policy year after year.

EXHIBIT 6.7

Comparison of Inventory Methods

	FIFO		Moving Weighted Average		Specific Identification	
	Units	$	Units	$	Units	$
Cost of Goods Sold (or Cost of Sales)	34	$3,535	34	$3,568	34	$3,562
Ending Inventory	11	1,265	11	1,232	11	1,238
Goods Available for Sale	45	$4,800	45	$4,800	45	$4,800

Inventory Costing and Technology

A perpetual inventory system can be kept in either electronic or manual form. A manual form is often too costly for businesses, especially those with many purchases and sales or many units in inventory. Advances in information technology and accounting software systems have greatly reduced the cost of an electronic perpetual inventory system, and many companies are now asking whether they can afford not to have one. This is because timely access to information is being used strategically by companies to gain a competitive advantage. Scanned sales data, for instance, can reveal crucial information on buying patterns, and can also help companies target promotional and advertising activities. These and other applications have greatly increased the use of the perpetual system.

DECISION INSIGHT

Loblaw's Corporate Grocery Stores Go Perpetual

Loblaw Companies Limited, identifies its upgrade of its IT infrastructure as a positive move to enable the company to develop a more precise estimate through a "system-generated average cost." The company estimates "the impact of this inventory measurement and other conversion differences associated with implementation of a perpetual inventory system to be a $190 million decrease to the value of the inventory."

SOURCES: http://www.loblaw.ca/English/Media-Centre/news-releases/news-release-details/2014/Loblaw-Companies-Limited-Reports-a-651-Increase-in-Adjusted-Operating-Income2-for-the-Second-Quarter-of-20141/default.aspx
http://www.marketwatch.com/story/loblaw-companies-limited-reports-a-651-increase-in-adjusted-operating-income2-for-the-second-quarter-of-20141-2014-07-24
http://www.retailingtoday.com/article/loblaw-embarks-its-next-chapter
http://www.prnewswire.com/news-releases/loblaw-companies-limited-reports-a-651-increase-in-adjusted-operating-income2-for-the-second-quarter-of-20141-268417412.html

CHECKPOINT

3. What fundamental accounting principle relates most closely with the costs allocations of cost of goods available for sale between ending inventory and cost of goods sold?

Do Quick Study questions: QS 6-5, QS 6-6, QS 6-7, QS 6-8

MID-CHAPTER DEMONSTRATION PROBLEM

Graphic Artz Co. uses a perpetual inventory system and had the following beginning inventory and purchases during January 2017:

Date		Units	Item X Unit Cost		Total Cost
Jan. 1	Inventory	300	@ $14	=	$ 4,200
16	Purchase	200	@ 15	=	3,000
20	Purchase	300	@ 16	=	4,800
	Total units and cost of goods available for sale	800			$12,000

Sales of units were as follows (all on credit):

Jan.	15	200 units at $30
	28	460 units at $35
	Total units sold.....................	660

Additional data for use in applying the specific identification method:
The specific units sold were:

Jan.	15	200 units from the January 1 units on hand
	28	75 units from the January 1 units on hand
		150 units from the January 16 purchase, and
		235 units from the January 20 purchase

Required

1. Calculate the ending inventory and the cost of goods sold under a perpetual inventory system by applying each of the three different methods of inventory costing:

   a. FIFO
   b. Moving weighted average
   c. Specific identification

2. Using your calculations from Part 1, record the purchase on January 16 and the sale on January 28 for each of:

   a. FIFO
   b. Moving weighted average
   c. Specific identification

Analysis Component:

A new supplier has approached Graphic Artz Co., offering to supply the merchandise inventory at a cost of $11 per unit. What should the company consider when deciding whether or not to change to the new supplier?

Planning the Solution

- Prepare a perpetual FIFO schedule showing the composition of beginning inventory and how the composition of inventory changes after each purchase of inventory and after each sale.

- Make a schedule of purchases and sales, recalculating the average cost of inventory after each purchase to arrive at the moving weighted average cost of ending inventory. Add up the average costs associated with each sale to determine the cost of goods sold using the moving weighted average method.

- Prepare a schedule showing the calculation of the cost of goods sold and ending inventory using the specific identification method. Use the information provided to determine the cost of the specific units sold and which specific units remain in inventory.

- Journalize the purchase on January 16 and the sale on January 28 by taking the relevant information from the schedules prepared in Part 1 for each method.

- Prepare an answer to the analysis question.

Solution

1a. FIFO Perpetual

Date	Purchases			Sales (at cost)			Inventory Balance		
	Units	**Unit Cost**	**Total Cost**	**Units**	**Unit Cost**	**Cost of Goods Sold**	**Units**	**Unit Cost**	**Total Cost**
Jan. 1	Beginning inventory				①		300 @	$14 =	$4,200
	300 @	$14 =	$ 4,200					②	
15				200 @	$14 =	$2,800	100 @	$14 =	$1,400
16	200 @	$15 =	$ 3,000				100 @	$14 =	$1,400
							200 @	$15 =	$3,000
20	300 @	$16 =	$ 4,800		③		100 @	$14 =	$1,400
							200 @	$15 =	$3,000
							300 @	$16 =	$4,800
28				100 @	$14 =	$1,400	④		
				200 @	$15 =	$3,000			
				160 @	$16 =	$2,560	140 @	$16 =	$2,240
Totals	**800**		**$12,000**	**660**		**$9,760**	**140**		**$2,240**

Cost of goods available for sale = Cost of goods sold + Ending inventory

① Under FIFO, units are assumed to be sold in the order acquired; therefore, the 200 units sold on January 15 come from beginning inventory.

② The 100 units remaining in inventory after the January 15 sale are from beginning inventory.

③ The 460 units sold on January 28 are assumed to be the 100 units from beginning inventory, plus the 200 units purchased on January 16, plus 160 units from the January 20 purchase.

④ All of the units remaining in inventory after the January 28 sale are from the January 20 purchase.

1b. Moving Weighted Average Perpetual

Date	Purchases			Sales (at cost)			Inventory Balance				Inventory Balance Calculations
	Units	Unit Cost	Total Cost	Units	Unit Cost	Cost of Goods Sold	(b) Units	(a) ÷ (b) Average Cost/Unit	(a) Total Cost		
Jan. 1	Beginning inventory 300 @ $14 = $4,200						300 @ $14.00 = $4,200.00				
15				200 @ $14.00 = $2,800.00			100 @ $14.00 = $1,400.00				300 $4,200.00 −200 @ $14.00 = −$2,800.00 100 $1,400.00
16	200 @ $15 = $3,000						300 @ $14.67 = $4,400.00				100 $1,400.00 +200 @ $15.00 = +$3,000.00 300 $4,400.00
20	300 @ $16 = $4,800						600 @ $15.33 = $9,200.00				300 $4,400.00 +300 @ $16.00 = +$4,800.00 600 $9,200.00
28				460 @ $15.33 = $7,051.80			140 @ $15.34* = $2,148.20				600 $9,200.00 −460 @ $15.33 = −$7,051.80 140 $2,148.20
Totals	**800**		**$12,000**	**660**		**$9,851.80**	**140**		**2,148.20**		

Cost of goods available for sale =   Cost of goods sold   +   Ending inventory

*Cost/unit changed due to rounding
① The most current average cost per unit is assigned to the units sold.
② The beginning balance less the units sold equals the remaining inventory.
③ The total cost remaining in inventory divided by the total units remaining equals the average unit cost. Notice that the average unit cost does not change because of a sale.

1c. Specific Identification

Date	Purchases			Sales (at cost)			Inventory Balance		
	Units	Unit Cost	Total Cost	Units	Unit Cost	Cost of Goods Sold	Units	Unit Cost	Total Cost
Jan. 1	Beginning inventory 300 @ $14 = $4,200						300 @	$14 = $4,200	
15				200 @	$14 =	$2,800	100 @	$14 = $1,400	
16	200 @ $15 = $3,000						100 @ 200 @	$14 = $1,400 $15 = $3,000	
20	300 @ $16 = $4,800						100 @ 200 @ 300 @	$14 = $1,400 $15 = $3,000 $16 = $4,800	
28				75 @ $14 = 150 @ $15 = 235 @ $16 =		$1,050 $2,250 $3,760	25 @ 50 @ 65 @	$14 = $ 350 $15 = $ 750 $16 = $1,040	
Totals	**800**		**$12,000**	**660**		**$9,860**	**140**		**$2,140**

Cost of goods available for sale   =   Cost of goods sold   +   Ending inventory

① 200 of the beginning inventory units were specifically identified as being sold on January 15. Therefore, the 100 units remaining on January 15 are identified as units from beginning inventory.
② The units sold on January 28 are specifically identified. The units sold determines exactly which units are remaining.

	a.	b.	c.
	FIFO	**Moving Weighted Average**	**Specific Identification**
2017			
Jan. 16 Merchandise Inventory............................	3,000	3,000	3,000
Accounts Payable	3,000	3,000	3,000
To record purchase of merchandise on credit.			
28 Accounts Receivable.................................	16,100	16,100	16,100
Sales...	16,100	16,100	16,100
To record credit sales; 460 units × $35 − $16,100.			
28 Cost of Goods Sold	6,960	7,052*	7,060
Merchandise Inventory.......................	6,960	7,052*	7,060
To record the sale of merchandise.			

*Rounded to nearest whole dollar for simplicity

Analysis Component:

Graphic Artz Co. should consider the following (as well as other possibilities):

- The quality of the merchandise inventory offered by the new supplier
- Whether the new supplier can meet the company's merchandise inventory quantity needs
- Whether the new supplier will deliver merchandise when required (dependable)
- The payment/delivery terms
- What kind of service the new supplier provides (customer support)
- Whether the new supplier can provide references (from satisfied customers; reputation)
- The duration of the $11 per unit offer and potential price increases

Financial Reporting and Inventory

LO3 Analyze the effects of the costing methods on financial reporting.

This section reviews the financial reporting issues related to inventory, including inventory disclosure, consistency, and prudence. As well, we look at the effects of inventory errors.

Financial Reporting

In our analysis of financial statements, it is important to know and understand inventory costing methods because the method used can have a material impact on the income statement and balance sheet, as illustrated in Exhibit 6.8. For this reason, the company's policy over inventory costing, including a description of the method used, must be *disclosed* in the notes to the financial statements as demonstrated previously for Amazon.com Inc., Lululemon Athletica Inc., Proctor & Gamble Company and Tiffany & Co.

EXHIBIT 6.8

Income Statement and Balance Sheet Effects of Inventory Costing Methods

MEC Income Statement—Mountain Bikes For Month Ended August 31, 2017			
	FIFO	**Moving Weighted Average**	**Specific Identification**
Sales..	$4,760	$4,760	$4,760
Cost of goods sold*.............................	3,535	3,568	3,562
Gross profit from sales.........................	$1,225	$1,192	$1,198
Operating expenses	374	374	374
Profit from operations..........................	$ 851	$ 818	$ 824

*From Exhibit 6.7

Partial Balance Sheet			
Assets			
Current assets:			
Merchandise inventory*..................	$1,265	$1,232	$1,238

*From Exhibit 6.7

When purchase prices do not change, the choice of an inventory costing method is unimportant. All methods assign the same cost amounts when prices remain constant. When purchase prices are rising or falling, however, the methods are likely to assign different cost amounts.

Because MEC's purchase prices rose in August, FIFO assigned the least amount to cost of goods sold. This led to the highest gross profit and the highest profit. This result will always occur in times of rising prices because the most recent and therefore most costly units are in ending inventory, assigning the least expensive units to cost of goods sold.[7]

ETHICS AND INVENTORY MANAGEMENT

Next to cash reserves, inventory is one of the most liquid assets held within a merchandising business and, as seen with Amazon in the chapter opening vignette, it is often one of the most significant in terms of dollar value of assets held. Fraudsters often target inventory either to generate schemes to take inventory for personal use, resell inventory on a secondary market, or attempt to modify inventory pricing through elaborate schemes. *The Wall Street Journal* reports that bar code scams, where consumers change the bar code to modify the cost of goods purchased, and store gift card scams are two ways that technology has negatively impacted the retail space.[8]

Corporations do well to ensure appropriate security measures and policies are in place to prevent theft of goods from the retail store as well as the shipping/receiving docks. To reduce the risk of fraud, employees who have access to the physical goods in the warehouse and retail space should not have access to modify the accounting records or authorize purchase orders. Chapter 7 further discusses appropriate measures to strengthen the organization's control environment.

---

7 The moving weighted average amount can be higher or lower than the FIFO amount depending on whether prices steadily increase or decrease.

8 http://www.wsj.com/articles/SB116174264881702894, accessed June 2015.

Companies should adopt the inventory costing method that best represents the actual cost flow of goods being brought in and sold out of inventory. Because the selection of inventory-costing methods can materially affect amounts on financial statements, some managers may want to adopt the method that provides the most favourable results. For example, if management's bonus plans were based on profit, managers might pick the method that results in the highest bonus each period. If managers were allowed to change methods each period, it would be even more difficult for users of financial statements to compare a company's financial statements from one period to the next. If profit increased, for instance, a user may believe it is due to successful operations and not realize it was due to the accounting method change. Fortunately, accounting standards prevent such questionable activities from occurring.

The **consistency principle** requires a company to use the same accounting methods period after period so that the financial statements are comparable across periods.[9] The consistency principle applies to all accounting methods.

The consistency principle *does not* require a company to use one method exclusively. It can use different methods to value different categories of inventory. As mentioned earlier, **Bombardier Inc.** uses two methods (specific identification and **weighted average**) to assign costs to various types of inventory. Also, the consistency principle does not mean that a company can never change from one accounting method to another. Instead, it means a company must argue that the method to which it is changing will improve its financial reporting. Under this circumstance, a change is acceptable; yet, when such a change is made, the full disclosure principle requires that the notes to the statements report the type of change, its justification, and its effect on profit.[10] A change in accounting policy of this type would also require restating prior period financial statements, demonstrating the overall impact of the change to prior years reported results.

Investors and banks track the working capital ratio of a company very closely and corporate debt covenants often require adherence to a specific working capital ratio (for example, a minimum of 2:1 current assets to current liabilities) or the outstanding principal on the debt becomes immediately due. Inventory balances need to be accurately reported and closely monitored.

 DECISION MAKER   Answer—End of chapter

Inventory Manager—Ethical Dilemma

You are the inventory manager for a trendy urban retail inventory merchandiser. Your compensation includes a bonus plan based on the amount of gross profit reported in the financial statements. Your supervisor comes to you and asks your opinion about changing the inventory costing method from moving weighted average to FIFO. Since costs have been rising and are expected to continue to rise, your superior predicts the company will be more attractive to investors because of the reported higher profit using FIFO. You realize this proposed change will likely increase your bonus as well. What do you recommend?

Exhibit 6.9 summarizes advantages and disadvantages for the cost flow assumptions discussed.

---

9   IFRS 2014, IAS 1, para. 45.

10   IFRS 2014, IAS 8, para. 14–18 and 28–31.

EXHIBIT 6.9

Advantages and Disadvantages of Cost Flow Assumptions

	FIFO	Moving Weighted Average	Specific Identification
Advantages:	Most current values are on the balance sheet as ending inventory	Smooths out purchase price changes.	Exactly matches costs and revenues.
	Matches the flow of goods for many businesses that attempt to sell older inventory first, such as a grocery retailer	Matches the flow of goods for businesses that have a large volume of small items that don't expire, such as a landscape centre selling stones/gravel	Works well for companies that sell differentiated products with a higher dollar value, such as a jewellery store
Disadvantages:	Cost of goods sold does not reflect current costs, so does not accurately match expenses to revenue	Averaging does not accurately match expenses to revenues	Relatively more costly to implement and maintain

CHECKPOINT

4. Give examples of types of businesses that might use specific identification despite the disadvantage indicated in Exhibit 6.9. Explain why these businesses might choose to use specific identification.
5. When costs and prices are rising, what effect does moving weighted average have on a balance sheet compared to FIFO?

Do Quick Study question: QS 6-9

Lower of Cost and Net Realizable Value (LCNRV)

LO4 Calculate the lower of cost and net realizable value of inventory.

The cost of inventory is not necessarily the amount always reported on a balance sheet. The *principle of faithful representation* provides the guidance in reporting inventory at the amount expected to be received on the sale of the inventory item, referred to as net realizable value, if it is lower than the cost of the item in inventory.[11] Merchandise inventory is then reported on the balance sheet at the **lower of cost and net realizable value (LCNRV)**. **Faithful representation** requires that information be complete, neutral, and free from error so that assets and profit are not overstated and liabilities and expenses are not understated.[12]

For example, assume on September 10 **Apple Inc.** announces the upcoming releases of its newest iPhone to be rolled out October 15. Immediately after the announcement, sales of the previous edition begin to plummet as consumers anticipate the new device has an improved feature set. Apple subsequently lowers the price of the older model in order to sell the items. As a result, inventory has to be written down from $50 million and reported at its new NRV of $20 million to ensure assets and profit are not overstated at year-end.

---

11   IFRS 2014, IAS 2, para. 28.
12   IFRS 2014, "Framework," para. QC 12.

If the NRV of the inventory were to recover after the balance sheet date, the inventory write-down would be reversed. The reversal is limited to the amount of the write-down to ensure that inventory is always reported at the lower of cost and NRV. The concept of inventory write-downs and reversals will be demonstrated in the next section.

Danier Leather reports that its inventories are valued at the lower of cost and NRV.

CALCULATING THE LOWER OF COST AND NET REALIZABLE VALUE (LCNRV)

The decline in merchandise inventory from cost to NRV is recorded in an adjusting entry at the end of the period. LCNRV is applied in one of two ways:

(1) Usually item by item, or, when not practicable,

(2) To groups of similar or related items.[13]

We show in Exhibit 6.10 how LCNRV is applied to the ending inventory of MEC.

EXHIBIT 6.10

LCNRV Calculations

Inventory Items	No. of Units	Cost/ Unit	Total Cost	NRV/ Unit	Total NRV	LCNRV applied to: Items	LCNRV applied to: Groups
Bicycles :							
Roadster.............	25	$ 750	$ 18,750	$ 790	$19,750	$ 18,750	
Sprint...............	60	1,100	66,000	1,100	66,000	66,000	
Group subtotal.........			$ 84,750		$85,750		$ 84,750
Kayaks:							
A1 Series............	21	$1,800	$ 37,800	$1,300	$27,300	$ 27,300	
Trax-4...............	29	2,200	63,800	2,250	65,250	63,800	
Group subtotal.........			$101,600		$92,550		$ 92,550
Total inventory........			$186,350			$175,850	$177,300

Using the information in Exhibit 6.10 to demonstrate the application of LCNRV on an item-by-item basis, we see that total LCNRV is $175,850. Therefore, $175,850 must be reported on the balance sheet. To achieve this, inventory needs to be reduced by $10,500, which is the difference between the total cost of $186,350 and total LCNRV of $175,850. The entry is:

Cost of Goods Sold	10,500	
Merchandise Inventory		10,500
To write inventory down to LCNRV;		
$186,350 − $175,850 = $10,500.		

After posting this entry, merchandise inventory would appear on the balance sheet as:

Current assets:	
Cash	$ x,xxx
Accounts receivable	x,xxx
Merchandise inventory, net	**175,850**

---

[13] IFRS 2014, IAS 2, para. 29.

Assume that the A1 Series kayaks in Exhibit 6.10 are still on hand at the end of the next accounting period. There is evidence that their NRV has increased to $1,450 per unit. The original write-down can be reversed (but is limited to the amount of the original write-down).[14] The entry is:

Merchandise Inventory...................................	3,150	
Cost of Goods Sold.............................		3,150
To reverse the inventory write-down;		
$1,450 − $1,300 = $150;		
$150 × 21 units = $3,150.		

Although international standards prefer the application of LCNRV on an item-by-item basis, in certain circumstances, accounting standards permit the application of LCNRV to groups.

To demonstrate the application of LCNRV to groups, refer to the information in Exhibit 6.10. The entry to write inventory down to LCNRV applied to groups is:

Cost of Goods Sold..	9,050	
Merchandise Inventory		9,050
To write inventory down to LCNRV;		
$186,350 − $177,300 = $9,050.		

CHECKPOINT

6. Refer to the information in Exhibit 6.10. Assume that LCNRV was applied to inventory on an item-by-item basis. In the next accounting period, the NRV of the A1 Series kayaks increased to $1,900 per unit because the factory burned down, causing a shortage in the marketplace. MEC had four of the previously written down A1 Series kayaks left in ending inventory a year after the original write-down. What entry, if any, is required in applying LCNRV to the remaining four units?

7. A company's ending inventory includes the following items:

Product	Units on Hand	Unit Cost	NRV Per Unit
A	20	$ 6	$ 5
B	40	9	8
C	10	12	15

Using LCNRV applied separately to individual items, calculate the reported amount for inventory.

Do Quick Study question: QS 6-10

Errors in Reporting Inventory

LO5 Analyze the effects of inventory errors on current and future financial statements—perpetual.

Companies must take care in calculating and taking a physical count of inventory. If inventory is reported in error, it causes misstatements of cost of goods sold, gross profit, profit, current assets, and equity. It also means misstatements will exist in the next period's statements. This is because ending inventory of one period is the beginning inventory of the next. An error carried forward causes

---

14 IFRS 2014, IAS 2, para. 33.

misstatements of the next period's cost of goods sold, gross profit, and profit. Since the inventory amount often is large, misstatements can reduce the usefulness of financial statements.

INCOME STATEMENT EFFECTS

The income statement effects of an inventory error are evident when looking at the components of cost of goods sold in each of the alternative presentations in Exhibit 6.11.

EXHIBIT 6.11

Cost of Goods Sold Components—Periodic

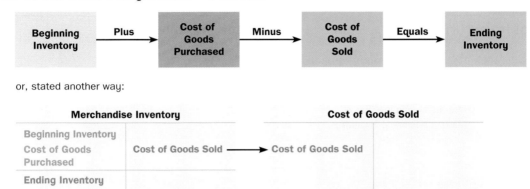

or, stated another way:

The effect of an inventory error on cost of goods sold is determined by calculating the inventory correctly and comparing the result to the result of the calculation when using the incorrect amount, as in Exhibit 6.12.

EXHIBIT 6.12

Effects of $2,000 Overstatement in Ending Inventory for 2017 on Three Periods' Income Statement Information—Perpetual

	For years ended December 31, 2017, 2018, 2019, the income statement information should have been reported as:	Income statement information actually reported for years ended December 31,		
		2017	2018	2019
Sales	$30,000	$30,000	$30,000	$30,000
Cost of goods sold	20,000	18,000	22,000	20,000
Gross profit from sales .	$10,000	$12,000	$ 8,000	$10,000
Operating expenses . . .	5,000	5,000	5,000	5,000
Profit	$ 5,000	$ 7,000	$ 3,000	$ 5,000

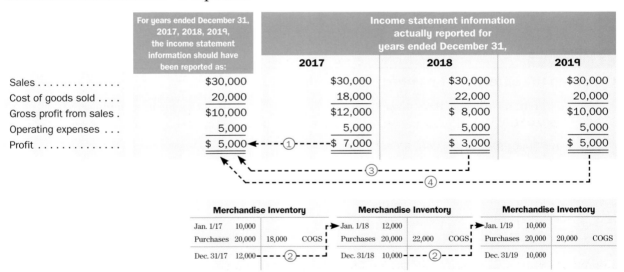

① 2017 profit and gross profit are overstated (too high) and cost of goods sold is understated (too low) when ending inventory is overstated (too high).
② Ending inventory for one period becomes the beginning inventory for the next period, carrying forward any errors that existed.
③ 2018 profit and gross profit are understated (too low) and cost of goods sold is overstated (too high) when beginning inventory is overstated (too high). Notice that the error has reversed itself in 2018, the second year.
④ An inventory error in the year 2017 does not affect 2019.

Exhibit 6.12 assumes that $2,000 of merchandise sold but awaiting delivery was incorrectly included in ending inventory on December 31, 2017. This ending inventory error carries over to the next period as a beginning inventory error yielding a reverse effect. We can see that overstating ending inventory will understate cost of goods sold. An understatement of cost of goods sold yields an overstatement of profit. We can do the same analysis with understating ending inventory and for an error in beginning inventory. Exhibit 6.13 shows the effects of inventory errors on the current period's income statement amounts.

EXHIBIT 6.13

Effect of Inventory Errors on This Period's Income Statement

Inventory Error	Cost of Goods Sold	Profit
Understate ending inventory	Overstated	Understated
Understate beginning inventory	Understated	Overstated
Overstate ending inventory	Understated	Overstated
Overstate beginning inventory	Overstated	Understated

> **Important Tip:** Notice that inventory errors yield opposite effects in cost of goods sold and profit.

Because an inventory error causes an offsetting error in the next period, it is sometimes said to be *self-correcting*. Do not think, however, that this makes inventory errors less serious. Managers, lenders, owners, and other users make important decisions on changes in profit and cost of goods sold. Imagine how a lender's decision would be affected by each of the graphs presented in Exhibit 6.14. Inventory errors must be avoided.

EXHIBIT 6.14

Graphing the Effects of Inventory Errors on Profit

BALANCE SHEET EFFECTS

Balance sheet effects of an inventory error are made evident by looking at the components of the accounting equation in Exhibit 6.15.

EXHIBIT 6.15

Accounting Equation

$$\text{Assets} = \text{Liabilities} + \text{Equity}$$

We can see, for example, that understating ending inventory will understate both current and total assets. An understatement of ending inventory also yields an understatement in equity because of the understatement of profit. We can do the same analysis with overstating ending inventory. Exhibit 6.16 shows the effects of inventory errors on the current period's balance sheet amounts.

EXHIBIT 6.16

Effects of Inventory Errors on This Period's Balance Sheet

Inventory Error	Assets	Equity
Understate ending inventory	Understated	Understated
Overstate ending inventory	Overstated	Overstated

Errors in beginning inventory do not yield misstatements in the balance sheet, but they do affect the end of period income statement, as the error results in a higher cost of goods sold and lower profit (illustrated in the year 2018 in Exhibit 6.12).

 **CHECKPOINT**

8. During 2018, a company discovered that the merchandise inventory reported on the 2017 balance sheet was overstated by $10,000. Did this error cause cost of goods sold to be overstated or understated in 2017? in 2018? By how much?

Do Quick Study question: QS 6-11

Estimating Inventory

This section describes methods to estimate inventory. Knowledge of these methods is important for preparers and users in understanding and analyzing financial information.

Gross Profit Method

LO6   Apply both the gross profit and retail inventory methods to estimate inventory.

The **gross profit method** estimates the cost of ending inventory by applying the *gross profit ratio* to net sales (at *retail*). Recall from Chapter 5 that the **gross profit ratio** measures how much of each sales dollar is gross profit. A need for the gross profit estimate can arise when inventory is destroyed, lost, or stolen. These cases need an estimate of inventory so a company can file a claim with its insurer. Users also apply this method to see if inventory amounts from either management or a physical count are reasonable. This method uses the historical relationship between cost of goods sold and net sales to estimate the proportion of cost of goods sold making up current sales. This cost of goods sold estimate is then subtracted from cost of goods available for sale to give us an estimate of ending inventory at cost.

To illustrate, assume the following in March of 2017 when the company's inventory is destroyed by fire:

Sales	$31,500
Sales returns	1,500
Inventory, January 1, 2017	12,000
Net cost of goods purchased	20,500
Gross profit ratio	30%

To estimate the inventory loss, we first need to recognize that each dollar of net sales is made up of gross profit and cost of goods sold. If this company's gross profit ratio is 30% as given, then 30% of each net sales dollar is gross profit and 70% is cost of goods sold. We show in Exhibit 6.17 how this 70% is used to estimate lost inventory.

For companies using a perpetual system, an important control policy includes having offsite data storage of its accounting records in the event of a fire or natural disaster, to ensure all company records are not destroyed. Some companies are moving to storage on the Cloud through an Internet connection to a remote database managed by a third party. Offsite storage is helpful to access detailed inventory records, which would provide a more accurate picture of inventory balances at the point of the disaster than an estimation through the gross profit method. Companies using the periodic inventory system would have to rely on the gross profit method to estimate destroyed inventory.

EXHIBIT 6.17

Calculating Inventory Using the Gross Profit Method

In Step 1 we use income statement relationships to calculate the dollar value of the estimated cost of goods sold.
In Step 2 we use our understanding of the cost of goods sold components as described earlier in Exhibit 6.11 to determine the estimated March inventory.

Step 1:

Sales	$31,500
Less: Sales returns...	1,500
Net sales	$30,000
Less: COGS*	**21,000**
Gross profit from sales	30%
	or $9,000

Step 2:

Inventory, January 1, 2017	$ 12,000
Add: Net cost of goods purchased	20,500
Less: COGS	**21,000**
Estimated March inventory	**$11,500**

*If gross profit equals 30% of net sales or $9,000 (30% × $30,000), then COGS must equal 70% of net sales or $21,000 (70% × $30,000).

Important Tip: Quick Method to Estimate Ending Inventory using the Gross Profit Method

Step 1: Calculate Cost of Goods Available for Sale: = Inventory + Purchases = 12,000 + 20,500 = 32,500
Step 2: Deduct Cost of Goods Sold: = Net Sales × COGS% = 30,000*(1 − 0.30) = 21,000
Difference = Estimated Ending Inventory = 32,500 − 21,000 = 11,500

Retail Inventory Method

Many companies prepare financial statements on a quarterly or monthly basis. The cost of goods sold information needed to prepare these interim financial reports is readily available if a perpetual inventory system is used. A periodic system, however, requires a physical inventory to determine cost of goods sold. To avoid the time-consuming and expensive process of taking a physical inventory each month or quarter, some companies use the **retail inventory method** to estimate cost of goods sold and ending inventory.

Some companies even use the retail inventory method to prepare the annual statements since it is acceptable for income tax purposes. **TJX Companies Inc.,** is the parent company for Winners, Homesense, Marshals, TJ Maxx, and Homegoods and online retailer Sierra Trading Post (STP). They operate in Canada, the United States, and Europe. The group reports in its February 1, 2014, annual report:

TJX Companies Inc. Feb 1, 2014 Annual Report Excerpt

SIGNIFICANT ACCOUNTING POLICIES NOTE F/S NOTE

Merchandise Inventories:

> Inventories are stated at the lower of cost or market. TJX uses the retail method for valuing inventories at all of its divi. sions, except STP, which results in a weighted average cost. TJX utilizes a permanent markdown strategy and lowers the cost value of the inventory that is subject to markdown at the time the retail prices are lowered in the stores. TJX accrues for inventory obligations at the time inventory is shipped. As a result, merchandise inventories on TJX's balance sheet include an accrual for in-transit inventory of $451.6 million at February 1, 2014 and $418.3 million at February 2, 2013. Comparable amounts were reflected in accounts payable at those dates.

CALCULATING THE RETAIL INVENTORY ESTIMATE

When the retail inventory method is used to estimate inventory, we need to gather information on the following data points:

- Amount of inventory a company had at the beginning of the period in both *cost* and *retail* amounts. Retail amount of inventory refers to its dollar amount measured using selling prices of inventory items.

- Net amount of goods purchased (minus returns, allowances, and discounts) during the period, both at cost and at retail.

- Dollar value of net sales at retail

A three-step process is used to estimate ending inventory after we calculate the amount of goods available for sale during the period both at cost and at retail. This process is demonstrated above in Exhibit 6.18.

EXHIBIT 6.18

Inventory Estimation Using Retail Inventory Method

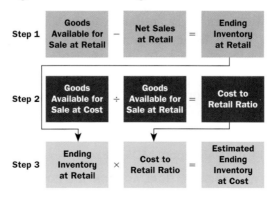

The reasoning behind the retail inventory method is that if we can get a good estimate of the cost to retail ratio, then we can multiply ending inventory at retail by this ratio to estimate ending inventory at cost. Assume TJX Group of Companies has identified the following information in its information system. Exhibit 6.19 illustrates how TJX Group can apply these steps to estimate ending inventory.

EXHIBIT 6.19

Example Calculation of Ending Inventory Using the Retail Inventory Method at TJX Group of Companies

		At Cost	At Retail
	Goods available for sale:		
	Beginning inventory	$20,500	$ 34,500
	Cost of goods purchased	39,500	65,500
	Goods available for sale.....................................	$60,000	$100,000
Step 1:	Less: Net sales at retail.....................................		70,000
	Ending inventory at retail....................................		$ 30,000
Step 2:	Cost to retail ratio: ($60,000 ÷ $100,000).........		× 60%
Step 3:	Estimated ending inventory at cost.....................		$ 18,000

ESTIMATING PHYSICAL INVENTORY AT COST

Items for sale by retailers, like TJX Group of Companies, usually carry price tags listing selling prices. When a retailer takes a physical inventory, it commonly totals inventory using selling prices of items on hand. It then reduces the dollar total of this inventory to a cost basis by applying the cost to retail ratio. This is done because selling prices are readily available and using the cost to retail ratio eliminates the need to look up invoice prices of items on hand.

Let's assume that the TJX Group in Exhibit 6.19 estimates its inventory by the retail method and takes a physical inventory using selling prices. If the retail value of this physical inventory is $29,600, then we can calculate the cost of this inventory by applying its cost to retail ratio as follows: $29,600 × 60% = $17,760. The $17,760 cost figure for ending physical inventory is an acceptable number for annual financial statements. It is also acceptable to CRA for tax reporting.

ESTIMATING INVENTORY SHORTAGE AT COST

The inventory estimate in Exhibit 6.19 is an estimate of the amount of goods on hand (at cost). Since it is calculated by deducting sales from goods available for sale (at retail), it does not reveal any shrinkage due to breakage, loss, or theft. However, we can estimate the amount of shrinkage by comparing the inventory calculated in Exhibit 6.19 with the amount from taking a physical inventory. In Exhibit 6.19, for example, we estimated ending inventory at retail as $30,000, but a physical inventory revealed only $29,600 of inventory on hand (at retail). The company has an inventory shortage (at retail) of $400, calculated as $30,000 − $29,600. The inventory shortage (at cost) is $240, calculated as $400 × 60%. The following excerpt outlines how TJX Companies Inc. handles the issue of shrinkage.

TJX Companies Inc. Feb 1, 2014 Annual Report MD&A Excerpt

MANAGEMENT DISCUSSION AND ANALYSIS: CRITICAL ACCOUNTING POLICIES F/S NOTE

Inventory Valuation:

> Inventory shrinkage requires estimating a shrinkage rate for interim periods, but we take a full physical inventory near the fiscal year-end to determine shrinkage at year-end.

CHECKPOINT

9. The following data pertain to a company's inventory during 2017:

	Cost	Retail
Beginning inventory	$324,000	$530,000
Cost of goods purchased	195,000	335,000
Net sales		320,000

Using the retail method, estimate the cost of ending inventory.

Do Quick Study questions: QS 6-12, QS 6-13, QS 6-14, QS 6-15

Financial Statement Analysis—Assess Inventory Management

LO7   Assess inventory management using both inventory turnover and days' sales in inventory.

Inventory Turnover and Days' Sales in Inventory

This section describes how we use information about inventory to assess a company's near-term liquidity and its management of inventory. Two measures useful for these assessments are defined and explained in this section.

Inventory Turnover

A company's ability to pay its near-term obligations depends, in part, on how quickly it sells its merchandise inventory. The **inventory turnover** is one ratio used to help analyze liquidity. It is also used to assess whether management is doing a good job of controlling the amount of inventory on hand. The inventory turnover is calculated as shown in Exhibit 6.20.

EXHIBIT 6.20

Inventory Turnover

$$\text{Inventory turnover} = \frac{\text{Cost of goods sold}}{\text{Average merchandise inventory}}$$

Average merchandise inventory is calculated by adding beginning and ending inventory and dividing the total by 2. If a company's sales vary within the year, it is often better to take an average of inventory amounts at the end of each quarter or month.

The inventory turnover ratio tells us how many *times* a company turns its inventory over during a period. For example, Exhibit 6.21 shows the merchandise turnover for Loblaw Companies Limited for its year ended December 28, 2013, in comparison to Lululemon Athletica Inc. for its year ended February 2, 2014.

As Exhibit 6.21 illustrates, Loblaw's turnover ratio suggests that the amount of inventory on hand is low and that it is sold more quickly than that of Lululemon. However, Loblaws sells foodstuffs, and is a different

EXHIBIT 6.21

Merchandise Turnovers Compared for Loblaw Companies Limited and Danier Leather

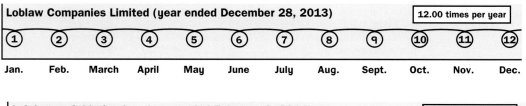

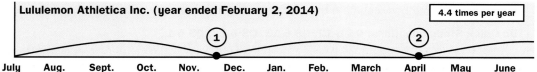

type of business than Lululemon. Loblaws is part of the grocery industry where it is critical to move merchandise quickly because of its perishable nature. Lululemon is in an industry where merchandise turnovers of 4.40 times per year for specialty retailers are typical. Ratio comparisons such as the preceding must be based on companies that are similar in order to be meaningful. There is no simple rule with merchandise turnover, except to say that a high ratio is preferable provided inventory is adequate to meet demand. It is imperative to look at comparisons to previous years results for a particular company and analyzing results against companies in a similar industry in order to perform an effective financial statement analysis.

Days' Sales in Inventory

To better interpret merchandise turnover, many users want a measure to determine if inventory levels can meet sales demand. **Days' sales in inventory** is a ratio that estimates how many days it will take to convert inventory on hand into accounts receivable or cash. Days' sales in inventory is calculated as shown in Exhibit 6.22

EXHIBIT 6.22

Days' Sales in Inventory

$$\text{Days' sales in inventory} = \frac{\text{Ending inventory}}{\text{Cost of goods sold}} \times 365$$

Notice the different focuses of days' sales in inventory and merchandise turnover. Days' sales in inventory focuses on ending inventory, whereas merchandise turnover focuses on average inventory. When looking at year-over-year comparatives for the same company or comparing results with a competitor company, a lower number of days in inventory is better.

CHECKPOINT

10. Company A and Company B sell similar merchandise. Company A has a merchandise turnover of 4.8, while this same ratio is 5.2 for Company B. Which company is more efficient at selling its inventory?

Do Quick Study questions: QS 6-16, QS 6-17

Refer to the Critical Thinking Challenge questions at the beginning of the chapter. Compare your answers to those suggested on Connect.

IFRS AND ASPE—THE DIFFERENCES

Difference	International Financial Reporting Standards (IFRS)	Accounting Standards for Private Enterprises (ASPE)
There are no significant differences between IFRS and ASPE related to this chapter.		

A Look Ahead

Chapter 7 takes a look at Internal Control and Cash with an introduction to the concept of internal controls, banking activities, accounting for petty cash funds and reconciling the differences between cash reported in the bank account and cash in the company's accounting records.

Summary

LO1 Identify the components and costs included in merchandise inventory. Merchandise inventory comprises goods owned by a company and held for resale. Goods in transit are reported in inventory of the company that holds ownership rights. Goods out on consignment are reported in inventory of the consignor; the consignee acts as an agent to sell the goods. Goods damaged or obsolete are reported in inventory at a conservative estimate of their net realizable value, calculated as sales price minus the selling costs. Costs of merchandise inventory include expenditures necessary, directly or indirectly, in bringing an item to a saleable condition and location (in other words, the invoice price minus any discount, plus any added or incidental costs necessary to put it in a place and condition for sale).

LO2 Calculate cost of goods sold and merchandise inventory using specific identification, moving weighted average, and FIFO—perpetual. Costs are assigned to the cost of goods sold account each time that a sale occurs in a perpetual system. Specific identification assigns cost by referring to the actual cost of the specific unit sold. Moving weighted average assigns a weighted average cost per unit calculated by taking the current balance in the merchandise inventory account and dividing it by the total items available for sale to determine the weighted average cost per unit. FIFO assigns cost assuming units purchased earliest are the first units sold.

LO3 Analyze the effects of the costing methods on financial reporting. When purchase prices are rising or falling, the inventory methods are likely to assign different cost amounts. Specific identification exactly matches costs and revenues. Moving weighted average smooths out price changes. FIFO assigns an amount to inventory closely approximating current replacement cost. The method(s) used must be disclosed in the notes to the financial statements and be consistent from period to period.

LO4 Calculate the lower of cost and net realizable value of inventory. Inventory is reported at net realizable value (NRV) when NRV is lower than cost. This is called the lower of cost and net realizable value (LCNRV) of inventory. LCNRV can be applied by item or by categories of similar or related items.

LO5 Analyze the effects of inventory errors on current and future financial statements—perpetual. An error in the amount of ending inventory affects assets (inventory), profit (cost of goods sold), and equity of that period. Since ending inventory is next period's beginning inventory, an error in ending inventory affects next period's cost of goods sold and profit. The financial statement effects of errors in one period are offset (reversed) in the next.

LO6 Apply both the gross profit and retail inventory methods to estimate inventory. The gross profit method involves two calculations: (1) net sales at retail multiplied by the gross profit ratio gives estimated cost of goods sold; and (2) goods available at cost minus estimated cost of goods sold gives estimated ending inventory at cost. The retail inventory method involves three calculations:

(1) goods available at retail minus net sales at retail gives ending inventory at retail; (2) goods available at cost divided by goods available at retail gives the cost to retail ratio; and (3) ending inventory at retail is multiplied by the cost to retail ratio to give estimated ending inventory at cost.

LO7 **Assess inventory management using both inventory turnover and days' sales in inventory.**

A high inventory turnover is preferred provided inventory is not out of stock and customers are not being turned away. We use days' sales in inventory to assess the likelihood of inventory being out of stock. Together, these ratios help us assess inventory management and evaluate a company's near-term liquidity.

Guidance Answer to DECISION MAKER

Inventory Manager

Your recommendation is a difficult one. Increased profits may attract investors but they will also increase your bonus. The question becomes one of motivation. That is, would the change really be better for the investors, or would the change take place only because your bonus would increase? This presents the classic conflict of interests. Another problem is that profits can be manipulated by changing accounting methods, and if this were the motivation the profession would frown on the change.

Guidance Answers to CHECKPOINT

1. Best Buy.
2. Total cost is $12,180, calculated as:
   $11,400 + $130 + $150 + $100 + $400.
3. The matching principle.
4. Businesses that sell unique, high dollar–value merchandise in relatively low volume levels might choose specific identification. Car dealerships are a good example because each car received as merchandise inventory is unique in terms of both features and identification number. Using specific identification allows the business to accurately tag each item coming in and going out.
5. Moving weighted average gives a lower inventory figure on the balance sheet as compared to FIFO. FIFO's inventory amount will approximate current replacement costs. Moving weighted average costs increase but more slowly because of the effect of averaging.
6. Because these units are the same ones that were originally written down, a reversal is appropriate and would be recorded as:

| Merchandise Inventory .... | 2,000 | |
| Cost of Goods Sold.................. | | 2,000 |

$1,800 − $1,300 = $500/unit
original write-down; $500 × 4 =
$2,000 maximum reversal

7. The reported inventory amount is $540, calculated as (20 × $5) + (40 × $8) + (10 × $12).
8. Cost of goods sold is understated by $10,000 in 2017 and overstated by $10,000 in 2018.
9. The estimated ending inventory (at cost) is $327,000 and is calculated as:

   Step 1: ($530,000 + $335,000) − $320,000 = $545,000

   Step 2: $\dfrac{\$324,000 + \$195,000}{\$530,000 + \$335,000} = 60\%$

   Step 3: $545,000 × 60% = $327,000
10. Company B is more efficient at selling its inventory because it has higher merchandise turnover.

DEMONSTRATION PROBLEM

Part 1

Assume the accounting department at **Swatch**, the Swiss Watch Company, prepared the following schedule comparing the total cost and NRV of its December 31, 2017, ending inventory:

	Total Cost	Total NRV	LCNRV applied to: Products	Group*
Product A	$ 29,000	$ 28,000		
Product B	46,000	36,000		
Product C	17,000	17,000		
Product D	31,000	30,000		
Product E	3,000	7,000		
Totals	$126,000	$118,000		

*Assume that all products are similar.

Required

a. Calculate the merchandise inventory value that should appear on Swatch's December 31, 2017, balance sheet. Apply LCNRV to each product and to inventory as a group by completing the schedule provided.

b. Based on your calculations in part (a), prepare the appropriate adjusting entry at year-end assuming LCNRV is applied to inventory as a group.

Analysis Component:

Assuming the adjustment in part (b) is not recorded, identify the over- or understatement of profit, assets, and equity.

Part 2

Assume Swiss Company, a competitor to Swatch, had $435,000 of sales during each of three consecutive years, and it purchased merchandise costing $300,000 during each of the years. It also maintained a $105,000 inventory from the beginning to the end of the three-year period. However, $15,000 of merchandise inventory purchased FOB shipping point on December 31, 2017, was accidentally excluded from the December 31, 2017, inventory. This error caused the company's ending 2017 inventory to appear on the statements at $90,000 rather than at the correct $105,000.

Required

1. Calculate the actual amount of the company's gross profit in each of the years.

2. Prepare a comparative income statement like Exhibit 6.12 to show the effect of this error on the company's cost of goods sold and gross profit in 2017, 2018, and 2019.

Solution

Part 1

a.

| | | | LCNRV applied to: | |
	Total Cost	Total NRV	Products	Group*
Product A	$ 29,000	$ 28,000	**$ 28,000**	
Product B	46,000	36,000	**36,000**	
Product C	17,000	17,000	**17,000**	
Product D	31,000	30,000	**30,000**	
Product E	3,000	7,000	**3,000**	
Totals	$126,000	$118,000	**$114,000**	**$118,000**

*Assume that all products are similar.

b.

2017			
Dec. 31	Cost of Goods Sold...	8,000	
	Merchandise Inventory		8,000
	To write inventory down to LCNRV.		

Analysis Component:

If the adjusting entry in part (b) is not recorded, profit would be overstated, assets would be overstated, and equity would also be overstated, each by $8,000.

Part 2

1. $435,000 - ($105,000 + $300,000 - $105,000) = $135,000

2.

	For years ended December 31, 2017, 2018, 2019, the income statement information should have been reported as:	Income statement information actually reported for years ended December 31,		
		2017	2018	2019
Sales............................	$435,000	$435,000	$435,000	$435,000
Cost of goods sold	300,000	315,000	285,000	300,000
Gross profit from sales ...	$135,000	$120,000	$150,000	$135,000

Merchandise Inventory			
Jan. 1/17	105,000		
Purchases	300,000	315,000	COGS
Dec. 31/17	90,000		

Merchandise Inventory			
Jan. 1/18	90,000		
Purchases	300,000	285,000	COGS
Dec. 31/18	105,000		

Merchandise Inventory			
Jan. 1/19	105,000		
Purchases	300,000	300,000	COGS
Dec. 31/19	105,000		

APPENDIX 6A

Assigning Costs to Inventory and Inventory Errors—Periodic System

LO8 Calculate cost of goods sold and merchandise inventory using FIFO—periodic, weighted average, and specific identification.

The aim of the periodic system is the same as the perpetual system: to assign costs to the inventory and the goods sold. The same three methods are used in assigning costs: first-in, first-out; weighted average; and specific identification. We use information from MEC to describe how we assign costs using these three methods with a periodic system. Data for sales and purchases are reported in the chapter in Exhibits 6.2 and 6.3 and are not repeated here.

First-In, First-Out

The first-in, first-out (FIFO) method of assigning cost to inventory and goods sold using the periodic system is shown in Exhibit 6A.1.

EXHIBIT 6A.1

FIFO Calculations—Periodic

Total cost of 45 units available for sale	$4,800
Less: **Ending inventory** priced using FIFO:	
11 units from August 17 purchase at $115 each	**1,265**
Cost of goods sold	**$3,535**

MEC's ending inventory reported on the balance sheet is $1,265 and its cost of goods sold reported on the income statement is $3,535. The assignment of costs to cost of goods sold and inventory using FIFO is the same for both the perpetual and periodic systems, as summarized in Exhibit 6A.4. This will always occur because the most recent purchases are in ending inventory under both systems.

Weighted Average

The **weighted average** inventory costing method involves three important steps, as illustrated in Exhibits 6A.2 and 6A.3. First, we multiply the unit cost for beginning inventory and each particular purchase by their corresponding number of units. Second, we add these amounts and divide by the total number of units available for sale to find the *weighted average cost per unit*.

EXHIBIT 6A.2

Weighted Average Cost Per Unit—Periodic

Step 1:

Aug.	1	Beginning inventory	10 units	@	$ 91	=	$ 910
	3	Purchased	15 units	@	106	=	1,590
	17	Purchased	20 units	@	115	=	2,300
			45 units available for sale				**$4,800** Total cost of goods available for sale

Step 2: $4,800/45 = **$106.67** weighted average cost per unit

The third step is to use the weighted average cost per unit to assign costs to inventory and to units sold:

EXHIBIT 6A.3

Weighted Average Calculations—Periodic

Step 3:

Total cost of 45 units available for sale..	$4,800
Less: **Ending inventory** priced on a weighted average cost basis:	
11 units at $106.67 each	**1,173***
Cost of goods sold (= 34 units × $106.67)	**$3,627***

45 united available for sale − 11 units in ending inventory = 34 units sold during the period

*Rounded to nearest whole dollar.

The assignment of costs to cost of goods sold and inventory using weighted average usually gives different results depending on whether a perpetual or periodic system is used, as shown in Exhibit 6A.4. This is because weighted average under a perpetual system recalculates the unit cost at the time of each item purchased. The periodic inventory system determines an average cost at the end of the period based on all items that were available for sale during the year and applies the cost to the number of items counted in ending inventory.

> **Important Tip:** Note that under the periodic inventory method, we do not recalculate the unit cost each time an item is purchased. Average cost is determined at the end of the period and is applied to the number of units in ending inventory (based on the year-end inventory count) and cost of goods sold.

EXHIBIT 6A.4

Comparison of Inventory Methods—Periodic and Perpetual

	FIFO		Weighted Average		Specific Identification	
	Perpetual	**Periodic**	**Perpetual**	**Periodic***	**Perpetual**	**Periodic**
COGS...................................	$3,535	$3,535	$3,568	$3,627	$3,562	$3,562
Ending Inventory.............................	1,265	1,265	1,232	1,173	1,238	1,238
Cost of Goods Available for Sale..	$4,800	$4,800	$4,800	$4,800	$4,800	$4,800

*Rounded to the nearest whole dollar for simplicity

Specific Identification

The amounts of cost assigned to inventory and cost of goods sold are the same under the perpetual and periodic systems as detailed in Exhibit 6A.4. This is because specific identification precisely defines which units are in inventory and which are sold.

Exhibit 6A.4 compares the inventory methods for both the periodic and perpetual systems.

Exhibit 6A.4 shows that the figures for specific identification and FIFO are identical under periodic and perpetual systems. However, the figures for weighted average will differ between the perpetual and periodic systems as explained above.

CHECKPOINT

11. A company uses a periodic inventory system and reports the following beginning inventory and purchases (and ends the period with 30 units on hand):

	Units	Cost Per Unit
Beginning Inventory	100	$10
Purchases #1	40	12
#2	20	14

a. Calculate ending inventory using FIFO

b. Calculate cost of goods sold using weighted average.

Do Quick Study question: *QS 6-18

Errors in Reporting Inventory

LO9   Analyze the effects of inventory errors on current and future financial statements—periodic.

Exhibits 6.11 and 6.12 were based on a perpetual inventory system. Those exhibits are reflected below under the assumption of a periodic inventory system.

Income Statement Effects of Inventory Errors

The income statement effects of an inventory error are evident when looking at the components of cost of goods sold in Exhibit 6A.5.

EXHIBIT 6A.5

Cost of Goods Sold Components—Periodic

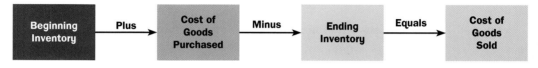

The effect of an inventory error on cost of goods sold is determined by calculating the inventory correctly and comparing it to the result of the calculation when using the incorrect amount, as in Exhibit 6A.6.

Exhibit 6A.6 assumes that $2,000 of merchandise sold but awaiting delivery was incorrectly included in ending inventory on December 31, 2017.

EXHIBIT 6A.6

Effects of $2,000 Overstatement in Ending Inventory for 2017 on Three Periods' Income Statement Information—Periodic

	For years ended December 31, 2017, 2018, 2019, the income statement information should have been reported as:	Income statement information actually reported for years ended December 31,		
		2017	**2018**	**2019**
Sales..............................	$30,000	$30,000	$30,000	$30,000
Cost of goods sold				
Beginning inventory......	$10,000	$10,000	$12,000	$10,000
Add: Purchases............	20,000	20,000	20,000	20,000
Less: Ending inventory...	10,000	12,000	10,000	10,000
Cost of goods sold	20,000	18,000	22,000	20,000
Gross profit.....................	$10,000	$12,000	$ 8,000	$10,000
Operating expenses.........	5,000	5,000	5,000	5,000
Profit	$ 5,000	$ 7,000	$ 3,000	$ 5,000

① 2017 profit and gross profit are overstated (too high) and cost of goods sold is understated (too low) when ending inventory is overstated (too high).

② Ending inventory for one period becomes the beginning inventory for the next period, carrying forward any errors that existed.

③ 2018 profit and gross profit are understated (too low) and cost of goods sold is overstated (too high) when beginning inventory is overstated (too high). Notice that the error has reversed itself in 2018, the second year.

④ An inventory error in the year 2017 does not affect 2019.

DEMONSTRATION PROBLEM

Abercrombie Company uses a periodic inventory system and had the following beginning inventory and purchases during January 2017:

		Units	Cost Per Unit		Total Cost
Jan. 1	Beginning inventory................	300	@ $ 14	=	$ 4,200
16	Purchased	200	@ 15	=	3,000
20	Purchased	300	@ 16	=	4,800
	Total goods available for sale..............	800			$12,000

Sales of units were as follows:

Jan. 15	200	units at $30
28	460	units at $35
Total units sold	660	

Additional data for use in applying the specific identification method:

The specific units sold were:

Jan.	15	200 units from the January 1 units on hand
	28	75 units from the January 1 units on hand
		150 units from the January 16 purchase, and
		235 units from the January 20 purchase

Required

Using the preceding information, calculate the ending inventory and the cost of goods sold for Abercrombie Company under a periodic inventory system by applying each of the three different methods of inventory costing:

a. FIFO

b. Weighted average, and

c. Specific identification

Planning the Solution

- Prepare a periodic FIFO schedule similar to Exhibit 6A.1 (recall that although the calculations differ, the results are the same under each of the periodic and perpetual systems for FIFO).

- Prepare a periodic weighted average schedule similar to Exhibits 6A.2 and 6A.3.

- Prepare a specific identification schedule similar to Exhibit 6.6 (recall that specific identification is calculated in the same manner under each of the perpetual and periodic systems for specific identification).

Solution

a. FIFO

Cost of goods available for sale	$12,000
Less: Ending inventory of 140 units:	
140 @ $16 = ...	2,240
Equals: Cost of goods sold	$ 9,760

b. Weighted Average

Cost of goods available for sale	$12,000
Less: Ending inventory of 140 units:	
140 × $15 avg. cost/unit*	2,100
Equals: Cost of goods sold	$ 9,900

*$12,000 ÷ 800 units = $15/unit avg. cost

c. Specific Identification

Cost of goods available for sale	$12,000
Less: Ending inventory of 140 units:	
25 @ $14 = $ 350	
50 @ $15 = 750	
65 @ $16 = 1,040	2,140
Equals: Cost of goods sold	$ 9,860

Summary of Appendix 6A

LO8 Calculate cost of goods sold and merchandise inventory using FIFO—periodic, weighted average, and specific identification. Periodic systems allocate the cost of goods available for sale between cost of goods sold and ending inventory *at the end of a period*. Specific identification and FIFO give identical results whether the periodic or perpetual system is used. Weighted average cost calculates cost per unit by taking the total cost of both beginning inventory and net purchases and dividing by the total number of units available. It then multiplies cost per

unit by the number of units sold to give cost of goods sold.

LO9 Analyze the effects of inventory errors on current and future financial statements—periodic. An error in the amount of ending inventory affects assets (inventory), profit (cost of goods sold), and equity of that period. Since ending inventory is next period's beginning inventory, an error in ending inventory affects next period's cost of goods sold and profit. The financial statement effects of errors in one period are offset (reversed) in the next.

Guidance Answers to CHECKPOINT

11. **a.** Ending inventory = (20 × $14) + (10 × $12) = $400

b. Cost of goods sold = [(100 × $10) + (40 × $12) + (20 × $14)]/160 × 30
= $11 × 30
= $330

Glossary

Consignee One who receives and holds goods owned by another party for the purpose of acting as an agent and selling the goods for the owner. The consignee gets paid a fee from the consignor for finding a buyer.

Consignor An owner of inventory goods who ships them to another party who will then find a buyer and sell the goods for the owner. The consignor retains title to the goods while they are held offsite by the consignee.

Consistency principle The accounting requirement that a company use the same accounting policies period after period so that the financial statements of succeeding periods will be comparable.

Days' sales in inventory A financial analysis tool used to estimate how many days it will take to convert the inventory on hand into accounts receivable or cash; calculated by dividing the ending inventory by cost of goods sold and multiplying the result by 365.

Faithful representation The accounting principle that requires information to be complete, neutral, unbiased, and free from error.

First-in, first-out (FIFO) The pricing of an inventory under the assumption that inventory items are sold in the order acquired; the first items received are the first items sold.

Gross profit method An estimate used for determining ending inventory in the event inventory is destroyed. The company's determined gross profit rate is used to estimate cost of goods sold, which is then subtracted from the cost of goods available for sale to determine the estimated ending inventory.

Gross profit ratio Measures how much of net sales is gross profit (net sales-cost of goods sold); calculated as gross profit divided by net sales; also known as the *gross margin ratio*.

Internal controls The policies and procedures used to protect assets, ensure reliable accounting, promote efficient operations, and urge adherence to company policies.

Inventory turnover A financial statement analysis tool used to determine the number of times a company's average inventory was sold during an accounting period, calculated by dividing cost of goods sold by the average merchandise inventory balance; also called *inventory turnover*.

Lower of cost and net realizable value (LCNRV) The required method of reporting merchandise inventory in the balance sheet where net realizable value is reported when net realizable value is lower than cost. This rule ensures inventory is not recorded at a higher value on the balance sheet than what the company can sell the item for.

Materiality principle This GAAP states that an amount may be ignored if its effect on the financial statements is not important to their users. Financial statement preparers need to assess whether the item would impact the decision of a user.

Moving weighted average A perpetual inventory pricing system in which the unit cost in inventory is recalculated at the time of each purchase by dividing the total cost of goods available for sale at that point in time by the corresponding total units available for sale. The most current moving weighted average cost per unit is multiplied by the units sold to determine cost of goods sold.

Net realizable value (NRV) The expected sales price of an item minus the cost of making the sale.

Physical count To count merchandise inventory for the purpose of reconciling goods actually on hand to the inventory control account in the general ledger; also called *taking an inventory*.

Retail price The selling price of merchandise inventory.

Retail inventory method A method used by retailers to estimate an ending inventory cost based on the ratio of the amount of goods for sale at cost to the amount of goods for sale at marked selling prices.

Specific identification The pricing of an inventory where the purchase invoice of each item in the ending inventory is identified and used to determine the cost assigned to the inventory.

Weighted average A periodic inventory pricing system in which the total cost of goods available for sale is divided by the total units available for sale. The resulting weighted average unit cost is multiplied by the units in ending inventory and then by the units that were sold.

Concept Review Questions

1. Caps Co., a store that sells baseball hats received a shipment of inventory. The purchase price of inventory is $2,000, a bulk discount of 40% off was received, the shipping charges were $200, and the import duties were $140. What is the total cost of inventory?

2. Give the meanings of the following when applied to inventory: (a) FIFO, and (b) cost.

3. If prices are falling, will the moving weighted average or the FIFO method of inventory valuation result in the lower cost of goods sold?

4. Where is merchandise inventory disclosed in the financial statements?

5. May a company change its inventory pricing method each accounting period?

6. Does the accounting principle of consistency disallow any changes from one accounting method to another?

7. What effect does the full disclosure principle have if a company changes from one acceptable accounting method to another?

8. What guidance for accountants is provided by faithful representation?

9. What is the usual meaning of NRV as it is used in determining the LCNRV for merchandise inventory?

10. What is meant when it is said that inventory errors correct themselves?

11. If inventory errors correct themselves, why be concerned when such errors are made?

12. Refer to **WestJet**'s financial statements in Appendix III. On December 31, 2014, what percentage of WestJet's assets was represented by what would be WestJet's inventory? Is this merchandise inventory?

13. Refer to Danier's financial statements in Appendix III. Is it possible to determine a cost of goods sold figure for Danier? If so, what is the cost of goods sold figure for Danier?

Quick Study

QS 6-1 Inventory ownership LO1

1. At year-end Carefree Company has shipped, FOB destination, $500 of merchandise that is still in transit to Stark Company. Which company should include the $500 as part of inventory at year-end?

2. Carefree Company has shipped goods to Stark and has an arrangement that Stark will sell the goods for Carefree. Identify the consignor and the consignee. Which company should include any unsold goods as part of inventory?

QS 6-2 Inventory ownership LO1

Say It Loud Cards, a distributor of fun and witty cards, operates out of owner Scott Arlen's home. At the end of the accounting period, Arlen has 1,500 units of products in his basement, 30 of which were damaged by water leaks and cannot be sold. He also has another 250 units in his van, ready to deliver to fill a customer order, terms FOB destination, and another 70 units out on consignment to a friend who owns a stationery store. How many units should be included in the end-of-period inventory?

QS 6-3 Inventory costs LO1

A car dealer acquires a used car for $3,000. Additional costs in obtaining and offering the car for sale include $150 for transportation-in, $200 for import duties, $50 for insurance during shipment, $25 for advertising, and $250 for sales staff salaries. For calculating inventory, what cost is assigned to the used car acquired?

QS 6-4 Inventory costs LO1

Owner of 555 Antiques, antique dealers, purchased a rare collection of superhero comic books for a bid price of $37,500. The terms of the purchase were FOB shipping point, and the cost of transporting the goods to 555 Antiques' warehouse was $1,200. 555 Antiques insured the shipment at a cost of $150. Prior to placing the goods in the store, they cleaned and refurbished some merchandise at a cost of $490 for labour and parts. Determine the cost of the inventory acquired in the purchase of the estate's contents.

QS 6-5 Calculating cost of goods available for sale LO2

A company has beginning inventory of 10 units at $50. Every week for four weeks an additional 10 units are purchased at respective costs of $51, $52, $55, and $60. Thirty-eight units were sold for $72 each. Calculate the total cost of goods that were available for sale and the total units that were available for sale.

QS 6-6 Inventory costing methods—perpetual LO2

A company had the following beginning inventory and purchases during January for a particular item. On January 28, 345 units were sold. What is the cost of the 140 units that remain in the ending inventory, assuming the following?

a. FIFO

b. Moving weighted average

Round numbers to the nearest cent. Assume a perpetual inventory system.

	Units	Unit Cost	Total Cost
Beginning inventory on January 1	310	$3.00	$ 930.00
Purchase on January 9......................................	75	3.20	240.00
Purchase on January 25....................................	100	3.35	335.00
Total available for sale	485		$1,505.00

QS 6-7 Specific identification inventory method LO2

Refer to the information in QS 6-6. Recall that 345 units were sold on January 28. The units specifically sold were:

- 250 units from beginning inventory
- 50 units from the January 9 purchase
- 45 units from the purchase on January 25

Calculate cost of goods sold and the cost of ending inventory

QS 6-8 Inventory costing methods—perpetual LO2

Bishr Company uses the moving weighted average method for inventory costing. You are to complete the following inventory sheet regarding Product XJ23789 (round calculations to two decimal places):

Date		Purchases/Transportation-In/ (Purchase Returns/Discounts)			Cost of Goods Sold/ (Returns to Inventory)			Balance in Inventory		
	Units	Cost/Unit	Total $	Units	Cost/Unit	Total $	Units	Avg Cost/Unit	Total $
Jan. 1		Brought Forward						10	$15.00	$150.00
3				6						
7	25	$18.50	$462.50							
8			50.00							
17			(46.25)							
18				14						

Note: January 8 reflects transportation costs regarding the January 7 purchase. The $46.25 on January 17 represents the discount taken regarding payment of the January 7 purchase within the discount period.

QS 6-9 Contrasting inventory costing methods LO3

Identify the inventory costing method most closely related to each of the following statements, assuming a period when the cost per unit is increasing:

    a. Current cost of inventory not reflected on income statement

    b. Results in a balance sheet inventory closest to replacement costs

    c. Is best when each unit of product has unique features that affect cost

QS 6-10 Applying LCNRV to inventories LO4

Thrifty Trading Co. has the following products in its ending inventory at December 31, 2017:

Product	Quantity	Per Unit Cost	Per Unit NRV
Aprons	9	$6.00	$5.50
Bottles	12	3.50	4.25
Candles	25	8.00	7.00

    a. Calculate LCNRV for the inventory as a whole, if applicable.

    b. Calculate LCNRV applied separately to each product.

    c. Prepare the appropriate adjusting entry, if any, assuming your calculations in (b).

QS 6-11 Inventory errors LO5,9

The Weston Company performed a physical inventory count at the end of 2017. It was later determined that certain units were counted twice. Explain how this error affects the following:

    a. 2017 cost of goods sold

    b. 2017 gross profit

    c. 2017 profit

    d. 2018 profit

    e. The combined two-year income

    f. Income in years after 2018

QS 6-12 Estimating inventories—gross profit method LO6

The inventory of Sixth Avenue Department Store was destroyed by a fire on September 10, 2017. The following 2017 data were found in the accounting records:

Jan. 1 inventory	$180,000
Jan. 1–Sept. 10 purchases (net)	$342,000
Jan. 1–Sept. 10 sales	$675,000
2017 estimated gross profit rate	42%

Estimate the cost of the inventory destroyed in the fire using the gross profit method.

QS 6-13 Estimating inventories—gross profit method LO6

During the past two months, management of Wallace Lake Computing Supplies was closely watching inventory levels due to suspected shrinkage caused by unknown factors. The physical count on July 31, the end of the current month, shows $48,000 of merchandise actually on hand. The accounting records for prior periods indicate that gross profit should be 30% of the $565,000 net sales for July. Inventory at June 30 was actually $65,000 and July purchases were $385,500. Calculate the estimated:

    a. Ending inventory

    b. Shrinkage

QS 6-14 Estimating ending inventory—retail method LO6

Best Stereo Centre showed the following selected information on August 31, 2017:

	Cost	Retail
Cost of goods available for sale	$67,600	$104,000
Net sales		82,000

Using the retail method, estimate the cost of the ending inventory.

QS 6-15 Estimating ending inventory—retail method LO6

Complete the following schedule by using the retail method to estimate ending inventory for September and October.

	September		October	
	Cost	Retail	Cost	Retail
Beginning inventory	$ 74,950	$112,000		
Cost of goods purchased	395,000	611,000	461,590	674,000
Goods available for sale				
Less: Net sales at retail........................		614,000		700,000
Ending inventory at retail				
Cost to retail ratio	────────	────────	────────	────────
Estimated ending inventory	════════	════════	════════	════════

QS 6-16 Inventory turnover LO7

Huff Company and Puff Company are similar firms that operate within the same industry. The following information is available.

	Huff			Puff		
	2017	2016	2015	2017	2016	2015
Inventory turnover.................	23.2	20.9	16.1	13.5	12.0	11.6

Required Based on the information provided, which company is managing inventory more efficiently? Explain.

QS 6-17 Inventory turnover and days' sales in inventory LO7

Mixon Company showed the following selected information for the years ended December 31, 2017, 2016, and 2015:

	2017	2016	2015
Cost of goods sold	$410,225	$344,500	$312,600
Merchandise inventory (December 31)	56,195	82,500	111,500

For the years ended 2017 and 2016, calculate:

    a. Days' sales in inventory

    b. Inventory turnover

Indicate if the change in the ratio from 2016 to 2017 is generally considered to be favourable (good) or unfavourable (not good). Round calculations to two decimal places.

*QS 6-18 Inventory costing methods—periodic LO8

Refer to the information in QS 6-6. Determine the cost of the 140 units that remain in ending inventory, assuming:

    a. FIFO

    b. Weighted average

Round numbers to the nearest cent and use a periodic inventory system.

An asterisk (*) identifies assignment material based on Appendix 6A.

Exercises

Exercise 6-1 **Inventory ownership** LO1

You are in charge of the year-end inventory count for OMG Luggage's December 31, 2017 year-end. OMG Luggage is known for its crazy luggage colours and designs. Assume the company uses a perpetual inventory system. Determine whether to include or exclude the following items and explain why. If OMG Luggage should include the inventory, determine the correct inventory cost.

a. On December 25, 2017, OMG Luggage purchased neon green luggage, FOB shipping from Baggage Co. The order had a purchase price of $2,500, shipping charges of $400, import duties of $300, and shipping insurance of $133. The products have not yet arrived at OMG Luggage, but Baggage Co. confirmed that the company shipped the order on December 27, 2017.

b. On December 31, 2017, OMG Luggage shipped leopard print luggage to a customer for a retail price of $777. This luggage had a cost of $500 and was shipped FOB destination. The shipping charges of $55 were paid by the appropriate party.

c. During the year, OMG luggage shipped inventory with a cost of $5,000 to a retailer on consignment. On December 31, 2017, the consignment store had sold $3,000 of the inventory and had paid OMG Luggage for the inventory sold.

d. On December 30, 2017, OMG Luggage sold yellow luggage to a customer with a price of $2,222 and a cost of $1,111. The customer paid for the luggage and arranged to pick up the inventory in person on January 4, 2018. As the inventory was still at the warehouse on December 31, 2017, the staff included this inventory in the final inventory listing.

Exercise 6-2 **Alternative cost flow assumptions—perpetual** LO2 e**X**cel

CHECK FIGURES: COGS a. $9,400.00; b. $9,417.90

Urban Glam Cosmetics made purchases of lipstick in the current year as follows:

Jan.	1	Beginning inventory..................	75 units	@	$12.00	=	$	900
Mar. 14		Purchased	250 units	@	$13.00	=		3,250
July 30		Purchased	500 units	@	$14.00	=		7,000
		Units available for sale............................	825 units					
		Cost of goods available for sale................						$11,150

Urban Glam Cosmetics made sales on the following dates at a selling price of $35 per unit:

Jan. 10	....	70 units
Mar. 15	....	180 units
Oct. 5	....	450 units
Total	....	700 units

Required The business uses a perpetual inventory system. Determine the costs that should be assigned to the ending inventory and to goods sold under:

a. FIFO

b. Moving weighted average (round to the nearest whole cent)

Also calculate the gross profit under each method.

Exercise 6-3 Specific identification cost flow assumption L02 e**X**cel

CHECK FIGURES: COGS = $9,427; Gross profit = $15,073

Refer to the data in Exercise 6-2. Assume that Urban Glam Cosmetics uses the specific identification method to cost inventory. The 700 units were specifically sold as follows:

Jan. 10:	70	units from beginning inventory
Mar. 15:	3	units from beginning inventory, and
	177	units from the March 14 purchase
Oct. 5:	50	units from the March 14 purchase, and
	400	units from the July 30 purchase

Calculate cost of goods sold and the gross profit.

Exercise 6-4 Alternative cost flow assumptions—perpetual inventory system L02 e**X**cel

Sport Box sells a wide variety of sporting equipment. The following is information on the purchases and sales of their top selling hockey stick. The hockey stick sells for $130.

	Description	Units	Unit Cost
Mar. 1	Beginning Inventory	5	$30
Mar. 3	Purchase	50	$35
Mar. 6	Purchase	100	$40
Mar. 17	Sale	45	
Mar. 23	Purchase	30	$40
Mar. 31	Sale	120	

Required

Calculate the cost of goods sold and ending inventory under the perpetual inventory system using

1. FIFO
2. Moving weighted average. Round all unit costs to two decimal places and round all other numbers to the nearest dollar

Exercise 6-5 Alternative cost flow assumptions—perpetual inventory system L02 e**X**cel

CHECK FIGURES: 3. COGS a. $4,610.00 b. $4,561.00

Car Armour sells car wash cleaners. Car Armour uses a perpetual inventory system and made purchases and sales of a particular product in 2017 as follows:

Jan. 1	Beginning inventory..................	120 units	@	$6.50	=	$ 780
Jan. 10	Sold	70 units	@	$15.00	=	1,050
Mar. 7	Purchased	250 units	@	$5.80	=	1,450
Mar. 15	Sold	125 units	@	$15.00	=	1,875
July 28	Purchased	500 units	@	$5.60	=	2,800
Oct. 3	Purchased	450 units	@	$5.50	=	2,475
Oct. 5	Sold	600 units	@	$15.00	=	9,000

Required

1. Calculate the total goods available for sale (in units and cost).

2. Calculate the number of units sold and units remaining in ending inventory.

3. Determine the share of the cost of goods available for sale calculated in Part 1 that should be assigned to ending inventory and to goods sold under:

   a. FIFO

   b. Moving weighted average

Exercise 6-6 Specific identification cost flow assumption LO2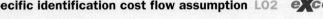

CHECK FIGURE: COGS = $4,529.50

Use the information in Exercise 6-5. Assume that Car Armour specifically sold the following units:

Jan. 10:	70	units from beginning inventory
Mar. 15:	25	units from beginning inventory, and
	100	units from the March 7 purchase
Oct. 5:	320	units from the July 28 purchase, and
	280	units from the October 3 purchase

Calculate cost to be assigned to ending inventory and cost of goods sold.

Exercise 6-7 Income statement effects of alternative cost flow assumptions LO3

Use the data in Exercises 6-5 and 6-6 to construct comparative income statements for Car Armour (year-end December 31, 2017), similar to those shown in Exhibit 6.8 in the chapter. Assume that operating expenses are $1,250.

1. Which method results in the highest profit?

2. If costs were rising instead of falling, which method would result in the highest profit?

Exercise 6-8 Moving weighted average cost flow assumption—perpetual LO2,3

Telamark Company uses the moving weighted average method for inventory costing. The following incomplete inventory sheet regarding Product W506 is available for the month of March 2017:

Date	Purchases/Transportation-In/ (Purchase Returns/Discounts)			Cost of Goods Sold/ (Returns to Inventory)			Balance in Inventory		
	Units	Cost/Unit	Total $	Units	Cost/Unit	Total $	Units	Avg Cost/Unit	Total $
Mar. 1		Brought Forward					60	$94.00	$5,640.00
2	35	$96.00							
3				22					
4				(2)					
7				65					
17	40	97.00							
28				43					

Note: March 4 reflects a return made by a customer of incorrect items shipped on March 3; these items were returned to inventory.

Required Complete the inventory sheet. Round all calculations to two decimal places.

Analysis Component: The gross profit realized on the sale of Product W506 during February 2017 was 32.16%. The selling price was $148 during both February and March. Calculate the gross profit ratio for Product W506 for March 2017 and determine whether the change is favourable or unfavourable from February. Identify the most probable cause of the change.

Exercise 6-9 Lower of cost and net realizable value LO4

CHECK FIGURES: a. $14,411; b. $13,802

Showtime Company's ending inventory at December 31, 2017, includes the following items: Calculate LCNRV for the inventory:

Product	Units on Hand	Unit Cost	Net Realizable Value Per Unit
BB	22	$110	$115
FM	15	145	138
MB	36	186	172
SL	40	78	92

a. As a whole (assuming the items are similar), and

b. Applied separately to each product.

c. Prepare the appropriate adjusting entry, if required, based on your calculations in (b).

Exercise 6-10 Analysis of inventory errors LO5,9

Assume that Volleyball Pro Equipment had $900,000 of sales during each of three consecutive years, and it purchased merchandise costing $500,000 during each of the years. It also maintained a $200,000 inventory from the beginning to the end of the three-year period. However, it made an error at the end of the first year, 2017, that caused its ending 2017 inventory to appear on its statements at $180,000 rather than the correct $200,000.

Required
1. Calculate the actual amount of the company's gross profit in each of the years.
2. Prepare a comparative income statement like Exhibit 6.12 (or Exhibit 6A.6) to show the effect of this error on the company's cost of goods sold and gross profit in 2017, 2018, and 2019.

Exercise 6-11 Estimating ending inventory—gross profit method LO6

On January 1, The Parts Store had a $450,000 inventory at cost. During the first quarter of the year, it purchased $1,590,000 of merchandise, returned $23,100, and paid freight charges on purchased merchandise totalling $37,600. During the past several years, the store's gross profit on sales has averaged 30%. Under the assumption the store had $2,000,000 of sales during the first quarter of the year, use the gross profit method to estimate its inventory at the end of the first quarter.

Exercise 6-12 Estimating ending inventory—retail method LO6

CHECK FIGURE: $71,941.68

During 2017, Harmony Co. sold $520,000 of merchandise at marked retail prices. At the end of 2017, the following information was available from its records:

	At Cost	At Retail
Beginning inventory	$127,600	$256,800
Net purchases	231,240	393,600

Use the retail method to estimate Harmony's 2017 ending inventory at cost. Round all calculations to two decimal places.

Exercise 6-13 Reducing physical inventory to cost—retail method LO6

Assume that in addition to estimating its ending inventory by the retail method, Harmony Co. of Exercise 6-10 also took a physical inventory at the marked selling prices of the inventory items at the end of 2017. Assume further that the total of this physical inventory at marked selling prices was $109,200.

    a. Determine the amount of this inventory at cost.

    b. Determine Harmony's 2017 inventory shrinkage from breakage, theft, or other causes at retail and at cost.

Round all calculations to two decimal places.

Exercise 6-14 Inventory turnover and days' sales in inventory LO7

From the following information for Russo Merchandising Co., calculate inventory turnover for 2018 and 2017 and days' sales in inventory at December 31, 2018, and 2017. Round answers to one decimal place.

	2018	2017	2016
Cost of goods sold	$643,825	$426,650	$391,300
Merchandise inventory (December 31)	96,400	86,750	91,500

Comment on Russo's efficiency in using its assets to support increasing sales from 2017 to 2018.

*Exercise 6-15 Alternative cost flow assumptions—periodic LO8

CHECK FIGURE: a. COGS = $12,672

Paddington Gifts made purchases of a particular product in the current year as follows:

Jan.	1	Beginning inventory...............	240 units	@	$6.00	=	$ 1,440
Mar.	7	Purchased	500 units	@	$5.60	=	2,800
July	28	Purchased	1,000 units	@	$5.00	=	5,000
Oct.	3	Purchased	900 units	@	$4.40	=	3,960
		Totals	2,640 units				$13,200

Required The business uses a periodic inventory system. Ending inventory consists of 120 units. Calculate the costs to be assigned to the ending inventory and to goods sold under:

    a. FIFO

    b. A weighted average cost basis

Which method provides the lower profit and why?

*Exercise 6-16 Alternative cost flow assumptions—periodic LO8

CHECK FIGURE: b. Ending inventory = $350.30

Jasper & Williams made purchases of a particular product in the current year as follows:

Jan.	1	Beginning inventory...................	120 units	@	$2.10	=	$ 252
Mar.	7	Purchased	250 units	@	$2.20	=	550
July	28	Purchased	500 units	@	$2.30	=	1,150
Oct.	3	Purchased	60 units	@	$2.45	=	147
		Totals	930 units				$2,099

An asterisk (*) identifies assignment material based on Appendix 6A or Appendix 6B.

Required Ending inventory consists of 155 units. Assuming a periodic system, determine the costs to be assigned to cost of goods sold and ending inventory under:

  a. FIFO

  b. Weighted average cost basis

Which method provides the lower profit, and why?

*Exercise 6-17 Specific identification cost flow assumption—periodic LO8

CHECK FIGURE: COGS = $1,761.20

Use the information in Exercise 6-16. Assume that the specific identification method is used to assign costs to cost of goods sold ending inventory. The units in ending inventory were specifically identified as follows:

- 80 units from beginning inventory

- 27 units from the March 7 purchase

- 48 units from the July 28 purchase

Required Determine the cost to be assigned to ending inventory and cost of goods sold.

Problems

Problem 6-1A **Inventory Ownership—perpetual** LO1

On December 31, 2017, Jen & Mink Clothing (J&M) performed the inventory count and determined the year-end ending inventory value to be $75,500. It is now January 8, 2018, and you have been asked to double-check the year-end inventory listing. J&M uses a perpetual inventory system. **Note:** Only relevant items are shown on the inventory listing.

		Jen & Mink Clothing Inventory Listing December 31, 2017			
#	**Inventory Number**	**Inventory Description**	**Quantity (units)**	**Unit Cost ($)**	**Total Value ($)**
1	7649	Blue jackets	100	20	2,000
2	10824	Black pants	300	15	5,000
...					. . .
				Total Inventory	$75,500

The following situations have been brought to your attention:

  a. On January 3, 2018, J&M received a shipment of $2,000 blue jackets (Item #7649). The inventory was purchased December 23, 2017, FOB destination from Global Threads. This inventory was included in J&M's inventory count and inventory listing.

  b. On December 29, 2017, J&M sold scarves (Item #5566) to a customer with a sale price of $700 and cost of $500, FOB shipping. The order was shipped on December 30, 2017. J&M has not included this inventory.

  c. Red Blazers (Item #6193) were purchased and shipped from International Co. on December 30, 2017, for $3,300, FOB shipping. The shipment arrived January 5, 2018, and the appropriate party paid for the shipping charges of $320. Additional costs were $220 for import duties and $60 for insurance during shipment. J&M has not included this inventory.

An asterisk (*) identifies assignment material based on Appendix 6A or Appendix 6B.

   d. At year-end, J&M is holding $5,000 of black pants (Item#10824) on consignment for designer Duke Co. This inventory was included in J&M's inventory count and inventory listing.

   e. On December 31, 2017, J&M shipped white shirts (Item #4291), FOB destination costing $1,000 to a customer. The customer was charged $1,400 and the customer received the goods on January 3, 2018. J&M has not included this inventory.

Required

1. In situations (a) to (e) determine whether inventory should be included or excluded in inventory at December 31, 2017, and explain why. If the inventory should be included, determine the correct inventory cost.

2. Determine the correct ending inventory value at December 31, 2017. Starting with the unadjusted inventory value of $75,500, add or subtract any errors based on your analysis in Part 1. Assume all items that are not shown in the inventory listing or discussed in situations (a) to (e) are recorded correctly.

Problem 6-2A Alternative cost flows—perpetual LO2 e**X**cel

CHECK FIGURES: 1. Ending inventory; a. $27,520.00; b. $27,279.00; 2. Ending inventory = $27,365.00

The Stilton Company has the following inventory and credit purchases during the fiscal year ended December 31, 2017.

Beginning	500 units	@	$85/unit
Feb. 10	250 units	@	$82/unit
Aug. 21	130 units	@	$95/unit

Stilton Company has two credit sales during the period. The units have a selling price of $145.00 per unit.

Sales	
Mar. 15	330 units
Sept. 10	235 units

Stilton Company uses a perpetual inventory system.

Required

1. Calculate the dollar value of cost of goods sold and ending inventory using:

   a. FIFO

   b. Moving weighted average. Round to two decimal places.

2. Calculate the dollar value of cost of goods sold and ending inventory using specific identification, assuming the sales were specifically identified as follows:

Mar. 15:	170	units from beginning inventory, and
	160	units from the February 10 purchase
Sept.10:	165	units from beginning inventory, and
	20	units from the February 10 purchase, and
	50	units from the August 21 purchase

3. Using information from your answers in Parts 1 and 2, journalize the credit purchase on February 10 and the credit sale on September 10 for each of:

   a. FIFO

   b. Moving weighted average

   c. Specific identification.

*Problem 6-3A Alternative cost flows—periodic LO8

CHECK FIGURES: Cost of goods sold: a. $47,830.00; b. $48,376.55

Use the data from Problem 6-2A and do Part 1, assuming Stilton Company uses a periodic inventory costing system. Round calculations to two decimal places.

Problem 6-4A Gross profit comparisons and cost flow assumptions—perpetual LO2,3

CHECK FIGURES: 1. Ending inventory: a. $9,600.00; b. $10,982.30

Gale Company has the following inventory and purchases during the fiscal year ended December 31, 2017.

Beginning inventory	280 units	@	$80/unit
Feb. 10 purchased.................	195 units	@	$84/unit
Feb. 20 sold..........................	360 units	@	$160/unit
Mar. 13 purchased	290 units	@	$78/unit
Sept. 5 purchased	255 units	@	$64/unit
Oct. 10 sold	510 units	@	$160/unit

Gale Company employs a perpetual inventory system.

Required

1. Calculate the dollar value of ending inventory and cost of goods sold using:

   a. FIFO

   b. Moving weighted average. Round all unit costs to two decimal places.

2. Using your calculations from Part 1, complete the following schedule:

	FIFO	Moving Weighted Average
Sales...		
Cost of goods sold		
Gross profit...		

Analysis Component: How would the gross profits calculated in Part 2 above change if Gale Company had been experiencing increasing prices in the acquisition of additional inventory?

*Problem 6-5A Alternative cost flows—periodic LO8

CHECK FIGURES: 1. Cost of goods sold; a. $68,120; b. $66,290

Use the data from Problem 6-4A and do Part 1 assuming Gale Company uses a periodic inventory costing system.

Problem 6-6A Alternative cost flows—perpetual LO2,3

Case Defence sells smart phone cases and uses the perpetual inventory system. The following is information on the purchases and sales of "Defender Box" cases. On October 1, Case Defence had 20 units with a unit cost of $14.

An asterisk (*) identifies assignment material based on Appendix 6A or Appendix 6B.

	Purchases		Sales	
Date	Units	Unit Cost	Units	Unit Price
Oct. 3	10	15		
Oct. 6			15	$50
Oct. 12	20	17		
Oct. 19			20	$50
Oct. 23	30	19		
Oct. 30			25	$50
Oct. 31	15	20		

Required

1. Calculate the dollar value of cost of goods sold and ending inventory for the month of October using the following methods.

   a. FIFO

   b. Moving weighted average. Round all unit costs to two decimal places and round all other numbers to the nearest dollar.

2. Using the calculations in Part 1, complete the following table:

	FIFO	Moving Weighted Average
Sales...		
Cost of goods sold		
Gross profit...		

3. Does using FIFO or Moving weighted average produce

   a. A higher gross profit?

   b. A higher ending inventory balance?

4. Calculate the gross profit percentage for FIFO and Moving weighted average for the month of October. Round to the nearest percentage.

Problem 6-7A Income statement comparisons and cost flow assumptions—perpetual LO2,3

CHECK FIGURE: a. Profit, FIFO = $199,400

During 2017, Fresh Express Company sold 2,500 units of its product on September 20 and 3,000 units on December 22, all at a price of $90 per unit. Incurring operating expenses of $14 per unit sold, it began the year with and made successive purchases of the product as follows:

January 1 beginning inventory	600 units	@	$35 per unit
Purchases:			
February 20	1,500 units	@	$37 per unit
May 16	700 units	@	$41 per unit
December 11	3,300 units	@	$42 per unit
Total	6,100 units		

Required Prepare a comparative income statement for the company, showing in adjacent columns the profits earned from the sale of the product, assuming the company uses a perpetual inventory system and prices its ending inventory on the basis of:

    a. FIFO

    b. Moving weighted average cost. Round all unit costs to two decimal places.

Analysis Component: If the manager of Fresh Express Company earns a bonus based on a percentage of gross profit, which method of inventory costing will she prefer?

*Problem 6-8A Income statement comparisons and cost flow assumptions—periodic LO8

CHECK FIGURE: Profit weighted average = $198,182

Use the data from Problem 6-7A and do the question assuming Fresh Express Company uses a periodic inventory costing system.

Problem 6-9A Analysis of inventory errors LO5,9

Shockley Co. reported the following amounts in its financial statements:

	Financial Statements for Year Ended December 31		
	2017	**2018**	**2019**
(a) Cost of goods sold..............................	$ 715,000	$ 847,000	$ 770,000
(b) Profit..	220,000	275,000	231,000
(c) Total current assets	1,155,000	1,265,000	1,100,000
(d) Equity	1,287,000	1,430,000	1,232,000

In making the physical counts of inventory, the following errors were made:

- Inventory on December 31, 2017: understated $70,000
- Inventory on December 31, 2018: overstated $32,000

Required For each of the preceding financial statement items—(a), (b), (c), and (d)—prepare a schedule similar to the following and show the adjustments that would have been necessary to correct the reported amounts.

	2017	**2018**	**2019**
Cost of goods sold:			
Reported..	_____	_____	_____
Adjustments: Dec. 31/17 error.........................	_____	_____	_____
Dec. 31/18 error.........................	_____	_____	_____
Corrected...	_____	_____	_____

Analysis Component: What is the error in the aggregate profit for the three-year period that resulted from the inventory errors? Explain why this result occurs. Also explain why the understatement of inventory by $70,000 at the end of 2017 resulted in an understatement of equity by the same amount that year.

An asterisk (*) identifies assignment material based on Appendix 6A or Appendix 6B.

Problem 6-10A **Analysis of inventory errors** LO5,9

While performing a detailed review of its financial records, Doors Unlimited noted the following ending inventory errors:

2017	2018	2019
Understated $52,000	Overstated $14,000	No errors

	2017	2018	2019
Ending inventory as reported........................	$ 345,000	$ 420,000	$ 392,000
Cost of goods sold as reported	1,300,000	1,750,000	2,100,000
Profit as reported	340,000	516,000	652,000

Required Calculate the corrected ending inventory and cost of goods sold amounts for each year by completing the following schedule:

	2017	2018	2019
Corrected ending inventory.............................			
Corrected cost of goods sold.........................			
Corrected profit			

Problem 6-11A **Lower of cost and net realizable value** LO4

CHECK FIGURES: 1a. $542,205; 1b. $527,855

The following information pertains to the physical inventory of Electronics Unlimited taken at December 31:

		Per Unit	
Product	Units on Hand	Cost	NRV
Audio equipment:			
Wireless audio receivers........................	335	$185	$196
Touchscreen MP3 players	250	220	200
Audio mixers	316	174	190
Audio stands..	194	100	82
Video equipment:			
Televisions...	470	295	250
5GB video cards......................................	281	180	168
Satellite video recorders	202	615	644
Car audio equipment:			
GPS navigators	175	142	168
Double-DIN Car Deck with iPod/			
iPhone Control & Aux Input	160	195	210

Required

1. Calculate the LCNRV:

   a. For the inventory by major group

   b. For the inventory, applied separately to each product.

2. Prepare the appropriate entry, if any, for (a) and (b).

Problem 6-12A Estimating ending inventory—gross profit method LO6

CHECK FIGURE: $177,470

The Navarre Company had a fire on February 10, 2017, that destroyed a major portion of its inventory. The salvaged accounting records contained the following information:

Sales, January 1 to February 10	$ 350,600
Net merchandise purchased Jan. 1 to Feb. 10	182,400
Additional information was determined from the 2016 annual report:	
Income statement:	
Sales	$3,200,225
Cost of goods sold	1,760,575
Balance sheet:	
Merchandise inventory	294,100

Navarre was able to salvage inventory with a cost of $106,200.

Required Determine the amount of inventory lost by Navarre as a result of the fire. Navarre has a December 31 year-end. *Round the gross profit ratio to the nearest whole percentage point.*

Problem 6-13A Gross profit method LO6

CHECK FIGURE: $483,022

Sporting Pro wants to prepare interim financial statements for the first quarter of 2017 but would like to avoid making a physical count of inventory. During the last five years, the company's gross profit rate has averaged 36%. The following information for the year's first quarter is available from its records:

January 1 beginning inventory	$300,260
Purchases	945,200
Purchase returns	13,050
Transportation-in	6,900
Sales	1,191,150
Sales returns	9,450

Required Use the gross profit method to prepare an estimate of the company's March 31 inventory.

Problem 6-14A Retail inventory method LO6

CHECK FIGURE: 2. Loss at cost = $41,392

The records of Earthly Goods provided the following information for the year ended December 31, 2017.

	At Cost	At Retail
January 1 beginning inventory	$ 471,350	$ 927,150
Purchases	3,328,830	6,398,700
Purchase returns	52,800	119,350
Sales		5,495,700
Sales returns		44,600

Required

1. Prepare an estimate of the company's year-end inventory by the retail method. Round all calculations to two decimal places.

2. Under the assumption the company took a year-end physical inventory at marked selling prices that totalled $1,675,800, prepare a schedule showing the store's loss from theft or other causes at cost and at retail.

Problem 6-15A Retail inventory method LO6

CHECK FIGURE: 2. $76,875

Petcetera had a robbery on the weekend in which a large amount of inventory was taken. The loss is covered completely by insurance. A physical inventory count determined that the cost of the remaining merchandise is $58,500. The following additional information is available:

	At Cost	At Retail
Beginning merchandise inventory	$ 75,000	$ 93,750
Purchase returns and allowances...............	15,000	20,000
Purchases...	1,275,000	1,731,250
Transportation-in.......................................	18,750	
Sales..		1,642,500
Sales returns and allowances		18,000

Required

1. Prepare an estimate of ending merchandise inventory using the retail method.

2. Calculate the cost of the stolen inventory.

Problem 6-16A Inventory ratios LO7

Using the **Indigo** financial statements in Appendix III, calculate the following ratios for the year ended March 29, 2014 and March 30, 2013. Comment on the change and consider whether the ratios make sense given the nature of the company's operations.

   a. Inventory turnover ratio (Round to two decimal places)

   b. Days sales in inventory (Round to the nearest day)

*Problem 6-17A Alternative cost flows—periodic LO8

CHECK FIGURES: 2. Cost of goods sold; a. $1,191,500; b. $1,231,250

Synergy Company began 2017 with 19,000 units of Product X in its inventory that cost $7.50 per unit, and it made successive purchases of the product as follows:

Mar.	7	26,000 units	@ $ 9.00 each
May	25	31,000 units	@ $11.00 each
Aug.	1	21,500 units	@ $12.00 each
Nov.	10	31,000 units	@ $13.50 each

The company uses a periodic inventory system. On December 31, 2017, a physical count disclosed that 15,000 units of Product X remained in inventory.

An asterisk (*) identifies assignment material based on Appendix 6A or Appendix 6B.

Required

1. Prepare a calculation showing the number and total cost of the units available for sale during 2017.

2. Prepare calculations showing the amounts that should be assigned to the 2017 ending inventory and to cost of goods sold, assuming:

   a. FIFO

   b. Weighted average cost basis (round the average cost per unit to two decimal places).

Alternate Problems

Problem 6-1B **Inventory ownership—perpetual** LO1

On November 30, 2017, York + Robin Shoes (Y+R) performed the annual inventory count and determined the year-end ending inventory value to be $49,222. It is now December 3, 2017, and you have been asked to double-check the inventory listing. Y+R uses a perpetual inventory system. Note: Only relevant items are shown on the inventory listing.

		York + Robin Shoes Inventory Listing Year-ended November 30, 2017			
#	**Inventory Number**	**Inventory Description**	**Quantity (units)**	**Unit Cost ($)**	**Total Value ($)**
1	A20	Men's brown dress shoes	74	$50	$3,700
2	B30	Women's black boots	50	30	1,500
...					...
				Total Inventory	$49,222

The following situations have been brought to your attention.

a. On November 28, 2017, Y+R received a customer order for men's sneakers (Item # D50) with a sale price of $1000 and cost of $600, FOB shipping. The order was shipped on November 30, 2017. Y+R did not include this inventory.

b. On December 2, 2018, Y+R received a shipment of $1,500 women's black boots (Item # B30). The inventory was purchased November 22, 2017, FOB destination from Global Threads. This inventory was included in Y+R's inventory count and inventory listing.

c. Women's sandals (Item # C40) were purchased and shipped from International Sole Co. on November 30, 2017 for $2,300, FOB shipping. The shipment arrived December 5, 2017 and the appropriate party paid for the shipping charges of $230. Additional costs were $161 for import duties and $86 for insurance during shipment.

d. On November 30, 2017, Y+R shipped women's flip flops (Item #E60) to a customer for $2,520, FOB destination. The inventory cost $1,800 and the customer received the goods on December 3, 2017. Y+R has not included this inventory.

e. Y+R had been holding $3,700 of men's brown dress shoes (Item# A20) on consignment for designer Blue Co. as at November 30, 2017. This inventory was included in Y+R's inventory count and inventory listing.

Required

1. In situations (a) to (e), determine whether each of the following should be included or excluded in inventory as at November 30, 2017 and explain why. If the inventory should be included, determine the inventory cost.

2. Determine the correct ending inventory value at November 30, 2017. Starting with the unadjusted inventory value of $49,222, add or subtract any errors based on your analysis in Part 1. Assume all items that are not shown in the inventory listing or discussed in situations (a) to (e) are recorded correctly.

Problem 6-2B **Alternative cost flows—perpetual** LO2 e**X**cel

CHECK FIGURES: 1. Ending inventory: a. $56,625.00; b. $55,309.25; 2. Ending inventory = $54,025.00

The Obama Company has the following inventory purchases during the fiscal year ended December 31, 2017.

Beginning.................................	600 units	@	$105/unit
Feb. 13	200 units	@	$109/unit
Aug. 5	345 units	@	$112/unit

Obama Company has two sales during the period. The units have a selling price of $165 per unit.

Sales	
Feb. 15	300 units
Aug. 10	335 units

Obama Company uses a perpetual inventory system.

Required

1. Calculate the dollar value of cost of goods sold and ending inventory using

   a. FIFO

   b. Moving weighted average method (round the average cost per unit to two decimal places)

2. Calculate the dollar value of cost of goods sold and ending inventory using specific identification assuming the sales were specifically identified as follows:

Feb. 15:	175	units from beginning inventory
	125	units from the February 13 purchase
Aug. 10:	15	units from beginning inventory
	320	units from the August 5 purchase

3. Using information from your answers in Parts 1 and 2, journalize the credit sale on February 15, and the credit purchase on August 5 for each of:

   a. FIFO

   b. Moving weighted average

   c. Specific identification

*Problem 6-3B Alternative cost flows—periodic L08

CHECK FIGURES: Cost of goods sold: a. $66,815.00; b. $68,456.90

Use the data from Problem 6-2B and do Part 1, assuming Obama Company uses a periodic inventory costing system. Round calculations to two decimal places.

Problem 6-4B Gross profit comparisons and cost flow assumptions—perpetual L02,3 **eXcel**

CHECK FIGURES: 1. Ending inventory; a. $875; b. $960

The Manson Company has the following sales, inventory, and purchases during the fiscal year ended December 31, 2017.

Beginning inventory	180 units	@	$30/unit
Feb. 20 sold...........................	145 units	@	$40/unit
Apr. 30 purchased	315 units	@	$29/unit
Oct. 5 purchased....................	225 units	@	$25/unit
Oct. 10 sold	540 units	@	$40/unit

Manson Company employs a perpetual inventory system.

Required

1. Calculate the dollar value of ending inventory and cost of goods sold using:

   a. FIFO

   b. Moving weighted average method. Round all unit costs to two decimal places.

2. Using your calculations from Part 1, complete the following schedule:

	FIFO	Moving Weighted Average
Sales...		
Cost of goods sold		
Gross profit..		

Analysis Component: How would the gross profits calculated in Part 2 above change if Manson Company had been experiencing increasing prices in the purchase of additional inventory?

*Problem 6-5B Alternative cost flows—periodic L08

CHECK FIGURES: Cost of goods sold: a. $19,285; b. $19,180

Use the data from Problem 6-4B and do Part 1 assuming Manson Company uses a periodic inventory costing system. Round calculations to two decimal places.

Problem 6-6B Alternative cost flows—perpetual L02,3

Tool Depot sells the latest selection of power tools and uses a perpetual inventory system. The following is information on the purchases and sales of the power drills, "M1500." On November 1, Tool Depot had 150 units with a unit cost of $49.

_____

An asterisk (*) identifies assignment material based on Appendix 6A or Appendix 6B.

	Purchases		Sales	
Date	Units	Unit Cost	Units	Unit Price
Nov. 4			100	$100
Nov. 6	200	47		
Nov. 16	350	45		
Nov. 20			275	$100
Nov. 24	150	40		
Nov. 28			250	$110
Nov. 30			100	$110

Required

1. Calculate the cost of goods sold and ending inventory using the following methods.

   a. FIFO

   b. Moving weighted average. Round all unit costs to two decimal places and round all other numbers to the nearest dollar.

2. Using your calculations from Part 1, complete the following schedule:

	FIFO	Moving Weighted Average
Sales...		
Cost of goods sold		
Gross profit...		

3. Does using FIFO or moving weighted average produce

   a. A higher gross profit?

   b. A higher ending inventory balance?

4. Calculate the gross profit percentage for both methods for the month of November. Round to the nearest percentage.

Problem 6-7B Income statement comparisons and cost flow assumptions—perpetual LO2,3

CHECK FIGURE: a. Profit, FIFO = $51,130

During 2017, the Blizzard Company sold 1,350 units of its product on May 20 and 1,700 units on October 25, all at a price of $51 per unit. Incurring operating expenses of $7 per unit in selling the units, it began the year with, and made successive purchases of, units of the product as follows:

January 1 Beginning inventory...............................	610 units costing $29 per unit		
Purchases:			
April 2	810 units	@	$28 per unit
June 14..	320 units	@	$27 per unit
Aug. 29..	1,340 units	@	$26 per unit
Total	3,080 units		

Required Prepare a comparative income statement for the company for 2017, showing in adjacent columns the profits earned from the sale of the product, assuming the company uses a perpetual inventory system and prices its ending inventory on the basis of:

    a. FIFO

    b. Moving weighted average cost. Round unit costs to two decimal places.

Analysis Component: If the Blizzard Company's manager earns a bonus based on a percentage of gross profit, which method of inventory costing will she prefer?

*Problem 6-8B Income statement comparisons and cost flow assumptions—periodic LO8

CHECK FIGURE: Profit, weighted average = $51,166.60

Use the data from Problem 6-5B and do the question assuming Blizzard Company uses a periodic inventory costing system.

Problem 6-9B Analysis of inventory errors LO5,9

Fireplace Company reported the following amounts in its financial statements:

	Financial Statements for Year Ended December 31		
	2017	**2018**	**2019**
(a) Cost of goods sold..................................	$102,600	$106,400	$ 98,015
(b) Profit..	87,400	105,635	91,955
(c) Total current assets	133,000	138,250	131,475
(d) Equity	152,000	158,000	168,000

In making the physical counts of inventory, the following errors were made:

- Inventory on December 31, 2017: overstated $8,100
- Inventory on December 31, 2018: understated $10,800

Required For each of the preceding financial statement items—(a), (b), (c), and (d)—prepare a schedule similar to the following and show the adjustments that would have been necessary to correct the reported amounts.

	2017	**2018**	**2019**
Cost of goods sold:			
Reported..	_____		_____
Adjustments: Dec. 31/17 error.........................	_____	_____	_____
Dec. 31/18 error.........................	_____	_____	_____
Corrected...	========	========	========

Analysis Component: What is the error in the aggregate profit for the three-year period that resulted from the inventory errors?

An asterisk (*) identifies assignment material based on Appendix 6A or Appendix 6B.

Problem 6-10B Analysis of inventory errors LO5,9

	Incorrect Income Statement Information For Years Ended December 31				Corrected Income Statement Information For Years Ended December 31			
	2017	%	2018	%	2017	%	2018	%
Sales..	$671,000	100	$835,000	100				
Cost of goods sold	402,600	60	417,500	50				
Gross profit.............................	$268,400	40	$417,500	50				

In comparing income statement information for the years ended December 31, 2017 and 2018, the owner noticed an increase in the gross profit. He was puzzled because he knew that inventory costs were increasing.

A detailed review of the records showed the following:

a. Goods with a cost of $37,500 were on consignment at another location. Through an error, they were not included in the inventory of December 31, 2017.

b. $16,000 of merchandise inventory purchased on December 25, 2018, was shipped FOB Shipping Point and received on January 6, 2019. It was not included in inventory on December 31, 2018, in error.

c. While performing the physical inventory count on December 31, 2018, a calculation error was discovered that caused inventory on hand to be overstated by $24,500.

Required

1. Using the information provided, complete the schedule showing the corrected income statement information (round percentages to the nearest whole number).

2. Does the new gross profit information reflect the owner's knowledge of increasing inventory costs?

Problem 6-11B Lower of cost and net realizable value LO4

CHECK FIGURES: 1a. $602,546; 1b. $579,744

The following information pertains to the physical inventory of Geo Furniture Company taken at December 31:

Product	Units on Hand	Per Unit Cost	Per Unit NRV
Office furniture:			
Desks..	430	$261	$305
Credenzas	290	227	256
Chairs	585	49	43
Bookshelves	320	93	82
Filing cabinets:			
Two-drawer..	215	81	70
Four-drawer...	400	135	122
Lateral..	178	104	118
Office equipment:			
Fax machines...	415	168	200
Copiers...	544	317	288
Typewriters	355	125	117

Required

1. Calculate the LCNRV for the:

   a. Inventory by major category

   b. Inventory, applied separately to each product.

2. Prepare the appropriate entry, if any, for (a) and (b).

Problem 6-12B **Estimating ending inventory—gross profit method** LO6

CHECK FIGURE: $81,380.50

The Zeon Company had a flood on July 5, 2017, that destroyed all of its inventory. The salvaged accounting records contained the following information:

Sales, January 1 to July 5...	$ 737,650
Net merchandise purchased Jan. 1 to July 5..	414,900
Additional information was determined from the 2016 annual report:	
Income statement:	
Sales...	$2,122,550
Cost of goods sold	1,337,175
Balance sheet:	
Merchandise inventory...	131,200

Zeon was unable to salvage any usable inventory after the water subsided.

Required Determine the amount of inventory lost by Zeon as a result of the flood. Zeon has a December 31 year-end. Round the gross profit ratio to the nearest whole percentage point.

Problem 6-13B **Gross profit method** LO6

CHECK FIGURE: $183,637.50

Belle Equipment Co. wants to prepare interim financial statements for the first quarter of 2017. The company uses a periodic inventory system but would like to avoid making a physical count of inventory. During the last five years, the company's gross profit rate has averaged 30%. The following information for the year's first quarter is available from its records:

January 1 beginning inventory	$ 376,440
Purchases..	1,066,050
Purchase returns	19,185
Transportation-in...	32,950
Sales...	1,855,125
Sales returns..	37,100

Required Use the gross profit method to prepare an estimate of the company's March 31, 2017, inventory.

Problem 6-14B Retail inventory method LO6

CHECK FIGURES: 2. Loss at cost = $2,040.27

The records of The Wilke Co. provided the following information for the year ended December 31, 2017:

	At Cost	At Retail
January 1 beginning inventory	$ 40,835	$ 57,305
Purchases	251,945	383,530
Purchase returns	5,370	7,665
Sales		393,060
Sales returns		2,240

Required

1. Prepare an estimate of the company's year-end inventory by the retail method. Round all calculations to two decimal places.

2. Under the assumption the company took a year-end physical inventory at marked selling prices that totalled $39,275, prepare a schedule showing the store's loss from theft or other causes at cost and at retail.

Problem 6-15B Retail inventory method LO6

CHECK FIGURE: Loss = $40,200

Poundmaker Company just had a fire in its warehouse that destroyed all of its merchandise inventory. The insurance company covers 80% of the loss. The following information is available regarding the year ended March 31, 2017:

	At Cost	At Retail
Beginning merchandise inventory	$ 75,000	$ 125,000
Purchases	1,050,000	1,750,000
Purchase returns and allowances	125,000	200,000
Transportation-in	5,000	
Sales		1,357,500
Sales returns and allowances		17,500

Required Prepare an estimate of the company's loss using the retail method.

Problem 6-16B Inventory Ratios LO7

Using the Danier Leather financial statements in Appendix III, calculate the following ratios for the year ended June 28, 2014, and June 29, 2013. At June 30, 2012, Danier had an ending inventories balance of $24,891,000 and Cost of sales of $71,513,000. Comment on the change.

    a. Inventory turnover ratio (Round to two decimal places)

    b. Days sales in inventory (Round to the nearest day)

*Problem 6-17B Alternative cost flows—periodic LO8

CHECK FIGURE: 2. COGS: a. $2,565,900; b. $2,487,060

Bonaire Co. began 2017 with 6,300 units of Product B in its inventory that cost $68 each, and it made successive purchases of the product as follows:

Jan.	4	....	10,500 units	@	$65 each
May	18	....	13,000 units	@	$62 each
July	9	....	12,000 units	@	$59 each
Nov.	21	....	15,500 units	@	$56 each

The company uses a periodic inventory system. On December 31, 2017, a physical count disclosed that 16,500 units of Product B remained in inventory.

Required

1. Prepare a calculation showing the number and total cost of the units available for sale during the year.

2. Prepare calculations showing the amounts that should be assigned to the ending inventory and to cost of goods sold assuming:

   a. FIFO

   b. Weighted average cost basis (round the average unit cost to two decimal places)

Analytical and Review Problem

A & R Problem 6-1

The records of Thomas Company as of December 31, 2017, show the following:

	Net Purchases	Net Income	Accounts Payable	Accounts Inventory
Balance per company's books	$325,000	$25,000	$31,000	$18,400
(a)				
(b)				
(c)				
(d)				
(e)				
Correct balances				

The accountant of Thomas Company discovers in the first week of January 2018 that the following errors were made by his staff.

   a. Goods costing $4,500 were in transit (FOB shipping point) and were not included in the ending inventory. The invoice had been received and the purchase recorded.

An asterisk (*) identifies assignment material based on Appendix 6A or Appendix 6B.

b. Damaged goods (cost $4,100) that were being held for return to the supplier were included in inventory. The goods had been recorded as a purchase and the entry for the return of these goods had also been made.

c. Inventory items costing $3,900 were incorrectly excluded from the final inventory. These goods had not been recorded as a purchase and had not been paid for by the company.

d. Goods that were shipped FOB destination had not yet arrived and were not included in inventory. However, the invoice had arrived on December 30, 2017, and the purchase for $2,700 was recorded.

e. Goods that cost $2,400 were segregated and not included in inventory because a customer expressed an intention to buy the goods. The sale of the goods for $4,200 had been recorded in December 2017.

Required Using the format provided above, show the correct amount for net purchases, profit, accounts payable, and inventory for Thomas Company as at December 31, 2017.

Ethics Challenge

EC 6-1

Diversion Inc. is a retail sports store carrying primarily women's golf apparel and equipment. The store is at the end of its second year of operations and, as new businesses often do, is struggling a bit to be profitable. The cost of inventory items has increased just in the short time the store has been in business. In the first year of operations the store accounted for inventory costs using the moving weighted average method. A loan agreement the store has with Dollar Bank, its prime source of financing, requires that the store maintain a certain gross profit and current ratio. The store's owner, Cindy Foor, is looking over Diversion's annual financial statements after year-end inventory has been taken. The numbers are not very favourable and the only way the store can meet the required financial ratios agreed upon with the bank is to change from the moving weighted average to the FIFO method of inventory. Cindy originally decided upon moving weighted average for inventory costing because she felt that moving weighted average yielded a better matching of costs to revenues. Cindy recalculates the ending inventory using FIFO and submits her income statement and balance sheet to the loan officer at the bank for the required bank review of the loan. As Cindy mails the financial statements to the bank, she thankfully reflects on the latitude she has as manager in choosing an inventory costing method.

Required
1. Why does Diversion's use of FIFO improve the gross profit ratio and current ratio?
2. Is the action by Diversion's owner ethical?

Focus on Financial Statements

FFS 6-1

CHECK FIGURES: 2a. Profit = $75,000; 2b. Profit = $79,000

The owner of Fardan Stereo Sales showed the following adjusted trial balance at December 31, 2017:

Account	Account Balance*
Cash..	16,000
Accounts receivable	27,000
Merchandise inventory..	?
Prepaid rent	36,000
Store fixtures	117,000
Accumulated depreciation, store fixtures	82,000
Trademark..	3,000
Accounts payable	18,000
Unearned sales revenue..	4,000
Notes payable, due in 2020...	22,000
Mikel Fardan, capital...	61,000
Mikel Fardan, withdrawals	44,000
Sales..	449,000
Sales discounts...	6,000
Cost of goods sold	?
Delivery expense	5,000
Rent expense	92,000
Salaries expense..	109,000
Interest expense..	2,000
Depreciation expense..	8,000

*Assume normal account balances.

The owner, Mikel Fardan, is analyzing the effect of the various merchandise inventory costing methods on his financial statements and has prepared the following schedule:

	FIFO	Moving Weighted Average
Merchandise inventory, December 31, 2016	12,000	12,000
Purchases..	159,000	159,000
Merchandise inventory, December 31, 2017	?	?
Cost of goods sold	152,000	148,000

Required

1. Calculate the merchandise inventory values at December 31, 2017, under each inventory costing method shown in the schedule above.

2. Prepare a single-step income statement (showing one line each for net sales, cost of goods sold, operating expenses, and interest expense) for the year ended December 31, 2017, along with a balance sheet at December 31, 2017, assuming:

   a. FIFO

   b. Moving weighted average

Analysis Component:

3. Does the schedule above reflect rising costs for merchandise inventory or falling costs? Explain how you know.

4. Based on your results in Part 2, which method should the owner use if he wants to:

   a. Maximize profit?

   b. Maximize assets?

FFS 6-2

Required Answer the following questions.

a. Refer to the balance sheets for WestJet and Danier in Appendix III at the end of the textbook. Both balance sheets include Inventory. Explain how Inventory is unique for each of these companies.

b. What method does Danier use to value its inventory? (Refer to the notes to Danier's financial statements in Appendix III at the end of the textbook.)

c. Inventory is classified on Danier's balance sheet as what type of asset?

d. Did the balance in Inventory for Danier increase or decrease from June 29, 2013, to June 28, 2014?

Critical Thinking Mini Case

The former CEO of Benton Beverages retired and you have been hired in her place. In reviewing the selected financial data shown below, you are puzzled given that industry information clearly shows that the cost of beverages has been on the rise. As you walk about the warehouse area for the first time, you observe that, as pallets of beverages are being moved to the loading dock, empty areas appear behind various rows. You question the forklift driver, who says that the CEO told him always to leave alternating empty rows when stacking pallets. You climb a ladder to get a better view of the inventory layout, gasp, climb down, and determine that an emergency report to the board of directors is required.

							Years Ended December 31,				
	2017		**2016**		**2015**		**2014**	
Sales	$900,000	100%	$750,000	100%	$690,000	100%	$640,000	100%
Cost of goods sold	459,000	51%	390,000	52%	372,600	54%	352,000	55%

Merchandise Inventory		**Merchandise Inventory**		**Merchandise Inventory**		**Merchandise Inventory**	
85,000[1]		73,000[1]		63,000[1]		45,000[1]	
345,000[2]	396,000[3]	306,000[2]	342,000[3]	312,600[2]	337,600[3]	330,000[2]	332,000[3]
63,000[4]		48,000[4]		35,000[4]		20,000[4]	
97,000[5]		85,000[5]		73,000[5]		63,000[5]	

1. Beginning inventory
2. Purchases during the period
3. Cost of goods sold
4. Year-end adjusting entry
5. Ending inventory

Required Incorporating the elements of critical thinking on the inside front cover, comment.

Internal Control and Cash

A Look Back

Chapter 5 and 6 focused how reporting merchandising activities differs from reporting service activities. We also analyzed and recorded merchandise purchases and sales transactions, explaining the adjustments and financial statement presentation for merchandisers. Concepts included which items are included in inventory, specific costs assigned, costing methods used, inventory valuation, and inventory estimation techniques.

A Look at This Chapter

This chapter provides an introduction to Internal Control and Cash with a detailed analysis of internal control guidelines, banking activities, accounting for petty cash funds, and reconciling the differences between cash reported in the bank account and cash in the company's accounting records.

© Feng Yu/Alamy

LEARNING OBJECTIVES

LO1 Define, explain the purpose of, and identify the principles of internal control.

LO2 Define cash and explain how it is reported.

LO3 Apply internal control to cash.

LO4   Explain and record petty cash fund transactions.

LO5   Explain and identify banking activities and the control features they provide.

LO6   Prepare a bank reconciliation and journalize any resulting adjustment(s).

LO7   Calculate the quick ratio and explain its use as an indicator of a company's liquidity.

What Is Cash? A Look at Today's Payment Options

Every year Canadians make approximately 24 billion payments worth more than $44 trillion, according to Lawrence Schembri, deputy governor of the Canadian Payments Association (CPA). Over the past several years Canada's payment system has undergone rapid and fundamental change. Technological innovation, convenience, and continued globalization are the key drivers behind the changes.

The CPA is mandated by Parliament to provide a leadership role in ensuring the safety and soundness of Canada's national clearing and settlement system for payments. The Minister of Finance has overall oversight of CPA activities. The association has a crucial role, as it allows millions of Canadians to conduct business transactions in a safe and efficient clearing system. The Canadian Payments System is continually investing in upgrading its infrastructure to meet changing payment trends, such as creating the framework to enable the deposit of cheques via smartphones. Other advances by the Association include the adoption of ISO-20022, which will enable Canadian companies conducting business in international financial markets to transact more efficiently using a standardized electronic payments language.

Globally, the CPA Environmental Report 2014 identifies the following trends and emerging factors:

- The digitization of payments—the replacement of cash and paper-based transactions with electronic transactions is transforming payment choices available to consumers and businesses.
- Mobile phone ownership and social and business networking (e.g., Facebook, LinkedIn) are important factors influencing payment processing platforms around the world. Mobile technology expands the reach of the Internet, and provides opportunities for cloud payments, and a greater demand for cloud computing applications. Advancements in computing power are making computers more mobile on the front end, and more powerful and smarter on the backend, where improved data processing power can improve fraud mitigation and risk management controls.
- The involvement of non-banks in retail payments systems has increased substantially in recent years, with these entities introducing highly impactful technological payment innovations. New players such as Amazon Payment, Google Checkout, PayPal, and Square are using technology to transform the experience for both consumers and businesses.

Mobile device payment options are also gaining momentum with entrants such as Apple Pay, Google Wallet, and retailer-issued payment options, including the Starbucks App. These Apps transmit financial data using a radio frequency, referred to as "near field communications" and rely on traditional financial infrastructures for the end payment.

Cryptocurrency uses cryptographic algorithms, which combines the fields of mathematics, computer science, and electrical engineering to enable secure transactions used by ATM cards and e-currency, such as Bitcoin and Peercoin. As e-currency providers are not linked to domestic currency and are not monitored by central banks, many critics consider them to be high risk and highly volatile; however, consumers are embracing the flexible payments trend. Businesses need to decide how to best implement appropriate controls over cash payments and cash receipts when the currency is moving to electronic money.

As is made evident by the following charts, Canadian businesses continue to rely on cheques as the most common form of payment for transactions (based on dollar value of transactions). Schembri indicates Canadian businesses are "still among the most cheque-reliant of the major economies."

(Continued)

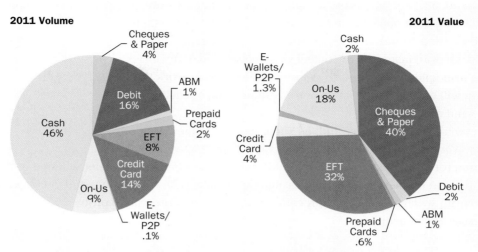

Figure A: Payment Categories Proportion of Total 2011 Canadian Payments

- Note: On-Us transactions refers to transactions conducted within the same bank. For example, a cheque written to a supplier that has a bank account at the same bank.

Sources: 2013 Annual Report, Canadian Payments Association; CPA Environmental Report 2014, Canadian Payments Association; http://www.bankofcanada.ca/2014/06/dual-vision-canadian-payments-system/; Canadian Payment Methods and Trends October 2012 report, Canadian Payments Association: https://www.cdnpay.ca/imis15/pdf/pdfs_publications/examining_canadian_payment_report_2012.pdf

Video Link: To learn more about the functions of the Canadian Payments Association, take a look at the following videos: http://videos.cdnpayannualreview.ca/en and https://vimeo.com/101633599

CRITICAL THINKING CHALLENGE If a debit card is used instead of currency to purchase a $10 item, would the journal entry for the buyer/seller be affected? Explain.

CHAPTER PREVIEW

As individuals, we are frequently reminded through media reports and personal experiences that we need to safeguard our personal assets from theft and our personal identity from fraud. We take advantage of security measures such as password protection, securing our wallets, cell phones and laptops, locking our doors and vehicles, installing alarm systems, and monitoring suspicious activity around us.

Businesses also need to develop systems and safeguards in order to effectively protect and manage their physical and technological assets. Many retailers offer online sales opportunities and have access to their customer's personal credit card information. Hackers and cybercriminals can attempt to access this data, requiring the development and continuous monitoring of the company's firewall, which is its network security system that functions to protect corporate data from outsiders.

Small companies can be the most vulnerable to occurrences of fraud, as they tend to have fewer formalized controls and procedures. For private companies, it is the owner's responsibility to set up policies and procedures to safeguard a company's assets, which is especially imperative for assets such as cash. It is critical that owners and employees understand and apply established policies and procedures of internal control to adequately safeguard the company's core resources, including both physical and technological assets. This chapter provides you with a foundation in internal control concepts and will enable you to identify instances of control weaknesses and deficiencies. If you apply principles taught in the chapter to your current work environment, you will be able to add value to the organization by identifying weaknesses and recommending improvement areas.

Cash is the most liquid asset and, as such, has the highest risk of theft. Common controls to protect cash resources are presented, including accounting for petty cash funds and reconciling bank accounts. Our understanding of these controls and procedures strengthens security in carrying out business. As was emphasized in the chapter opening vignette, security with respect to cash receipts and payments is crucial to protect the financial lifeline of both businesses and consumers.

Internal Control

This section introduces internal control and its fundamental principles. We also discuss the impact of computing technology on internal control and the limitations of control procedures.

Purpose of Internal Control

LO1 Define, explain the purpose of, and identify the principles of internal control.

Owners of small businesses often have their eyes, ears, and physical presence in the entire operation. They participate in all activities from hiring and managing employees to signing all cheques. These owners know from personal contact and observation whether the business is actually receiving the assets and services being paid for. Many of these owners have a clear picture of how much cash is in the bank on a daily basis and monitor their cash needs carefully. The larger the operation, the more senior management must delegate responsibilities and rely on formal procedures rather than personal contact in controlling and knowing all operations of the business.

These executives place a high priority on internal control systems to monitor and control operations. This is because a well-developed control system can prevent avoidable losses, help managers plan operations, and monitor company and human performance. An **internal control system** is all policies and procedures used to:

- Protect assets
- Ensure reliable accounting
- Promote efficient operations
- Encourage adherence to company policies

> **Important Tip:** Remember the CAR principle. Attributes of a strong control system can be broken into an easily remembered acronym: C.A.R. This stands for Custody, Authorization, and Recording of assets. These three duties must always be performed by separate individuals to ensure adequate controls and prevent occurrences of fraud. A control weakness can be identified when two or more of these tasks are performed by the same or related individuals.

Principles of Internal Control

Internal control policies and procedures depend on the nature and size of the business. The fundamental **principles of internal control** are the following:

1. ESTABLISH A SEPARATION OF DUTIES.

A **separation of duties** involves dividing responsibility for related transactions between two or more individuals or departments. Specifically the *custody, authorization* and *recording* of assets should be performed by different individuals.

- *Authorization and custody of assets* need to be separate to prevent theft of goods. Having an independent person check incoming goods for quality and quantity encourages more care and attention to detail than when they are checked by the person who placed the order and helps to ensure items received are not stolen and the original order is not modified to hide the theft. Requiring two signatures on cheques also works to verify that disbursements comply with policies and procedures.

- *Recordkeeping* should be separated from the *custody of assets* to ensure a person who controls or has access to an asset is not responsible for maintaining that asset's accounting records. The risk of theft or waste is reduced since the person with control over the asset knows that records are kept by another person. The recordkeeper does not have access to the asset and has no reason to falsify records. In situations where recordkeeping is separate from the custody of assets, *collusion* is necessary to hide theft from the records. **Collusion** is not likely because it means two or more people must agree to commit a fraud.

- Authorization and recordkeeping, if performed by the same individual, can lead to misappropriation of assets. For example, an individual could authorize a purchase transaction from a fictitious vendor and process a payment for goods that were never received. Better control is maintained if, for instance, the person designing and programming the IT system does not serve as the operator. Cheque-writing activities should not be controlled by a computer operator in order to avoid risk of fraud.

2. ENSURE TRANSACTIONS AND ACTIVITIES ARE AUTHORIZED.

Establish responsibilities for each task clearly for each position in the company. Approvals must be made by authorized individuals. When two salesclerks share access to the same cash register, for instance, neither clerk can prove or disprove any alleged shortage. Assigning responsibility for a separate cash drawer for each clerk provides a better opportunity to monitor misappropriation of cash. Having a manager review employee timesheets helps to ensure accuracy and prevents paying employees for hours not worked.

3. MAINTAIN RECORDS.

Maintain adequate records to help protect assets by ensuring that employees use prescribed procedures. When detailed records of manufacturing equipment and tools are kept, for instance, lost or stolen items are readily noticed. Similarly, the use of a chart of accounts encourages the correct recording of transactions that improves the accuracy of reports.

Preprinted forms are an important control to ensure required information is tracked and help to ensure employees do not miss recording important information. For example, when sales receipts are prenumbered and automatically generated by the cash register, a salesperson is not able to pocket cash by making a sale and destroying the sales slip. Computerized point-of-sale systems achieve the same control results.

4. INSURE ASSETS AND BOND KEY EMPLOYEES.

Insure assets and bond key employees to reduce risk of loss from casualty and theft. To **bond** an employee is to purchase an insurance policy, or a bond, against losses from theft by that employee. Bonding reduces the risk of loss suffered from theft in addition to discouraging theft by the bonded employee.

463

5. APPLY TECHNOLOGICAL CONTROLS.

Cash registers with a locked-in tape or electronic file make a record of each cash sale. A time clock registers the exact time an employee arrives at and departs from the job. Passwords limit access to sensitive information. Change and currency counting machines can quickly and accurately count amounts. Personal identification scanners, such as iris scanners or fingerprint scanners, can limit access to only those individuals who are authorized. All of these and other technological controls are effective parts of many internal control systems. For example, gold and gem mines incorporate security measures including cameras, X-ray machines, and body searches to prevent theft of their inventory.

6. PERFORM INTERNAL AND EXTERNAL AUDITS.

Perform regular and independent reviews to ensure that internal control procedures are followed. No internal control system is entirely effective, for various reasons such as employee turnover, human error and intentional circumventing of controls. Reviews are preferably done by internal auditors who are employees not directly involved in operations and who report directly to senior management or the audit committee of the board of directors. An independent evaluation of the controls ensures the established policies and procedures are being followed.

Many companies also pay for audits by independent external auditors who are professional accountants. These external auditors are required to document the controls for every financial statement line item and test existing controls. The auditors perform a detailed analysis of the company's financial records and give an opinion as to whether the company's financial statements are presented fairly in accordance with the applicable set of generally accepted accounting principles. In the process of their evaluation, they often identify internal controls that need improvement.

> **Important Tip:** **Solving problems related to controls.** To ensure you provide a full analysis of a control issue it is helpful to remember the acronym W.I.R. First identify the *weakness* (could be due to a C.A.R. issue), then explain the *implication* of how the weak control will cause issues/errors, and provide a *recommendation* to resolve the identified weakness.

Three Drivers of Fraud

The following diagram highlights a standard framework developed for fraud investigators in the 1950s by criminologist Dr. Donald Cressey that, despite over half a century of technological advancement, has proven to be a useful tool for today's leading forensic investigators.

A 2013 KPMG Study, "Global Profiles of the Fraudster: White Collar Crime—Present and Future'" revealed the following regarding the components of the fraud triangle:

Opportunity:

- 54% of the frauds committed were facilitated by weak internal controls

- Frauds were found to frequently occur because of a failure to have a basic control in place, such as checking supporting documentation before authorizing a transaction.

- Capability: the more senior the executive position held by the fraudster, the greater ability he or she has to get past the controls. Management's ability to override controls is a key area of risk.

● Deterrent: A focus on fraud prevention is key; continuously evaluating the controls in place and strengthening identified weaknesses (including adequate supervision of employees) will help prevent several of the occurrences.

Motivation:

○ Out of 1,082 fraudsters surveyed, 57% claimed to be motivated by greed, financial gain, and financial difficulty. Approximately 10% were motivated to meet business targets.

● Deterrent: More and more companies are increasing the linkage between management compensation and their company's financial performance and decreasing the portion of their fixed salary.

Rationale:

○ Fraudsters will often rationalize their acts: 44% of executive directors felt they were above the rules regulating the workplace, indicating a sense of superiority; and 16% indicated being under-remunerated as a contributor.

● Deterrent: KPMG International indicated the reason for the fraud is broadly determined by the ethical and cultural context; the study indicates that Singapore, for example, has stringent enforcement and as a result has less corruption.

The study comments with respect to the fraud triangle that "people commit fraud when the three elements occur simultaneously, the perfect storm; motivation, opportunity, and ability to rationalize the act." The study revealed the following key characteristics of the fraudsters that participated in the study:

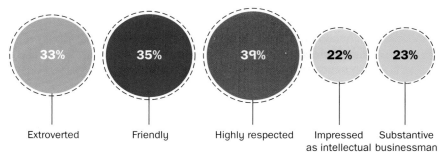

Source: Global profiles of the fraudster, KPMG International 2013, White collar crime- present and future. www.kpmg.com/fraudster

REDUCED PROCESSING ERRORS

Provided the software and data entries are correct, the risk of mechanical and mathematical errors is nearly eliminated because of technology. Yet mistakes happen and one must be alert to that possibility. The decreasing human involvement in later data processing can cause data entry errors to go undiscovered. Similarly, errors in software can produce consistent erroneous processing of transactions.

MORE EXTENSIVE TESTING

Auditors and others need to test not only samples of data from the electronic accounting system but also the controls over the system itself. The results of the review of the controls over the accounting system will affect the scope of the samples of data tested.

LIMITED EVIDENCE OF PROCESSING

Because many data processing steps are increasingly done by computer, fewer "hard copy" items of documentary evidence are available for review. Yet technologically advanced systems can store additional evidence. They can, for instance, record information such as who made the entries, the date and time, and the source of their entry. Technology can also be designed to require use of passwords or other identification before access to the system is granted. This means that internal control depends more on the design and operation of the information system and less on analysis of the documents left behind by the system.

INCREASED ECOMMERCE

Technology has encouraged the growth of ecommerce. **Amazon.ca** and **Kijiji.ca** are examples of companies that have successfully exploited ecommerce, and most companies today have at least some ecommerce transactions. All such transactions involve at least three risks. (1) *Credit card number theft* is a risk of using, transmitting, and storing such data online. This increases the cost of e-commerce. (2) *Computer viruses* are malicious programs that attach themselves to innocent files for purposes of infecting and harming other files and programs. (3) *Impersonation* online can result in charges of sales to bogus accounts, purchases of inappropriate materials, and the inadvertent surrender of confidential information to hackers. To combat some of these risks, companies use both firewalls (points of entry to a system that require passwords to continue) and encryption (a mathematical process to rearrange contents that cannot be read without the process code).

DECISION INSIGHT

Warning Signs

There are clues to internal control violations. Warning signs from accounting include (1) an increase in customer refunds (could be fake), (2) missing documents (could be used for fraud), (3) differences between bank deposits and cash receipts (could be embezzled cash), and (4) delayed recording (could reflect fraudulent records). Warning signs from employees include (1) lifestyle changes (could be embezzlement), (2) too close with suppliers (could signal fraudulent transactions), and (3) failure to leave job, even for vacations (could conceal fraudulent activities).

Limitations of Internal Control

All internal control policies and procedures have limitations. Probably the most serious source of these limitations is the human element that we can categorize as either (1) human error, or (2) human fraud.

Human error is a factor whenever internal control policies and procedures are carried out by people. Human error can occur from negligence, fatigue, misjudgment, lack of training, or confusion. Human fraud involves intent by people to defeat internal controls for personal gain. This human element highlights the importance of establishing an *internal control environment* that conveys management's attitude and commitment to internal control.

Another important limitation of internal control is the *cost–benefit trade-off*. This means the costs of internal controls must not exceed their benefits. Analysis of costs and benefits must consider all factors, including the impact on morale. Most companies, for instance, have a legal right to read employees' e-mail. Yet companies seldom exercise that right unless confronted with evidence of potential harm to the company. The same holds for drug testing, phone tapping, and hidden cameras. The bottom line is that no internal control system is perfect and that managers must establish internal control policies and procedures with a net benefit to the company.

The preceding discussion is an introduction to internal controls. The study of *auditing* takes a detailed look at internal controls.

Cybercriminals Hit ATMs—A Massive $45M Modern-Day Bank Heist

An organized group of criminals recently executed "one of the most sophisticated cyberattacks on bank machines ever conducted." A crime ring of hackers withdrew $45 million from ATMs from 21 countries around the world prior to being arrested. According to *The Globe and Mail*, prosecutors labelled the crime a "massive 21st-century bank heist that reached across the Internet and stretched around the globe." How did they do it? The criminals "allegedly hacked into prepaid debit-card networks, boosted balances, then successfully erased daily withdrawal limits, giving them the ability to drain money from the accounts." This is another reason that companies need to constantly be working to defend themselves from hackers and organized crime; today's bank robbers are able to hide behind laptops and no longer show up with a pistol and a mask. The attached video link demonstrates how the hackers were able to accomplish the robbery.

Sources: http://www.theglobeandmail.com/report-on-business/eight-men-charged-in-massive-worldwide-atm-heist/article11844090/, accessed October 20, 2014; http://www.nbcnews.com/tech/security/6-arrested-45-million-global-atm-bank-cyberheist-f2D11617858, accessed June 23, 2015; http://www.forbes.com/sites/josephsteinberg/2013/05/13/a-message-for-every-business-owner-from-criminals-who-stole-45-million/., accessed June 23, 2015.

Video Link: http://money.cnn.com/2013/05/09/technology/security/cyber-bank-heist/

DECISION MAKER

Answer—End of chapter

Campaign Manager

You are leading a campaign to influence the government to improve the health care system. Your funding is limited and you try hiring people who are committed to your cause and will work for less. A systems analyst recently volunteered her services and put together a web strategy to attract supporters. She also strongly encouraged you to force all employees to take at least one week of vacation per year. Why does she feel so strongly about a "forced vacation" policy?

CHECKPOINT

1. Fundamental principles of internal control state that (choose the correct statement):
   a. Responsibility for a series of related transactions (such as placing orders for, receiving, and paying for merchandise) should be assigned to one person.
   b. Responsibility for all tasks should be shared by two or more employees so that one serves as a check on the other.
   c. Employees who handle cash and negotiable assets are bonded.
2. What are some impacts of computing technology on internal control?

Do Quick Study question: QS 7-1

Cash

LO2 Define cash and explain how it is reported.

Cash is the most important asset companies need to manage. It is not only the most liquid asset, but also the most fraudulently misappropriated. Companies need to maintain adequate cash levels to pay off upcoming current liabilities, as was presented in Chapter 4 with our analysis of the current ratio, also referred to as working capital ratio. Due to the high risk of theft, it is essential that companies implement effective controls over cash handling, cheque processing, and electronic payments. Good accounting systems support both goals by managing how much cash is on hand and controlling who has access to it.

Cash Defined

The financial statement line item **cash** includes items such as currency, coins, amounts on deposit in bank accounts, chequing accounts, and most cash savings accounts.[1] Cash also includes items that are acceptable for deposit in these accounts, such as customers' cheques, cashier's cheques, certified cheques, money orders, e-currency, and deposits made through electronic funds transfer (EFT).

Many companies invest idle cash in short-term investments called *cash equivalents* to increase earnings. Because cash equivalents are similar to cash, many companies combine them with cash as a single item on the balance sheet. **Amazon.com Inc.,** for instance, reports the following on its December 31, 2013, balance sheet:

Cash and cash equivalents..............................$8,658 (Million)

Amazon.com Inc. discloses its accounting policy over the category Cash and Cash Equivalents in its 2013 Annual Report as:

Cash and Cash Equivalents

We classify all highly liquid instruments with an original maturity of three months or less at the time of purchase as cash equivalents.

LIQUIDITY

Cash is the usual means of payment when paying for other assets, services, or liabilities. **Liquidity** refers to how easily an asset can be converted into another asset or used in paying for services or obligations. Cash and cash equivalents are called **liquid assets** because they are converted easily into other assets or used in paying for services or liabilities. A company must maintain a certain level of liquid assets so it has the capacity to pay bills on time and can make cash purchases when necessary.

Quotable Quotes:

"Cash is king. No matter how many good opportunities come your way, do not invest all your cash. If you run out of reserves, the smallest or foolish of things may bring you down. Companies with millions in assets have gone bankrupt because they cannot make a $25,000 payment."

— Mauricio Chaves Mesén, *12 Laws of Great Entrepreneurs*

Control of Cash

LO3 Apply internal control to cash.

It is important that we apply principles of good internal control to cash. Cash is the most liquid of all assets and is easily hidden and transported. A good system of internal control for cash provides adequate procedures for protecting both cash receipts and cash disbursements. Because cash is the most liquid of

---

[1] IFRS 2014, IAS 7, para. 6.

assets, specific controls need to be in place over the handing (**c**ustody) of cash. These procedures should meet three basic guidelines:

1. **Separate handling of cash from recordkeeping of cash.** When duties are separated, it requires two or more people to collude for cash to be stolen and the theft to be concealed in the accounting records. (**C**ustody and **R**ecording).

2. **Deposit cash receipts promptly (daily) in a bank.** Immediate (daily) deposits of all cash receipts produces a timely independent test of the accuracy of the count of cash received. It also reduces cash theft or loss, and it reduces the risk of an employee personally using the money before depositing it. (**C**ustody and **R**ecording).

3. **Make cash disbursements by cheque.** Paying expenses by cheque, when possible, develops a bank record of cash disbursements. This guideline also reduces the risk of cash theft. If possible it is best if two signatures are required to ensure that legitimate invoices are being paid. (**A**uthorization and **R**ecording)

One exception to the third guideline is to allow small disbursements of currency and coins from a petty cash fund. We describe a petty cash fund later in this chapter. Another important point is that the deposit of cash receipts and the use of cheques for cash disbursements allow a company to use bank records as a separate external record of cash transactions. We then explain how using externally prepared bank records enables a company to confirm the accuracy of its internal records using an effective control tool called a bank reconciliation.

Control of Cash Receipts

Internal control of cash receipts ensures that all cash received is accurately recorded and deposited. Cash receipts arise from many transactions, including cash sales, collections of customers' accounts, receipts of interest and rent, bank loans, sale of assets, and owners' investments. This section explains internal control over two important types of cash receipts: over-the-counter and mail.

OVER-THE-COUNTER CASH RECEIPTS

For purposes of internal control, over-the-counter cash sales should be recorded on a cash register at the time of each sale for internal control. To help ensure that correct amounts are entered, each register should be positioned so customers can read the amounts entered. The design of each cash register should provide a permanent, locked-in record of each transaction. Many software programs facilitate point-of-sale cash register transactions and enter them in accounting records. Less technology-dependent registers simply print a record of each transaction on a paper tape or electronic file locked inside the register.

Custody over cash should be separate from its recordkeeping; therefore, the clerk who has access to cash in the register should not have access to modify its locked-in record. The register should open only when a sale is recorded to prevent employees from accessing the till between transactions. Exhibit 7.1 summarizes the cash receipt controls that help to protect cash.

At the end of the clerk's work period, the clerk should count the cash in the register, record the amount, and turn over the cash and a record of the cash balance to an employee in the cashier's office. The employee in the cashier's office, like the clerk, has access to the cash as he or she prepares the bank deposit and should not have access to modify accounting records (or the register tape or file). A third employee compares the record of total register transactions (or the register tape or file) with a copy of the deposit slip and cash receipts summary reported by the cashier's office. This record (or register tape or file) is the basis for a journal entry recording over-the-counter cash sales.

EXHIBIT 7.1

Cash Receipt Controls

Cash register ——————————————————→ **Cashier** ——————————————————→**Computer**

© Zavgsg/Dreamstime.com/GetStock.com

© Mario Beauregard/The Canadian Press

© Ds011photo/Dreamstime.com/GetStock.com

Note that the third employee has access to the records for cash but not to the actual cash. The clerk and the employee from the cashier's office have access to cash but not to the accounting records. This means the accuracy of cash records and amounts is automatically checked. The process described above significantly reduces the risk of error or diversion of cash without the difference being revealed.

CASH OVER AND SHORT

Sometimes errors in making change are discovered when there is a difference between the cash in a cash register and the record of the amount of cash sales. This difference is reported in the **Cash Over and Short account**. This income statement account, included under general and administrative expenses, records the effects of cash overages and cash shortages to profit from errors in making change and missing petty cash receipts. The journal entries to record cash over and short are illustrated later in this chapter.

CASH RECEIPTS BY MAIL

Control of cash receipts[2] that arrive through the mail starts with the person who opens the mail. In a large business, two people are assigned the task and are present when opening the mail. The person opening the mail makes a list of money received. This list should contain a record of each sender's name, the amount, invoice number, and an explanation for what purpose the money is sent. Copies of the list are sent with the money to the cashier to prepare the bank deposit, and to the accounting department to adjust the customer accounts and record the cash receipt. The cashier deposits the money in the bank, and the recordkeeper records amounts received in the accounting records. In a small business, the owner should assume responsibility for cash.

Control of Cash Disbursements

Control of cash disbursements is especially important for companies. Most large thefts occur from payments of fictitious invoices. The key to controlling cash disbursements is to require that all expenditures be made by cheque, with two signatures if possible when not signed by the owner. The **three-way match** is a good control for cash disbursements. A copy of the approved purchase order, receiving report, and invoice must be "matched" or present before any cash disbursement is approved. The only exception is for small payments from petty cash. Another key is that when the authority to sign cheques is assigned to a person other than the owner, that person must not have access to modify the accounting records. This separation of duties helps prevent an employee from hiding fraudulent disbursements in the accounting records. It is best to have two signatories on all cheques if possible to prevent a single person from writing him- or herself a cheque.

---

2   Cash receipts by mail are normally in the form of cheques. Cheques are equivalent to cash and would therefore be recorded as cash.

The manager of a small business often signs cheques and knows from personal contact that the items being paid for are actually received. This arrangement is impossible in large businesses. Instead, internal control procedures must be substituted for personal contact. These controls are achieved through a *voucher system*. Briefly, the voucher system of control requires that a number of procedures be performed and documents collected to support the validity of each disbursement. These procedures are designed to assure the cheque signer that the obligations recorded were properly incurred and should be paid.

The exact procedures used to achieve control over cash vary across companies. They depend on factors such as company size, number of employees, volume of cash transactions, and sources of cash. We must therefore view the procedures described in this section as illustrative of those in practice today.

DECISION INSIGHT

The Bank of Canada is charged with the issuance of currency and is responsible for the design, issuance, and distribution of Canadian bank notes (bills). The image below identifies the security measures incorporated into the design of the Canadian bills printed by the Bank of Canada. Why do you think the bank develops currency with such a wide range of security measures? In

supplying bank notes, the Bank ensures they are difficult to counterfeit and easy to authenticate, ensuring businesses can easily identify true Canadian currency. As counterfeiters work to reproduce currency, banks need to incorporate more and more security into the manufacture of the notes to prevent fraud. Follow the link below to view a video presentation by the Bank of Canada, summarizing the features of the new polymer notes and demonstrating how to handle situations when you identify counterfeit currency.

Video Link: http://www.bankofcanada.ca/multimedia/counterfeit-prevention/

PHOTO SOURCE: © Bank of Cananda. http://www.bankofcanada.ca/banknotes/image-gallery/

CHECKPOINT

3. Good internal control procedures for cash receipts imply that (choose one):
   a. All cash disbursements, other than those for very small amounts, are made by cheque.
   b. An accounting employee should count cash received from sales and promptly deposit receipts.
   c. Cash receipts by mail should be opened by an accounting employee who is responsible for recording and depositing receipts.

Do Quick Study questions: QS 7-2, QS 7-3

PETTY CASH SYSTEM OF CONTROL

 Explain and record petty cash fund transactions.

A basic principle for controlling cash disbursements is that all payments are made by cheque. An exception to this rule is made for petty cash disbursements. Petty cash disbursements are the *small amount*

payments required in most companies for items such as postage, courier fees, repairs, and supplies. To avoid writing cheques for small amounts, a company usually sets up a petty cash fund and uses the money in this fund to make small payments.

OPERATING A PETTY CASH FUND

Establishing a petty cash fund requires estimating the total amount of small payments likely to be made during a short period such as a week or month. A cheque is then drawn by the company cashier's office for an amount slightly in excess of this estimate. To illustrate, assume the trendy messenger bag company, Demano, established a petty cash fund on November 1, 2017, in the amount of $75. A $75 cheque was drawn, cashed, and its proceeds turned over to Milani Taylor, an office employee designated as the *petty cashier* or *petty cash custodian*. The **petty cashier** is responsible for safekeeping of the cash, for making payments from this fund, and for keeping accurate records. The entry to record the set-up of this petty cash fund is:

Nov.	1	Petty Cash...	75	
		Cash...		75
		To establish a petty cash fund.		

This entry transfers $75 from the regular Cash account to the Petty Cash account. After the petty cash fund is established, the *Petty Cash account is not debited or credited again unless the size of the total fund is changed.*

The petty cashier should keep petty cash in a locked box in a safe place. As each disbursement is made, the person receiving payment signs a *petty cash receipt* or *petty cash ticket* as illustrated in Exhibit 7.2.

EXHIBIT 7.2

Petty Cash Receipt

Petty Cash Receipt	No. 6
For _____ Delivery charges _____	Date _____ Nov.18, 2017 _____
Charge to _____ Delivery expense _____	Amount _____ $5.00 _____
Approved by _____ *Jim Gibbs* _____	Received by _____ *Dick Pitch* _____

The petty cash receipt is then placed in the petty cash box with the remaining money. When the cash is nearly gone, the fund should be reimbursed. When it is time to reimburse the petty cash fund, the petty cashier should sort the receipts by type and prepare a summary as shown in Exhibit 7.3.

This summary and all petty cash receipts are presented to the company's cashier. The company's cashier stamps all receipts paid so they cannot be reused, files them for recordkeeping, records the reimbursement, and gives the petty cashier a cheque for a sum *equal to the fund size less the cash remaining*. In our example, Jim Gibbs had only $2.20 cash remaining in the fund at the end of November. Therefore, the reimbursement cheque is for $72.80 (= $75.00 − $2.20). Notice that Exhibit 7.3 shows total receipts for

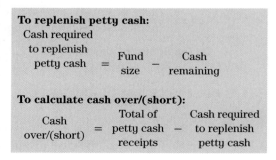

To replenish petty cash:
$$\text{Cash required to replenish petty cash} = \text{Fund size} - \text{Cash remaining}$$

To calculate cash over/(short):
$$\text{Cash over/(short)} = \text{Total of petty cash receipts} - \text{Cash required to replenish petty cash}$$

EXHIBIT 7.3

Petty Cash Payments Report

DEMANO					
Petty Cash Payments Report					
Receipts:					
Office maintenance					
Nov. 2 Washing windows			$10.00		
17 Washing windows			10.00		
27 Computer repairs..			26.50	$46.50	
Transportation-in					
Nov. 5 Delivery of merchandise purchased...............................			$ 6.75		
20 Delivery of merchandise purchased...............................			8.30	15.05	
Delivery expense					
Nov. 28 Customer's package delivered				5.00	
Office supplies					
Nov. 15 Purchased office supplies				4.75	
Total receipts..					$71.30
Fund total				$75.00	
Less: Cash remaining				2.20	
Equals: Cash required to replenish petty cash...............................					$72.80
Cash over/(short)...					($ 1.50)

$71.30. The difference between the total receipts and the reimbursement cheque represents a cash shortage of $1.50 (= $71.30 − $72.80) due to an error. The reimbursement cheque is recorded as follows:

Nov.	27	Office Maintenance Expenses.........................	46.50	
		Merchandise Inventory...................................	15.05	
		Delivery Expense	5.00	
		Office Supplies Expense	4.75	
		Cash Over and Short......................................	1.50	
		Cash..		72.80
		To reimburse petty cash.		

In the case of an overage in the petty cash fund, a credit to Cash Over and Short is recorded in the reimbursing entry.

When the reimbursement cheque is cashed and the money returned to the cash box, the total money in the box is restored to its original amount of $75.00 (= $72.80 + $2.20). The fund is now ready to begin a new cycle of operations.

INCREASING OR DECREASING PETTY CASH FUND

A decision to increase or decrease a petty cash fund is often made when the fund is being reimbursed. To illustrate, let us assume that Demano decides to increase the petty cash fund by $25, from $75 to $100, on November 27 when it reimburses the fund. This is recorded as follows:

Nov.	27	Petty Cash..	25.00	
		Office Maintenance Expenses.........................	46.50	
		Merchandise Inventory...................................	15.05	
		Delivery Expense	5.00	
		Office Supplies Expense	4.75	
		Cash Over and Short......................................	1.50	
		Cash..		97.80
		To reimburse petty cash and increase it		
		by $25.00.		

DECISION MAKER

Answer—End of chapter

Internal Auditor

You just graduated and have been hired as an internal audit trainee for a company. As part of your training, your supervisor has instructed you to make surprise counts of three $200 petty cash funds. You arrive at the office of one of the petty cashiers while she is on the telephone. You explain the purpose of your visit, and the petty cashier asks politely that you come back after lunch so that she can finish the business she's conducting by long distance. You agree and return after lunch. The petty cashier opens the petty cash box and shows you nine new $20 bills with consecutive serial numbers plus receipts totalling $20. Do you take further action or comment on these events in your report to your supervisor?

CHECKPOINT

4. Why are some cash payments made from a petty cash fund?
5. Why should a petty cash fund be reimbursed at the end of an accounting period?
6. What are three results of reimbursing the petty cash fund?

Do Quick Study questions: QS 7-4, QS 7-5, QS 7-6

MID-CHAPTER DEMONSTRATION PROBLEM

Castillo Company, an HR Consulting firm, established a $250 petty cash fund on February 10. On February 28, the fund had $180.14 remaining in cash and receipts for these expenditures: postage, $10.51; office supplies, $50.00; and repair expenses, $10.50. Prepare:

   a. The February 10 entry to establish the fund,

   b. The February 28 entry to record the fund transactions and replenish it, and

   c. Independent of (b), the February 28 entry to record the fund transactions and reduce the fund to $100.

Analysis Component:

Assume that there was no receipt for the $50.00 of office supplies. Should this amount be reimbursed? Explain why or why not.

Planning the Solution

   - Total petty cash receipts.
   - Calculate cash required to replenish petty cash.
   - Calculate cash over/(short), if any.
   - Prepare journal entries as required.
   - Prepare an answer to the analysis question.

Solution

a.	Feb. 10	Petty Cash Fund...	250.00	
		Cash		250.00
		To establish petty cash fund.		
b.	28	Postage Expense..	10.51	
		Office Supplies Expense	50.00	
		Repair Expense	10.50	
		Cash...		69.86[1]
		Cash Over and Short..........................		1.15[2]
		To reimburse petty cash fund.		

Calculations:

[1]Total of petty cash receipts = \$10.51 + \$50.00 + \$10.50 = $\underline{\underline{\$71.01}}$

Cash required to replenish petty cash = Fund size − Cash remaining

$$= \$250 - \$180.14$$
$$= \underline{\$69.86}$$

[2]Cash over/(short) = Receipt totals − Cash required

$$= \$71.01 - \$69.86$$
$$= \underline{\underline{\$1.15}}$$

c.	28	Cash	80.14[3]	
		Postage Expense..	10.51	
		Office Supplies Expense	50.00	
		Repair Expense	10.50	
		Petty Cash...		150.00
		Cash Over and Short..................................		1.15
		To reimburse petty cash fund and		
		decrease it to \$100.		

Calculation:

[3]Cash required to replenish petty cash = New fund size − Cash remaining

$$= \$100.00 - \$180.14$$
$$= \underline{\underline{-\$80.14}} \text{ (therefore, instead of a credit to Cash, debit Cash)}$$

Analysis Component:

The \$50.00 should not be reimbursed without a receipt for two reasons. First, it is a basic internal control measure to ensure that only valid expenditures are reimbursed. If receipts were not required, individuals could request reimbursement for fictitious expenditures. Second, GAAP require that transactions be recorded based on verifiable evidence (which is related to internal controls).

Banking Activities as Controls

LO5 Explain and identify banking activities and the control features they provide.

From the first moment a business is established, the ability to efficiently make and receive payments forms the lifeblood of the business. Banks safeguard cash, provide detailed and independent records of cash transactions, and are a source of cash financing. This section highlights the key services and documents provided by banking activities that increase management's control over cash and enable businesses to transact efficiently.

Basic Bank Services

This first section outlines key bank services, including bank accounts, bank deposits, and cheques. Each of these services contributes to the control or safeguarding of cash.

BANK ACCOUNT

A bank account is a record set up by a bank for a customer, permitting this customer to deposit money for safeguarding and providing the opportunity to make payments through cheque, cash, and electronic fund transfer (EFT) withdrawals. To control access to a bank account, all persons authorized to use a bank account must sign a signature card. A **signature card** includes the signature of each person authorized to sign cheques from the account. Bank employees use signature cards to verify signatures on cheques. This lowers the risk of loss from forgery for both banks and customers. Many businesses require dual signatures on cheques to strengthen control over cash payments. Many companies have more than one bank account for various reasons such as a payroll account dedicated to issuing payments for wages to employees or for special transactions.

BANK DEPOSIT

Each bank deposit is supported by a *deposit slip*. Companies use **deposit slips** to list the items such as currency, coins, and cheques included in the deposit along with each of their dollar amounts. When the deposit is brought to the bank, the company is provided a copy of the deposit slip or a deposit receipt as proof of the deposit. Exhibit 7.4 shows an example of a deposit slip.

EXHIBIT 7.4

Deposit Slip

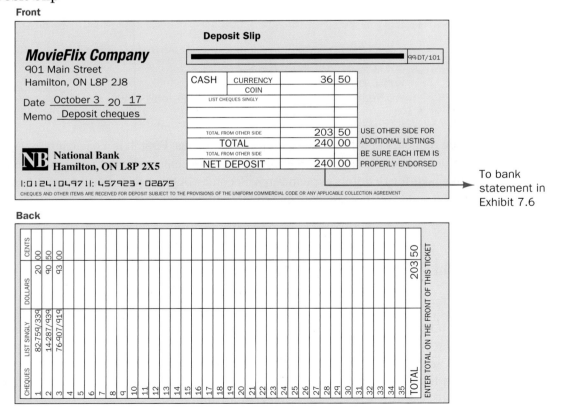

BANK CHEQUE

To withdraw money from an account, a customer uses a *cheque*. A **cheque** is a document signed by the depositor instructing the bank to pay a specified amount of money to a designated recipient. As mentioned in the chapter opening vignette, cheques are the most common method of payment used by Canadian businesses. A cheque involves three parties: a drawer (also referred to as payor or remitter) who signs the cheque, a *payee* who is the recipient, and a *bank* on which the cheque is drawn. The bank provides a depositor with cheques that are serially numbered and imprinted with the name and address of both the depositor and the bank. Both cheques and deposit slips are imprinted with identification codes in magnetic ink for computer processing. Exhibit 7.5 shows an example cheque. This cheque is accompanied by an optional *remittance advice* giving an explanation for the payment. When a remittance advice is unavailable, the memo line is often used for a brief explanation.

ELECTRONIC FUNDS TRANSFER

Electronic funds transfer (EFT) is the use of electronic communication to transfer cash from one party to another. No paper documents are necessary. Banks simply transfer cash from one account to another with a journal entry. Companies are increasingly using EFT because of its convenience and low cost. It can cost, for instance, up to a dollar to process a cheque through the banking system, whereas the EFT cost is near zero. We see items such as payroll, rent, utilities, insurance, interest payments being handled by EFT. For example, Alberta Blue Cross issues more than 110,000 cheques per month, but this number is declining as more payments are being made by direct deposit. The bank statement lists cash withdrawals by EFT with cheques and other deductions. Cash receipts by EFT are listed with deposits and other additions. A bank statement is sometimes a depositor's only notice of an EFT.

EXHIBIT 7.5

Cheque with Remittance Advice

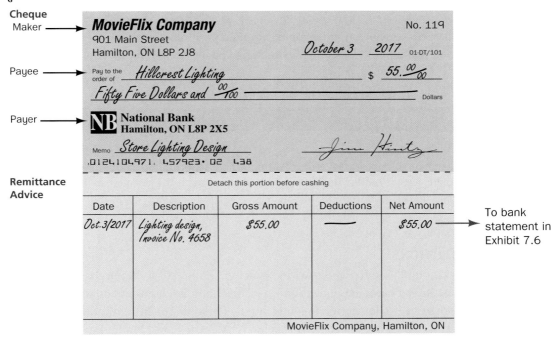

CREDIT CARD TRANSACTIONS

Many companies allow customers to use credit cards such as Visa, MasterCard, or American Express to pay for purchases. The customer has the convenience of using the credit card instead of using cash or cheques. The retailer enjoys the benefits of being paid by the credit card company. The payment to the retailer normally occurs faster than if the retailer had to collect credit sales personally and the risk of credit customers who do not pay is transferred to the credit card company. The credit card company issues the customer a monthly statement detailing the customer's transactions and follows up with the customer for payment. The customer pays the credit card company directly and can be charged interest based on the credit terms on the statement.

The seller pays a fee for the services provided by the credit card company. The fee covers costs incurred by the credit card company including credit checks on credit card customers, cost of collections, and, of course, a profit margin. Therefore, when the fee is deducted, the cash received by the retailer is less than 100% of the sales value of the transaction. The fee charged by the credit card company can be calculated as a percentage of sales or it may vary depending on the volume of sales. For simplicity, we will assume in this textbook that the credit card fee is based on a percentage of the sales value.

When a credit card is used, the retailer receives cash, net of the credit card fee, immediately upon deposit of the credit card sales receipt at the bank or when the credit card is processed electronically at the point of sale. For instance, if TechCom has $100 of credit card sales with a 4% fee and cash is received immediately, the entry is (assume cost of sales is $40):

Aug.	15	Cash	96	
		Credit Card Expense	4	
		Sales		100
		To record credit card sales less a 4% credit card expense.		
	15	Cost of Goods Sold.......................................	40	
		Merchandise Inventory		40
		To record cost of sales.		

Some firms report credit card expense on the income statement as a type of discount deducted from sales to arrive at net sales. Other companies classify it as a selling expense or even as an administrative expense.

DECISION MAKER   Answer—End of chapter

Entrepreneur

You are the owner of a small retail store. You are considering allowing customers to purchase merchandise using credit cards. Until now, your store accepted only cash and cheques. What forms of analysis do you use to make this decision?

DEBIT CARD TRANSACTIONS

The use of **debit cards** is common and popular with consumers. Payment for a purchase is electronically transferred from the customer's bank account to the vendor's bank account immediately at the point of sale. The customer authorizes the transaction by entering the Personal Identification Number (PIN). Normally, the bank charges the retailer a fee for this service. The entries are identical to a credit card sale.

For example, assume a customer purchases a $100 service on October 1 and pays using a debit card. If the bank charges the retailer $0.40 per debit card transaction, the entry is:

Oct.	1	Cash	99.60	
		Debit Card Expense	0.40	
		Service Revenue		100.00
		To record a debit card transaction.		

INTERAC FLASH

Interac debit cards have evolved with the introduction of *Interac* Flash—the contactless enhancement of traditional debit. In 2011, **RBC, Scotiabank**, and **TD Canada Trust** began issuing *Interac* Flash debit cards that allow customers to pay using contactless debit technology. By holding an *Interac* Flash card at the contactless reader, a purchase is quickly and securely processed.

The advantages? Convenience, for one: Merchants can serve customers more efficiently. The need for efficiency at the point of sale is significant because of the huge volumes of transactions now being handled electronically. The Consumers' Association of Canada reported that between 2008 and 2009, debit card transactions in Canada increased from $3.7 billion to $3.9 billion, and this number continues to grow.

Security is another advantage. Security is a growing concern given the increase in electronic payments and related increase in fraud. For example, in June 2011, a bank machine gang located in the Greater Toronto area was charged with fraud that cost financial institutions $245,000. In terms of credit and debit card fraud, the RCMP report that organized crime costs Canadians an estimated $5 billion a year.

The new *Interac* Flash card is reported to enhance protection against security issues like skimming, counterfeiting, transaction replay types of fraud, and electronic pickpocketing. Controls have been put in place to limit the risk of other types of losses. For example, RBC requires that cardholders enter their PIN after every $200 of Flash purchases to validate the cardholders' identity. In terms of additional security, the *Interac* Zero Liability Policy* automatically protects the debit card user from unauthorized transactions.

*All *Interac* cardholders are protected from losses resulting from circumstances beyond their control under the *Interac* Zero Liability Policy.

Note: *Interac, Interac* Flash, and *Interac* e-Transfer are trademarks of Interac Inc. Used under licence.

CHECKPOINT

7. What is a benefit to the retailer of accepting credit and debit cards?

Do Quick Study questions: QS 7-7, QS 7-8

Bank Statement

At least once a month, the bank sends the depositor a bank statement showing the activity in the accounts during the month; a company can also access its banking activity online at any time. Different banks use a variety of formats for their bank statements; however, they all include the following information:

1. Beginning-of-month balance of the depositor's account.
2. Cheques and other debits decreasing the account during the month.
3. Deposits and other credits increasing the account during the month.
4. End-of-month balance of the depositor's account.

The information reported on the bank statement reflects the bank's records of the activity in the bank account during the reported month. Exhibit 7.6 shows an example bank statement for MovieFlix.

Bank Statement

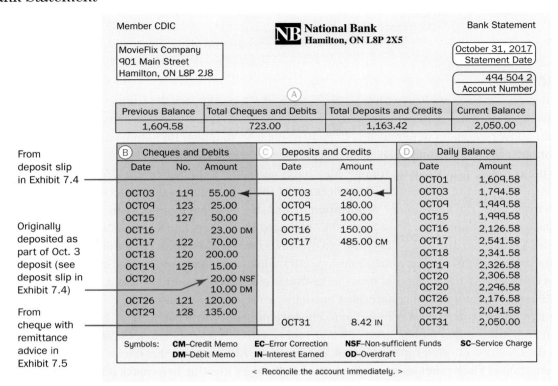

From deposit slip in Exhibit 7.4

Originally deposited as part of Oct. 3 deposit (see deposit slip in Exhibit 7.4)

From cheque with remittance advice in Exhibit 7.5

(A) Summarizes changes in the account.

(B) Lists paid cheques in date order along with other debits (or decreases).

(C) Lists deposits and credits (increases) to the account.

(D) Shows the daily account balances.

Important Tip: Notice that deposits are called credits and cheques are called debits on the bank statement. This is because the bank statement reports information from the bank's point of view—*that a depositor's account is a liability on the bank's records since the money belongs to the depositor and not the bank.*

When Capri Jones, a customer of the bank, puts money into the bank, the bank debits cash and *credits* the bank's liability account to Jones. Hence, *credit memos* show the bank's increasing liability to Jones. When Jones withdraws money from the bank, the bank records it as a credit to cash and *debits* the bank's liability account for Jones. Therefore, *debit memos* reflect decreases in the bank's liability to Jones.[3]

---

3 Recall that a bank records transactions in an identical manner to any other business. For example, on October 3 the bank cashed a cheque written by MovieFlix. This was recorded by the bank as:

MovieFlix Customer Account [a liability to the bank]	55	
Cash [an asset to the bank]		55

Notice on the bank statement in Exhibit 7.6 that this cheque is reported to MovieFlix as a debit because the bank has decreased its liability to MovieFlix. As a second example, on October 3 MovieFlix deposited $240 into its bank account; this was recorded by the bank as:

Cash	240	
MovieFlix Customer Account [a liability to the bank]		240

The bank statement reports this deposit to MovieFlix as a credit because the bank's liability to MovieFlix has increased.

Enclosed with a bank statement are the depositor's cancelled cheques and any debit or credit memos affecting the account. **Cancelled cheques** are cheques the bank has paid and deducted from the customer's account during the month. Other deductions also often appear on a bank statement and include (1) service charges and fees assessed by the bank, (2) customers' cheques deposited that are uncollectible, (3) corrections of previous errors, (4) withdrawals through automated teller machines (ATMs)[4], and (5) periodic payments arranged in advance by a depositor such as insurance and lease payments. Except for service charges, the bank notifies the depositor of each deduction with a debit memo when the bank reduces the balance. A copy of each debit memo is usually sent with the monthly statement.

While deposits increase a depositor's bank balance, there are other transactions that increase the depositor's account. Examples are amounts the bank collects on behalf of the depositor and corrections of previous errors. Credit memos notify the depositor of all increases recorded by the bank. A copy of each credit memo is often sent with the bank statement. Another item added to the bank balance is interest earned by the depositor. Many chequing accounts pay the depositor interest based on the average cash balance maintained in the account. The bank computes the amount of interest earned and credits it to the depositor's account each month. In Exhibit 7.6, for instance, the bank credits $8.42 of interest to the account of MovieFlix. We describe the methods used to calculate interest for notes receivable in Chapter 8.

Bank Reconciliation

LO6 Prepare a bank reconciliation and journalize any resulting adjustment(s).

When a company deposits all receipts intact and when all payments except petty cash payments are by cheque, the bank statement serves as a device for proving the accuracy of the depositor's cash records. We test the accuracy by preparing a *bank reconciliation*. A **bank reconciliation** is a form of internal control over cash that explains the difference between the balance of a chequing account according to the depositor's records and the balance reported on the bank statement.

PURPOSE OF BANK RECONCILIATION

The balance of a chequing account reported on the bank statement is rarely equal to the balance in the depositor's accounting records. This is usually due to information that one party has that the other does not. We must therefore prove the accuracy of both the depositor's records and those of the bank. This means we must *reconcile* the two balances and explain or account for the differences in these two balances.

Required Adjustments to the Bank's Period End Statement Balance:

Several adjustments need to be made to the bank balance to reflect transactions that occurred in the accounting records cash balance that at year-end have not yet been reflected in the bank statement. These adjustments are due to timing differences of items being captured in the bank statement and do not require adjustments as they are already reflected in the accounting records of the company and include:

Among the factors causing the bank statement balance to differ from the depositor's book balance are:

1. *Unrecorded deposits* (also known as *deposits in transit* or *outstanding deposits*). These are deposits made and recorded by the depositor but not yet captured on the bank statement. For example, companies often make deposits at the end of a business day, after the bank is closed. A deposit in the bank's night depository on the last day of the month is not recorded by the bank until the next business day and does not appear on the bank statement for that month.

---

4   Because of a desire to make all disbursements by cheque, most business chequing accounts do not allow ATM withdrawals.

2. *Outstanding cheques.* These are cheques written (or drawn) for outstanding payables and expenses, resulting in a decrease in the company's Cash account. The cheque has been mailed to the payee; however, the payee has not yet deposited the cheque in its bank, so the cash in the bank statement has not been reduced.

3. *Errors.* Both banks and depositors can make errors. For example, a bank error might include a cheque written by *MovieMax* Company mistakenly charged against the account of *MovieFlix* Company or a deposit made by *MovieFlix* Company accidentally posted to the account of *Digital Access Inc.*

Required Adjustments to the Cash Book Balance:

Several adjustments need to be made to the book balance to reflect transactions that occurred to the bank's record of the company's cash balance that have not yet been captured in the company's G/L cash account. These adjustments require journal entries to book the changes to the accounting records and include:

1. *Additions for collections, electronic transfers and interest.* Banks sometimes act as collection agents for their depositors by collecting notes and other items. Banks can also receive electronic funds transfers to the depositor's account. When a bank collects an item, it adds it to the depositor's account, less any service fee. Some banks notify the company by way of a credit memo to notify them of the transaction. At the time a memo is received, it should be recorded by the depositor. Often these transactions remain unrecorded until the time of the bank reconciliation.

   Many bank accounts earn interest on the average cash balance in the account during the month. If an account earns interest, the bank statement includes a credit for the amount earned during the past month. The bank statement provides notification of earned interest.

2. *Deductions for uncollectible items and for services.* A company sometimes deposits a customer's cheque that is uncollectible. This usually is because the balance in the customer's account is not large enough to cover the cheque. This cheque is called a *non-sufficient funds (NSF)* cheque. The bank initially credited the depositor's account for the amount of the deposited cheque. When the bank learns that the cheque is uncollectible, it debits (reduces) the depositor's account for the full amount of that cheque. The bank may also charge the depositor a fee for processing an uncollectible cheque and some banks notify the depositor of the deduction by sending a debit memo. While each deduction should be recorded by the depositor when a debit memo is received, notification of the NSF cheque may not take place and an entry is sometimes not made until the bank reconciliation is prepared.

3. *Other possible bank charges* to a depositor's account reported on a bank statement include the printing of new cheques and a service charge for maintaining the account. Notification of these charges is *not* provided until the statement is mailed. All of these items must be recorded as an adjustment to the *balance per books*.

4. *Errors.* A depositor error might involve a cheque actually written for $102 but recorded in error in the cash disbursements journal as $120. These kinds of errors might not be discovered until the depositor prepares a bank reconciliation.

STEPS IN RECONCILING A BANK BALANCE

The employee who prepares the bank reconciliation should not be responsible for cash receipts, processing cheques, or maintaining cash records. This employee needs to gather information from the bank statement and from other records. A reconciliation requires this person to:

Step 1   Identify the end of month bank balance of the cash account as reported on the bank statement.

Step 2   Compare deposits on the bank statement with deposits in the accounting records (cash receipts journal and last month's bank reconciliation). Identify any discrepancies and determine which is correct. List any errors or unrecorded deposits.

Step 3   Identify and list any outstanding cheques through the following steps:

● Compare cancelled cheques on the bank statement with actual cheques returned with the statement. For each cheque, make sure the bank deducts the correct amount and the returned cheque is properly charged to the account. List any discrepancies or errors.

● Compare cancelled cheques on the bank statement with cheques recorded in the books (cash disbursements journal). List any outstanding cheques. Also, while companies with good internal controls would rarely write a cheque without recording it, we should inspect and list any cancelled cheques that are unrecorded in the books.

● Identify any outstanding cheques listed on the previous month's bank reconciliation that are not included in the cancelled cheques on this month's bank statement. List these cheques that remain outstanding at the end of the current month. Send the list to the cashier's office for follow-up with the payees to see if the cheques were actually received.

Step 4   Calculate the adjusted bank balance.

Step 5   Identify the company's cash balance in the General Ledger Cash Account.

Step 6   Inspect all additions (credits) on the bank statement and determine whether each is recorded in the books. These items include collections by the bank, correction of previous bank statement errors, and interest earned by the depositor. List any unrecorded items.

Step 7   Inspect all deductions (debits) to the account on the bank statement and determine whether each is recorded in the books. These include bank charges for newly printed cheques, NSF cheques, and monthly service charges. List items not yet recorded.

Step 8   Calculate the adjusted book balance.

Step 9   Check to ensure adjusted bank balance and adjusted book balance are equal. If they are not equal, investigate for mathematical accuracy and missing information.

ILLUSTRATING A BANK RECONCILIATION

We illustrate a bank reconciliation by preparing one for MovieFlix as of October 31. We use the guidelines listed above and follow nine specific steps. Follow each step to the corresponding Exhibits 7.6 to 7.9 to see where the information comes from and how it is shown on the bank reconciliation in Exhibit 7.10.

① Identify the bank balance of the cash account at October 31 (balance per bank).
   – *Bank balance shown on the bank statement is $2,050 (from Exhibit 7.6).*

② Identify and list any unrecorded deposits* and any bank errors.* Add them to the bank balance on the bank reconciliation.
   – *A $145 deposit was placed in the bank's night depository on October 31 and is not recorded on the bank statement (from Exhibit 7.7).*

③ Identify and list any outstanding cheques* and any bank errors.* Deduct them from the bank balance on the bank reconciliation.
   – *A comparison of cancelled cheques with the company's books showed two cheques outstanding: #124 for $150 and #126 for $200 (from Exhibit 7.8).*

④ Calculate the *adjusted bank balance*, also called *corrected* or *reconciled* balance.
   – *See Exhibit 7.10.*

⑤ Identify the company's balance of the cash account (book balance).
   – *Cash balance shown in the accounting records is $1,404.58 (from Exhibit 7.9).*

⑥ Identify and list any unrecorded credit memos from the bank statement, such as interest earned and errors.* Add them to the book balance on the bank reconciliation.

ⓐ *Enclosed with the bank statement is a credit memo showing that the bank collected a note receivable for the company on October 17. The note's proceeds of $500 (minus a $15 collection fee) were credited to the company's account. This credit memo is not yet recorded by the company (from Exhibit 7.6).*

ⓑ *The bank statement shows a credit of $8.42 for interest earned on the average cash balance in the account. There was no prior notification of this item and it is not yet recorded on the company's books (from Exhibit 7.6).*

⑦ Identify and list any unrecorded debit memos from the bank, such as service charges and errors.[5] Deduct them from the book balance on the bank reconciliation.

– *Debits on the bank statement that are not recorded on the books include* ⓐ *a $23 charge for cheques printed by the bank, and* ⓑ *an NSF cheque for $20 plus* ⓒ *a related $10 processing fee. The NSF cheque is from a customer, Frank Heflin, and was originally included as part of the October 3 deposit (from Exhibit 7.6).*

*For simplicity, this example includes no errors and assumes that there were no outstanding cheques or deposits on last month's bank reconciliation. The End-of-Chapter Demonstration Problem illustrates these additional complexities.

EXHIBIT 7.6

Bank Statement (repeated from earlier page for ease of reference)

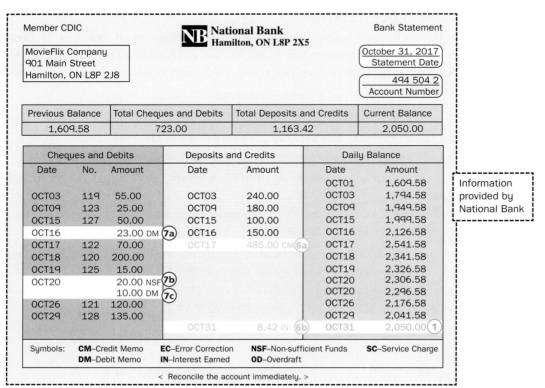

⑧ Calculate the *adjusted book balance*, also called the *corrected* or *reconciled* balance.
 – *See Exhibit 7.10.*

⑨ Verify that the two adjusted balances from Steps 4 and 8 are equal. If so, they are reconciled. If not, check for mathematical accuracy and missing data.
 – *See Exhibit 7.10.*

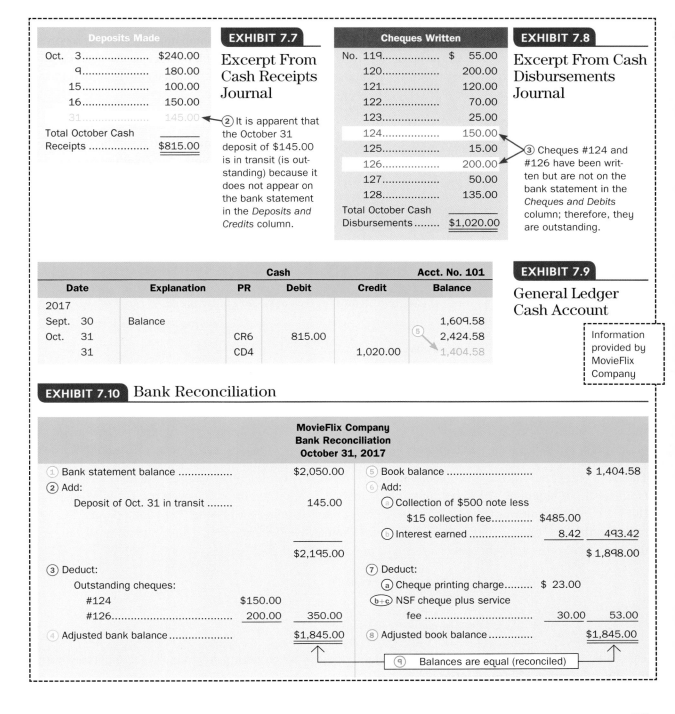

EXHIBIT 7.7 Excerpt From Cash Receipts Journal

Deposits Made	
Oct. 3	$240.00
9	180.00
15	100.00
16	150.00
31	145.00
Total October Cash Receipts	$815.00

② It is apparent that the October 31 deposit of $145.00 is in transit (is outstanding) because it does not appear on the bank statement in the *Deposits and Credits* column.

EXHIBIT 7.8 Excerpt From Cash Disbursements Journal

Cheques Written	
No. 119	$ 55.00
120	200.00
121	120.00
122	70.00
123	25.00
124	150.00
125	15.00
126	200.00
127	50.00
128	135.00
Total October Cash Disbursements	$1,020.00

③ Cheques #124 and #126 have been written but are not on the bank statement in the *Cheques and Debits* column; therefore, they are outstanding.

EXHIBIT 7.9 General Ledger Cash Account

Cash — Acct. No. 101

Date	Explanation	PR	Debit	Credit	Balance
2017					
Sept. 30	Balance				1,609.58
Oct. 31		CR6	815.00		2,424.58 ⑤
31		CD4		1,020.00	1,404.58

Information provided by MovieFlix Company

EXHIBIT 7.10 Bank Reconciliation

MovieFlix Company
Bank Reconciliation
October 31, 2017

① Bank statement balance		$2,050.00
② Add:		
Deposit of Oct. 31 in transit		145.00
		$2,195.00
③ Deduct:		
Outstanding cheques:		
#124	$150.00	
#126	200.00	350.00
④ Adjusted bank balance		$1,845.00

⑤ Book balance		$ 1,404.58
⑥ Add:		
ⓐ Collection of $500 note less $15 collection fee	$485.00	
ⓑ Interest earned	8.42	493.42
		$ 1,898.00
⑦ Deduct:		
ⓐ Cheque printing charge	$ 23.00	
ⓑ⁺ⓒ NSF cheque plus service fee	30.00	53.00
⑧ Adjusted book balance		$1,845.00

⑨ Balances are equal (reconciled)

When the reconciliation is complete, the employee sends a copy to the accounting department to record any needed journal entries. For instance, entries are needed to record any adjustments made to the balance per books to reflect items such as unrecorded debit and credit memos and any company mistakes. The entries resulting from MovieFlix's bank reconciliation are illustrated in the next section. Another copy goes to the cashier's office. This is especially important if the bank has made an error that needs correction.

RECORDING ADJUSTING ENTRIES IDENTIFIED FROM THE BANK RECONCILIATION

A bank reconciliation helps locate errors by either the bank or the depositor. It also identifies unrecorded items that need recording on the company's books. In MovieFlix's reconciliation, for instance, the adjusted balance of $1,845.00 is the correct balance as of October 31. But the company's accounting records show a $1,404.58 balance. We must prepare journal entries to adjust the book balance to the correct balance. It is important to remember that only the items reconciling the book balance side require adjustment. This means that the following four entries are required for MovieFlix:

1. COLLECTION OF NOTE

The first entry is to record the net proceeds of MovieFlix's note receivable collected by the bank, the expense of having the bank perform that service, and the reduction in the Notes Receivable account:

Oct.	31	Cash	485.00	
		Collection Expense	15.00	
		Notes Receivable		500.00
		To record collection fee and proceeds of a note collected by the bank.		

2. INTEREST EARNED

The second entry records the interest credited to MovieFlix's account by the bank:

	31	Cash	8.42	
		Interest Income		8.42
		To record interest earned on the average Cash balance in the chequing account.		

Interest earned is a type of income, and the entry recognizes both the profit and the related increase in Cash.

3. NSF CHEQUE

The third entry records the NSF cheque that is returned as uncollectible. The $20 cheque was received from Heflin in payment of his account and deposited. When the cheque cleared the banking system, Heflin's bank account was found to have insufficient funds to cover the cheque. The bank charged $10 for handling the NSF cheque and deducted $30 total from MovieFlix's account. The company must reverse the entry made when the cheque was received and also record the $10 fee:

	31	Accounts Receivable—Frank Heflin	30.00	
		Cash..		30.00
		To charge Frank Heflin's account for his NSF cheque and the bank's fee.		

This entry reflects business practice by adding the NSF $10 fee to Heflin's account. The company will try to collect the entire $30 from Heflin.

4. CHEQUE PRINTING

The fourth entry debits Office Supplies Expense for the printing of cheques:

31	Office Supplies Expense	23.00	
	Cash..		23.00
	Cheque printing charge.		

After these four entries are recorded, the balance of Cash is increased to the correct amount of $1,845 (= $1,404.58 + $485 + $8.42 − $30 − $23).

 **DECISION INSIGHT**

The Financial Transactions and Reports Analysis Centre of Canada, or FINTRAC, is Canada's financial intelligence unit created to collect, analyze, and disclose financial information and intelligence on suspected money laundering and terrorist financing activities. Banks, among others identified in the Proceeds of Crime (Money Laundering) and Terrorist Financing Act and Regulations, are required to report certain transactions to FINTRAC. When there are reasonable grounds to suspect that the information is relevant to threats to the security of Canada, FINTRAC will disclose that information to the Canadian Security and Intelligence Service (CSIS).

SOURCE: http://www.fintrac.gc.ca/

 **CHECKPOINT**

8. What is a bank statement?

9. What is the meaning of the phrase *to reconcile a bank balance*?

10. Why do we reconcile the bank statement balance of cash and the depositor's book balance of cash?

11. List items affecting the bank side of a reconciliation and indicate if the items are added or subtracted.

12. List items affecting the book side of a reconciliation and indicate if the items are added or subtracted.

Do Quick Study questions: QS 7-9, QS 7-10, QS 7-11

Financial Statement Analysis

Quick Ratio

LO7 Calculate the quick ratio and explain its use as an indicator of a company's liquidity.

We learned in Chapter 5 that merchandise inventory often makes up a large portion of current assets for merchandising companies. We know that merchandise inventory must be sold and any resulting accounts receivable need to be collected before cash is available. This often means that a large part of current assets is not readily available for paying liabilities because it is in the form of merchandise inventory.

We explained in Chapter 4 how the current ratio, calculated as total current assets divided by total current liabilities, is useful in assessing a company's ability to pay current liabilities. Because some current assets, specifically merchandise inventories and prepaids, are not readily available as a source of payment for current liabilities, we look to a measure other than the current ratio to obtain a stricter measure of a company's ability to cover current liabilities: the *acid-test ratio*.

The *acid-test ratio* differs from the current ratio by excluding current assets that are *less liquid*, such as inventory and prepaids. The **quick ratio**, also called the **acid-test ratio**, is defined as shown in Exhibit 7.11.

EXHIBIT 7.11

Quick Ratio

$$\text{Quick ratio} = \frac{\text{Quick assets*}}{\text{Current liabilities}}$$

*Quick assets are assets that can be readily converted to cash and include cash, short-term investments, and receivables.

Exhibit 7.12 shows both the quick and current ratios of **WestJet**.

EXHIBIT 7.12

Current and Quick Ratios Compared

	At December 31,				
	2013	2012	2011	2010	2009
Current Ratio............................	1.085	1.39	1.51	1.53	1.48
Quick Ratio	0.95	1.24	1.41	1.44	1.37

The quick ratio is interpreted in a similar manner as the current ratio. In Exhibit 7.12, WestJet's current ratio at December 31, 2013, shows $1.085 of current assets available to cover each $1.00 of current liability as it comes due. As a stricter measure, the quick ratio tells us WestJet had $0.95 of quick assets to cover each $1.00 of current obligations at December 31, 2013. A quick ratio equal to or greater than 1 is generally considered favourable (good). December 2013 saw a significant decline in the current ratio and the quick ratio for WestJet's compared to prior years. WestJet's main current liabilities that increased included accounts payable and advance ticket sales. As the advance ticket sales represent a unearned revenue liability balance, for this portion of the current liabilities no real cash obligation exists, indicating the company will still be able to meet the liabilities that require cash settlement. Companies need to manage their liquid asset positions cautiously, as too much cash on hand can also signal inefficient use of company resources. Investors will want to monitor WestJet's quick and current ratios to ensure the decreasing trend does not put the company at a significant of a risk of failing to meet current obligations.

 **CHECKPOINT**

13. ABC Company had quick ratios of 1.4 and 1.6 for 2017 and 2016, respectively. Is the change in the ratio favourable or unfavourable?

Do Quick Study question: QS 7-12

CRITICAL THINKING CHALLENGE

Refer to the Critical Thinking Challenge questions at the beginning of the chapter. Compare your answers to those suggested on Connect.

IFRS AND ASPE—THE DIFFERENCES

Difference	International Financial Reporting Standards (IFRS)	Accounting Standards for Private Enterprises (ASPE)
There are no significant differences between IFRS and ASPE related to this chapter.		

A Look Ahead

Chapter 8 takes a look at accounting for customer accounts receivable and short-term notes receivable balances, specifically investigating tools such as A/R aging reports, methods to estimate bad debts, and using the accounts receivable turnover ratio and days' sales uncollected ratios to evaluate financial statements.

For further study on some topics of relevance to this chapter, please see the following Extend Your Knowledge supplements:

EYK 7-1 Accounting for Debt and Share Investments

EYK 7-2 Voucher System of Control

EYK 7-3 Global Profiles of the Fraudster

EYK 7-4 Examples of Bank Documents (bank statement, cheque, deposit slip)

Summary

LO1 Define, explain the purpose of, and identify the principles of internal control. An internal control system consists of the policies and procedures that managers use to protect assets, ensure reliable accounting, promote efficient operations, and encourage adherence to company policies. It is a key part of systems design, analysis, and performance. It can prevent avoidable losses and help managers both plan operations and monitor company and human performance. Principles of good internal control include establishing responsibilities to ensure custody, authorization, and recording of assets are performed by separate individuals. Important controls include maintaining adequate records, insuring assets and bonding employees, dividing responsibilities for related transactions, applying technological controls, and performing regular independent reviews.

LO2 Define cash and explain how it is reported. Cash consists of cash on hand and demand deposits, including currency and coins, and amounts on deposit in bank, chequing, and some savings accounts. It also includes items that are acceptable for deposit in these accounts. Cash equivalents or short-term investments are similar to cash; therefore, most companies combine them with cash as a single item on the balance sheet. Cash and cash equivalents are liquid assets because they are converted easily into other assets or used in paying for services or liabilities.

LO3 Apply internal control to cash. Internal control of cash receipts ensures that all cash received is properly recorded and deposited. Cash receipts arise from cash sales, collections of customers' accounts, receipts of interest and rent, bank loans, sale of assets, and owner investments. Good internal control for cash receipts by mail includes at least two people being assigned to open the mail and prepare a list with each sender's name, amount of money received, and explanation.

LO4 Explain and record petty cash fund transactions. To avoid writing cheques for small amounts, a company sets up one or more petty cash funds to pay for items such as postage, courier fees, repairs, and supplies. A petty cashier is responsible for safekeeping of the cash, for making payments from this fund, and for keeping receipts and records. A Petty Cash account is debited when the fund is established or increased in size. The cashier presents all paid receipts to the company's cashier for reimbursement to restore petty cash to its full amount. Petty cash disbursements are recorded whenever the fund is replenished with debits to expense accounts reflecting receipts and a credit to cash.

LO5 Explain and identify banking activities and the control features they provide. Banks offer several services—such as the bank account, the bank deposit, and chequing—that promote the control or safeguarding of cash. A bank account is set up by a bank and permits a customer to deposit money for safeguarding and cheque withdrawals. A bank deposit is money added to the account with a deposit slip as proof. A cheque is a document signed by the depositor instructing the bank to pay a specified amount of money to a designated recipient. Sales resulting from debit card and credit card transactions are usually deposited into the bank account immediately, less a fee. Electronic funds transfer (EFT) uses electronic communication to transfer cash from one party to another, and it decreases certain risks. Companies increasingly use it because of its convenience and low cost.

LO6 Prepare a bank reconciliation and journalize any resulting adjustment(s). A bank reconciliation is prepared to prove the accuracy of the depositor's and the bank's records. In completing a reconciliation, the bank statement balance is adjusted for items such as outstanding cheques and unrecorded deposits made on or before the bank statement date but not reflected on the statement. The depositor's Cash account balance also often requires adjustment. These adjustments include items such as service charges, bank collections for the depositor, and interest earned on the account balance.

LO7 Calculate the quick ratio and explain its use as an indicator of a company's liquidity. The quick ratio (also known as acid-test ratio) is calculated as quick assets (cash, short-term investments, and receivables) divided by current liabilities. It is an indicator of a company's ability to pay its current liabilities with its existing quick assets. A ratio equal to or greater than 1 is often considered adequate.

Guidance Answers to DECISION MAKER

Campaign Manager

A forced vacation policy is part of a system of good internal controls. When employees are forced to take vacations, their ability to hide any fraudulent behaviour decreases. This is because someone must take on the responsibilities of the person on vacation, and the replacement employee potentially can uncover fraudulent behaviour or records. A forced vacation policy is especially important for employees in more sensitive positions of handling money or other easily transferable assets.

Internal Auditor

You inform your supervisor, who emphasizes that the purpose of the surprise visit was defeated because you allowed another employee to interfere with and influence your actions; this was a valuable first lesson! Your problem is now whether to accept the situation or to dig further to see if the petty cashier is abusing petty cash. Since you were asked to postpone your count and the fund consists of new $20 bills, you have legitimate concerns about whether money is being borrowed for personal use. You should conduct a further investigation. One result might show that the most recent reimbursement of the fund was for $180 (= 9 × $20) or more. In that case, this reimbursement can leave the fund with sequentially numbered $20 bills. But if the most recent reimbursement was for less than $180, the presence of nine sequentially numbered $20 bills suggests that the $180 of new $20 bills was obtained from a bank as replacement for bills that had been removed. Neither situation shows that the cashier is stealing money. Yet the second case indicates that the cashier "borrowed" the cash and later replaced it after the auditor showed up. In writing your report, you must not conclude that the cashier is unethical unless evidence along with your knowledge of company policies supports it. Your report must present facts according to the evidence.

Entrepreneur

Your analysis of allowing credit card sales should estimate the benefits against the costs. The primary benefit is the potential to increase sales by attracting customers who prefer the convenience of credit cards. The primary cost is the fee charged by the credit card company for providing this service to your store. Your analysis should therefore estimate the expected increase in sales dollars from allowing credit card sales and then subtract (1) the normal costs and expenses, and (2) the credit card fees associated with this expected increase in sales dollars. If your analysis shows an increase in profit from allowing credit card sales, your store should probably allow them.

Guidance Answers to CHECKPOINT

1. c

2. Technology reduces processing errors, allows more extensive testing of records, limits the amount of hard evidence of processing steps, and highlights the importance of maintaining separation of duties.

3. a

4. If all cash payments are made by cheque, numerous cheques for small amounts must be written. Because this practice is expensive and time consuming, a petty cash fund is established to make small cash payments.

5. If the petty cash fund is not reimbursed at the end of an accounting period, the transactions in petty cash are not yet recorded in the accounts and the petty cash asset is overstated. But these amounts are rarely large enough to affect users' decisions based on financial statements.

6. First, when the petty cash fund is reimbursed, the petty cash transactions are recorded in their proper accounts. Second, reimbursement also gives money that allows the fund to continue being used. Third, reimbursement identifies any cash shortage or overage in the fund.

7. The retailer receives payment faster than if it had to collect credit sales, and the risk of

uncollectible customer accounts is transferred to the credit card company and bank.

8. A bank statement is a detailed report prepared by the bank outlining the activities in a depositor's account over the period of time, generally monthly.

9. To reconcile a bank balance means to outline the difference between the cash balance in the depositor's accounting records and the balance on the bank statement.

10. The purpose of the bank reconciliation is to determine if any errors have been made by the bank or by the depositor and to determine if the bank has completed any transactions affecting the depositor's account that the depositor has not recorded. It is also an internal control mechanism to ensure that the company's cash system is operating properly.

11. Outstanding cheques—subtracted
   Unrecorded deposits—added

12. Bank service charges—subtracted
   Debit memos—subtracted
   NSF cheques—subtracted
   Interest earned—added
   Credit memos—added

13. Unfavourable.

DEMONSTRATION PROBLEM

Required

Consider the following information and prepare a bank reconciliation, along with any resulting journal entries, for TJ Company , an online retailer that specializes in digital device accessories at April 30, 2017.

Analysis Component:

Assume that you are the owner of TJ Company and have just read an online article about employee accounting fraud. As a result, you have decided to review the bank reconciliation prepared for April 30. You notice that cheque #808 for $850 is not included with the cancelled cheques that are returned by the bank with the bank statement. Your office is small and is managed by one employee, Brent Wicker. When questioned, Brent cannot locate the missing cheque. What do you do, if anything? Explain.

The bank reconciliation prepared by TJ Company on March 31, 2017, follows:

	TJ Company Bank Reconciliation March 31, 2017			
Bank statement balance		$7,670	Book balance.......................................	$8,590
Add:				
Deposit of March 31 in transit		1,100		
		$8,770		
Deduct:				
Outstanding cheques:				
#797:	$ 60			
#804:	120	180		
Adjusted bank balance................................		$8,590	Adjusted book balance	$8,590

The following bank statement is available for April:

Bank Statement					
To: TJ Company				April 30, 2017 Bank of Nova Scotia	
Cheques/Charges/Debits			Deposits/Credits		Balance
					7,670
#811	04/03	834	04/03	1,100	7,936
#807	04/07	375	04/07	810	8,371
#810	04/13	208	04/13	690	8,853
NSF	04/18	450	04/18	680	9,083
#808	04/23	850	04/23	355	8,588
#797	04/27	60	04/27	750	9,278
#814	04/30	550	04/30	620	9,348
#813	04/30	372	INT	47	9,023
#809	04/30	124			8,899
SC	04/30	32	04/30		8,867
NSF = Not Sufficient Funds		SC = Service Charge		INT = Interest	

A list of deposits made and cheques written during April, taken from the cash receipts journal and cash disbursements journal, is shown below:

Deposits Made			Cheques Written	
April 7.....................................	$ 810		No. 807......................................	$ 375
13...................................	690		808...................................	850
18...................................	680		809...................................	124
23...................................	355		810...................................	208
27...................................	750		811...................................	348
30...................................	620		812...................................	207
30...................................	770		813...................................	372
Total April Cash Receipts............	$4,675		814...................................	550
			815...................................	405
			816...................................	602
			Total April Cash Disbursements ..	$4,041

General Ledger Cash Account:

			Cash			Acct. No. 101
Date	Explanation	PR	Debit		Credit	Balance
2017						
March 31	Balance					8,590
April 30		CR12	4,675			13,265
30		CD14			4,041	9,224

In reviewing cheques returned by the bank, the bookkeeper discovered that cheque #811, for delivery expense, was recorded in the cash disbursements journal incorrectly as $348. The NSF cheque for $450 was that of customer A. Hussain, deposited in April.

Planning the Solution

- Set up a schedule like Exhibit 7.10 with a bank side and a book side for the reconciliation.
- Follow the nine steps used in the chapter to prepare the bank reconciliation.
- For every reconciling item on the book side, prepare an entry, if required.
- Prepare an answer to the analysis component.

Solution

TJ Company
Bank Reconciliation
April 30, 2017

Bank statement balance		$8,867	Book balance		$9,224
Add:			Add:		
Deposit of April 30 in transit		770	Interest income		47
		$9,637			$9,271
Deduct:			Deduct:		
Outstanding cheques:			Error (cheque #811 for delivery exp).....	$486	
#804:	$120		NSF cheque	450	
#812:	207		Service charge	32	968
#815:	405				
#816:	602	1,334			
Adjusted bank balance.....................		$8,303	Adjusted book balance		$8,303

Required Entries

April	30	Cash	47	
		Interest income......................................		47
		To record interest earned.		
	30	Delivery Expense	486	
		Cash...		486
		To correct accounting error on cheque #811.		
	30	Accounts Receivable—A. Hussain	450	
		Cash...		450
		To reinstate customer account due to NSF cheque.		
	30	Bank Service Charges Expense......................	32	
		Cash...		32
		To record bank service charges.		

Analysis Component:

Several things need to be done. A review of prior months' bank reconciliations needs to be conducted to determine if this is an anomaly or a recurring event. The journal entry regarding cheque #808 needs to be reviewed to determine the payee. The payee, if identifiable, needs to be contacted to verify the purchase. If this cannot be done, the bank needs to be contacted to determine if its records are able to verify the payee on the cheque. Hopefully, Brent made an honest mistake and misplaced the cheque. However, in the future, the owner of TJ Company should review each bank reconciliation and ensure that the cheques being paid are scrutinized to ensure they are for business-related payments.

Glossary

Acid-test ratio *See quick ratio.*

Bank reconciliation An analysis that explains the difference between the balance of a chequing account shown in the depositor's records and the balance reported on the bank statement.

Bond An insurance policy purchased by a company to protect against losses from theft by that employee.

Cancelled cheques Cheques that the bank has paid and deducted from the customer's account during the month.

Cash Consists of cash on hand and demand deposits, including currency, coins, and amounts on deposit in bank chequing or savings accounts.

Cash Over and Short account An income statement account used to record cash shortages and cash overages arising from omitted petty cash receipts and from errors in making change.

Cheque A document signed by the depositor instructing the bank to pay a specified amount of money to a designated recipient.

Collusion An act in which two or more people agree to commit a fraud.

Debit cards Cards used at point of sale to transfer payment for a purchase immediately from the customer's to the vendor's bank account.

Deposit slip Bank document that lists the items such as currency, coins, and cheques deposited along with each of their dollar amounts.

Electronic funds transfer (EFT) The use of electronic communication to transfer cash from one party to another.

Interest income interest earned on outstanding customer notes receivable and investments in interest-bearing debt.

Internal control system All the policies and procedures managers use to protect assets, ensure reliable accounting, promote efficient operations, and urge adherence to company policies.

Liquid assets Assets such as cash that are easily converted into other types of assets or used to buy services or to pay liabilities.

Liquidity A characteristic of an asset that refers to how easily the asset can be converted into cash or another type of asset or used in paying for services or obligations.

Petty cashier Employee responsible for safekeeping of the cash, making payments from this fund, and keeping accurate records.

Principles of internal control Fundamental principles of internal control that apply to all companies requiring management to ensure transactions and activities are authorized, maintain records, insure assets, separate recordkeeping and custody of assets, establish a separation of duties, apply technological controls, and perform internal and external audits.

Quick assets Those current assets that are most liquid, specifically cash, short-term investments, and receivables.

Quick ratio A ratio used to assess a company's ability to cover its current debts with existing assets calculated as quick assets (cash, short-term investments, and receivables) divided by current liabilities; also called *acid-test ratio.*

Separation of duties An internal control principle requiring the division of responsibility for related transactions between two or more individuals or departments.

Signature card Bank document that includes the signature of each person authorized to sign cheques from the account.

Three-way match A special control over cash disbursements to prevent payment of invoices for which the goods have not yet been received or were not approved internally. Three documents—purchase order, receiving report, and invoice—must be present and the information must agree or be "matched" before any payment is made to the supplier.

Concept Review Questions

1. List the following assets from most liquid to least liquid: merchandise inventory, building, accounts receivable, cash?

2. Why are internal controls important in a business? List the fundamental principles of internal control.

3. Eddie works at a clothing store in the mall. He sees that his manager is very busy. At the end of the day, Eddie offers to count the cash in the cash register, deposit it at the bank, and record the accounting journal entries. What is the risk in this situation? Explain using the concept of separation of duties.

4. Internal control procedures are important in every business, but at what stage in the development of a business do they become critical?

5. The bartender at a restaurant performs a monthly inventory count for the wine, beer, and other liquor and will update the accounting records for any differences between the inventory records and the physical inventory count. Identify the weaknesses, implications, and recommendations (W.I.R).

6. Using the three components of the fraud triangle, explain why a student may cheat on an exam.

7. When merchandise is purchased for a large store, why are department managers not permitted to deal directly with suppliers?

8. What is a petty cash receipt? Who signs a petty cash receipt?

9. Refer to **Danier**'s balance sheet in Appendix III. What is its cash balance as at June 28, 2014?

10. WestJet Airlines showed cash and cash equivalents on December 31, 2014, of $1,358,071,000. What percentage is this of total assets?

Quick Study

QS 7-1 Internal control objectives LO1

You are currently part of a university work experience program. Your job placement is at the municipal transit centre. Your supervisor is responsible for the recording and distribution of monthly transit passes to authorized vendors throughout the city. The vendors pay $50 per bus pass and sell them for $55. Your work experience job is to prepare a monthly reconciliation of the transit passes including the quantity sold, the number actually distributed, the unsold passes, and the cash proceeds. You are unable to reconcile the past two months. The bus passes are sequentially numbered and, in checking the sequence, you notice that numbers 9750 to 9820, 11012 to 11750, and 22000 to 22440 cannot be accounted for. You bring this to the attention of the supervisor, who tells you that reconciliations are never done; the job was created by her superior "to give you something to do," and not to worry about it.

    a. What is the main objective of internal control and how is it accomplished?

    b. Why should recordkeeping for assets be separated from custody over the assets?

    c. Do you report your findings?

QS 7-2 Reporting cash and other current assets LO2

Prepare the current asset section based on the following alphabetized post-closing trial balance information at March 31, 2017, for Whiteagle Company:

Account	Debits	Credits
Accounts payable		$ 7,000
Accounts receivable	$ 4,500	
Accumulated depreciation		9,900
Cash	15,000	
Isaac Whiteagle, capital		25,800
Notes payable, due 2023		14,000
Petty cash	600	
Prepaid rent	3,200	
Property, plant and equipment	38,000	
Unearned revenue		4,600

QS 7-3 Internal controls for cash LO3

The treasurer of a local not-for-profit organization was found guilty today of defrauding the organization of thousands of dollars. Among the individual's many responsibilities were the recording of cash deposits, the writing of cheques, and the preparation of the bank reconciliation. A member of the organization suspected wrongdoing when the treasurer reported total cash collections of $2,800 regarding the sale of nonsequentially numbered raffle tickets; the member submitted $1,600 to the treasurer and knew that other members had collectively sold in excess of $3,000. The police were consulted and an investigation revealed that not only had the treasurer pocketed an undisclosed amount of cash over a two-year period but also had made cash withdrawals from the bank and destroyed the debit memos when returned with the bank statement.

Required

Identify three weaknesses of how cash is handled. For each weakness, explain the implication of the weakness and make a recommendation to the organization for the future.

QS 7-4 Petty cash LO4

The petty cash fund of the Wee Ones Agency was established on May 1, 2017, at $75. At the end of the month, the fund contained $12.74 and had the following receipts: film rentals, $19.40; refreshments for meetings, $22.81 (both expenditures to be classified as Entertainment Expense); postage, $6.95; and printing, $13.10.

1. Prepare the journal entry to record the establishment of the fund.
2. Prepare a summary of the petty cash payments similar to Exhibit 7.3, and then record the reimbursement on May 31.
3. Explain when the Petty Cash account would be credited in a journal entry.

QS 7-5 Petty cash LO4

WilsonArt set up a petty cash fund of $200 on March 1, 2017. On March 17, the petty cash box contained $19 and the following receipts: $75 for printing, $48 for taxi fare, and $55 for delivery expense. Record the reimbursement of the fund on March 17.

QS 7-6 Petty cash LO4

Canmore Consulting established a $100 petty cash fund on September 1, 2017. On September 23, the petty cash box contained $7 and receipts for the following expenses: $32 for entertainment expense (lunch with a client), $45 for computer repair, and $18 for delivery expense. Record the reimbursement of the fund on September 23.

QS 7-7 Credit card transactions LO5

Journalize the following transactions (assume a perpetual inventory system):

February	1	Recorded $75,000 of sales (cost $62,000) to customers using MasterCard. MasterCard charges the retailer 2.5% for credit card transactions.
February	10	Sold merchandise to customers who paid $28,000 in cash (cost $23,000).

QS 7-8 Debit card transactions LO5

Journalize the following transactions (assume a perpetual inventory system):

Oct.	1	Recorded sales of $14,000 (cost $8,000) to customers using debit cards. Assume the bank charges 0.25% for all debit card transactions.
	7	Sold merchandise to customers who paid $3,500 in cash (cost $2,800).

QS 7-9 Bank reconciliation LO6

1. Identify whether each of the following items affects the bank or book side of the reconciliation and indicate if the amount represents an addition or a subtraction:

   a. Deposits in transit.

   b. Interest on average monthly balance.

   c. Credit memos.

   d. Bank service charges.

   e. Outstanding cheques.

   f. Debit memos.

   g. NSF cheques.

2. Which of the previous items require a journal entry?

QS 7-10 Bank reconciliation LO6

Bolton Company's October 31, 2017, bank statement showed a cash balance of $15,400, while the company's general ledger Cash account for the same date showed a balance of $13,150. A bank deposit of October 31 for $1,200 does not appear on the bank statement. Cheques #150 for $980 and #169 for $2,515, both written in October, had not cleared the bank during October. Bank service charges for the month were $45. Prepare a bank reconciliation at October 31, 2017, and prepare the necessary entries.

QS 7-11 Bank reconciliation LO6

Your accountant has been asked to prepare the bank reconciliation for Ultimate Discs (UD), a store that sells frisbees.

- You login to the online bank statement and note that the bank balance is $66,362 as at March 31. 2017. The amount of cash recorded in the accounting records (the books) is $64,800.

- You go through the online bank statement and notice an electronic fund transfer from a customer for $2,300. This customer had purchased goods on account.

- UD earned $48 of interest income, but was also charged a $25 service charge as the cash balance dropped below the minimum balance of $70,000 this month.

- The bank notified you that one of the cheques you had deposited had insufficient funds in that customer's bank account. The cheque and bank charges are $761.

Required

   a. Prepare a bank reconciliation at March 31, 2017.

   b. Prepare the necessary journal entries.

QS 7-12 Quick ratio LO7

Your company has a policy of granting credit only to customers whose quick ratio is greater than or equal to 1. Based on this policy, determine if the following companies would be granted credit (round to two decimal places). Why or why not?

	Company A	Company B
Cash	$1,200	$1,200
Accounts receivable	2,700	2,700
Inventory	5,000	5,000
Prepaid expenses	600	600
Accounts payable	3,100	4,750
Other current liabilities	250	950

Exercises

Exercise 7-1 Analyzing internal control LO1

Lombard Company is a young business that has grown rapidly. The company's bookkeeper, who was hired two years ago, left town suddenly after the company's manager discovered that a great deal of money had disappeared over the past 18 months. An audit disclosed that the bookkeeper had written and signed several cheques made payable to the bookkeeper's brother and then recorded the cheques as salaries expense. The brother, who cashed the cheques but had never worked for the company, left town with the bookkeeper. As a result, the company incurred an uninsured loss of $84,000.

Evaluate Lombard Company's internal control system and identify violations of the principles of internal control.

Exercise 7-2 Internal control objectives LO3

As a member of the city's internal audit team, you have been instructed to observe the procedures regarding the collection of coins from the municipally owned parking meters. You accompany the civic employee on the collection route. The employee uses a key to open the locked coin compartment of the meter and empties its contents into a canvas bag that closes with a drawstring. When the bag is full, the employee closes it, and places it in the vehicle, which is parked along the route. At the end of the day, the civic employee delivers the bags to two individuals in a municipal office who are jointly responsible for counting the contents.

Required Write a brief report identifying three weaknesses in the above situation. For each weakness, identify the implication of the weakness and make a recommendation.

Exercise 7-3 Recommending internal control procedures LO3

What internal control procedures would you recommend in each of the following situations?

    a. A concession company has one employee who sells T-shirts and sunglasses at the beach. Each day, the employee is given enough shirts and sunglasses to last through the day and enough cash to make change. The money is kept in a box at the stand.

    b. An antique store has one employee who is given cash and sent to garage sales each weekend. The employee pays cash for merchandise to be resold at the antique store.

Exercise 7-4 Internal control over cash receipts LO3

Some of Fannin Co.'s cash receipts from customers are sent to the company in the mail. Fannin's bookkeeper opens the letters and deposits the cash received each day. What internal control problem do you see in this arrangement? What changes would you recommend?

Exercise 7-5 Petty cash fund LO4

Cameron Co. established a $150 petty cash fund on January 1, 2017. One week later, on January 8, the fund contained $29.25 in cash and receipts for these expenditures: postage, $42.00; transportation-in, $27.00; store supplies, $32.75; and a withdrawal of $19.00 by Jim Cameron, the owner. Cameron uses the perpetual method to account for merchandise inventory.

    a. Prepare the journal entry to establish the fund on January 1.

    b. Prepare a summary of the petty cash payments similar to Exhibit 7.3 and record the entry to reimburse the fund on January 8.

Analysis Component: If the January 8 entry to reimburse the fund were not recorded and financial statements were prepared for the month of January, would profit be over- or understated?

Exercise 7-6 Petty cash fund LO4

Willard Company established a $400 petty cash fund on September 9, 2017. On September 30, the fund had $159.40 in cash along with receipts for these expenditures: transportation-in, $32.45; office supplies, $113.55; and repairs expense, $87.60. Willard uses the perpetual method to account for merchandise inventory. The petty cashier could not account for the $7.00 shortage in the fund.

a. Prepare the September 9 entry to establish the fund.

b. Prepare a summary of the petty cash payments similar to Exhibit 7.3 and record the entry on September 30 to reimburse the fund and reduce it to $250.

Analysis Component: You are the senior marketing manager and are reviewing the unadjusted account balances for your division. You notice the $7.00 cash shortage recorded on September 30 regarding petty cash. The current petty cash custodian has been in place for three months. What should be done, if anything? Explain.

Exercise 7-7 Petty cash fund LO4

Conway Designs established a $200 petty cash fund on October 1, 2017. Prepare the entry to replenish the fund at the end of each of the following months of activity:

a. The petty cash box contained $23 on October 31 along with receipts for $100 for cleaning, $26 for postage, and $45 for delivery expense.

b. On November 30, the petty cash box contained only two receipts, for a $78 computer repair and a $95 entertainment expense. The petty cash custodian counted cash remaining of $32.

c. The petty cash box contained $18 on December 31 plus receipts for $49 for gas expense, $92 for office supplies, and $41 for entertainment expense. In addition to replenishing the fund, it was increased by $50.

Exercise 7-8 Credit card and debit card transactions LO5

Journalize the following transactions for Stillwater Spa Consultants:

Oct.	1	Sold services for $160,000 to customers using debit cards. Assume the bank charges 0.5% for all debit card transactions.
	7	Sold services to customers for $19,000 cash.
	8	Recorded Visa credit card sales totalling $92,000. Visa applies fees of 2%.
	10	Sold $68,000 of services to Edson Community Health Clinic, terms 2/15, n/30.
	25	Collected the amount owing regarding the October 10 sale.

Exercise 7-9 Credit card and debit card transactions LO5

On January 15, Tundra Co. sold merchandise to customers for cash of $42,000 (cost $28,500). Merchandise costing $10,500 was sold to customers for $15,800 on January 17; terms 2/10, n/30. Sales totalling $296,000 (cost $198,000) were recorded on January 20 to customers using MasterCard, a credit card that charges a 2% fee. On January 25, sales of $72,000 (cost $48,200) were made to debit card customers. The bank charges Tundra a flat fee of 0.5% on all debit card transactions.

Required Prepare journal entries for each of the transactions described (assume a perpetual inventory system).

Analysis Component: Identify the advantages and disadvantages of each type of sale: cash sale, credit sale, credit card sale, or debit card sale. Explain why Tundra would likely accept all these types of sales.

Exercise 7-10 Preparation of bank reconciliation LO6

CHECK FIGURE: 1. Adjusted book balance = $11,203

The bank reconciliation prepared by Winfield Construction on June 30, 2017, appeared as follows:

Winfield Construction Bank Reconciliation June 30, 2017			
Bank statement balance	$ 9,200	Book balance	$9,770
Add:			
Deposit of June 30 in transit........................	1,350		
	$10,550		
Deduct:			
Outstanding cheque #14	780		
Adjusted bank balance	$ 9,770	Adjusted book balance	$9,770

The Cash account in the general ledger appeared as follows on July 31:

Cash					Acct. No. 101
Date	Explanation	PR	Debit	Credit	Balance
2017					
June 30	Balance				9,770
July 31		CR3	5,040		14,810
31		CD6		3,142	11,668

A list of deposits made and cheques written during July, taken from the cash receipts journal and cash disbursements journal, is shown below:

Deposits Made		Cheques Written	
July 8.....................................	$1,280	No. 52.....................................	$1,796
11.....................................	1,675	53.....................................	964
24.....................................	1,445	54.....................................	382
31.....................................	640		
Total July Cash Receipts	$5,040	Total July Cash Disbursements...	$3,142

The following bank statement is available for July:

Bank Statement					
To: Winfield Construction					July 31, 2017 Bank of Montreal
Cheques/Charges			Deposits/Credits		Balance
					9,200
NSF	07/02	465	07/02	1,350	10,085
#52	07/08	1,796	07/08	1,280	9,569
#96	07/11	420	07/11	1,675	10,824
			07/24	1,445	12,269
#54	07/31	382	07/31		11,887
NSF = Not Sufficient Funds		SC = Service Charge	PMT = Principal Payment	INT = Interest	

In reviewing cheques returned by the bank, the bookkeeper noted that cheque #96 written by Winburn Construction in the amount of $420 was charged against Winfield's account in error by the bank. The NSF cheque was regarding a customer account, Jim Anderson.

Required

1. Prepare a bank reconciliation at July 31.
2. Prepare the necessary journal entries to bring the general ledger Cash account into agreement with the adjusted balance on the bank reconciliation.

Analysis Component: If the journal entries in Part 2 were not recorded, what financial statement elements (profit, assets, liabilities, and equity) would be over- or understated?

Exercise 7-11 Bank reconciliation LO6

CHECK FIGURE: Adjusted book balance = $11,090

Kesler Co. deposits all receipts intact on the day received and makes all payments by cheque. On July 31, 2017, after all posting was completed, its Cash account showed an $11,042 debit balance. However, Kesler's July 31 bank statement showed only $9,860 on deposit in the bank on that day along with the following information.

   a. Outstanding cheques, $2,695.

   b. Included with the July cancelled cheques returned by the bank was a $42 debit memo for bank services.

   c. Cheque #919, returned with the cancelled cheques, was correctly drawn for $892 in payment of the utility bill and was paid by the bank on July 15. However, it had been recorded with a debit to Utilities Expense and a credit to Cash as though it were for $982.

   d. The July 31 cash receipts, $3,925, were placed in the bank's night depository after banking hours on that date and were unrecorded by the bank at the time the July bank statement was prepared.

Required

   a. Prepare a bank reconciliation for Kesler Co. at July 31.

   b. Give the journal entries that Kesler Co. should make as a result of having prepared the bank reconciliation in part (a).

Analysis Component: Identify whether profit, assets, liabilities, and equity would be over- or understated if the journal entires in part (b) were not recorded.

Exercise 7-12 Bank reconciling items and required entries LO6

Set up a table with the following headings for a bank reconciliation as of September 30:

Bank Balance		Book Balance			Not Shown on the Reconciliation
Add	Deduct	Add	Deduct	Must Adjust	

For each item that follows, place an X in the appropriate columns to indicate whether the item should be added to or deducted from the book or bank balance, or whether it should not appear on the reconciliation. If the book balance is to be adjusted, place a Dr. or Cr. in the Must Adjust column to indicate whether the Cash balance should be debited or credited.

1. Interest income earned on the account.

2. Deposit made on September 30 after the bank was closed.

3. Cheques outstanding on August 31 that cleared the bank in September.

4. NSF cheque from customer returned on September 15 but not recorded by the company.

5. Cheques written and mailed to payees on September 30.

6. Deposit made on September 5 that was processed on September 8.

7. Bank service charge.

8. Cheques written and mailed to payees on October 5.

9. Cheques written by another company but charged against the company's account in error.

10. Customer payment through electronic fund transfer received in the bank but not recorded in the company's books.

11. Bank charge for collection of electronic fund transfer in Item 10.

12. Cheque written against the account and cleared by the bank; not recorded by the bookkeeper.

Exercise 7-13 Quick ratio LO7

Calculate the quick ratio in each of the following cases:

	Case X	Case Y	Case Z
Cash	$ 800	$ 910	$1,100
Current investments	-0-	-0-	500
Receivables	-0-	990	800
Inventory	2,000	1,000	4,000
Prepaid expenses	1,200	600	900
Total current assets	$4,000	$3,500	$7,300
Current liabilities	$2,200	$1,100	$3,650

Required Which case is in the best position to meet short-term obligations most easily? Explain your choice. *Round calculations to two decimal places.*

Problems

Problem 7-1A Principles of internal control LO1

For the following five scenarios, identify the principle of internal control that is violated. Next, make a recommendation as to what the business should do to ensure adherence to principles of internal control.

1. At Stratford Iron Company, Jill and Joan alternate lunch hours. Normally Jill is the petty cash custodian, but if someone needs petty cash when Jill is at lunch, Joan fills in as custodian.

2. Nadine McDonald does all the posting of patient charges and payments at the Northampton Medical Clinic. Every night, Nadine backs up the computerized accounting system to a tape and stores the tape in a locked file at her desk.

3. Jack Mawben prides himself on hiring quality workers who require little supervision. As office manager, Jack gives his employees full discretion over their tasks and has seen no reason to perform independent reviews of their work for years.

4. Bill Clark's manager has told him to "reduce overhead" no matter what! Bill decides to raise the deductible on the plant's property insurance from $5,000 to $10,000. This cuts the property insurance premium in half. In a related move, he decides that bonding of the plant's employees is really a waste of money since the company has not experienced any losses due to employee theft. Bill saves the entire amount of the bonding insurance premium by dropping the bonding insurance.

5. Catherine Young records all incoming customer cash receipts for her employer and also posts the customer payments to their accounts.

Problem 7-2A Establishing, reimbursing, and increasing the petty cash fund LO4

Milton Consulting completed the following petty cash transactions during February 2017:

Feb.	2	Prepared a $400 cheque, cashed it, and gave the proceeds and the petty cash box to Nick Reed, the petty cashier.
	5	Purchased paper for the copier, $22.45.
	9	Paid $36.80 COD charges on merchandise purchased for resale. *Assume Milton Consulting uses the perpetual method to account for merchandise inventory.*
	12	Paid $15.65 postage to express mail a contract to a client.
	14	Reimbursed Kim Marn, the manager of the business, $135.00 for business auto expenses.
	20	Purchased stationery, $58.70.
	23	Paid a courier $32.45 to deliver merchandise sold to a customer.
	25	Paid $37.80 COD charges on merchandise purchased for resale.
	28	Paid $50.00 for stamps.
	28	Reed sorted the petty cash receipts by accounts affected and exchanged them for a cheque to reimburse the fund for expenditures. However, there was only $8.15 in cash in the fund. In addition, the size of the petty cash fund was increased to $500.

Required

1. Prepare a journal entry to record establishing the petty cash fund.

2. Prepare a summary of petty cash payments, similar to Exhibit 8.2 that has these categories: delivery expense, auto expense, postage expense, merchandise inventory, and office supplies. Sort the payments into the appropriate categories and total the expenditures in each category.

3. Prepare the journal entry to record the reimbursement and the increase of the fund.

Analysis Component: One of your responsibilities as an employee with Milton Consulting is to handle the petty cash fund. You are concerned about the auto expense claims made regularly by Kim Marn, the manager who hired you: Kim tells you how much the expenditures were and you give her the cash out of petty cash. Kim has never given you receipts to substantiate her claims. The owner of the business is visiting and asks you how things are going. What should you do, if anything? Explain.

Problem 7-3A Petty cash fund reimbursement and analysis of errors LO4

Capital Irrigation has only a general journal in its accounting system and uses it to record all transactions. However, the company recently set up a petty cash fund to facilitate payments of small items. The following petty cash transactions were noted by the petty cashier as occurring during April 2017:

Apr.   1   Received a company cheque for $300 to establish the petty cash fund.

       15   Received a company cheque to replenish the fund for the following expenditures made since April 1 and to increase the fund to $400.

            a.   Paid $82 for janitorial service.

            b.   Purchased office supplies for $78.15.

            c.   Purchased postage stamps for $25.00.

            d.   Paid $92.50 to *The County Crier* for an advertisement in the newspaper.

            e.   Discovered that $24.35 remained in the petty cash box.

       30   The petty cashier noted that $244.95 remained in the fund and decided that the April 15 increase in the fund was too large. Therefore, a company cheque was issued to replenish the fund for the following expenditures made since April 15 and to reduce the fund to $350.

            f.   Purchased office supplies for $94.65.

            g.   Reimbursed office manager for business auto, $45.60.

            h.   Paid $14.80 courier charges to deliver merchandise to a customer.

Required Prepare journal entries to record the establishment of the fund on April 1 and its replenishments on April 15 and April 30.

Analysis Component: Explain how the company's financial statements would be affected if the petty cash fund were not replenished and no entry were made on April 30. (*Hint: The amount of office supplies that appears on a balance sheet is determined by a physical count of the supplies on hand.*)

Problem 7-4A Preparation of bank reconciliation and recording adjustments LO6

CHECK FIGURE: Adjusted book balance = $2,401.54

The bank reconciliation prepared by Gatz Company on May 31, 2017, appeared as follows:

Gatz Company
Bank Reconciliation
May 31, 2017

Bank statement balance		$ 9,564.35	Book balance..........................		$20,056.03
Add:					
Deposit of April 30 in transit ...		982.17			
		$10,546.52			
Deduct:			Deduct:		
Outstanding cheques:			NSF cheque plus service		
#876	$ 655.99		charge............................	$11,900.50	
#882:	1,800.00	2,455.99	Bank service charge	65.00	11,965.50
Adjusted bank balance		$ 8,090.53	Adjusted book balance		$ 8,090.53

The Cash account in the general ledger appeared as follows on June 30 (Gatz uses only a general journal to record transactions):

Cash						Acct. No. 101
Date	Explanation	PR	Debit	Credit	Balance
2017					
May 31	Balance				8,090.53
June 1	Cheque #883	GJ16		1,865.30	6,225.23
1	Cheque #884	GJ16		112.70	6,112.53
3	Cheque #885	GJ16		650.84	5,461.69
4	Cheque #886	GJ16		2,018.45	3,443.24
9	Deposit	GJ16	4,285.26		7,728.50
12	Cheque #887	GJ16		425.15	7,303.35
12	Cheque #888	GJ16		3,040.60	4,262.75
12	Cheque #889	GJ16		974.12	3,288.63
18	Deposit	GJ16	3,515.60		6,804.23
20	Cheque #890	GJ16		2,640.00	4,164.23
21	Cheque #891	GJ16		1,406.24	2,757.99
24	Cheque #892	GJ16		2,590.81	167.18
26	Cheque #893	GJ16		75.99	91.19
29	Deposit	GJ16	1,845.35		1,936.54

The following bank statement is available for June:

Bank Statement					
To: Gatz Company				June 30, 2017 Bank of Montreal	
Cheques/Charges			Deposits/Credits		Balance
			05/31		9,564.35
#884	06/01	112.70	06/01	982.17	10,433.82
#883	06/04	1,865.30			8,568.52
#876	06/09	655.99	06/09	4,285.26	12,197.79
#889	06/12	974.12			11,223.67
#882	06/14	1,800.00			9,423.67
#887	06/18	245.15	06/18	3,515.60	12,694.12
#885	06/20	650.84			12,043.28
#891	06/21	1,046.24			10,997.04
#886	06/29	2,018.45			8,978.59
SC	06/30	75.00	06/30		8,903.59
NSF = Not Sufficient Funds	SC = Service Charge		PMT = Principal Payment	INT = Interest	

Required

a. Prepare a bank reconciliation at June 30, 2017. Assume that any errors made were by the bookkeeper (cheque #887 was for office supplies; cheque #891 was for utilities expense).

b. Prepare the necessary entries resulting from the bank reconciliation.

Analysis Component: You have been employed with Gatz Company since June 1, 2017, and part of your job is writing and recording cheques as well as preparing the bank reconciliation. To your surprise, the person you replaced brought in the June bank statement as it had been mailed to her home. While preparing the June bank reconciliation, you notice that cheque #882 for $1,800 cleared the bank in June but is not among the cancelled cheques. What should you do? Explain.

Problem 7-5A Preparation of bank reconciliation and recording adjustments LO6

CHECK FIGURE: a. Adjusted book balance = $7,193

The bank reconciliation prepared by Gemma Tours on March 31, 2017, appeared as follows:

Gemma Tours				
Bank Reconciliation				
March 31, 2017				
Bank statement balance		$14,800	Book balance.................................	$32,710
Add:				
Deposit of March 31 in transit.......		21,050		
		$35,850		
Deduct:				
Outstanding cheques:				
#79	$1,250			
#84:	1,890	3,140		
Adjusted bank balance.................		$32,710	Adjusted book balance	$32,710

The Cash account in the general ledger appeared as follows on April 30:

			Cash		Acct. No. 101
Date	**Explanation**	**PR**	**Debit**	**Credit**	**Balance**
2017					
March 31	Balance				32,710.00
April 30		CR11	34,049.00		66,759.00
30		CD14		43,643.00	23,116.00

A list of deposits made and cheques written during April, taken from the cash receipts journal and cash disbursements journal, is shown below:

Deposits Made		Cheques Written	
April 7..	$14,200	No. 91......................................	$ 1,200
13..	850	92......................................	5,230
18..	13,600	93......................................	2,590
23..	945	94......................................	3,452
27..	1,890	95......................................	2,900
30..	2,564	96......................................	1,811
Total April Cash Receipts............	$34,049	97......................................	8,470
		98......................................	2,900
		99......................................	8,590
		100......................................	6,500
		Total April Cash Disbursements ..	$43,643

The following bank statement is available for April:

Bank Statement					
To: Gemma Tours				**April 30, 2017**	
				Bank of Montreal	
Cheques/Charges			**Deposits/Credits**		**Balance**
					14,800
#93	04/02	2,509	04/03	21,050	33,341
#92	04/07	5,230	04/07	14,200	42,311
#84	04/13	1,890	04/13	850	41,271
NSF	04/18	6,540	04/18	13,600	48,331
#95	04/23	2,900	04/23	945	46,376
#99	04/27	8,590	04/27	1,890	39,676
#96	04/30	1,811	04/30	2,564	40,429
#97	04/30	8,470	04/30	46	32,005
#94	04/30	3,452			28,553
PMT	04/30	9,420			19,133
INT	04/30	35			19,098
SC	04/30	55			**19,043**
NSF = Not Sufficient Funds		SC = Service Charge	PMT = Principal Payment		INT = Interest

In reviewing cheques returned by the bank, the bookkeeper discovered that cheque #93, for delivery expense, was recorded in the cash disbursements journal incorrectly as $2,590. The NSF cheque was that of customer Laura Clark, deposited in April.

Required

   a. Prepare a bank reconciliation at April 30.

   b. Prepare the necessary journal entries to bring the general ledger Cash account into agreement with the adjusted balance on the bank reconciliation.

Problem 7-6A **Preparation of bank reconciliation and recording adjustments** LO6

CHECK FIGURE: 1. Adjusted book balance = $32,439

The following information was available to reconcile Montrose Company's book balance of Cash with its bank statement balance as of October 31, 2017:

   a. After all posting was completed on October 31, the company's Cash account had a $13,254 debit balance, but its bank statement showed a $29,436 balance.

   b. Cheques #296 for $1,340 and #307 for $12,809 were outstanding on the September 30 bank reconciliation. Cheque #307 was returned with the October cancelled cheques, but cheque #296 was not. It was also found that cheque #315 for $897 and cheque #321 for $2,010, both written in October, were not among the cancelled cheques returned with the statement.

   c. In comparing the cancelled cheques returned by the bank with the entries in the accounting records, it was found that cheque #320 for the October rent was correctly written for $3,070 but was erroneously entered in the accounting records as $3,700.

   d. A credit memo enclosed with the bank statement indicated that there was an electronic fund transfer related to a customer payment for $22,000. A $120 bank service charge was deducted. This transaction was not recorded by Montrose before receiving the bank statement.

e. A debit memo for $3,250 listed a $3,200 NSF cheque plus a $50 NSF charge. The cheque had been received from a customer, Jefferson Tyler. Montrose had not recorded this bounced cheque before receiving the statement.

f. Also enclosed with the statement was a $75 debit memo for bank services. It had not been recorded because no previous notification had been received.

g. The October 31 cash receipts, $7,250, were placed in the bank's night depository after banking hours on that date and this amount did not appear on the bank statement.

Required

1. Prepare a bank reconciliation for the company as of October 31, 2017.

2. Prepare the general journal entries necessary to bring the company's book balance of Cash into agreement with the reconciled balance.

Analysis Component: Assume that an October 31, 2017, bank reconciliation for the company has already been prepared and some of the items were treated incorrectly in preparing the reconciliation. For each of the following errors, explain the effect of the error on (1) the final balance that was calculated by adjusting the bank statement balance, and (2) the final balance that was calculated by adjusting the Cash account balance.

a. The company's Cash account balance of $13,254 was listed on the reconciliation as $12,354.

b. The electronic fund transfer for the collection of a customer's payment of $22,000 less the $120 collection fee was added to the bank statement balance.

Problem 7-7A **Preparation of bank reconciliation and recording adjustments** LO6

CHECK FIGURE: 1. Adjusted book balance, $4,871.89

Pelzer Company reconciled its bank and book statement balances of Cash on **August 31** and showed two cheques outstanding at that time, #5888 for $6,220.00 and #5893 for $1,485.65.

The following information was available for the September 30, 2017, reconciliation:

From the September 30, 2017, bank statement

BALANCE OF PREVIOUS STATEMENT ON AUG. 31/17...........	10,674.50
6 DEPOSITS AND OTHER CREDITS TOTALLING.................	22,417.05
9 CHEQUES AND OTHER DEBITS TOTALLING...................	26,296.05
CURRENT BALANCE AS OF SEPT. 30/17.........................	6,795.50

Chequing Account Transactions

Date	Amount	Transaction Description	Date	Amount	Transaction Description
Sept. 05	5,643.20	+Deposit	Sept. 25	4,230.60	+Deposit
12	2,561.45	+Deposit	30	45.00	+Interest
17	1,176.50	−NSF cheque	30	3,500.00	+Credit memo
21	6,436.80	+Deposit			

Date	Cheque No.	Amount	Date	Cheque No.	Amount
Sept. 03	5904	9,340.55	Sept. 22	5888	6,220.00
07	5901	1,450.00	24	5909	2,140.40
08	5905	338.25	28	5907	3324.60
10	5903	1320.15	29	5902	985.60

From Pelzer Company's accounting records:

			Cash		Acct. No. 101
Date	Explanation	PR	Debit	Credit	Balance
2017					
Aug. 31	Balance				2,968.85
Sept. 30		CR12	20,005.75		22,974.60
30		CD23		15,071.21	7,903.39

Deposits Made			Cheques Written		
Sept. 5.................................	$ 5,643.20		No. 5901...........................	$ 1,450.00	
12................................	2,561.45		5902...........................	985.60	
21................................	6,436.80		5903...........................	1,320.15	
25................................	4,230.60		5904...........................	3,940.55	
30................................	1,133.70		5905...........................	338.25	
Total Sept. Cash Receipts	$20,005.75		5906...........................	715.26	
			5907...........................	3 ,324.60	
			5908...........................	856.40	
			5909...........................	2,140.40	
			Total Sept. Cash		
			Disbursements	$15,071.21	

- Cheque #5904 was correctly written for $9,340.55 to pay for computer equipment; however, the bookkeeper misread the amount and entered it in the accounting records with a debit to Computer Equipment and a credit to Cash as though it were for $3,940.55. The NSF cheque was originally received from a customer, Lisa Willis, in payment of her account. Its return was not recorded when the bank first notified the company.

- The credit memo resulted from an electronic fund transfer of $3,550 for a customer payment. The bank had deducted a $50 bank service charge. The collection has not been recorded.

Required

1. Prepare a September 30 bank reconciliation for the company.
2. Prepare the general journal entries needed to adjust the book balance of cash to the reconciled balance.

Analysis Component: The preceding bank statement discloses three places where the cancelled cheques returned with the bank statement are not numbered sequentially. In other words, some of the prenumbered cheques in the sequence are missing. Several possible situations would explain why the cancelled cheques returned with a bank statement might not be numbered sequentially. Describe three possible explanations.

Problem 7-8A Preparation of a bank reconciliation and recording adjustments LO6

CHECK FIGURE: a. Adjusted book balance = $100,488

Stewart Recording Studio, owned by Ron Stewart, showed the following bank reconciliation at March 31:

Stewart Recording Studio Bank Reconciliation March 31, 2017				
Bank statement balance		$22,100	Book balance..	$30,945
Add:				
Deposit of March 31 in transit........		10,000		
		$32,100		
Deduct:				
Outstanding cheques:				
#14	$840			
#22	315	1,155		
Adjusted bank balance......................		$30,945	Adjusted book balance	$30,945

	Cash				Acct. No. 101
Date	Explanation	PR	Debit	Credit	Balance
2017					
Mar. 31	Balance				30,945
Apr. 30		CR17	71,440		102,385
30		CD13		91,172	11,213

A list of deposits made and cheques written during April, taken from the cash receipts journal and cash disbursements journal, is shown below:

Deposits Made		Cheques Written	
April 7.................................	$ 690	No. 23	$ 5,200
13.................................	4,600	24	3,150
18.................................	5,900	25	940
23.................................	13,900	26	310
27.................................	1,750	27	4,230
30.................................	44,600	28	4,900
Total April Cash Receipts........	$71,440	29	19,630
		30	41,000
		31	412
		32	11,400
		Total April Cash Disbursements ..	$91,172

The following bank statement is available for April:

Bank Statement					
To: Stewart Recording Studio				April 30, 2017 Bank of Canada	
Cheques/Charges			**Deposits/Credits**		**Balance**
					22,100
#31	04/03	412	04/03	10,000	31,688
#28	04/07	9,400	04/07	690	22,978
#26	04/13	310	04/13	4,600	27,268
NSF	04/18	14,200	04/18	5,900	18,968
#24	04/23	3,150	04/23	13,900	29,718
#23	04/27	5,200	04/27	1,750	26,268
#29	04/30	19,630	04/30	120,000	126,638
PMT	04/30	15,900			110,738
INT	04/30	450			110,288
SC	04/30	175			**110,113**
NSF = Not Sufficient Funds		SC = Service Charge	PMT = Payment of Principal on the Loan		INT = Interest on Bank Loan

- In reviewing cheques returned by the bank, the bookkeeper discovered that cheque #28, for delivery expense, was recorded in the cash disbursements journal correctly as $4,900.
- The NSF cheque for $14,200 was that of customer Oprah Winney, deposited in March.
- On the bank statement, the payment for $15,900 is regarding a note payable.
- There is also a deposit of $120,000 dated April 30. It is an investment made by the owner into the business (the bank transferred the funds electronically from the owner's personal account to his business account, which is why it was not recorded in the cash receipts journal).

Required

a. Prepare a bank reconciliation for Stewart Recording Studio at April 30.

b. Prepare the necessary journal entries to bring the general ledger Cash account into agreement with the adjusted balance on the bank reconciliation.

Problem 7-9A **Preparation of a bank reconciliation and recording adjustments** LO6

CHECK FIGURE: a. Adjusted book balance = $82,994.99

Presented below is information related to Simalan Dive Company. The balance according to the books at October 31, 2017, was $99,657.29; cash receipts recorded during November were $64,805.69; and cash disbursements recorded for November were $76,850.30. The balance according to the bank statement on November 30, 2017, was $82,370.68.

The following cheques were outstanding at November 30:

Cheque	Amount
#920	947.29
#991	2,843.50
#1030	1,971.34
#1064	824.66

Included with the November bank statement and not recorded by the company were a bank debit memo for $32.26 covering bank charges for the month, a debit memo for $5,200.75 for a customer's cheque (Marnie Wiesen) returned and marked NSF, and a credit memo for $615.32 representing interest collected by the bank for Simalan Dive Company. Cash on hand at November 30, which has been recorded and is awaiting deposit, amounted to $7,211.10.

Required

    a. Prepare a bank reconciliation at November 30, 2017.

    b. Prepare any journal entries required to adjust the Cash account at November 30.

Problem 7-10A **Preparation of a bank reconciliation and recording adjustments** LO6

CHECK FIGURE: 1. Adjusted book balance = $28,250

The following is information for Dundee Realty:

    a. Balance per the bank statement dated October 31, 2017, is $26,830.

    b. Balance of the Cash account on the company books as of October 31, 2017, is $5,575.

    c. $14,680 of customer deposits were outstanding as of September 30; this amount had been deposited to Dundee's account in October.

    d. Cheques written in October that had not cleared the bank as of October 31 were:

        #8700, $985

        #8709, $12,600

        #8801, $620

        #8815, $145.

    e. The bank charged Dundee's account for a $2,350 cheque of the E-Zone Networks; the cheque was found among the cancelled cheques returned with the bank statement.

    f. Bank service charges for October amount to $65.

    g. A customer's cheque (Teresa Krant) for $7,050 had been deposited in the bank correctly but was recorded in the accounting records as $7,500.

    h. Among the cancelled cheques is one for $260 given in payment of an account payable to Decker Company; the bookkeeper had recorded the cheque incorrectly at $620 in the company records.

    i. The bank statement showed an electronic fund transfer of $22,880 for a customer payment. A bank service fee of $50 was charged.

    j. A bank deposit of October 31 for $13,420 does not appear on the bank statement.

Required

  1. Prepare a bank reconciliation statement as of October 31, 2017.

  2. Prepare the necessary entries to make the Cash account agree with the bank reconciliation adjusted Cash balance as of October 31.

Analysis Component: Identify the effects on the income statement and balance sheet if the entries in Part 2 were not recorded.

Alternate Problems

Problem 7-1B Principles of internal control LO1

For the following five scenarios, identify the principle of internal control that is violated. Next, recommend what the business should do to ensure adherence to principles of internal control.

1. Tamerick Company is a fairly small organization but has segregated the duties of cash receipts and cash disbursements. However, the employee responsible for cash disbursements also reconciles the bank account monthly.

2. Stan Spencer is the most computer literate employee in his company. His boss has recently asked him to put password protection on all the office computers. Stan's main job at the company is to process payroll. Stan has put a password in place that now allows only his boss access to the file where pay rates are changed and personnel are added or deleted from the company payroll.

3. Starlight Theatre has a computerized order-taking system for its tickets. The system is active all week and backed up every Friday night.

4. Trek There Company has two employees handling acquisitions of inventory. One employee places purchase orders and pays vendors. The second employee receives the merchandise.

5. The owner of Holiday Helper uses a cheque protector to perforate cheques, making it difficult for anyone to alter the amount of the cheque. The cheque protector sits on the owner's desk in an office that houses company cheques and is often unlocked.

Problem 7-2B Establishing, reimbursing, and increasing the petty cash fund LO4

Stihl Repairs completed the following petty cash transactions during July 2017:

July	5	Prepared a $500 cheque, cashed it, and turned the proceeds and the petty cash box over to Bob Stuart, the petty cashier.
	6	Paid $108.00 COD charges on merchandise purchased for resale. *Stihl Repairs uses the perpetual inventory method to account for merchandise inventory.*
	11	Paid $23.75 delivery charges on merchandise sold to a customer.
	12	Purchased file folders, $8.50.
	14	Reimbursed Collin Dodge, the manager of the business, $8.26 for office supplies purchased.
	18	Purchased paper for printer, $12.15.
	27	Paid $21.60 COD charges on merchandise purchased for resale.
	28	Purchased stamps, $23.00.
	30	Reimbursed Collin Dodge $64.80 for business car expenses.
	31	Bob Stuart sorted the petty cash receipts by accounts affected and exchanged them for a cheque to reimburse the fund for expenditures. However, there was $233.94 in cash in the fund. In addition, the size of the petty cash fund was decreased to $300.

Required

1. Prepare a general journal entry to record establishing the petty cash fund.

2. Prepare a summary of petty cash payments similar to Exhibit 8.2 that has these categories: delivery expense, auto expense, postage expense, merchandise inventory, and office supplies.

3. Prepare the general journal entry to record the reimbursement and the increase of the fund.

Analysis Component: You supervise Bob Stuart, the petty cashier, and while reviewing the accounts you notice that the Cash Over/Short Expense account has a balance for the seven months ended July 31, 2017, of $300. Given the size of the petty cash account, does this balance appear to be unusual? Explain and identify any concerns that you might have.

Problem 7-3B Petty cash fund; reimbursement and analysis of errors LO4

The accounting system used by Dartmouth Sales and Service requires that all entries be journalized in a general journal. To facilitate payments for small items, Dartmouth established a petty cash fund. The following transactions involving the petty cash fund occurred during February 2017.

Feb.	3	A company cheque for $200 was prepared and made payable to the petty cashier to establish the petty cash fund.
	14	A company cheque was prepared to replenish the fund for the following expenditures made since February 3 and to increase the fund to $250.

   a.   Purchased office supplies, $65.82.

   b.   Paid $75.00 COD charges on merchandise purchased for resale. Dartmouth uses the perpetual method to account for merchandise inventory.

   c.   Paid $36.40 to Data Services for minor repairs to a computer.

   d.   Paid $15.23 for postage expenses.

   e.   Discovered that only $5.55 remained in the petty cash box.

| | 28 | The petty cashier noted that $39.30 remained in the fund, and decided that the February 14 increase in the fund was not large enough. A company cheque was prepared to replenish the fund for the following expenditures made since February 14, and to increase it to $300. |

   f.   Paid $45 to *The Smart Saver* for an advertisement in a monthly newsletter.

   g.   Paid $96.35 for office supplies.

   h.   Paid $69.35 to Best Movers for delivery of merchandise to a customer.

Required Prepare general journal entries to record the establishment of the fund on February 3 and its replenishment on February 14 and February 28.

Analysis Component: Explain how the company's financial statements would be affected if the petty cash fund is not replenished and no entry is made on February 28. (*Hint: The amount of Office Supplies that appears on a balance sheet is determined by a physical count of the supplies on hand.*)

Problem 7-4B Preparing a bank reconciliation and recording adjustments LO6

CHECK FIGURE: Adjusted book balance = $2,837.06

Mae Telford, the controller of the Baylor Company, provided the following information:

Baylor Company Bank Reconciliation October 31, 2017					
Bank statement balance		$19,687.60	Book balance...........................		$45,548.66
Add:			Deduct:		
Deposit of Oct. 31 in transit....		4,280.45	NSF cheque plus		
		$23,968.05	service charge	$25,140.95	
Deduct:			Bank service charges...........	130.00	25,270.95
Outstanding cheques:			Adjusted book balance		$20,277.71
#537	$ 725.00				
#542	2,965.34	3,690.34			
Adjusted bank balance		$20,277.71			

The Cash account in the general ledger appeared as follows on November 30 (Baylor Company uses only a general journal to record transactions):

					Cash		Acct. No. 101
Date		Explanation	PR	Debit		Credit	Balance
2017							
Oct.	31	Balance					20,277.71
Nov.	1	Cheque #543	GJ5			6,505.12	13,772.59
	1	Cheque #544	GJ5			854.71	12,917.88
	1	Cheque #545	GJ5			1,156.94	11,760.94
	1	Cheque #546	GJ5			2,564.24	9,196.70
	1	Cheque #547	GJ5			1,345.68	7,851.02
	1	Cheque #548	GJ6			56.45	7,794.57
	1	Cheque #549	GJ6			564.23	7,230.34
	9	Deposit	GJ6	1,548.97			8,779.31
	9	Cheque #550	GJ6			3,457.15	5,322.16
	9	Cheque #551	GJ6			985.64	4,336.52
	18	Deposit	GJ6	5,649.85			9,986.37
	20	Cheque #552	GJ6			5,556.71	4,429.66
	27	Cheque #553	GJ6			964.25	3,465.41
	29	Deposit	GJ6	1,250.65			4,716.06

The following bank statement is available for November 2017:

		Bank Statement				
To: Baylor Company					**November 30, 2017**	
					Bank of Canada	
	Cheques/Charges			**Deposits/Credits**		**Balance**
						9,200
#543	11/02	6,505.12				16,898.70
#549	11/01	564.23	11/01		4,280.45	23,403.82
#537	11/07	725.00				16,173.70
#551	11/09	985.64	11/09		1,584.97	16,773.03
#542	11/12	2,965.34				13,807.69
#544	11/14	854.71				12,952.98
#547	11/18	3,145.68	11/18		5,649.85	15,457.15
#545	11/20	1,156.94				14,300.21
#546	11/29	2,564.24				11,735.97
SC	11/30	115.00	11/30			**11,620.97**

NSF = Not Sufficient Funds	SC = Service Charge	PMT = Principal Payment	INT = Interest

Required

a. Prepare a bank reconciliation for Baylor Company for the month of November 2017. Assume that any errors made were by the bookkeeper (cheque #547 was for advertising expense; the deposit of November 9 was regarding a credit customer, Val Pacino).

b. Prepare the necessary entries resulting from the bank reconciliation.

Analysis Component: You have been employed with Baylor Company since November 1, 2017, and part of your job is writing and recording cheques as well as preparing the bank reconciliation. In reviewing the cheques returned by the bank, you notice that the payee on cheque #543 is the employee you recently replaced. You investigate further and find that the journal entry recording cheque #543 debited Office Supplies Expense. What should you do? Explain.

Problem 7-5B Preparing a bank reconciliation and recording adjustments LO6

CHECK FIGURE: a. Adjusted book balance = $13,929

The bank reconciliation prepared by Village-on-the-Lake Condos on May 31, 2017, is shown below:

Village-on-the-Lake Condos Bank Reconciliation May 31, 2017					
Bank statement balance		$ 2,060	Book balance..		$3,910
Add:					
Deposit of May 31 in transit		12,500			
		$14,560			
Deduct:					
Outstanding cheques:					
#103	$6,520				
#120	4,130	10,650			
Adjusted bank balance..................		$ 3,910	Adjusted book balance		$3,910

The Cash account in the general ledger appeared as follows on June 30:

Cash						Acct. No. 101
Date		Explanation	PR	Debit	Credit	Balance
2017						
May	31	Balance				3,910
June	30		CR21	38,680		42,590
	30		CD16		31,861	10,729

A list of deposits made and cheques written during June, taken from the cash receipts journal and cash disbursements journal, is shown below:

Deposits Made			Cheques Written	
June 5.......................................	$ 590		No. 127.....................................	$ 2,100
10.......................................	1,120		128.....................................	450
15.......................................	5,690		129.....................................	680
20.......................................	4,510		130.....................................	9,750
27.......................................	7,830		131.....................................	196
30.......................................	12,600		132.....................................	6,420
30.......................................	6,340		133.....................................	4,550
Total June Cash Receipts	$38,680		134.....................................	6,780
			135.....................................	820
			136.....................................	115
			Total June Cash Disbursements..	$31,861

The following bank statement is available:

Bank Statement					
To: Village-on-the-Lake Condos					June 30, 2017
					Bank of Nova Scotia
Cheques/Charges			**Deposits/Credits**		**Balance**
					2,060
#133	06/02	4,550	06/02	12,500	10,010
#136	06/05	115	06/05	590	10,485
#129	06/10	680	06/10	1,120	10,925
#130	06/15	9,750	06/15	5,690	6,865
#103	06/20	6,520	06/20	4,510	4,855
#134	06/27	6,780	06/27	7,830	5,905
#128	06/30	450	06/30	16,200	21,655
SC	06/30	400			21,255
NSF = Not Sufficient Funds		SC = Service Charge	PMT = Principal Payment		INT = Interest

In reviewing deposits recorded by the bank, the bookkeeper discovered that the deposit from customer Darla Smith dated June 30, recorded in the cash receipts journal incorrectly as $12,600, was recorded by the bank correctly as $16,200.

Required

a. Prepare a bank reconciliation at June 30.

b. Prepare the necessary journal entries to bring the general ledger Cash account into agreement with the adjusted balance on the bank reconciliation.

Problem 7-6B **Preparing a bank reconciliation and recording adjustments** LO6

CHECK FIGURE: 1. Adjusted book balance = $20,374

The following information was available to reconcile Frogbox Moving's book Cash balance with its bank statement balance as of December 31, 2017:

a. The December 31 Cash balance according to the accounting records was $12,644, and the bank statement balance for that date was $13,650.

b. Cheque #3115 for $1,213 and cheque #3201 for $694, both written and entered in the accounting records in December, were not among the cancelled cheques returned. Two cheques, #3207 for $3,260 and #3221 for $984, were outstanding on November 30 when the bank and book statement balances were last reconciled. Cheque #3207 was returned with the December cancelled cheques, but cheque #3221 was not.

c. When the December cheques were compared with entries in the accounting records, it was found that cheque #3199 had been correctly written for $3,910 to pay for office supplies, but was erroneously entered in the accounting records as though it were written for $9,310.

d. Two debit memos were included with the returned cheques and were unrecorded at the time of the reconciliation. One of the debit memos was for $1,620 and dealt with an NSF cheque for $1,570 that had been received from a customer, Tork Industries, in payment of its account. It also assessed a $50 fee for processing. The second debit memo covered cheque printing and was for $35. These transactions had not been recorded by Frogbox before receiving the statement.

e. A credit memo indicated the receipt of an electronic fund transfer of $4,000 for a customer payment. A $15 bank service charge was deducted. This transaction was not recorded by Frogbox before receiving the statement.

f. The December 31 cash receipts, $9,615, had been placed in the bank's night depository after banking hours on that date and did not appear on the bank statement.

Required

1. Prepare a bank reconciliation for the company as of December 31.

2. Prepare the general journal entries necessary to bring the company's book balance of Cash into conformity with the reconciled balance.

Analysis Component: Explain the nature of the messages conveyed by a bank to one of its depositors when the bank sends a debit memo and a credit memo to the depositor.

Problem 7-7B Preparing a bank reconciliation and recording adjustments LO6

CHECK FIGURE: 1. Adjusted book balance = $35,201.35

Yardworx reconciled its book balance of Cash with its bank statement balance on April 30 and showed two cheques outstanding at that time, #1771 for $15,463.10 and #1780 for $955.65.

The following information is available for the May 31, 2017, reconciliation:

From the May 31, 2017, bank statement:

Balance of previous statement on Apr. 30/17	$61,045.95
5 deposits and other credits totalling..............................	26,088.10
9 cheques and other debits totalling...............................	57,005.40
Current balance as of this statement..............................	30,128.65

Chequing Account Transactions

Date	Amount	Transaction Description	Date	Amount	Transaction Description
May 04	14,662.30	+Deposit	May 25	5,200.00	+Credit memo
14	849.25	+Deposit	26	4,210.10	+Deposit
18	15,600.40	−NSF cheque	31	135.00	−Service charge
22	1,166.45	+Deposit			

Date	Cheque No.	Amount	Date	Cheque No.	Amount
May 01	1784	7,600.00	May 26	1785	620.15
02	1783	1,465.80	28	1771	15,463.10
15	1787	2,334.75	29	1788	985.65
16	1782	12,800.55			

From Yardworx's accounting records:

Date		Explanation	PR	Debit	Credit	Balance
2017						
Apr.	30	Balance				44,627.20
May	31		CR7	29,289.05		73,916.25
	31		CD8		28,089.50	45,826.75

Cash — Acct. No. 101

Deposits Made		Cheques Written	
May 4 .... $14,662.30		No. 1782 .... $12,800.55	
14 .... 849.25		1783 .... 1,465.80	
22 .... 1,166.45		1784 .... 7,600.00	
26 .... 4,210.10		1785 .... 620.15	
31 .... 8,400.95		1786 .... 974.35	
Total May Cash Receipts $29,289.05		1787 .... 2,334.75	
		1788 .... 895.65	
		1789 .... 1,398.25	
		Total May Cash Disbursements $28,089.50	

- Cheque #1788 was correctly written for $985.65 to pay for May utilities; however, the bookkeeper misread the amount and entered it in the accounting records with a debit to Utilities Expense and a credit to Cash as though it were for $895.65. The bank paid and deducted the correct amount.

- The NSF cheque was originally received from a customer, Gertie Mayer, in payment of her account. Its return was unrecorded.

- The credit memo resulted from a $5,300 electronic fund transfer for the collection of a customer payment. The bank had deducted a $100 bank service charge fee. The collection has not been recorded in the company's books.

Required

1. Prepare a bank reconciliation for Yardworx.
2. Prepare the general journal entries needed to adjust the book balance of Cash to the reconciled balance.

Analysis Component: The preceding bank statement discloses two places where the cancelled cheques returned with the bank statement are not numbered sequentially. In other words, some of the prenumbered cheques in the sequence are missing. Several possible situations would explain why the cancelled cheques returned with a bank statement might not be numbered sequentially. Describe three possible reasons that this might occur.

Problem 7-8B Preparing a bank reconciliation and recording adjustments LO6

CHECK FIGURE: 1. Adjusted book balance = $31,532

Lyryx Co. reconciled its bank statement balances of Cash on October 31 and showed two cheques outstanding at that time, #1388 for $14,650 and #1393 for $9,800. The following information was available for the November 30, 2017, reconciliation:

From the November 30 bank statement:

Balance of previous statement on Oct. 31/17	106,980
5 deposits and other credits totalling	63,568
9 cheques and other debits totalling.................................	123,873
Current balance as of November 30/17...........................	46,675

		Chequing Account Transactions			
Date	Amount	Transaction Description	Date	Amount	Transaction Description
Nov. 05	21,640	+Deposit	Nov. 25	29,008	+Deposit
12	956	+Deposit	30	250	+Interest
17	1,810	−NSF cheque	30	10,550	+Credit memo
21	1,164	+Deposit			

Date	Cheque No.	Amount	Date	Cheque No.	Amount
Nov. 03	1402	9,325	Nov. 17	1409	12,125
04	1403	11,500	20	1405	14,850
08	1388	14,650	27	1407	38,412
12	1401	18,600	29	1404	2,601

From Lyryx Co.'s accounting records:

		Cash			Acct. No. 101
Date	Explanation	PR	Debit	Credit	Balance
2017					
Oct. 31	Balance				82,530
Nov. 30		CR12	86,145		168,675
30		CD23		149,733	18,942

Deposits Made		Cheques Written	
Nov. 5................................	$21,640	No. 1401	$ 18,600
12...............................	956	1402	9,325
21...............................	1,164	1403	11,500
25...............................	29,008	1404	6,201
30...............................	33,377	1405	14,850
Total November Cash		1406	12,980
Receipts	$86,145	1407	38,412
		1408	25,740
		1409	12,125
		Total November Cash	
		Disbursements	$149,733

- Cheque #1404 was correctly written for $2,601 to pay for computer equipment: however, the bookkeeper misread the amount and entered it in the accounting records with a debit to Computer Equipment and a credit to Cash as though it were for $6,201.

- The NSF cheque was originally received from a customer, Jerry Skyles, in payment of his account. Its return was not recorded when the bank first notified the company.

- The credit memo resulted from receiving an electronic fund transfer of $10,700 for a customer payment. The bank had deducted a $150 bank service charge fee. The collection has not been recorded in the books.

Required

1. Prepare a November 30 bank reconciliation for the company.

2. Prepare the general journal entries needed to adjust the book balance of Cash to the reconciled balance.

Problem 7-9B Preparing a bank reconciliation and recording adjustments LO6

CHECK FIGURE: 1. Adjusted book balance = $24,370

The following information was available to reconcile Shanghai Company's book balance of Cash with its bank statement balance as of February 28, 2017.

a. The bank statement at February 28 indicated a balance of $23,620. The general ledger account for Cash showed a balance at February 28 of $9,400.

b. Of the cheques issued in February, the following were still outstanding:

Cheque	Amount
#202	$ 960
#205	1,075
#213	610
#240	840

c. Two cheques, #136 for $1,036 and #200 for $2,600, were outstanding on Jan. 31 when the bank and book balances were last reconciled. Cheque #136 was returned with the February cancelled cheques but cheque #200 was not.

d. Included with the February bank statement was an NSF cheque for $6,250 that had been received from a customer, Mrs. Loni Fung, in payment of her account.

e. Cheque #219 was correctly written for $1,910 in payment for office supplies but was erroneously entered as $9,110 in the cash payments journal.

f. A debit memo for $35 was enclosed with the bank statement. This charge was for printing the chequebook for Shanghai Company.

g. Included with the bank statement was a $120 credit memo for interest earned on the bank account in February.

h. The February 28 cash receipts amounting to $6,835 had been placed in the bank's night depository after banking hours on that date and did not appear among the deposits on the February bank statement.

i. Included with the bank statement was a credit memo for an electronic fund transfer of $14,000 for the collection of a customer payment. A bank service charge of $65 was deducted.

Required

1. Prepare a bank reconciliation for the Shanghai Company as of February 28, 2017.

2. Prepare the entries needed to adjust the book balance of Cash to the reconciled balance.

Problem 7-10B **Preparing a bank reconciliation and recording adjustments** LO6

CHECK FIGURE: 1. Adjusted book balance = $60,580

The following is information for the Timbits Cafe:

    a. Balance per the bank statement dated December 31, 2017, is $50,860.

    b. Balance of Cash account on the company books as of December 31, 2017, is $57,285.

    c. A cheque from customer Della Armstrong for $7,860 that had been deposited in the bank was erroneously recorded by the bookkeeper as $8,760.

    d. A cheque made out by Neon Company for $10,140 deposited on December 21 is returned by the bank marked NSF; no entry has been made on the company records to reflect the returned cheque.

    e. Among the cancelled cheques is one for $692 given in payment of an account payable to CT Financial; the bookkeeper had incorrectly recorded the cheque at $962 in the company records.

    f. Bank service charges for December amount to $35.

    g. The bank erroneously charged the Timbits Cafe account for a $5,000 cheque of HRD Company; the cheque was found among the cancelled cheques returned with the bank statement.

    h. The bank had collected a $14,150 electronic fund transfer for a customer payment; $14,150 was credited to the Timbits Cafe's bank account; a collection fee of $50 was debited to the Timbits Cafe's bank account.

    i. The bank deposit of December 31 for $6,860 does not appear on the bank statement.

    j. Outstanding cheques as of December 31: #197, $920; #199, $1,220.

Required

1. Prepare a bank reconciliation as of December 31, 2017.

2. Prepare the necessary entries to make the Cash account agree with the bank reconciliation adjusted Cash balance as of December 31.

Analysis Component: Identify the effects on the income statement and balance sheet if the adjustments in Part 2 were not recorded.

Analytical and Review Problems

A & R Problem 7-1

CHECK FIGURE: 1. Adjusted book balance = $20,552

You are a college student and have just been hired to work part-time in the accounting department of Candy's Cleaning Services. The person you are replacing had difficulty preparing the bank reconciliation for April 30, which is shown below.

Candy's Cleaning Services						
Bank Reconciliation						
April 30, 2017						
Bank balance		$33,452	Book balance..........................			$28,934
			Add:			
Deduct:			Interest................................	$47		
NSF, customer Bonne	$ 412		Error Chq #93	99		146
						$29,080
Outstanding cheques:			Deduct:			
#879	2,600		Service Charge....................			40
#100	1,400	4,412	Adjusted book balance			$29,040
Adjusted bank balance......................		$29,040				

In comparing the bank reconciliation to the Cash account in the general ledger, you notice a problem. You investigate further and come up with some additional information as follows:

a. The Cash account in the general ledger showed the following:

Cash						**Acct. No. 101**
Date	**Explanation**	**PR**	**Debit**		**Credit**	**Balance**
2017						
March 31	Balance					28,934
April 30		CR16	56,000			84,934
30		CD21			63,883	21,051

b. The error in cheque #93, for Utilities Expense, resulted from the bank incorrectly debiting our account for $99; the correct amount entered in the accounting records is $199.

c. The bank statement showed interest expense of $47; there was no other interest.

d. The bank debited our account for cheque #879 written by Candy's Hair Salon.

e. Cheque #86 for $14,000 listed as outstanding on last month's bank reconciliation was not returned with the April 30 bank statement.

Required

1. Prepare a corrected bank reconciliation for April 30, 2017.

2. Record the journal entries resulting from the corrected bank reconciliation.

A & R Problem 7-2

CHECK FIGURE: 1. Adjusted book balance = $10,014

Your assistant prepared the following bank reconciliation statement. It appears that the statement is unacceptable and the task of preparing a proper reconciliation falls upon you.

Brandon Company Bank Reconciliation May 31, 2017		
Balance per books May 31...		$ 9,500
Add:		
Electronic Fund Transfer..	$ 1,060	
Deposit in transit...	2,455	3,515
		$13,015
Deduct:		
Bank charges..	$ 10	
NSF cheque, Rhonda Teal	500	
Outstanding cheques...	1,800	

Error in cheque #78: correctly issued and processed
     by the bank for $762, but incorrectly recorded
     in the books as $726 (Accounts Payable–Delta Co.).....................
	36	2,346

Indicated bank balance		$10,669
Balance per bank statement..		9,359
Discrepancy		$ 1,310

Required

1. Prepare a proper bank reconciliation showing the true Cash balance.

2. Prepare the necessary journal entries.

A & R Problem 7-3

Wanda White acquired a sports equipment distribution business with a staff of six salespeople and two clerks. Because of the trust that Wanda had in her employees—after all, they were all her friends and just like members of the family—she believed that an honour system in regard to the operation of the petty cash fund was adequate. Consequently, Wanda placed $300 in a coffee jar, which, for convenience, was kept in a cupboard in the common room. All employees had access to the petty cash fund and withdrew amounts as required. No vouchers were required for withdrawals. As required, additional funds were placed in the coffee jar and the amount of the replenishment was charged to "miscellaneous selling expense."

Required

1. From the internal control point of view, discuss the weaknesses of the petty cash fund operation and suggest steps necessary for improvement.

2. Does the petty cash fund operation as described above violate any of the generally accepted accounting principles? If yes, which one(s), and how are the principles violated?

Ethics Challenge

EC 7-1

Marge Page, Dot Night, and Colleen Walker work for a dentist, Dr. Linda Thomen, who is in a private practice. Dr. Thomen is fairly knowledgeable about sound office management practices and has segregated the cash receipt duties as follows. Marge opens the mail and prepares a triplicate list of money received. She sends one copy of the list to Dot, the cashier, who deposits the receipts daily in the bank. Colleen, the recordkeeper, also receives a copy of the list and posts payments to patients' accounts. About once a month the office clerks decide to have an expensive lunch compliments of Dr. Thomen. Dot endorses a patient's cheque in Dr. Thomen's name and cashes it at the bank. Marge destroys the remittance advice accompanying the cheque. Colleen posts the payment to the customer's account as a miscellaneous credit. The clerks justify their actions given their relatively low pay and knowing that Dr. Thomen will likely never miss the payment.

Required

1. Who would be the best person in Dr. Thomen's office to reconcile the bank statement?
2. Would a bank reconciliation detect the office fraud scheme?
3. What are some ways of uncovering this type of scheme?
4. Suggest additional internal controls that Dr. Thomen might want to implement.

Focus on Financial Statements

FFS 7-1

CHECK FIGURES: Current assets = $68,190, Total assets = $112,540

Ellis Worton, the owner of Worton Consulting, showed the following unadjusted account balances at December 31, 2017, the business's year-end (accounts have been listed in alphabetical order):

Account	Account Balance*
Accounts payable	$ 31,500
Accounts receivable	46,250
Accumulated depreciation, store fixtures	61,000
Cash	19,340
Cost of goods sold	469,000
Delivery expense	11,330
Ellis Worton, capital	89,560
Ellis Worton, withdrawals	69,000
Interest expense	2,240
Notes payable (principal of $20,000 to be paid in 2018)	56,000
Petty cash	350
Prepaid rent	16,200
Rent expense	11,250
Salaries expense	213,000
Salaries payable	17,750
Sales	721,400
Sales returns and allowances	6,000
Store fixtures	113,250
*Assume normal account balances.	

Other information:

1. There were two reconciling items on the bank reconciliation: an outstanding cheque in the amount of $620 and an NSF cheque for $2,835.

2. A review of the Prepaid Rent account showed that the unexpired portion was $2,250.

3. Annual depreciation on the store fixtures is $7,900.

Required
Prepare the December 31, 2017, classified balance sheet.

Analysis Component:

a. Calculate Worton Consulting's current ratio and quick-test ratio at December 31, 2017. Compare and comment. Round calculations to two decimal places.

b. Recalculate the current ratio and quick-test ratio assuming the current portion of the note payable was reported as part of the long-term liabilities. Compare your results to part (a) and comment. Round calculations to two decimal places.

FFS 7-2

Refer to WestJet's December 31, 2014, balance sheet in Appendix III at the end of the textbook.

Required
Answer the following questions.

1. WestJet shows cash and cash equivalents on its December 31, 2014, balance sheet. Explain the meaning of cash and cash equivalents.

2. How much cash and cash equivalents did WestJet have on December 31, 2014?

3. By how much did WestJet's cash and cash equivalents increase or decrease from December 31, 2013, to December 31, 2014?

Analysis Component: Is it possible for there to be excessive cash and cash equivalents? Explain.

Critical Thinking Mini Case

You are the newly elected vice-president of campus life for the business students' association at your institution. The first big event of the year is a party that has three live bands playing from 5:00 p.m. to midnight; tickets are $20 (cash only). A number of people are helping you sell tickets during the two weeks prior to the event. At the end of each day, you collect the cash from each seller and reconcile it against the tickets sold (the tickets are sequentially numbered). You place your records and the cash in a locked filing cabinet in your office, which is always locked. In less than two weeks, all of the tickets are sold. After collecting the cash from the ticket sellers on the day of the sellout, you're feeling terrific about the success of the sales campaign you organized for the event and go to your office, unlock the door, and immediately notice that the filing cabinet has been tampered with ... all of the money is gone ... over $35,000!

Required Using the elements of critical thinking described on the inside front cover, comment.

Receivables

A Look Back

Chapter 7 provides an introduction to Internal Control and Cash with a detailed analysis of internal control guidelines, banking activities, accounting for petty cash funds, and reconciling the differences between cash reported in the bank account and cash in the company's accounting records.

A Look at This Chapter

Chapter 8 takes a look at accounting for customer accounts receivable and short-term notes receivable, specifically investigating tools such as initial recognition of the receivables and subsequent measurement at the end of the accounting period. Valuation is assessed through methods to estimate bad debts, including the benefits of an A/R aging report, and using the accounts receivable turnover ratio and days' sales uncollected ratios to evaluate financial statements.

Used by permission of WN Pharmaceuticals.

LEARNING OBJECTIVES

LO1 Describe accounts receivable and how they occur and are recorded.

LO2 Apply the allowance method to account for uncollectible accounts receivable.

LO3 Estimate uncollectible accounts receivable using approaches based on sales and accounts receivable.

LO4   Describe and record a short-term note receivable and calculate its maturity date and interest.

LO5   Calculate accounts receivable turnover and days' sales uncollected to analyze liquidity.

*Appendix 8A

LO6   Explain how receivables can be converted to cash before maturity.

Effective Receivables Management Tools Strengthen Corporate Health

WN Pharmaceuticals is one of North America's largest manufacturers of health products and its well-known brand Webber Naturals vitamin, mineral, and herbal supplements. The company headquarters is in Coquitlam, B.C. It has experienced significant growth over the past 50 years from its first product—topical vitamin E—to over 230 products today.

The company relies on leading-edge manufacturing technologies to extract the purest of nutrients for use in its products. Ingredients are sourced both domestically and globally and are rigorously tested using pharmaceutical standards for purity, potency, pesticides and contaminants, and quality. Natural health products are subject to very strict regulations set out by the Canadian Food and Drug Association and the United States Food and Drug Association. Finished products are tested in WN Pharmaceuticals' laboratories for weight, uniformity, and potency levels to ensure all products sold meet the company's quality standards.

The company sells its vitamins to pharmacies, grocery stores, and major retailers throughout North America. The wide range of retailers results in varying trade terms depending on the risk level of the retailer, history with the company, volume purchases made, or special promotional campaigns. In order to care for these large mass distribution centre accounts, the receivable department clerks are assigned a group of customers to care for, and to maintain and reconcile outstanding balances for. The clerks handle questions with respect to invoice discrepancies, requests for credit on promotions, and issues with shipments and invoice discrepancies. Continuous monitoring and follow-up is essential to the timely collection of claims and payment deductions, as many customers will not take the time required to research claims past 90–120 days. Detailed analysis is done on all accounts to identify the average days it takes to clear invoices, and increase the efficiency of collections.

Specialized reports are created, incorporating data from sales, marketing, and accounts receivable, to monitor closely the promotional activity of large chain accounts and to incorporate and translate that information into cash flow forecasting and budgeting. Aging reports are used to identify possible issues or invoices that have been missed, or not received by customers, and are used as collection lists for collections on smaller chains and independent customers. The days' sales outstanding and accounts receivable turnover ratio are used by the department to determine how effectively they are managing collections. These ratios are described later in the chapter. At Webber Naturals, the receivables department is a major player in collecting and managing the cash receipts process, significantly impacting the overall cash flow of the company.

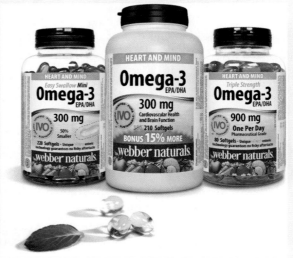

Used by permission of WN Pharmaceuticals.

CRITICAL THINKING CHALLENGE   Why is assessing customer credit critical to the overall success of businesses like WN Pharmaceuticals?

CHAPTER PREVIEW

Accounts receivable management is a critical aspect of managing a company's cash resources. This chapter focuses on accounting practices for both accounts receivable and short-term notes receivable. The chapter provides a detailed description for each of these assets, identifies their use in practice, demonstrates how they are accounted for and reported in financial statements, and analyzes how to handle valuation issues and account for bad debts.

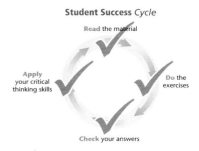

Student Success *Cycle*

Accounts Receivable

LO1 Describe accounts receivable and how they occur and are recorded.

A *receivable* refers to an amount due from another party. The two most common receivables are accounts receivable and notes receivable. Other receivables include interest receivable, rent receivable, tax refund receivable, and amounts due from other parties such as officers and employees.

Accounts receivable are amounts due from customers and result from non-cash sales to customers. They are also referred to as **trade receivables** because they result from customers with whom we engage in *trade*. This section begins by describing how accounts receivable arise and their various sources. These sources include sales when customers use the seller's credit cards, and when a company gives credit directly to customers. When a company extends credit directly to customers, it must (1) maintain a separate account receivable for each customer and (2) account for bad debts from credit sales.

Recognizing Accounts Receivable

Accounts receivable arise from credit sales to customers. Recognition of accounts receivable is directly linked to revenue recognition at the time of the sales transaction. In general, revenue from a sale of goods can be recorded when the following key criteria are met[1]:

- *Performance:* A company can recognize revenue when it transfers the product or service to the customer, meaning the customer obtains control of the specific asset purchased or receives the benefit of the service provided. This generally involves the company physically transferring the asset to the customer, meaning the customer is now responsible for the risks and rewards of ownership of the asset and the customer accepts the asset.

- *Measurement:* The amount of cash or cash equivalents it expects to receive based on the sale of the product or service can be determined. The transaction price to be recorded is determined by the customer agreement or contract[2].

- *Collectability:* The company has an enforceable right to receive payment, as performance has been completed to date and it is probable the company will collect any outstanding balances from the customer. The enforceable right is generally linked to an agreement or formal contract with the customer.

---

1 IFRS 2014, IAS 18, para. 14. IFRS 15 Revenue from Contracts with Customers: http://www.ifrs.org/Current-Projects/IASB-Projects/Revenue-Recognition/Documents/IFRS-15/Revenue-from-Contracts-Project-summary-Feedback-Statement-May-2014.pdf, (accessed October 2014).

2 IFRS 2015, IFRS 15, para. 9, 31.

If the above conditions are not met, the sale of the product or service cannot be recognized under generally accepted accounting principles, including the related customer's accounts receivable.

The amount of credit sales over cash sales has increased in recent years, reflecting several factors including an efficient banking system and a sound economy. Exhibit 8.1 shows the dollar amounts of accounts receivable and their percentage of total assets for seven companies. Notice how Lululemon Athletica Inc. has less than 1% of its total assets as receivables and Amazon has nearly 12% of total assets as receivables.

EXHIBIT 8.1

Accounts Receivable Analysis for Selected Companies as a Percentage of Total Assets

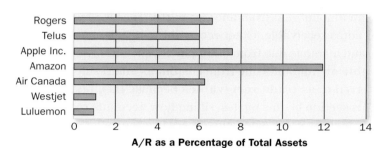

Note the above information is based on December 31, 2013, financial results for all companies except Lululemon Athletica Inc. at February 2, 2014, and Apple Inc. at September 27, 2014.

SALES ON CREDIT

To review how accounts receivable from credit sales are recognized, we will record two transactions in the accounting records for TechCom, a small electronics wholesaler. TechCom's accounts receivable controlling account in the general ledger and accounts receivable subledger prior to recording these transactions are illustrated in Exhibit 8.2.

EXHIBIT 8.2

Accounts Receivable Controlling Account and the Accounts Receivable Subledger

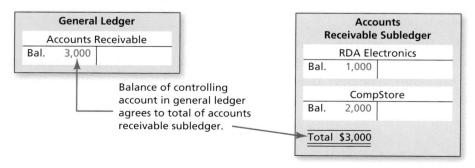

The first transaction to be recorded on July 15 is a credit sale of $950 to CompStore (cost of sales to TechCom is $630 assuming a perpetual inventory system). The second is a collection of $720 from RDA Electronics from prior credit sales. Both transactions are reflected in Exhibit 8.3. Note that these transactions would typically be recorded in the appropriate sales and cash receipts journals. We use the general journal format here for simplicity.

Accounts Receivable Transactions

July	15	Accounts Receivable—CompStore..................	950	
		Sales		950
		To record credit sales.		
	15	Cost of Goods Sold.......................................	630	
		Merchandise Inventory		630
		To record cost of sales.		
	15	Cash	720	
		Accounts Receivable—RDA Electronics.....		720
		To record collection of credit sales.		

Exhibit 8.4 shows the Accounts Receivable controlling account and the accounts receivable subledger after posting these two transactions.

Accounts Receivable Controlling Account and the Accounts Receivable Subledger

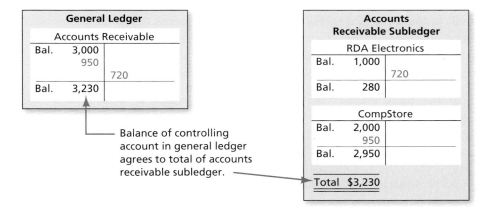

Like many companies, TechCom grants credit directly to qualified customers. Many large retailers such as **Canadian Tire Corporation Ltd.** and **Hudson's Bay Company** issue credit to retail customers. Once credit has been granted to approved customers, the company will earn interest on any outstanding balances. The company also avoids paying a transaction fee charged by the credit card company. Canadian Tire has a separate Financial Services segment that manages the credit granting and receivables collection process. The receivables fall under the financial statement line item "Loans Receivable" under the category of current assets. The entries in this case are the same as those above except for the possibility of added interest income. If a customer owes interest on the bill, then Canadian Tire debits Loans Receivable and credits Interest income for this amount.

DECISION INSIGHT

Canadian Banking: Rogers Canada and Walmart Canada Apply for Permission to Operate as Financial Institutions

Both **Rogers Canada** and **Walmart Canada** recently applied under the federal Bank Act to get permission to operate as a financial institution in Canada. Both companies were granted permission. According to Rogers, the decision to enter financial services markets is to provide the company with the option to issue credit cards and have the ability to provide mobile banking opportunities with its Suretap mobile wallet to its customers in the future. Walmart Financial Services has already marketed its cobranded MasterCard credit cards to customers and provides opportunities for money transfers at its customer service desks.

SOURCE: http://www.theglobeandmail.com/globe-investor/rogers-sets-sights-on-banking-business/article1360602, accessed October 2014; http://www.mobilepaymentstoday.com/articles/when-a-telco-turns-to-banking (accessed October 2014); www.walmartfinancial.ca

CHECKPOINT

1. Where on the balance sheet are accounts receivable reported?

Do Quick Study question: QS 8-1

Credit Risk Analysis Accounts Receivable

Assessing the creditworthiness of customers is an important task and has a significant impact on the company's cash resources and ability to meet expenses. Each company needs to develop its own procedures for assessing creditworthiness of its customers. It is in the company's best interest to treat the granting of credit in the form of a receivable in a similar likeness to a loan, assessing the company's history, reputation, and financial strength.

According to Canadian Tire Corporation's 2013 Annual Report, the following describes the risk management process employed by the company when extending credit to its customers:

Consumer credit risk

Financial Services grants credit to its customers on Canadian Tire credit cards, personal loans and lines of credit. With the granting of credit, Financial Services assumes certain risks such as the failure to accurately predict the willingness of its customers to repay debt. Financial Services manages credit risk to maintain and improve the quality of its consumer lending portfolio by:

- Employing sophisticated credit-scoring models to constantly monitor the creditworthiness of customers;
- Using the latest technology to make informed credit decisions for each customer account to limit credit risk exposure;
- Adopting technology to improve the effectiveness of the collection process; and
- Monitoring the macroeconomic environment, especially with respect to consumer debt levels, interest rates, employment levels and profit levels.

Accounts Receivable Control Considerations

Ensuring appropriate controls are in place is essential to mitigate the risk of fraudulent activities and enable an efficient use of resources. As discussed in Chapter 7, separation of certain responsibilities in an organization can minimize the risk of misappropriation of assets. For example, it is imperative that the individuals responsible for the sales of products to customers are not also responsible for the granting of credit. It would not be in the best interest of Audi Canada if its car salespeople who get commission on vehicle sales had the final say on which customers were approved for vehicle financing; customers with weak credit and an inability to meet future car payment obligations may be approved by a salesperson interested in maximizing his or her commission.

Below are a couple of recommendations by BDO Consulting to strengthen the control environment for customer collections in its "Segregation of Duties Checklist." BDO adds a fourth element to the "CAR Principle" introduced in Chapter 7. Along with separation of duties associated with Custody, Authorization and Recording of Assets, BDO includes reconciliation of the bank statement and other records. Control considerations for customer payments include the following:

- Any employee responsible for receipt of cash should not have access to record or authorize transactions in the A/R ledger or customer accounts.
- Any employee receiving the cash or preparing the deposit should not be able to record cash transactions or prepare the bank reconciliation.
- The bank reconciliation should not be prepared by an employee who is involved in either cash receipts (collections) or disbursements (payments).
- Write-offs and adjustments to receivables should be performed by an employee who does not have the ability to record transactions.

Source: http://www.financialexecutives.org/ferf/download/2009%20Final/2009-018.pdf (accessed November 2014).

Valuing Accounts Receivable

When a company grants credit to its customers, there are usually a few customers who do not end up paying what they promised at the point of the sales or service transaction. The accounts of these customers are **uncollectible accounts**, commonly referred to as **bad debts**. The total amount of uncollectible accounts is an expense of selling on credit. Why do companies sell on credit if it is likely some accounts will prove uncollectible? Companies believe granting credit will substantially increase revenues and profits, which offsets the negative impact of bad debts. Also, in order to remain competitive, many companies are required to grant credit to customers, especially if it is an industry standard of practice.

Two main methods are commonly used by companies to account for uncollectible accounts: (1) allowance method, and (2) direct write-off method. Exhibit 8.5 summarizes these methods.

Allowance Method

LO2 Apply the allowance method to account for uncollectible accounts receivable.

The matching principle requires that expenses be reported in the same accounting period as the sales they helped produce. The **allowance method of accounting for bad debts** satisfies the matching principle by recording any estimated bad debt expense that is connected to the current period sales in the same period the related revenue is earned. How is this accomplished? Since the seller is unable to identify in advance which specific customer receivables will become uncollectible, an estimate is based on the company's past experience combined with future expectations based on both the industry and economic climates. This requires professional judgment and a big-picture perspective. As a result, an experienced accountant usually determines the end-of-period adjustment. Recording too low of an estimate for the allowance would result in an overstatement of assets and could cause users of the financial statements to make inappropriate investment decisions.

EXHIBIT 8.5

Methods for Writing Off Bad Debts

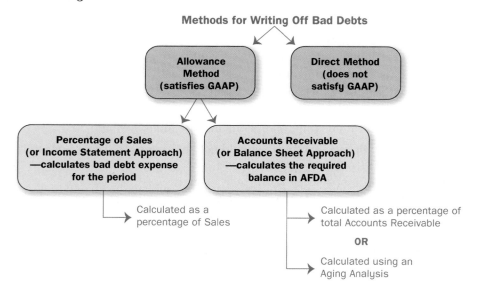

Recording Estimated Bad Debt Expense

The allowance method estimates bad debt expense at the end of each accounting period and records it with an adjusting entry. TechCom, for instance, had credit sales of approximately $300,000 during its first year of operations. At the end of the first year, $20,000 of credit sales remained uncollected. Based on the experience of similar businesses, TechCom estimated bad debt expense to be $1,500. This estimated expense is recorded with the following adjusting entry at the end of the accounting period:

Dec.	31	Bad Debt Expense	1,500	
		Allowance for Doubtful Accounts		1,500
		To record estimated bad debts.		

The debit in this entry means the estimated bad debt expense of $1,500 from selling on credit is matched on the income statement with the $300,000 of sales it helped produce. The credit in this entry is to a contra asset called **Allowance for Doubtful Accounts**. A contra account is used because at the time of the adjusting entry, we do not know which customers will not pay. Because specific uncollectible accounts are not determinable at the time of the end of period adjusting entry, the expected amounts cannot be removed from the accounts receivable subledger. Instead, the valuation adjustment is reflected as a credit to the Allowance for Doubtful Accounts.

BAD DEBTS AND RELATED ACCOUNTS IN FINANCIAL STATEMENTS

Recall that TechCom has $20,000 of outstanding accounts receivable at the end of its first year of operations. After the bad debt adjusting entry is posted, TechCom's Accounts Receivable, Allowance for Doubtful Accounts, and Bad Debt Expense have balances as shown in Exhibit 8.6.

EXHIBIT 8.6

General Ledger Balances After Bad Debts Adjustment

Accounts Receivable and *Allowance for Doubtful Accounts* are BOTH balance sheet accounts shown under current assets.

Accounts Receivable		Allowance for Doubtful Accounts	
Dec. 31 20,000			1,500 Dec. 31

Bad Debt Expense is an income statement account and is normally listed as a selling expense.

Bad Debt Expense	
Dec. 31 1,500	

Although $20,000 is legally owed to TechCom by its credit customers, $18,500 (= $20,000 − $1,500) is the **realizable value**, or the estimated amount to be realized in cash collections from customers.

On the balance sheet, the Allowance for Doubtful Accounts is subtracted from Accounts Receivable to show the realizable value. This information is often reported as shown in Exhibit 8.7.

EXHIBIT 8.7

Balance Sheet Presentation of Allowance for Doubtful Accounts

Current assets:
Accounts receivable	$20,000	
Less: Allowance for doubtful accounts..	1,500	18,500

Often the contra account to Accounts Receivable is not reported as a separate line item. This alternative presentation is shown in Exhibit 8.8.

EXHIBIT 8.8

Alternative Presentation of Allowance for Doubtful Accounts

Current assets:
Accounts receivable (net of $1,500 estimated uncollectible accounts)	$18,500

WRITING OFF BAD DEBT FOR A SPECIFIC CUSTOMER

When specific accounts receivable are identified as uncollectible, they must be removed from accounts receivable. This is done by writing these accounts off against the Allowance for Doubtful Accounts. For instance, after spending a year trying to collect from Jack Kent, TechCom finally decides that his $520 account is uncollectible and makes the following entry to write it off:

Jan.	23	Allowance for Doubtful Accounts	520	
		Accounts Receivable—Jack Kent		520
		To write off an uncollectible account.		

After this entry is posted, the general ledger accounts appear as shown in Exhibit 8.9.

EXHIBIT 8.9

General Ledger Balances After Posting Write-Off

Accounts Receivable				Allowance for Doubtful Accounts			
Dec. 31	20,000					1,500	Dec. 31
		520	Jan. 23	Jan. 23	520		
Balance	19,480					980	Balance

Note that the expense account is not debited, because bad debt expense is previously estimated and recorded with an adjusting entry at the end of the period in which the sale occurred. While the write-off removes the amount of the account receivable from the ledgers, it does not affect the estimated realizable value of TechCom's net accounts receivable as shown in Exhibit 8.10.

EXHIBIT 8.10		

Realizable Value Before and After Write-Off

	Before Write-Off (Dec. 31)	After Write-Off (Jan. 23)
Accounts receivable...	$20,000	$19,480
Less: Allowance for doubtful accounts..	1,500	980
Estimated realizable accounts receivable...	$18,500	$18,500

Neither total assets nor profit is affected by the write-off of a specific account. But both total assets and profit are affected by recognizing the year's bad debt expense in the adjusting entry.

RECOVERY OF A BAD DEBT—THE CUSTOMER MAKES A PAYMENT

When a customer fails to pay and the account is written off, his or her credit standing is jeopardized. The customer sometimes chooses to pay all or part of the amount owed after the account is written off as uncollectible. This payment helps restore credit standing. When a recovery of a bad debt occurs, it is recorded in the customer's subsidiary account where this information is retained for use in future credit evaluation.

On March 11, Jack Kent pays in full his account that TechCom previously wrote off. The first entry reinstates the accounts receivable balance:

Mar.	11	Accounts Receivable—Jack Kent.....................	520	
		Allowance for Doubtful Accounts		520
		To reinstate the account of Jack Kent previously written off.		

The second entry reflects the cash receipt and the customer payment of the outstanding balance.

	11	Cash	520	
		Accounts Receivable—Jack Kent.............		520
		In full payment of account.		

Jack Kent paid the entire amount previously written off, but in some cases a customer may pay only a portion of the amount owed. A question then arises of whether the entire balance of the account is returned to accounts receivable or just the amount paid. The answer is a matter of judgment. If we believe this customer will later pay in full, the entire amount owed is returned to accounts receivable. But only the amount paid is returned if we expect no further collection.

To summarize, the transactions discussed in this chapter[3] that cause changes in Accounts Receivable and Allowance for Doubtful Accounts are illustrated using T-accounts in Exhibit 8.11.

---

3 Remember that Sales Returns and Allowances also cause Accounts Receivable to decrease.

EXHIBIT 8.11

Summary of Accounts Receivable and Allowance for Doubtful Accounts Transactions

Accounts Receivable		Allowance for Doubtful Accounts	
(a) Sales on credit	(b) Collections received from credit customers		
	(c) Write-off of accounts receivable identified as uncollectible	(c) Write-off of accounts receivable identified as uncollectible	
(d) Recovery (reinstatement of accounts previously written off)	(e) Recovery (collection of reinstated accounts)		(d) Recovery (reinstatement of accounts previously written off)
			(f) Adjusting entry to estimate uncollectible accounts

CHECKPOINT

2. Why does the matching principle require that bad debt expenses be estimated?

3. What term describes the balance sheet valuation of accounts receivable less the allowance for doubtful accounts?

4. Why is estimated bad debt expense credited to a contra account rather than to the Accounts Receivable controlling account?

5. Record entries for the following transactions:

January 10, 2017	The $300 account of customer Cool Jam is determined to be uncollectible.
April 12, 2017	Cool Jam pays in full its account that was deemed uncollectible on January 10, 2017.

Do Quick Study questions: QS 8-2, QS 8-3

Alternative Methods for Estimating Bad Debt

LO3 Estimate uncollectible accounts receivable using approaches based on sales and accounts receivable.

There are two general approaches for estimating bad debt expense. These were introduced briefly in Exhibit 8.5.

ACCOUNTS RECEIVABLE APPROACH

The **accounts receivable approach**, also known as the **balance sheet approach**, uses balance sheet relationships (Accounts Receivable and the Allowance for Doubtful Accounts) to estimate bad debts. It is based on the idea that some portion of the end-of-period accounts receivable balance is not collectible. The objective for the bad debt adjusting entry is to make the Allowance for Doubtful Accounts balance equal to the portion of outstanding accounts receivable estimated to be uncollectible. To obtain this required balance for the

Allowance for Doubtful Accounts account, we compare its balance before the adjustment with the required balance. The difference between the two is debited to Bad Debt Expense and credited to Allowance for Doubtful Accounts. Estimating this required balance for the allowance account is done in one of two ways:

1. By using a simple percentage estimate of uncollectible accounts from the total outstanding accounts receivable, or

2. By applying a unique percentage estimate to each category of the aged accounts receivable listing.

1. *PERCENTAGE OF ACCOUNTS RECEIVABLE*

Estimating the required balance in the Allowance for Doubtful Accounts by using the **percentage of accounts receivable approach** assumes that a percentage of a company's outstanding receivables is uncollectible. This estimated percentage is based on past experience and is also affected by recent economic conditions and difficulties faced by customers. The total dollar amount of all outstanding receivables is multiplied by an estimated percentage to get the estimated dollar amount of uncollectible accounts. This is the amount to be reported in the balance sheet as the balance for Allowance for Doubtful Accounts. To accomplish this, we prepare the adjusting entry in the amount necessary to give us the required balance in Allowance for Doubtful Accounts.

For example, assume Modern Office, an office furniture supplier, has $50,000 of outstanding accounts receivable on December 31. Past experience suggests that 5% of outstanding receivables are uncollectible.

Therefore, we want the Allowance for Doubtful Accounts to show a $2,500 credit balance (5% of $50,000). Assume that the unadjusted balance in the Allowance for Doubtful Accounts at December 31 is currently a $500 credit.

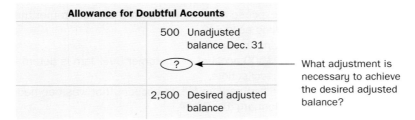

The adjusting entry to give the required $2,500 balance is:

Dec.	31	Bad Debt Expense	2,000	
		Allowance for Doubtful Accounts		2,000
		To record estimated bad debts.		

After this entry is posted, the allowance has a $2,500 credit balance as shown in Exhibit 8.12.

EXHIBIT 8.12

Allowance for Doubtful Accounts After Bad Debt Adjusting Entry

Allowance for Doubtful Accounts

	500 Unadjusted balance Dec. 31
	2,000 From Dec. 31 adjusting entry
	2,500 Adjusted balance Dec. 31

Accounts receivable would then be reported as follows on Modern Office's balance sheet:

Current assets:
  Accounts receivable $50,000
  Less: Allowance for doubtful accounts...   2,500 $47,500

or

Current assets:
  Accounts receivable (net of $2,500 estimated uncollectible accounts)...................................... $47,500

2. AGING OF ACCOUNTS RECEIVABLE

Normally, the older the account receivable is outstanding, the more likely that it will become uncollectible. An **accounts receivable aging analysis** estimates uncollectible accounts by grouping accounts receivable according to how much time has passed since they were created. Grouping categories used depends depend on the judgment of management but are often based on 30-day periods. Estimated rates of uncollectible amounts are applied to each class and totalled to get the required balance of the Allowance for Doubtful Accounts. This calculation is illustrated in Exhibit 8.13 for DeCor, an interior design company whose total outstanding accounts receivable at December 31 were $49,900.

EXHIBIT 8.13

Aging of Accounts Receivable

	DeCor Schedule of Accounts Receivable by Age December 31, 2017					
Customer's Name	**Total**	**Not Yet Due**	**1 to 30 Days Past Due**	**31 to 60 Days Past Due**	**61 to 90 Days Past Due**	**Over 90 Days Past Due**
Chloe Arden	$ 450	$ 450				
Luca Fontana...........	710			$ 710		
Jasmine Kasu..........	500	300	$ 200			
Amy Ma	740				$ 100	$ 640
ZZ Services.............	1,000	810	190			
Totals	$49,900	$37,000	$6,500	$3,500	$1,900	$1,000
Percentage Uncollectible		× 2%	× 5%	× 10%	× 25%	× 40%
Estimated Uncollectible Accounts................	$ 2,290	$ 740	$ 325	$ 350	$ 475	$ 400

Notice the percentage of estimated uncollectible receivables increases with the age of the accounts to reflect the increasing risk of not collecting these accounts

The total in the first column tells us the adjusted balance in DeCor's Allowance for Doubtful Accounts should be $2,290 (= $740 + $325 + $350 + $475 + $400). Because DeCor's allowance account as shown below has an unadjusted *debit balance* of $200, the required adjustment to the Allowance for Doubtful Accounts needs to be calculated as follows:

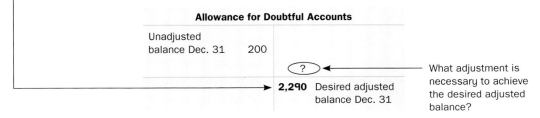

Allowance for Doubtful Accounts

Unadjusted balance Dec. 31   200

(?)

2,290   Desired adjusted balance Dec. 31

What adjustment is necessary to achieve the desired adjusted balance?

DeCor records the following adjusting entry:

Dec.	31	Bad Debt Expense	2,490	
		Allowance for Doubtful Accounts		2,490
		To record estimated bad debts;		
		$2,290 + $200 = $2,490.		

On the balance sheet, DeCor's accounts receivable would be reported as follows:

Current assets:			
Accounts receivable		$49,900	
Less: Allowance for doubtful accounts..		2,290	$47,610

or

Current assets:	
Accounts receivable (net of $2,290 estimated uncollectible accounts)......................................	$47,610

PERCENTAGE OF SALES APPROACH

The **percentage of sales approach** (or **income statement approach**) uses income statement relations to estimate bad debts. It is based on the idea that a percentage of a company's credit sales for the period are uncollectible.[4] To demonstrate, assume MusicLand has credit sales of $400,000 in 2017. Based on experience, MusicLand estimates 0.6% of credit sales to be uncollectible. Using this prediction, MusicLand expects $2,400 of bad debt expense from 2017's sales ($400,000 × 0.006 = $2,400). The adjusting entry to record this estimated expense is:

Dec.	31	Bad Debt Expense	2,400	
		Allowance for Doubtful Accounts		2,400
		To record estimated bad debts.		

For demonstration purposes, assume that the Allowance for Doubtful Accounts (AFDA) had an unadjusted credit balance of $200 on December 31. Bad Debt Expense and Allowance for Doubtful Accounts would appear as in Exhibit 8.14 *after* the December 31 adjustment.

EXHIBIT 8.14

Accounts Receivable and Allowance for Doubtful Accounts Balances After the December 31 Adjustment

Bad Debt Expense			Allowance for Doubtful Accounts	
			200	Unadjusted Balance Dec. 31
Dec. 31 Adjustment	2,400		2,400	Dec. 31 Adjustment
Adjusted Balance Dec. 31	2,400		2,600	Adjusted Balance Dec. 31

---

4 Note that the focus is on credit sales. Cash sales do not produce bad debts, and they are generally not used in this estimation. But if cash sales are relatively small compared to credit sales, there is no major impact of including them.

Note that the unadjusted balance of AFDA could be a zero balance, a credit balance, or a debit balance depending on the circumstances. If MusicLand were in its first period of operations, the AFDA would have a zero beginning balance. In the next accounting periods, if write-offs are *greater* than what had been estimated, a *debit* unadjusted balance will result. If *fewer* write-offs occur than what was estimated, as in Exhibit 8.14, a *credit* unadjusted balance will result. If the estimate for bad debts is too high or too low, the percentage used to estimate bad debts can be adjusted in future periods.

Exhibit 8.15 summarizes the principles guiding the estimation approaches and their focus of analysis.

EXHIBIT 8.15

Approaches to Estimate Bad Debts

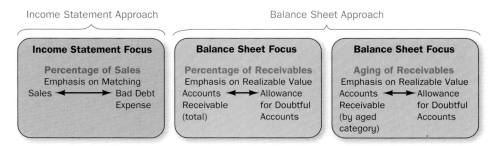

Using an aging of receivables is the most reliable of the three calculations because it is based on a more detailed examination of the basket of outstanding receivables. In many cases, the aging analysis is supplemented with information about the current economic conditions and information about specific customers, allowing management to decide whether those accounts should be classified as uncollectible. This analysis is often best performed by the sales and credit department managers.

 **CHECKPOINT**

6. SnoBoard Company's end-of-period December 31, 2017, balance in the Allowance for Doubtful Accounts is a credit of $440. It estimates from an aging of accounts receivable that $6,142 is uncollectible. Prepare SnoBoard's year-end adjusting entry for bad debts.

Do Quick Study questions: QS 8-4, QS 8-5, QS 8-6, QS 8-7

DIRECT WRITE-OFF METHOD

Another approach to writing off bad debt is referred to as the *direct write-off method*. This method is permitted only in circumstances where the total reported accounts receivable balance is insignificant to the financial statements as a whole. The **direct write-off method** records the loss from an uncollectible account receivable at the time it is determined to be uncollectible. No attempt is made to estimate uncollectible accounts or bad debt expense. For example, if TechCom determines on January 23 that it cannot collect $520 owed by an individual named Jack Kent, this loss is recognized using the direct write-off method in the following entry:

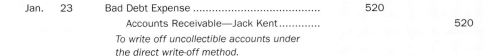

Jan.	23	Bad Debt Expense	520	
		Accounts Receivable—Jack Kent.............		520
		To write off uncollectible accounts under		
		the direct write-off method.		

The allowance method satisfies the requirement for faithful representation and matching; the direct write-off method does not.

1. An aspect of faithful representation demands that caution be exercised to prevent the over-statement of assets and profit. Overstated assets and/or profit could result in bad lending or investing decisions. By estimating uncollectible accounts, the allowance method is recognizing that less than 100% of the accounts receivable will be collected (Accounts Receivable less Allowance for Doubtful Accounts), ensuring receivables are not overstated. Under the direct write-off method, Accounts Receivable are reported on the balance sheet at 100% of the customer's outstanding balance, which is more than what will typically be collected.

2. The matching principle requires that expenses be reported in the period in which the related revenue was recorded. Often, an uncollectible account receivable is not discovered until the next accounting period. The allowance method attempts to match the expense of uncollectible accounts to the period in which the revenue was recorded by recording an estimate at the end of the period. The direct write-off method does *not* achieve matching since the expense is recorded when an account is identified as uncollectible, which is normally *not* in the period in which the revenue was recorded.

Although the direct write-off method is not in accordance with faithful representation and matching, *a business may choose to use it* instead of the allowance method. As mentioned above, this would occur when uncollectible accounts are not material. The materiality principle states that an amount can be ignored if its effect on the financial statements is unimportant to users. The materiality principle permits the matching principle to be ignored when bad debt expenses are very small in relation to a company's other financial statement items. So the direct write-off method would be used when bad debt expense is unimportant for decisions made by users of the company's financial statements.

CHECKPOINT

7. The direct write-off method is recorded by debiting Bad Debt Expense and crediting the Allowance for Doubtful Accounts.
   a. True
   b. False

Do Quick Study question: QS 8-8

DECISION MAKER ◦

Answer—End of chapter

Labour Union Negotiation

You are representing your employee union in contract negotiations with management. One week prior to contract discussions, management released financial statements showing zero growth in earnings. This is far below the 10% growth predicted earlier. In your review of the financial statements, you find the company increased its "allowance for uncollectible accounts" from 1.5% to 4.5% of accounts receivable. Apart from this change, earnings would show a 9% growth. Does this information affect your negotiations?

MID-CHAPTER DEMONSTRATION PROBLEM

Maxo Industries, a distributor of electrical supplies, had outstanding accounts receivable on December 31, 2017, of $450,000 aged as follows:

Customer's Name	Total	Not Yet Due	1 to 30 Days Past Due	31 to 60 Days Past Due	61 to 90 Days Past Due	Over 90 Days Past Due
Maxo Industries — Schedule of Accounts Receivable by Age — December 31, 2017						
Alton Group	$ 90,000		$ 90,000			
Filby's Electrical Service	48,000			$22,000	$26,000	
GDP Servicing..	162,000	$120,000	42,000			
Parker's Electrical	80,000	80,000				
Trenton Construction	15,000					$15,000
Xeon Developments	55,000	30,000	25,000			
Totals...	$450,000	$230,000	$157,000	$22,000	$26,000	$15,000
Percentage uncollectible..................................		× 1%	× 4%	× 8%	× 25%	× 60%
Estimated uncollectible accounts						

During the year 2017, the company had sales of $3,720,000, of which $38,000 were cash sales. The Allowance for Doubtful Accounts had an unadjusted debit balance on December 31, 2017, of $3,050.

Required

Prepare the adjusting entry to estimate uncollectible accounts on December 31, 2017, under each of the following independent assumptions, and show the resulting balance sheet presentation for accounts receivable:

a. Bad debts are estimated to be 0.6% of credit sales.

b. Bad debts are estimated to be 4% of outstanding accounts receivable.

c. Bad debts are based on an aging analysis (part of the required information is provided in the schedule above).

Analysis Component:

d. If Maxo did not record the adjusting entry to estimate uncollectible accounts receivable, what effect would this have on current assets, equity, and profit?

e. Assume Maxo's competitors report uncollectible accounts receivable of 1% of outstanding receivables. How does Maxo's experience compare?

Solution

a. 0.6% × ($3,720,000 − $38,000 = $3,682,000 credit sales) = $22,092

2017				
Dec. 31	Bad Debt Expense		22,092	
	Allowance for Doubtful Accounts			22,092
	To record estimated bad debts.			

Current assets:

Accounts receivable $450,000

Less: Allowance for doubtful accounts.. 19,042* $430,958

or

Current assets:

Accounts receivable (net of $19,042* estimated uncollectible accounts)................................. $430,958

*$22,092 credit adjustment − $3,050 debit balance = $19,042.

b. The required balance in the Allowance for Doubtful Accounts is $18,000 (= 4% × $450,000)

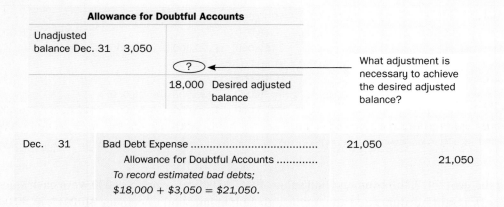

Allowance for Doubtful Accounts

Unadjusted balance Dec. 31	3,050		
		?	
		18,000	Desired adjusted balance

What adjustment is necessary to achieve the desired adjusted balance?

Dec. 31	Bad Debt Expense	21,050	
	Allowance for Doubtful Accounts		21,050
	To record estimated bad debts;		
	$18,000 + $3,050 = $21,050.		

Current assets:

Accounts receivable $450,000

Less: Allowance for doubtful accounts.. 18,000 $432,000

or

Current assets:

Accounts receivable (net of $18,000 estimated uncollectible accounts)................................ $432,000

c. First, calculate total estimated uncollectible accounts by completing the bottom of the aging schedule as follows:

	Total	Not Yet Due	1–30 days Past Due	31–60 Days Past Due	61–90 Days Past Due	Over 90 Days Past Due
Totals	$450,000	$230,000	$157,000	$22,000	$26,000	$15,000
Percentage uncollectible		× 1%	× 4%	× 8%	× 25%	× 60%
Estimated uncollectible accounts.............	$ 25,840	$ 2,300	$ 6,280	$ 1,760	$ 6,500	$ 9,000

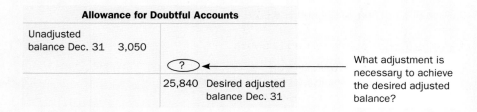

Allowance for Doubtful Accounts

Unadjusted balance Dec. 31	3,050		
		?	
		25,840	Desired adjusted balance Dec. 31

What adjustment is necessary to achieve the desired adjusted balance?

Second, determine what adjustment is necessary to achieve the desired balance of $25,840 in the Allowance for Doubtful Accounts as follows:

Dec. 31	Bad Debt Expense	28,890	
	Allowance for Doubtful Accounts		28,890
	To record estimated bad debts;		
	$25,840 + $3,050.		

Current assets:		
Accounts receivable	$450,000	
Less: Allowance for doubtful accounts...	25,840	$424,160

or

Current assets:	
Accounts receivable (net of $25,840 estimated uncollectible accounts).....................................	$424,160

Analysis Component:

d. If Maxo did not record the adjusting entry to estimate uncollectible accounts receivable, current assets would be overstated, equity would be overstated, and profit would be overstated.

e. Maxo's competitors are experiencing a lower rate of uncollectible accounts receivable, which, on the surface, appears to be favourable. However, additional information is required. Perhaps Maxo has an aggressive credit policy, granting credit to a wider range of customers, which increases revenues but at the same time increases the risk of the balance not being collected but overall increases profit. It may also be that Maxo's experience is the result of weak credit policies that grant credit to riskier customers (regarding collectability).

Short-Term Notes Receivable

LO4 Describe and record a short-term note receivable and calculate its maturity date and interest.

A **promissory note**, as illustrated in Exhibit 8.16, is a written promise to pay a specified amount of money either on demand or at a definite future date. A **short-term note receivable** (or **note receivable**) is a promissory note that becomes due within the next 12 months or within the business's operating cycle if greater than 12 months.

Calculations for Notes

We need to know two calculations related to notes:

1. How to determine the maturity date, and
2. How to calculate interest.

EXHIBIT 8.16

Terminology Related to a Promissory Note

* Note: The due date of a note is also referred to as the maturity date. The **period of this note** is 90 days, the time from the *date of the note* to its *maturity date* or *due date*.

MATURITY DATE

A note dated on July 10 with a specified maturity date of July 15 is a five-day note (calculated as July 15 − July 10 = 5 days). A 10-day note dated July 10 would have a maturity date of July 20 (calculated as July 10 + 10 days = July 20). The promissory note dated July 10 in Exhibit 8.16 is a 90-day note and the maturity date is calculated as shown in Exhibit 8.17.

EXHIBIT 8.17

Maturity Date Calculation

Days in July...	31
Minus date of note..	10
Days remaining in July	21
Add days in August	31
Add days in September	30
Days to equal 90 days or **Maturity Date, October 8**	8
Period of the note in days...	90

The period of a note is sometimes expressed in months or years. When months are used, the note matures and is payable in the month of its maturity on the *same day of the month* as its original date. A three-month note dated July 10, for instance, is payable on October 10. The same analysis applies when years are used.

INTEREST CALCULATION

Interest is an annual rate unless otherwise stated. The formula for calculating interest is shown in Exhibit 8.18.

EXHIBIT 8.18

Formula for Calculating Interest

		Principal		Annual		Time		
Interest	=	of the note	×	interest rate	×	Expressed in years	or	$i = Prt$

Interest on a $1,000, 6%, six-month note is calculated as:

$$\$1{,}000 \times 6\% \times \frac{6}{12} = \$30$$

Using the promissory note in Exhibit 8.16 where the *term of the note is in days*, interest is calculated as follows:

$$\text{Interest} = \text{Principal} \times \text{Rate} \times \frac{\text{Exact days}}{365}$$

or

$$\$1,000 \times 6\% \times \frac{90}{365} = \$14.79$$

> **Important Tip:** Unless otherwise instructed, you are to solve problems using the specific number of days and a 365-day year. Interest calculations should be rounded to the nearest whole cent.

Receipt of a Note

To illustrate recording the receipt of a note, we use the $1,000, 90-day, 6% promissory note in Exhibit 8.16. Assume that TechCom receives this note at the time of a product sale to Julia Browne (cost of sales $630). This transaction is recorded as (assuming a perpetual inventory system):

July	10	Notes Receivable...	1,000	
		Sales		1,000
		Sold merchandise in exchange for		
		a 90-day, 6% note.		
	10	Cost of Goods Sold..	630	
		Merchandise Inventory		630
		To record cost of inventory sold.		

A note receivable can also arise when a company accepts a note from an overdue customer as a way of granting a time extension on a past-due account receivable. When this occurs, a company may collect part of the past-due balance in cash. This partial payment forces a concession from the customer, reduces the customer's debt (and the seller's risk), and produces a note for a smaller amount. TechCom, for instance, agreed to accept $1,000 in cash and a $3,000, 60-day, 6% note on December 16 from Jo Cook to settle her $4,000 past-due account. TechCom made the following entry to record receipt of this cash and conversion of the remaining A/R balance to a note receivable:

Dec.	16	Cash	1,000	
		Notes Receivable...	3,000	
		Accounts Receivable—Jo Cook................		4,000
		Received cash and note in settlement		
		of account.		

End-of-Period Interest Adjustment

When notes receivable are outstanding at the end of an accounting period, accrued interest is calculated and recorded. This recognizes both the interest income when it is earned and the added asset (interest receivable) owned by the note's holder. When TechCom's accounting period ends on December 31, $7.40 of interest accrues on the note dated December 16 ($3,000 × 6% × 15/365). The following adjusting entry records this revenue:

Dec.	31	Interest Receivable	7.40	
		Interest Income		7.40
		To record accrued interest.		

This adjusting entry means that interest income appears on the income statement of the period when it is earned. It also means that interest receivable appears on the balance sheet as a current asset.

Honouring a Note—Customer Payment of Note

When the note dated December 16 is paid on the maturity date of February 14, the maker of the note, Jo Cook, is **honouring a note receivable**. TechCom's entry to record the cash receipt is:

Feb.	14	Cash..	3,029.59	
		Interest Income...		22.19
		Interest Receivable		7.40
		Notes Receivable		3,000.00
		Received payment of a note and its interest.		

Total interest earned on this note is $29.59 (= $3,000 × 6% × 60/365). On February 14, Interest Receivable is credited for $7.40 to record the collection of the interest accrued on December 31. The interest income in this period is $22.19 (= $29.59 total interest less $7.40 interest accrued on December 31) and reflects TechCom's revenue from holding the note from January 1 to February 14.

Dishonouring a Note—Customer Neglects to Pay at Maturity

Sometimes the maker of a note does not pay the note at maturity; this is known as **dishonouring a note receivable**. The act of dishonouring does not relieve the maker of the obligation to pay. The payee should use every legitimate means to collect. Assume Julia Browne did not pay the note dated July 10 when it matured on October 8. TechCom removes the amount of the note from the Notes Receivable account and charges it back to an account receivable from its maker as follows:

Oct.	8	Accounts Receivable—Julia Browne	1,014.79	
		Interest Income...		14.79
		Notes Receivable		1,000.00
		To charge the account of Julia Browne		
		for a dishonoured note including interest;		
		$1,000 × 6% – 90/365.		

Charging a dishonoured note back to the account of its maker serves three purposes. *First,* it removes the amount of the note from the Notes Receivable account, leaving in the account only notes that have not matured, and records the dishonoured note in the maker's account. *Second,* and most important, if the maker of the dishonoured note applies for credit in the future, his or her account will show all past dealings, including the dishonoured note. *Third,* restoring the account also reminds the company to continue collection efforts for both principal and interest. As accounts receivable, the customer's outstanding balance will then be included in the end of period A/R assessment when determining the appropriate allowance provision. If the restored account receivable is later identified as being uncollectible, it is written off as follows:

Oct.	31	Allowance for Doubtful Accounts	1,014.79	
		Accounts Receivable—Julia Browne..........		1,014.79
		To write off an uncollectible account.		

It is important to note that once the note has reached maturity and has not been paid off by the customer, accrual of interest is usually no longer recorded, as interest income should be recorded only if it is determined to be collectible. In the circumstance of a dishonoured note, collectability of the underlying interest is not reasonably assured.

CHECKPOINT

8. Brad purchases $7,000 of merchandise from Stamford Company on December 16, 2017. Stamford accepts Brad's $7,000, 90-day, 12% note as payment. Stamford's annual accounting period ends on December 31 and it doesn't make reversing entries. Prepare entries for Stamford Company on December 16, 2017, and December 31, 2017.

9. Using the information in Checkpoint 8, prepare Stamford's March 16, 2018, entry if Brad dishonours the note.

Do Quick Study questions: QS 8-9, QS 8-10, QS 8-11

Financial Statement Analysis—Accounts Receivable Turnover and Days' Sales Uncollected

LO5 Calculate accounts receivable turnover and days' sales uncollected to analyze liquidity.

For a company selling on credit, we want to assess both the *quality* and *liquidity* of its accounts receivable to assess performance and risk. Quality of receivables refers to the likelihood of collection without loss. Experience shows that the longer receivables are outstanding beyond their due date, the lower the likelihood of collection. Liquidity of receivables refers to the speed or efficiency of collection. Therefore, tools to help monitor receivables are critical to their timely collection.

Accounts Receivable Turnover

The **accounts receivable turnover** is a measure of both the quality and liquidity of accounts receivable. It indicates how often, on average, receivables are received and collected during the period. Accounts receivable turnover also helps us evaluate how well management is doing in granting credit to customers in a desire to increase sales revenues. A high turnover in comparison with competitors suggests that management should consider using more liberal credit terms to increase sales. A low turnover suggests management should consider more strict credit terms and more aggressive collection efforts to avoid having its resources tied up in accounts receivable.

The formula for this ratio is shown in Exhibit 8.19.

EXHIBIT 8.19

Accounts Receivable Turnover Formula

$$\text{Accounts receivable turnover} = \frac{\text{Net sales}}{\text{Average accounts receivable}}$$

Although the numerator of this ratio is more precise if credit sales are used, total net sales are usually used by external users because information about credit sales is typically not reported. The denominator includes accounts receivable and all short-term receivables (including notes receivable) from customers. Average accounts receivable is calculated by adding the balances at the beginning and end of the period and dividing the sum by 2. Some users prefer using gross accounts receivable, before subtracting the allowance for doubtful accounts, but many balance sheets report only the net amount of accounts receivable.

DECISION MAKER

Answer—End of chapter

Private Health Care Investor

You have invested in a private diagnostic imaging clinic so you and your fellow investors hire a health care analyst. The analyst highlights several points including the following: "Accounts receivable turnover is too low. Tighter credit policies are recommended along with discontinuing service to those most delayed payments." How do you interpret these recommendations? What actions do you take?

Days' Sales Uncollected

We use the number of **days' sales uncollected** (also known as **days' sales in receivables**) to assess the liquidity of receivables by estimating how much time is likely to pass before we receive cash from credit sales equal to the *current amount* of accounts receivable.[5] The formula for this ratio is shown in Exhibit 8.20.

EXHIBIT 8.20

Days' Sales Uncollected Formula

$$\text{Days' sales uncollected} = \frac{\text{Accounts receivable}}{\text{Net sales}} \times 365$$

Days' sales uncollected is more meaningful if we know the company's credit terms. A rough guideline is that days' sales uncollected should not exceed one and one-third times the days in its (1) credit period, if discounts are not offered; (2) discount period, if discounts are offered.

Analysis

To perform an analysis using the receivable ratios, we select data from the annual reports of two Canadian food manufacturers, **High Liner Foods Incorporated**, and **Maple Leaf Foods Inc.**, as shown in Exhibit 8.21.

EXHIBIT 8.21

Comparison of Accounts Receivable Turnover and Days' Sales Uncollected for High Liner Foods Incorporated and Maple Leaf Foods Inc.

		($ thousands)	
		December 31, 2013	**January 1, 2013**
High Liner Foods Inc.	Accounts receivable..	$ 89,860	$ 74,100
	Net sales...	947,300	N/A
Maple Leaf Foods Inc.	Accounts receivable..	111,034	117,533
	Net sales...	4,406,450	N/A

Results for December 31, 2013		
	Accounts Receivable Turnover	**Days' Sales Uncollected**
High Liner	$\dfrac{\$947,300}{(\$89,860 + \$74,100)/2} = 11.56$ times	$\dfrac{\$89,860}{\$947,300} \times 365 = 34.62$ days
Maple Leaf	$\dfrac{\$4,406,450}{(\$111,034 + \$117,533)/2} = 38.56$ times	$\dfrac{\$111,034}{\$4,406,450} \times 365 = 9.20$ days

---

5   When days' sales uncollected is calculated using *average* accounts receivable, the result tells us how many days, *on average*, it takes to collect receivables. The formula in Exhibit 8.20 tells us how many days it will take to collect the current receivables balance.

Maple Leaf Foods' accounts receivable turnover of 38.56 times tells us that in 2013 it collected receivables more than four times as fast as High Liner Foods. The days' sales uncollected ratio indicates that High Liner Foods will take 34.62 days to collect the January 1, 2013, balance in accounts receivable as compared to Maple Leaf's 9.20 days to collect its receivables balance on December 31, 2013. Although both companies are in a similar industry, their credit management appears to be significantly different based on a review of the receivables ratios.

10. WebCor reported an accounts receivable turnover at March 31, 2017, of 11. The industry average is 10 for the same date. At March 31, 2016, WebCor reported an accounts receivable turnover of 13. Did WebCor improve regarding its collection of receivables?

Do Quick Study questions: QS 8-12, QS 8-13, QS 8-14

CRITICAL THINKING CHALLENGE

Refer to the Critical Thinking Challenge question at the beginning of the chapter. Compare your answers to those suggested on Connect.

IFRS AND ASPE—THE DIFFERENCES

Difference	International Financial Reporting Standards (IFRS)	Accounting Standards for Private Enterprises (ASPE)
There are no significant differences between IFRS and ASPE related to this chapter.		

A Look Ahead

Chapter 9, the first chapter of Volume 2, investigates accounting issues for fixed assets under the following major categories: property, plant and equipment, and intangible assets. The chapter focuses on identifying all items that are included in their asset cost and analyzes options for matching their usage costs over their useful lives. Other considerations such as how to handle asset disposals, exchanges, and sales are analyzed.

Summary

LO1 Describe accounts receivable and how they occur and are recorded. Accounts receivable are amounts due from customers for credit sales. The subledger lists the amounts owed by individual customers. Credit sales arise from at least two sources: (1) sales on credit and (2) non-bank credit card sales. Sales on credit refers to a company granting credit directly to customers. Non-bank credit card sales involve use of a third party issuing a credit card.

LO2 Apply the allowance method to account for uncollectible accounts receivable. Under the allowance method, bad debt expense is estimated at the end of the accounting period by debiting Bad Debt Expense and crediting the Allowance for Doubtful

Accounts. This method is required under generally accepted accounting principles as it matches the expense to the associated revenue. When accounts are later identified as being uncollectible, they are written off by debiting the Allowance for Doubtful Accounts and crediting Accounts Receivable.

LO3 Estimate uncollectible accounts receivable using approaches based on sales and accounts receivable. Uncollectibles are estimated by focusing on either (a) the income statement relationship between bad debt expense and credit sales or (b) the balance sheet relationship between Accounts Receivable and the Allowance for Doubtful Accounts (AFDA). The first approach emphasizes the matching principle for the income statement. The second approach can include either a simple percentage of accounts receivable or a percentage of each category of the aged accounts receivable listing. Accounts receivable is presented net of the AFDA at its realizable value on the balance sheet. The direct write-off method debits Bad Debt Expense and credits Accounts Receivable when accounts are determined to be uncollectible. It is used when the amount of bad debt expense is immaterial.

LO4 Describe and record a short-term note receivable and calculate its maturity date and interest. A short-term note receivable is a written promise to pay a specified amount of money either on demand or at a definite future date, normally within the next 12 months or the business's operating cycle if greater than one year. The maturity date of a note is the day the note (principal and interest) must be repaid. Interest rates are typically stated in annual terms. When a note's time to maturity is more or less than one year, the amount of interest on a note is calculated by expressing time as a fraction of one year and multiplying the note's principal by this fraction and the annual interest rate. It is recorded at its principal amount by

debiting the Notes Receivable account and is credited to the asset or related revenue associated with the issuance of the note. Interest earned is accrued at period-end. When a note is honoured, the payee debits the money received and credits both Notes Receivable and Interest Income. Dishonoured notes are credited to Notes Receivable and Interest Income and debited to Accounts Receivable.

LO5 Calculate accounts receivable turnover and days' sales uncollected to analyze liquidity. Accounts receivable turnover and days' sales uncollected are measures of both the quality and liquidity of accounts receivable. The accounts receivable turnover indicates how often, on average, receivables are received and collected during the period and is calculated as sales divided by average accounts receivable for the period. Days' sales uncollected is calculated as (Accounts receivable $\div$ Net sales) $\times$ 365 and is used to estimate how much time is likely to pass before cash receipts from net sales are received equal to the average amount of accounts receivable. Both ratios are compared to those for other companies in the same industry, and with prior years' estimates.

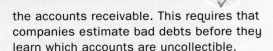

Guidance Answer to DECISION MAKER

Labour Union Negotiator

Yes, this information is likely to affect your negotiations. The obvious question is why the company increased the allowance to such a large extent. This major increase in allowance means a substantial increase in bad debt expense *and* a decrease in earnings. Also, this change coming immediately prior to labour contract discussions raises concerns since it

reduces the union's bargaining power for increased compensation. You want to ask management for supporting documentation justifying this increase. Also, you want data for two or three prior years, and similar data from competitors. These data should give you some sense of whether the change in the allowance for uncollectibles is justified or not.

Private Health Care Investor

The recommendations are twofold. First, the analyst suggests more stringent screening of clients' credit standing. Second, the analyst suggests dropping clients who are most overdue in payments. You are likely bothered by both suggestions. They are probably financially wise recommendations but you are troubled by

eliminating services to those less able to pay. One alternative is to follow a care program directed at clients less able to pay for services. This allows you to continue services to clients less able to pay and lets you discontinue services to clients able but unwilling to pay.

Guidance Answers to CHECKPOINT

1. Accounts receivable are typically due within the current accounting period so would be reported on the balance sheet as a current asset.

2. Bad debt expense must be estimated to match it with the sales that gave rise to

the accounts receivable. This requires that companies estimate bad debts before they learn which accounts are uncollectible.

3. Realizable value.

4. The estimated amount of bad debt expense cannot be credited to the Accounts Receivable

account because the specific customer accounts that will prove uncollectible cannot be identified and removed from the accounts receivable subledger. If the controlling account were credited directly, its balance would not equal the sum of the subsidiary account balances.

5.

2017			
Jan. 10	Allowance for Doubtful Accounts ...	300	
	Accounts Receivable— Cool Jam		300
	To record write-off of uncollectible account.		
Apr. 12	Accounts Receivable—Cool Jam....	300	
	Allowance for Doubtful Accounts		300
	To reinstate account previously written off.		
12	Cash..	300	
	Accounts Receivable— Cool Jam		300
	To record collection.		

6.

2017			
Dec. 31	Bad Debt Expense	5,702	
	Allowance for Doubtful Accounts		5,702
	To record estimated bad debts; $6,142 − $440.		

7. False. The direct write-off method is recorded by debiting Bad Debt Expense and crediting Accounts Receivable.

8.

2017			
Dec. 16	Notes Receivable.................	7,000.00	
	Sales		7,000.00
	To record 90-day, 12% note.		
31	Interest Receivable	34.52	
	Interest Income.............		34.52
	To record accrued interest; $7,000 × 12% × 15/365.		

9.

2018			
Mar. 16	Accounts Receivable—Brad....	7,207.12	
	Interest Income.............		172.60
	Interest Receivable........		34.52
	Notes Receivable		7000.00
	To record dishonouring of a bad note; $7,000 × 12% × 90/365 = $207.12.		

10. At March 31, 2017, WebCor collected its receivables faster than what was reported for the industry average. However, in comparison to its performance in the previous year, WebCor's efficiency in its collection of receivables decreased.

DEMONSTRATION PROBLEM

GardenWorks Co. had a number of transactions involving receivables during the year 2017. Each of them follows.

Required

Prepare journal entries to record these independent transactions on the books of GardenWorks Co.. GardenWorks Co.'s year-end is December 31.

a. On November 15, 2017, GardenWorks Co. agreed to accept $500 in cash and a $2,000, 90-day, 8% note from Argo Company to settle its $2,500 past-due account. Determine the maturity date and record the entry on November 15, on December 31, and on the date of maturity.

b. GardenWorks Co. held a $1,800, 6%, 45-day note of Altamira Industries. At maturity, December 15, Altamira dishonoured the note. Record the dishonouring of the Note Receivable.

c. GardenWorks Co. estimates bad debts to be 3.5% of net credit sales. During 2017, total sales were $6,200,000, of which 35% were for cash. Sales returns and allowances for the year were $128,000, all related to credit sales. Accounts receivable in the amount of $130,000 were identified as uncollectible and written off during 2017. Calculate the adjusted balance in the allowance for doubtful accounts at December 31, 2017, assuming a credit balance on January 1, 2017, of $160,000.

Analysis Component:

In (b) the note receivable was dishonoured. How should this be classified on the balance sheet?

Planning the Solution

* Examine each item to determine which accounts are affected and perform the required calculations.
* Prepare required journal entries.
* Prepare an answer to the analysis component.

Solution

a.

Days in November	30
Minus date of note	15
Days remaining in November	15
Add days in December	31
	46
Add days in January	31
Days to equal 90 days or Maturity date, February 13	13
Period of the note in days	90

2017				
Nov.	15	Cash	500.00	
		Notes Receivable	2,000.00	
		Accounts Receivable—Argo Company		2,500.00
		Received cash and note in settlement of account.		
Dec.	31	Interest Receivable	20.16	
		Interest Income		20.16
		To record accrued interest;		
		$2,000 × 46/365 × 8% = $20.16.		
2018				
Feb.	13	Cash	2,039.45	
		Interest Receivable		20.16
		Interest Income		19.29
		Notes Receivable		2,000.00
		Collected note with interest;		
		$2,000 × 90/365 × 8% = $39.45.		

b.

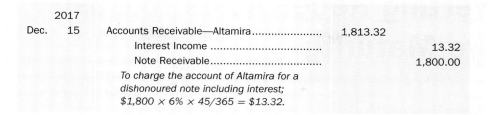

	2017			
Dec.	15	Accounts Receivable—Altamira......................	1,813.32	
		Interest Income		13.32
		Note Receivable...................................		1,800.00

To charge the account of Altamira for a
dishonoured note including interest;
$1,800 × 6% × 45/365 = $13.32.

c.

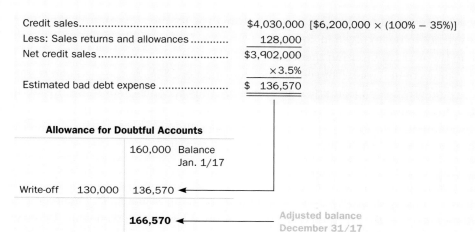

Credit sales..	$4,030,000 [$6,200,000 × (100% − 35%)]
Less: Sales returns and allowances	128,000
Net credit sales	$3,902,000
	×3.5%
Estimated bad debt expense	$ 136,570

Allowance for Doubtful Accounts

		160,000	Balance Jan. 1/17
Write-off	130,000	136,570	◄
		166,570 ◄	Adjusted balance December 31/17

Analysis Component:

The dishonoured note receivable in (b) is technically recorded as a current asset on December 15. However, given the high risk of this receivable not being collected, the Allowance for Doubtful Accounts should be adjusted appropriately or the account should be written off or some other appropriate course of action should be taken to ensure that accounts receivable are not overstated at year-end because of this note.

APPENDIX 8A

Converting Receivables to Cash Before Maturity

LO6 Explain how receivables can be converted to cash before maturity.

Sometimes companies convert receivables to cash before they are due. Reasons for this include the need for cash or a desire not to be involved in collection activities. Converting receivables is usually done either (1) by selling them or (2) by using them as security for a loan. A recent survey showed that about 20% of large companies obtain cash from either the sale of receivables or the pledging of receivables as security. In some industries, such as textiles and furniture, this is common practice. Recently, this practice has spread to other industries, especially the apparel industry. Also, many small companies use sales of receivables as an immediate source of cash. This is especially the case for those selling to companies and government agencies that often delay payment.

Selling Accounts Receivable

A company can sell its accounts receivable to a finance company or bank. The buyer, called a **factor**, charges the seller a *factoring fee* and then collects the receivables as they come due. By incurring a factoring fee, the seller receives cash earlier and passes the risk of bad debts to the factor. The seller also avoids costs of billing and accounting for the receivables.

If TechCom, for instance, sells $20,000 of its accounts receivable on August 15 and is charged a 2% factoring fee, it records this sale as:

Aug.	15	Cash..	19,600	
		Factoring Fee Expense	400	
		Accounts Receivable		20,000
		Sold accounts receivable for cash, less a 2% factoring fee.		

Pledging Accounts Receivable as Loan Security

A company can also raise cash by borrowing money and then *pledging* its accounts receivable as security for the loan. Pledging receivables does not transfer the risk of bad debts to the lender. The borrower retains ownership of the receivables. But if the borrower defaults on the loan, the lender has a right to be paid from cash receipts as the accounts receivable are collected. When TechCom borrowed $35,000 and pledged its receivables as security, it recorded this transaction as:

Aug.	20	Cash..	35,000	
		Notes Payable		35,000
		Borrowed money with the note secured by pledging accounts receivable.		

Because pledged receivables are committed as security for a specific loan, the borrower's financial statements should disclose the pledging of accounts receivable. TechCom, for instance, includes the following note with its financial statements regarding its pledged receivables: "Accounts receivable in the amount of $40,000 are pledged as security for a $35,000 note payable to First National Bank."

Discounting Notes Receivable

Notes receivable can be converted to cash before they mature. Companies that may need cash sooner to meet their obligations can discount (or sell) notes receivable at a financial institution or bank. TechCom, for instance, discounted a $3,000, 90-day, 10% note receivable at First National Bank. TechCom held the note for 50 of the 90 days before discounting it. The bank applied a 12% rate in discounting the note. Tech-Com received proceeds of $3,033.55 from the bank calculated as:

Principal of Note	$3,000.00
+ Interest from Note ($3,000 × 10% × 90/365)	73.97
= Maturity Value	$3,073.97
− Bank Discount ($3,073.97 × 12% × 40/365)	40.42
= Proceeds	$3,033.55

TechCom recorded the discounting of this note as:

Aug.	25	Cash	3,033.55	
		Interest Income		33.55
		Notes Receivable		3,000.00
		Discounted a note receivable.		

Computer programs are used in practice to calculate bank proceeds easily. Notes receivable are discounted without recourse or with recourse. When a note is discounted *without recourse*, the bank assumes the risk of a bad debt loss and the original payee does not have a *contingent liability*. A **contingent liability**[6] is a potential obligation dependent on an uncertain future event that has arisen due to a past business event (such as an employee-related lawsuit). A note discounted without recourse is like an outright sale of an asset. If a note is discounted *with recourse* and the original maker of the note fails to pay the bank when it matures, the original payee of the note must pay for it. This means a company discounting a note with recourse has a contingent liability until the bank is paid. A company should disclose contingent liabilities in notes to its financial statements. TechCom included the following note: "The Company is contingently liable for a $3,000 note receivable discounted with recourse."

Full Disclosure

The disclosure of contingent liabilities in notes is consistent with the full disclosure principle. Contingent liabilities are discussed in more detail in Chapter 10.

 **CHECKPOINT**

11. A company needs cash and has substantial accounts receivable. What alternatives are available for getting cash from its accounts receivable prior to receiving payments from credit customers?

Do Quick Study questions: QS 8-15, QS 8-16

---

6 IFRS 2014, IAS 37, para. 10.

Summary of Appendix 8A

LO6 Explain how receivables can be converted to cash before maturity. There are three usual means to convert receivables to cash before maturity. First, a company can sell accounts receivable to a factor, which charges a factoring fee. Second, a company can borrow money by signing a note payable that is secured by pledging the accounts receivable. Third, notes receivable can be discounted at a bank, with or without recourse. The full disclosure principle requires companies to disclose the amount of receivables pledged and the contingent liability for notes discounted with recourse.

Guidance Answers to CHECKPOINT

11. Alternatives are:

1. Selling their accounts receivable to a factor,

2. Pledging accounts receivable as loan security, and

3. Discounting notes receivable at a bank with or without recourse.

Glossary

Accounts receivable Amounts due from customers for credit sales. Also referred to as *trade receivables*.

Accounts receivable approach A method of estimating bad debts using balance sheet relationships. Also known as the *balance sheet approach*.

Accounts receivable aging analysis A process of classifying accounts receivable in terms of how long they have been outstanding for the purpose of estimating the amount of uncollectible accounts.

Accounts receivable turnover A measure of both the quality and liquidity of accounts receivable; it indicates how often, on average, receivables are received and collected during the period; calculated by dividing credit sales (or net sales) by the average accounts receivable balance.

Allowance for Doubtful Accounts A contra asset account with a balance equal to the estimated amount of accounts receivable that will be uncollectible; also called the *Allowance for Uncollectible Accounts*.

Allowance method of accounting for bad debts An accounting procedure that (1) estimates and reports bad debt expense from credit sales during the period of the sales, and (2) reports accounts receivable as the amount of cash proceeds that are expected from their collection (their estimated realizable value).

Bad debts The accounts of customers who fail to pay what they have committed to pay at the time of the sale of goods or provision of service. It is the total dollar value of the unpaid accounts receivables balance. Once determined to be uncollectible, the amount is booked as bad debt expense; also called *uncollectible accounts*.

Balance sheet approach See *accounts receivable approach*.

Contingent liability A potential liability that depends on a future event arising out of a past event.

Creditor See *payee*.

Date of a note The date on which interest begins to accrue.

Days' sales uncollected A measure of the liquidity of receivables calculated by taking the balance of receivables and dividing by the credit (or net) sales over the year just completed, and then multiplying by 365 (the number of days in a year); also called *days' sales in receivables*.

Days' sales in receivables See *days' sales uncollected*.

Debtor See *maker of a note*.

Direct write-off method A method of accounting for bad debts that is not compliant with IFRS and ASPE. The loss from an uncollectible account receivable is recorded at the time it is determined to be uncollectible; no attempt is made to estimate uncollectible accounts or bad debt expense.

Dishonouring a note receivable When a note's maker is unable or refuses to pay at maturity.

Due date of a note See *maturity date*.

Factor The buyer of accounts receivable.

Honouring a note receivable When the maker of the note pays the note in full at maturity.

Income statement approach See *percentage of sales approach*.

Interest rate The charge for using (not paying) money until a later date.

Maker of a note One who signs a note and promises to pay it at maturity.

Maturity date of a note The date on which a note and any interest are due and payable.

Note receivable See *short-term note receivable*.

Payee of a note The one to whom a promissory note is made payable.

Percentage of accounts receivable approach A method of estimating bad debts that assumes a percentage of outstanding receivables is uncollectible.

Percentage of sales approach Uses income statement relations to estimate bad debts. Also known as the *income statement approach*.

Period of a note The time from the issue date of the note to its maturity date or due date.

Principal of a note The amount that the signer of a promissory note agrees to pay back when it matures, not including the interest.

Promissory note A written promise to pay a specified amount of money either on demand or at a definite future date.

Realizable value The expected proceeds from converting assets into cash.

Short-term note receivable A promissory note that becomes due within the next 12 months or within the business's operating cycle if greater than 12 months.

Trade receivables See *accounts receivable*.

Uncollectible accounts See *bad debts*.

Concept Review Questions

1. Identify and explain the criteria that must be met before recording accounts receivable and revenue.

2. Identify three roles or responsibilities that should be segregated within the accounts receivable process.

3. Explain why writing off a bad debt against the allowance account does not reduce the estimated realizable value of a company's accounts receivable.

4. Why does the Bad Debt Expense account usually not have the same adjusted balance as the Allowance for Doubtful Accounts?

5. Why does the direct write-off method of accounting for bad debts commonly fail to match revenues and expenses?

6. What is the essence of the accounting principle of materiality?

7. Why might a business prefer a note receivable to an account receivable?

8. Review the balance sheet for **Danier Leather** in Appendix III. Did accounts receivable increase or decrease from 2013 to 2014 and by how much?

*9. What does it mean to sell a receivable without recourse?

Quick Study

QS 8-1 Entries for sale on credit and subsequent collection LO1

Journalize the following transactions for Kimmel Company (assume a perpetual inventory system):

    a. On March 1, Kimmel Company sold $40,000 of merchandise costing $32,000 on credit terms of n/30 to JP Holdings.

    b. On March 27, JP Holdings paid its account in full.

QS 8-2 Recognizing accounts receivable and revenue LO1

Trophy Services is in the business of selling trophies, medals, and plaques. On May 15, Central High School ordered plaques and medals to reward students with high academic and extracurricular achievement. Trophy Services shipped the goods with a cost of $450 on May 25. Central High School received the

---

An asterisk (*) identifies assignment material based on Appendix 8A.

goods on June 1. Upon inspecting the invoice, the order came to a price of $900 with shipping terms FOB destination and the balance is due within 30 days of receiving the goods.

    a. When has Trophy Services finished delivering the products?

    b. Is the related accounts receivable and revenue measurable in this transaction?

    c. Is it probable that Trophy Services will collect the amount owed from Central High School?

    d. Based on your analysis, conclude when Trophy Services should recognize the accounts receivable and revenue for the transaction with Central High School.

QS 8-3 Bad debts, write-off, recovery LO2

Record the following selected transactions for Allistar Company during its first two months of operations:

Mar.	4	Performed services for various customers on account; $165,000.
	15	Collected $80,000 from credit customers.
	20	Determined that Tom Williams, a credit customer, would not be paying his $5,000 account; wrote it off.
	25	Tom Williams came into an inheritance and paid Allistar the amount written off on March 20.
Apr.	2	Performed services for various customers on account; $280,000.
	9	Collected $110,000 from credit customers.
	30	Allistar estimated bad debt expense to be $8,000.

QS 8-4 Balance sheet presentation LO2

From the following alphabetized list of adjusted account balances, prepare the current asset section of Biatech's December 31, 2017, balance sheet.

Account	Debit	Credit
Accounts receivable..	29,000	
Allowance for doubtful accounts		1,300
Bad debt expense	800	
Cash	10,000	
Machinery	52,000	
Office supplies..	400	
Prepaid insurance	950	

QS 8-5 Adjusting entry to estimate bad debts—percentage of sales LO2,3

Lexton Company uses the allowance method to account for uncollectible accounts receivable. At year-end, October 31, it was estimated that 0.6% of net credit sales were uncollectible based on past experience. Net sales were $690,000, of which 2/3 were on credit. Record the entry at year-end to estimate uncollectible receivables.

QS 8-6 Adjusting entry to estimate bad debts—percentage of receivables LO2,3

Dim Sum Foods has accounts receivable of $260,000 and the allowance for doubtful accounts has a credit balance of $6,000. Based on analyzing the aging of the accounts receivable, management determined that the appropriate ending balance in the allowance for doubtful accounts at year-end, December 31, should be $26,000.

    a. Draw a T-account for the allowance for doubtful account and fill it in with all of the given information.

    b. Determine the amount of bad debt expense that needs to be recorded.

    c. Prepare the adjusting journal entry to record the estimated bad debts at year-end.

QS 8-7 Adjusting entry to estimate bad debts—percentage of receivables LO2,3

Foster Company uses the allowance method to account for uncollectible accounts receivable. At year-end, December 31, the unadjusted balance in the Allowance for Doubtful Accounts was $450 credit. Based on past experience, it was estimated that 2.5% of the Accounts Receivable balance of $640,000 was uncollectible. Record the adjusting entry to estimate bad debts at December 31.

QS 8-8 Accounts receivable allowance method of accounting for bad debts LO2,3

Duncan Company's year-end trial balance shows accounts receivable of $89,000, allowance for doubtful accounts of $500 (credit), and net credit sales of $270,000. Uncollectibles are estimated to be 1.5% of outstanding accounts receivable.

    a. Prepare the December 31 year-end adjustment.

    b. What amount would have been used in the year-end adjustment had the allowance account had a year-end debit balance of $200?

    c. Assume the same facts, except that Duncan estimates uncollectibles as 1% of net credit sales. What amount would be used in the adjustment?

QS 8-9 Aging analysis LO2,3

Delcom had total accounts receivable on December 31, 2017, of $160,000 aged as follows:

December 31, 2017 Accounts Receivable	Age of Accounts Receivable	Expected Percentage Uncollectible
$110,000	Not due (under 45 days)	2%
40,000	1 to 30 days past due	5%
10,000	Over 30 days past due	40%

Prepare the December 31, 2017, adjusting entry to estimate uncollectible accounts receivable assuming an unadjusted credit balance in Allowance for Doubtful Accounts of $800.

QS 8-10 Direct write-off method LO3

Winston Abbott operates Abbott Small Engine Repair on his cattle farm, greatly supplementing his farm profit. Most of his customers pay cash, so he uses the direct write-off method to account for uncollectible accounts receivable. On March 28, 2017, he determined that the $1,100 account for Jim Patterson is uncollectible. Record the write-off

QS 8-11 Notes receivable LO4

On August 2, 2017, SLM Company received a $5,500, 90-day, 5% note from customer Will Carr as payment on his account. Determine the maturity date and prepare the August 2 and maturity date entries, assuming the note is honoured by Carr.

QS 8-12 Notes receivable LO4

Seaver Company's December 31 year-end trial balance shows an $8,000 balance in Notes Receivable. This balance is from one note dated December 1, with a term of 45 days and 4.5% interest. Determine the maturity date and prepare the December 31 and maturity date entries, assuming the note is honoured.

QS 8-13 Dishonouring of a note receivable LO4

Ajax Company had a $17,000, 7%, 30-day note of Beatrice Inc. At maturity, April 4, Beatrice dishonoured the note. Record the entry on April 4.

QS 8-14 **Accounts receivable turnover and days' sales uncollected** LO5

Mega Company and Holton Company are similar firms that operate within the same industry. The following information is available:

| | Industry Average | Mega Company | | | Holton Company | | |
		2017	**2016**	**2015**	**2017**	**2016**	**2015**
Accounts receivable turnover	12	14.9	12.2	11.5	10.6	13.1	13.5
Days' sales uncollected	30	24.5	29.9	31.7	34.4	27.9	27.1

a. Which company has the *more favourable* accounts receivable turnover in 2017?

b. Which company has the *greater* number of days in uncollected accounts in 2017? Is this generally favourable or unfavourable?

c. Which company is showing an *unfavourable* trend in terms of managing accounts receivable?

*QS 8-15 **Sale of accounts receivable** LO6

On June 4, Maltex sold $108,000 of its accounts receivable to a collection agency, which charges a 2.5% factoring fee. Record the entry on June 4.

*QS 8-16 **Discounting a note receivable** LO6

Tallcrest discounted a $50,000, 45-day, 5% note receivable on August 10 at the local bank, which applies an 8% discount rate. Tallcrest had held the note for 25 days before discounting it. Record the entry on August 10.

Exercises

Exercise 8-1 **Subledger accounts** LO1

Wallace Contracting recorded the following transactions during November 2017:

Nov.	3	Accounts Receivable—ABC Shop	8,500	
		Sales*		8,500
	8	Accounts Receivable—Colt Enterprises	2,600	
		Sales*		2,600
	11	Accounts Receivable—Red McKenzie	1,560	
		Sales*		1,560
	19	Sales Returns and Allowances*	214	
		Accounts Receivable—Red McKenzie		214
	28	Accounts Receivable—ABCShop	4,980	
		Sales*		4,980

*Cost of goods sold (or COGS) has been ignored for the purpose of maintaining focus on accounts receivable.

Required

1. Open a general ledger having T-accounts for Accounts Receivable, Sales, and Sales Returns and Allowances. Also, open an accounts receivable subledger having a T-account for each customer. Post the preceding entries to the general ledger accounts and the customer accounts.

2. List the balances of the accounts in the subledger, total the balances, and compare the total with the balance of the Accounts Receivable controlling account.

An asterisk (*) identifies assignment material based on Appendix 8A or Appendix 8B.

Exercise 8-2 Recognizing accounts receivable and revenue LO1

You and your friends are taking a two-week trip to Paris, France, from June 1 to 15, 2017. On May 1, 2017, you booked and prepaid for your stay at Hotel de Paris for $300 per night for 14 nights. Based on the hotel policies, the booking is non-refundable.

1. What product or service is being sold? When does Hotel de Paris fulfill its performance of providing its product or service?

2. Can Hotel de Paris measure the amount of accounts receivable and revenue for the above transaction? Explain.

3. Is it probable that Hotel de Paris will collect payment from you and your friends for your hotel booking? Explain.

4. Based on your analysis, determine when Hotel de Paris should recognize the accounts receivable and revenue.

Exercise 8-3 Accounts receivable control considerations LO1

Carolyn owns a small business, Snappy Frames, that sells picture frames. Carolyn says, "I let most of my employees be the CEO of their responsibilities. Trust is the key to my success!" Once customers place their order online and the products are shipped, customers will send their payment in the mail or by electronic fund transfer. Quinn, accounts receivable clerk, posts the journal entries to record the customer payments (Dr. Cash Cr. Accounts Receivable). Quinn files the payments received in the mail in the office and deposits them on a monthly basis. As Quinn helped to set up the bank account years ago, she is responsible for making deposits and withdrawals. Every month, Quinn prepares a bank reconciliation and keeps them on file. When accounts receivable are overdue by greater than 90 days, Quinn cleans up the books by writing off the accounts receivable. Carolyn recently decided to follow up on some of the greater than 90-day accounts. Oddly enough, four of the customers she called with accounts receivable accounts greater than 90 days insisted that they had paid their account in full.

1. Identify four control weaknesses. For each, explain the implication of the weakness and make a recommendation of a control that would prevent or detect error or fraud.

2. Describe what fraud may have occurred in the above situation.

Exercise 8-4 Write-off and subsequent partial recovery LO2

Foster Company uses the allowance method to account for uncollectibles. On October 31, it wrote off a $1,200 account of a customer, Gwen Rowe. On December 9, it received an $800 payment from Rowe.

      a. Make the appropriate entry or entries for October 31.

      b. Make the appropriate entry or entries for December 9.

Exercise 8-5 Allowance for doubtful accounts LO2,3

At the end of its annual accounting period, Midi Company estimated its bad debts as 0.75% of its $1,750,000 of credit sales made during the year. On December 31, Midi made an addition to its Allowance for Doubtful Accounts equal to that amount. On the following February 1, management decided that the $2,600 account of Catherine Hicks was uncollectible and wrote it off as a bad debt. Four months later, on June 5, Hicks unexpectedly paid the amount previously written off. Give the journal entries required to record these transactions.

Exercise 8-6 Bad debt expense LO2,3

CHECK FIGURE: b. Bad Debt Expense = $7,515

At the end of each year, Deutch Supply Co. uses the simplified balance sheet approach (i.e., percentage of accounts receivable) to estimate bad debts. On December 31, 2017, it has outstanding accounts receivable of $159,000 and estimates that 3.5% will be uncollectible.

Required

    a. Give the entry to record bad debt expense for 2017 under the assumption that the Allowance for Doubtful Accounts has a $1,950 credit balance before the adjustment.

    b. Give the entry under the assumption that the Allowance for Doubtful Accounts has a $1,950 debit balance before the adjustment.

Exercise 8-7 Receivables, allowance for doubtful accounts, write-off, and subsequent recovery LO1,2,3

Outdoor Equipment (OE) sells camping equipment. On December 1, the accounts receivable account had a balance of $50,000, the bad debt expense account had a balance of $0, and the allowance for doubtful account had a credit balance of $5,000. Journalize the remaining journal entries for the 2017 year.

Dec.	2	Sold tents for $5,000 on account with a cost of $2,500.
	20	Determined that the total accounts of Rocky Co. with an accounts receivable balance of $1,200 and Grouse Co. with an accounts receivable balance of $2,500 were uncollectible and needed to be written off.
	23	Unexpectedly received payment from Grouse Co. for $2,500.
	31	Estimated that 10% of accounts receivable recorded to date would be uncollectible.

Required

1. Prepare journal entries to record the transactions.

2. Draw and fill in the T-account for accounts receivable, bad debt expense, and allowance for doubtful accounts. Determine the ending balance for each account.

Exercise 8-8 Analyzing receivables and allowance for doubtful accounts LO1,2,3

Accounts Receivable				Allowance for Doubtful Accounts			
Dec. 31/16						2,900	Dec. 31/16
Balance	78,000						Balance
	420,000	448,000				210	
		3,250			3,250	2,600	
	210	210				2,460	
Dec. 31/17							Dec. 31/17
Balance	46,750						Balance

Required Analyzing the information presented in the T-accounts above, identify the dollar value related to each of the following:

    a. Credit sales during the period.

    b. Collection of credit sales made during the period.

    c. Write-off of an uncollectible account.

    d. Recovery of the account previously written off.

    e. The adjusting entry to estimate bad debts.

Exercise 8-9 Balance sheet presentation LO2,4

From the following alphabetized list of adjusted account balances, prepare the current asset section of LisTel's March 31, 2017, balance sheet.

Account	Balance*
Accounts receivable	$110,000
Accumulated depreciation, building	29,000
Allowance for doubtful accounts	2,350
Bad debt expense	2,100
Building	375,000
Cash	19,000
Merchandise inventory	82,000
Notes receivable, due May 1, 2019	61,000
Notes receivable, due Nov. 30, 2017	14,300
Supplies	5,260

*Assume all balances are normal.

Exercise 8-10 Estimating bad debt expense—percentage of sales LO3

CHECK FIGURE: d. Accounts receivable (net) = $232,700

Selected unadjusted account balances at December 31, 2017, are shown below for Demron Servicing.

Account	Debit	Credit
Accounts receivable	$70,000	
Allowance for doubtful accounts		$ 1,100
Sales (all on credit)		480,000
Sales discounts	8,000	

Required

a. Demron estimates that 1.5% of net credit sales will prove to be uncollectible. Prepare the adjusting entry required on December 31, 2017, to estimate uncollectible receivables.

b. During 2018, credit sales were $620,000 (cost of sales $406,500); sales discounts of $12,000 were taken when accounts receivable of $440,000 were collected; and accounts written off during the year totalled $10,000. Prepare the entries for these transactions.

c. Record the adjusting entry required on December 31, 2018, to estimate uncollectible receivables, assuming it is based on 1.5% of net credit sales.

d. Show how accounts receivable would appear on the December 31, 2018, balance sheet.

Analysis Component: Comment on the advantages and disadvantages of using the income statement approach for estimating uncollectibles.

Exercise 8-11 Estimating bad debt expense—percentage of receivables LO3

CHECK FIGURE: d. Accounts receivable (net) = $235,200;

Refer to the information in Exercise 8-10.

Required

    a. Assume that Demron estimates uncollectible accounts as 2% of receivables. Prepare the adjusting entry required on December 31, 2017, to estimate uncollectible receivables.

    b. During 2018, credit sales were $620,000 (cost of sales $406,500); sales discounts taken were $12,000; accounts receivable collected were $440,000; and accounts written off during the year totalled $10,000. Prepare the entries to record these transactions.

    c. Record the adjusting entry required on December 31, 2018, to estimate uncollectible receivables, assuming it is based on 2% of receivables.

    d. Show how accounts receivable would appear on the December 31, 2018, balance sheet.

Analysis Component: Comment on the advantages and disadvantages of using the balance sheet approach for estimating uncollectibles.

Exercise 8-12 Aging analysis LO3

CHECK FIGURE: c. Accounts receivable (net) = $332,600

Winfrey Designs had an unadjusted credit balance in its Allowance for Doubtful Accounts at December 31, 2017, of $1,800.

Required

    a. Prepare the adjusting entry assuming that Winfrey estimates uncollectible accounts based on an aging analysis as follows:

December 31, 2018 Accounts Receivable	Age of Accounts Receivable	Expected Percentage Uncollectible
$240,000	Not due (under 30 days)	0.75%
75,000	1 to 30 days past due	4%
20,000	31 to 60 days past due	10%
11,000	Over 60 days past due	60%

    b. During 2018, credit sales were $1,200,000; sales discounts taken were $22,000; accounts receivable collected were $995,000; and accounts written off during the year totalled $24,000. Prepare the adjusting entry required on December 31, 2018, to estimate uncollectible receivables assuming it is based on the following aging analysis.

December 31, 2017 Accounts Receivable	Age of Accounts Receivable	Expected Percentage Uncollectible
$120,000	Not due (under 30 days)	0.75%
35,000	1 to 30 days past due	4%
8,000	31 to 60 days past due	10%
2,000	Over 60 days past due	60%

    c. Show how accounts receivable would appear on the December 31, 2018, balance sheet.

Analysis Component: Comment on the advantages and disadvantages of using an aging analysis for estimating uncollectible accounts.

Exercise 8-13 Direct write-off method LO3

Delores Cooper operates Cooper Garden Designs. Most of her customers pay cash so she uses the direct write-off method to account for uncollectible accounts receivable. On May 3, 2017, she determined that the $2,600 account for Wilma Benz was uncollectible. During 2017, she had total credit sales of $265,000. The December 31, 2017, balance in accounts receivable was $42,000.

Required Record the May 3 write-off using the direct write-off method.

Analysis Component: Delores wants to compare the effect of using the allowance method versus the direct write-off method for recording uncollectible accounts. If uncollectible accounts were estimated at (a) 2% of credit sales or (b) 4% of outstanding accounts receivable, prepare a comparison of the effects on profit of using the allowance methods versus the direct write-off method.

Exercise 8-14 End-of-period interest adjustment for note receivables LO4

Outer Armour (OA) is a company that sells high quality outerwear. OA has accepted two notes receivables from customers and has a December 31, 2017, year-end.

Note Receivable A	On September 1, 2017, OA accepted a $500,000, 6 months notes receivable with an interest rate of 6%. Interest and the principal balance are due at maturity.
Note Receivable B	On October 31, 2017 OA accepted a $300,000 note receivable with an interest rate of 4.5%. Interest is paid the first day of each following month and the principal is due at maturity on June 30, 2018.

Required
1. Outer Armour is preparing the financial statements as at December 31, 2017. Explain why interest income needs to be recorded up to December 31 even though Note Receivable A and B do not need to be fully paid off until 2018.

2. How many months need to be accrued for Note Receivable A and B as of December 31, 2017?

3. Prepare the adjusting journal entries to accrue the interest for Note Receivable A and Note Receivable B as at December 31, 2017.

Exercise 8-15 Dishonouring a note LO4

Prepare journal entries to record these transactions:

Mar.	21	Accepted a $6,200, six-month, 4% note dated today from Bradley Brooks in granting a time extension on his past-due account.
Sept.	21	Brooks dishonoured his note when presented for payment.
Dec.	31	After exhausting all legal means of collection, wrote off Brooks's account against the Allowance for Doubtful Accounts.

Exercise 8-16 Honouring a note LO4

Prepare journal entries to record these transactions (round the answer to two decimal places):

Oct.	31	Accepted a $15,000, six-month, 4.5% note dated today from Leann Grimes in granting a time extension on her past-due account.
Dec.	31	Adjusted the books for the interest due on the Grimes note.
Apr.	30	Grimes honoured her note when presented for payment.

Exercise 8-17 **Accounting for notes receivable transactions** LO4

CHECK FIGURE: May 31, 2018: Interest income = $78.90

Following are transactions of the Barnett Company (round the answer to two decimal places):

2017		
Dec.	16	Accepted a $22,000, 60-day, 5% note dated this day in granting Carmel Karuthers a time extension on her past-due account.
	31	Made an adjusting entry to record the accrued interest on the Karuthers note.
	31	Closed the Interest income account.
2018		
Feb.	14	Received Karuthers' payment for the principal and interest on the note dated December 16.
Mar.	2	Accepted an $8,000, 4%, 90-day note dated this day in granting a time extension on the past-due account of ATW Company.
	17	Accepted a $3,200, 30-day, 4.5% note dated this day in granting Leroy Johnson a time extension on his past-due account.
May	31	Received ATW's payment for the principal and interest on the note dated March 2.

Required Prepare journal entries to record the Barnett Company's transactions.

Exercise 8-18 **Accounts receivable turnover and days' sales uncollected** LO5

The following information was taken from the December 31, 2017, annual report of WestCon Developments.

	($ millions)				Industry Average
	2017	**2016**			
Net sales	$7,280	$5,410	Accounts receivable turnover		16.2
Accounts receivable	598	486	Days' sales uncollected		21.0

Required

1. Calculate accounts receivable turnover and days' sales uncollected for the year 2017.*

2. Compare your calculations in (1) to the industry average and comment on WestCon's relative performance as F (Favourable) or U (Unfavourable).*

*Round the answer to two decimal places.

***Exercise 8-19** **Selling and pledging accounts receivable** LO6

On July 31, Konrad International had $125,900 of accounts receivable. Prepare journal entries to record the following August transactions. Also, prepare any footnotes to the August 31 financial statements that should be reported as a result of these transactions.

2017		
Aug.	2	Sold merchandise to customers on credit, $6,295. Cost of sales was $3,150.
	7	Sold $18,770 of accounts receivable to Fidelity Bank. Fidelity charges a 1.5% fee.
	15	Received payments from customers, $3,436.
	25	Borrowed $10,000 from Fidelity Bank, pledging $14,000 of accounts receivable as security for the loan.

An asterisk (*) identifies assignment material based on Appendix 8A or Appendix 8B.

*Exercise 8-20 Discounting notes receivable LO6

CHECK FIGURE: Feb. 19: Interest income = $487.58

Prepare journal entries to record the following transactions by Ericton Industries:

2017

Jan.	20	Accepted a $170,000, 90-day, 9% note dated this day in granting a time extension on the past due account of Steve Soetart.
Feb.	19	Discounted the Steve Soetart note at the bank at 11.5%.

Problems

Problem 8-1A Recognizing accounts receivable and revenue LO1

A major source of revenue for Google Inc. is advertising. With Google AdWords, advertisers can pay on a cost-per-click basis (Google, 2013). This means that the advertisers pay every time a customer clicks on one of their ads. Assume that Tech Experts create an AdWord account with Google on October 1, 2017. Tech Expert starts advertising on a cost-per-click basis for the month of November 2017. In November, 300 users clicked on their ad at a rate of $0.30 per click. Google billed and Tech Experts pays for the advertising services in December 2017. Assume Google prepares financial statements on a monthly basis.

Required

Analyze and determine what month Google should recognize the accounts receivable and revenue for Tech Experts using the revenue recognition criteria of performance, measurability and collectability.

Source: https://investor.google.com/pdf/20131231_google_10K.pdf (accessed November 2014).

Problem 8-2A Estimating bad debt expense LO2,3

CHECK FIGURES: 1b. Bad Debt Expense = $138,000; 2. Accounts receivable (net) = $1,962,000

On December 31, 2017, Corotel Company's year-end, the unadjusted trial balance included the following items:

Account	Debit	Credit
Accounts receivable..	$2,100,000	
Allowance for doubtful accounts	33,000	
Sales ($2,850,000 cash sales)...		$11,400,000

Required

1. Prepare the adjusting entry needed in Corotel's books to recognize bad debts under each of the following independent assumptions:

   a. Bad debts are estimated to be 2% of credit sales.

   b. An analysis suggests that 5% of outstanding accounts receivable on December 31, 2017, will become uncollectible.

2. Show how Accounts Receivable and the Allowance for Doubtful Accounts would appear on the December 31, 2017, balance sheet given the facts in requirement 1(a).

3. Show how Accounts Receivable and the Allowance for Doubtful Accounts would appear on the December 31, 2017, balance sheet given the facts in requirement 1(b).

Analysis Component: If bad debts are not adjusted for at the end of the accounting period, identify which GAAP are violated and why.

An asterisk (*) identifies assignment material based on Appendix 8A or Appendix 8B.

Problem 8-3A **Aging accounts receivable** LO2,3   e**X**cel

CHECK FIGURE: 2. Bad Debt Expense = $60,205

On December 31, 2017, Toro Company's Allowance for Doubtful Accounts had an unadjusted credit balance of $31,000. The accountant for Toro has prepared a schedule of the December 31, 2017, accounts receivable by age and, on the basis of past experience, has estimated the percentage of the receivables in each age category that will become uncollectible. This information is summarized as follows:

December 31, 2017 Accounts Receivable	Age of Accounts Receivable	Expected Percentage Uncollectible
$1,500,000	Not due (under 30 days)	1.25%
708,000	1 to 30 days past due	2.00
152,000	31 to 60 days past due	6.50
98,000	61 to 90 days past due	32.75
24,000	Over 90 days past due	68.00

Required

1. Calculate the amount that should appear in the December 31, 2017, balance sheet as the allowance for doubtful accounts.

2. Prepare the journal entry to record bad debt expense for 2017.

Analysis Component: On June 30, 2018, Toro Company concluded that a customer's $7,500 receivable (created in 2017) was uncollectible and that the account should be written off. What effect will this action have on Toro's 2018 profit? Explain your answer.

Problem 8-4A **Accounts receivable transactions and bad debt adjustments** LO1,2,3

CHECK FIGURES: 2. Bad Debt Expense = $20,460; 5. Bad Debt Expense = $7,200

BeleVu Supplies showed the following selected adjusted balances at its December 31, 2016, year-end:

Accounts Receivable		Allowance for Doubtful Accounts	
Dec. 31/16			16,400 Dec. 31/16
Balance 490,000			Balance

During the year 2017, the following selected transactions occurred:

   a. Sales totalled $2,800,000, of which 25% were cash sales (cost of sales $1,804,000).
   b. Sales returns were $108,000, half regarding credit sales. The returned merchandise was scrapped.
   c. An account for $24,000 was recovered.
   d. Several accounts were written off; $26,000.
   e. Collections from credit customers totalled $1,790,000 (excluding the recovery in (c) above).

Part A

Required

1. Journalize transactions (a) through (e). You may find it useful to post your entries to T-accounts for Accounts Receivable and Allowance for Doubtful Accounts.

Part B

Required

2. Prepare the December 31, 2017, adjusting entry to estimate bad debts assuming that uncollectible accounts are estimated to be 1% of net credit sales.

3. Show how accounts receivable will appear on the December 31, 2017, balance sheet.

4. What will bad debt expense be on the income statement for the year ended December 31, 2017?

Part C (independent of Part B)

Required

5. Prepare the December 31, 2017, adjusting entry to estimate bad debts assuming that uncollectible accounts are estimated to be 3% of outstanding receivables.

6. Show how accounts receivable will appear on the December 31, 2017, balance sheet.

7. What will bad debt expense be on the income statement for the year ended December 31, 2017?

Problem 8-5A Recording accounts receivable transactions and bad debt adjustments LO1,2,3

CHECK FIGURES: d. Bad Debt Expense = $47,290; h. Bad Debt Expense = $63,155

Peru Industries began operations on January 1, 2017. During the next two years, the company completed a number of transactions involving credit sales, accounts receivable collections, and bad debts (assume a perpetual inventory system). These transactions are summarized as follows:

2017

    a. Sold merchandise on credit for $2,250,000, terms n/30 (COGS = $1,240,000).

    b. Wrote off uncollectible accounts receivable in the amount of $34,000.

    c. Received cash of $1,330,000 in payment of outstanding accounts receivable.

    d. In adjusting the accounts on December 31, concluded that 1.5% of the outstanding accounts receivable would become uncollectible.

2018

    e. Sold merchandise on credit for $2,940,000, terms n/30 (COGS = $1,592,000).

    f. Wrote off uncollectible accounts receivable in the amount of $53,000.

    g. Received cash of $2,210,000 in payment of outstanding accounts receivable.

    h. In adjusting the accounts on December 31, concluded that 1.5% of the outstanding accounts receivable would become uncollectible.

Required Prepare journal entries to record Peru's 2017 and 2018 summarized transactions and the adjusting entries to record bad debt expense at the end of each year.

Problem 8-6A Uncollectible accounts LO2,3

CHECK FIGURES: b. Accounts receivable (net) = $126,450; d. Accounts receivable (net) = $140,600

Aaron Servicing showed the following partial unadjusted results at October 31, 2017, its year-end:

Account	Debit	Credit
Sales		$1,650,000
Accounts receivable...	$148,000	
Allowance for doubtful accounts	3,200	

Part 1

Required

    a. Assuming Aaron estimates bad debts to be 1.5% of sales, prepare the adjusting entry at October 31, 2017.

    b. Show how accounts receivable would be shown on the October 31, 2017, balance sheet using your calculations in (a).

Part 2

Required

    c. Instead of (a), assume that Aaron estimates bad debts to be 5% of outstanding accounts receivable. Prepare the adjusting entry at October 31, 2017.

    d. Show how accounts receivable would be shown on the October 31, 2017, balance sheet using your calculations in (c).

Problem 8-7A **Bad debt expense** LO3

CHECK FIGURES: 1. Bad Debt Expense = $8,200; 2. Bad Debt Expense = $5,100

The following is information taken from the June 30, 2017, balance sheet of Tippleton Company:

Accounts receivable	$320,000	
Less: Allowance for doubtful accounts...	14,000	$306,000

Part 1

During July, Tippleton Company recorded total sales of $850,000, all on credit. There were $30,000 of sales returns and allowances. Collections during July were $920,000. Total receivables identified as being uncollectible and written off during July were $15,000. Tippleton estimates bad debts as 1% of net credit sales.

Required Prepare the adjusting entry to record estimated bad debts for July.

Part 2

During August, total sales of $845,000 were recorded, all on credit. Sales returns and allowances totalled $14,000. Collections during the month were $710,000, which included the recovery of $1,950 from a customer account written off in a previous month. No accounts were written off during August. Tippleton Company changed its method of estimating bad debts to the balance sheet approach because the new accountant said it more accurately reflected uncollectible accounts. The resulting aging analysis determined total estimated uncollectible accounts at August 31 to be $14,250.

Required Prepare the August 31 adjusting entry to record estimated bad debts for August.

Problem 8-8A **Estimating bad debts** LO3 e**X**cel

CHECK FIGURE: a. Total estimated uncollectible accounts = $12,450

The following information is available regarding the outstanding accounts receivable of Mufu Contracting at September 30, 2017:

| | Month of Credit Sale* | | | | |
Customer	May	June	July	Aug.	Sept.
B. Axley	$32,000	$ -0-	$ -0-	$ -0-	$ -0-
T. Holton	-0-	-0-	68,000	33,000	15,000
W. Nix	-0-	21,000	-0-	9,000	11,000
C. Percy	-0-	-0-	5,000	-0-	14,000
K. Willis	-0-	-0-	-0-	-0-	82,000

*All services are performed on terms of n/30. Assume all sales occurred on the last day of the month.

Mufu estimates bad debts using the following rates:

Not yet due	1 to 29 days past due	30 to 59 days past due	60 to 89 days past due	90 to 119 days past due	Over 119 days past due
0.5%	1%	4%	10%	20%	50%

Required

a. Complete a Schedule of Accounts Receivable by Age at September 30, 2017 (similar to Exhibit 8.13).

b. The Allowance for Doubtful Accounts showed an unadjusted balance on September 30, 2017, of $1,600. Record the adjusting entry at September 30, 2017, to estimate uncollectible accounts.

Problem 8-9A Uncollectible accounts LO3

CHECK FIGURE: Dec. 31, 2018: Bad debt expense = $19,560

At year-end, December 31, 2017, Corolla Sales showed unadjusted balances of: $394,000 in Accounts Receivable; $13,800 debit in Allowance for Doubtful Accounts; and $1,940,000 in Sales. Uncollectible accounts are estimated to be 2.5% of sales.

Unadjusted balances at December 31, 2018, were Accounts Receivable, $514,000; Allowance for Doubtful Accounts, $1,000 credit; and Sales, $3,280,000. Corolla Sales changed the method of estimating uncollectible accounts to 4% of outstanding accounts receivable.

At December 31, 2019, the general ledger showed unadjusted balances of: $460,000 in Accounts Receivable; $700 debit in Allowance for Doubtful Accounts; and $3,400,000 in Sales. Corolla prepared an aging analysis on December 31, 2019, that estimated total uncollectible accounts to be $26,500.

Required Prepare the 2017, 2018, and 2019 year-end adjusting entries to estimate uncollectible accounts.

Analysis Component: On December 31, 2017, the unadjusted balance in Allowance for Doubtful Accounts was a debit of $13,800. What is the normal balance for the Allowance for Doubtful Accounts account? What would cause Allowance for Doubtful Accounts to have an unadjusted debit balance?

Problem 8-10A **Notes receivable** LO4

CHECK FIGURES: d. Interest income = $454.93 e. Cash = $90,499.32

Vauxall Holdings showed the following information regarding its notes receivable:

Note	Date of Note	Principal	Interest Rate	Term	Maturity Date	Days of Accrued Interest at Dec. 31, 2017	Accrued Interest at Dec. 31, 2017*
1	Nov. 1/13	$240,000	4.0%	180 days			
2	Jan. 5/14	100,000	5.0%	90 days			
3	Nov. 20/14	90,000	4.5%	45 days			
4	Dec. 10/14	120,000	5.5%	30 days			

*Round calculations to the nearest whole cent.

Required For each note:

   a. Determine the maturity date.

   b. Calculate the *days* of accrued interest, if any, at December 31, 2017 (Vauxall Holdings' year-end).

   c. Calculate the *amount* of accrued interest, if any, at December 31, 2017.

For Note 3:

   d. Prepare the entry to record the accrued interest at December 31, 2017.

   e. Prepare the entry to record the collection on the maturity date. Assume that both interest and principal are collected at maturity.

Problem 8-11A **Accrued interest calculation and dishonouring note receivable** LO4

CHECK FIGURE: b. May 31, 2017

Following are transactions of the Purple Onion Company (round calculations to the nearest whole cent):

2016

Dec.	16	Accepted a $20,000, 60-day, 5.5% note dated this day in granting Hal Krueger a time extension on his past-due account.
	31	Made an adjusting entry to record the accrued interest on the Krueger note.
	31	Closed the Interest income account.

2017

Feb.	14	Received Krueger's payment for the principal and interest on the note dated December 16.
Mar.	2	Accepted a $15,000, 3.75%, 90-day note dated this day in granting a time extension on the past-due account of ARC Company.
	17	Accepted a $6,500, 30-day, 4% note dated this day in granting Penny Bobek a time extension on her past-due account.
Apr.	16	Bobek dishonoured her note when presented for payment.

Required

   a. Prepare journal entries to record the Purple Onion's transactions.

   b. Determine the maturity date of the note dated March 2. Prepare the entry on the maturity date, assuming ARC Company honours the note.

Problem 8-12A **Short-term notes receivable** LO4

CHECK FIGURES: d. July 14, 2017: Interest income = $783.56 e. November 1, 2017: Interest income = $989.58

Seerden Servicing monitors its accounts receivable carefully. A review determined that a customer, John Daley, was unable to pay his $130,000 past-due account. Seerden accepted a 90-day promissory note dated April 15, 2017, bearing interest of 5% in exchange for Daley's account. Another customer, ABC Drilling, signed a 4.75%, six-month note dated May 1 in place of its $50,000 past-due accounts receivable. On May 31, Seerden's year-end, accrued interest was recorded on the notes receivable. John Daley honoured his note on the maturity date. ABC Drilling dishonoured its note on the maturity date. On November 15, Seerden Servicing wrote off ABC Drilling's account as it was determined to be uncollectible.

Required Prepare Seerden Servicing's entries for each of the following dates (round calculations to the nearest whole cent):

a. April 15, 2017

b. May 1, 2017

c. May 31, 2017

d. Maturity date of John Daley's note

e. Maturity date of ABC Drilling's note

f. November 15, 2017

Analysis Component: Assuming a $4,000 debit balance in the Allowance for Doubtful Accounts on November 14, 2017, calculate the balance after posting the entry in (f) above. Comment on the adequacy of the Allowance for Doubtful Accounts.

Problem 8-13A **Accounts Receivable Ratios** LO5

Using the **Indigo** financial statements in Appendix III, calculate the following ratios for the years ended March 29, 2014, and March 30, 2013. Comment on the change.

a. Accounts receivable turnover ratio (round to two decimal places)

b. Days sales uncollected (round to the nearest day)

*Problem 8-14A **Discounting notes receivable** LO6

CHECK FIGURE: Sept. 18: Interest expense = $25.00

Required Prepare entries to record the following transactions of Wipe-Out Company:

Mar.	2	Accepted a $10,240, 5%, 90-day note dated this day in granting a time extension on the past-due account of JNC Company.
Apr.	21	Discounted, with recourse, the JNC Company note at BancFirst at a cost of $50.
June	2	Received notice from BancFirst that JNC Company defaulted on the note due May 31. Paid the bank the principal plus interest due on the note. *(Hint: Create an account receivable for the maturity value of the note.)*
July	16	Received payment from JNC Company for the maturity value of its dishonoured note plus interest for 45 days beyond maturity at 5%.
Sept.	3	Accepted a $4,160, 60-day, 5% note dated this day in granting Cecile Duval a time extension on her past-due account.
	18	Discounted, without recourse, the Duval note at BancFirst at a cost of $25.

Analysis Component: What reporting is necessary when a business discounts notes receivable with recourse and these notes have not reached maturity by the end of the fiscal period? Explain the reason for this requirement and what accounting principle is being satisfied.

An asterisk (*) identifies assignment material based on Appendix 8A or Appendix 8B.

*Problem 8-15A Discounting notes receivable LO6

CHECK FIGURES: Jan. 10, 2018: Cash = $15,060.80; Mar. 29, 2018: Cash = $4,507.09

Required Prepare general journal entries to record the following transactions of Leduc Company:

2017

Dec.	11	Accepted a $15,000, 6%, 60-day note dated this day in granting Fred Calhoun a time extension on his past-due account.
	31	Made an adjusting entry to record the accrued interest on the Fred Calhoun note.
	31	Closed the Interest income account.

2018

Jan.	10	Discounted the Fred Calhoun note at the bank at 7%.
Feb.	10	The Fred Calhoun note was dishonoured. Paid the bank the maturity value of the note plus a $30 fee.
Mar.	5	Accepted a $4,500, 5.5%, 60-day note dated this day in granting a time extension on the past-due account of Donna Reed.
	29	Discounted the Donna Reed note at the bank at 7.5%.
May	7	The Donna Reed note had been received by the bank and paid by Donna Reed.
June	9	Accepted a $6,750, 60-day, 5% note dated this day in granting a time extension on the past-due account of Jack Miller.
Aug.	8	Received payment of the maturity value of the Jack Miller note.
	11	Accepted an $8,000, 60-day, 5% note dated this day in granting Roger Addison a time extension on his past-due account.
	31	Discounted the Roger Addison note at the bank at 6.5%.
Oct.	12	The Roger Addison note was dishonoured. Paid the bank the maturity value of the note plus a $30 fee.
Nov.	19	Received payment from Roger Addison of the maturity value of his dishonoured note, the fee, and interest on both for 40 days beyond maturity at 5%.
Dec.	23	Wrote off the Fred Calhoun account against Allowance for Doubtful Accounts.

Alternate Problems

Problem 8-1B **Recognizing accounts receivable and revenue** LO1

A major source of revenue for Google Inc. is advertising. With Google AdSense, advertisers pay on a cost-per-impression basis (Google, 2013). This means that the advertisers pay each time their ads are displayed on websites. Ramen Noodle House is a Japanese noodle restaurant. The company creates an account with Google on March 1, 2017. Ramen Noodle House launches an advertisement that will be displayed on selected websites three times per day at a rate of $0.50 per time the ad is displayed for the full month of April 2017. Google bills and Raman Noodle House pays for the advertising services in May 2017. Assume that Google prepares financial statements on a monthly basis.

Required

Analyze and determine when Google should recognize the accounts receivable and revenue using the revenue recognition criteria of performance, measurability, and collectability.

Source: https://investor.google.com/pdf/20131231_google_10K.pdf (accessed November 2014).

Problem 8-2B **Estimating bad debt expense** LO2,3

CHECK FIGURES: 1b. Bad Debt Expense = $11,240 2. Accounts receivable (net) = $216,160

An asterisk (*) identifies assignment material based on Appendix 8A or Appendix 8B.

On December 31, 2017, Stilton Service Company's year-end, the unadjusted trial balance included the following items:

Account	Debit	Credit
Accounts receivable..	$239,000	
Allowance for doubtful accounts		$ 3,100
Sales ($470,000 cash sales)...		1,128,000

Required

1. Prepare the adjusting entry on the books of Stilton Service Company to estimate bad debts under each of the following independent assumptions:

   a. Bad debts are estimated to be 3% of credit sales.

   b. An analysis suggests that 6% of outstanding accounts receivable on December 31, 2017, will become uncollectible.

2. Show how Accounts Receivable and the Allowance for Doubtful Accounts would appear on the December 31, 2017, balance sheet given the facts in requirement 1(a).

3. Show how Accounts Receivable and the Allowance for Doubtful Accounts would appear on the December 31, 2017, balance sheet given the facts in requirement 1(b).

Analysis Component: Would you recommend to Stilton that it use the income statement or the balance sheet approach to estimate uncollectible accounts receivable? Explain why, identifying advantages and disadvantages for each approach.

Problem 8-3B Aging accounts receivable LO2,3   eXcel

CHECK FIGURE: 2. Bad Debt Expense = $43,860

On December 31, 2017, RCA Company's Allowance for Doubtful Accounts had an unadjusted debit balance of $7,800. The accountant for RCA has prepared a schedule of the December 31, 2017, accounts receivable by age and, on the basis of past experience, has estimated the percentage of the receivables in each age category that will become uncollectible. This information is summarized as follows:

December 31, 2017 Accounts Receivable	Age of Accounts Receivable	Expected Percentage Uncollectible
$620,000	Not due (under 30 days)	1.75%
355,600	1 to 30 days past due	2.5
91,000	31 to 60 days past due	8.5
11,500	61 to 90 days past due	35
7,600	Over 90 days past due	60

Required

1. Calculate the amount that should appear in the December 31, 2017, balance sheet as the Allowance for Doubtful Accounts.

2. Prepare the journal entry to record bad debt expense for 2017.

Analysis Component: On July 31, 2018, RCA concluded that a customer's $4,200 receivable (created in 2017) was uncollectible and that the account should be written off. What effect will this action have on RCA's 2018 profit? Explain your answer.

Problem 8-4B Accounts receivable transactions and bad debt adjustments LO1,2,3

CHECK FIGURES: 2. Bad Debt Expense = $118,160; 5. Bad Debt Expense = $35,940

Wondra Supplies showed the following selected adjusted balances at its December 31, 2016, year-end:

Accounts Receivable		Allowance for Doubtful Accounts	
Dec. 31/16 Balance 490,000		12,300 Dec. 31/16 Balance	

During the year 2017, the following selected transactions occurred:

a. Sales totalled $1,800,000, of which 85% were credit sales (cost of sales $987,000).

b. Sales returns were $31,000, all regarding credit sales. The returned merchandise was scrapped.

c. An account for $29,000 was recovered.

d. Several accounts were written off, including one very large account; the total was $65,500.

e. Collected accounts receivable of $1,630,000 (excluding the recovery in (c) above). Sales discounts of $22,000 were taken.

Part A

Required

1. Journalize transactions (a) through (e). You may find it useful to post your entries to T-accounts for Accounts Receivable and Allowance for Doubtful Accounts.

Part B

Required

2. Prepare the December 31, 2017, adjusting entry to estimate bad debts, assuming uncollectible accounts are estimated to be 8% of net credit sales.

3. Show how accounts receivable will appear on the December 31, 2017, balance sheet.

4. What will bad debt expense be on the income statement for the year ended December 31, 2017?

Part C (independent of Part B)

Required

5. Prepare the December 31, 2017, adjusting entry to estimate bad debts, assuming uncollectible accounts are estimated to be 4% of outstanding receivables.

6. Show how accounts receivable will appear on the December 31, 2017, balance sheet.

7. What will bad debt expense be on the income statement for the year ended December 31, 2017?

Problem 8-5B Recording accounts receivable transactions and bad debt adjustments LO1,2,3

CHECK FIGURES: d. Bad Debt Expense = $12,075; h. Bad Debt Expense = $12,834

Selzer Products Co. began operations on January 1, 2017, and completed a number of transactions during 2017 and 2018 that involved credit sales, accounts receivable collections, and bad debts. Assume a perpetual inventory system. These transactions are summarized as follows:

2017

a. Sold merchandise on credit for $1,640,000, terms n/30 (COGS = $1,070,000).

b. Received cash of $1,175,000 in payment of outstanding accounts receivable.

   c. Wrote off uncollectible accounts receivable in the amount of $7,500.

   d. In adjusting the accounts on December 31, concluded that 1% of the outstanding accounts receivable would become uncollectible.

2018

   e. Sold merchandise on credit for $1,876,000, terms n/30 (COGS = $1,224,000).

   f. Received cash of $1,444,000 in payment of outstanding accounts receivable.

   g. Wrote off uncollectible accounts receivable in the amount of $8,600.

   h. In adjusting the accounts on December 31, concluded that 1% of the outstanding accounts receivable would become uncollectible.

Required Prepare general journal entries to record the 2017 and 2018 summarized transactions of Selzer Products Co., and the adjusting entries to record bad debt expense at the end of each year.

Problem 8-6B Uncollectible accounts LO2,3

CHECK FIGURES: b. Accounts receivable (net) = $108,700; d. Accounts receivable (net) = $126,440

Littlerock Surveying showed the following partial unadjusted results at May 31, 2017, its month-end:

Account	Debit	Credit
Sales		$860,000
Accounts receivable...	$132,000	
Allowance for doubtful accounts		1,800

Part 1

Required

   a. Assuming Littlerock estimates bad debts to be 2.5% of sales, prepare the adjusting entry at May 31, 2017.

   b. Show how accounts receivable would be shown on the May 31, 2017, balance sheet using your calculations in (a).

Part 2

Required

   c. Instead of (a) above, prepare the adjusting entry at May 31, 2017, assuming that Littlerock estimates bad debts to be based on the following aging analysis.

May 31, 2017 Accounts Receivable	Age of Accounts Receivable	Expected Percentage Uncollectible
$98,000	Not due (under 30 days)	1%
27,000	1 to 30 days past due	4%
7,000	Over 60 days past due	50%

   d. Show how accounts receivable would be shown on the May 31, 2017, balance sheet using your calculations in (c).

Problem 8-7B Bad debt expense LO3

CHECK FIGURES: 1. Bad Debt Expense = $8,730; 2. Bad Debt Expense = $2,820

The following is information regarding adjusted account balances for Leonardo Painters at September 30, 2017:

Accounts Receivable		Allowance for Doubtful Accounts	
235,000			13,700

Part 1

During October, Leonardo Painters recorded $1,746,000 in total revenues, all on credit. Collections during October were $1,532,000. Included in the $1,532,000 collections was the recovery of $6,100 from a customer account written off in September. Total receivables identified as being uncollectible and written off during October were $14,700. Leonardo Painters estimates bad debts to be 0.5% of net credit revenues.

Required Prepare the adjusting entry to record estimated bad debts for October.

Part 2

During November, revenues totalled $1,680,000, all on credit. Collections during the month were $1,890,000. An account for $5,400 was identified as being uncollectible and written off on November 28. It was recommended to Leonardo Painters that the method of estimating bad debts be changed to the balance sheet approach. As a result, it was estimated that 5% of the November 30 accounts receivable balance was uncollectible.

Required Prepare the adjusting entry to record estimated bad debts for November.

Problem 8-8B Estimating bad debts LO3

CHECK FIGURE: a. Total estimated uncollectible accounts = $29,010

The following information is available regarding the accounts receivable of Club Fit Holdings at August 31, 2017:

	Month of Credit Sale*				
Customer	April	May	June	July	Aug.
A. Leslie	$ -0-	$ 24,000	$ -0-	$ 58,000	$32,000
T. Meston	52,000	-0-	-0-	-0-	-0-
P. Obrian	-0-	-0-	-0-	104,000	42,000
L. Timms	-0-	126,000	52,000	-0-	28,000
W. Victor	-0-	-0-	166,000	122,000	64,000

*All services are performed on terms of n/60. Assume all sales occurred on the last day of the month.

Club Fit estimates uncollectibility of accounts receivable using the following rates:

Not yet due	1 to 29 days past due	30 to 59 days past due	60 to 89 days past due	90 to 119 days past due	Over 119 days past due
1.5%	2%	5%	20%	35%	50%

Required

    a. Complete a Schedule of Accounts Receivable by Age at August 31, 2017, similar to Exhibit 8.13.

    b. The Allowance for Doubtful Accounts showed an unadjusted balance on August 31, 2017, of $9,600 (debit). Record the adjusting journal entry at August 31, 2017, to estimate uncollectible accounts.

Problem 8-9B **Uncollectible accounts** LO3

CHECK FIGURE: Mar. 31, 2018: Bad debt expense = $17,290

At year-end, March 31, 2017, Waterton Contractors showed unadjusted balances of $243,000 in Accounts Receivable; $1,100 debit in Allowance for Doubtful Accounts; and $4,640,000 in Sales. Uncollectible accounts are estimated to be 0.4% of sales.

Unadjusted balances at March 31, 2018, were Accounts Receivable, $298,000; Allowance for Doubtful Accounts, $900 debit; and Sales, $3,971,000. Waterton changed the method of estimating uncollectible accounts to 5.5% of outstanding accounts receivable.

At March 31, 2019, the general ledger showed unadjusted balances of: $253,000 in Accounts Receivable; $4,600 credit in Allowance for Doubtful Accounts; and $3,750,000 in Sales. Waterton prepared an aging analysis on March 31, 2019, that estimated total uncollectible accounts to be $12,900.

Required Prepare the 2017, 2018, and 2019 year-end adjusting entries to estimate uncollectible accounts.

Analysis Component: List the adjusted balances in Allowance for Doubtful Accounts for each of March 31, 2017, 2018, and 2019. Beside each, show the respective Accounts Receivable and Sales balances. Comment on the change in Allowance for Doubtful Accounts and Accounts Receivable relative to the change in Sales.

Problem 8-10B **Notes receivable** LO4

CHECK FIGURES: d. Interest income = $170.96; e. Interest income = $223.56

Shostak showed the following details regarding its notes receivable:

Note	Date of Note	Principal	Interest Rate	Term	Maturity Date	Days of Accrued Interest at Dec. 31, 2017	Accrued Interest at Dec. 31, 2017
1	Sept. 20/16	$490,000	3.0%	120 days			
2	June 01/17	240,000	3.5%	45 days			
3	Nov. 23/17	164,000	4.5%	90 days			
4	Dec. 18/17	120,000	4.0%	30 days			

*Round calculations to the nearest whole cent.

Required

For each note:

    a. Determine the maturity date.

    b. Calculate the *days* of accrued interest, if any, at December 31, 2017, Shostak's year-end.

    c. Calculate the *amount* of accrued interest, if any, at December 31, 2017.

For Note 4:

d. Prepare the entry to record the accrued interest at December 31, 2017.

e. Prepare the entry to record the collection on the maturity date. Assume that interest and principal are collected at maturity.

Problem 8-11B Accrued interest calculation and dishonouring note receivable LO4

CHECK FIGURE: b. Interest income = $484.11

Following are transactions of Rural Company (round calculations to the nearest whole cent):

2017		
Nov.	16	Accepted a $74,000, 90-day, 4% note dated this day in granting Bess Parker a time extension on her past-due account.
Dec.	31	Made an adjusting entry to record the accrued interest on the Parker note.
	31	Closed the Interest income account.
2018		
Feb.	14	Received Parker's payment for the principal and interest on the note dated November 16.
	28	Accepted a $36,000, 5.5%, 30-day note dated this day in granting a time extension on the past-due account of The Simms Co.
Mar.	1	Accepted a $62,000, 60-day, 4.75% note dated this day in granting Bedford Holmes a time extension on his past-due account.
	30	The Simms Co. dishonoured its note when presented for payment.

Required

a. Prepare journal entries to record Rural's transactions.

b. Determine the maturity date of the note dated March 1. Prepare the entry at maturity assuming Bedford Holmes honours the note.

Problem 8-12B Short-term notes receivable LO4

CHECK FIGURES: d. February 15, 2018: Interest income = $203.43; e. April 1, 2018: Interest income = $330.00

Asiatic Electroplating analyzes its accounts receivable weekly. On November 17, 2017, Asiatic accepted a 5.5%, 90-day, $90,000 note receivable from RoadWorks in exchange for its past-due account. On December 1, Ellen Huskey's $36,000 overdue account was converted to a four-month, 5.5% note receivable. On January 31, 2018, Asiatic's year-end accrued interest was recorded on the notes. RoadWorks honoured its note on the maturity date but Ellen Huskey's note was dishonoured. Huskey's account was determined to be uncollectible and written off on July 15, 2018.

Required Prepare Asiatic Electroplating's entries for each of the following dates:

a. November 17, 2017   **d.** Maturity date of RoadWorks' note

b. December 1, 2017   **e.** Maturity date of Huskey's note

c. January 31, 2018   **f.** July 15, 2018

Analysis Component: Assuming a $50,000 credit balance in the Allowance for Doubtful Accounts on July 14, 2018, calculate the balance after posting the entry in (f) above. Assuming no additional write-offs were made prior to year-end, comment on the adequacy of the Allowance for Doubtful Accounts.

Problem 8-13B Accounts receivable ratios LO5

Using the **Danier Leather** financial statements in Appendix III, calculate the following ratios for the years ended June 28, 2014 and June 29, 2013. At June 30, 2012, Danier had an accounts receivable balance of $517,000 and net sales of $148,219,000. Comment on the change.

      c. Accounts receivable turnover ratio (Round to two decimal places)

      d. Days sales in inventory (Round to the nearest day)

*Problem 8-14B Discounting notes receivable LO6

CHECK FIGURE: July 5: Interest expense = $475

Required Prepare entries to record the following transactions of Ibscon Company:

Mar.	1	Accepted a $50,000, 60-day, 4.5% note dated this day in granting Bolton Company a time extension on its past-due account.
	23	Discounted, without recourse, the Bolton note at Security Bank at a cost of $100.
June	21	Accepted a $22,000, 90-day, 5% note dated this day in granting Vince Soto a time extension on his past-due account.
July	5	Discounted, with recourse, the Soto note at Security Bank at a cost of $475.
Sept.	25	Received notice from Security Bank that the Soto note had been paid.

Analysis Component: What reporting is necessary when a business discounts notes receivable with recourse and these notes have not reached maturity by the end of the fiscal period? Explain the reason for this requirement and what accounting principle is being satisfied.

*Problem 8-15B Discounting notes receivable LO6

CHECK FIGURES: Mar. 28: Cash = $2,088.15; July 24: Cash = $1,304.51

Required Prepare general journal entries to record the following transactions of Billington Company.

2017		
Jan	10	Accepted a $3,000, 60-day, 6% note dated this day in granting a time extension on the past-due account of David Huerta.
Mar.	14	David Huerta dishonoured his note when presented for payment.
	19	Accepted a $2,100, 90-day, 5% note dated this day in granting a time extension on the past-due account of Rose Jones.
	28	Discounted the Rose Jones note at the bank at 8%.
Jun.	20	Received word from the bank that the Rose Jones note had been paid.
	27	Accepted $700 in cash and a $1,300, 60-day, 6% note dated this day in granting a time extension on the past-due account of Jake Thomas.
July	24	Discounted the Jake Thomas note at the bank at 7%.
Aug.	29	The Jake Thomas note was dishonoured. Paid the bank the maturity of the note plus a $10 fee.
Sept.	4	Accepted a $1,500, 60-day, 5.5% note dated this day in granting a time extension on the past-due account of Ginnie Bauer.
Oct.	13	Discounted the Ginnie Bauer note at the bank at 7%.
Nov.	6	The Ginnie Bauer note was dishonoured. Paid the bank the maturity value of the note plus a $10 fee.
Dec.	6	Received payment from Ginnie Bauer of the maturity value of her dishonoured note, the fee, and interest at 5.5% on both for 30 days beyond maturity.
	28	Decided the accounts of David Huerta and Jake Thomas were uncollectible and wrote them off against Allowance for Doubtful Accounts.

An asterisk (*) identifies assignment material based on Appendix 8A or Appendix 8B.

Analytical and Review Problems

A & R Problem 8-1

CHECK FIGURE: g. Bad Debt Expense = $18,000

Reproduced below from Farthington Supply's accounting records is the accounts receivable subledger along with selected general ledger accounts.

General Ledger

Accounts Receivable

Dec. 31/16 Balance	158,500		
		7,000	Jan. 4/17
Credit sales in 2017	????	????	Collections in 2017
		14,000	July 15/17
Dec. 31/17 Balance	????		

Allowance for Doubtful Accounts

		200	Dec. 31/16 Balance
July 15/17	14,000		
		????	Dec. 31/17
		????	Dec. 31/17 Balance

Accounts Receivable Subledger

JenStar Company

Dec. 31/16 Balance	48,000		
		48,000	Jan. 20/17
Nov. 15/17	????		
Dec. 31/17 Balance	104,000		

Indigo Developments

Dec. 31/16 Balance	-0-		
Mar. 1/17	17,000	17,000	Mar. 20/17
Nov. 28/17	39,000		
Dec. 2/17	4,000		
Dec. 31/17 Balance	43,000		

Lomas Industries

Dec. 31/16 Balance	????		
		7,000	Jan. 4/17
		????	Jan. 7/17
Apr. 21/17	52,000	52,000	May 5/17
Dec. 7/17	21,000		
Dec. 31/17 Balance	21,000		

PDQ Servicing

Dec. 31/16 Balance	14,000		
		14,000	July 15/17
Dec. 31/17 Balance	-0-		

During the year 2017, there were no recoveries of accounts previously written off. Only one account that of PDQ Servicing, was identified as being uncollectible on July 15, 2017. On January 4, 2017, Farthington issued a $7,000 credit memo to Lomas Industries regarding damaged goods returned.

Required Analyzing the accounts, determine the following amounts:

   a. The December 31, 2016, balance in Lomas Industries' account.

   b. The January 7, 2017, collection from Lomas Industries.

   c. The December 31, 2017, balance in the Accounts Receivable controlling account.

   d. The November 15, 2017, transaction in JenStar Company's account.

   e. Collections during 2017.

f. Credit sales during 2017.

g. Adjusting entry on December 31, 2017, to estimate uncollectible accounts based on a rate of 2.5% of outstanding receivables.

h. The December 31, 2017, balance in the Allowance for Doubtful Accounts.

i. Show how accounts receivable should appear on the balance sheet on December 31, 2017.

Analysis Component: Why does Farthington maintain an accounts receivable subledger? What other subledgers might the company be using and why?

A & R Problem 8-2

CHECK FIGURES: a. April 30, 2017, and Feb. 1, 2018 b. May 7, 2017, credit card expense = $710

Sullivan Equipment Sales showed the following.

2017		
Jan.	15	Sold $25,000 of merchandise for $29,000 to JanCo; terms 3/5, n/15.
	16	Wrote off Fedun's account in the amount of $15,000.
	20	Collected the amount owing from the January 15 sale.
Mar.	1	Accepted a $12,000, 60-day, 7% note dated this day in granting Parker Holdings a time extension on its past-due account.
Apr.	15	Sold merchandise costing $62,000 for $71,000 to customers who used their Visa credit cards. Visa charges a 1% fee and deposits the cash electronically into the retailer's account immediately at the time of sale.
	?	Parker Holdings honoured the note dated March 1.
Nov.	1	Accepted a $24,000, three-month, 6% note dated this day in granting Grant Company a time extension on its past-due account.
Dec.	31	Sullivan's year-end. Interest was accrued on outstanding notes receivable.
	31	Bad debts are based on an aging analysis that estimated $9,700 of accounts receivable are uncollectible. Allowance for Doubtful Accounts showed an unadjusted credit balance of $1,600 on this date.
2018		
	?	Grant Company dishonoured its note dated November 1, 2017.
Mar.	5	Recovered $1,500 from Derek Holston that was previously written off.
	14	Wrote off the Grant Company account.

Required

a. Determine the maturity dates of the March 1 and November 1 notes.

b. Prepare entries as appropriate for each date.

Analysis Component: Sullivan's receivable turnovers at December 31, 2017 and 2018, were 7 and 7.5, respectively. Explain what this ratio measures and whether the change in the ratio for Sullivan was favourable or unfavourable.

Ethics Challenge

EC 8-1

Randy Meyer is the chief executive officer of a medium-sized company in Regina, Saskatchewan. Several years ago, Randy persuaded the board of directors of his company to base a percentage of his compensation on the profit the company earns each year. Each December, Randy estimates year-end financial figures in anticipation of the bonus he will receive. If the bonus is not as high as he would like, he offers several accounting recommendations to his controller for year-end adjustments. One of his favourite recommendations is for the controller to reduce the estimate of doubtful accounts. Randy has used this technique with success for several years.

1. What effect does lowering the estimate for doubtful accounts have on the income statement and balance sheet of Randy's company?

2. Do you think Randy's recommendations to adjust the allowance for doubtful accounts is within his right as CEO or do you think this action is an ethics violation? Justify your response.

3. What type of internal control might be useful for this company in overseeing the CEO's recommendations for accounting changes?

Focus on Financial Statements

FFS 8-1

CHECK FIGURES: Total current assets = $61,900; Total assets = $199,900; Total current liabilities = $25,100

Clara Dover, the owner of Dover Plumbing Sales and Service, showed the following adjusted account balances for the year ended March 31, 2017 (listed alphabetically):

Account	Account Balance*
Accounts payable	$ 6,900
Accounts receivable	28,000
Accumulated depreciation, tools	11,000
Accumulated depreciation, truck	14,000
Allowance for doubtful accounts	1,800
Bad debt expense	5,600
Cash	16,000
Cash over/short expense	20**
Clara Dover, capital	248,770
Clara Dover, withdrawals	72,000
Cost of goods sold	103,000
Depreciation expense, tools	2,000
Depreciation expense, truck	5,000
Insurance expense	7,100
Interest expense	250
Merchandise inventory	9,000
Notes payable, due August 31, 2020	17,000
Notes payable, due February 1, 2018	6,000
Notes receivable, due December 1, 2019	14,000
Petty cash	400
Plumbing revenue	121,000
Prepaid insurance	3,800
Prepaid rent	6,500
Rent expense	23,000
Salaries expense	118,000
Salaries payable	3,200
Sales	124,000
Tools	82,000
Truck	67,000
Unearned plumbing revenue	9,000

*Assume all account balances are normal unless otherwise stated.
**Debit balance.

Required Prepare a classified balance sheet based on the information provided.

Analysis Component: Dover Plumbing had total *Plumbing revenue* for the year ended March 31, 2016, of $86,000 and net accounts receivable at March 31, 2016, of $21,200. Calculate and compare days' sales uncollected for March 31, 2016, and March 31, 2017. Round calculations to two decimal places.

FFS 8-2

Refer to **Danier Leather**'s balance sheet and income statement in Appendix III.

Required Answer the following questions.

1. The balance sheet shows accounts receivable of $638,000 at June 28, 2014, and $1,197,000 at June 29, 2013. What type of asset is accounts receivable? Explain how accounts receivable arise.

2. Refer to the income statement. Does the change in receivables appear to correspond to the change in total sales? Explain your answer.

Critical Thinking Mini Case

You are the finance officer at a bank where the owner of Delta Designs is applying for a $600,000 loan. In reviewing the account information for the year ended June 30, 2017 you are concerned by the following selected adjusted account information:

Account	Debit	Credit
Accounts receivable[1]	$472,000	
Allowance for doubtful accounts		$ 7,080
Sales[2]		3,980,000

[1] 85% of this balance represents receivables that are not yet due. Delta Designs offers credit terms of 2/10, n/30.

[2] All sales are on credit and sales occur evenly throughout the year.

Required Using the elements of critical thinking described on the inside front cover, respond.

Payroll Liabilities

© Lobby/Dreamstime.com/GetStock.com

LEARNING OBJECTIVES

LO1 Identify the taxes and other items frequently withheld from employees' wages.

LO2 Make the calculations necessary to prepare a payroll register and prepare the entries to record and pay payroll liabilities.

LO3 Calculate the payroll costs levied on employers and prepare the entries to record the accrual and payment of these amounts.

LO4 Calculate and record employee fringe benefit costs.

Guilty

The Canada Revenue Agency (CRA) announced that a dentist was fined $3,000 in Edmundston, New Brunswick, provincial court after pleading guilty to three charges of failing to remit over $8,000 in monies deducted and withheld from wages and salaries paid to employees.

In Montreal a director on the board of two companies was fined $541,870 and sentenced to a 12-month prison term following a CRA investigation that showed payroll deductions from the salaries of employees were not remitted to the Receiver General for Canada.

In each of the above cases, unpaid deductions had to be paid in addition to the fines. Failure to do so would result in imprisonment. The CRA takes non-payment of source deductions very seriously, as the amounts deducted from employees are deemed to be held in trust until remitted to CRA on the employees' behalf. Canadians have to be confident that the tax system is fair, and know that CRA will prosecute those individuals who cheat.

CRITICAL THINKING CHALLENGE If payroll liabilities are not recorded, what is the effect on the financial statements?

APPENDIX PREVIEW

Wages or salaries generally amount to one of the largest expenses incurred by a business. Accounting for employees' wages and salaries is one task that is shared by almost all business entities.

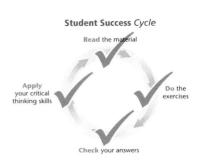

Student Success *Cycle*

Payroll accounting:

- Records cash payments to employees
- Provides valuable information regarding labour costs
- Accounts for amounts withheld from employees' pay
- Accounts for employee (fringe) benefits and payroll costs paid by the employer
- Provides the means to comply with governmental regulations on employee compensation

As you study this appendix, you will learn the general processes that all businesses follow to account for these items.

Items Withheld from Employees' Wages

LO1 Identify the taxes and other items frequently withheld from employees' wages.

An understanding of payroll accounting and the design and use of payroll records requires some knowledge of the laws and programs that affect payrolls. Many of these require **payroll deductions**, amounts withheld from the wages of employees, and are discussed in the first portion of this appendix.

DECISION INSIGHT

The Canadian Payroll Association (CPA) represents more than 10,000 members of the professional payroll community in Canada, the United States, and abroad. With over 18 million Canadian employees paid through CPA member companies, its mission is to provide payroll leadership through advocacy and education. The two qualifications granted through the country's only nationally recognized Payroll Management Certificate Program are Payroll Compliance Practitioner (PCP) and Certified Payroll Manager (CPM).

SOURCE: www.payroll.ca.

Withholding Employees' Income Tax

Employers are required to calculate, collect, and remit to the Receiver General for Canada the income taxes of their employees. Historically, when the first federal income tax law became effective in 1917, it applied to only a few individuals having high earnings. It was not until the Second World War that income taxes were levied on almost all wage earners. At that time, Parliament recognized that many individual wage earners could not be expected to save the money needed to pay their income taxes once each year, so Parliament began a system of pay-as-you-go withholding of taxes at the source each payday. This pay-as-you-go withholding of employee income taxes requires an employer to act as a tax-collecting agent of the federal government. Failure to cooperate results in litigation and potential criminal charges.

The amount of income taxes to be withheld from an employee's wages is determined by his or her wages and the amount of **personal tax credits**. Based on rates in effect January 1, 2015, each individual is entitled, in 2015, to some or all of the following annual amounts that are subject to tax credits (as applicable):

1. Basic Personal Amount .... $11,327[1]
2. Married or Equivalent 11,327
   (with maximum earnings stipulated)

The total of each taxpayer's personal tax credits is deducted directly from income to determine the level of income tax deductions from the individual's gross pay. Additional personal credits, beyond the basic personal amount, are provided for items such as being a caregiver to dependent children, tuition dues paid, and unused personal amounts of a spouse/common-law partner. For example, based on rates effective January 1, 2015, a Saskatchewan resident with a gross weekly salary of $400 and personal tax credits of $11,327 (2015 net claim code 1[2] on the *TD1* form) would have $28.75 of total income taxes withheld. Another individual with the same gross salary but with personal tax credits of $16,000 (claim code 4) would have only $4.75 withheld.

Employers withhold income tax owed by each employee every payday based on an employee's completed Personal Tax Credits Return, Form **TD1**. There are federal and provincial/territorial TD1 forms. The taxpayer must file revised TD1 forms each time the exemptions change during a year.

In determining the amounts of income taxes to be withheld from the wages of employees, employers use payroll deductions tables provided by the Canada Revenue Agency (CRA). The to-be-withheld amounts include both federal and provincial income taxes except for the province of Quebec, which levies and collects its own income tax and its own pension plan contributions. Provincial income tax rates vary from province to province. Therefore, for consistency, all examples and problems making use of tax tables in this appendix will be based on Saskatchewan's tables. Employers are required to remit the withheld taxes to the Receiver General for Canada each month.

Canada (or Quebec) Pension Plan (CPP or QPP)

Every working person between the ages of 18 and 70 with few exceptions must make contributions in required amounts to the **Canada Pension Plan** (CPP) or Quebec Pension Plan (QPP).

Effective for the 2015 annual reporting period, contributions are based on earnings as follows:

Canada Pension Plan Contributions		
Effective	Employee Contributions	Employer Contributions
Rate	4.95%*	4.95%*
Maximum	$2,479.95	$2,479.95
*4.95% of earnings greater than $3,500 and less than $53,600.		

Employers are responsible for making the proper deductions from their employees' earnings. They remit these deductions each month, together with their own contributions, to the Receiver General for Canada.

Self-employed individuals pay the combined rate for employees and employers, or 9.9% on annual earnings between $3,500 and the exempt ceiling of $53,600.

Employment Insurance (EI)

To assist the unemployed, the federal government began an employee/employer-financed unemployment insurance plan. Under the revised 1996 *Employment Insurance Act*, compulsory **Employment**

---

1 Source: http://www.cra-arc.gc.ca/E/pbg/tf/td1/td1-15e.pdf

2 For more information on claim codes visit the following CRA resource: http://www.cra-arc.gc.ca/tx/bsnss/tpcs/pyrll/t4032/2015/t4032-sk-15eng.pdf

Insurance (EI) coverage was extended to all Canadian workers who are not self-employed. Over 13 million employees, including teachers, hospital workers, and top-level executives, are covered by the insurance plan.

The Employment Insurance fund from which benefits are paid is jointly financed by employees and their employers. At January 1, 2015, employers are required to deduct from their employees' wages 1.88% of insured earnings, to add a contribution of 1.4 times the amount deducted from employees' wages, and to remit both amounts to the Receiver General for Canada. The system is summarized as follows:

Employment Insurance Contributions		
Effective Jan. 1, 2015	Employee Contributions	Employer Contributions
Rate	1.88%	1.4 times employee rate
Maximum	$930.60	$1,302.84
Note: maximum insurable earnings for 2015 are $49,500.		

Insured earnings, in most instances, refer to gross earnings. An employee may receive taxable benefits or allowances that would be included in gross earnings but would not be considered insurable earnings. However, in this text, gross earnings will be insurable earnings.

The *Employment Insurance Act* also requires that an employer complete a "record of employment" in cases of termination of employment, illness, injury, or pregnancy and keep a record for each employee that shows among other things wages subject to employment insurance and taxes withheld.

Use of Withholding Tables

Employers may use **wage bracket withholding tables** in determining Canada Pension Plan and Employment Insurance to be withheld from employees' gross earnings. These tables are available from CRA.

Alternatively, determining the amount of withholdings from an employee's gross wages is quite easy when the CRA Payroll Deductions Online Calculator is used. The Payroll Deductions Online Calculator can be found at http://www.cra-arc.gc.ca/pdoc.

THE T-4 FORM

Employers are required to report wages and deductions both to each employee and to the local office of CRA. On or before the last day of February, the employer must give each employee a T-4 statement that tells the employee:

- Total wages for the preceding year
- Taxable benefits received from the employer
- Income taxes withheld
- Deductions for registered pension plan
- Canada Pension Plan contributions
- Employment Insurance deductions

On or before the last day of February the employer must forward to the district taxation office copies of the employee's T-4 statements plus a T-4 that summarizes the information contained on the employee's T-4 statements. The T-4 form is shown in Exhibit AI.1. CRA publishes a guide to direct employers in filling out the T4 form. For more information refer to the CRA website: www.cra-arc.gc.ca.[3]

---

3 Fillable PDF forms can be found at http://www.cra-arc.gc.ca/E/pbg/tf/t4/t4-fill-14e.pdf.

EXHIBIT A1.1

2015 T-4 Form

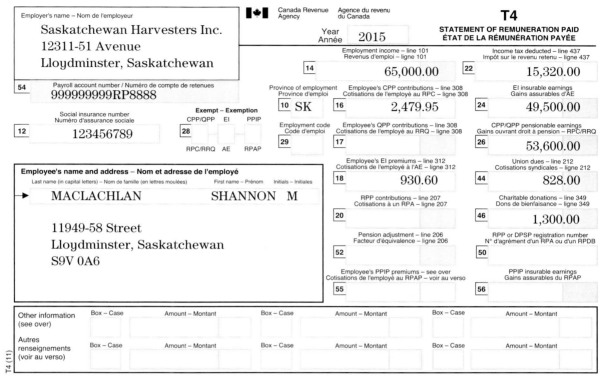

Reproduced with permission of the Minister of Public Works and Government Services Canada, 2015.

WAGES, HOURS, AND UNION CONTRACTS

All provinces have laws establishing maximum hours of work and minimum pay rates. And, while the details vary with each province, generally employers are required to pay an employee for hours worked in excess of 40 in any one week at the employee's regular pay rate plus an overtime premium of at least one-half of his or her regular rate. In addition, employers commonly operate under contracts with their employees' union that provide even better terms.

In addition to specifying working hours and wage rates, union contracts often provide that the employer shall deduct dues from the wages of each employee and remit the amounts deducted to the union.

Other Payroll Deductions

Employees may individually authorize additional deductions such as:

1. Deductions to accumulate funds for the purchase of Canada Savings Bonds
2. Deductions to pay health, accident, hospital, or life insurance premiums
3. Deductions to repay loans from the employer or the employees' credit union
4. Deductions to pay for merchandise purchased from the company
5. Deductions for donations to charitable organizations such as United Way

CHECKPOINT

1. What is the purpose of the federal Employment Insurance scheme?
2. When must T-4 statements be given to employees?
3. What are other typical non-mandatory payroll deductions?

Do Quick Study question: QS AI-1

The Payroll Register

LO2 Make the calculations necessary to prepare a payroll register and prepare the entries to record and pay payroll liabilities.

Each pay period the total hours worked are summarized in a payroll register, an example of which is shown in Exhibit AI.2. The illustrated register is for a weekly pay period and shows the payroll data for each employee on a separate line.

In Exhibit AI.2, the columns under the heading Daily Time show the hours worked each day by each employee. The total of each employee's hours is entered in the column headed Total Hours. If hours include overtime hours, these are entered in the column headed O.T. Hours.

EXHIBIT A1.2

Payroll Register

Payroll Week Ended

Employees	Clock Card No.	Daily Time M	T	W	T	F	S	S	Total Hours	O.T. Hours	Earnings: Reg. Pay Rate	Regular Pay	O.T. Premium Pay	Gross Pay	
Auer, John	118	8	8	8	8	8			40		10.00	400.00		400.00	1
Cheung, Joen	109	0	8	8	8	8	8		40		12.00	480.00		480.00	2
Daljit, Moe	121	8	8	8	8	8	8	4	52	12	15.00	780.00	90.00	870.00	3
Lee, Shannon	104	8	8		8	8	8	4	44	4	14.00	616.00	28.00	644.00	4
Prasad, Sunil	108		8	8	8	8	4	8	44	4	15.00	660.00	30.00	690.00	5
Rupert, Allan	105	8	8	8	8	8			40		12.00	480.00		480.00	6
Totals												3,416.00	148.00	3,564.00	

Register March 9, 2015

	Gross Pay	Deductions: EI Premium	Income Taxes	Hospital Insurance	CPP	Total Deductions	Payment: Net Pay	Cheque Number	Distribution: Sales Salaries	Office Salaries
1	400.00	7.52	28.75	18.00	16.47	70.74	329.26	754	400.00	
2	480.00	9.02	48.45	18.00	20.43	95.90	384.10	755	480.00	
3	870.00	16.36	142.85	24.00	39.73	222.94	647.06	756		870.00
4	644.00	12.11	87.90	18.00	28.55	146.56	497.44	757		644.00
5	690.00	12.97	99.30	24.00	30.82	167.09	522.91	758	690.00	
6	480.00	9.02	48.45	18.00	20.43	95.90	384.10	759	480.00	
	3,564.00	67.00	455.70	120.00	156.43	799.13	2,764.87		2,050.00	1,514.00

The Regular Pay Rate column shows the hourly pay rate of each employee. Total hours worked multiplied by the regular pay rate equals regular pay. Overtime hours multiplied by the overtime premium rate (50% in this case) equals overtime premium pay (O.T. Premium Pay column). And regular pay plus overtime premium pay is the **employee's gross pay**.

The amounts withheld from each employee's gross pay are recorded in the Deductions columns of the payroll register. For example, you determine the income tax deductions by matching the gross pay of each employee to the tax deduction tables and then enter the results in the tax deduction column. Income tax deductions are based on the gross pay less the amounts deducted for EI and CPP (or QPP). The tax tables allow for these adjustments and separate books are available for each province. Exhibit AI.2 assumes that income tax deductions are based on the tables provided in Exhibit AI.3 and assumes the employees reside in Saskatchewan.

For example, you can use the tables in Exhibit AI.3 to determine the appropriate CPP, EI, and income tax deductions for John Auer's $400 pay. In the CPP table, under the *Pay* column, find $400. The CPP deduction according to the table is $16.47 for the pay range $399.93–$400.12. Using the EI table, go to the *Insurable Earnings* column and find $400. The table shows that the EI deduction for the range $399.74–$400.26 is $7.52. Finally, using each of the federal and provincial tax deductions tables, go to the Pay column and find $400. Now follow the numbers across to the claim code 1 column (*assume a claim code of 1 unless otherwise specified*). The tables show a total income tax to be deducted of $28.75[4] (federal tax of $20.55 + provincial tax of $8.70). You can use the tables to determine the CPP, EI, and income tax deductions for the remaining employees.

The column headed Hospital Insurance in Exhibit AI.2 shows the amounts withheld to pay for hospital insurance for the employees and their families. The total withheld from all employees is a current

EXHIBIT A1.3

Excerpts From CPP, EI, and Income Tax Tables Effective January 1, 2015

Canada Pension Plan Contributions
Weekly (52 pay periods a year)

Pay			Pay			Pay			Pay		
From	To	CPP	From	To	CPP	From	To	CPP	From	To	CPP
370.84 -	371.03	15.03	385.39 -	385.58	15.75	399.93 -	400.12	16.47	414.48 -	414.67	17.19
371.04 -	371.23	15.04	385.59 -	385.78	15.76	400.13 -	400.33	16.48	414.68 -	414.87	17.20
371.24 -	371.44	15.05	385.79 -	385.98	15.77	400.34 -	400.53	16.49	414.88 -	415.07	17.21
371.45 -	371.64	15.06	385.99 -	386.18	15.78	400.54 -	400.73	16.50	415.08 -	415.27	17.22
371.65 -	371.84	15.07	386.19 -	386.39	15.79	400.74 -	400.93	16.51	415.28 -	415.48	17.23
371.85 -	372.04	15.08	386.40 -	386.59	15.80	400.94 -	401.13	16.52	415.49 -	415.68	17.24
372.05 -	372.24	15.09	386.60 -	386.79	15.81	401.14 -	401.34	16.53	415.69 -	415.88	17.25
372.25 -	372.45	15.10	386.80 -	386.99	15.82	401.35 -	401.54	16.54	415.89 -	416.08	17.26
372.46 -	372.65	15.11	387.00 -	387.19	15.83	401.55 -	401.74	16.55	416.09 -	416.28	17.27
479.93 -	480.12	20.43	494.48 -	494.67	21.15	509.02 -	509.21	21.87	523.57 -	523.76	22.59
480.13 -	480.33	20.44	494.68 -	494.87	21.16	509.22 -	509.42	21.88	523.77 -	523.96	22.60
480.34 -	480.53	20.45	494.88 -	495.07	21.17	509.43 -	509.62	21.89	523.97 -	524.16	22.61
480.54 -	480.73	20.46	495.08 -	495.27	21.18	509.63 -	509.82	21.90	524.17 -	524.37	22.62
480.74 -	480.93	20.47	495.28 -	495.48	21.19	509.83 -	510.02	21.91	524.38 -	524.57	22.63
480.94 -	481.13	20.48	495.49 -	495.68	21.20	510.03 -	510.22	21.92	524.58 -	524.77	22.64
481.14 -	481.34	20.49	495.69 -	495.88	21.21	510.23 -	510.43	21.93	524.78 -	524.97	22.65
481.35 -	481.54	20.50	495.89 -	496.08	21.22	510.44 -	510.63	21.94	524.98 -	525.17	22.66
481.55 -	481.74	20.51	496.09 -	496.28	21.23	510.64 -	510.83	21.95	525.18 -	525.38	22.67

---

4 The Payroll Deductions Online Calculator produces marginally more accurate results since the table values are based on ranges vs. specific dollar amounts.

EXHIBIT A1.3

Excerpts From CPP, EI, and Income Tax Tables Effective January 1, 2015 (continued)

Canada Pension Plan Contributions
Weekly (52 pay periods a year)

Pay From		Pay To	CPP	Pay From		Pay To	CPP	Pay From		Pay To	CPP	Pay From		Pay To	CPP
599.93	-	600.12	26.37	614.48	-	614.67	27.09	629.02	-	629.21	27.81	643.57	-	643.76	28.53
600.13	-	600.33	26.38	614.68	-	614.87	27.10	629.22	-	629.42	27.82	643.77	-	643.96	28.54
600.34	-	600.53	26.39	614.88	-	615.07	27.11	629.43	-	629.62	27.83	643.97	-	644.16	28.55
600.54	-	600.73	26.40	615.08	-	615.27	27.12	629.63	-	629.82	27.84	644.17	-	644.37	28.56
600.74	-	600.93	26.41	615.28	-	615.48	27.13	629.83	-	630.02	27.85	644.38	-	644.57	28.57
600.94	-	601.13	26.42	615.49	-	615.68	27.14	630.03	-	630.22	27.86	644.58	-	644.77	28.58
601.14	-	601.34	26.43	615.69	-	615.88	27.15	630.23	-	630.43	27.87	644.78	-	644.97	28.59
601.35	-	601.54	26.44	615.89	-	616.08	27.16	630.44	-	630.63	27.88	644.98	-	645.17	28.60
601.55	-	601.74	26.45	616.09	-	616.28	27.17	630.64	-	630.83	27.89	645.18	-	645.38	28.61
823.57	-	823.76	37.44	838.11	-	838.31	38.16	852.66	-	852.85	38.88	867.20	-	867.40	39.60
823.77	-	823.96	37.45	838.32	-	838.51	38.17	852.86	-	853.05	38.89	867.41	-	867.60	39.61
823.97	-	824.16	37.46	838.52	-	838.71	38.18	853.06	-	853.25	38.90	867.61	-	867.80	39.62
824.17	-	824.37	37.47	838.72	-	838.91	38.19	853.26	-	853.46	38.91	867.81	-	868.00	39.63
824.38	-	824.57	37.48	838.92	-	839.11	38.20	853.47	-	853.66	38.92	868.01	-	868.20	39.64
824.58	-	824.77	37.49	839.12	-	839.32	38.21	853.67	-	853.86	38.93	868.21	-	868.41	39.65
824.78	-	824.97	37.50	839.33	-	839.52	38.22	853.87	-	854.06	38.94	868.42	-	868.61	39.66
824.98	-	825.17	37.51	839.53	-	839.72	38.23	854.07	-	854.26	38.95	868.62	-	868.81	39.67
825.18	-	825.38	37.52	839.73	-	839.92	38.24	854.27	-	854.47	38.96	868.82	-	869.01	39.68

Employee's maximum CPP contribution for the year 2015 is $2,479.95

Employment Insurance Premiums

Insurable Earnings From		To	EI premium	Insurable Earnings From		To	EI premium	Insurable Earnings From		To	EI premium	Insurable Earnings From		To	EI premium
321.02	-	321.54	6.04	359.31	-	359.84	6.76	397.61	-	398.13	7.48	435.91	-	436.43	8.20
321.55	-	322.07	6.05	359.85	-	360.37	6.77	398.14	-	398.67	7.49	436.44	-	436.96	8.21
322.08	-	322.60	6.06	360.38	-	360.90	6.78	398.68	-	399.20	7.50	436.97	-	437.49	8.22
322.61	-	323.13	6.07	360.91	-	361.43	6.79	399.21	-	399.73	7.51	437.50	-	438.03	8.23
323.14	-	323.67	6.08	361.44	-	361.96	6.80	399.74	-	400.26	7.52	438.04	-	438.56	8.24
323.68	-	324.20	6.09	361.97	-	362.49	6.81	400.27	-	400.79	7.53	438.57	-	439.09	8.25
324.21	-	324.73	6.10	362.50	-	363.03	6.82	400.80	-	401.32	7.54	439.10	-	439.62	8.26
324.74	-	325.26	6.11	363.04	-	363.56	6.83	401.32	-	401.86	7.55	439.63	-	440.15	8.27
325.27	-	325.79	6.12	363.57	-	364.09	6.84	401.87	-	402.39	7.56	440.16	-	440.69	8.28
478.99	-	479.52	9.01	517.29	-	517.81	9.73	555.59	-	556.11	10.45	593.89	-	594.41	11.17
479.53	-	480.05	9.02	517.82	-	518.35	9.74	556.12	-	556.64	10.46	594.42	-	594.94	11.18
480.06	-	480.58	9.03	518.36	-	518.88	9.75	556.65	-	557.18	10.47	594.95	-	595.47	11.19
480.59	-	481.11	9.04	518.89	-	519.41	9.76	557.19	-	557.71	10.48	595.48	-	596.01	11.20
481.12	-	481.64	9.05	519.42	-	519.94	9.77	557.72	-	558.24	10.49	596.02	-	596.54	11.21
481.65	-	482.18	9.06	519.95	-	520.47	9.78	558.25	-	558.77	10.50	596.55	-	597.07	11.22
482.19	-	482.71	9.07	520.48	-	521.01	9.79	558.78	-	559.30	10.51	597.08	-	597.60	11.23
482.72	-	483.24	9.08	521.02	-	521.54	9.80	559.31	-	559.84	10.52	597.61	-	598.13	11.24
483.25	-	483.77	9.09	521.55	-	522.07	9.81	559.85	-	560.37	10.53	598.14	-	598.67	11.25
641.76	-	642.28	12.07	680.06	-	680.58	12.79	718.36	-	718.88	13.51	756.65	-	757.18	14.23
642.29	-	642.81	12.08	680.59	-	681.11	12.80	718.89	-	719.41	13.52	757.19	-	757.71	14.24
642.82	-	643.35	12.09	681.12	-	681.64	12.81	719.42	-	719.94	13.53	757.72	-	758.24	14.25
643.36	-	643.88	12.10	681.65	-	682.18	12.82	719.95	-	720.47	13.54	758.25	-	758.77	14.26
643.89	-	644.41	12.11	682.19	-	682.71	12.83	720.48	-	721.01	13.55	758.78	-	759.30	14.27
644.42	-	644.94	12.12	682.72	-	683.24	12.84	721.02	-	721.54	13.56	759.31	-	759.84	14.28
644.95	-	645.47	12.13	683.25	-	683.77	12.85	721.55	-	722.07	13.57	759.85	-	760.37	14.29
645.48	-	646.01	12.14	683.78	-	684.30	12.86	722.08	-	722.60	13.58	760.38	-	760.90	14.30
646.02	-	646.54	12.15	684.31	-	684.84	12.87	722.61	-	723.13	13.59	760.91	-	761.43	14.31
790.16	-	790.69	14.86	828.46	-	828.98	15.58	866.76	-	867.28	16.30	905.06	-	905.58	17.02
790.70	-	791.22	14.87	828.99	-	829.52	15.59	867.29	-	867.81	16.31	905.59	-	906.11	17.03
791.23	-	791.75	14.88	829.53	-	830.05	15.60	867.82	-	868.35	16.32	906.12	-	906.64	17.04
791.76	-	792.28	14.89	830.06	-	830.58	15.61	868.36	-	868.88	16.33	906.65	-	907.18	17.05
792.29	-	792.81	14.90	830.59	-	831.11	15.62	868.89	-	869.41	16.34	907.19	-	907.71	17.06
792.82	-	793.35	14.91	831.12	-	831.64	15.63	869.42	-	869.94	16.35	907.72	-	908.24	17.07
793.36	-	793.88	14.92	831.65	-	832.18	15.64	869.95	-	870.47	16.36	908.25	-	908.77	17.08
793.89	-	794.41	14.93	832.19	-	832.71	15.65	870.48	-	871.01	16.37	908.78	-	909.30	17.09
794.42	-	794.94	14.94	832.72	-	833.24	15.66	871.02	-	871.54	16.38	909.31	-	909.84	17.10

Yearly maximum insurable earnings are $49,500
Yearly maximum employee premiums are $930.60
The premium rate for 2015 is 1.88 %

EXHIBIT A1.3

Excerpts From CPP, EI, and Income Tax Tables Effective January 1, 2015 (continued)

Federal tax deductions
Effective January 1, 2015
Weekly (52 pay periods a year)
Also look up the tax deductions in the provincial table

Pay From	Less than	CC 0	CC 1	CC 2	CC 3	CC 4	CC 5	CC 6	CC 7	CC 8	CC 9	CC 10
383	387	51.00	18.35	15.20	8.95	2.70						
387	391	51.55	18.90	15.75	9.50	3.30						
391	395	52.10	19.45	16.30	10.10	3.85						
395	399	52.70	20.00	16.90	10.65	4.40						
399	403	53.25	20.55	17.45	11.20	4.95						
463	467	62.20	29.50	26.40	20.15	13.90	7.65	1.40				
467	471	62.75	30.05	26.95	20.70	14.45	8.20	1.95				
471	475	63.30	30.60	27.50	21.25	15.00	8.80	2.55				
475	479	63.85	31.20	28.05	21.80	15.60	9.35	3.10				
479	483	64.40	31.75	28.60	22.40	16.15	9.90	3.65				
623	631	84.80	52.15	49.05	42.80	36.55	30.30	24.05	17.80	11.55	5.35	
631	639	85.95	53.25	50.15	43.90	37.65	31.40	25.15	18.95	12.70	6.45	.20
639	647	87.05	54.40	51.25	45.00	38.80	32.55	26.30	20.05	13.80	7.55	1.30
647	655	88.15	55.50	52.40	46.15	39.90	33.65	27.40	21.15	14.95	8.70	2.45
655	663	89.30	56.60	53.50	47.25	41.00	34.75	28.55	22.30	16.05	9.80	3.55
863	871	118.90	86.20	83.10	76.85	70.60	64.35	58.10	51.85	45.65	39.40	33.15
871	879	120.55	87.90	84.75	78.50	72.30	66.05	59.80	53.55	47.30	41.05	34.80
879	887	122.25	89.55	86.45	80.20	73.95	67.70	61.45	55.25	49.00	42.75	36.50
887	895	123.90	91.25	88.10	81.90	75.65	69.40	63.15	56.90	50.65	44.40	38.20
895	903	125.60	92.90	89.80	83.55	77.30	71.05	64.85	58.60	52.35	46.10	39.85

Saskatchewan provincial tax deductions
Effective January 1, 2015
Weekly (52 pay periods a year)
Also look up the tax deductions in the federal table

Pay From	Less than	CC 0	CC 1	CC 2	CC 3	CC 4	CC 5	CC 6	CC 7	CC 8	CC 9	CC 10
398	400	41.25	8.20	6.05	1.80							
400	402	41.45	8.40	6.25	2.00							
402	404	41.65	8.60	6.45	2.20							
404	406	41.85	8.80	6.65	2.40							
406	408	42.10	9.00	6.85	2.60							
468	472	48.55	15.45	13.30	9.05	4.80	.55					
472	476	48.95	15.85	13.75	9.50	5.20	.95					
476	480	49.35	16.25	14.15	9.90	5.65	1.35					
480	484	49.75	16.70	14.55	10.30	6.05	1.80					
484	488	50.20	17.10	14.95	10.70	6.45	2.20					
628	632	64.95	31.85	29.70	25.45	21.20	16.95	12.70	8.45	4.15		
632	636	65.35	32.25	30.15	25.85	21.60	17.35	13.10	8.85	4.60	.30	
636	640	65.75	32.65	30.50	26.30	22.00	17.75	13.50	9.25	5.00	.75	
640	644	66.15	33.10	30.95	26.70	22.45	18.20	13.90	9.65	5.40	1.15	
644	648	66.55	33.50	31.35	27.10	22.85	18.60	14.35	10.05	5.80	1.55	
848	856	87.80	54.70	52.55	48.30	44.05	39.80	35.55	31.30	27.00	22.75	18.50
856	864	88.75	55.70	53.55	49.30	45.05	40.80	36.50	32.25	28.00	23.75	19.50
864	872	89.75	56.65	54.55	50.25	46.00	41.75	37.50	33.25	29.00	24.70	20.45
872	880	90.70	57.65	55.50	51.25	47.00	42.75	38.50	34.20	29.95	25.70	21.45
880	888	91.70	58.60	56.50	52.25	47.95	43.70	39.45	35.20	30.95	26.70	22.40

Reproduced with the permission of the Minister of Public Works and Government Services, 2015.

liability of the employer until paid to the insurance company. Likewise, the total withheld for employees' union dues is a current liability until paid to the union.

Additional columns may be added to the payroll register for any other deductions that occur sufficiently often to warrant special columns. For example, a company that regularly deducts amounts from its employees' pay for Canada Savings Bonds may add a special column for this deduction.

An employee's gross pay less total deductions is the **employee's net pay** and is entered in the Net Pay column. The total of this column is the amount the employees are to be paid. The numbers of the cheques used to pay the employees are entered in the column headed Cheque Number.

The Distribution columns are used to classify the various salaries in terms of different kinds of expense. Here you enter each employee's gross salary in the proper column according to the type of work performed. The column totals then indicate the amounts to be debited to the salary expense accounts.

Recording the Payroll

The entry to record the payroll shown in Exhibit AI.2 is:

March 10	Sales Salaries Expense	2,050.00	
	Office Salaries Expense	1,514.00	
	EI Payable		67.00
	Employees' Income Taxes Payable		455.70
	Employees' Hospital Insurance Payable		120.00
	CPP Payable		156.43
	Salaries Payable		2,764.87
	To record the March 10 payroll.		

The debits of the entry were taken from the payroll register's distribution column totals. They charge the employees' gross earnings to the proper salary expense accounts. The credits to EI Payable, Employees' Income Taxes Payable, Employees' Hospital Insurance Payable, and CPP Payable record these amounts as current liabilities. The credit to Salaries Payable (also called Payroll Payable, Wages Payable, or Accrued Salaries Payable, etc.) records as a liability the net amount to be paid to the employees.

 **CHECKPOINT**

4. What constitutes the employee's gross pay?

5. What is the employee's net pay?

Do Quick Study questions: QS AI-2, QS AI-3, QS AI-4, QS AI-5, QS AI-6

Paying the Employees

Almost every business pays its employees by cheque or through electronic funds transfer (EFT). Employers give each employee an earnings statement each payday showing the hours worked, gross pay, deductions, and net pay, as shown in Exhibit AI.4.

EXHIBIT A1.4

A Payroll Cheque

Employee	Total Hours	O.T. Hours	Reg. Pay Rate	Reg-ular Pay	O.T. Prem. Pay	Gross Pay	EI Pre-mium	Income Taxes	CP Plan	Hosp. Ins.	Total Deduc-tions	Net Pay
John Auer	40		10.00	400.00		400.00	7.32	32.00	16.47	18.00	73.79	326.21

STATEMENT OF EARNINGS AND DEDUCTIONS FOR EMPLOYEE'S RECORDS—DETACH BEFORE CASHING CHEQUE

GRASSLAND INDUSTRIES
Loon Lake, Saskatchewan

No. 1517

PAY TO THE
ORDER OF ___John Auer___   Date _March 6, 2017_ $ ___326.21___

___Three hundred twenty-six dollars and twenty-one cents___ – – – – – – – – – –

Lloydminster Credit Union
Lloydminster, Saskatchewan

GRASSLAND INDUSTRIES

Jane R. Morris

Employee's Individual Earnings Record

An **employee's individual earnings record**, as shown in Exhibit AI.5, provides for each employee, in one record, a full year's summary of the employee's working time, gross earnings, deductions, and net pay. In addition, it accumulates information that:

1. Serves as a basis for the employer's payroll tax returns

2. Indicates when an employee's earnings have reached the maximum amounts for CPP and EI deductions

3. Supplies data for the T4 slip, which must be given to the employee at the end of the year

The payroll information on an employee's individual earnings record is posted from the payroll register. Note the last column of the record. It shows an employee's earnings to date and is used to determine when the earnings reach maximum amounts and are no longer subject to the various deductions such as CPP and EI.

EXHIBIT A1.5

Employee's 2015 Individual Earnings Record

Employee's Name __John Auer__   SIN No. __123-456-789__   Employee No. __114__

Home
Address __Box 68, Loon Lake__   Notify in Case
of Emergency __Margaret Auer__   Phone
No. __555-964-9834__

Employed __May 15, 1999__   Date of
Termination _____   Reason _____

Date of
Birth __June 6, 1972__   Date
Becomes 65 __June 6, 2037__   Male (X)
Female ( )   Married ( )
Single (X)   Number of
Exemptions __0__   Pay
Rate __$10.00__

Occupation __Clerk__   Place __Warehouse__

Date			Time Lost		Time Worked												
Per. Ends	Paid	Hrs.	Rea-son	Total	O.T. Hours	Reg. Pay	O.T. Pay	Gross Pay	EI Prem	Income Taxes	Hosp. Ins.	CPP	Total Deduc-tions	Net Pay	Cheque No.	Cumu-lative Earnings
6-Jan	6-Jan			40		400.00		400.00	7.52	28.75	18.00	16.47	70.74	329.26		400.00
13-Jan	13-Jan			40		400.00		400.00	7.52	28.75	18.00	16.47	70.74	329.26		800.00
20-Jan	20-Jan			40		400.00		400.00	7.52	28.75	18.00	16.47	70.74	329.26		1,200.00
27-Jan	27-Jan	4	Sick	36		360.00		360.00	6.77	19.15	18.00	14.49	58.41	301.59		1,560.00
3-Feb	3-Feb			40		400.00		400.00	7.52	28.75	18.00	16.47	70.74	329.26		1,960.00
10-Feb	10-Feb			40		400.00		400.00	7.52	28.75	18.00	16.47	70.74	329.26		2,360.00
25-May	25-May			40		400.00		400.00	7.52	28.75	18.00	16.47	70.74	329.26		8,400.00

DECISION MAKER

Answer—End of chapter

Landscape Maintenance Technician

You take a summer job working for a family friend who runs a small landscaping service. When the time arrives for your first paycheque, the owner slaps you on the back, gives you full payment in cash, winks, and adds: "No need to pay those high taxes, eh?" What are your responsibilities in this case? Do you take any action?

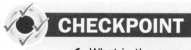

CHECKPOINT

6. What is the purpose of the employee's individual earnings record?

Do Quick Study questions: QS AI-7, QS AI-8

MID-APPENDIX DEMONSTRATION PROBLEM

On January 27, the end of its fourth weekly pay period in 2015, Moosejaw Micro Brew Co.'s payroll record showed that its one office employee and two sales employees had earned $481 (claim code 2), $645 (claim code 3), and $868 (claim code 4), respectively. Each employee has $40 of hospital insurance premiums withheld plus $15 of union dues.

Required

a. Prepare a schedule similar to the register in Exhibit AI.2 to summarize deductions by employee and in total. Use the tables in Exhibit AI.3 to determine the appropriate CPP, EI, and income tax to be withheld.

b. Give the journal entry to record the payroll on January 27.

Analysis Component:

What effect does the entry in part (b) have on the balance sheet?

Solution

a.

				Deductions					Payment		Distribution	
CC	Gross Pay	EI Premium	Income Taxes	Hospital Insurance	CPP	Union Dues	Total Deductions	Net Pay	Cheque Number	Sales Salaries	Office Salaries
2	481.00	9.04	43.15	40.00	20.48	15.00	127.67	353.33	754	481.00	
4	645.00	12.13	61.65	40.00	28.60	15.00	157.38	487.62	758		645.00
4	868.00	16.32	116.60	40.00	39.63	15.00	227.55	640.45	759		868.00
	1,994.00	37.49	221.40	120.00	88.71	45.00	512.60	1,481.40		481.00	1,513.00

b.

January	27	Office Salaries Expense	481.00	
		Sales Salaries Expense.................................	1,513.00	
		EI Payable		37.49
		Employees' Income Taxes Payable		221.40
		Employees' Hospital Insurance Payable...		120.00
		CPP Payable		88.71
		Employees' Union Dues Payable		45.00
		Salaries Payable		1,481.40
		To record payroll deductions for pay period ending January 27.		

Analysis Component:

The entry in part (b) will cause liabilities, specifically current liabilities, to increase and equity to decrease.

Payroll Deductions Required of the Employer

LO3   Calculate the payroll costs levied on employers and prepare the entries to record the accrual and payment of these amounts.

Under the previous discussion of the Canada (or Quebec) Pension Plan (CPP or QPP), it was pointed out that pension deductions are required in like amounts on both employed workers and their employers. A covered employer is required by law to deduct from the employees' pay the amounts of their CPP (or QPP), but in addition, the employer must pay an amount equal to the sum of the employees' CPP (or QPP). Commonly, the amount deducted by the employer is recorded at the same time as the payroll to which it relates is recorded. Also, since both the employees' and employer's shares are reported on the same form and are paid in one amount, the liability for both is normally recorded in the same liability account, the CPP (or QPP) Payable account.

An employer is also required to pay Employment Insurance (EI) that is 1.4 times the sum of the employees' EI deductions. Most employers record both of these payroll deductions with a journal entry that is made at the time of recording the payroll to which they relate. For example, the entry to record the employer's amounts on the payroll in Exhibit AI.2 is:

March 10	EI Expense (1.4 × $67.00)	93.80	
	CPP (or QPP) Expense	156.43	
	EI Payable		93.80
	CPP (or QPP) Payable		156.43
	To record the employer's payroll taxes.		

The debit in the entry records as an expense the payroll taxes levied on the employer, and the credits record the liabilities for the taxes.

Paying the Payroll Deductions

Income tax, EI, and CPP (or QPP) amounts withheld each payday from the employees' pay plus the employer's portion of EI and CPP (or QPP) are current liabilities until paid to the Receiver General for Canada. The normal method of payment is to pay the amounts due at any chartered bank or remit them directly to the Receiver General for Canada. Payment of these amounts is usually required to be made before the 15th of the month following the month that deductions were made from the earnings of the employees. Large employers are required to remit on the 10th and 25th of each month.

For simplicity, we assume the payment of the March 10 amounts recorded above is made the following day. Recall, however, that the employer must remit the amounts withheld from the employee as determined in Exhibit AI.2 *plus* the employer's portion recorded above. The following T-accounts summarize all of these amounts:

EI Payable		Employees' Income Taxes Payable	
	67.00*		455.70*
	93.80**		
	160.80	**CPP (or QPP) Payable**	
			156.43*
Hospital Insurance Payable			156.43**
	120.00*		312.86

*Employees' portion per Exhibit AI.2   ** Employer's portion

The entry to record remittance to the Receiver General for Canada is then:

March 11	EI Payable..	160.80	
	Employees' Income Taxes Payable.................	455.70	
	CPP (or QPP) Payable....................................	312.86	
	Cash..		929.36
	To record the remittance of payroll liabilities to the Receiver General for Canada.		

The entry to record remittance to the hospital insurance plan authority is then:

March 11	Employment Hospital Insurance Payable........	120.00	
	Cash..		120.00
	To record the remittance of employees' hospital insurance premiums.		

Notice that the payment of payroll liabilities is recorded in the same manner as payment of any other liabilities.

Accruing Payroll Deductions on Wages

Mandatory payroll deductions are levied *only on wages actually paid*. Accrued wages are not subject to payroll deductions until they are paid. However, to satisfy the matching principle, both accrued wages and the related accrued deductions should be recorded at the end of an accounting period. In reality, because the amounts of such deductions vary little from one accounting period to the next and often are small in amount, many employers apply the materiality principle and do not accrue payroll deductions.

 **CHECKPOINT**

7. When are the payments for employee deductions due to the Receiver General for Canada?

Do Quick Study questions: QS A-9, QS A-10

Employee (Fringe) Benefit Costs

LO4 Calculate and record employee fringe benefit costs.

Many companies pay for a variety of benefits called **employee fringe benefits** in addition to the wages earned by employees and the related amounts paid by the employer. For example, an employer may pay for part (or all) of the employees' medical insurance, life insurance, and disability insurance. Another typical employee benefit involves employer contributions to a retirement income plan. Workers' compensation and vacation pay are required to be paid by employers according to the legislation in each province.

Workers' Compensation

Legislation is in effect in all provinces for payments to employees for an injury or disability arising out of or in the course of their employment. Under the provincial workers' compensation acts, employers are required to insure their employees against injury or disability that may arise as a result of employment. Premiums are normally based on (1) accident experience of the industrial classification to which each business is assigned and (2) the total payroll.

Procedures for payment are as follows:

1. At the beginning of each year, every covered employer is required to submit to the Workers' Compensation Board[5] an estimate of the expected payroll for the coming year.

2. Provisional premiums are then established by the board relating estimated requirements for disability payments to estimated payroll. Provisional premium notices are then sent to all employers.

3. Provisional premiums are normally payable in three to six installments during the year.

4. At the end of each year, actual payrolls are submitted to the board, and final assessments are made based on actual payrolls and actual payments. Premiums are normally between 1% and 3% of gross payroll and are borne by the employer.

Employer Contributions to Employee Insurance and Retirement Plans

The entries to record employee benefits costs depend on the nature of the benefit. Some employee retirement plans are quite complicated and involve accounting procedures that are too complex for discussion in this introductory course. In other cases, however, the employer simply makes periodic cash contributions to a retirement fund for each employee and records the amounts contributed as expense. Other employee benefits that require periodic cash payments by the employer include employer payments of insurance premiums for employees.

In the case of employee benefits that simply require the employer to make periodic cash payments, the entries to record the employer's obligations are similar to those used for payroll deductions.[6] For example, assume that an employer with five employees has agreed to pay medical insurance premiums of $40 per month for each employee. The employer will also contribute 10% of each employee's salary to a retirement program. If each employee earns $2,500 per month, the entry to record these employee benefits for the month of March is:

March 31	Benefits Expense...	1,450	
	Employees' Medical		
	Insurance Payable		200
	Employees' Retirement Program		
	Payable..		1,250
	To record employee benefits;		
	($2,500 × 5) × 10% = $1,250.		

---

5 In Ontario, the Workers' Compensation Board is called the Workplace Safety and Insurance Board (WSIB). In BC, it is called WorkSafeBC.

6 Some payments of employee benefits must be added to the gross salary of the employee for the purpose of calculating income tax, CPP, and EI payroll deductions. However, in this chapter and in the problems at the end of the chapter, the possible effect of employee benefit costs on payroll taxes is ignored to avoid undue complexity in the introductory course.

Vacation Pay

Employers are required to allow their employees paid vacation time (at a minimum rate of 4% of gross earnings) as a benefit of employment. For example, many employees receive two weeks' vacation in return for working 50 weeks each year. The effect of a two-week vacation is to increase the employer's payroll expenses by 4% (2/50 = 0.04). After five years of service, most employees are entitled to a three-week vacation (i.e., 3/49 = 6.12%). However, new employees often do not begin to accrue vacation time until after they have worked for a period of time, perhaps as much as a year. The employment contract may say that no vacation is granted until the employee works one year, but if the first year is completed, the employee receives the full two weeks. Contracts between the employer and employee may allow for vacation pay in excess of the 4% minimum.

To account for vacation pay, an employer should estimate and record the additional expense during the weeks the employees are working and earning the vacation time. For example, assume that a company with a weekly payroll of $20,000 grants two weeks' vacation after one year's employment. The entry to record the estimated vacation pay is:

Date	Benefits Expense..	800	
	Estimated Vacation Pay Liability..............		800
	To record estimated vacation pay;		
	$20,000 × 0.04 = $800.		

As employees take their vacations and receive their vacation pay, the entries to record the vacation payroll take the following general form:

Date	Estimated Vacation Pay Liability	xxx	
	EI and CPP (or QPP) Payable		xxx
	Employees' Income Taxes Payable		xxx
	Other Withholding Liability Accounts		
	Such as Employees' Hospital		
	Insurance Payable		xxx
	Salaries Payable		xxx
	To record payroll.		

Mandatory payroll deductions and employee benefits costs are often a major category of expense incurred by a company. They may amount to well over 25% of the salaries earned by employees.

CHECKPOINT

8. How is the cost of Workers' Compensation determined?

Do Quick Study question: QS AI-11

CRITICAL THINKING CHALLENGE

Refer to the Critical Thinking Challenge question at the beginning of the appendix. Compare your answers to those suggested on Connect.

Summary

LO1 Identify the taxes and other items frequently withheld from employees' wages. Amounts withheld from employees' wages include federal income taxes, Canada (or Quebec) Pension Plan (CPP or QPP), and Employment Insurance (EI). Payroll costs levied on employers include EI and CPP (or QPP).

An employee's gross pay may be the employee's specified wage rate multiplied by the total hours worked plus an overtime premium rate multiplied by the number of overtime hours worked. Alternatively, it may be the given periodic salary of the employee. Taxes withheld and other deductions for items such as union dues, insurance premiums, and charitable contributions are subtracted from gross pay to determine the net pay.

LO2 Make the calculations necessary to prepare a payroll register and prepare the entries to record and pay payroll liabilities. A payroll register is used to summarize all employees' hours worked, regular and overtime pay, payroll deductions, net pay, and distribution of gross pay to expense accounts during each pay period. It provides the necessary information for journal entries to record the accrued payroll and to pay the employees.

LO3 Calculate the payroll costs levied on employers and prepare the entries to record the accrual and payment of these amounts. When a payroll is accrued at the end of each pay period, payroll deductions and levies should also be accrued with debits and credits to the appropriate expense and liability accounts.

LO4 Calculate and record employee fringe benefit costs. Fringe benefit costs that involve simple cash payments by the employer should be accrued with an entry similar to the one used to accrue payroll levies. Legislated employee benefits related to Workers' Compensation and vacation pay are paid for by the employer.

Guidance Answer to DECISION MAKER

Landscape Maintenance Technician

You need to be concerned about being an accomplice to unlawful payroll activities. Not paying federal and provincial taxes on wages earned is unlawful and unethical. Such payments won't provide CPP and EI contributions.

The best course of action is to request payment by cheque. If this fails to change the owner's payment practices, you must consider quitting this job.

Guidance Answers to CHECKPOINT

1. Employment Insurance is designed to alleviate hardships caused by interruptions in earnings through unemployment.

2. On or before the last day in February.

3. Deductions for Canada Savings Bonds, health or life insurance premiums, loan repayments, and donations to charitable organizations.

4. Regular pay plus overtime pay.

5. Gross pay less all the deductions.

6. An employee's individual earnings record serves as a basis for the employer's tax returns, indicates when the maximum CPP (or QPP) and EI deductions have been reached, and supplies the data for the employees' T-4 slips.

7. Normally by the 15th of the following month; large employers must remit on the 10th and 25th of each month.

8. Premiums are based on the accident experience in the specific industry and on the size of the employer's payroll.

DEMONSTRATION PROBLEM

Presented below are various items of information for three part-time employees of the Saskatchewan Consulting Company for the week ending March 30, 2015.

	Billings	Dephir	Singe
Wage rate (per hour)	$ 75.00	$ 60.00	$ 18.00
Overtime premium (when >40 hours).........	50%	50%	50%
Annual vacation	2.5 weeks	2.5 weeks	2.5 weeks
Cumulative wages as of March 30, 2015:....................................	$28,500.00	$52,600.00	$10,800.00
For the week (pay period) ended March 30, 2015:			
Hours worked......................................	8	22	48
Medical insurance:			
Employer's contribution	$ 25.00	$ 25.00	$ 25.00
Withheld from employee.................	18.00	18.00	18.00
Union dues withheld	50.00	70.00	50.00
Income tax withheld............................	77.80	298.35	165.80
Employment Insurance withheld	10.98	—	17.18
Canada Pension withheld....................	26.37	—	43.00
Payroll deduction rates:			
Employment Insurance	1.88% to an annual maximum of $930.60		
Canada Pension Plan............................	4.95% less annual exemption of $3,500; maximum per year is $2,479.95		

Required

In solving the following requirements, round all amounts to the nearest whole penny. Prepare schedules that determine, for each employee and for all employees combined, the following information:

1. Wages earned for the week, total overtime pay (if any), and gross wages.

2. Vacation pay accrued for the week.

3. Costs imposed on the employer.

4. Employees' net pay for the week.

5. Employer's total payroll-related cost (wages, mandatory deductions, and fringe benefits).

Present journal entries to record the following:

6. Payroll expense.

7. Payroll deductions and employees' benefits expense.

8. Remittance to the Receiver General for Canada on April 15.

Analysis Component:

What percentage of the total payroll-related cost to the employer represents deductions and fringe benefits versus gross pay? Round your answers to two decimal places.

Planning the Solution

- Calculate the gross pay for each employee.
- Calculate the amounts deducted for all employees and their net pay.
- Calculate the employer's share of payroll deductions.
- Prepare the necessary journal entries.
- Address the analysis component.

Solution

1. The gross wages (including overtime) for the week:

	Billings	Dephir	Singe	Total
Regular wage rate	$ 75.00	$ 60.00	$ 18.00	
Regular hours	× 8	× 22	× 48	
Regular pay	$600.00	$1,320.00	$864.00	$2,784.00
Overtime premium	$ 37.50	$ 30.00	$ 9.00	
Overtime hours	-0-	× -0-	× 8	
Total overtime pay	$ -0-	$ -0-	$ 72.00	$ 72.00
Gross wages	$600.00	$1,320.00	$936.00	$2,856.00

2. The vacation pay accrued for the week:

	Billings	Dephir	Singe	Total
Annual vacation	2.5 weeks	2.5 weeks	2.5 weeks	
Weeks worked in year	49.5 weeks	49.5 weeks	49.5 weeks	
Vacation pay as a percentage of regular pay	5.05%	5.05%	5.05%	
Regular pay this week	× $600.00	× $1,320.00	× $936.00	
Vacation pay this week	$ 30.30	$ 66.66	$ 47.27	$144.23

The information in the following table is needed for part 3:

			Earnings Subject to	
Employees	Earnings Through March 30	Earnings This Week	CPP	Employment Insurance
Billings	$28,500.00	$ 600.00	$ 532.69[3]	$ 600.00
Dephir[1]	52,600.00	1,320.00	—	—
Singe[2]	10,800.00	936.00	868.69[3]	936.00
Totals		$2,856.00	$1,402.00	$1,536.00

[1]Dephir's earnings have exceeded the CPP maximum of $53,600 and EI maximum of $45,900 and the maximum deductions of $2,479.95 (CPP) and $930.60 (EI). Therefore, neither CPP nor EI is deducted.

[2]Deductions would cease when the yearly maximum deduction of $930.60 was reached.

[3]Recall that the first $3,500 of income is exempt from CPP. This represents $67.31/week (= $3,500/52 weeks).

3. The costs imposed on the employer.

	Billings	Dephir	Singe	Total
CPP (1.0)	$26.37	—	$43.00	$ 69.37
Employment Insurance (1.4)...................	15.79	—	24.63	40.42
Totals..	$42.16	—	$67.63	$109.79

4. The net amount paid to the employees:

	Billings	Dephir	Singe	Total
Regular pay..	$600.00	$1,320.00	$864.00	$2,784.00
Overtime pay...	-0-	-0-	72.00	72.00
Gross pay	$600.00	$1,320.00	$936.00	$2,856.00
Withholdings:				
Income tax withholding.........................	$ 77.80	$ 298.35	$165.80	$ 541.95
CPP withholding................................	26.37	—	43.00	69.37
EI withholding....................................	11.28	—	17.60	28.88
Medical insurance	18.00	18.00	18.00	54.00
Union dues	50.00	70.00	50.00	170.00
Total withholdings	$183.45	$ 386.35	$294.40	$ 864.20
Net pay to employees...........................	$416.55	$ 933.65	$641.60	$1,991.80

5. The total payroll-related cost to the employer.

	Billings	Dephir	Singe	Total
Regular pay...	$600.00	$1,320.00	$ 864.00	$2,784.00
Overtime pay...	-0-	-0-	72.00	72.00
Gross pay	$600.00	$1,320.00	$ 936.00	$2,856.00
Deductions and fringe benefits:				
CPP	$ 26.37	$ —	$ 43.00	$ 69.37
EI	15.79	—	24.63	40.42
Vacation...	30.30	66.66	47.27	144.23
Medical insurance................................	25.00	25.00	25.00	75.00
Total deductions and fringe benefits......	$ 97.76	$ 91.66	$ 139.90	$ 329.02
Total payroll-related cost	$697.76	$1,411.66	$1,075.90	$3,185.02

6. Journal entry for payroll expense:

2015				
March 27	Salary Expense		2,856.00	
	Employees' Income Taxes Payable			541.95
	CPP Payable			69.37
	EI Payable			28.88
	Employees' Medical Insurance Payable ...			54.00
	Employees' Union Dues Payable			170.00
	Salaries Payable.....................................			1,991.80
	To record payroll expense.			

7. Journal entry for payroll deductions and employees' benefit expense:

2015				
March	27	CPP Expense	69.37	
		EI Expense	40.42	
		Benefits Expense	219.23	
		CPP Payable		69.37
		EI Payable		39.42
		Accrued Vacation Pay Payable		144.23
		Employees' Medical Insurance Payable		75.00

To record employer's share of payroll deductions and benefits expense.

8. Journal entry to record the remittance to the Receiver General for Canada:

2015				
Apr.	15	EI Payable[1]	69.30	
		CPP Payable[2]	138.74	
		Employees' Income Taxes Payable	541.95	
		Cash		749.99

Calculations:

1. $28.88 (Employees' Portion) + $40.42 (Employer's Portion) = $69.30
2. $69.37 (Employees' Portion) + $69.37 (Employer's Portion) = $138.74

Analysis Component:

Deductions and fringe benefits represent 10.30% (= $328.02/$3,184.02) of total payroll-related costs, and gross pay is 89.70% (= $2,856.00/$3,184.02).

Glossary

Canada Pension Plan A national contributory retirement pension scheme.

Employee fringe benefits Payments by an employer, in addition to wages and salaries, that are made to acquire employee benefits such as insurance coverage and retirement income.

Employee's gross pay The amount an employee earns before any deductions for taxes or other items such as union dues or insurance premiums.

Employee's individual earnings record A record of an employee's hours worked, gross pay, deductions, net pay, and certain personal information about the employee.

Employee's net pay The amount an employee is paid, determined by subtracting from gross pay all deductions for taxes and other items that are withheld from the employee's earnings.

Employment Insurance An employee/employer–financed unemployment insurance plan.

Payroll deductions Amounts deducted from an employee's pay, usually based on the amount of an employee's gross pay.

Personal tax credits Amounts that may be deducted from an individual's income taxes and that determine the amount of income taxes to be withheld.

TD1 A form, known as the Personal Tax Credit Return, that determines how much income tax is to be withheld by the employer based on the employee's exemptions.

Wage bracket withholding table A table showing the amounts to be withheld from employees' wages at various levels of earnings.

Concept Review Questions

1. Who pays the contributions to the Canada Pension Plan?

2. Who pays premiums under the Workers' Compensation laws?

3. Who pays federal Employment Insurance? What is the rate?

4. What are the objectives of Employment Insurance laws?

5. To whom and when are payroll deductions remitted?

6. What determines the amount that must be deducted from an employee's wages for income taxes?

7. What is a tax withholding table?

8. What is the Canada Pension Plan deduction rate for self-employed individuals?

9. What information is accumulated on an employee's individual earnings record? Why must this information be accumulated? For what purposes is the information used?

10. What payroll charges are levied on the employer? What amounts are deducted from the wages of an employee?

11. What are employee fringe benefits? Name some examples.

Note: For consistency, assume all companies used in the questions are based in Saskatchewan. All questions making use of tax tables in this appendix will be based on Saskatchewan's tables.

Quick Study

QS AI-1 **Payroll expenses** L01

A company deducts $260 in Employment Insurance and $205 in Canada Pension from the weekly payroll of its employees. How much is the company's expense for these items for the week?

QS AI-2 **Preparing payroll journal entries** L02

Trax Ltd. has six employees, each of whom earns $3,000 per month. Income taxes are 20% of gross pay and the company deducts EI and CPP. Prepare the March 31 journal entry to record payroll for the month.

QS AI-3 **Paying employees** L02

Use the information in QS AI-2 to record the payment of the wages to the employees for March.

QS AI-4 **Completing a payroll register** L02 e**X**cel

		Deductions			Pay		Distribution	
Employee	Gross Pay	EI Premium	Income Taxes	CPP	Total Deductions	Net Pay	Office Salaries	Sales Salaries
Johnson, S.	1,200.00	22.56	256.35	56.07				
Waverley, N.	530.00	9.96	60.05	22.90				
Zender, B.	675.00	12.69	95.40	30.08				
Totals	2,405.00	45.21	411.80	109.05				

Required Prairie Rigging's three employees are paid weekly. Waverley works in the office and Johnson and Zender are sales representatives. Complete the payroll register above for the week ended March 9, 2015.

QS AI-5 Completing a payroll register using tables LO2 e**X**cel

		Deductions					Pay	
Employee	Gross Pay	EI Premium	Income Taxes	CPP	Total Deductions	Net Pay	Salaries Expense
Bentley, A.	2,010.00						
Craig, T.	2,115.00						
Totals	4,125.00						

Required Meadow Lake Groceries has two employees who are paid monthly. Using the payroll deduction tables at the end of the appendix, complete the payroll register above for the month ended March 31, 2015, assuming both employees' TD1 claim code is 1. For the complete CPP, EI, and federal and provincial tax deduction tables, please go to Connect.

QS AI-6 Completing a payroll register by calculating deductions LO2 e**X**cel

		Deductions				Pay	Distribution	
Employee	Gross Pay	EI Premium	Income Taxes	CPP	Total Deductions	Net Pay	Office Salaries	Sales Salaries
Withers, S.	2,500.00						2,500.00	
Volt, C.	1,800.00							1,800.00
Totals								

Required Maidstone Plumbing Services' two employees are paid biweekly. Assuming a tax rate of 30%, complete the payroll register above for the two-week period ended February 24, 2015.

QS AI-7 Payroll journal entry LO2

Games Co. has eight employees, each of whom earns $3,500 per month. Income taxes are 20% of gross pay and the company deducts EI and CPP. Prepare the March 31, 2015, journal entry to record Games Co.'s salaries expenses for the month.

QS AI-8 Payroll journal entry LO2

Chandler Tailors pays its three part-time employees monthly. The following information is available for the February 2015 payroll:

		Deductions				Pay	Distribution	
Employee	Gross Pay	EI Premium	Income Taxes	CPP	Total Deductions	Net Pay	Office Salaries	Sales Salaries
Berkley, M.	575.00	10.81	0.00	14.03	24.84	550.16	575.00	
Chandler, O.	840.00	15.79	0.00	27.14	42.93	797.07		840.00
Meister, P.	1,020.00	19.18	0.00	36.05	55.23	964.77		1,020.00
Totals	2,435.00	45.78	0.00	77.22	123.00	2,312.00	575.00	1,860.00

Required Prepare the journal entry to record payroll expenses for the month.

QS AI-9 Recording employer's payroll deductions LO3

Refer to the information in QS AI-8. Prepare a journal entry to record Chandler Tailors' share of payroll deductions.

QS AI-10 Payment of payroll deductions LO3

Refer to the information in QS AI-8 and QS AI-9. Prepare a journal entry to record payment by Chandler Tailors to the Receiver General for Canada on March 15.

QS AI-11 Recording fringe benefit costs LO4

Games Co. (see QS AI-7) contributes 8% of an employee's salary to a retirement program, pays medical insurance premiums of $60 per employee, and pays vacation allowance equivalent to 5% of the employee's salary. Prepare a journal entry to record the fringe benefit costs for March.

Exercises

Exercise AI-1 **Calculating gross and net pay** LO2

CHECK FIGURE: Net pay = $1,844.27

Julie Leung, an employee of the Import Company, worked 172 hours during the month of January 2015. Her pay rate is $12.50 per hour, and her wages are subject to no deductions other than income taxes, EI, and CPP. The overtime premium is 50% and is applicable to any time greater than 160 hours per month. Calculate her regular pay, overtime premium pay, gross pay, total deductions, and net pay (assume claim code 1). For the complete CPP, EI, and federal and provincial tax deduction tables, please go to Connect.

Exercise AI-2 **Calculating payroll deductions and recording the payroll** LO2 e**X**cel

CHECK FIGURE: Total EI withholding = $72.57

The following information as to earnings and deductions for the weekly pay period ended March 9 was taken from a company's payroll records:

Employees' Names	Weekly Gross Pay	Earnings to End of Previous Week	Income Taxes	Health Insurance Deductions
Hellen Craig	$ 720	$12,510	$106.20	$ 24.00
Joseph Lim............	610	10,320	79.70	24.00
Dino Patelli............	830	15,500	132.25	36.00
Sharleen McFee.....	1,700	29,500	432.55	24.00
	$3,860		$750.70	$108.00

Required Calculate the amounts paid to each employee, and the employees' EI and CPP withholdings, and prepare a general journal entry to record the payroll. Assume all employees work in the office.

Exercise AI-3 Completing a payroll register LO2 e**X**cel

CHECK FIGURE: Total deductions = $2,479.53

Lendrum Servicing's four employees are paid every two weeks. Atkins runs the office and the remaining employees are sales representatives.

		Deductions				Pay		Distribution	
Employee	Gross Pay	EI Premium	Income Taxes	United Way	CPP	Total Deductions	Net Pay	Admin. Salaries	Sales Salaries
Atkins, D.	1,900.00	35.72	338.55	80.00	87.39				
Nesbitt, M.	1,260.00	23.69	167.75	50.00	55.71				
Trent, F.	1,680.00	31.58	272.00	40.00	76.50				
Vallot, M.	3,000.00	56.40	722.40	300.00	141.84				
Totals	7,840.00	147.39	1,500.70	470.00	361.44				

Required Complete the payroll register above for the biweekly period ended March 16, 2015.

Exercise AI-4 Completing a payroll register using tables LO2

CHECK FIGURE: Total EI premiums = $156.32 e**X**cel

D&D Stockyards' four employees are paid monthly. Each employee donates 5% of gross pay to United Way through payroll deductions. Crimson and Peterson purchase Canada Savings Bonds through monthly payroll deductions of $150 and $200 respectively.

		Deductions					Pay		Distribution	
Employee	Gross Pay	EI Premium	Income Taxes	Canada Saving Bonds	CPP	United way	Total Deductions	Net Pay	Office Salaries	Sales Salaries
Crimson, L.	1,995.00								1,995.00	
Long, M.	2,040.00									2,040.00
Morris, P.	2,000.00									2,000.00
Peterson, B.	2,280.00									2,280.00
Totals										

Required Using the payroll tables, complete the payroll register above for the monthly pay period ended February 29, 2015, assuming the following TD1 claim codes for each employee: Crimson (2), Long (1), Morris (1), and Peterson (3). For the complete CPP, EI, and federal and provincial tax deduction tables, please go to Connect.

Exercise AI-5 Completing a payroll register by calculating deductions LO2 e**X**cel

CHECK FIGURE: Total deductions = $1,556.83

		Deductions					Pay		Distribution	
Employee	Gross Pay	EI Premium	Income Taxes	Medical Ins.	CPP	United way	Total Deductions	Net Pay	Office Salaries	Guide Salaries
Wynn, L.	1,200.00			65.00		40.00				1,200.00
Short, M.	950.00			65.00		100.00			950.00	
Pearl, P.	1,150.00			65.00		-0-				1,150.00
Quincy, B.	875.00			65.00		50.00				875.00
Totals										

Required Piperel Lake Resort's four employees are paid weekly. Assume an income tax rate of 20%. Complete the payroll register above for the month ended January 31, 2015.

Exercise AI-6 Other payroll deductions LO2

CHECK FIGURE: Monthly United Way contribution = $34.50

Sharon Von Hatton is the only employee of a self-employed businessperson. She earned a monthly salary of $2,050 in February 2015, her first month of employment. In response to a citywide effort to obtain charitable contributions to the local United Way programs, Von Hatton has requested that her employer withhold 2% of her salary (after CPP, EI, and income taxes have been deducted).

Required Prepare the journal entry to record payroll expenses for the month of February 2015. Use the tables to determine CPP, EI, and income tax deductions (assume claim code 1). For the complete CPP, EI, and federal and provincial tax deduction tables, please go to Connect.

Exercise AI-7 Payroll journal entry LO2

Paradise Hills Berry Farm has 25 employees who are paid biweekly. The payroll register showed the following payroll deductions for the pay period ending March 23, 2015.

Gross Pay	EI Premium	Income Taxes	CPP	Medical Ins.	United Way
65,950.00	1,207.00	9,095.00	3,097.93	1,150.00	1,319.00

Required Using the information provided, prepare the journal entry to record the payroll expenses.

Exercise AI-8 Recording employer's payroll deductions LO3

Refer to the information in Exercise AI-7. Prepare a journal entry to record the employer's share of payroll deductions.

Exercise AI-9 Payment of payroll deductions LO3

Refer to the information in Exercise AI-7 and Exercise AI-8. Prepare a journal entry to record payment by the employer to the Receiver General for Canada on April 15.

Exercise AI-10 Calculating and recording payroll deductions LO3,4

Use the information provided in Exercise AI-2 to complete the following requirements:

1. Prepare a general journal entry to record the employer's payroll costs resulting from the payroll.
2. Prepare a general journal entry to record the following employee benefits incurred by the company: (a) health insurance costs equal to the amounts contributed by each employee and (b) contributions equal to 10% of gross pay for each employee's retirement income program.

Exercise AI-11 Analyzing total labour costs LO2,3,4

CHECK FIGURE: Total CPP contributions = $12,092.85

O'Riley Company's payroll costs and fringe benefit expenses include the normal CPP and EI contributions, retirement fund contributions of 10% of total earnings, and health insurance premiums of $120 per employee per month. Given the following list of employees' projected 2015 annual salaries, payroll costs and fringe benefits are what percentage of salaries?

Doherty	$ 52,000
Fane	61,000
Kahan	59,000
Martin	49,000
Leung	76,000
Total	$297,000

Exercise AI-12 Calculating and recording payroll costs (using tables) LO2,3,4

Milly's Drive-In's 12 employees earn a gross pay of $2,050 each per month. Milly's Drive-In contributes 8% of gross pay to a retirement program for employees and pays an extended–medical insurance premium of $50 per month per employee.

Required Prepare the entries to record the employer's payroll costs for the month of March 2015. Use the payroll tables to determine CPP, EI, and income tax deductions (assume claim code 1). For the complete CPP, EI, and federal and provincial tax deduction tables, please go to Connect.

Exercise AI-13 Calculating fringe benefits costs LO4

Bellward Company grants vacation time of two weeks to those employees who have worked for the company one complete year. After 10 years of service, employees receive four weeks of vacation. The monthly payroll for January totals $320,000, of which 70% is payable to employees with 10 or more years of service. On January 31, record the January expense arising from the vacation policy of the company. Round calculations to the nearest whole dollar.

Problems

Problem AI-1A Payroll register and payroll deductions LO2,3

CHECK FIGURE: Total deductions = $2,298.42

The payroll records of Brownlee Company provided the following information for the weekly pay period ended March 23, 2015:

												Earnings to End of
	Employee	Daily Time							Pay	Hospital	Union	Previous
Employees	No.	M	T	W	T	F	S	S	Rate	Insurance	Dues	Week
Ray Loran	11	8	8	8	8	8	4	0	40.00	40.00	16.00	43,000
Kathy Sousa	12	7	8	6	7	8	4	0	36.00	40.00	15.00	46,000
Gary Smith	13	8	8	0	8	8	4	4	32.00	40.00	14.00	21,000
Nicole Parton	14	8	8	8	8	8	0	0	40.00	40.00	16.00	32,000
Diana Wood	15	0	6	6	6	6	8	8	36.00	40.00	15.00	36,000
Totals										200.00	76.00	

Payroll Week Ended March 23, 2015

Required

1. Enter the relevant information in the proper columns of a payroll register and complete the register; calculate CPP and EI deductions. Charge the wages of Kathy Sousa to Office Wages Expense

and the wages of the remaining employees to Service Wages Expense. Calculate income tax deductions at 20% of gross pay. Employees are paid an overtime premium of 50% for all hours in excess of 40 per week.

2. Prepare general journal entries to record the payroll register information, including the employer's expenses.

Problem AI-2A Payroll register and journal entries LO2,3

On January 13, at the end of the second weekly pay period of the year, a company's payroll register showed that its 30 employees had earned $19,570 of sales salaries and $6,230 of office salaries. Assume withholdings from the employees' salaries were to include $446.34 of EI, $1,177.14 of CPP, $5,310 of income taxes, $930 of hospital insurance, and $420 of union dues.

Required

1. Prepare the general journal entry to record the January 13 payroll.

2. Prepare a general journal entry to record the employer's payroll expenses resulting from the January 13 payroll.

Problem AI-3A Journal entries—payroll taxes, and employee fringe benefits LO2,3,4

A company showed the following information in its payroll register for the week ended March 16, 2015:

		Deductions						Pay	Distribution	
EI Premium	Income Taxes	Medical Insurance	CPP	Union Dues	Total Deductions	Net Pay	Sales Salaries Expense	Office Salaries Expense	Shop Salaries Expense
22.56	256.35	47.50	56.07	90.00	472.48	727.52	1,200.00		
26.32	326.25	52.50	65.97	105.00	576.04	823.96			1,400.00
31.96	432.55	25.00	80.82	127.50	697.83	1,002.17			1,700.00
19.74	205.15	35.00	48.64	78.75	387.28	662.72		1,050.00	
100.58	**1,220.30**	**160.00**	**251.50**	**401.25**	**2,133.63**	**3,216.37**	**1,200.00**	**1,050.00**	**3,100.00**

1. Prepare a general journal entry to record the payroll register information.

2. Prepare a general journal entry to record the employer's payroll expenses resulting from the payroll.

3. Prepare general journal entries to accrue employee fringe benefit costs for the week. Assume that the company matches the employees' payments for medical insurance and contributes an amount equal to 8% of each employee's gross pay to a retirement program. Also, each employee accrues vacation pay at the rate of 6% of the wages and salaries earned. The company estimates that all employees eventually will be paid their vacation pay.

Problem AI-4A Journal entries for payroll transactions LO2,3,4

A company has three employees, each of whom has been employed since January 1, earns $2,600 per month, and is paid on the last day of each month. On March 1, the following accounts and balances appeared in its ledger.

    a. Employees' Income Taxes Payable, $1,006.05 (liability for February).

    b. EI Payable, $351.94 (liability for February).

    c. CPP Payable, $685.56 (liability for February).

    d. Employees' Medical Insurance Payable, $1,560.00 (liability for January and February).

During March and April, the company completed the following related to payroll.

Mar.   17   Issued cheque #320 payable to the Receiver General for Canada. The cheque was in payment of the February employee income taxes, EI, and CPP amounts due.

31   Prepared a general journal entry to record the March payroll register, which had the following column totals:

EI	Income Taxes	CPP	Medical Insurance	Total Deductions	Net Pay	Office Salaries	Shop Salaries
$146.64	$1,006.05	$342.78	$390.00	$1,885.47	$5,914.53	$2,600	$5,200

31   Recorded the employer's $390.00 liability for its 50% contribution to the medical insurance plan of employees and 6% vacation pay accrued to the employees.

31   Prepared a general journal entry to record the employer's costs resulting from the March payroll.

Apr.   17   Issued cheque #375 payable to the Receiver General for Canada in payment of the March mandatory deductions.

17   Issued cheque #376 payable to All Canadian Insurance Company in payment of the employee medical insurance premiums for the first quarter.

Required Prepare the entries to record the transactions.

Alternate Problems

Problem AI-1B   Payroll register and payroll deductions LO2,3

CHECK FIGURE: Total deductions = $2,003.83

The payroll records of Wailee Company provided the following information for the weekly pay period ended March 23, 2015:

												Payroll Week Ended March 23, 2015	
Employees	Employee No.	M	T	W	T	F	S	S	Pay Rate	Hospital Insurance	Union Dues	Earnings to End of Previous Week	
Ben Amoko	31	8	8	8	8	8	0	0	34.00	30.00	12.00	43,000	
Auleen Carson	32	7	8	8	7	8	4	0	36.00	30.00	12.00	42,100	
Mark Cheng	33	8	8	0	8	8	4	4	36.00	30.00	12.00	28,000	
Gene Deszca	34	8	8	8	8	8	0	0	30.00	30.00	12.00	32,000	
Ysong Tan	35	0	6	6	6	6	8	8	30.00	30.00	12.00	36,000	
Totals										150.00	60.00		

Required

1. Enter the relevant information in the proper columns of a payroll register and complete the register; calculate CPP and EI deductions. Charge the wages of Auleen Carson to Office Wages Expense and the wages of the remaining employees to Service Wages Expense. Calculate income tax deductions at 20% of gross pay. Employees are paid an overtime premium of 50% for all hours in excess of 40 per week.

2. Prepare general journal entries to record the payroll register information, including the employer's expenses.

Problem AI-2B Payroll register and journal entries LO2,3

On January 13, at the end of the second weekly pay period of the year, a company's payroll register showed that its 45 employees had earned $23,400 of sales salaries and $5,820 of office salaries. Assume withholdings from the employees' salaries were to include $505.51 of EI, $1,296.46 of CPP, $6,180 of income taxes, $920 of hospital insurance, and $490 of union dues.

Required

1. Prepare the general journal entry to record the January 13 payroll.

2. Prepare a general journal entry to record the employer's payroll expenses resulting from the January 13 payroll.

Problem AI-3B Journal entries—payroll taxes, and employee fringe benefits LO2,3,4

A company showed the following information in its payroll register for the week ended March 16, 2015:

			Deductions						Pay	Distribution	
EI Premium	Income Taxes	Medical Insurance	CPP	Union Dues	Total Deductions	Net Pay	Sales Salaries Expense	Office Salaries Expense	Shop Salaries Expense
27.26	344.60	47.50	68.44	90.00	577.80	872.20	1,450.00		
37.22	539.95	52.50	94.68	105.00	829.35	1,150.65			1,980.00
33.09	452.60	25.00	83.79	127.50	721.98	1,038.02			1,760.00
32.34	439.30	35.00	81.81	78.75	667.19	1,052.81		1,720.00	
129.91	**1776.45**	**160.00**	**328.72**	**401.25**	**2,796.33**	**4,113.67**	**1,450.00**	**1,720.00**	**3,740.00**

1. Prepare a general journal entry to record the payroll register information.

2. Prepare a general journal entry to record the employer's payroll expenses resulting from the payroll.

3. Prepare general journal entries to accrue employee fringe benefit costs for the week. Assume that the company matches the employees' payments for medical insurance and contributes an amount equal to 8% of each employee's gross pay to a retirement program. Also, each employee accrues vacation pay at the rate of 6% of the wages and salaries earned. The company estimates that all employees eventually will be paid their vacation pay.

Problem AI-4B Journal entries for payroll transactions LO2,3,4

A company has three employees, each of whom has been employed since January 1, earns $3,000 per month, and is paid on the last day of each month. On March 1, the following accounts and balances appeared in its ledger.

  a. Employees' Income Taxes Payable, $1,298.25 (liability for February).

  b. EI Payable, $406.08 (liability for February).

  c. CPP Payable, $804.36 (liability for February).

  d. Employees' Medical Insurance Payable, $1,380.00 (liability for January and February).

During March and April, the company completed the following related to payroll:

Mar.	17	Issued cheque #635 payable to the Receiver General for Canada. The cheque was in payment of the February employee income taxes, EI, and CPP amounts due.
	31	Prepared a general journal entry to record the March payroll register, which had the following column totals:

EI	Income Taxes	CPP	Medical Insurance	Total Deductions	Net Pay	Office Salaries	Shop Salaries
$169.20	$1,298.25	$402.18	$345.00	$2,214.63	$6,785.37	$3,000	$6,000

	31	Recorded the employer's $345.00 liability for its 50% contribution to the medical insurance plan of employees and 6% vacation pay accrued to the employees.
	31	Prepared a general journal entry to record the employer's payroll costs resulting from the March payroll.
Apr.	14	Issued cheque #764 payable to the Receiver General for Canada in payment of the March mandatory deductions.
	14	Issued cheque #765 payable to National Insurance Company in payment of the employee medical insurance premiums for the first quarter.

Required Prepare the entries to record the transactions.

Analytical and Review Problems

A & R Problem AI-1

Using the current year's withholding tables for Canada Pension Plan, Employment Insurance, and income tax, update the payroll register of Exhibit A.2. In calculating income tax withholdings, state your assumption as to each employee's personal deductions. Assume that hospital insurance deductions continue at the same amounts as in Exhibit A.2.

A & R Problem AI-2

The following data were taken from the payroll register of Eastcoastal Company:

Gross Salary	xxx
Employees' Income Tax Deductions	xxx
EI Deductions	xxx
CPP Deductions	xxx
Hospital Insurance Deductions	xxx
Union Dues Deductions	xxx

Eastcoastal contributes an equal amount to the hospital insurance plan, in addition to the statutory payroll taxes, and 6% of the gross salaries to a pension retirement program.

Required Record in general journal form the payroll, payment of the employees, and remittance to the appropriate persons amounts owing in connection with the payroll. (Note: All amounts are to be indicated as xxx.)

Ethics Challenge

EC AI-1

Moe Daljit is the accountant for Valley Sales Company, which is currently experiencing a cash shortage because its Pacific Rim customers have not been paying their accounts on a timely basis. The owner has been unable to arrange adequate bank financing to cover the cash shortage and has suggested that Moe delay sending the amounts withheld from employees to the Receiver General for Canada for a few months, "until things clear up." Then he adds, "After all, we will be sending the money to the Receiver General eventually."

Required

1. What are the company's responsibilities with respect to amounts withheld from employees' wages and salaries?

2. What are the ethical factors in this situation?

3. Would you recommend that Moe follow the owner's "suggestion"?

4. What alternatives might be available to the owner if Moe does not delay sending the amounts to the Receiver General for Canada?

Critical Thinking Mini Case

Delta Yard Maintenance offers a variety of services to its customers, including lawn and garden care, tree pruning, exterior painting, fence building/installation, eavestrough cleaning, snow removal, and other miscellaneous tasks. Delta employs five full-time salaried individuals and 15 to 20 part-time wage employees. During the year just ended, $194,392 was paid in cash to the part-time employees "under the table," meaning that cash was paid to the employees and no payroll deductions were withheld. The part-time wage employees would not have paid income tax on the cash received because Delta would not have issued T4 slips. To cover up these payments, Delta claimed $194,392 in various other expenses that were not supported by documentation. You have just been hired by Delta as one of the five full-time individuals—the office manager. One of your many duties will be to keep the accounting records, including payroll.

Required Using the elements of critical thinking described on the inside front cover, comment.

For the complete CPP, EI, and Federal and Provincial tax deduction tables, please click here or go to Connect.

Accounting Information Systems

The Accounting Information Systems Appendix can be accessed online through Connect.

Financial Statement Information

This appendix includes financial statement information from **Danier Leather Inc., WestJet Airlines Ltd., Indigo Books & Music Inc.,** and **Telus Corporation.** All of this information is taken from their annual reports. An **annual report** is a summary of the financial results of a company's operations for the year and its future plans. It is directed at external users of financial information, but also affects actions of internal users.

An annual report is also used by a company to showcase itself and its products. Many include attractive pictures, diagrams, and illustrations related to the company. But the *financial section* is its primary objective. This section communicates much information about a company, with most data drawn from the accounting information system.

The layout of the annual reports' financial sections that are included in this appendix for Danier and WestJet are:

- Management's report
- Auditor's report
- Financial statements
- Notes to financial statements

In addition, selected portions of the Indigo and Telus annual reports have also been incorporated. These include the following:

- Auditor's report
- Financial statements

There are questions at the end of each chapter that refer to information in this appendix. We encourage readers to spend extra time with these questions as they are especially useful in reinforcing and showing the relevance and diversity of financial reporting.

More current financial information about these and other Canadian corporations can be found online at www.sedar.com.

DANIER

ANNUAL REPORT 2014

MANAGEMENT'S RESPONSIBILITY FOR FINANCIAL STATEMENTS

The accompanying financial statements and other financial information contained in this Annual Report are the responsibility of management and have been approved by the Board of Directors of Danier Leather Inc. The financial statements have been prepared by management in conformity with International Financial Reporting Standards using management's best estimates and judgments based on currently available information, where appropriate. The financial information contained elsewhere in this Annual Report has been reviewed to ensure consistency with that in the financial statements.

Management is also responsible for a system of internal controls which is designed to provide reasonable assurance that assets are safeguarded, liabilities are recognized and that financial records are properly maintained to provide timely and accurate financial reports.

The Board of Directors is responsible for ensuring that management fulfills its responsibility in respect of financial reporting and internal control. The Audit Committee of the Board, which is comprised solely of unrelated and outside directors, meets regularly to review significant accounting and auditing matters with management and the independent auditors and to review the interim and annual financial statements.

The financial statements have been audited by PricewaterhouseCoopers LLP, the independent auditors, in accordance with Canadian generally accepted auditing standards on behalf of the shareholders. The Auditor's Report outlines the nature of their examination and their opinion on the financial statements. PricewaterhouseCoopers LLP have full and unrestricted access to the Audit Committee to discuss their audit and related findings as to the integrity of the financial reporting.

Jeffrey Wortsman
President and CEO

Bryan Tatoff, CPA, CA
Executive Vice-President, CFO and Secretary

INDEPENDENT AUDITOR'S REPORT TO SHAREHOLDERS

To the Shareholders of Danier Leather Inc.

We have audited the accompanying consolidated financial statements of Danier Leather Inc. and its subsidiaries, which comprise the consolidated balance sheets as at June 28, 2014 and June 29, 2013 and the consolidated statements of earnings (loss) and comprehensive earnings (loss), cash flow, and changes in shareholders' equity for the 52-week period ended June 28, 2014 and 52-week period ended June 29, 2013, and the related notes, which comprise a summary of the significant accounting policies and other explanatory information.

Management's responsibility for the consolidated financial statements
Management is responsible for the preparation and fair presentation of these consolidated financial statements in accordance with International Financial Reporting Standards, and for such internal control as management determines is necessary to enable the preparation of consolidated financial statements that are free from material misstatement, whether due to fraud or error.

Auditor's responsibility
Our responsibility is to express an opinion on these consolidated financial statements based on our audits. We conducted our audits in accordance with Canadian generally accepted auditing standards. Those standards require that we comply with ethical requirements and plan and perform the audits to obtain reasonable assurance about whether the consolidated financial statements are free from material misstatement.

An audit involves performing procedures to obtain audit evidence about the amounts and disclosures in the consolidated financial statements. The procedures selected depend on the auditor's judgment, including the assessment of the risks of material misstatement of the consolidated financial statements, whether due to fraud or error. In making those risk assessments, the auditor considers internal control relevant to the entity's preparation and fair presentation of the consolidated financial statements in order to design audit procedures that are appropriate in the circumstances, but not for the purpose of expressing an opinion on the effectiveness of the entity's internal control. An audit also includes evaluating the appropriateness of accounting policies used and the reasonableness of accounting estimates made by management, as well as evaluating the overall presentation of the consolidated financial statements.

We believe that the audit evidence we have obtained in our audits is sufficient and appropriate to provide a basis for our audit opinion.

Opinion
In our opinion, the consolidated financial statements present fairly, in all material respects, the financial position of Danier Leather Inc. and its subsidiaries as at June 28, 2014 and June 29, 2013 and their financial performance and their cash flows for the 52-week period ended June 28, 2014 and the 52-week period ended June 29, 2013 in accordance with International Financial Reporting Standards.

PricewaterhouseCoopers LLP

Chartered Professional Accountants, Licensed Public Accountants
Toronto, Ontario
August 13, 2014

CONSOLIDATED STATEMENTS OF EARNINGS (LOSS) & COMPREHENSIVE EARNINGS (LOSS)

(thousands of Canadian dollars, except per share amounts and number of shares)

	Years Ended	
	June 28, 2014	June 29, 2013
	52 weeks	52 weeks
Revenue	$141,930	$154,995
Cost of Sales (Note 13)	73,697	76,579
Gross profit	68,233	78,416
Selling, general and administrative expenses (Note 13)	79,086	76,620
Interest income	(118)	(236)
Interest expense	59	51
Earnings (loss) before income taxes	(10,794)	1,981
Provision for (recovery of) income taxes (Note 14)	(3,131)	570
Net earnings (loss) and comprehensive earnings	($7,663)	$1,411
Net earnings (loss) per share:		
Basic	($2.00)	$0.34
Diluted	($2.00)	$0.33
Weighted average number of shares outstanding:		
Basic	3,840,319	4,180,829
Diluted	3,948,336	4,323,619
Number of shares outstanding at period end	3,854,168	3,832,168

See accompanying notes to the consolidated financial statements

CONSOLIDATED BALANCE SHEETS

(thousands of Canadian dollars)

	June 28, 2014	June 29, 2013
Assets		
Current Assets		
Cash	$ 13,507	$ 24,541
Accounts receivable	638	1,197
Income taxes recoverable	3,461	358
Inventories (Note 5)	21,721	22,810
Prepaid expenses	643	803
	39,970	49,709
Non-current Assets		
Property and equipment (Note 6)	16,826	16,034
Computer software (Note 7)	1,459	1,143
Deferred income tax asset (Note 14)	2,374	2,163
	$ 60,629	$ 69,049
Liabilities		
Current Liabilities		
Payables and accruals (Note 9)	$ 9,185	$ 10,101
Deferred revenue	1,511	1,548
Sales return provision (Note 10)	94	99
	10,790	11,748
Non-current Liabilities		
Deferred lease inducements and rent liability	1,432	1,392
	12,222	13,140
Shareholders' Equity		
Share capital (Note 11)	11,772	11,533
Contributed surplus	1,040	954
Retained earnings	35,595	43,422
	48,407	55,909
	$ 60,629	$ 69,049

Contingencies, Guarantees and Commitments (Notes 16 and 17)

Approved by the Board of Directors
August 13, 2014

Jeffrey Wortsman
Jeffrey Wortsman, Director

Edwin F. Hawken, Chairman

See accompanying notes to the consolidated financial statements

CONSOLIDATED STATEMENTS OF CASH FLOW (thousands of Canadian dollars)

	Years Ended	
	June 28, 2014	June 29, 2013
	52 weeks	52 weeks
Cash provided by (used in)		
Operating Activities		
Net earnings (loss)	($7,663)	$1,411
Adjustments for:		
Amortization of property and equipment	3,517	3,149
Amortization of computer software	791	412
Impairment loss on property and equipment	663	327
Amortization of deferred lease inducement	(75)	(100)
Straight line rent expense	115	121
Stock-based compensation	209	131
Interest income	(118)	(236)
Interest expense	59	51
Provision for (refund of) income taxes	(3,131)	570
Changes in working capital (Note 15)	883	1,348
Interest paid	(107)	(12)
Interest received	133	244
Income taxes (paid) recovered	(183)	(664)
Net cash generated from (used in) operating activities	**(4,907)**	**6,752**
Financing Activities		
Subordinate voting shares issued	227	183
Subordinate voting shares repurchased (Note 11)	(275)	(11,399)
Net cash used in financing activities	**(48)**	**(11,216)**
Investing Activities		
Acquisition of property and equipment	(4,972)	(4,498)
Acquisition of computer software	(1,107)	(829)
Net cash used in investing activities	**(6,079)**	**(5,327)**
Decrease in cash	(11,034)	(9,791)
Cash, beginning of period	24,541	34,332
Cash, end of period	**$13,507**	**$24,541**

See accompanying notes to the consolidated financial statements

CONSOLIDATED STATEMENTS OF CHANGES IN SHAREHOLDERS' EQUITY
(thousands of Canadian dollars)

	Share Capital	Contributed Surplus	Accumulated Other Comprehensive Income	Retained Earnings	Total
Balance - June 29, 2013	$11,533	$954	$ -	$43,422	$55,909
Net loss	-	-	-	(7,663)	(7,663)
Stock based compensation related to stock options	-	209	-	-	209
Exercise of stock options	350	(123)	-	-	227
Share repurchases (net of tax)	(111)	-	-	(164)	(275)
Balance - June 28, 2014	$11,772	$1,040	$ -	$35,595	$48,407

	Share Capital	Contributed Surplus	Accumulated Other Comprehensive Income	Retained Earnings	Total
Balance - June 30, 2012	$15,040	$925	$ -	$49,526	$65,491
Net earnings	-	-	-	1,411	1,411
Stock based compensation related to stock options	-	131	-	-	131
Exercise of stock options	285	(102)	-	-	183
Share repurchases	(3,792)	-	-	(7,515)	(11,307)
Balance - June 29, 2013	$11,533	$954	$ -	$43,422	$55,909

See accompanying notes to the consolidated financial statements

NOTES TO CONSOLIDATED FINANCIAL STATEMENTS

For the Years Ended June 28, 2014 and June 29, 2013
(unless otherwise stated, all amounts are in thousands of Canadian dollars)

1. GENERAL INFORMATION:

Danier Leather Inc. and its subsidiaries ("Danier" or the "Company") comprise a vertically integrated designer, manufacturer, distributor and retailer of leather apparel and accessories. Danier Leather Inc. is a corporation existing under the Business Corporations Act (Ontario) and is domiciled in Canada. The Company's subordinate voting shares (the "Subordinate Voting Shares") are listed on the Toronto Stock Exchange (the "TSX") under the symbol "DL". The address of its registered head office is 2650 St. Clair Avenue West, Toronto, Ontario, M6N 1M2, Canada.

The Company's operations are focused on the design, manufacture, distribution and retail of leather apparel and accessories in Canada. As such, the Company presents one operating segment in its consolidated financial statements.

Due to the seasonal nature of the retail business and the Company's product line, the results of operation for any interim period are not necessarily indicative of the results of operations to be expected for the fiscal year. A significant portion of the Company's sales and earnings are typically generated during the second fiscal quarter, which includes the holiday selling season. Sales are usually lowest and losses are typically experienced during the period from April to September.

2. BASIS OF PREPARATION:

(a) Statement of Compliance

These consolidated financial statements have been prepared in accordance with International Financial Reporting Standards ("IFRS") as issued by the International Accounting Standards Board ("IASB") and using the accounting policies described herein. These consolidated financial statements were approved by the Board of Directors of the Company on August 13, 2014.

(b) Basis of Presentation

These consolidated financial statements have been prepared on a going concern basis, under the historical cost convention, except for the following items which are measured at fair value:

- Financial instruments at fair value through profit and loss; and
- Liabilities for cash-settled share-based compensation plans.

(c) Functional and Presentation Currency

These consolidated financial statements are presented in Canadian dollars ("C$"), the Company's functional currency. All financial information is presented in thousands, except per share amounts, which are presented in whole dollars, and number of shares, which are presented as whole numbers.

(d) Use of Estimates, Judgments and Assumptions

The preparation of these consolidated financial statements in accordance with IFRS requires management to make certain judgments, estimates and assumptions that affect the application of accounting policies and the reported amounts of assets and liabilities and disclosure of contingent liabilities at the date of the consolidated financial statements, and the reported amounts of revenues and expenses during the period.

Judgment is commonly used in determining whether a balance or transaction should be recognized in the consolidated financial statements, and estimates and assumptions are more commonly used in determining the measurement of recognized transactions and balances. However, judgments and estimates are often interrelated.

Management has applied its judgment in its assessment of the classification of leases and financial instruments, the recognition of tax provisions, determining the tax rates used for measuring deferred taxes, and identifying the indicators of impairment of property and equipment.

Estimates are used when estimating the useful lives of property and equipment and computer software for the purposes of depreciation and amortization, when determining the number of share-based payments that will ultimately vest, when accounting for or measuring items such as inventory provisions, gift card breakage, assumptions underlying income taxes, sales and use taxes and sales return provisions, certain fair value measures including those related to the valuation of share-based payments and financial instruments and when testing assets for impairment. These estimates depend upon subjective and complex judgments about matters that may be uncertain, and changes in those estimates could materially impact the consolidated financial statements. Volatile equity, foreign currency and energy markets, the potential illiquidity of credit markets and unpredictable changes in consumer spending have combined to increase the uncertainty inherent in such estimates and assumptions. As future events and their effects cannot be determined with precision, actual results may differ significantly from such estimates and assumptions.

Estimates and underlying assumptions are reviewed on an ongoing basis. Revisions to accounting estimates are recognized in the period in which the estimates are revised and in any future periods affected.

3.   SIGNIFICANT ACCOUNTING POLICIES:

The accounting policies described below have been applied consistently to all periods presented in these consolidated financial statements.

(a)   Basis of Measurement:

The consolidated financial statements have been prepared on a going concern basis, under the historical cost convention as modified by the revaluation of certain financial assets and financial liabilities (including derivative instruments) at fair value through profit and loss.

(b)   Basis of Consolidation:

The consolidated financial statements include the accounts of Danier Leather Inc. consolidated with those of its wholly-owned subsidiaries, 1333677 Ontario Inc., Danier International Corporation and Danier Leather (USA) Inc. 1333677 Ontario Inc. was incorporated in Ontario, Canada on December 22, 1998 to hold vacant land next to the Company's Toronto head office. Danier International Corporation was incorporated in Barbados on April 7, 2006 to hold the international intellectual property of Danier. Danier Leather (USA), Inc. is currently inactive and was incorporated in Delaware, U.S.A. on September 8, 1998 to operate Danier stores in the United States, which operations have since been discontinued. On consolidation, all intercompany transactions, balances, revenue and expenses have been eliminated.

(c)   Year-End:

The fiscal year end of the Company consists of a 52 or 53 week period ending on the last Saturday in June each year. The current fiscal year for the consolidated financial statements is the 52-week period ended June 28, 2014 and, comparatively, the 52-week period ended June 29, 2013.

(d)   Foreign Currency Translation:

Items included in the financial statements of each wholly-owned consolidated entity in the Danier Leather Inc. group are measured using the currency of the primary economic environment in which the entity operates (the "functional currency"). The consolidated financial statements are presented in Canadian dollars, which is the Company's presentation currency.

Accounts in foreign currencies are translated into Canadian dollars. Monetary financial position items are translated at the foreign currency exchange rate in effect at the balance sheet date and non-monetary items are measured at historical cost. Revenues and expenses are translated into Canadian dollars at foreign currency exchange rates that approximate the rates in effect at the dates when such items are transacted. Revenues and expenses are translated at the foreign currency exchange rate in effect on the transaction dates or at the average foreign currency exchange rate for the reporting period. The resulting net gain or loss is included as part of selling, general and administrative expenses ("SG&A") in the consolidated statement of earnings (loss).

(e)   Revenue Recognition:

Revenue comprises the fair value of the consideration received or receivable for the sale of merchandise and services in the ordinary course of the Company's activities inclusive of amounts invoiced for alteration services and shipping. Revenue is shown net of sales tax and estimated returns.

The Company recognizes revenue when the amount can be reliably measured, it is probable that future economic benefits will flow to the Company and when specific criteria have been met for each of the Company's activities as described below. The Company bases estimates on historical results, taking into consideration the type of activity and the specifics of each arrangement.

Retail Sales

Revenue for merchandise sold to customers through the Company's stores is recognized at the time of purchase. Alteration revenue is recorded at the time the buyer takes possession of the merchandise.

Online Sales

Revenue for online customers is recognized upon estimated receipt of the merchandise by the customer.

Third Party Distributor

Revenue for merchandise sold through a third party distributor is recognized when the significant risks and rewards of ownership have been transferred to the buyer, which is at the time the distributor ships the merchandise to their customer.

Gift Cards

Gift cards sold are recorded as deferred revenue and revenue is recognized at the time of redemption or in accordance with the Company's accounting policy for breakage. Breakage income represents the estimated value of gift cards that are not expected to be redeemed by customers where the unredeemed balance is more than two years old from the date of issuance. Historically, breakage has not been material.

(f)   Share-Based Compensation Plans:

The Company maintains an equity-settled Stock Option Plan and cash-settled Restricted Share Unit ("RSU") and Deferred Share Unit ("DSU") share-based compensation plans.

For the equity-settled Stock Option Plan, where options to purchase Subordinate Voting Shares are issued to directors, officers, employees or service providers (further details of which are described in Note 12(a)), the expense is based on the fair value of the awards granted, excluding the impact of any non-market service conditions (for example, continued employment over a specified time period). Non-market vesting conditions are considered in making assumptions about the number of awards that are expected to vest. The fair value of options granted is estimated at the date of grant using the Black-Scholes Option Pricing Model. The expense is recognized on a graded vesting basis over the vesting period of the stock options, which is generally three years.

When stock options are subsequently exercised, share capital is increased by the sum of the consideration paid together with the related portion previously added to contributed surplus when compensation costs were charged against income.

For the cash-settled RSU plan, where RSUs are issued to eligible directors, officers or employees and vest over a period of up to three years (further details of which are described in Note 12(c)), the expense is recognized on a graded vesting schedule and is determined based on the fair value of the liability incurred at each balance sheet date until the award is settled. The fair value of the liability is measured at each balance sheet date by applying the Black-Scholes Option Pricing Model, taking into account the extent to which participants have rendered services to date.

For the cash-settled DSU plan, where DSUs are issued to directors and vest immediately and can only be redeemed once the director leaves the Board of Directors of the Company (further details of which are described in Note 12(b)), the expense is recognized on the grant date based on the fair value of the award by applying the Black-Scholes Option Pricing Model. The fair value of the liability is measured at each balance sheet date by applying the Black-Scholes Option Pricing Model until the award is settled.

At each balance sheet date, the Company reassesses its estimates of the number of awards that are expected to vest and recognizes the impact of any revisions in the statement of earnings (loss) with a corresponding adjustment to equity or liabilities, as appropriate.

(g)   Cash:

Cash consists of cash on hand and bank balances.

(h)   Financial Instruments:

(i) Classification of Financial Instruments

Financial instruments are classified into one of the following three categories: fair value through profit and loss; loans and receivables or financial liabilities at amortized cost. The classification determines the accounting treatment of the instrument. The classification is determined by the Company when the financial instrument is initially recorded, based on the underlying purpose of the instrument.

The Company's financial instruments are classified and measured as follows:

Financial Asset/Liability	Category	Measurement
Cash	Loans and receivables	Amortized cost
Accounts receivable	Loans and receivables	Amortized cost
Payables and accruals	Financial liabilities	Amortized cost
Sales return provision	Financial liabilities	Amortized cost
Foreign currency option contract derivatives[1]	Fair value through profit and loss	Fair value through profit and loss

(1) The carrying value of the Company's derivatives are included in the consolidated balance sheet as accounts receivable (if the fair value is an unrealized gain) or payables and accruals (if the fair value is an unrealized loss).

Loans and receivables are initially recognized at fair value and then subsequently at amortized cost using the effective interest method, less any impairment losses recognized in the statement of earnings (loss) in the period in which the impairment is recognized. Financial liabilities are initially recognized at the amount required to be paid less, when material, a discount to reduce the payables to fair value. Subsequently, financial liabilities are measured at amortized cost using the effective interest method. Changes in fair value of financial instruments classified as held for trading are recorded in the statement of earnings (loss) in the period of change.

The Company categorizes its financial assets and financial liabilities that are recognized in the balance sheets at fair value using the fair value hierarchy. The fair value hierarchy has the following levels:

•   Level 1 – quoted market prices in active markets for identical assets or liabilities;

•   Level 2 – inputs other than quoted market prices included in Level 1 that are observable for the asset or liability, either directly (as prices) or indirectly (derived from prices); and

•   Level 3 – unobservable inputs such as inputs for the asset or liability that are not based on observable market data.

The level in the fair value hierarchy within which the fair value measurement is categorized in its entirety is determined on the basis of the lowest level input that is significant to the fair value measurement in its entirety.

(ii) Transaction Costs

Transaction costs are added to the initial value of financial assets and liabilities when those financial assets and liabilities are not measured at fair value subsequent to initial measurement. Transaction costs are recorded in SG&A using the effective interest method.

(iii) Derivative Financial Instruments

The Company uses derivatives in the form of foreign currency option contracts and forwards, which are used to manage risks related to its inventory purchases, which are primarily denominated in United States dollars. All derivatives have been classified as fair value through profit and loss, are not designated as hedges, are included in the balance sheets as accounts receivable or payables and accruals, and are classified as current or non-current based on the contractual terms specific to the instrument. Gains and losses on re-measurement are included in SG&A.

(iv) Fair Value

The fair value of a financial instrument is the estimated amount that the Company would receive to sell an asset or pay to transfer a liability in an orderly transaction between market participants at the measurement date. These estimates are subjective in nature, often involve uncertainties and the exercise of significant judgment and are made at a specific point in time using available information about the financial instrument and may not reflect fair value in the future. The estimated fair value amounts can be materially affected by the use of different assumptions or methodologies.

The methods and assumptions used in estimating the fair value of the Company's financial instruments are as follows:

- The derivative financial instruments, which consist of foreign currency option contracts and forwards, have been marked-to-market and are categorized as Level 2 in the fair value hierarchy. Factors included in the determination of fair value include the spot rate, forward rates, estimates of volatility, present value factor, strike prices, credit risk of the Company and credit risk of counterparties. As at June 28, 2014, a $364 unrealized loss (June 29, 2013 – $822 unrealized gain) was recorded in SG&A for the contracts outstanding.

- Given their short-term maturity, the fair value of cash, accounts receivable, payables and accruals and sales return provision approximates their carrying values.

(i) Impairment of Financial Assets:

At each reporting date, the Company assesses whether there is objective evidence that a financial asset is impaired. Evidence of impairment may include: indications that a debtor or a group of debtors are experiencing significant financial difficulty; default or delinquency in interest or principal payments; and observable data indicating that there is a measurable decrease in the estimated future cash flows. If such evidence exists, the Company recognizes an impairment loss.

For financial assets carried at amortized cost, the loss is the difference between the amortized cost of the receivable and the present value of the estimated future cash flows, discounted using the instrument's original effective interest rate. The carrying amount of the asset is reduced by this amount either directly or indirectly through the use of an allowance account. Impairment losses on financial assets carried at amortized cost are reversed in subsequent periods if the amount of the loss decreases and the decrease can be related objectively to an event occurring after the impairment was recognized.

(j) Inventories:

Merchandise inventories are valued at the lower of cost, using the weighted average cost method, and net realizable value. For inventories manufactured by the Company, cost includes direct labour, raw materials, manufacturing and distribution centre costs related to inventories and transportation costs that are directly incurred to bring inventories to their present location and condition. For inventories purchased from third party vendors, cost includes the cost of purchase, duty and brokerage, quality assurance costs, distribution centre costs related to inventories and transportation costs that are directly incurred to bring inventories to their present location and condition.

The Company estimates the net realizable value as the amount at which inventories are expected to be sold, taking into account fluctuations in retail prices due to seasonality, age, excess quantities, condition of the inventory, nature of the inventory and the estimated variable costs necessary to make the sale. Inventories are written down to net realizable value when the cost of inventories is not estimated to be recoverable due to obsolescence, damage or declining selling prices. When circumstances that previously caused inventories to be written down below cost no longer exist, the amount of the write-down previously recorded is reversed.

Storage costs, administrative overheads and selling costs related to the inventories are expensed in the period in which the costs are incurred.

(k) Property and Equipment:

Property and equipment are recorded at cost less accumulated amortization and accumulated impairment losses, if any. Cost includes expenditures that are directly attributable to the acquisition of the asset. Borrowing costs attributable to the acquisition, construction or production of qualifying assets are added to the cost of those assets, until such time as the assets are substantially ready for their intended use. Qualifying assets are those assets that take longer than nine months to be substantially ready for their intended use. All other borrowing costs are recognized as interest expense in the statement of earnings (loss) in the period in which they are incurred.

Subsequent costs are included in the asset's carrying amount or recognized as a separate asset, as appropriate, only when it is probable that future economic benefits can be measured reliably. The carrying amount of a replaced asset is de-recognized when replaced. Repair and maintenance costs are

charged to the statement of earnings (loss) during the period in which they are incurred.

Depreciation of an asset begins once it is available for use. The Company allocates the amount initially recognized in respect of an item of property and equipment to its significant parts and depreciates each such part separately. The depreciable amount of an asset, being the cost of an asset less the residual value, if any, is allocated on a straight-line basis over the estimated useful life of the asset. Residual value is estimated to be zero unless the Company expects to dispose of the asset at a value that exceeds the estimated disposal costs. Gains and losses on disposals of property and equipment, if any, are determined by comparing the proceeds with the carrying amount of the asset and are included as part of SG&A in the statement of earnings (loss).

The major categories of property and equipment, their methods of amortization and useful lives for the fiscal years ended June 28, 2014 and June 29, 2013 are as follows:

Building	25 years straight-line
Roof	20 years straight-line
HVAC equipment	5 to 15 years straight-line
Computer hardware	4 to 7 years straight-line
Furniture and equipment (non-retail)	5 to 7 years straight-line
Leasehold improvements, furniture and fixtures (retail locations)	Term of lease not to exceed 10 years

The residual values, useful lives and amortization methods applied to assets are reviewed annually based on relevant market information and management considerations.

Property and equipment is derecognized either upon disposal or when no future economic benefits are expected from their use. Any gain or loss arising on derecognition is included as part of SG&A in the statement of earnings (loss).

(l) Computer Software:

Computer software is recorded at cost less accumulated amortization and accumulated impairment losses, if any. Amortization commences when the computer software application is available for its intended use. Residual value is estimated to be zero unless the Company expects to dispose of the asset at a value that exceeds the estimated disposal costs. The residual values, useful lives and amortization methods applied to computer software are reviewed annually based on relevant market information and management considerations. Computer software costs are capitalized and amortized on a straight line basis over the period of its expected useful life which ranges from 4 to 7 years. The assets are reviewed for impairment whenever events or circumstances indicate that the carrying amount may not be recoverable.

Computer software is derecognized either upon disposal or when no future economic benefit is expected from its use. Any gain or loss arising on derecognition is included as part of SG&A in the statement of earnings (loss).

(m) Impairment of Non-Financial Assets:

Property and equipment and computer software with finite lives are tested for impairment at each reporting date and whenever events or changes in circumstances indicate that the carrying amount may not be recoverable. Events or changes in circumstances which may indicate impairment include: a significant change to the Company's operations, a significant decline in performance or a change in market conditions which adversely affects the Company.

An impairment loss is recognized for the amount by which the asset's carrying amount exceeds its recoverable amount. For purposes of measuring recoverable amounts, assets are grouped at the lowest levels for which there are separately identifiable cash flows (cash-generating units or CGUs), which is at the individual store level for the Company. The recoverable amount is the greater of an asset's fair value less costs to sell and value in use (being the present value of the expected future cash flows of the relevant asset or CGU). The Company evaluates impairment losses for potential reversals when events or circumstances warrant such consideration.

(n) Leased Assets:

Leases are classified as either operating or finance, based on the substance of the transaction at inception of the lease. Classification is re-assessed if the terms of the lease are changed.

Leases in which a significant portion of the risks and rewards of ownership are not assumed by the Company are classified as operating leases. The Company enters into leases of varying terms for the operation of its stores, which are accounted for as operating leases. Payments under an operating lease are recognized in SG&A on the statement of earnings (loss) on a straight-line basis over the term of the lease. When a lease contains a predetermined fixed escalation of the minimum rent, the Company recognizes the related rent expense on a straight-line basis and records the difference between the recognized rental expense and the amount payable under the lease as deferred rent, which is included in deferred lease inducements and rent liability on the balance sheet. Contingent rentals (rent as a percentage of sales above a predetermined sales threshold) are recognized in SG&A in the period in which they are incurred.

Tenant allowances are recorded as deferred lease inducements and amortized as a reduction of rent expense over the term of the related leases.

(o) Provisions:

Provisions represent liabilities to the Company for which the amount or timing is uncertain. Provisions are recognized when the Company has a present legal or constructive obligation as a result of past events, it is probable that an outflow of resources will be required to settle the obligation and the amount can be reliably estimated. The sales return provision primarily comprises customer returns of unworn and undamaged purchases for a full refund within the time period provided by Danier's return policy, which is generally 14 days after the purchase date. The sales return provision is estimated based on historical experience and, since the time period of the provision is of relatively short duration, the present value of the expenditure expected to be required to settle the obligation approximates the actual provision estimate. The provision is reviewed at each balance sheet date and updated to reflect management's latest best estimate. However, actual returns could vary from these estimates.

(p) Deferred Lease Inducements and Rent Liability

Deferred lease inducements represent cash benefits received from landlords pursuant to store lease agreements. These lease inducements are amortized against rent expense over the term of the lease, not exceeding 10 years.

Rent liability represents the difference between minimum rent as specified in the lease and rent calculated on a straight-line basis.

(q) Income Taxes:

Income tax comprises current and deferred tax. The Company's income tax expense is based on tax rules and regulations that are subject to interpretation and require estimates and assumptions that may be challenged by taxation authorities.

Current income tax is the expected tax payable on the taxable income for the year using tax rates enacted or substantially enacted at the end of the reporting period and any adjustments to tax payable in respect of previous years. A weighted average of rates across provinces or categories of income is used if it is a reasonable approximation of the effect of using more specific rates. The Company's estimates of current income tax are periodically reviewed and adjusted as circumstances warrant, such as for changes to tax laws and administrative guidance and the resolution of uncertainties through either the conclusion of tax audits or expiration of prescribed time limits within the relevant statutes. The final results of government tax audits and other events may vary materially compared to estimates and assumptions used by management in determining income tax expense and in measuring current income tax.

In general, deferred tax is recognized in respect of temporary differences arising between the tax bases of assets and liabilities and their carrying amounts in the consolidated financial statements. Deferred income tax is determined on a non-discounted basis using tax rates and laws that have been enacted or substantially enacted at the balance sheet date and are expected to apply when the deferred tax asset or liability is settled. The effect on deferred income tax assets and liabilities of a change in tax rates are included in net earnings in the period that the laws have been enacted or substantially enacted. Deferred tax assets are recognized to the extent that it is probable that the assets can be recovered.

Estimation of income taxes includes evaluating the recoverability of deferred tax assets based on an assessment of the Company's ability to utilize the underlying future tax deductions against future taxable income before they expire. As described above, the Company's assessment is based upon substantially enacted tax rates and laws that are expected to apply when the assets are expected to be realized, as well as on estimates of future taxable income. If the assessment of the Company's ability to utilize the underlying future tax deductions changes, the Company would be required to recognize more or fewer of the tax deductions or assets, which would decrease or increase (respectively) the income tax expense in the period in which this is determined. Deferred income tax assets are recognized on the balance sheet under non-current assets, irrespective of the expected date of realization or settlement.

Significant judgment is required in determining the provision for taxation. There are many transactions and calculations for which the ultimate tax determination is uncertain during the ordinary course of business. The Company assesses the need for provisions for uncertain tax positions using best estimates of the amounts that would be expected to be paid based on a qualitative assessment of all relevant factors. However, it is possible that at some future date an additional liability could result from audits such differences will affect the tax provisions in the period in which such determination is made.

(r) Earnings Per Share:

Basic earnings per share is calculated by dividing the net earnings available to shareholders by the weighted average number of shares outstanding during the year (see Note 11(c)). Diluted earnings per share is calculated using the treasury stock method, which assumes that all outstanding stock options with an exercise price below the average monthly market price of the Subordinate Voting Shares on the TSX are exercised and the assumed proceeds are used to purchase the Company's Subordinate Voting Shares at the average monthly market price on the TSX during the fiscal year.

(s) Share Capital:

Subordinate Voting Shares are classified as equity. When Subordinate Voting Shares are purchased for cancellation, the carrying amount of the Subordinate Voting Shares is recognized as a deduction from share capital. The excess of the purchase price over the carrying amount of the Subordinate Voting Shares is charged to retained earnings.

(t) Accounting Standards Implemented During Fiscal 2014:

The Company adopted the following new accounting standards in preparing these annual consolidated financial statements:

(i) **Financial Instruments – Offsetting Financial Assets and Financial Liabilities:** The IASB issued an amendment to IFRS 7, Financial Instruments: Offsetting Financial Assets and Financial Liabilities ("IFRS 7") which was effective for annual periods beginning on or after January 1, 2013 and was adopted by the Company on June 30, 2013. Amendments to IFRS 7 increased the disclosure requirement related to offsetting of financial assets and liabilities. The implementation of IFRS 7 did not have a significant impact on the Company.

(ii) **Fair Value Measurement:** The IASB issued a new standard, IFRS 13, Fair Value Measurement ("IFRS 13"), which was required to be adopted for annual periods beginning on or after January 1, 2013 and was prospectively adopted by the Company on June 30, 2013. IFRS 13 provides a standard definition of fair value, sets out a framework for measuring fair value and provides for specific disclosures about fair value. IFRS 13 defines fair value as the price that would be received to sell an asset or paid to transfer a liability, in an orderly transaction between market participants at the measurement date. The Company determined that the adoption of IFRS 13 had no measurement impact on the Company's consolidated financial statements. The Company has included the disclosures required by this standard in Note 18.

4. FUTURE ACCOUNTING STANDARDS:

A number of new standards, and amendments to standards and interpretations, are not yet effective for the year ended June 28, 2014 and have not been applied in preparing these annual consolidated financial statements. New standards and amendments to standards and interpretations that are currently under review include:

IFRS 9 – Financial Instruments

On November 12, 2009, the IASB issued a new standard, IFRS 9, Financial Instruments ("IFRS 9"), which will ultimately replace IAS 39, Financial Instruments: Recognition and Measurement ("IAS 39"). The replacement of IAS 39 is a multi-phase project with the objective of improving and simplifying the reporting for financial instruments and the issuance of IFRS 9 is a part of the first phase.

On November 19, 2013, the IASB published IFRS 9, Hedge Accounting, which is a part of the third phase of its replacement of IAS 39. The new requirements allow entities to better reflect their risk management activities in the financial statements. As part of the amendments, entities may change the accounting for liabilities that they have elected to measure at fair value before applying any of the requirements in IFRS 9. This change in accounting would mean that gains caused by a worsening in an entity's own credit risk on such liabilities would no longer be recognized in profit or loss.

Because the impairment phase of the IFRS 9 project is not yet completed, the IASB decided that a mandatory effective date of January 1, 2015 would not allow sufficient time for entities to prepare to apply IFRS 9. Accordingly, the IASB determined to apply a later mandatory effective date, which will be determined when IFRS 9 is closer to completion. However, entities may still choose to apply IFRS 9 immediately. IFRS 9 must be applied retrospectively, however, hedge accounting is to be applied prospectively (with some exceptions). At the present time, Danier does not expect to apply IFRS 9 earlier than the date required by the IASB. The Company is assessing the potential impact of IFRS 9.

IAS 32 – Financial Instruments: Presentation ("IAS 32")

The IASB issued an amendment to IAS 32 which provides further guidance on the requirements for offsetting financial instruments. The amendments to IAS 32 are effective for annual periods beginning on or after January 1, 2014 and must be applied retrospectively. The Company will apply IAS 32 beginning in the first quarter of fiscal 2015 and no significant impact on the consolidated financial statements is expected.

IAS 36 – Impairment of Assets: Recoverable Amount Disclosures for Non-Financial Assets ("IAS 36")

The IASB issued amendments to IAS 36 which reduces the circumstances in which the recoverable amount of assets or cash generating units is required to be disclosed, clarifies the disclosure required and introduces an explicit requirement to disclose the discount rate in determining impairment or reversals where the recoverable amount (based on fair value less costs of disposal) is determined using a present value technique. The amendments to IAS 36 are effective for annual periods beginning on or after January 1, 2014 and must be applied retrospectively. The Company will apply IAS 36 beginning in the first quarter of fiscal 2015 and no significant impact on the consolidated financial statements is expected.

IFRIC 21 – Levies ("IFRIC 21")

The IFRS Interpretations Committee ("IFRIC") of the IASB issued IFRIC 21 which addresses the accounting for a liability to pay a levy to a government. IFRIC applies to levy liabilities within the scope of IAS 37 – Provisions, Contingent Liabilities and Contingent Assets, and to levy liabilities when the timing and amount is uncertain. IFRIC 21 is effective for years beginning on or after January 1, 2014 and must be applied retrospectively. The Company will apply IFRIC 21 beginning in the first quarter of fiscal 2015 and no significant impact on the consolidated financial statements is expected.

A number of other standards have been adopted by the IASB but currently have no impact on the Company.

5. INVENTORIES:

	June 28, 2014	June 29, 2013
Raw materials	$1,026	$2,594
Work-in-process	198	222
Finished goods	20,497	19,994
	$21,721	$22,810

	June 28, 2014	June 29, 2013
Cost of inventory recognized as an expense	$73,084	$75,805
Write-downs of inventory due to net realizable value being lower than cost	$2,589	$1,632
Write-downs recognized in previous periods that were reversed	$9	$30

6. PROPERTY AND EQUIPMENT:

Year Ended June 28, 2014

Cost	Land	Building	Roof	HVAC	Leasehold Improvements	Furniture & Equipment	Computer Hardware	Total
At June 29, 2013	$1,000	$6,063	$308	$840	$22,679	$9,957	$3,348	$44,195
Additions	-	-	-	-	3,078	1,671	223	4,972
Disposals	-	-	-	-	(2,451)	(270)	(280)	(3,001)
At June 28, 2014	$1,000	$6,063	$308	$840	$23,306	$11,358	$3,291	$46,166

Accumulated amortization and impairment losses

	Land	Building	Roof	HVAC	Leasehold Improvements	Furniture & Equipment	Computer Hardware	Total
At June 29, 2013	-	$2,508	$216	$625	$15,322	$6,754	$2,736	$28,161
Amortization for the period	-	154	16	49	1,865	1,005	428	3,517
Impairment losses	-	-	-	-	661	2	-	663
Disposals	-	-	-	-	(2,451)	(270)	(280)	(3,001)
At June 28, 2014	-	$2,662	$232	$674	$15,397	$7,491	$2,884	$29,340

Net carrying value

	Land	Building	Roof	HVAC	Leasehold Improvements	Furniture & Equipment	Computer Hardware	Total
At June 28, 2014	$1,000	$3,401	$76	$166	$7,909	$3,867	$407	$16,826

Capital work in progress included above
At June 28, 2014: $56 (Leasehold Improvements), $81 (Computer Hardware), $137 (Total)

Year Ended June 29, 2013

Cost	Land	Building	Roof	HVAC	Leasehold Improvements	Furniture & Equipment	Computer Hardware	Total
At June 30, 2012	$1,000	$6,063	$308	$793	$22,208	$9,088	$3,386	$42,846
Additions	-	-	-	47	2,970	1,333	148	4,498
Disposals	-	-	-	-	(2,499)	(464)	(186)	(3,149)
At June 29, 2013	$1,000	$6,063	$308	$840	$22,679	$9,957	$3,348	$44,195

Accumulated amortization and impairment losses

	Land	Building	Roof	HVAC	Leasehold Improvements	Furniture & Equipment	Computer Hardware	Total
At June 30, 2012	-	$2,354	$201	$578	$15,875	$6,321	$2,505	$27,834
Amortization for the period	-	154	15	47	1,669	847	417	3,149
Impairment losses	-	-	-	-	277	50	-	327
Disposals	-	-	-	-	(2,499)	(464)	(186)	(3,149)
At June 29, 2013	-	$2,508	$216	$625	$15,322	$6,754	$2,736	$28,161

Net carrying value

	Land	Building	Roof	HVAC	Leasehold Improvements	Furniture & Equipment	Computer Hardware	Total
At June 29, 2013	$1,000	$3,555	$92	$215	$7,357	$3,203	$612	$16,034

Capital work in progress included above
At June 29, 2013: $299 (Leasehold Improvements), $19 (Furniture & Equipment), $318 (Total)

The Company conducted an impairment test for its property and equipment and determined that there were impairments at some non-performing stores in the amount of $663 for the year ended June 28, 2014 ($327 for the year ended June 29, 2013) and recorded in SG&A during the third and fourth quarters of fiscal 2014. The recoverable amount of the CGU was estimated based on value-in-use calculations as this was determined to be higher than fair value less costs to sell. These calculations use cash flow projections based on actual performance during the past 12 months which are then extrapolated over each CGU's remaining lease term and then discounted using an estimated discount rate. The key assumptions for the value-in-use calculations include discount rates, growth rates and expected cash flows. Management estimates discount rates using pre-tax rates that reflect a current market assessment of the time value of money and the risks specific to the CGUs. Changes in revenues and direct costs are based on past experience and expectations of future changes in the market.

The pre-tax discount rate used to calculate the value-in-use range is 12% (11% during the year ended June 29, 2013) and is dependent on the specific risks in relation to the CGU. The discount rate is derived from retail industry comparable post-tax weighted average cost of capital.

If management's cash flow estimate were to decrease by 10%, the impairment would have increased by $128 (unchanged for the year ended June 29, 2013). Similarly, if the discount rate were to increase by 100 basis points, the impairment would have increased by $36 (unchanged for the year ended June 29, 2013).

7. COMPUTER SOFTWARE:

	Year Ended	
Cost	June 28, 2014	June 29, 2013
Beginning of fiscal year	$4,684	$3,994
Additions	1,107	829
Disposals	(752)	(139)
End of Period	5,039	4,684

Accumulated amortization	June 28, 2014	June 29, 2013
Beginning of fiscal year	$3,541	$3,268
Amortization for the period	791	412
Disposals	(752)	(139)
End of Period	$3,580	$3,541

Net carrying value		
End of period	$1,459	$1,143
Beginning of fiscal year	$1,143	$726

Capital work in progress include at end of period	$2	$702

8.   BANK FACILITIES:

The Company has an operating credit facility for working capital and for general corporate purposes to a maximum amount of $25 million that is committed until June 25, 2016 and bears interest at prime plus 0.75%. The Company also has a revolving term credit facility ("term capex facility") to be used exclusively for capital expenditures in the amount of $4 million that is committed until June 25, 2016 and bears interest at prime plus 0.75%. At the end of each quarter, repayments equal to 6.25% of the aggregate principal amount of all borrowings under the term capex facility must be paid.

Standby fees of 0.50% are paid on a quarterly basis for any unused portion of the operating credit facility and term capex facility. The operating credit facility and term capex facility are subject to certain covenants and other limitations that, if breached, could cause a default and may result in a requirement for immediate repayment of amounts outstanding. Security provided includes a security interest over all personal property of the Company's business and a mortgage over the land and building comprising the Company's head office/distribution facility.

The Company also has an uncommitted letter of credit facility to a maximum amount of $10 million and an uncommitted demand overdraft facility in the amount of $0.5 million to be used exclusively for issuance of letters of credit for the purchase of inventory. Any amounts outstanding under the overdraft facility will bear interest at the bank's prime rate. In addition, the Company has a US$4.05 million foreign exchange line available to hedge foreign currency exposure not exceeding 12 months. The foregoing facilities and exchange line are secured by the Company's personal property from time to time financed with the proceeds drawn thereunder.

9.   PAYABLES AND ACCRUALS:

	June 28, 2014	June 29, 2013
Trade payables	$ 1,250	$ 1,840
Accruals	5,089	4,981
RSU/DSU liability	1,591	2,516
Commodity and capital taxes	891	764
Derivative financial instruments	364	-
	$ 9,185	$ 10,101

10.   SALES RETURN PROVISION:

The provision for sales returns primarily relates to customer returns of unworn and undamaged purchases for a full refund within the time period provided by Danier's return policy, which is generally 14 days after the purchase date. Since the time period of the provision is of relatively short duration, all of the provision is classified as current. The following transactions occurred during the years ended June 28, 2014 and June 29, 2013, respectively, with respect to the sales return provision:

	Year Ended	
	June 28, 2014	June 29, 2013
Beginning of period	$99	$124
Amount provided during the period	1,996	2,049
Utilized or released during the period	(2,001)	(2,074)
End of period	$94	$99

11.   SHARE CAPITAL:

(a)   Authorized

1,224,329 Multiple Voting Shares

Unlimited Subordinate Voting Shares

Unlimited Class A and B Preference Shares

(b)   Issued

Multiple Voting Shares	Number	Consideration
Balance June 30, 2012	1,224,329	Nominal
Balance June 29, 2013	1,224,329	Nominal
Balance June 28, 2014	1,224,329	Nominal

Subordinate Voting Shares	Number	Consideration
Balance June 30, 2012	3,422,573	$ 15,040
Shares repurchased	(862,801)	(3,792)
Shares issued upon exercising of stock options	48,067	285
Balance June 29, 2013	2,607,839	$ 11,533
Shares repurchased	(25,000)	(111)
Shares issued upon exercising of stock options	47,000	350
Balance June 28, 2014	2,629,839	$ 11,772

The Multiple Voting Shares and Subordinate Voting Shares have identical attributes except that the Multiple Voting Shares entitle the holder to 10 votes per share and the Subordinate Voting Shares entitle the holder to one vote per share. Each Multiple Voting Share is convertible at any time, at the holder's option, into one fully paid and non-assessable Subordinate Voting Share. The Multiple Voting Shares are subject to provisions whereby, if a triggering event occurs, then each Multiple Voting Share is converted into one fully paid and non-assessable Subordinate Voting Share. A triggering event may occur if, among other things, Mr. Jeffrey Wortsman, President and Chief Executive Officer: (i) dies; (ii) ceases to be a senior officer of the Company; (iii) ceases to own 5% or more of the aggregate number of Multiple Voting Shares and Subordinate Voting Shares outstanding; or (iv) owns less than 918,247 Multiple Voting Shares and Subordinate Voting Shares combined.

(c)   Earnings Per Share

Basic and diluted per share amounts are based on the following weighted average number of shares outstanding:

	Fiscal Year Ended	
	June 28, 2014	June 29, 2013
Weighted average number of shares for basic earnings per share calculations	3,840,319	4,180,829
Effect of dilutive options outstanding	108,017	142,790
Weighted average number of shares for diluted earnings per share calculations	3,948,336	4,323,619

The computation of dilutive options outstanding only includes those options having exercise prices below the average market price of Subordinate Voting Shares on the TSX during the period. The number of options excluded was 111,200 as at June 28, 2014 and 26,200 as at June 29, 2013.

(d)   Issuer Bids

During the fiscal year ended June 29, 2013, the Company announced its intention to commence a substantial issuer bid (the "Offer"). The Offer was formally commenced on October 24, 2012 by filing and mailing a formal offer to purchase and accompanying circular, pursuant to which the Company offered to purchase for cancellation up to $10 million of its Subordinate Voting Shares from shareholders for cash by way of a "modified Dutch Auction" at a range of Offer prices between $12.55 and $13.30 per share. The Offer expired on November 28, 2012 and a total of 1,748,470 Subordinate Voting Shares were validly deposited and not withdrawn under the Offer. Pursuant to the terms of the Offer, the Company determined the purchase price to be $12.70 per share. As the aggregate value of Subordinate Voting Shares deposited under the Offer exceeded the $10 million maximum value of consideration payable by the Company pursuant to the Offer, a pro-ration factor of 0.9852 was applied to deposited Subordinate Voting Shares (except for odd lot deposits, which were not subject to pro-ration), and the Company repurchased for cancellation 787,401 Subordinate Voting Shares at a purchase price of $12.70 per share. Approximately $3,460 of the purchase price, representing the average paid-in value of the shares, was charged to share capital, and approximately $6,973, which included the excess paid-in value of the shares as well as the transaction costs (net of tax) associated with the Offer, was charged to retained earnings.

During the past several years, the Company has from time to time received approval from the TSX to commence various normal course issuer bids ("NCIBs"). On February 12, 2014, the Company announced that the TSX had accepted a notice of its intention to proceed with its seventh NCIB (the "2014 NCIB"). Pursuant to the 2014 NCIB, the Company may purchase for cancellation up to a maximum of 145,496 Subordinate Voting Shares. The maximum number of Subordinate Voting Shares that may be purchased pursuant to the 2014 NCIB represents approximately 10% of the "public float" of the Subordinate Voting Shares outstanding as at the date of the notice of its intention to proceed with the 2014 NCIB. The 2014 NCIB commenced on February 14, 2014 and will terminate on February 13, 2015, or on such earlier date as the Company may complete its purchases under the 2014 NCIB.

The following Subordinate Voting Shares were repurchased for cancellation under the Offer and NCIBs then in effect during the years ended June 28, 2014 and June 29, 2013, respectively:

The following table summarizes the distribution of these options and the remaining contractual life as at June 28, 2014:

		Options Outstanding			Options Exercisable	
Exercise Prices	# Outstanding	Weighted Average Remaining Contractual Life	Weighted Average Exercise Price		Shares	Weighted Average Exercise Price
$3.15	83,600	4.3 years	$3.15		83,600	$3.15
$6.25	50,000	4.0 years	$6.25		50,000	$6.25
$7.80	28,000	2.6 years	$7.80		28,000	$7.80
$8.68	15,000	2.8 years	$8.68		15,000	$8.68
$10.99	25,000	9.6 years	$10.99		-	$10.99
$11.21	25,000	9.6 years	$11.21		-	$11.21
$11.56	35,000	9.3 years	$11.56		-	$11.56
$12.97	26,200	8.6 years	$12.97		8,732	$12.97
	287,800	5.9 years	$7.73		185,332	$5.60

During the year ended June 28, 2014, the Company granted an aggregate of 85,000 stock options with exercise prices ranging from $10.99 to $11.56 per stock option (June 29, 2013 – 26,200 stock options were granted with an exercise price of $12.97 per stock option). The estimated fair value at the date of grant for the options granted during the year ended June 28, 2014 was between $3.74 and $4.10 per stock option (June 29, 2013 – $6.57 per stock option). The fair value of each option granted was estimated on the date of grant using the Black-Scholes Options Pricing Model with the following assumptions:

		Year Ended June 28, 2014		Year Ended June 29, 2013
Grant date	Oct 30, 2013	Feb 7, 2014	Feb 12, 2014	Feb 7, 2013
Number of options granted	35,000	25,000	25,000	26,200
Expected option life	5 years	5 years	5 years	10 years
Risk free rate	1.7%	1.6%	1.6%	2.0%
Expected stock price volatility	36%	36%	36%	38%
Dividend yield	-	-	-	-
Estimated forfeiture rate	0%	0%	0%	0%
Share price at grant date	$11.56	$11.21	$10.99	$12.97
Weighted average fair value of options granted	$4.10	$3.82	$3.74	$6.57

The risk free rate was based on the Government of Canada benchmark bond yield on the date of grant for a term equal to the expected life of the options. Expected volatility was determined by calculating the historical volatility of the Company's share price over a period equal to the expected life of the options. The expected contractual life was based on the contractual life of the awards and adjusted, based on management's best estimate and historical redemption rates. The estimated forfeiture rate was estimated based on forfeiture rates for options granted between January 2007 and December 2013.

The Black-Scholes Option Pricing Model was developed for use in estimating the fair value of traded options, which have no black-out or vesting restrictions and are fully transferable. In addition, the Black-Scholes Option Pricing Model requires the use of subjective assumptions, including the expected stock price volatility. As a result of the Company's Stock Option Plan having characteristics different from those of traded options, and because changes in the subjective assumptions can have a material effect on the fair value estimate, the Black-Scholes Option Pricing Model does not necessarily provide a reliable single measure of the fair value of options granted.

(b) Deferred Share Unit Plan

The cash-settled DSU Plan, as amended, was established for non-management directors. Under the DSU Plan, non-management directors of the Company may receive an annual grant of DSUs at the discretion of the Board of Directors on the advice of the Committee, and can also elect to receive their annual retainers and meeting fees in DSUs. A DSU is a notional unit equivalent in value to one Subordinate Voting Share of the Company based on the five-day average high and low board lot trading prices of the Company's Subordinate Voting Shares on the TSX immediately prior to the date on which the value of the DSU is determined.

Upon retirement from the Board of Directors, a participant in the DSU Plan receives a cash payment equal to the market value of the accumulated DSUs in their account. The fair value of the liability is measured at each balance sheet date by applying the Black-Scholes Option Pricing Model until the award is settled.

	Fiscal Year Ended	
	June 28, 2014	June 29, 2013
Number of shares repurchased under Offer	-	787,404
Number of shares repurchased under NCIBs	25,000	75,400
Amount charged to share capital	$111	$3,792
Amount charged to retained earnings representing the excess over the average paid-in value	$164	$7,515
Total cash consideration	**$275**	**$11,307**
Income tax related to Offer that was recorded directly to Shareholders' Equity	-	$92

12. SHARE-BASED COMPENSATION:

The Company's net share-based compensation expense recognized in SG&A related to its stock option, RSU and DSU plans is presented below:

	Fiscal Year Ended	
	June 28, 2014	June 29, 2013
Stock option plan expense	$209	$131
RSU plan expense	296	693
DSU plan expense	(157)	75
	$348	$899

The carrying amount of the Company's share-based compensation arrangements including stock option, RSU and DSU plans are recorded on the consolidated balance sheet as follows:

	Fiscal Year Ended	
	June 28, 2014	June 29, 2013
Payables and accruals	$1,591	$2,516
Contributed surplus	1,040	954
	$2,631	$3,470

(a) Stock Option Plan

The Company maintains a Stock Option Plan, as amended, for the benefit of directors, officers, employees and service providers, pursuant to which granted options are exercisable for Subordinate Voting Shares. As at June 28, 2014, the Company has reserved 525,100 Subordinate Voting Shares for issuance under its Stock Option Plan. The granting of options and the related vesting periods are at the discretion of the Board of Directors, on the advice of the Governance, Compensation, Human Resources and Nominating Committee of the Board (the "Committee"), at exercise prices determined as the weighted average of the trading prices of the Company's Subordinate Voting Shares on the TSX for the five trading days preceding the effective date of the grant. In general, options granted to officers, employees and service providers under the Stock Option Plan typically vest over a period of three years from the grant date and expire no later than the tenth anniversary of the date of grant (subject to extension in accordance with the Stock Option Plan if the options would otherwise expire during a black-out period).

A summary of the status of the Company's Stock Option Plan as of June 28, 2014 and June 29, 2013 and changes during the fiscal years ended on those dates is presented below:

	June 28, 2014		June 29, 2013	
Stock Option	Shares	Weighted Average Exercise Price	Shares	Weighted Average Exercise Price
Outstanding at beginning of year	277,900	$6.45	357,767	$7.14
Granted	85,000	$11.29	26,200	$12.97
Exercised	(47,000)	$4.83	(48,067)	$3.80
Forfeited	(28,100)	$10.68	(58,000)	$15.85
Outstanding at end of year	287,800	$7.73	277,900	$6.45
Options exercisable at end of year	185,332	$5.60	232,966	$5.37

The following transactions occurred during each of the years ended June 28, 2014 and June 29, 2013, respectively, with respect to the DSU Plan:

	Year Ended	
	June 28, 2014	June 29, 2013
Outstanding at beginning of year	83,136	103,920
Granted	-	-
Redeemed	-	(20,784)
Outstanding at end of period	83,136	83,136
Danier stock price at end of period	$9.41	$11.31
Liability at end of period	$782	$940

(c) Restricted Share Unit Plan

The Company has established a cash-settled RSU Plan, as amended, as part of its overall compensation plan. An RSU is a notional unit equivalent in value to one Subordinate Voting Share of the Company. The RSU Plan is administered by the Board of Directors, with the advice of the Committee. Under the RSU Plan, certain eligible officers, employees and directors of the Company are eligible to receive a grant of RSUs that generally vest over periods not exceeding three years, as determined by the Committee. Upon the exercise of the vested RSUs, a cash payment equal to the market value of the exercised vested RSUs will be paid to the participant. The market value is based on the average daily closing prices of the Subordinate Voting Shares on the TSX immediately prior to the applicable payment date. RSU expense is recognized on a graded vesting schedule and is determined based on the fair value of the liability incurred at each balance sheet date until the award is settled. The fair value of the liability is measured by applying the Black-Scholes Option Pricing Model, taking into account the extent to which participants have rendered services to date.

The following transactions occurred during each of the years ended June 28, 2014 and June 29, 2013, respectively, with respect to the RSU Plan:

	Year Ended	
	June 28, 2014	June 29, 2013
Outstanding at beginning of period	174,605	167,536
Granted	45,000	46,600
Redeemed	(91,647)	(36,063)
Forfeited	(4,569)	(3,468)
Outstanding at end of period	123,389	174,605
RSUs vested at end of period	14,785	39,331
Liability at end of period	$809	$1,576

13. AMORTIZATION AND IMPAIRMENT LOSS:

Amortization of property and equipment and computer software and impairment loss on property and equipment included in cost of sales and SG&A is summarized as follows:

	Year Ended	
	June 28, 2014	June 29, 2013
Cost of sales	$165	$168
SG&A	4,806	3,720
End of period	$4,971	$3,888

14. INCOME TAXES:

The Company's income tax expense is comprised as follows:

	Year Ended	
	June 28, 2014	June 29, 2013
Current tax expense		
Current period	($2,856)	$746
Adjustment for prior years	(64)	(14)
Current tax expense	($2,920)	$732
Deferred tax expense		
Recognition and reversal of temporary differences	($158)	($156)
Changes in tax rates	(6)	(7)
Adjustment for prior years and other	(47)	1
Deferred tax expense	($211)	($162)
Total income tax expense	**($3,131)**	**$570**

The Company's effective income tax rate consists of the following:

	Year Ended	
	June 28, 2014	June 29, 2013
Combined basic federal and provincial average statutory rate	26.5%	26.4%
Current year losses applied to prior year	2.6%	-
Non-deductible expenses	(1.1%)	4.2%
Future federal and provincial rate changes	0.1%	(0.3%)
Adjustment for prior years	1.1%	(0.7%)
Other	(0.2%)	(0.8%)
	29.0%	28.8%

Deferred income tax asset is summarized as follows:

	Year Ended	
	June 28, 2014	June 29, 2013
Amortization	$1,190	$1,041
Stock based compensation	421	667
Deferred lease inducements and rent liability	380	369
Federal and provincial tax credits	308	-
Other deferred expenses	75	86
	$2,374	$2,163

15. CHANGES IN WORKING CAPITAL ITEMS:

	Year Ended	
	June 28, 2014	June 29, 2013
Decrease (increase) in:		
Accounts receivable	559	(680)
Inventories	1,089	2,081
Prepaid expenses	193	(53)
Increase (decrease) in:		
Payables and accruals	(916)	(60)
Deferred revenue	(37)	85
Sales return provision	(5)	(25)
	$883	$1,348

16.   CONTINGENCIES AND GUARANTEES:

(a)   Legal proceedings

In the course of its business, the Company from time to time becomes involved in various claims and legal proceedings. In the opinion of management, all such claims and suits are adequately covered by insurance, or if not so covered, the results are not expected to materially affect the Company's financial position.

(b)   Guarantees

The Company has provided the following guarantees to third parties and no amounts have been accrued in the consolidated financial statements for these guarantees:

(i)   In the ordinary course of business, the Company has agreed to indemnify its lenders under its credit facilities against certain costs or losses resulting from changes in laws and regulations or from a default in repaying a borrowing. These indemnifications extend for the term of the credit facilities and do not provide any limit on the maximum potential liability. Historically, the Company has not made any indemnification payments under such agreements.

(ii)   In the ordinary course of business, the Company has provided indemnification commitments to certain counterparties in matters such as real estate leasing transactions, director and officer indemnification agreements and certain purchases of non-inventory assets and services. These indemnification agreements generally require the Company to compensate the counterparties for costs or losses resulting from legal action brought against the counterparties related to the actions of the Company. The terms of these indemnification agreements will vary based on the contract and generally do not provide any limit on the maximum potential liability.

17.   COMMITMENTS:

(a)   Operating leases:

The Company leases various store locations, a distribution warehouse and equipment under non-cancellable operating lease agreements. The leases are classified as operating leases since there is no transfer of risks and rewards inherent to ownership.

The leases have varying terms, escalation clauses and renewal rights. Minimum lease payments are recognized on a straight-line basis. Leases run for varying terms that generally do not exceed 10 years, with options to renew (if any) that do not exceed five years. The majority of real estate leases are net leases, which require additional payments for the cost of insurance, taxes, common area maintenance and utilities. Certain rental agreements include contingent rent, which is based on revenue exceeding a minimum amount. Minimum rentals, excluding rentals based upon revenue, are as follows:

Not later than one year	$10,978
Later than one year and not later than five years	$30,740
Later than five years	$14,793
Total	$56,511

Minimum lease payments and contingent rentals recognized as an expense are summarized as follows:

	Year Ended	
	June 28, 2014	June 29, 2013
Minimum lease payments	$11,875	$11,550
Contingent rentals	$289	$292

(b)   Letters of credit:

As at June 28, 2014, the Company had outstanding letters of credit in the amount of $7,146 (June 29, 2013 – $8,743) for the importation of finished goods inventories to be received.

18.   FINANCIAL INSTRUMENTS:

(a)   Fair value disclosure

The following table presents the carrying amount and the fair value of the Company's financial instruments:

	Classification	Maturity	June 28, 2014		June 29, 2013	
			Carrying Value	Fair Value	Carrying Value	Fair Value
Cash	Loans and receivables	Short-term	$13,507	$13,507	$24,541	$24,541
Accounts receivable	Loans and receivables	Short-term	$638	$638	$375	$375
Payables and accruals	Financial liabilities	Short-term	$8,821	$8,821	$10,101	$10,101
Sales return provision	Financial liabilities	Short-term	$94	$94	$99	$99
Derivative financial instruments[1]	Fair value through profit and loss	Short-term	($364)	($364)	$822	$822

(1) Included in payables and accruals for the fiscal year ended June 28, 2014 and included in accounts receivable for the fiscal year ended June 29, 2013

The fair value of a financial instrument is the estimated amount that the Company would receive or pay to transfer an asset or pay to transfer a liability in an orderly transaction between market participants at the measurement date. These estimates are subjective in nature, often involve uncertainties and the exercise of significant judgment and are made at a specific point in time using available information about the financial instrument and may not reflect fair value in the future. The estimated fair value amounts can be materially affected by the use of different assumptions or methodologies.

The principal methodologies and assumptions used in estimating the fair value of the Company's financial instruments are as follows:

- The derivative financial instruments, which consist of foreign exchange contracts, have been marked-to-market and are categorized as Level 2 in the fair value hierarchy. Factors included in the determination of fair value include the spot rate, forward rates, estimates of volatility, present value factor, strike prices, credit risk of the Company and credit risk of counterparties. As at June 28, 2014, a $364 unrealized loss (June 29, 2013 – $822 unrealized gain) was recorded in SG&A for the foreign exchange contracts outstanding.
- Given their short-term maturity, the fair value of cash, accounts receivable, payables and accruals and sales return provision approximate their carrying values. There were no transfers between Level 1 and 2 during the year.

(b)   Financial instrument risk management

Foreign Currency Risk

Foreign currency risk is the risk that the fair value or future cash flows of a financial instrument will fluctuate because of changes in foreign currency exchange rates.

The Company purchases a significant portion of its leather and finished goods inventory from foreign vendors with payment terms in U.S. dollars. The Company uses a combination of foreign exchange contracts and spot purchases to manage its foreign exchange exposure on cash flows related to these purchases. A foreign exchange contract represents an option with a counterparty to buy or sell a foreign currency to meet its obligations. Credit risk exists in the event of a failure by a counterparty to fulfill its obligations. The Company reduces this risk by mainly dealing with highly-rated counterparties such as major Canadian financial institutions.

During the years ended June 28, 2014 and June 29, 2013, the Company entered into foreign exchange contracts with Canadian financial institutions as counterparties with U.S. dollar notional amounts as listed below. Foreign exchange contracts outstanding as at June 28, 2014 expired or will expire at various times between July 3, 2014 and April 24, 2015 and the foreign exchange contracts that were outstanding as at June 29, 2013 expired or will expire between July 8, 2013 and August 29, 2014.

	Year Ended	
	June 28, 2014	June 29, 2013
Notional amount outstanding at beginning of period (US$000)	$32,700	$21,000
Notional amount of foreign exchange contracts entered into during the period (US$000)	21,800	38,200
Notional amount of foreign exchange contracts expired during the period (US$000)	(29,000)	(26,500)
Notional amount outstanding at end of period (US$000)	$25,500	$32,700
Maturing in less than 1 year (US$000)	$25,500	$29,000
Maturing from 1 to 2 years (US$000)	–	$3,700
Fair value of foreign exchange contracts – gain/(loss) – (CDN$000)	($364)	$822

As at June 28, 2014, a sensitivity analysis was performed on the Company's U.S. dollar denominated financial instruments, which principally consist of US$17 million of cash, to determine how a change in the U.S. dollar exchange rate would impact net earnings. A 500 basis point rise or fall in the Canadian dollar against the U.S. dollar, assuming that all other variables, in particular interest rates, remain the same, would have resulted in a $62 decrease or increase in the Company's net loss for the year ended June 28, 2014.

Liquidity Risk

Liquidity risk is the risk that the Company will not be able to meet its financial obligations as they become due. The Company's approach to managing liquidity risk is to ensure, to the extent possible, that it will have sufficient liquidity to meet its liabilities when due. As at June 28, 2014, the Company had $13.5 million of cash, an operating credit facility of $25 million and term capex facility of $4 million that are committed until June 25, 2016; and a $10 million uncommitted letter of credit facility which includes an uncommitted demand overdraft facility in the amount of $0.5 million and an uncommitted foreign exchange credit line in the amount of US$4.05 million related thereto. The credit facilities are used to finance seasonal working capital requirements for merchandise purchases and other corporate purposes. The Company expects that the majority of its payables and accruals and deferred revenue will be discharged within 90 days.

Interest Rate Risk

Interest rate risk is the risk that the fair value or future cash flows of a financial instrument will fluctuate because of changes in market interest rates. The Company's exposure to interest rate fluctuations is primarily related to cash borrowings under its existing credit facility, which bears interest at floating rates, and interest earned on its cash balances. The Company has performed a sensitivity analysis on interest rate risk at June 28, 2014 to determine how a change in interest rates would have impacted net loss. As at June 28, 2014, the Company's cash available for investment was approximately $13.5 million. A 100 basis point change in interest rates would have increased or decreased net loss by approximately $0.1 million for the year ended June 28, 2014. This analysis assumes that all other variables, in particular foreign currency exchange rates, remain constant.

Equity Price Risk

Equity price risk is the risk that the fair value or future cash flows of a financial instrument will fluctuate because of changes in market equity prices. The Company's exposure to equity price fluctuations is primarily related to the RSU and DSU liability included in payables and accruals. The value of the vested DSU and RSU liability is adjusted to reflect changes in the market value of the Company's Subordinate Voting Shares on the TSX. The Company has performed a sensitivity analysis on equity price risk as at June 28, 2014 to determine how a change in the price of the Company's Subordinate Voting Shares would have impacted net loss. As at June 28, 2014, a total of 123,389 RSUs and 83,136 DSUs have been granted and are outstanding. An increase or decrease of $1.00 in the market price of the Company's Subordinate Voting Shares would have increased or decreased net loss by approximately $0.2 million for the year ended June 28, 2014. This analysis assumes that all RSUs and DSUs were fully vested and all other variables remain constant.

Credit Risk

Credit risk is the risk that a customer or counterparty to a financial instrument will cause a financial loss to the Company by failing to meet its obligations. The Company's financial instruments that are exposed to concentrations of credit risk are primarily cash, accounts receivable and foreign exchange option contracts. The Company limits its exposure to credit risk with respect to cash by investing in short-term deposits with major Canadian financial institutions. The Company's accounts receivable, excluding derivative financial instruments, consist primarily of credit card receivables from the last few days of the fiscal period end, which are settled within the first few days of the new fiscal period. Accounts receivable also consist of accounts receivable from distributors and corporate customers. Accounts receivable are net of applicable allowance for doubtful accounts, which is established based on the specific credit risks associated with the distributor and each corporate customer and other relevant information. The allowance for doubtful accounts is assessed on a quarterly basis. Concentration of credit risk with respect to accounts receivable from distributors and corporate customers is limited due to the relatively insignificant balances outstanding and the number of different customers comprising the Company's customer base. Credit risk for foreign exchange option contracts exists in the event of a failure by a counterparty to fulfill its obligations. The Company reduces this risk by mainly dealing with highly-rated counterparties such as major Canadian financial institutions.

As at June 28, 2014, the Company's exposure to credit risk for these financial instruments was cash of $13.5 million, accounts receivable of $0.6 million and foreign exchange option contracts that had a notional value of US$25.5 million.

19. CAPITAL DISCLOSURE:

The Company defines its capital as shareholders' equity. The Company's objectives in managing capital are to:

- Ensure sufficient liquidity to support its current operations and execute its business plans;
- Enable the internal financing of capital projects; and
- Maintain a strong capital base so as to maintain investor, creditor and market confidence.

The Company's primary uses of capital are to finance non-cash working capital along with capital expenditures for new store additions, existing store renovation or relocation projects, information technology software and hardware purchases and production machinery and equipment purchases. The Company maintains a $25 million operating credit facility, a $4 million term capex facility and a $10 million uncommitted letter of credit facility which includes an uncommitted demand overdraft facility in the amount of $0.5 million and an uncommitted foreign exchange credit line in the amount of US$4.05 million related thereto, that it uses to finance seasonal working capital requirements for merchandise purchases and other corporate purposes. The Company does not have any long-term debt and therefore net earnings generated from operations are available for reinvestment in the Company.

The Board of Directors does not establish quantitative return on capital criteria for management, but rather promotes year-over-year sustainable profitable growth. On a quarterly basis, the Board of Directors monitors share repurchase program activities. Decisions on whether to repurchase shares are made on a specific transaction basis and depend on the Company's cash position, estimates of future cash requirements, market prices and regulatory restrictions, among other things. The Company does not currently pay dividends.

Externally-imposed capital requirements include a debt-to-equity ratio covenant as part of the operating credit facility. The Company was in compliance with this covenant as at June 28, 2014 and June 29, 2013. There has been no change with respect to the overall capital risk management strategy during the year ended June 28, 2014.

20. RELATED PARTIES:

Key management personnel are those individuals having authority and responsibility for planning, directing and controlling the activities of the Company, including members of the Company's Board of Directors. The Company considers key management to be the Company's Board of Directors and its five most highly compensated executive officers. Compensation awarded to key management included:

	Year Ended	
	June 28, 2014	June 29, 2013
Salaries and short-term benefits	$2,090	$2,000
Termination benefits	457	-
Share-based compensation	249	810
	$2,796	$2,810

The Company's subsidiaries are described in Note 3(b).

21. EXPENSE ANALYSIS:

Selling, general and administrative expenses include the following:

	Year Ended	
	June 28, 2014	June 29, 2013
Selling expense	$60,168	$60,464
General and administrative expense	18,918	16,156
	$79,086	$76,620

Selling expense comprises costs incurred to operate the Company's stores including wages and benefits for store management and staff, rent and occupancy, advertising, credit card fees, amortization of store property and equipment and computer software and other store operating expenses.

General and administrative expense includes the cost of design, merchandising, sourcing, merchandise planning, marketing, store administrative support, finance, loss prevention, information technology, human resource and executive functions.

22. EMPLOYEE BENEFITS EXPENSE:

Selling, general and administrative expenses include the following:

	Year Ended	
	June 28, 2014	June 29, 2013
Wages, salaries and bonus	$27,523	$27,783
Short-term benefits expense	4,125	4,295
Termination benefits	783	237
Share-based compensation	348	898
	$32,779	$33,213

Executing on our strategies

WestJet Annual Report 2014

MANAGEMENT'S REPORT TO THE SHAREHOLDERS

The consolidated financial statements have been prepared by management in accordance with International Financial Reporting Standards. When a choice between accounting methods exists, management has chosen those they deem most appropriate in the circumstances. Financial statements will, by necessity, include certain amounts based on judgments and estimates. Management has determined such amounts on a reasonable basis so that the consolidated financial statements are presented fairly in all material respects. All information in this report is the responsibility of management.

Management has established systems of internal control, including disclosure controls and procedures and internal controls over financial reporting, which are designed and operated to provide reasonable assurance that financial and non-financial information disclosed in a timely, complete, relevant and accurate manner. These systems of internal control also serve to safeguard the Corporation's assets. The systems of internal control are monitored by management and are further supported by an internal audit department whose functions include reviewing internal controls and their applications.

The Board of Directors is responsible for the overall stewardship and governance of the Corporation, including ensuring management fulfills its responsibilities for financial reporting and internal control, and reviewing and approving the consolidated financial statements. The Board carries out these responsibilities principally through its Audit Committee.

The Audit Committee of the Board of Directors, composed of independent Directors, meets regularly with management, the internal auditors and the external auditors to satisfy itself that each is properly discharging its responsibilities and to review the consolidated financial statements and management's discussion and analysis. The Audit Committee reports its findings to the Board of Directors prior to the approval of the consolidated financial statements and management's discussion and analysis for issuance to the shareholders. The Audit Committee also recommends, for review by the Board of Directors and approval of shareholders, the reappointment of the external auditors. The internal and external auditors have full and free access to the Audit Committee.

The consolidated financial statements have been audited by KPMG LLP, the independent external auditors, in accordance with Canadian Generally Accepted Auditing Standards on behalf of the shareholders. The auditors' report outlines the scope of their examination and sets forth their opinion.

Gregg Saretsky
President and
Chief Executive Officer

Vito Culmone
Executive Vice-President, Finance and
Chief Financial Officer

February 2, 2015
Calgary, Canada

INDEPENDENT AUDITORS' REPORT

To the Shareholders of WestJet Airlines Ltd.

We have audited the accompanying consolidated financial statements of WestJet Airlines Ltd., which comprise the consolidated statements of financial position at December 31, 2014 and December 31, 2013, the consolidated statements of earnings, changes in equity, cash flows and comprehensive income for the years then ended, and notes, comprising a summary of significant accounting policies and other explanatory information.

Management's Responsibility for the Consolidated Financial Statements

Management is responsible for the preparation and fair presentation of these consolidated financial statements in accordance with International Financial Reporting Standards and for such internal controls as management determines are necessary to enable the preparation of consolidated financial statements that are free from material misstatement, whether due to fraud or error.

Auditors' Responsibility

Our responsibility is to express an opinion on these consolidated financial statements based on our audits. We conducted our audits in accordance with Canadian Generally Accepted Auditing Standards. Those standards require that we comply with ethical requirements and plan and perform the audit to obtain reasonable assurance about whether the consolidated financial statements are free from material misstatement.

An audit involves performing procedures to obtain audit evidence about the amounts and disclosures in the consolidated financial statements. The procedures selected depend on our judgment, including the assessment of the risks of material misstatement of the consolidated financial statements, whether due to fraud or error. In making those risk assessments, we consider internal controls relevant to the entity's preparation and fair presentation of the consolidated financial statements in order to design audit procedures that are appropriate in the circumstances, but not for the purpose of expressing an opinion on the effectiveness of the entity's internal controls. An audit also includes evaluating the appropriateness of accounting policies used and the reasonableness of accounting estimates made by management as well as evaluating the overall presentation of the consolidated financial statements.

We believe that the audit evidence we have obtained in our audits is sufficient and appropriate to provide a basis for our audit opinion.

Opinion

In our opinion, the consolidated financial statements present fairly, in all material respects, the consolidated financial position of WestJet Airlines Ltd. at December 31, 2014 and December 31, 2013, and its consolidated financial performance and its consolidated cash flows for the years then ended in accordance with International Financial Reporting Standards.

KPMG LLP

Chartered Accountants

February 2, 2015
Calgary, Canada

WESTJET

Consolidated Statement of Earnings
For the years ended December 31
(Stated in thousands of Canadian dollars, except per share amounts)

	Note	2014	2013
Revenue:			
Guest		3,599,157	3,337,569
Other		377,395	324,628
		3,976,552	3,662,197
Operating expenses:			
Aircraft fuel		1,090,330	1,039,448
Airport operations		507,743	460,566
Flight operations and navigational charges		458,146	408,951
Sales and distribution		376,676	356,988
Depreciation and amortization		226,740	200,840
Marketing, general and administration		224,783	222,567
Maintenance		193,685	169,197
Aircraft leasing expense		182,450	175,646
Inflight expense		171,741	176,907
Employee profit share		68,787	51,577
		3,501,081	3,262,687
Earnings from operations		475,471	399,510
Non-operating income (expense):			
Finance income		17,070	17,848
Finance cost		(51,838)	(43,447)
Gain (loss) on foreign exchange		(2,064)	1,136
Loss on disposal of property and equipment	7	(48,332)	(2,962)
		(85,164)	(27,425)
Earnings before income tax		390,307	372,085
Income tax expense (recovery):			
Current		114,521	154,964
Deferred		(8,171)	(51,601)
		106,350	103,363
Net earnings	11	283,957	268,722
Earnings per share:			
Basic		2.22	2.05
Diluted		2.20	2.03

The accompanying notes are an integral part of the consolidated financial statements.

WESTJET

Consolidated Statement of Financial Position
At December 31
(Stated in thousands of Canadian dollars)

	Note	2014	2013
Assets			
Current assets:			
Cash and cash equivalents	5	1,358,071	1,256,005
Restricted cash	6	58,149	58,106
Accounts receivable	18	54,950	42,164
Prepaid expenses, deposits and other	18	144,192	133,263
Inventory	18	36,658	36,722
Assets held for sale	7	78,306	–
		1,730,326	1,526,260
Non-current assets:			
Property and equipment	7	2,793,194	2,487,734
Intangible assets	8	60,623	58,691
Other assets	18	62,290	70,778
Total assets		4,646,433	4,143,463
Liabilities and shareholders' equity			
Current liabilities:			
Accounts payable and accrued liabilities	18	502,432	543,167
Advance ticket sales	18	575,781	551,022
Non-refundable guest credits	18	45,434	46,975
Current portion of maintenance provisions	9	54,811	76,105
Current portion of long-term debt	10	159,843	189,191
		1,338,301	1,406,460
Non-current liabilities:			
Maintenance provisions	9	191,768	142,411
Long-term debt	10	1,028,820	689,204
Other liabilities	18	13,150	8,834
Deferred income tax	11	296,892	306,714
Total liabilities		2,868,931	2,553,623
Shareholders' equity:			
Share capital	12	603,287	603,861
Equity reserves		75,094	69,079
Hedge reserves		(3,179)	105
Retained earnings		1,102,300	916,795
Total shareholders' equity		1,777,502	1,589,840
Commitments	16		
Total liabilities and shareholders' equity		4,646,433	4,143,463

The accompanying notes are an integral part of the consolidated financial statements.

On behalf of the Board:

Gregg Saretsky, Director   Hugh Bolton, Director

WESTJET✈

Consolidated Statement of Cash Flows
For the years ended December 31
(Stated in thousands of Canadian dollars)

	Note	2014	2013
Operating activities:			
Net earnings		283,957	268,722
Items not involving cash:			
Depreciation and amortization		226,740	200,840
Change in maintenance provisions		8,413	26,610
Change in other liabilities		(529)	1,782
Amortization of hedge settlements		1,400	1,400
Loss on disposal of property and equipment	12	48,332	2,962
Share-based payment expense		18,626	14,533
Deferred income tax recovery		(8,171)	(51,601)
Unrealized foreign exchange gain		(10,634)	(12,020)
Change in non-cash working capital		208,595	298,697
Change in restricted cash		(43)	(6,484)
Change in other assets		(6,833)	(1,374)
Cash interest received		17,243	19,079
Cash taxes paid		(204,489)	(147,868)
Purchase of shares pursuant to compensation plans		(10,989)	(7,131)
		571,618	608,147
Investing activities:			
Aircraft additions		(694,200)	(639,734)
Aircraft disposals		75,655	142
Other property and equipment and intangible additions		(46,586)	(75,580)
		(665,131)	(715,172)
Financing activities:			
Increase in long-term debt		613,885	318,075
Repayment of long-term debt		(303,573)	(178,647)
Shares repurchased	12	(39,431)	(112,362)
Dividends paid	13	(61,313)	(52,188)
Issuance of shares pursuant to compensation plans		96	106
Cash interest paid		(39,507)	(36,677)
Change in non-cash working capital		4,866	146
		175,023	(61,547)
Cash flow from operating, investing and financing activities		81,510	(168,572)
Effect of foreign exchange on cash and cash equivalents		20,556	16,378
Net change in cash and cash equivalents		102,066	(152,194)
Cash and cash equivalents, beginning of year		1,256,005	1,408,199
Cash and cash equivalents, end of year	5	1,358,071	1,256,005

The accompanying notes are an integral part of the consolidated financial statements.

WESTJET✈

Consolidated Statement of Changes in Equity
For the years ended December 31
(Stated in thousands of Canadian dollars)

	Note	2014	2013
Share capital:			
Balance, beginning of year		603,861	614,899
Issuance of shares pursuant to compensation plans		6,177	11,027
Shares repurchased		(6,751)	(22,065)
	12	603,287	603,861
Equity reserves:			
Balance, beginning of year		69,079	69,856
Share-based payment expense		18,626	14,533
Issuance of shares pursuant to compensation plans	12	(12,611)	(15,310)
		75,094	69,079
Hedge reserves:			
Balance, beginning of year		105	(5,746)
Other comprehensive income		(3,284)	5,851
		(3,179)	105
Retained earnings:			
Balance, beginning of year		916,795	793,296
Dividends declared	13	(61,313)	(52,188)
Shares repurchased	12	(32,680)	(90,297)
Purchase of shares pursuant to compensation plans		(4,459)	(2,738)
Net earnings		283,957	268,722
		1,102,300	916,795
Total shareholders' equity		**1,777,502**	**1,589,840**

The accompanying notes are an integral part of the consolidated financial statements.

![WestJet logo]

Notes to Consolidated Financial Statements

As at and for the years ended December 31, 2014 and 2013
(Stated in thousands of Canadian dollars, except percentage, ratio, share and per share amounts)

1. Statement of significant accounting policies

The annual consolidated financial statements of WestJet Airlines Ltd. (the Corporation) for the years ended December 31, 2014 and 2013, were authorized for issue by the Board of Directors on February 2, 2015. The Corporation is a public company incorporated and domiciled in Canada. The Corporation provides airline service and travel packages. The Corporation's shares are publicly traded on the Toronto Stock Exchange (TSX) under the symbols WJA and WJA.A. The principal business address is 22 Aerial Place N.E., Calgary, Alberta, T2E 3J1 and the registered office is Suite 2400, 525 - 8 Avenue SW, Calgary, Alberta, T2P 1G1.

(a) Basis of presentation

These annual consolidated financial statements and the notes hereto have been prepared in accordance with International Financial Reporting Standards (IFRS) as issued by the International Accounting Standards Board (IASB).

These annual consolidated financial statements have been prepared on an historical cost basis except for certain financial assets and liabilities, including derivative financial instruments that are measured at fair value. Where applicable, these differences have been described in the notes hereto.

Amounts presented in these annual consolidated financial statements and the notes hereto are in Canadian dollars, the Corporation's reporting currency, unless otherwise stated. The Corporation's functional currency is the Canadian dollar.

(b) Principles of consolidation

The accompanying consolidated financial statements include the accounts of the Corporation and its subsidiaries. Subsidiaries consist of entities over which the Corporation is exposed to, or has rights to, variable returns as well as the ability to affect those returns through the power to direct the relevant activities of the entity. A description of the Corporation's subsidiaries is provided in note 17. All intercompany balances and transactions between the Corporation and its subsidiaries have been eliminated.

(c) Seasonality

The airline industry is sensitive to general economic conditions and the seasonal nature of air travel. The Corporation experiences increased domestic travel in the summer months and more demand for transborder and international travel over the winter months, thus reducing the effects of seasonality on net earnings.

(d) Revenue recognition

(i) Guest

Guest revenue, including the air component of vacation packages, is recognized when air transportation is provided. Tickets sold but not yet used are reported in the consolidated statement of financial position as advance ticket sales.

(ii) Other

Other revenue includes items such as net revenue from the sale of the land component of vacation packages, ancillary fees as well as cargo and charter revenue.

Revenue for the land component of vacation packages is generated from providing agency services equal to the amount paid by the guest for products and services, less payment to the travel supplier, and is reported at the net amount received. Revenue from the land component is deferred as advance ticket sales and recognized in earnings on completion of the vacation.

Ancillary revenue is recognized when the services and products are provided to the guest. Ancillary revenues include items such as fees associated with guest itinerary changes or cancellations, baggage fees, buy-on-board sales, pre-reserved seating fees and breakage from the WestJet Rewards Program.

![WestJet logo]

Consolidated Statement of Comprehensive Income
For the years ended December 31
(Stated in thousands of Canadian dollars)

	2014	2013
Net earnings	283,957	268,722
Items to be reclassified to net earnings:		
Other comprehensive income, net of tax:		
Amortization of hedge settlements to aircraft leasing	1,400	1,400
Net unrealized loss on foreign exchange derivatives[(i)]	8,652	6,660
Reclassification of net realized gain on foreign exchange derivatives[(ii)]	(7,023)	(3,514)
Net unrealized gain (loss) on interest rate derivatives[(iii)]	(8,697)	522
Reclassification of net realized loss on interest rate derivatives[(iv)]	2,384	783
	(3,284)	5,851
Total comprehensive income	280,673	274,573

(i)   Net of income taxes of $3,048 (2013 – $(2,347)).
(ii)   Net of income taxes of $2,475 (2013 – $1,238).
(iii) Net of income taxes of $3,065 (2013 – $(183)).
(iv)   Net of income taxes of $(841) (2013 – $(275)).

The accompanying notes are an integral part of the consolidated financial statements.

WESTJET

Notes to Consolidated Financial Statements
As at and for the years ended December 31, 2014 and 2013
(Stated in thousands of Canadian dollars, except percentage, ratio, share and per share amounts)

1. Statement of significant accounting policies (continued)

(d) Revenue recognition (continued)

(iii) WestJet Rewards Program

The Corporation has a rewards program that allows guests to accumulate credits based on their WestJet travel spend to be used towards future flights and vacation packages. Revenue received in relation to credits issued is deferred as a liability at fair value until the credit is utilized and air transportation is provided, at which time it is recognized in guest revenue. Revenue associated with credits expected to expire (breakage) is recognized in other revenue at the time the credit is issued.

The Corporation also has a co-branded MasterCard with the Royal Bank of Canada (RBC). RBC issues reward credits to cardholders as a percentage of their total retail spend. Revenue related to new credit cards issued is recognized in other revenue immediately upon activation.

(iv) Non-refundable guest credits

The Corporation issues future travel credits to guests for flight changes and cancellations. Where appropriate, travel credits are also issued for flight delays, missing baggage and other inconveniences. All credits are non-refundable and have expiry dates dependent upon the nature of the credit. The Corporation records a liability at face value for credits issued for flight changes and cancellations. Revenue related to flight changes and cancellations is recorded in guest revenue when air transportation is provided. No liability is recorded for travel credits related to flight delays, missing baggage or other inconveniences as these credits are issued as goodwill gestures by the Corporation and do not represent a performance obligation. Credits issued as a sign of goodwill are recorded as a reduction to guest revenue when the credit is utilized.

(e) Financial instruments

A financial instrument is any contract that gives rise to a financial asset to one entity and a financial liability to another entity or equity instrument of another entity. Financial assets and liabilities, including derivatives, are recognized in the consolidated statement of financial position at the time the Corporation becomes a party to the contractual provisions. Upon initial recognition, financial instruments are measured at fair value. Subsequent measurement is based on designation in one of the following five categories: at fair value through profit or loss, held-to-maturity, loans and receivables, available-for-sale or other financial liabilities.

The following table lists the Corporation's financial instruments and the method of measurement subsequent to initial recognition:

Financial instrument	Category	Measurement method
Cash and cash equivalents	At fair value through profit or loss	Fair value
Restricted cash	At fair value through profit or loss	Fair value
Deposits	At fair value through profit or loss	Fair value
Accounts receivable	Loans and receivables	Amortized cost
Accounts payable and accrued liabilities	Other financial liabilities	Amortized cost
Long-term debt	Other financial liabilities	Amortized cost
Derivative instruments	At fair value through profit or loss	Fair value

Financial assets and liabilities at fair value through profit or loss include financial assets classified as held-for-trading and financial assets and liabilities designated upon initial recognition at fair value through profit or loss. Financial assets and liabilities are classified as held-for-trading if they are acquired for the purpose of selling or repurchasing in the near term. This category includes derivative financial instruments entered into by the Corporation that are not designated as effective hedging instruments. At December 31, 2014 and 2013, the Corporation did not hold any financial instruments classified as held-for-trading. Financial assets and liabilities designated upon initial recognition at fair value through profit or loss are initially measured at fair value with subsequent changes in fair value recorded in net earnings. The Corporation uses trade-date accounting for initial recognition of financial instruments in this category.

Financial assets classified as loans and receivables are measured at amortized cost using the effective interest method. Impairment, if any, is recorded in net earnings.

WESTJET

Notes to Consolidated Financial Statements
As at and for the years ended December 31, 2014 and 2013
(Stated in thousands of Canadian dollars, except percentage, ratio, share and per share amounts)

1. Statement of significant accounting policies (continued)

(e) Financial instruments (continued)

Other financial liabilities are measured at amortized cost using the effective interest method and include all liabilities other than derivatives, which are designated as cash flow hedges.

The Corporation may, from time to time, use various financial derivatives to reduce market risk exposure from changes in foreign exchange rates, interest rates and jet fuel prices. Derivatives are recorded at fair value on the consolidated statement of financial position with changes in fair value recorded in net earnings unless designated as effective hedging instruments. Similarly, embedded derivatives are recorded at fair value on the consolidated statement of financial position with the changes in fair value recorded in the consolidated statement of earnings unless exempted from derivative treatment as a normal purchase and sale or the host contract and derivative are deemed to be clearly and closely related. When financial assets and liabilities are designated as part of a hedging relationship and qualify for hedge accounting, they are subject to measurement and classification requirements as cash flow hedges. The Corporation's policy is not to utilize derivative financial instruments for trading or speculative purposes.

At each reporting period, the Corporation will assess whether there is any objective evidence that a financial asset, other than those classified at fair value through profit or loss, is impaired.

The Corporation offsets qualifying transaction costs incurred in relation to the acquisition of financial assets and liabilities not measured at fair value through profit or loss against those same financial assets and liabilities.

(f) Cash flow hedges

The Corporation uses various financial derivative instruments such as forwards and swaps to manage fluctuations in foreign exchange rates and interest rates.

The Corporation's derivatives that have been designated and qualify for hedge accounting are classified as cash flow hedges. The Corporation formally documents all relationships between hedging instruments and hedged items as well as the risk-management objective and strategy for undertaking the hedge transaction. This process includes linking all derivatives that are designated in a cash flow hedging relationship to a specific firm commitment or forecasted transaction. The Corporation also formally assesses, both at inception and at each reporting date, whether derivatives used in hedging transactions have been highly effective in offsetting changes in cash flows of hedged items and whether those derivatives may be expected to remain highly effective in future periods.

Under cash flow hedge accounting, the effective portion of the change in the fair value of the hedging instrument is recognized in other comprehensive income (OCI) and presented within shareholders' equity in hedge reserves. The ineffective portion of the change in fair value is recognized in non-operating income (expense). Upon maturity of the financial derivative instrument, the effective gains and losses previously accumulated in hedge reserves within shareholders' equity are recorded in net earnings under the same caption as the hedged item.

The Corporation excludes time value from the measurement of effectiveness; accordingly, changes in time value are recognized in non-operating income (expense) during the period the change occurs.

If the hedging relationship ceases to qualify for cash flow hedge accounting, any change in fair value of the instrument from the point it ceases to qualify is recorded in non-operating income (expense). Amounts previously accumulated in hedge reserves within shareholders' equity will remain in shareholders' equity until settlement, at which time, the amount is recorded in net earnings under the same caption as the hedged item. If the transaction is no longer expected to occur, amounts previously accumulated in hedge reserves within shareholders' equity will be reclassified to non-operating income (expense).

(g) Foreign currency

Monetary assets and liabilities, denominated in foreign currencies, are translated into Canadian dollars at the rate of exchange in effect at the consolidated statement of financial position date, with any resulting gain or loss recognized in net earnings. Non-monetary assets, non-monetary liabilities, revenue and expenses arising from transactions denominated in foreign currencies are translated into Canadian dollars at the rates prevailing at the time of the transaction.

(h) Cash and cash equivalents

Cash and cash equivalents consist of cash and short-term investments that are highly liquid in nature and have maturity dates of up to 91 days.

WESTJET

Notes to Consolidated Financial Statements
As at and for the years ended December 31, 2014 and 2013
(Stated in thousands of Canadian dollars, except percentage, ratio, share and per share amounts)

1. Statement of significant accounting policies (continued)

(i) Inventory

Inventories are valued at the lower of cost and net realizable value, with cost being determined on a first-in, first-out basis and a specific item basis depending on the nature of the inventory. The Corporation's inventory balance consists of aircraft fuel, de-icing fluid, retail merchandise and aircraft expendables.

(j) Property and equipment

Property and equipment is stated at cost and depreciated to its estimated residual value. Expected useful lives and depreciation methods are reviewed annually.

Asset class	Basis	Rate
Aircraft, net of estimated residual value	Straight-line	15 to 20 years
Engine, airframe and landing gear overhaul	Straight-line	5 to 15 years
Ground property and equipment	Straight-line	3 to 25 years
Spare engines and rotables, net of estimated residual value	Straight-line	15 to 20 years
Buildings	Straight-line	40 years
Leasehold improvements	Straight-line	5 years/Term of lease

Estimated residual values of the Corporation's aircraft range between $2,500 and $6,000 per aircraft. Spare engines have an estimated residual value equal to 10% of the original purchase price. Residual values, where applicable, are reviewed annually against prevailing market rates at the consolidated statement of financial position date.

Major overhaul expenditures are capitalized and depreciated over the expected life between overhauls. All other costs relating to the maintenance of fleet assets are charged to the consolidated statement of earnings on consumption or as incurred.

Rotable parts are purchased, depreciated and disposed of, on a pooled basis. When parts are purchased, the cost is added to the pool and depreciated over its useful life of 15 to 20 years. The cost to repair rotable parts is recognized in maintenance expense as incurred.

(k) Assets held for sale

The Corporation classifies a non-current asset as held for sale if the carrying amount of the asset will be recovered principally through a sale transaction instead of through continuing use. The Corporation measures any asset held for sale at the lower of: (i) its carrying amount, or (ii) fair value less costs to sell. Assets held for sale are not depreciated or amortized and are classified as a current asset on the consolidated statement of financial position until the sale is complete. If the asset is considered a separate component of the Corporation, then the operating results of this component will be classified as discontinued operations on the consolidated statement of earnings. If the asset is not considered a separate component, then the operating results continue to be included in earnings from continuing operations until the time of sale. Any subsequent changes to the fair value less costs to sell after classification as held for sale are recognized in profit or loss, not to exceed the original carrying amount of the assets held for sale.

At December 31, 2014, the Corporation has recognized five aircraft as held for sale. These aircraft form part of a transaction for the sale of 10 Boeing 737-700 series aircraft. The Boeing 737-700 series aircraft were not assessed to be a separate component of the entity as they are not managed separately from the entire fleet and therefore, the operating results of these aircraft continue to be included in earnings from continuing operations on the consolidated statement of earnings until such time that they are delivered. The five undelivered 737-700 series aircraft are classified as current assets on the consolidated statement of financial position at the contracted purchase price with the buyer less costs to sell. The difference between the carrying amounts and contracted purchase price was recorded as a loss on disposal of property and equipment. The Corporation has recorded the aircraft at the contracted Canadian dollar equivalent proceeds using the period end US-dollar foreign exchange rate.

WESTJET

Notes to Consolidated Financial Statements
As at and for the years ended December 31, 2014 and 2013
(Stated in thousands of Canadian dollars, except percentage, ratio, share and per share amounts)

1. Statement of significant accounting policies (continued)

(l) Intangible assets

Included in intangible assets are costs related to software, landing rights and other. Software and landing rights are carried at cost, less accumulated amortization and are amortized on a straight-line basis over their respective useful lives of five to 20 years. Expected useful lives and amortization methods are reviewed annually.

(m) Impairment

Property and equipment and intangible assets are grouped into cash generating units (CGU) and reviewed for impairment when events or changes in circumstances indicate that the carrying value of the CGU may not be recoverable. When events or circumstances indicate that the carrying amount of the CGU may not be recoverable, the long-lived assets are tested for recoverability by comparing the recoverable amounts, defined as the greater of the CGU's fair value less cost to sell or value-in-use, with the carrying amount of the CGU. Fair value is defined as the amount an asset could be exchanged, or a liability settled, between consenting parties, in an arm's length transaction. Value-in-use is defined as the present value of the cash flows expected from the future use or eventual sale of the asset at the end of its useful life. If the carrying value of the CGU exceeds the greater of the fair value less cost to sell and value-in-use, an impairment loss is recognized in net earnings for the difference. Impairment losses may subsequently be reversed and recognized in earnings due to changes in events and circumstances, but only to the extent of the original carrying amount of the asset, net of depreciation or amortization, had the original impairment not been recognized.

(n) Maintenance

(i) Provisions

Provisions are made when it is probable that an outflow of economic benefits will be required to settle a present legal or constructive obligation in respect of a past event and where the amount of the obligation can be reliably estimated.

The Corporation's aircraft operating lease agreements require leased aircraft to be returned to the lessor in a specified operating condition. This obligation requires the Corporation to record a maintenance provision liability for certain return conditions specified in the operating lease agreements. Certain obligations are based on aircraft usage and the passage of time, while others are fixed amounts. Expected future costs are estimated based on contractual commitments and company-specific history. Each period, the Corporation recognizes additional maintenance expense based on increased aircraft usage, the passage of time and any changes to judgments or estimates, including discount rates and expected timing and cost of maintenance activities. The unwinding of the discounted present value is recorded as a finance cost on the consolidated statement of earnings. The discount rate used by the Corporation is the current pre-tax risk-free rate approximated by the corresponding term of a Government of Canada Bond to the remaining term until cash outflow. Any difference between the provision recorded and the actual amount incurred at the time the maintenance activity is performed is recorded to maintenance expense.

(ii) Reserves

A certain number of aircraft leases also require the Corporation to pay a maintenance reserve to the lessor. Payments are based on aircraft usage. The purpose of these deposits is to provide the lessor with collateral should an aircraft be returned in an operating condition that does not meet the requirements stipulated in the lease agreement. Maintenance reserves are refunded to the Corporation when qualifying maintenance is performed, or if not refunded, act to reduce the end of lease obligation payments arising from the requirement to return leased aircraft in a specified operating condition. Where the amount of maintenance reserves paid exceeds the estimated amount recoverable from the lessor, the non-recoverable amount is recorded as maintenance expense in the period it is incurred. Non-recoverable amounts previously recorded as maintenance expense may be recovered and capitalized based on changes to expected overhaul costs and recoverable amounts over the term of the lease.

(iii) Power-by-the-hour maintenance contracts

The Corporation is party to certain power-by-the-hour aircraft maintenance agreements, whereby the Corporation makes ongoing payments to maintenance providers based on flight hours flown. Payments are capitalized when they relate to qualifying capital expenditures such as major overhauls, otherwise, payments are recorded to maintenance expense on the consolidated statement of earnings when payment is incurred.

WESTJET

Notes to Consolidated Financial Statements
As at and for the years ended December 31, 2014 and 2013
(Stated in thousands of Canadian dollars, except percentage, ratio, share and per share amounts)

1. Statement of significant accounting policies (continued)

(o) Leases

The determination of whether an arrangement is, or contains, a lease is made at the inception of the arrangement based on the substance of the arrangement and whether (i) fulfillment of the arrangement is dependent on the use of a specific asset and (ii) whether the arrangement conveys a right to use the asset.

Operating leases do not result in the transfer of substantially all risks and rewards incidental to ownership. Non-contingent lease payments are recognized as an expense in the consolidated statement of earnings on a straight-line basis over the term of the lease. The Corporation has a variety of operating leases including, but not limited to, those for aircraft, land, hangar space and airport operations.

(p) Borrowing costs

Interest and other borrowing costs are capitalized to a qualifying asset provided they are directly attributable to the acquisition, construction or production of the qualifying asset. For specific borrowings, any investment income on the temporary investment of borrowed funds is offset against the capitalized borrowing costs. The Corporation capitalizes interest related to the acquisition of aircraft.

(q) Income taxes

Current tax assets and liabilities are recognized based on amounts receivable from or payable to a tax authority within the next 12 months. A current tax asset is recognized for a benefit relating to an unused tax loss or unused tax credit that can be carried back to recover current tax of a previous period.

Deferred tax assets and liabilities are recognized for temporary differences between the tax and accounting bases of assets and liabilities on the consolidated statement of financial position using the tax rates that are expected to apply in the period in which the deferred tax asset or liability is expected to settle. The tax rates that are expected to be applied in future periods are based on the enacted or substantively enacted rates known at the end of the reporting period. Deferred tax assets are only recognized to the extent that it is probable that a taxable profit will be available when the deductible temporary differences can be utilized. A deferred tax asset is also recognized for any unused tax losses and unused tax credits to the extent that it is probable that future taxable profit will be available for use against the unused tax losses and unused tax credits. Deferred tax assets and liabilities are not discounted.

Current and deferred tax benefit or expense is recognized in the same period as the related transaction or event is recognized in net earnings. Current and deferred tax benefit or expense related to transactions or events in OCI or equity are recognized directly in those accounts.

Current tax assets and liabilities are offset on the consolidated statement of financial position to the extent the Corporation has a legally enforceable right to offset and the amounts are levied by the same taxation authority or when the Corporation has the right to offset and intends to settle on a net basis or realize the asset and settle the liability simultaneously. Deferred tax assets and liabilities are classified as long-term.

(r) Share-based payment plans

Equity-settled share-based payments to employees are measured at the fair value of the equity instrument granted. An option valuation model is used to fair value stock options issued to employees on the date of grant. The market value of the Corporation's voting shares on the date of the grant is used to determine the fair value of the equity-based share units issued to employees.

The cost of the equity-settled share-based payments is recognized as compensation expense with a corresponding increase in equity reserves over the related service period provided to the Corporation. The service period may commence prior to the grant date with compensation expense recognition being subject to specific vesting conditions and the best estimate of equity instruments expected to vest. Estimates related to vesting conditions are reviewed regularly with any adjustments recorded to compensation expense. On the vesting date, the Corporation revises, if necessary, the estimate to equal the number of equity instruments ultimately vested and adjusts the corresponding compensation expense and equity reserves accordingly.

Market conditions attached to certain equity-settled share-based payments are taken into account when estimating the fair value of the equity instruments granted.

Upon exercise or settlement of equity-based instruments, consideration received, if any, together with amounts previously recorded in the equity reserves, are recorded as an increase in share capital.

Cash-settled share-based payments are measured based on the fair value of the cash liability. The amount determined is recorded as compensation expense at the date of grant. The liability is remeasured each period with a corresponding adjustment to the related compensation expense until the date of settlement.

WESTJET

Notes to Consolidated Financial Statements
As at and for the years ended December 31, 2014 and 2013
(Stated in thousands of Canadian dollars, except percentage, ratio, share and per share amounts)

1. Statement of significant accounting policies (continued)

(s) Earnings per share

Basic earnings per share is calculated by dividing net earnings attributable to equity holders by the weighted average number of voting shares outstanding during the period, accounting for any changes to the number of voting shares outstanding, except those transactions affecting the number of voting shares outstanding without a corresponding change in resources.

Diluted earnings per share is calculated by dividing net earnings attributable to equity holders by the weighted average number of voting shares outstanding adjusted for the effects of all potential dilutive voting shares. Potential dilutive voting shares are only those shares that would result in a decrease to earnings per share or increase to loss per share. The calculation of potential dilutive voting shares assumes the exercise of all dilutive instruments at the average market price during the period with the proceeds received from exercise assumed to reduce the number of dilutive voting shares otherwise issued.

(t) Critical accounting judgments and estimates

The preparation of these consolidated financial statements in conformity with IFRS requires management to make judgments and estimates that could materially affect the amounts recognized in the consolidated financial statements. By their nature, judgments and estimates may change in light of new facts and circumstances in the internal and external environment. The following judgments and estimates are those deemed by management to be material to the Corporation's consolidated financial statements.

Judgments

(i) Componentization

The componentization of the Corporation's assets, namely aircraft, are based on management's judgment of what components constitute a significant cost in relation to the total cost of an asset and whether these components have similar or dissimilar patterns of consumption and useful lives for purposes of calculating depreciation and amortization. Management has considered the market value, depreciation rates and industry practices in determining the level of componentization.

(ii) Depreciation and amortization

Depreciation and amortization methods for aircraft and related components as well as other property and equipment and intangible assets are based on management's judgment of the most appropriate method to reflect the pattern of an asset's future economic benefit expected to be consumed by the Corporation. Among other factors, these judgments are based on industry standards, manufacturers' guidelines and company-specific history and experience.

(iii) Impairment

Assessment of impairment is based on management's judgment of whether there are sufficient internal and external factors that would indicate that an asset or CGU is impaired. The determination of a CGU is also based on management's judgment and is an assessment of the smallest group of assets that generate cash inflows independently of other assets. Management has assessed WestJet as one CGU and considered factors such as whether an active market exists for the output produced by the asset or group of assets as well as how management monitors and makes decisions about the Corporation's operations to conclude that there is no impairment at December 31, 2014.

(iv) Lease classification

Assessing whether a lease is a finance lease or an operating lease is based on management's judgment of the criteria applied in IAS 17 – Leases. The most prevalent leases of the Corporation are those for aircraft. Management has determined that all of the Corporation's leased aircraft are operating leases.

(v) Unconsolidated structured entities

The classification of the Corporation's participation in nine Canadian Fuel Facility Corporations (FFCs), two US FFCs and one Canadian De-Icing Facility Corporation (DFC) as interests in unconsolidated structured entities is based on management's judgement of each entity including contractual relationships and the absence of equity ownership. Management considered the restricted, narrow and well-defined objectives and activities of each FFC and DFC, the financial dependence of each FFC and DFC on the contracting airlines, and the contractual terms of each FFC and DFC preventing any single airline from having control or significant influence. Refer to note 17 for additional disclosures of the Corporation's interest in unconsolidated structured entities.

(vi) Operating and reportable segments

The assessment of the Corporation as one operating and reportable segment is based on management's judgement that resource allocation decisions and performance assessments are done at a consolidated company and fleet level with a view that the Corporation manages an integrated network of markets with a consolidated fleet of different sized aircraft.

WESTJET

Notes to Consolidated Financial Statements
As at and for the years ended December 31, 2014 and 2013
(Stated in thousands of Canadian dollars, except percentage, ratio, share and per share amounts)

1. Statement of significant accounting policies (continued)

(t) Critical accounting judgments and estimates (continued)

Judgments (continued)

(vii) Assets held for sale

The classification of five Boeing 737-700 series aircraft as held for sale is based on judgements applied by management in determining the probability of the sale, the timing of when the asset is available for sale and whether the asset comprises a separate operating component of the entity. Among other items, management considered the condition of the asset subject to sale, the presence of a buyer and whether the asset is considered a separate line of business, geographic segment or subsidiary. Based on these considerations, the Corporation has recognized five Boeing 737-700 series aircraft as held for sale at December 31, 2014. A key judgement, amongst other factors, that resulted in the aircraft being classified as held for sale on the consolidated statement of financial position and presented in continuing operations on the consolidated statement of earnings was the identification of the major aircraft components to be delivered with each aircraft and the aircraft not being managed as a separate component from the fleet as a whole.

Estimates

(viii) Depreciation and amortization

Depreciation and amortization are calculated to write-off the cost, less estimated residual value, of assets on a systematic and rational basis over their expected useful lives. Estimates of residual value and useful lives are based on data and information from various sources including vendors, industry publications, and company-specific history. Expected useful lives and residual values are reviewed annually for any change to estimates and assumptions.

(ix) Maintenance provisions

The Corporation has a legal obligation to adhere to certain maintenance conditions set out in its aircraft operating lease agreements relating to the condition of the aircraft when it is returned to the lessor. To fulfill these obligations, a provision is made during the lease term. Estimates related to the maintenance provision include the likely utilization of the aircraft, the expected future cost of the maintenance, the point in time at which maintenance is expected to occur, the discount rate used to present value the future cash flows and the lifespan of life-limited parts. These estimates are based on data and information obtained from various sources including the lessor, current maintenance schedules and fleet plans, contracted costs with maintenance service providers, other vendors and company-specific history.

(x) Income taxes

Deferred tax assets and liabilities contain estimates about the nature and timing of future permanent and temporary differences as well as the future tax rates that will apply to those differences. Changes in tax laws and rates as well as changes to the expected timing of reversals may have a significant impact on the amounts recorded for deferred tax assets and liabilities. Management closely monitors current and potential changes to tax law and bases its estimates on the best available information at each reporting date.

(xi) Fair value of equity-settled share-based payments

The Corporation uses an option pricing model to determine the fair value of certain share-based payments. Inputs to the model are subject to various estimates relating to volatility, interest rates, dividend yields and expected life of the units issued. Fair value inputs are subject to market factors as well as internal estimates. The Corporation considers historic trends together with any new information to determine the best estimate of fair value at the date of grant.

Separate from the fair value calculation, the Corporation is required to estimate the expected forfeiture rate of equity-settled share-based payments. The Corporation has assessed forfeitures to be insignificant based on the underlying terms of its payment plans.

(xii) Fair value of derivative instruments

The fair value of derivative instruments is estimated using inputs, including forward prices, foreign exchange rates, interest rates and historical volatilities. These inputs are subject to change on a regular basis based on the interplay of various market forces. Consequently, the fair value of the Corporation's derivative instruments are subject to regular changes in fair value each reporting period.

WESTJET

Notes to Consolidated Financial Statements
As at and for the years ended December 31, 2014 and 2013
(Stated in thousands of Canadian dollars, except percentage, ratio, share and per share amounts)

2. New accounting standards and interpretations

The IASB and International Financial Reporting Interpretations Committee (IFRIC) have issued the following standards that have not been applied in preparing these consolidated financial statements as their effective dates fall within annual periods beginning subsequent to the current reporting period.

Proposed standards	Description	Previous standard	Effective date[1]
IFRS 15 – Revenue from Contracts with Customers	Provides a single revenue recognition model which will improve comparability over a range of industries, companies and geographical boundaries	IAS 11 - Construction contracts; IAS 18 – Revenue; IFRIC 13 - Customer Loyalty Programmes; IFRIC 15 - Agreements for the Construction of Real Estate; IFRIC 18 - Transfers of Assets from Customers; SIC-31 - Revenue - Barter Transactions Involving Advertising Services	January 1, 2017
IFRS 9 – Financial Instruments	A single financial instrument accounting standard addressing: classification and measurement (Phase 1), impairment (Phase II) and hedge accounting (Phase III).	IAS 39; IAS 32; IFRS 7 – Financial Instruments: Recognition and Measurement; Presentation; Disclosures	January 1, 2018

(1) Effective for annual periods beginning on or after the stated date.

Management has not yet evaluated the impact of these new standards on the Corporation's financial statement measurements and disclosures. The Corporation does not anticipate early adopting these standards.

WESTJET

Notes to Consolidated Financial Statements
As at and for the years ended December 31, 2014 and 2013
(Stated in thousands of Canadian dollars, except percentage, ratio, share and per share amounts)

3. Capital management

The Corporation's policy is to maintain a strong capital base in order to maintain investor, creditor and market confidence and to sustain the future development of the airline. The Corporation manages its capital structure and makes adjustments in light of changes in economic conditions and the risk characteristics of the underlying assets.

In order to maintain the capital structure, the Corporation may, from time to time, purchase shares for cancellation pursuant to normal course issuer bids, issue new shares, pay dividends and adjust current and projected debt levels.

In the management of capital, the Corporation includes shareholders' equity (excluding hedge reserves), long-term debt, cash and cash equivalents and the Corporation's off-balance-sheet obligations related to its aircraft operating leases, all of which are presented in detail below.

The Corporation monitors its capital structure on a number of bases, including cash to trailing 12 months revenue, adjusted debt-to-equity and adjusted net debt to earnings before net finance cost, taxes, depreciation and amortization and aircraft leasing (EBITDAR). EBITDAR is a non-GAAP financial measure commonly used in the airline industry to evaluate results by excluding differences in tax jurisdictions and in the method an airline finances its aircraft. In addition, the Corporation will adjust EBITDAR for non-operating gains and losses on derivatives and foreign exchange. The calculation of EBITDAR is a measure that does not have a standardized meaning prescribed under IFRS and therefore may not be comparable to similar measures presented by other issuers. The Corporation adjusts debt to include its off-balance-sheet aircraft operating leases. To derive a present-value debt equivalent, common industry practice is to multiply the trailing 12 months of aircraft leasing expense by a multiplier. The Corporation uses a multiplier of 7.5. The Corporation defines adjusted net debt as adjusted debt less cash and cash equivalents. The Corporation defines equity as total shareholders' equity, excluding hedge reserves.

	2014	2013	Change
Cash to trailing 12 months revenue			
Cash and cash equivalents	1,358,071	1,256,005	102,066
Trailing 12 months revenue	3,976,552	3,662,197	314,355
Cash to trailing 12 months revenue(v)	34.2%	34.3%	(0.1pts)
Adjusted debt-to-equity			
Long-term debt(i)	1,188,663	878,395	310,268
Off-balance-sheet aircraft leases(ii)	1,368,375	1,317,345	51,030
Adjusted debt	2,557,038	2,195,740	361,298
Total shareholders' equity	1,777,502	1,589,840	187,662
Add: Hedge reserves	3,179	(105)	3,284
Adjusted equity	1,780,681	1,589,735	190,946
Adjusted debt-to-equity(v)	1.44	1.38	4.3%
Adjusted net debt to EBITDAR			
Adjusted debt (as above)	2,557,038	2,195,740	361,298
Less: Cash and cash equivalents	(1,358,071)	(1,256,005)	(102,066)
Adjusted net debt	1,198,967	939,735	259,232
Net earnings	283,957	268,722	15,235
Add:			
Net finance cost(iii)	34,768	25,599	9,169
Taxes	106,350	103,363	2,987
Depreciation and amortization	226,740	200,840	25,900
Aircraft leasing	182,450	175,646	6,804
Other(iv)	2,064	(1,136)	3,200
EBITDAR	836,329	773,034	63,295
Adjusted net debt to EBITDAR(v)	1.43	1.22	17.2%

(i) At December 31, 2014, long-term debt includes the current portion of long-term debt of $159,843 (December 31, 2013 – $189,191) and long-term debt of $1,028,820 (December 31, 2013 – $689,204).

(ii) Off-balance-sheet aircraft leases is calculated by multiplying the trailing 12 months of aircraft leasing expense by 7.5. At December 31, 2014, the trailing 12 months of aircraft leasing costs totaled $182,450 (December 31, 2013 – $175,646).

(iii) At December 31, 2014, net finance cost includes the trailing 12 months of finance income of $17,070 (December 31, 2013 – $17,848) and the trailing 12 months of finance cost of $51,838 (December 31, 2013 – $43,447).

(iv) At December 31, 2014, other includes the trailing 12 months foreign exchange loss of $2,064 (December 31, 2013 – gain of ($1,136)).

(v) The Corporation has internal guidelines for a cash to trailing 12 months revenue of approximately 30 per cent, an adjusted debt-to-equity measure of less than 3.00 and an adjusted net debt to EBITDAR measure of less than 3.00. The Corporation's internal guidelines are not related to any covenants.

WESTJET

Notes to Consolidated Financial Statements
As at and for the years ended December 31, 2014 and 2013
(Stated in thousands of Canadian dollars, except percentage, ratio, share and per share amounts)

4. Employee counts and compensation

The Corporation employed 8,698 full-time equivalent employees at December 31, 2014 (2013 – 8,000). The following table reconciles the Corporation's compensation expense items to where the amounts are presented on the consolidated statement of earnings:

	Note	2014	2013
Salaries and benefits(i)		626,373	582,225
Employee share purchase plan(i)	12	79,942	73,010
Employee profit share		68,787	51,577
Share-based payment expense(i)	12	18,626	14,533
		793,728	721,345
Airport operations		109,754	97,986
Flight operations and navigational charges		254,018	218,483
Sales and distribution		70,992	65,452
Marketing, general and administration		95,301	95,156
Inflight		133,183	137,990
Maintenance		61,693	54,701
Employee profit share		68,787	51,577
		793,728	721,345

(i) Classified in the consolidated statement of earnings based on the related nature of the service performed.

5. Cash and cash equivalents

	December 31, 2014	December 31, 2013
Bank balances(i)	400,808	394,984
Short-term investments(i)	957,263	861,021
	1,358,071	1,256,005

(i) Included in these balances, at December 31, 2014, the Corporation has US-dollar cash and cash equivalents totaling US $124,394 (2013 – US $106,749), GBP-dollar cash and cash equivalents totaling GBP $8 (2013 - GBP nil), and EUR-dollar cash and cash equivalents totaling EUR 309 (2013 – EUR nil).

6. Restricted cash

	December 31, 2014	December 31, 2013
Cash held in trust for WestJet Vacations Inc.	47,811	48,530
Security on facilities for letters of guarantee	9,515	8,322
Passenger facility charges	823	1,254
	58,149	58,106

WESTJET⟡

Notes to Consolidated Financial Statements
As at and for the years ended December 31, 2014 and 2013
(Stated in thousands of Canadian dollars, except percentage, ratio, share and per share amounts)

7. Property and equipment

	January 1 2014	Net additions	Depreciation	Transfers	December 31 2014
Aircraft(i)	1,747,319	122,609(ii)	(184,123)	247,481	1,933,286
Ground property and equipment	62,547	10,817	(13,901)	689	60,152
Spare engines and rotables	130,202	13,449	(12,630)	13,014	144,035
Deposits on aircraft	418,348	329,358	-	(238,022)	509,684
Buildings	112,450	428	(3,444)	-	109,434
Leasehold improvements	11,371	488	(2,082)	683	10,460
Assets under development	5,497	44,491	-	(23,845)	26,143
	2,487,734	521,640	(216,180)	-	2,793,194

	January 1 2013	Net additions	Depreciation	Transfers	December 31 2013
Aircraft(i)	1,477,388	304,479	(162,128)	127,580	1,747,319
Ground property and equipment	57,115	14,958	(14,088)	4,562	62,547
Spare engines and rotables	101,709	32,840	(10,391)	6,044	130,202
Deposits on aircraft	208,602	327,244	-	(117,498)	418,348
Buildings	115,899	(42)	(3,436)	29	112,450
Leasehold improvements	11,002	157	(1,751)	1,963	11,371
Assets under development	13,884	14,293	-	(22,680)	5,497
	1,985,599	693,929	(191,794)	-	2,487,734

(i) Aircraft includes (a) engine, (b) airframe, airframe and landing gear core components (c) engine, airframe and landing gear overhaul components, and (d) live satellite television equipment. For the year ended December 31, 2014, total aircraft depreciation expense was $184,123 (December 31, 2013 – $162,128). Included in total aircraft depreciation for the year ended December 31, 2014, was depreciation for overhaul components of $63,892 (December 31, 2013 – $56,523).

(ii) The Corporation has an agreement to sell 10 Boeing 737-700 aircraft with delivery dates scheduled to occur between October 2014 and May 2015. The Corporation has recorded the aircraft at the contracted Canadian dollar equivalent proceeds using the period end US-dollar foreign exchange rate. The difference between these proceeds and the carrying amount of the 10 aircraft resulted in a $47,919 loss on disposal of property and equipment on the consolidated statement of earnings for the year ended December 31, 2014. At December 31, 2014, $78,306 for the remaining five undelivered aircraft are recorded as assets held for sale on the consolidated statement of financial position.

December 31, 2014	Cost	Accumulated depreciation	Net book value
Aircraft	3,024,219	(1,090,933)	1,933,286
Ground property and equipment	158,078	(97,926)	60,152
Spare engines and rotables	216,051	(72,016)	144,035
Deposits on aircraft	509,684	-	509,684
Buildings	136,338	(26,904)	109,434
Leasehold improvements	19,768	(9,308)	10,460
Assets under development	26,143	-	26,143
	4,090,281	(1,297,087)	2,793,194

December 31, 2013	Cost	Accumulated depreciation	Net book value
Aircraft	2,985,722	(1,238,403)	1,747,319
Ground property and equipment	154,986	(92,439)	62,547
Spare engines and rotables	185,308	(55,106)	130,202
Deposits on aircraft	418,348	-	418,348
Buildings	135,910	(23,460)	112,450
Leasehold improvements	18,597	(7,226)	11,371
Assets under development	5,497	-	5,497
	3,904,368	(1,416,634)	2,487,734

The net book value of the property and equipment pledged as collateral for the Corporation's long-term debt was $1,522,978 at December 31, 2014 (2013 – $1,640,952).

WESTJET⟡

Notes to Consolidated Financial Statements
As at and for the years ended December 31, 2014 and 2013
(Stated in thousands of Canadian dollars, except percentage, ratio, share and per share amounts)

8. Intangible assets

	January 1 2014	Net additions	Amortization	Transfers	December 31 2014
Software	25,833	2,892	(9,583)	7,853	26,995
Landing rights	16,372	-	(889)	-	15,483
Other	5,785	-	(88)	-	5,697
Assets under development	10,701	9,600	-	(7,853)	12,448
	58,691	12,492	(10,560)	-	60,623

	January 1 2013	Net additions	Amortization	Transfers	December 31 2013
Software	18,970	5,337	(8,102)	9,628	25,833
Landing rights	17,261	-	(889)	-	16,372
Other	4,956	880	(51)	-	5,785
Assets under development	9,621	10,708	-	(9,628)	10,701
	50,808	16,925	(9,042)	-	58,691

December 31, 2014	Cost	Accumulated amortization	Net book value
Software	73,598	(46,603)	26,995
Landing rights	17,781	(2,298)	15,483
Other	5,836	(139)	5,697
Assets under development	12,448	-	12,448
	109,663	(49,040)	60,623

December 31, 2013	Cost	Accumulated amortization	Net book value
Software	69,050	(43,217)	25,833
Landing rights	17,781	(1,409)	16,372
Other	5,836	(51)	5,785
Assets under development	10,701	-	10,701
	103,368	(44,677)	58,691

WESTJET

Notes to Consolidated Financial Statements
As at and for the years ended December 31, 2014 and 2013
(Stated in thousands of Canadian dollars, except percentage, ratio, share and per share amounts)

9. Maintenance provisions and reserves

The Corporation's operating aircraft lease agreements require leased aircraft to be returned to the lessor in a specified operating condition. The maintenance provision liability represents the present value of the expected future cost. A maintenance expense is recognized over the term of the provision based on aircraft usage and the passage of time, while the unwinding of the present value discount is recognized as a finance cost. The majority of the Corporation's maintenance provision liabilities are recognized and settled in US dollars. Where applicable, all amounts have been converted to Canadian dollars at the period end foreign exchange rate.

	2014	2013
Opening balance	218,516	179,791
Additions	34,863	32,740
Change in estimate[(i)]	3,281	(1,055)
Foreign exchange	20,052	12,115
Accretion[(i)]	2,246	1,990
Settled	(32,379)	(7,065)
Ending balance	246,579	218,516
Current portion	(54,811)	(76,105)
Long-term portion	191,768	142,411

(i) Reflects changes to the timing and scope of maintenance activities and the discount rate used to present value the liability.

(ii) At December 31, 2014, the Corporation's aircraft lease maintenance provisions are discounted using a weighted average risk-free rate of approximately 0.91% (2013 – 0.99%) to reflect the weighted average remaining term of approximately 30 months (2013 – 27 months) until cash outflow.

A certain number of operating aircraft leases also require the Corporation to pay a maintenance reserve to the lessor. Maintenance reserves are either refunded when qualifying maintenance is performed or offset against end of lease obligations for returning leased aircraft in a specified operating condition. Where the amount of maintenance reserves paid exceeds the estimated amount recoverable from the lessor, the non-recoverable amount is recorded as maintenance expense in the period it is incurred. Non-recoverable amounts previously recorded as maintenance expense may be recovered and capitalized based on changes to expected overhaul costs and recoverable amounts over the term of the lease. The Corporation's maintenance reserves are recognized and settled in US dollars. Where applicable, all amounts have been converted to Canadian dollars at the period end foreign exchange rate.

At December 31, 2014, the current portion of maintenance reserves included in prepaid expenses, deposits and other is $54,466 (2013 – $49,810) and the long-term portion of maintenance reserves included in other assets is $8,110 (2013 – $11,851).

10. Long-term debt

	2014	2013
Term loans – purchased aircraft[(i)]	343,056	510,764
Term loans – purchased aircraft[(ii)]	218,425	238,964
Term loans – purchased aircraft[(iii)]	229,270	128,667
Senior unsecured notes[(iv)]	397,912	–
Ending balance	1,188,663	878,395
Current portion	(159,843)	(189,191)
Long-term portion	1,028,820	689,204

(i) 42 individual term loans, amortized over a 12-year term, repayable in quarterly principal instalments totalling $31,737, at an effective weighted average fixed rate of 5.93%, maturing between 2015 and 2020. These facilities are guaranteed by Export-Import Bank of the United States (Ex-Im Bank) and secured by 42 Boeing 737 Next Generation aircraft. At December 31, 2013 – 52 individual term loans, amortized over a 12-year term, repayable in quarterly principal instalments totalling $40,676, at an effective weighted average fixed rate of 5.95%, maturing between 2014 and 2020 and secured by 52 737 Next Generation aircraft. There are no financial covenants related to these term loans.

(ii) Seven individual term loans, amortized over a 12-year term, repayable in quarterly principal instalments totalling $5,576, in addition to a floating rate of interest at the three month Canadian Dealer Offered Rate plus a basis point spread, with an effective weighted average floating interest rate of 2.87% at December 31, 2014, maturing between 2024 and 2025. The Corporation has fixed the rate of interest on these seven term loans using interest rate swaps. These facilities are guaranteed by Ex-Im Bank and secured by seven Boeing 737 Next Generation aircraft. No changes from December 31, 2013, other than weighted average floating interest rate of 2.85%. There are no financial covenants related to these term loans.

(iii) 15 individual term loans, amortized over a 12-year term, repayable in quarterly principal instalments totalling $4,269, at an effective weighted average fixed rate of 3.87%, maturing in 2025 and 2026. These loans are secured by 15 Bombardier Q400 aircraft. At December 31, 2013 – eight individual term loans, amortized over a 12-year term, repayable in quarterly principal instalments totalling $2,231, at an effective weighted average fixed rate of 4.02%, maturing in 2025. There are no financial covenants related to these term loans.

(iv) 3.287% Senior Unsecured Notes with semi-annual interest payments and an effective interest rate of 3.30%, at December 31, 2014, with principal due upon maturity in July 2019. The notes rank equally in right of payment with all other existing and future unsubordinated debt of the Corporation, but are effectively subordinate to all of the Corporation's existing and future secured debt to the extent of the value of the assets securing such debt. There are no financial covenants related to these senior unsecured notes.

WESTJET

Notes to Consolidated Financial Statements
As at and for the years ended December 31, 2014 and 2013
(Stated in thousands of Canadian dollars, except percentage, ratio, share and per share amounts)

10. Long-term debt (continued)

Future scheduled repayments of long-term debt at December 31, 2014 are as follows:

Within 1 year	159,843
1 – 3 years	237,778
3 – 5 years	538,341
Over 5 years	252,701
	1,188,663

In June 2014, the Corporation entered into a credit agreement with a syndicate of banks whereby the Corporation has access to an unsecured, revolving $250,000 syndicated credit facility maturing in June 2017. The credit facility is available for general corporate purposes, including the funding of future aircraft acquisitions, and matures in June 2017 with an option to extend the three year term on an annual basis. Funds from the revolving credit facility can be drawn by way of: (i) Canadian dollar prime loans, (ii) US dollar base rate loans, (iii) US dollar LIBOR loans, (iv) Canadian dollar bankers' acceptances, and (v) Canadian or US dollar fronted letters of credit. Interest is calculated by reference to the applicable base rate plus an applicable pricing margin based on the Corporation's debt rating. The Corporation also pays a standby fee for the undisbursed portion of the revolving credit facility. At December 31, 2014, the Corporation has $nil (December 31, 2013 – not applicable) drawn on the facility. The credit facility contains two financial covenants: (i) minimum pooled asset coverage ratio of 1.5 to 1, and (ii) minimum fixed charge coverage ratio of 1.25 to 1. At December 31, 2014, the Corporation has met both covenants.

On July 23, 2014, the Corporation successfully completed a private placement offering for $400,000 3.287% Senior Unsecured Notes. The Corporation used a portion of the net proceeds from the sale of these notes to repay the amounts drawn under its revolving credit facility during the year with the balance to be used for general corporate purposes, including the funding of future aircraft acquisitions.

The Corporation has an $820,000 loan agreement with Export Development Canada for the future purchase of Bombardier Q400 NextGen aircraft. The Corporation is charged a non-refundable commitment fee of 0.2 per cent per annum on the undisbursed portion of the loan. The undisbursed portion of the loan at December 31, 2014, is $575,088 (December 31, 2013 – $688,973). Availability of any undrawn amount expires on December 31, 2018. The expected amount available for each aircraft is up to 80 per cent of the net price with a term to maturity of up to 12 years, repayable in quarterly instalments, including interest at a floating or fixed rate, determined at the inception of the loan.

11. Income taxes

(a) Reconciliation of total income tax expense

The effective rate on the Corporation's earnings before income tax differs from the expected amount that would arise using the combined Canadian federal and provincial statutory income tax rates. A reconciliation of the difference is as follows:

	2014	2013
Earnings before income tax	390,307	372,085
Combined Canadian federal and provincial income tax rate	25.96%	26.02%
Expected income tax provision	101,324	96,817
Add (deduct):		
Non-deductible expenses	3,931	3,694
Non-deductible share-based payment expense	1,985	1,920
Effect of tax rate changes	–	1,829
Other	(890)	(897)
Actual income tax provision	106,350	103,363
Effective tax rate	27.25%	27.78%

WESTJET

Notes to Consolidated Financial Statements
As at and for the years ended December 31, 2014 and 2013
(Stated in thousands of Canadian dollars, except percentage, ratio, share and per share amounts)

11. Income taxes (continued)

(b) Deferred tax

Components of the net deferred tax liability are as follows:

	2014	2013
Deferred tax liability:		
Property and equipment	(251,444)	(255,969)
Deferred partnership income	(45,785)	(49,464)
Net unrealized gain on derivatives designated in a hedging relationship	–	(1,314)
Deferred tax asset:		
Net unrealized loss on derivatives designated in a hedging relationship	337	–
Non-capital losses	–	33
	(296,892)	(306,714)

12. Share capital

(a) Authorized

Unlimited number of common voting shares

The common voting shares may be owned and controlled only by Canadians and shall confer the right to one vote per common voting share at all meetings of shareholders of the Corporation.

If a common voting share becomes beneficially owned or controlled by a person who is not a Canadian, such common voting share shall be converted into one variable voting share automatically and without any further act of the Corporation or the holder.

Unlimited number of variable voting shares

The variable voting shares may be beneficially owned and controlled only by a person who is not Canadian and are entitled to one vote per variable voting share unless (i) the number of issued and outstanding variable voting shares exceed 25% of the total number of all issued and outstanding variable voting shares and common voting shares collectively, including securities currently convertible into such a share and currently exercisable options and rights to acquire such shares (or any higher percentage the Governor in Council may specify pursuant to the *Canada Transportation Act*) or (ii) the total number of votes cast by, or on behalf of, the holders of variable voting shares at any meeting exceeds 25% (or any higher percentage the Governor in Council may specify pursuant to the *Canada Transportation Act*) of the total number of votes cast that may be cast at such meeting.

If either of the thresholds described in the paragraph above is surpassed at any time, the vote attached to each variable voting share will decrease automatically and without further act or formality to equal the maximum permitted vote per variable voting share. In the circumstance described in (i) in the paragraph above, the variable voting shares as a class cannot carry more than 25% (or any higher percentage the Governor in Council may specify pursuant to the *Canada Transportation Act*) of the aggregate votes attached to all variable voting shares and common voting shares collectively, including securities currently convertible into such a share and currently exercisable options and rights to acquire such shares. In the circumstance described in (ii) in the paragraph above, the variable voting shares as a class cannot, for a given shareholders' meeting, carry more than 25% (or any higher percentage the Governor in Council may specify pursuant to the *Canada Transportation Act*) of the total number of votes that can be exercised at the meeting.

Each issued and outstanding variable voting share shall be automatically converted into one common voting share without any further intervention on the part of the Corporation or of the holder if (i) the variable voting share is or becomes owned and controlled by a Canadian or if (ii) the provisions contained in the *Canada Transportation Act* relating to foreign ownership restrictions are repealed and not replaced with other similar provisions in applicable legislation.

WESTJET

Notes to Consolidated Financial Statements
As at and for the years ended December 31, 2014 and 2013
(Stated in thousands of Canadian dollars, except percentage, ratio, share and per share amounts)

12. Share capital (continued)

(a) Authorized (continued)

Unlimited number of non-voting shares and unlimited number of non-voting first, second and third preferred shares

The non-voting shares and non-voting preferred shares may be issued, from time to time in one or more series, each series consisting of such number of non-voting shares and non-voting preferred shares as determined by the Corporation's Board of Directors who may also fix the designations, rights, privileges, restrictions and conditions attached to the shares of each series of non-voting shares and non-voting preferred shares. There are no non-voting shares or non-voting preferred shares issued and outstanding.

(b) Issued and outstanding

	2014		2013	
	Number	Amount	Number	Amount
Common and variable voting shares:				
Balance, beginning of year	128,625,420	603,861	132,256,794	614,899
Issuance of shares pursuant to compensation plans	500,598	6,177	1,086,336	11,027
Shares repurchased	(1,435,150)	(6,751)	(4,717,710)	(22,065)
Balance, end of year	127,690,868	603,287	128,625,420	603,861

At December 31, 2014, the number of common voting shares outstanding was 107,998,929 (December 31, 2013 – 107,062,008) and the number of variable voting shares was 19,691,939 (December 31, 2013 – 21,563,412).

On May 5, 2014, the Corporation filed a notice with the TSX to make a normal course issuer bid to purchase outstanding shares on the open market. As approved by the TSX, the Corporation is authorized to purchase up to 2,000,000 common voting shares and variable voting shares (representing approximately 1.6 per cent of the Corporation's issued and outstanding shares at the time of the bid) during the period May 8, 2014 to May 7, 2015, or until such time as the bid is completed or terminated at the Corporation's option. Any shares purchased under this bid are purchased on the open market through the facilities of the TSX at the prevailing market price at the time of the transaction. Common voting shares and variable voting shares acquired under this bid are cancelled.

On February 14, 2013, the Corporation filed a notice with the TSX to make a normal course issuer bid to purchase outstanding shares on the open market. As approved by the TSX, the Corporation was authorized to purchase up to 6,616,543 common voting shares and variable voting shares (representing approximately five per cent of the Corporation's issued and outstanding shares at the time of the bid) during the period February 19, 2013, to February 18, 2014, or until such time as the bid was completed or terminated at the Corporation's option. Any shares purchased under this bid were purchased on the open market through the facilities of the TSX at the prevailing market price at the time of the transaction. Common voting shares and variable voting shares acquired under this bid were cancelled. The bid expired on February 18, 2014, with the Corporation purchasing and cancelling a total of 5,672,550 shares out of a possible 6,616,543 shares.

During the year ended December 31, 2014, the Corporation purchased and cancelled 480,310 shares under the May 2014 bid and 954,840 shares under February 2013 bid for a total of 1,435,150 shares (December 31, 2013 – 4,717,710) for total consideration of $39,431 (December 31, 2013 – $112,362). The average book value of the shares repurchased was $4.70 per share (December 31, 2013 – $4.68) and was charged to share capital. The excess of the market price over the average book value, including transaction costs, was $32,680 (December 31, 2013 – $90,297) and was charged to retained earnings.

(c) Stock option plan

The Corporation has a stock option plan, whereby at December 31, 2014, 9,248,957 (2013 – 9,749,555) voting shares were reserved for issuance to officers and employees of the Corporation, subject to the following limitations:

(i) the number of common voting shares reserved for issuance to any one optionee will not exceed 5% of the issued and outstanding voting shares at any time;

(ii) the number of common voting shares reserved for issuance to insiders shall not exceed 10% of the issued and outstanding voting shares; and

(iii) the number of common voting shares issuable under the stock option plan, which may be issued within a one-year period, shall not exceed 10% of the issued and outstanding voting shares at any time.

Stock options are granted at a price equal to the five day weighted average market value of the Corporation's voting shares preceding the date of grant and vest completely on or on a graded basis on the first, second and third anniversary from the date of grant. Stock options expire no later than seven years from the date of grant.

WESTJET

Notes to Consolidated Financial Statements
As at and for the years ended December 31, 2014 and 2013
(Stated in thousands of Canadian dollars, except percentage, ratio, share and per share amounts)

12. Share capital (continued)

(c) Stock option plan (continued)

The fair value of the options is expensed over the service period, with an offsetting entry to equity reserves. The fair value of each option grant is estimated on the date of grant using the Black-Scholes option pricing model. Upon the exercise of stock options, consideration received, together with amounts previously recorded in equity reserves, is recorded as an increase to share capital.

The fair value of options granted and the assumptions used in their determination:

	2014	2013
Weighted average fair value per option	4.55	4.54
Weighted average risk-free interest rate	1.5%	1.3%
Weighted average expected volatility	27%	29%
Expected life of options (years)	3.8	3.9
Weighted average dividend yield	1.6%	1.6%

Changes in the number of options and their weighted average exercise price:

	2014		2013	
	Number of options	Weighted average exercise price	Number of options	Weighted average exercise price
Stock options outstanding, beginning of year	2,834,639	19.20	3,850,898	14.45
Granted	2,353,474	23.94	1,722,013	21.92
Exercised	(1,447,250)	18.82	(2,668,440)	14.24
Forfeited	(2,149)	22.90	(67,796)	14.05
Expired	-	-	(2,036)	13.55
Stock options outstanding, end of year	3,738,714	22.33	2,834,639	19.20
Exercisable, end of year	912,772	19.38	637,292	14.57

Under the terms of the Corporation's stock option plan, with the approval of the Corporation, option holders can either (i) elect to receive shares by delivering cash to the Corporation in the amount of the exercise price of the options, or (ii) choose a cashless settlement alternative, whereby they can elect to receive a number of shares equivalent to the market value of the options over the exercise price. For the year ended December 31, 2014, option holders exercised 1,442,006 options (2013 – 2,660,717 options) on a cashless settlement basis and received 495,354 shares (2013 – 1,064,373 shares). For the year ended December 31, 2014, 5,244 options were exercised on a cash basis and option holders received 5,244 shares (2013 – 7,723 options and 7,723 shares, respectively).

Options outstanding and exercisable at December 31, 2014:

	Outstanding options			Exercisable options	
Range of exercise prices	Number outstanding	Weighted average remaining life (years)	Weighted average exercise price	Number exercisable	Weighted average exercise price
13.85-20.00	502,547	2.99	14.94	330,361	14.89
20.01-23.00	883,768	3.66	21.92	582,411	21.92
23.01-26.00	2,312,389	4.12	23.87	-	-
26.01-30.97	40,010	6.50	28.01	-	-
	3,738,714	3.89	22.33	912,772	19.38

WESTJET

Notes to Consolidated Financial Statements
As at and for the years ended December 31, 2014 and 2013
(Stated in thousands of Canadian dollars, except percentage, ratio, share and per share amounts)

12. Share capital (continued)

(d) Key employee plan

The Corporation has a key employee plan (KEP), whereby restricted share units (RSU) are issued to senior management and pilots of the Corporation. The fair market value of the RSUs at the time of grant is equal to the weighted average trading price of the Corporation's voting shares for the five trading days immediately preceding the date of grant. Each RSU entitles the employee to receive payment upon vesting in the form of voting shares of the Corporation. The Corporation intends to settle all RSUs with shares either through the purchase of voting shares on the open market or the issuance of new shares from treasury; however, wholly at its own discretion, the Corporation may settle the units in cash. The RSU's time vest at the end of a two or three-year period, with compensation expense being recognized in net earnings over the service period. At December 31, 2014, 944,738 (2013 – 944,738) voting shares of the Corporation were reserved for issuance under the KEP plan. For the year ended December 31, 2014, the Corporation settled nil RSUs with shares issued from treasury and 217,623 RSUs through the open market (December 31, 2013 – 2,660 and 156,610, respectively).

	2014		2013	
	Number of units	Weighted fair value	Number of units	Weighted fair value
Units outstanding, beginning of year	476,103	17.39	465,417	14.52
Granted	126,759	23.93	168,571	21.92
Units, in lieu of dividends	7,207	27.38	7,612	24.75
Settled	(217,623)	15.05	(159,270)	14.27
Forfeited	(1,416)	19.34	(6,227)	14.49
Units outstanding, end of year	391,030	20.99	476,103	17.39

(e) Executive share unit plan

The Corporation has an equity-based executive share unit (ESU) plan, whereby RSUs and performance share units (PSU) may be issued to senior executive officers. At December 31, 2014, 1,011,927 (2013 – 1,011,927) voting shares of the Corporation were reserved for issuance under the ESU plan.

The fair market value of the RSUs and PSUs at the time of grant is equal to the weighted average trading price of the Corporation's voting shares for the five trading days immediately preceding the grant date.

Each RSU entitles the senior executive officers to receive payment upon vesting in the form of voting shares of the Corporation. RSUs time vest over a period of up to three years, with compensation expense being recognized in net earnings over the service period.

Each PSU entitles the senior executive officers to receive payment upon vesting in the form of voting shares of the Corporation. PSUs time vest over a period of up to three years and incorporate performance criteria established at the time of grant. Compensation expense is recognized in net earnings over the service period based on the number of units expected to vest.

The Corporation intends to settle all RSUs and PSUs with shares either through the purchase of voting shares on the open market or the issuance of new shares from treasury; however, wholly at its own discretion, the Corporation may settle the units in cash.

	2014				2013			
	RSUs		PSUs		RSUs		PSUs	
	Number of units	Weighted fair value	Number of units	Weighted fair value	Number of units	Weighted fair value	Number of units	Weighted fair value
Units outstanding, beginning of year	192,084	17.35	243,567	17.18	214,168	14.54	243,567	14.41
Granted	60,338	24.34	144,559	24.33	68,205	21.82	82,635	21.89
Units, in lieu of dividends	1,689	28.17	3,207	28.54	713	25.24	959	24.97
Settled	(74,221)	17.22	(69,713)	15.44	(71,765)	14.00	(68,893)	13.64
Forfeited	-	-	-	-	(19,237)	14.70	(25,649)	14.70
Units outstanding, end of year	179,890	19.85	321,620	20.88	192,084	17.35	243,567	17.18

WESTJET

Notes to Consolidated Financial Statements
As at and for the years ended December 31, 2014 and 2013
(Stated in thousands of Canadian dollars, except percentage, ratio, share and per share amounts)

12. Share capital (continued)

(f) Share-based payment expense

Share-based payment expense for the Corporation's equity-based plans:

	2014	2013
Stock option plan	11,449	7,706
Key employee plan	3,039	3,602
Executive share unit plan	4,138	3,225
Total share-based payment expense	18,626	14,533
Flight operations and navigational charges	9,781	7,580
Marketing, general and administration	8,845	6,953
Total share-based payment expense	18,626	14,533

(g) Deferred share units

The Corporation has a cash-settled deferred share unit (DSU) plan as an alternative form of compensation for independent members of the Corporation's Board of Directors. Each DSU entitles a participant to receive cash equal to the market value of the equivalent number of shares of the Corporation. The number of DSUs granted is determined based on the closing price of the Corporation's common shares on the trading day immediately prior to the date of grant. Total compensation expense is recognized at the time of grant. Fluctuations in the market value are recognized in compensation expense in the period in which the fluctuations occur. For the year ended December 31, 2014, 18,913 (2013 – 23,887) DSUs were granted, with $1,782 (2013 – $1,848) of expense included in marketing, general and administration expense. During the years ended December 31, 2014 and 2013, the Corporation did not settle any DSUs. The carrying amount of the liability, included in trade and other payables, relating to the cash-settled DSUs at December 31, 2014 is $4,874 (2013 – $3,542). At December 31, 2014, 146,096 (2013 – 127,183) DSUs are vested and outstanding. DSUs are redeemable upon the Director's retirement from the Board.

(h) Employee share purchase plan

The Corporation has an employee share purchase plan (ESPP), whereby the Corporation matches the contributions made by employees. Under the terms of the ESPP, employees may, dependent on their employment agreement, contribute up to a maximum of 10% or 20% of their gross salary to acquire voting shares of the Corporation at the current fair market value. The contributions are matched by the Corporation and are required to be held within the ESPP for a period of one year. Employees may offer to sell ESPP shares, which have not been held for at least one year, to the Corporation, at a purchase price equal to 50% of the weighted average trading price of the Corporation's voting shares for the five trading days immediately preceding the employee's notice to the Corporation, to a maximum of four times per year.

Under the terms of the ESPP, the Corporation acquires voting shares on behalf of employees through open market purchases.

The Corporation's share of the contributions in 2014 amounted to $79,942 (2013 – $73,010) and is recorded as compensation expense within the related business unit (refer to note 4).

13. Dividends

During the year ended December 31, 2014, the Corporation declared quarterly cash dividends of $0.12 per share on its common voting shares and variable voting shares. For the year ended December 31, 2014, the Corporation paid dividends totaling $61,313 (2013 – $52,188).

WESTJET

Notes to Consolidated Financial Statements
As at and for the years ended December 31, 2014 and 2013
(Stated in thousands of Canadian dollars, except percentage, ratio, share and per share amounts)

14. Earnings per share

Share data used in the computation of basic and diluted earnings per share:

	2014	2013
Weighted average number of shares outstanding – basic	127,858,259	130,974,532
Effect of dilution:		
Employee stock options	680,507	454,574
Key employee – RSUs	320,162	380,470
Executive – RSUs	118,449	129,077
Executive – PSUs	165,563	135,349
Weighted average number of shares outstanding – diluted	129,142,940	132,074,002

For the year ended December 31, 2014, 36,499 employee stock options (2013 – 372,349) and 849 (2013 – nil) restricted share units were not included in the calculation of dilutive potential shares as the result would have been anti-dilutive.

15. Financial instruments and risk management

(a) Fair value of financial assets and financial liabilities

The Corporation's financial assets and liabilities consist primarily of cash and cash equivalents, accounts receivable, derivatives designated in an effective hedging relationship, interest bearing deposits, accounts payable and accrued liabilities and long-term debt. The following tables set out the Corporation's classification and carrying amount, together with the fair value, for each type of financial asset and financial liability at December 31, 2014 and 2013:

	Fair value		Amortized cost		Total	
December 31, 2014	Through profit or loss	Derivatives	Loans and receivables	Other financial liabilities	Carrying amount	Fair value
Asset (liability):						
Cash and cash equivalents(i)	1,416,220	–	–	–	1,416,220	1,416,220
Accounts receivable	–	–	54,950	–	54,950	54,950
Foreign exchange derivatives(iii)	–	6,360	–	–	6,360	6,360
Interest rate derivatives(iii)	–	(7,654)	–	–	(7,654)	(7,654)
Deposits(iv)	25,204	–	–	–	25,204	25,204
Accounts payable and accrued liabilities(v)	–	–	–	(412,704)	(412,704)	(412,704)
Long-term debt(vi)	–	–	–	(1,188,663)	(1,188,663)	(1,225,907)
	1,441,424	(1,294)	54,950	(1,601,367)	(106,287)	(143,531)

	Fair value		Amortized cost		Total	
December 31, 2013	Through profit or loss	Derivatives	Loans and receivables	Other financial liabilities	Carrying amount	Fair value
Asset (liability):						
Cash and cash equivalents(i)	1,314,111	–	–	–	1,314,111	1,314,111
Accounts receivable	–	–	42,164	–	42,164	42,164
Foreign exchange derivatives(iii)	–	4,158	–	–	4,158	4,158
Interest rate derivatives(iii)	–	883	–	–	883	883
Deposits(iv)	32,021	–	–	–	32,021	32,021
Accounts payable and accrued liabilities(v)	–	–	–	(480,836)	(480,836)	(480,836)
Long-term debt(vi)	–	–	–	(878,395)	(878,395)	(924,570)
	1,346,132	5,041	42,164	(1,359,231)	34,106	(12,069)

(i) Includes restricted cash of $58,149 (2013 – $58,106).
(ii) Includes $6,409 (2013 – $4,187) classified in prepaid expenses, deposits and other, and $49 (2013 – $29) classified in accounts payable and accrued liabilities.
(iii) Includes $2,809 (2013 – $3,220) classified in accounts payable and accrued liabilities and $4,845 classified in other long-term liabilities (2013 – $4,103 in long-term assets).
(iv) Includes $17,585 (2013 – $19,355) classified in prepaid expenses, deposits and other, and $7,619 (2013 – $12,666) classified in other long-term assets.
(v) Excludes deferred WestJet Rewards program revenue of $86,870 (2013 – $59,082), foreign exchange derivative liabilities of $49 (2013 – $29), and interest rate derivative liabilities of $2,809 (2013 – $3,220).
(vi) Includes current portion of long-term debt of $159,843 (2013 – $189,191) and long-term debt of $1,028,820 (2013 – $689,204).

WESTJET

Notes to Consolidated Financial Statements
As at and for the years ended December 31, 2014 and 2013
(Stated in thousands of Canadian dollars, except percentage, ratio, share and per share amounts)

15. Financial instruments and risk management (continued)

(a) Fair value of financial assets and financial liabilities (continued)

The following items shown in the consolidated statement of financial position at December 31, 2014 and 2013, are measured at fair value on a recurring basis using level 1 or level 2 inputs. The fair value of the financial assets and liabilities at December 31, 2014, using level 3 inputs, was $nil (2013 – $nil).

December 31, 2014	Level 1	Level 2	Total
Asset (liability):			
Cash and cash equivalents(i)	1,416,220	–	1,416,220
Foreign exchange derivatives	–	6,360	6,360
Interest rate derivatives	–	(7,654)	(7,654)
Deposits	25,204	–	25,204
	1,441,424	(1,294)	1,440,130

December 31, 2013	Level 1	Level 2	Total
Asset (liability):			
Cash and cash equivalents(i)	1,314,111	–	1,314,111
Foreign exchange derivatives	–	4,158	4,158
Interest rate derivatives	–	883	883
Deposits	32,021	–	32,021
	1,346,132	5,041	1,351,173

(i) Includes restricted cash of $58,149 (2013 – $58,106).

During the years ended December 31, 2014 and 2013, there were no transfers between level 1, level 2 and level 3 financial assets and liabilities measured at fair value.

Cash and cash equivalents: Consist of bank balances and short-term investments, primarily highly liquid instruments, with terms up to 91 days. Classified in level 1 as the measurement inputs are derived from observable, unadjusted quoted prices in active markets. Interest income is recorded in the consolidated statement of earnings as finance income. Due to their short-term nature, the carrying value of cash and cash equivalents approximates their fair value.

Foreign exchange derivatives: Consist of foreign exchange forward contracts where the fair value of the forward contracts is measured based on the difference between the contracted rate and the current forward price obtained from the counterparty. Classified in level 2 as the significant measurement inputs used in the valuation models are observable in active markets. At December 31, 2014, the weighted average contracted rate on the forward contracts was 1.1187 (2013 – 1.1025) Canadian dollars to one US dollar, and the weighted average forward rate used in determining the fair value was 1.1640 (December 31, 2013 – 1.0683) Canadian dollars to one US dollar.

Interest rate derivatives: Consist of interest rate swap contracts that exchange a floating rate of interest with a fixed rate of interest. The fair value of the interest rate swaps is determined by measuring the difference between the fixed contracted rate and the forward curve for the applicable floating interest rates obtained from the counterparty. Classified in level 2, as the significant measurement inputs used in the valuation models are observable in active markets. At December 31, 2014, the Corporation's swap contracts have a weighted average fixed interest rate of 2.60% (2013 – 2.59%). The December 31, 2013, weighted average forward interest rate curve for the three month Canadian Dealer Offered Rate over the term of the debt was 1.96% (2013 – 2.76%).

Deposits: Relate to purchased aircraft and airport operations and earn a floating market rate of interest. Classified in level 1 as the measurement inputs are unadjusted, observable inputs in active markets.

Accounts receivable and accounts payable and accrued liabilities: The Corporation designates accounts receivable and accounts payable and accrued liabilities as loans and receivables and other financial liabilities, respectively. These items are initially recorded at fair value and subsequently measured at amortized cost. Due to their short-term nature, the carrying value of accounts receivable and accounts payable and accrued liabilities approximate their fair value.

Long-term debt: The fair value of the Corporation's fixed-rate long-term debt is determined by discounting the future contractual cash flows under the current financing arrangements at discount rates presently available to the Corporation for loans with similar terms and remaining maturities. At December 31, 2014, the rates used in determining the fair value ranged from 1.30% to 3.44% (2013 – 1.28% to 4.10%). The fair value of the Corporation's floating-rate debt approximates its carrying value.

WESTJET

Notes to Consolidated Financial Statements
As at and for the years ended December 31, 2014 and 2013
(Stated in thousands of Canadian dollars, except percentage, ratio, share and per share amounts)

15. Financial instruments and risk management (continued)

(b) Risk management related to financial instruments

The Corporation is exposed to market, credit and liquidity risks associated with its financial assets and liabilities. From time to time, the Corporation may use various financial derivatives to reduce exposures from changes in foreign exchange rates, interest rates and jet fuel prices. The Corporation does not hold or use any derivative instruments for trading or speculative purposes.

The Corporation's Board of Directors has responsibility for the establishment and approval of the Corporation's overall risk management policies, including those related to financial instruments. Management performs continuous assessments so that all significant risks related to financial instruments are reviewed and addressed in light of changes to market conditions and the Corporation's operating activities.

Market risk

Market risk is the risk that the fair value or future cash flows of a financial instrument will fluctuate due to changes in market prices. The Corporation's significant market risks relate to fuel price risk, foreign exchange risk and interest rate risk.

(i) Fuel price risk

The airline industry is inherently dependent upon jet fuel to operate and, therefore, the Corporation is exposed to the risk of volatile fuel prices. Fuel prices are impacted by a host of factors outside the Corporation's control, such as significant weather events, geopolitical tensions, refinery capacity, and global demand and supply. For the year ended December 31, 2014, aircraft fuel expense represented approximately 31% (2013 – 32%) of the Corporation's total operating expenses.

(ii) Foreign exchange risk

The Corporation is exposed to foreign exchange risks arising from fluctuations in exchange rates on its US-dollar-denominated monetary assets and liabilities and its US dollar operating expenditures, mainly aircraft fuel, aircraft leasing expense, the land component of vacations packages and certain maintenance and airport operations costs.

US dollar monetary assets and liabilities

The gain or loss on foreign exchange included in the Corporation's consolidated statement of earnings is mainly attributable to the effect of the changes in the value of the Corporation's US-dollar-denominated monetary assets and liabilities. At December 31, 2014, US-dollar-denominated net monetary assets totaled approximately US $6,073 (2013 – US $256 net liabilities).

The Corporation estimates that a one-cent change in the value of the US dollar versus the Canadian dollar at December 31, 2014, would have increased or decreased net earnings for the year ended December 31, 2014, by $44 (2013 – $2), as a result of the Corporation's US-dollar-denominated net monetary asset balance.

US dollar aircraft leasing costs

At December 31, 2014, the Corporation has entered into foreign exchange forward contracts for an average of US $11,689 (2013 – US $13,439) per month for the period of January to December 2014 for a total of US $140,273 (2013 – US $161,273) at a weighted average contract price of 1.1187 (2013 – 1.1025) Canadian dollars to one US dollar to offset a portion of its US-dollar-denominated aircraft lease payments. At December 31, 2014, no portion of the forward contracts was considered ineffective.

Upon proper qualification, the Corporation accounts for its foreign exchange derivatives as cash flow hedges.

The following table presents the financial impact and statement presentation of the Corporation's foreign exchange derivatives on the consolidated statement of financial position:

	Statement presentation	2014	2013
Fair value	Prepaid expenses, deposits and other	6,409	4,187
Fair value	Accounts payable and accrued liabilities	(49)	(29)
Unrealized gain	Hedge reserves (before tax)	6,360	4,158

The following table presents the financial impact and statement presentation of the Corporation's foreign exchange derivatives on the consolidated statement of earnings:

	Statement presentation	2014	2013
Realized gain	Aircraft leasing	9,498	4,752

A one-cent change in the US-dollar exchange rate for the year ended December 31, 2014, would impact OCI, net of taxes, by $1,037 (2013 – $1,192) as a result of the Corporation's foreign exchange derivatives.

WESTJET

Notes to Consolidated Financial Statements
As at and for the years ended December 31, 2014 and 2013
(Stated in thousands of Canadian dollars, except percentage, ratio, share and per share amounts)

15. Financial instruments and risk management (continued)

(b) Risk management related to financial instruments (continued)

Market risk (continued)

(iii) Interest rate risk

Interest rate risk is the risk that the value or future cash flows of a financial instrument will fluctuate as a result of changes in market interest rates.

Cash and cash equivalents

The Corporation is exposed to interest rate fluctuations on its short-term investments, included in cash and cash equivalents. A change of 50 basis points in the market interest rate would have an approximate impact on net earnings of $4,673 (2013 – $4,639) as a result of the Corporation's short-term investment activities.

Deposits

The Corporation is exposed to interest rate fluctuations on its deposits that relate to certain purchased aircraft and airport operations, which, at December 31, 2014, totaled $25,204 (2013 – $32,021). A reasonable change in market interest rates at December 31, 2014, would not have significantly impacted the Corporation's net earnings due to the small size of these deposits.

Long-term debt

The Corporation is exposed to interest rate risks arising from fluctuations in market interest rates on its variable rate debt. The fixed-rate nature of the majority of the Corporation's long-term debt mitigates the impact of interest rate fluctuations over the term of the outstanding debt. The Corporation accounts for its long-term fixed-rate debt at amortized cost, and therefore, a change in interest rates at December 31, 2014, would not impact net earnings.

At December 31, 2014, the Corporation had seven interest rate swap contracts outstanding with a 12-year term to fix the interest rate on seven variable interest rate term loans at a weighted average contracted rate of 2.60%, inclusive of a basis point spread. The term loans were used to finance the purchase of aircraft.

Upon proper qualification, the Corporation accounts for its interest rate swap derivatives as cash flow hedges.

The following table presents the financial impact and statement presentation of the Corporation's interest rate derivatives on the consolidated statement of financial position:

	Statement presentation	2014	2013
Fair value	Accounts payable and accrued liabilities	(2,809)	(3,220)
Fair value	Other assets	–	4,103
Fair value	Other liabilities	(4,845)	–
Unrealized gain (loss)	Hedge reserves (before tax)	(7,654)	883

The following table presents the financial impact and statement presentation of the Corporation's interest rate derivatives on the consolidated statement of earnings:

	Statement presentation	2014	2013
Realized loss	Finance cost	(3,225)	(1,058)

A change of 50 basis points in market interest rates at December 31, 2014, would impact OCI, net of taxes, by $4,214 (2013 – $4,926) as a result of the Corporation's interest rate derivatives.

WESTJET

Notes to Consolidated Financial Statements
As at and for the years ended December 31, 2014 and 2013
(Stated in thousands of Canadian dollars, except percentage, ratio, share and per share amounts)

15. Financial instruments and risk management (continued)

(b) Risk management related to financial instruments (continued)

Credit risk

Credit risk is the risk that one party to a financial instrument will cause a financial loss for the other party by failing to discharge an obligation. At December 31, 2014, the Corporation's credit exposure consists primarily of the carrying amounts of cash and cash equivalents, restricted cash, accounts receivable, deposits and the fair value of derivative financial assets.

The Corporation's maximum exposure to credit risk is represented by the balances in the aforementioned accounts:

	2014	2013
Cash and cash equivalents[i]	1,358,071	1,256,005
Restricted cash[i]	58,149	58,106
Accounts receivable[ii]	54,950	42,164
Deposits[iii]	25,204	32,021
Derivative financial assets[iv]	6,409	11,568

(i) Consist of bank balances and short-term investments with terms of up to 91 days. Credit risk associated with cash and cash equivalents and restricted cash is minimized substantially by ensuring that these financial assets are invested primarily in debt instruments with highly rated financial institutions, some with provincial-government-backed guarantees. The Corporation manages its exposure by assessing the financial strength of its counterparties and by limiting the total exposure to any one individual counterparty.

(ii) All significant counterparties, both current and new, are reviewed and approved for credit on a regular basis under the Corporation's credit management policies. The Corporation does not hold any collateral as security, however, in some cases the Corporation requires guaranteed letters of credit with certain of its counterparties. Trade receivables are generally settled within 30 to 60 days. Industry receivables are generally settled in less than 30 days.

(iii) The Corporation is not exposed to counterparty credit risk on its deposits that relate to purchased aircraft, as the funds are held in a security trust separate from the assets of the financial institution. While the Corporation is exposed to counterparty credit risk on its deposit relating to airport operations, it considers this risk to be remote because of the nature and size of the counterparty.

(iv) Derivative financial assets consist of foreign exchange forward contracts and interest rate swap contracts. The Corporation reviews the size and credit rating of both current and any new counterparties in addition to limiting the total exposure to any one counterparty.

There were no new bad debts recorded for the year ended December 31, 2014 (2013 – $69). For the year ended December 31, 2014, the Corporation revised its estimate for its allowance for doubtful accounts relating to value-added tax (VAT) in a foreign jurisdiction. The effect of recording this change in estimate for the year ended December 31, 2014, is a reduction to *Aircraft fuel* and *Airport operations* expense on the consolidated statement of earnings by $20,234 and $2,869, respectively. The Corporation's change in estimate is based on the successful outcome of filed VAT returns. The Corporation has no remaining VAT amounts recorded in its allowance for doubtful accounts.

Liquidity risk

Liquidity risk is the risk that the Corporation will encounter difficulty in meeting obligations associated with financial liabilities. The Corporation maintains a strong liquidity position and sufficient financial resources to meet its obligations as they fall due.

The table below presents a maturity analysis of the Corporation's undiscounted contractual cash flows for its non-derivative and derivative financial liabilities at December 31, 2014. The analysis is based on foreign exchange and interest rates in effect at the consolidated statement of financial position date, and includes both principal and interest cash flows for long-term debt.

	Total	Within 1 year	1–3 years	3–5 years	Over 5 years
Accounts payable and accrued liabilities[i]	412,704	412,704	–	–	–
Derivative financial liabilities[ii]	7,703	2,858	4,845	–	–
Long-term debt	1,363,817	205,626	307,446	588,961	261,784
	1,784,224	621,188	312,291	588,961	261,784

(i) Excludes deferred WestJet Rewards liability of $86,870, foreign exchange derivative liabilities of $49 and interest rate derivative liabilities of $2,809.

(ii) Derivative financial liabilities consist of foreign exchange forward contracts of $49 and interest rate derivative contracts of $7,654. The Corporation reports long-term interest rate derivatives at their net position. At December 31, 2014, net long-term interest rate derivative liabilities were $4,845.

A portion of the Corporation's cash and cash equivalents balance relates to cash collected with respect to advance ticket sales, for which the balance at December 31, 2014, was $575,781 (2013 – $551,022). The Corporation has cash and cash equivalents on hand to have sufficient liquidity to meet its liabilities, when due, under both normal and stressed conditions. At December 31, 2014, the Corporation had cash and cash equivalents on hand of 2.36 times (2013 – 2.28) the advance ticket sales balance.

The Corporation aims to maintain a current ratio, defined as current assets over current liabilities, of at least 1.00. At December 31, 2014, the Corporation's current ratio was 1.29 (2013 – 1.09). At December 31, 2014, the Corporation has not been required to post collateral with respect to any of its outstanding derivative contracts.

WESTJET

Notes to Consolidated Financial Statements

As at and for the years ended December 31, 2014 and 2013
(Stated in thousands of Canadian dollars, except percentage, ratio, share and per share amounts)

16. Commitments

(a) Purchased aircraft and spare engines

At December 31, 2014, the Corporation is committed to purchase 18 737 Next Generation aircraft for delivery between 2015 and 2017 as well as 65 737 MAX aircraft for delivery between 2017 and 2027. The Corporation is also committed to purchase 15 Q400 NextGen aircraft for delivery between 2015 and 2016 and a total of 10 spare engines for our Boeing and Bombardier aircraft for delivery between 2015 and 2026.

The remaining estimated amounts to be paid in deposits and purchase prices for the 98 aircraft and 10 spare engines are presented in the table below. Where applicable, US dollar commitments are translated at the period end foreign exchange rate.

Within 1 year	573,294
1 – 3 years	878,247
3 – 5 years	952,857
Over 5 years	2,318,142
	4,722,540

(b) Leases and contractual commitments

The Corporation has entered into leases and other contractual commitments for aircraft, land, buildings, equipment, computer hardware, software licenses and inflight entertainment. At December 31, 2014, the future payments under these commitments are presented in the table below. Where applicable, US dollar commitments are translated at the period end foreign exchange rate.

Within 1 year	287,447
1 – 3 years	431,880
3 – 5 years	233,264
Over 5 years	166,082
	1,118,673

(c) Letters of guarantee

At December 31, 2014, the Corporation has a revolving letter of credit facility with a Canadian Chartered Bank totaling $30,000 (2013 – $30,000). The facility requires funds to be assigned and held in cash security for the full value of letters of guarantee issued by the Corporation. At December 31, 2014, $9,515 (2013 – $8,322) letters of guarantee were issued under the facility by assigning restricted cash of $9,515 (2013 – $8,322).

WESTJET

Notes to Consolidated Financial Statements

As at and for the years ended December 31, 2014 and 2013
(Stated in thousands of Canadian dollars, except percentage, ratio, share and per share amounts)

17. Related parties

(a) Interests in subsidiaries

The consolidated financial statements of WestJet Airlines Ltd., the parent company, include the accounts of the Corporation and its following four directly wholly-owned subsidiaries incorporated in Canada, as well as an indirectly wholly-owned Alberta partnership:

WestJet Investment Corp. (WIC)
WestJet Operations Corp. (WOC)
WestJet Vacations Inc. (WVI)
WestJet Encore Ltd. (Encore)
WestJet, An Alberta Partnership (Partnership)

The Partnership is the primary operating entity of the Corporation. WIC, WOC, WVI and Encore were created for legal, tax and marketing purposes and do not operate independently of the Partnership. Their relationship is such that they depend critically on the Partnership for a variety of resources including financing, human resources and systems and technology. There are no legal or contractual restrictions on the Corporation's and subsidiaries' ability to access or use assets or settle liabilities of the consolidated group.

(b) Interests in consolidated structured entities

The Corporation also controls and consolidates six structured entities in which the Corporation has no equity ownership but controls and has power over all relevant activities and is exposed to and has rights to variable returns by means of contractual relationships. These entities were established for legal purposes to facilitate the financing of aircraft. These entities do not conduct any operations except to hold legal title to specific aircraft and their related debt obligations. Through these contractual relationships, the Corporation is required to fund all of the aircraft debt obligations of these entities. There are no legal or contractual restrictions between the Corporation and these entities that limit the access or use of assets or the settlement of liabilities. The full amount of the aircraft debt obligations are reported as long-term debt on the Corporation's consolidated statement of financial position. The nature of the risks associated with these entities is limited to specific tax legislation in Canada and the U.S. Although considered remote by Management, the potential for future changes to Canadian and U.S. tax legislation affecting these entities could have potential adverse tax effects on the Corporation.

(c) Interests in unconsolidated structured entities

The Corporation is a party to 11 FFCs and one DFC for the purpose of obtaining cost effective into-plane fuel services and aircraft de-icing services at select Canadian and US airports. These operating costs are recorded in aircraft fuel and airport operations, respectively, on the consolidated statement of earnings. At December 31, 2014, the Corporation has $1,812 in operating deposits with the FFCs and DFC classified in prepaids, deposits and other on the consolidated statement of financial position. The Corporation has no equity ownership and no control or significant influence in the FFCs or DFC. The financing and operating costs of these entities are shared amongst numerous contracting airlines based on a variety of contractual terms including fuel volume consumption and qualifying flights. The Corporation classifies its monthly operating cost obligations to the FFCs and DFC as other financial liabilities and these obligations are included in accounts payable and accrued liabilities on the consolidated statement of financial position. At November 30, 2014, the 11 FFCs and one DFC have combined total assets of approximately $492,726 and liabilities of $454,556. In the event any or all contracting airlines default and withdraw from the FFCs and DFC and no amounts are recovered through legal recourse, the Corporation and any remaining contracting airlines are liable for the outstanding obligations of the FFCs and DFC. These obligations represent the Corporation's maximum exposure to loss from the FFCs and DFC.

(d) Key management personnel

The Corporation has defined key management personnel as Senior Executive Officers and the Board of Directors, as they have the collective authority and responsibility for planning, directing and controlling the activities of the Corporation. The following table outlines the total compensation expense for key management personnel for the years ended December 31, 2014 and 2013.

	2014	2013
Salaries, benefits and other compensation[i]	5,845	5,428
Share-based payment expense[ii]	6,835	5,657
	12,680	11,085

(i) Other compensation includes the employee share purchase plan, profit share, cash compensation paid to the Board of Directors and payments under the Corporation's short-term incentive plan to Senior Executive Officers.

(ii) Includes amounts expensed pursuant to the stock option plan, executive share unit plan and deferred share unit plan.

WESTJET

Notes to Consolidated Financial Statements
As at and for the years ended December 31, 2014 and 2013
(Stated in thousands of Canadian dollars, except percentage, ratio, share and per share amounts)

18. Additional financial information

(a) Assets

	Note	2014	2013
Accounts receivable:			
Trade and industry[i]		43,454	43,198
Other		13,864	1,403
Allowance		(2,368)	(2,437)
		54,950	42,164
Prepaid expenses, deposits and other:			
Prepaid expenses[ii]		48,533	43,628
Short-term deposits[iii]		34,472	35,438
Maintenance reserves – current portion	9	54,466	49,810
Derivatives	15	6,409	4,187
Other		312	200
		144,192	133,263
Inventory:			
Fuel		21,309	24,365
Aircraft expendables		12,539	9,749
De-icing fluid		454	900
Other		2,356	1,708
		36,658	36,722
Other Assets:			
Aircraft deposits[iv]		45,740	47,615
Maintenance reserves – long term	9	8,110	11,851
Derivatives	15	–	4,103
Other[v]		8,440	7,209
		62,290	70,778

(i) Trade receivables include receivables relating to airport operations, fuel rebates, marketing programs and ancillary revenue products and services. Industry receivables include receivables relating to travel agents, interline agreements with other airlines and partnerships. All significant counterparties are reviewed and approved for credit on a regular basis. Trade receivables are generally settled in 30 to 60 days. Industry receivables are generally settled in less than 30 days.

(ii) Includes prepaid expenses for insurance, vacation package vendors and other operating costs.

(iii) Includes deposits relating to aircraft fuel, airport operations, deposits on leased aircraft and other operating costs.

(iv) Includes long-term deposits with lessors for leased aircraft.

(v) Includes long-term deposits for airport operations and long-term prepaid financing costs.

(b) Liabilities

	Note	2014	2013
Accounts payable and accrued liabilities:			
Trade and industry		337,458	330,836
Taxes payable		20,431	109,674
WestJet Rewards		86,870	59,082
Derivatives	15	2,858	3,249
Other		54,815	40,326
		502,432	543,167
Other current liabilities:			
Advance ticket sales		575,781	551,022
Non-refundable guest credits		45,434	46,975
Other liabilities:			
Deferred contract incentives[i]		8,305	8,834
Derivatives	15	4,845	–
		13,150	8,834

(i) Deferred contract incentives relate to discounts received on aircraft related items as well as the net effect of rent free periods and cost escalations on land leases. Incentives, rent free periods and cost escalations are amortized over the terms of the related contracts.

"We are what we repeatedly do. Excellence, then, is not an act, but a habit."

— *Aristotle*

!ndigo

Enrich your life™

Indigo   Chapters   Coles   indigo.ca

Independent Auditors' Report

To the Shareholders of Indigo Books & Music Inc.

We have audited the accompanying consolidated financial statements of Indigo Books & Music Inc., which comprise the consolidated balance sheets as at March 29, 2014, March 30, 2013, and April 1, 2012, and the consolidated statements of earnings (loss) and comprehensive earnings (loss), changes in equity and cash flows for the 52 week periods then ended March 29, 2014 and March 30, 2013 and a summary of significant accounting policies and other explanatory information.

Management's responsibility for the consolidated financial statements

Management is responsible for the preparation and fair presentation of these consolidated financial statements in accordance with International Financial Reporting Standards, and for such internal control as management determines is necessary to enable the preparation of consolidated financial statements that are free from material misstatement, whether due to fraud or error.

Auditors' responsibility

Our responsibility is to express an opinion on these consolidated financial statements based on our audits. We conducted our audits in accordance with Canadian generally accepted auditing standards. Those standards require that we comply with ethical requirements and plan and perform the audit to obtain reasonable assurance about whether the consolidated financial statements are free from material misstatement.

An audit involves performing procedures to obtain audit evidence about the amounts and disclosures in the consolidated financial statements. The procedures selected depend on the auditors' judgment, including the assessment of the risks of material misstatement of the consolidated financial statements, whether due to fraud or error. In making those risk assessments, the auditors consider internal control relevant to the entity's preparation and fair presentation of the consolidated financial statements in order to design audit procedures that are appropriate in the circumstances, but not for the purpose of expressing an opinion on the effectiveness of the entity's internal control. An audit also includes evaluating the appropriateness of accounting policies used and the reasonableness of accounting estimates made by management, as well as evaluating the overall presentation of the consolidated financial statements.

We believe that the audit evidence we have obtained in our audits is sufficient and appropriate to provide a basis for our audit opinion.

Opinion

In our opinion, the consolidated financial statements present fairly, in all material respects, the financial position of Indigo Books & Music Inc. as at March 29, 2014, March 30, 2013 and April 1, 2012 and its financial performance and its cash flows for the 52 week periods then ended March 29, 2014 and March 30, 2013 in accordance with International Financial Reporting Standards.

Ernst & Young LLP

Toronto, Canada   Chartered Accountants
May 27, 2014   Licensed Public Accountants

Consolidated Balance Sheets

(thousands of Canadian dollars)	As at March 29, 2014	As at March 30, 2013 restated (notes 4 and 22)	As at April 1, 2012 restated (notes 4 and 22)
ASSETS			
Current			
Cash and cash equivalents (note 6)	157,578	210,562	206,718
Accounts receivable	5,582	7,126	12,810
Inventories (note 7)	218,979	216,533	229,199
Prepaid expenses	5,184	4,153	3,692
Total current assets	387,323	438,374	452,419
Property, plant and equipment (note 8)	58,476	58,903	66,928
Intangible assets (note 9)	21,587	22,164	22,810
Equity investment (note 20)	598	968	961
Deferred tax assets (note 10)	44,604	48,731	48,633
Total assets	512,588	569,140	591,751
LIABILITIES AND EQUITY			
Current			
Accounts payable and accrued liabilities (note 19)	136,428	150,177	173,416
Unredeemed gift card liability (note 19)	46,827	47,169	42,711
Provisions (note 11)	928	2,168	232
Deferred revenue	12,860	13,733	11,234
Income taxes payable	—	11	65
Current portion of long-term debt (notes 12 and 18)	584	773	1,060
Total current liabilities	197,627	214,031	228,718
Long-term accrued liabilities (note 19)	2,896	4,004	5,800
Long-term provisions (note 11)	164	78	460
Long-term debt (notes 12 and 18)	227	705	1,141
Total liabilities	200,914	218,818	236,119
Equity			
Share capital (note 13)	203,812	203,805	203,373
Contributed surplus (note 14)	8,820	8,128	7,039
Retained earnings	99,042	138,389	145,220
Total equity	311,674	350,322	355,632
Total liabilities and equity	512,588	569,140	591,751

See accompanying notes

On behalf of the Board:

Heather Reisman
Director

Michael Kirby
Director

Consolidated Statements of Earnings (Loss) and Comprehensive Earnings (Loss)

(thousands of Canadian dollars, except per share data)	52-week period ended March 29, 2014	52-week period ended March 30, 2013 restated (notes 4 and 22)
Revenues	867,668	878,785
Cost of sales	(493,955)	(495,099)
Gross profit	373,713	383,686
Operating, selling and administrative expenses (notes 8, 9 and 15)	(403,693)	(383,319)
Operating profit (loss)	(29,980)	367
Interest on long-term debt and financing charges	(95)	(101)
Interest income on cash and cash equivalents	2,377	2,609
Share of earnings from equity investment (note 20)	789	1,315
Earnings (loss) before income taxes	(26,909)	4,190
Income tax recovery (expense) (note 10)		
Current	37	—
Deferred	(4,127)	98
Net earnings (loss) and comprehensive earnings (loss) for the period	(30,999)	4,288
Net earnings (loss) per common share (note 16)		
Basic	$(1.21)	$0.17
Diluted	$(1.21)	$0.17

See accompanying notes

Consolidated Statements of Changes in Equity

(thousands of Canadian dollars)	Share Capital	Contributed Surplus	Retained Earnings	Total Equity
Balance, March 31, 2012	203,373	7,039	145,220	355,632
Earnings for the 52-week period ended March 30, 2013	–	–	4,288	4,288
Exercise of options (notes 13 and 14)	417	(85)	–	332
Directors' deferred share units converted (note 13)	15	(15)	–	–
Stock-based compensation (note 14)	–	743	–	743
Directors' compensation (note 14)	–	446	–	446
Dividends paid (note 13)	–	–	(11,119)	(11,119)
Balance, March 30, 2013	203,805	8,128	138,389	350,322
Balance, March 30, 2013	203,805	8,128	138,389	350,322
Loss for the 52-week period ended March 29, 2014	–	–	(30,999)	(30,999)
Exercise of options (notes 13 and 14)	7	–	–	7
Directors' deferred share units converted (note 13)	–	1,242	–	1,242
Stock-based compensation (note 14)	–	425	–	425
Directors' compensation (note 14)	–	–	(8,348)	(8,348)
Dividends paid (note 13)	–	(975)	–	(975)
Repurchase of options (note 14)				
Balance, March 29, 2014	203,812	8,820	99,042	311,674

See accompanying notes

Consolidated Statements of Cash Flows

(thousands of Canadian dollars)	52-week period ended March 29, 2014	52-week period ended March 30, 2013 restated (notes 4 and 22)
CASH FLOWS FROM OPERATING ACTIVITIES		
Net earnings (loss) for the period	(30,999)	4,288
Add (deduct) items not affecting cash		
Depreciation of property, plant and equipment (note 8)	16,358	17,638
Amortization of intangible assets (note 9)	11,123	10,245
Net impairment of capital assets (note 8)	2,604	250
Loss on disposal of capital assets	302	65
Stock-based compensation (note 14)	1,242	743
Directors' compensation (note 14)	425	446
Deferred tax assets (note 10)	4,127	(98)
Other	(206)	(482)
Net change in non-cash working capital balances (note 17)	(19,196)	1,089
Interest on long-term debt and financing charges	95	101
Interest income on cash and cash equivalents	(2,377)	(2,609)
Income taxes received	26	32
Share of earnings from equity investment (note 20)	(789)	(1,315)
Cash flows from (used in) operating activities	(17,265)	30,393
CASH FLOWS FROM INVESTING ACTIVITIES		
Purchase of property, plant and equipment (note 8)	(18,700)	(9,441)
Addition of intangible assets (note 9)	(10,546)	(9,621)
Distributions from equity investment (note 20)	1,159	1,308
Interest received	2,463	2,691
Cash flows used in investing activities	(25,624)	(15,063)
CASH FLOWS FROM FINANCING ACTIVITIES		
Notes payable (note 21)	–	190
Repayment of long-term debt	(814)	(1,200)
Interest paid	(110)	(160)
Proceeds from share issuances (note 13)	7	332
Dividends paid (note 13)	(8,348)	(11,119)
Repurchase of options (note 14)	(975)	–
Cash flows used in financing activities	(10,240)	(11,957)
Effect of foreign currency exchange rate changes on cash and cash equivalents	145	471
Net increase (decrease) in cash and cash equivalents during the period	(52,984)	3,844
Cash and cash equivalents, beginning of period	210,562	206,718
Cash and cash equivalents, end of period	157,578	210,562

See accompanying notes

each and every day

14 annual report

TELUS
the future is friendly®

Report of management on internal control over financial reporting

Management of TELUS Corporation (TELUS, or the Company) is responsible for establishing and maintaining adequate internal control over financial reporting and for its assessment of the effectiveness of internal control over financial reporting.

TELUS' President and Chief Executive Officer and Executive Vice-President and Chief Financial Officer have assessed the effectiveness of the Company's internal control over financial reporting as of December 31, 2014, in accordance with the criteria established in *Internal Control – Integrated Framework (2013)* issued by the Committee of Sponsoring Organizations of the Treadway Commission. Internal control over financial reporting is a process designed by, or under the supervision of, the President and Chief Executive Officer and the Executive Vice-President and Chief Financial Officer and effected by the Board of Directors, management and other personnel to provide reasonable assurance regarding the reliability of financial reporting and the preparation of financial statements for external purposes in accordance with generally accepted accounting principles.

Due to its inherent limitations, internal control over financial reporting may not prevent or detect misstatements on a timely basis. Also, projections of any evaluation of the effectiveness of internal control over financial reporting to future periods are subject to the risk that the controls may become inadequate because of changes in conditions, or that

the degree of compliance with the policies or procedures may deteriorate. Based on this assessment, management has determined that the Company's internal control over financial reporting is effective as of December 31, 2014. In connection with this assessment, no material weaknesses in the Company's internal control over financial reporting were identified by management as of December 31, 2014.

Deloitte LLP, an Independent Registered Public Accounting Firm, audited the Company's Consolidated financial statements for the year ended December 31, 2014, and as stated in the Report of Independent Registered Public Accounting Firm, they have expressed an unqualified opinion on the effectiveness of the Company's internal control over financial reporting as of December 31, 2014.

John R. Gossling
Executive Vice-President
and Chief Financial Officer
February 12, 2015

Joe Natale
President
and Chief Executive Officer
February 12, 2015

Report of independent registered public accounting firm

To the Board of Directors and Shareholders of TELUS Corporation

We have audited the accompanying consolidated financial statements of TELUS Corporation and subsidiaries (the Company), which comprise the consolidated statements of financial position as at December 31, 2014, and December 31, 2013, and the consolidated statements of income and other comprehensive income, changes in owners' equity and cash flows for the years ended December 31, 2014, and December 31, 2013, and a summary of significant accounting policies and other explanatory information.

Management's Responsibility for the Consolidated Financial Statements

Management is responsible for the preparation and fair presentation of these consolidated financial statements in accordance with International Financial Reporting Standards as issued by the International Accounting Standards Board, and for such internal control as management determines is necessary to enable the preparation of consolidated financial statements that are free from material misstatement, whether due to fraud or error.

Auditors' Responsibility

Our responsibility is to express an opinion on these consolidated financial statements based on our audits. We conducted our audits in accordance with Canadian generally accepted auditing standards and the standards of the Public Company Accounting Oversight Board (United States). Those standards require that we comply with ethical requirements and plan and perform the audit to obtain reasonable assurance about whether the consolidated financial statements are free from material misstatement.

An audit involves performing procedures to obtain audit evidence about the amounts and disclosures in the consolidated financial statements. The procedures selected depend on the auditor's judgment, including the assessment of the risks of material misstatement of the consolidated financial statements, whether due to fraud or error. In making those risk assessments, the auditor considers internal control relevant to the entity's preparation and fair presentation of the consolidated financial statements in order to design audit procedures that are appropriate in the circumstances. An audit also includes evaluating the appropriateness of accounting policies used and the reasonableness of accounting estimates made by management, as well as evaluating the overall presentation of the consolidated financial statements.

We believe that the audit evidence we have obtained in our audits is sufficient and appropriate to provide a basis for our audit opinion.

Opinion

In our opinion, the consolidated financial statements present fairly, in all material respects, the financial position of TELUS Corporation and subsidiaries as at December 31, 2014, and December 31, 2013, and their financial performance and their cash flows for each of the years ended December 31, 2014, and December 31, 2013, in accordance with International Financial Reporting Standards as issued by the International Accounting Standards Board.

Other Matter

We have also audited, in accordance with the standards of the Public Company Accounting Oversight Board (United States), the effectiveness of the Company's internal control over financial reporting as at December 31, 2014, based on the criteria established in *Internal Control – Integrated Framework (2013)* issued by the Committee of Sponsoring Organizations of the Treadway Commission and our report dated February 12, 2015, expressed an unqualified opinion on the Company's internal control over financial reporting.

Deloitte LLP

Deloitte LLP
Chartered Accountants
Vancouver, Canada
February 12, 2015

Report of independent registered public accounting firm

We have audited the internal control over financial reporting of TELUS Corporation and subsidiaries (the Company) as of December 31, 2014, based on the criteria established in *Internal Control – Integrated Framework (2013)* issued by the Committee of Sponsoring Organizations of the Treadway Commission. The Company's management is responsible for maintaining effective internal control over financial reporting and for its assessment of the effectiveness of internal control over financial reporting, included in the accompanying Report of Management on Internal Control over Financial Reporting. Our responsibility is to express an opinion on the Company's internal control over financial reporting based on our audit.

We conducted our audit in accordance with the standards of the Public Company Accounting Oversight Board (United States). Those standards require that we plan and perform the audit to obtain reasonable assurance about whether effective internal control over financial reporting was maintained in all material respects. Our audit included obtaining an understanding of internal control over financial reporting, assessing the risk that a material weakness exists, testing and evaluating the design and operating effectiveness of internal control based on the assessed risk, and performing such other procedures as we considered necessary in the circumstances. We believe that our audit provides a reasonable basis for our opinion.

A company's internal control over financial reporting is a process designed by, or under the supervision of, the company's principal executive and principal financial officers, or persons performing similar functions, and effected by the company's board of directors, management, and other personnel to provide reasonable assurance regarding the reliability of financial reporting and the preparation of financial statements for external purposes in accordance with generally accepted accounting principles. A company's internal control over financial reporting includes those policies and procedures that (1) pertain to the maintenance of records that, in reasonable detail, accurately and fairly reflect the transactions and dispositions of the assets of the company; (2) provide reasonable assurance that transactions are recorded as

necessary to permit preparation of financial statements in accordance with generally accepted accounting principles, and that receipts and expenditures of the company are being made only in accordance with authorizations of management and directors of the company; and (3) provide reasonable assurance regarding prevention or timely detection of unauthorized acquisition, use, or disposition of the company's assets that could have a material effect on the financial statements.

Because of the inherent limitations of internal control over financial reporting, including the possibility of collusion or improper management override of controls, material misstatements due to error or fraud may not be prevented or detected on a timely basis. Also, projections of any evaluation of the effectiveness of the internal control over financial reporting to future periods are subject to the risk that the controls may become inadequate because of changes in conditions, or that the degree of compliance with the policies or procedures may deteriorate.

In our opinion, the Company maintained, in all material respects, effective internal control over financial reporting as of December 31, 2014, based on the criteria established in *Internal Control – Integrated Framework (2013)* issued by the Committee of Sponsoring Organizations of the Treadway Commission.

We have also audited, in accordance with Canadian generally accepted auditing standards and the standards of the Public Company Accounting Oversight Board (United States), the consolidated financial statements as at and for the year ended December 31, 2014, of the Company and our report dated February 12, 2015, expressed an unqualified opinion on those financial statements.

Deloitte LLP

Deloitte LLP
Chartered Accountants
Vancouver, Canada
February 12, 2015

Consolidated statements of income and other comprehensive income

Years ended December 31 (millions except per share amounts)	Note	2014	2013
Operating Revenues			
Service		$ 11,108	$ 10,601
Equipment		819	735
Revenues arising from contracts with customers		11,927	11,336
Other operating income	6	75	68
		12,002	11,404
Operating Expenses			
Goods and services purchased		5,299	4,962
Employee benefits expense	7	2,487	2,424
Depreciation	16	1,423	1,380
Amortization of intangible assets	17(a)	411	423
		9,620	9,189
Operating Income		2,382	2,215
Financing costs	8	456	447
Income Before Income Taxes		1,926	1,768
Income taxes	9	501	474
Net Income		1,425	1,294
Other Comprehensive Income			
Items that may subsequently be reclassified to income	10		
Change in unrealized fair value of derivatives designated as cash flow hedges		1	–
Foreign currency translation adjustment arising from translating financial statements of foreign operations		10	4
Change in unrealized fair value of available-for-sale financial assets		(4)	(13)
		7	(9)
Item never subsequently reclassified to income			
Employee defined benefit plan re-measurements		(445)	998
		(438)	989
Comprehensive Income		$ 987	$ 2,283
Net Income Per Equity Share	11		
Basic		$ 2.31	$ 2.02
Diluted		$ 2.31	$ 2.01
Total Weighted Average Equity Shares Outstanding			
Basic		616	640
Diluted		618	643

The accompanying notes are an integral part of these consolidated financial statements.

Consolidated statements of financial position

As at December 31 (millions)	Note	2014	2013
Assets			
Current assets			
Cash and temporary investments, net		$ 60	$ 336
Accounts receivable	25(a)	1,483	1,461
Income and other taxes receivable		97	32
Inventories	25(a)	320	326
Prepaid expenses		199	168
Current derivative assets	4(h)	27	6
		2,186	2,329
Non-current assets			
Property, plant and equipment, net	16	9,123	8,428
Intangible assets, net	17	7,797	6,531
Goodwill, net	17	3,757	3,737
Real estate joint ventures	18	21	11
Other long-term assets	25(a)	333	530
		21,031	19,237
		$ 23,217	$ 21,566
Liabilities and Owners' Equity			
Current liabilities			
Short-term borrowings	19	$ 100	$ 400
Accounts payable and accrued liabilities	25(a)	2,019	1,735
Income and other taxes payable		2	102
Dividends payable	12	244	222
Advance billings and customer deposits	25(a)	753	729
Provisions	20	126	110
Current maturities of long-term debt	21	255	–
Current derivative liabilities	4(h)	–	1
		3,499	3,299
Non-current liabilities			
Provisions	20	342	219
Long-term debt	21	9,055	7,493
Other long-term liabilities	25(a)	931	649
Deferred income taxes	9(b)	1,936	1,891
		12,264	10,252
Liabilities		15,763	13,551
Owners' equity			
Common equity	22	7,454	8,015
		$ 23,217	$ 21,566
Commitments and Contingent Liabilities	23		

The accompanying notes are an integral part of these consolidated financial statements.

Approved by the Directors:

W. A. MacKinnon
William A. MacKinnon
Director

Darren Entwistle
Director

Consolidated statements of changes in owners' equity

(millions except number of shares)	Note	Common Shares		Non-Voting Shares[1]		Contributed surplus	Retained earnings	Accumulated other comprehensive income	Total
		Number of shares	Share capital	Number of shares	Share capital				
Balance as at January 1, 2013		349,821,092	$ 2,219	302,104,972	$ 3,360	$ 163	$ 1,904	$ 40	$ 7,686
Net income		–	–	–	–	–	1,294	–	1,294
Other comprehensive income	10	–	–	–	–	–	998	(9)	989
Dividends	12	–	–	–	–	–	(866)	–	(866)
Share option award expense	13(a)	–	–	–	–	6	–	–	6
Shares issued pursuant to cash exercise of share options	13(b)	–	–	200	–	–	–	–	–
Shares issued pursuant to use of share option award net-equity settlement feature	13(b)	2,534,586	18	152,160	2	(20)	–	–	–
Shareholder-approved and court-approved exchange of shares		302,257,332	3,362	(302,257,332)	(3,362)	–	–	–	–
Costs related to share transactions		–	(19)	–	–	–	–	–	(19)
Normal course issuer bid purchase of Common Shares	22(d)	(31,180,612)	(266)	–	–	–	(734)	–	(1,000)
Liability for automatic share purchase plan commitment pursuant to the 2014 normal course issuer bid for Common Shares		–	(18)	–	$ –	–	(57)	–	(75)
Balance as at December 31, 2013		623,432,398	$ 5,296	–	–	$ 149	$ 2,539	$ 31	$ 8,015
Balance as at January 1, 2014		623,432,398	$ 5,296			$ 149	$ 2,539	$ 31	$ 8,015
Net income		–	–			–	1,425	–	1,425
Other comprehensive income	10	–	–			–	(445)	7	(438)
Dividends	12	–	–			–	(935)	–	(935)
Share option award expense	13(a)	–	–			3	–	–	3
Shares issued pursuant to use of share option award net-equity settlement feature	13(b)	1,447,207	11			(11)	–	–	–
Normal course issuer bid purchase of Common Shares	22(d)	(15,855,171)	(135)			–	(480)	–	(615)
Liability for automatic share purchase plan commitment pursuant to normal course issuer bids for Common Shares	22(d)								
Reversal of opening liability		–	18			–	57	–	75
Recognition of closing liability		–	(15)			–	(60)	–	(75)
Other		–	–			–	(1)	–	(1)
Balance as at December 31, 2014		609,024,434	$ 5,175			$ 141	$ 2,100	$ 38	$ 7,454

(1) At our annual and special meeting held May 9, 2013, our shareholders approved the elimination of the Non-Voting Shares from our authorized share structure and the elimination of all references to Non-Voting Shares from our Articles.

The accompanying notes are an integral part of these consolidated financial statements.

Consolidated statements of cash flows

Years ended December 31 (millions)	Note	2014	2013
Operating Activities			
Net income		$ 1,425	$ 1,294
Adjustments to reconcile net income to cash provided by operating activities:			
Depreciation and amortization		1,834	1,803
Deferred income taxes	9(b)	188	21
Share-based compensation expense	13(a)	74	24
Net employee defined benefit plans expense	14(b)-(c)	87	108
Employer contributions to employee defined benefit plans		(88)	(200)
Other		(49)	9
Net change in non-cash operating working capital	25(b)	(64)	187
Cash provided by operating activities		3,407	3,246
Investing Activities			
Cash payments for capital assets, excluding spectrum licences	25(b)	(2,373)	(2,035)
Cash payments for spectrum licences		(1,171)	(67)
Cash payments for acquisitions and related investments	25(b)	(49)	(261)
Real estate joint ventures advances and contributions	18(c)	(57)	(24)
Real estate joint venture receipts	18(c)	4	1
Proceeds on dispositions		7	12
Other		(29)	(15)
Cash used by investing activities		(3,668)	(2,389)
Financing Activities			
Dividends paid to holders of equity shares	25(b)	(913)	(852)
Purchase of Common Shares for cancellation	22(d), 25(b)	(612)	(1,000)
Issuance and repayment of short-term borrowings	19	(300)	(2)
Long-term debt issued	21, 25(b)	7,273	4,619
Redemptions and repayment of long-term debt	21, 25(b)	(5,450)	(3,375)
Other		(13)	(18)
Cash used by financing activities		(15)	(628)
Cash Position			
Increase (decrease) in cash and temporary investments, net		(276)	229
Cash and temporary investments, net, beginning of period		336	107
Cash and temporary investments, net, end of period		$ 60	$ 336
Supplemental Disclosure of Operating Cash Flows			
Interest paid	25(b)	$ (412)	$ (364)
Interest received		$ 2	$ 4
Income taxes paid, net	9	$ (464)	$ (438)

The accompanying notes are an integral part of these consolidated financial statements.

Chart of Accounts

Note: The blanks in the account names below allow students to specify account names.

Assets

CURRENT ASSETS
101   Cash
102   Petty cash
103   Investments
104   _____ investments
106   Accounts receivable
107   Allowance for doubtful accounts
108   GST receivable
109   Interest receivable
110   Rent receivable
111   Notes receivable
119   Merchandise inventory
120   _____ inventory
124   Office supplies
125   Store supplies
126   _____ supplies
128   Prepaid insurance
129   Prepaid _____
131   Prepaid rent

NON-CURRENT INVESTMENTS
141   Investment in _____ shares
142   Investment in _____ bonds
144   Investment in _____

PROPERTY, PLANT, AND EQUIPMENT (PPE)
151   Automobiles/Car/Vehicle
152   Accumulated depreciation, automobiles/Car/Vehicle
153   Trucks
154   Accumulated depreciation, trucks
159   Library
160   Accumulated depreciation, library
161   Furniture
162   Accumulated depreciation, furniture
163   Office equipment
164   Accumulated depreciation, office equipment
165   Store equipment
166   Accumulated depreciation, store equipment
167   _____ equipment
168   Accumulated depreciation, _____ equipment
169   Machinery
170   Accumulated depreciation, machinery
173   Building _____
174   Accumulated depreciation, building _____
175   Land
176   Leasehold improvements
179   Land improvements, _____
180   Accumulated depreciation, land improvements _____

INTANGIBLE ASSETS
191   Patents
192   Accumulated amortization, patents
193   Leasehold
194   Accumulated amortization, leasehold
195   Franchise
196   Accumulated amortization, franchise
197   Copyright
198   Accumulated amortization, copyright
199   Brand name

GOODWILL
200   Goodwill

Liabilities

CURRENT LIABILITIES
201   Accounts payable
202   Insurance payable
203   Interest payable
204   Legal fees payable
205   Short-term notes payable
206   Rent payable
207   Salaries payable
208   Wages payable
209   Estimated warranty liability
210   Income taxes payable
211   Common dividends payable
212   Preferred dividends payable
213   EI payable
214   CPP payable
215   Employees' medical insurance payable
216   PST payable
217   GST payable
218   _____ payable

UNEARNED REVENUES
230   Unearned consulting revenue
231   Unearned revenue
232   Unearned _____ / Unearned _____ revenue

LONG-TERM LIABILITIES
250   Long-term notes payable
251   Long-term lease liability
252   Bonds payable
253   Discount on bonds payable
254   Premium on bonds payable

Equity
301   _____, capital
302   _____, withdrawals

CORPORATE CONTRIBUTED CAPITAL
307   Common shares
310   Common share dividends distributable

313 Contributed capital from the retirement of common shares
315 Preferred shares

318 Retained earnings
319 Cash dividends
320 Share dividends

401 _____ revenue
403 _____ services revenue
405 Commission revenue
406 Rent revenue
407 Dividends income
408 Earnings from investment in _____
409 Interest income
413 Sales
414 Sales returns and allowances
415 Sales discounts

500 Cost of goods sold
501 Purchases
502 Purchases returns and allowances
503 Purchases discounts
504 Transportation-in/freight-in

600 Depreciation expense, automobiles/Car/Vehicle
602 Depreciation expense, _____

603 Amortization expense, copyrights
604 Amortization expense, _____

620 Office salaries expense
621 Sales salaries expense
622 Salaries expense
623 _____ wages expense
624 Employees' benefits expense

630 Cash over and short
633 Interest expense
634 Transaction fees

636 Insurance expense, building
637 Insurance expense, _____

640 Rent expense
641 Rent expense, office space
642 Rent expense, _____

650 Office supplies expense
651 _____ supplies expense

655 Advertising expense
656 Bad debts expense
659 Collection expense
661 Debit Card Expense

662 Credit card expense
663 Delivery expense/ freight-out expense
667 Equipment expense
668 Food and drinks expense
671 Gas and oil expense
673 Janitorial expense
674 Legal fees expense
676 Mileage expense
682 Postage expense
683 Property taxes expense
684 Repairs expense, _____
688 Telephone/Cell phone expense
689 Travel and entertaining expense
690 Utilities expense
691 Warranty expense
695 Income taxes expense
696 _____ expense

701 Gain on retirement of bonds
702 Gain on sale of machinery
703 Investment income
705 Gain on _____
805 Loss on retirement of bonds
806 Loss on sale of investments
807 Loss on sale of machinery
809 Loss on _____

901 Income summary

Index

SUMMARY OF FOCUS ON FINANCIAL STATEMENT ONLINE COMPANIES—VOLUME 1

EXTEND YOUR KNOWLEDGE (EYK) INDEX—VOLUME 1